Arms Control Law

The International Law of Peace and Security
Series Editor: Nigel D. White

Arms Control Law

Edited by

Daniel H. Joyner

University of Alabama, USA

ASHGATE

Published by
Ashgate Publishing Limited
Wey Court East
Union Road
Farnham
Surrey GU9 7PT
England

Ashgate Publishing Company
Suite 420
101 Cherry Street
Burlington
VT 05401-4405
USA

www.ashgate.com

British Library Cataloguing in Publication Data
Arms control law. – (The international law of peace and
    security)
    1. Arms control. 2. Nuclear nonproliferation–
    International cooperation. 3. Weapons of mass destruction
    (International law)
    I. Series II. Joyner, Daniel.
    341.7'33–dc22

Library of Congress Control Number: 2011930000

ISBN 9780754629535

MIX
Paper from
responsible sources
FSC
www.fsc.org   FSC® C013056

Printed and bound in Great Britain by
TJ International Ltd, Padstow, Cornwall.

Contents

PART III   CHEMICAL AND BIOLOGICAL WEAPONS

PART IV   MISSILES

PART V   THE UN SECURITY COUNCIL AND NONPROLIFERATION LAW

Acknowledgements

The editor and publishers wish to thank the following for permission to use copyright material.

Ashgate Publishing Limited for the essays: Alexander Kelle (2006), 'CBW Export Controls: Towards Regime Integration?', in Daniel H. Joyner (ed.), *Non-Proliferation Export Controls: Origins, Challenges and Proposals for Strengthening*, Aldershot: Ashgate, pp. 101–18; Scott Jones (2006), 'Emptying the Haunted Air: The Current and Future Missile Control Regime', in Daniel H. Joyner (ed.), *Non-Proliferation Export Controls: Origins, Challenges and Proposals for Strengthening*, Aldershot: Ashgate, pp. 75–99.

Brill N.V. for the essay: Eric P.J. Myjer (2001), 'The Organization for the Prohibition of Chemical Weapons: Moving Closer towards an International Arms Control Organization? A Quantum Leap in the Institutional Law of Arms Control', in E.P.J. Myjer (ed.), *Issues of Arms Control and the Chemical Weapons Convention: Obligations Inter Se and Supervisory Mechanisms*, Netherlands: Kluwer, pp. 61–139.

Cambridge University Press for the essay: Rein Müllerson (2001), 'The ABM Treaty: Changed Circumstances, Extraordinary Events, Supreme Interests and International Law', *International and Comparative Law Quarterly*, **50**, pp. 509–39. Copyright © 2001 British Institute of International and Comparative Law.

Copyright Clearance Center for the essays: David A. Koplow (1992), 'The Jurisprudence of Non-Proliferation: Taking International Law Seriously', *Transnational Law and Contemporary Problems*, **2**, pp. 357–83. Copyright © 1992 Transnational Law and Contemporary Problems; Mason Willrich (1967–68), 'The Treaty on Non-Proliferation of Nuclear Weapons: Nuclear Technology Confronts World Politics', *Yale Law Journal*, **77**, pp. 1447–519. Copyright © 1967–68 Yale Law Journal Company, Inc.; George Bunn and Roland M. Timerbaev (1995), 'Nuclear Disarmament: How Much Have the Five Nuclear Powers Promised in the Non-Proliferation Treaty?', in John Rhinelander and Adam Scheinman (eds), *At the Nuclear Crossroads*, Lanham, MD: University Press of America, pp. 11–29 & notes. Copyright © 1995 University Press of America; Daniel H. Joyner (2010), 'Why Less Is More: Law and Policy Considerations on the Iranian Nuclear Issue', *Harvard Law and Policy Review (Online)*, **4**, pp. 1–12. http://hlpronline.com/2010/03/joyner_iran/. Copyright © 2010 Harvard University Law School; Jack M. Beard (2007), 'The Shortcomings of Indeterminacy in Arms Control Regimes: The Case of the Biological Weapons Convention', *American Journal of International Law*, **101**, pp. 271–321. Copyright © 2007 American Society of International Law.

David P. Fidler (2004), 'International Law and Weapons of Mass Destruction: End of the Arms Control Approach?', *Duke Journal of Comparative and International Law*, **14**, pp. 39–88. Copyright © 2004 David P. Fidler.

Series Preface

The essays collected in the four volumes of this reprint series, The International Law of Peace and Security, focus on a number of facets of international law concerned with peace and security. Clearly there are existing volumes in the Library of Essays on International Law (series editor Robert McCorquodale) that are essential reading for anyone interested in this area of international law, primarily *Collective Security Law*, edited by Nigel White, and *International Peacekeeping*, edited by Boris Kondoch. However, the aim of this series is not simply to develop and deepen the reader's understanding of international law in the area of peace and security, but to introduce new areas and concepts, namely the international laws that purport to govern and regulate arms control, counter-terrorism, the use of force, and peace-building. The focus will be on peace and security rather than on conflict, as the law of armed conflict has already been covered in the aforementioned series, in *Humanitarian Law* edited by Judith Gardam.

The international laws in the area of peace and security are essentially different from those that apply in conflicts – basically, the difference is between the law of peace and the law of war. Simply put, the law of war is concerned with regulating warfare – its means, methods, and issues of targeting and protecting persons – thereby upholding principles of humanity while recognizing the dictates of military necessity. The law of peace and security is about preventing conflicts and wars, and is increasingly concerned with rebuilding a situation of peace and security on the other side of the conflict following a ceasefire and peace agreement. Of course, it is not always possible to maintain a clear line between the *jus ad bellum*, *jus in bello* and *jus post bellum* – an issue raised by the controversial 'war on terror', but coming through more practically in specific instances such as the application of international humanitarian law to peacekeepers. In addition, the series only considers issues of international criminal justice when analysing the rebuilding of a post-conflict state or as an element of counter-terrorism, thus giving rise to little overlap with the collection in the aforementioned series, *The International Criminal Court* edited by Olympia Bekou and Robert Cryer.

The focus of these four volumes is essentially on the law of peace, more specifically those laws and legal regimes that underpin peace by means of controlling the spread of dangerous weapons and by limiting the occasions when states can use force on the international stage, or restoring it when that peace has been broken. In times of peace the main fear is of sudden attacks, possibly by the use of WMD or by terrorists, signifying that arms control law, the law regulating the use of force and anti-terrorist laws are all potentially applicable. In post-conflict situations, peace is being restored usually with the involvement of international actors, which raises a whole host of legal issues, including the applicability of human rights law within the unstable post-conflict state and the principles governing international intervention and involvement. The presence of the UN Security Council, as principal international guarantor and guardian of peace and security, in each of the four volumes is not only illustrative of the unifying theme of peace and security, but also raises concerns and issues about the central role of this most political of bodies in this area of law.

In considering the four volumes in this series individually, it can be seen that the volume edited by Dan Joyner – *Arms Control Law* – is a pretty unique collection of secondary sources collected from both legal and non-legal areas. The essays in this collection review and analyse the major arms control treaties and institutions including the Security Council. The contribution of arms control law to international peace and security is a key theme.

In *The Use of Force in International Law*, Tarcisio Gazzini and NicholasTsagourias have carefully selected essays from a vast range of literature to reflect the debates and controversies of this most fundamental, but much contested, area. The rules on when states and organizations can use or authorize the use of force is not only confined to the primary international treaty governing peace and security – the UN Charter – but also includes different viewpoints on controversial (customary) exceptions such as humanitarian intervention, as well as the more recent debates on the responsibility to protect. All this again requires attention to be given to the Security Council.

In *Counter-Terrorism and International Law*, Katja Samuel and Nigel White consider the problem of international terrorism (embodied in the struggle to define it) and the range of responses crafted by states and international organizations in order to try to respond to it, ranging from declaring 'war' to consensual cooperative criminal justice-type measures. The role of the Security Council in developing the legal regimes here, by use for example of targeted sanctions, is considered against the backdrop of existing conventions and practices. The contribution of these measures to the goals of peace and security embodied in the UN Charter is central to this collection.

Finally, *Post-Conflict Rebuilding and International Law*, edited by Ray Murphy, comprises an interesting collection of essays illustrating the phenomenon of rebuilding peace within different regions, followed by a consideration of the general normative framework including the arguments for and against recognizing (the need for) a *jus post bellum*. The essays review and analyse various types, stages and institutions involved in post-conflict peace-building from an international law perspective. They include discussion of rebuilding and peace operations (a much wider concept than peacekeeping operations), electoral support, humanitarian assistance and rule-of-law capacity-building. Post-conflict accountability mechanisms (amnesties, truth commissions, criminal tribunals) and their contribution to peace-building, as well as the wider restoration of peace and security, are also covered. Because this area is new and still developing there will be a need to identify the applicable principles of international law (for example, human rights including economic, social and cultural rights and the right of self-determination, but also the right to security), and the possible development of a *jus post bellum*, but Ray Murphy identifies a number of other challenges to this most difficult of tasks – rebuilding peace.

Each volume of collected essays is of immense value in itself, but each is also supplemented by an introduction by the volume editors and a selected bibliography, both of which add considerably to the usefulness of the collections to the reader.

NIGEL D. WHITE
Series Editor
University of Nottingham

Introduction

I was asked by Nigel White, the general editor of this series, to produce a volume entitled 'Arms Control Law'. Stipulating the title in my original charge was actually a great mercy to me, though I doubt Nigel knew it at the time. It spared me from what would otherwise have been considerable anguishing over the title of this volume. Let me begin this introduction by explaining why there is such anguish to be had in the semantics of placing a name upon the area of law which this book seeks to represent, and to which I have devoted the last nine years of my professional life.

There are three terms which vie for an author's favour when he discusses sources of international law related to weapons of mass destruction (WMD) that is, nuclear, chemical and biological weapons. These terms have in some significant ways separate, but in other ways significantly overlapping, meaning and descriptive usefulness. They are: 'arms control law'; 'nonproliferation law'; and 'disarmament law'. In my discussions with colleagues working in this area, I have found that there are significant variations of thought as to the respective definitions of these terms, and as to the propriety of their use in referring to selected sets of legal issues. I have come to the conclusion that there are, in fact, no orthodox or universally accepted understandings of the definitions of these terms and their relationship to each other. This fact is at once liberating to the analyst, in that he or she may therefore come to his/ her own conclusion regarding their definition and use; and at the same time the cause of sometimes distracting disagreement with other writers in the same field.

When I am pressed for definitions of these terms, I respond as follows: arms control law, to my mind, encompasses within it all sources of international law whose object and purpose is to limit or completely stop the further development, acquisition and spread of weapons technologies both conventional and non-conventional, and/or whose object and purpose is to reverse trends of weapons proliferation and stockpiling by providing for a reduction in existing weapons arsenals. The term 'arms control law' was the preferred term in official circles for many decades, including the decades of the Cold War, for generally referring to all things weapons-law-related, in both the conventional and non-conventional contexts. Due to this traditional popularity, 'arms control law' has remained in the general perception the most appropriate term for the area of law this book seeks to cover.

'Disarmament law' is more of a niche term to my mind, meaning that it carries with it a significantly more restricted definition. 'Disarmament law' encompasses those sources of international law which relate specifically to what is sometimes termed vertical proliferation, or the possession and stockpiling of weapons within a state. To my mind this term does not include sources or provisions of law which seek to limit or prohibit horizontal proliferation, or the spread of weapons technologies from one state or non-state actor to other states or actors. Thus, when one speaks of disarmament law, one really speaks only of arms reduction and prohibition treaties or treaty provisions, where states agree to decrease or eliminate their current stockpiles of specified weapons. Disarmament law as a term is almost always used exclusively in the context of non-conventional weapons (WMD).

'Nonproliferation law' is a term of more recent ascendance in popularity of use, and one which has come into vogue in official and academic circles really only in the last 10–15 years. My own view is that the first Gulf War in 1990–91 was the primary catalyst for the rising to prominence of this term, as this was the first instance of Western powers going to war with a state not a member of the group of five 'sanctioned' nuclear powers, to which somehow WMD technologies had proliferated, and which was threatening the use of those weapons against Western coalition soldiers. I think the term also suited US administrations in the post-Cold War decades, as their concern switched from primarily worrying about one large antipathetic state with thousands of nuclear weapons, to instead primarily worrying about many smaller antipathetic states and non-state actors who seemed to be seeking and sometimes acquiring nuclear weapons at an alarming rate (for example, Pakistan, North Korea, Libya, Iran). 'Nonproliferation law' as a term focused legal attention on the spread of WMD technologies, and especially nuclear weapons, outside of the chosen and sanctioned five. Which is precisely where the focus belonged in their opinion, and not, as US officials made clear, upon Western powers' rather unimpressive track record in upholding their own vertical disarmament obligations. When one refers to nonproliferation law, one is clearly referring only to legal sources relevant to WMD proliferation, and not to conventional weapons regulation/ disarmament. This is perhaps the chief distinction between nonproliferation law and arms control law as descriptive terms. Nonproliferation law is thus in essence a lesser included concept within the broader concept of arms control law.

As I understand the term nonproliferation law – and this is an understanding borne from examination of the fundamental nonproliferation legal instruments, including the 1968 Nuclear Nonproliferation Treaty (NPT), the 1972 Biological Weapons Convention (BWC) and the 1993 Chemical Weapons Convention (CWC) – refers to both horizontal proliferation and vertical proliferation. All of these cornerstone nonproliferation legal instruments address both vectors of proliferation of their subject weapons technologies within their terms. In fact in all three cornerstone treaties, there are provisions either prohibiting outright their subject weapons technologies (BWC, CWC) or requiring their eventual elimination through processes of good faith negotiation and implementing action (NPT). Thus, in my view, nonproliferation law as a term properly understood, subsumes within its descriptive scope the entirety of the descriptive scope of the term disarmament law, as well as the descriptive scope of the term arms control law, *with the significant exception* of arms control law's definitional extension to additionally covering conventional weapons issues.

This is why in my writings I have generally favoured employing the term nonproliferation law, and have used it to refer to all legal sources relevant to both horizontal and vertical proliferation of WMD, inclusive of disarmament. So, this is a long-winded way of saying that, if I had chosen a title for this volume, I would have chosen the title 'Nonproliferation Law', because the volume seeks to provide a coherent and concise survey of some of the best scholarly writing on exactly this scope of legal sources. However, I realize that this term is less broadly recognized outside of the nonproliferation studies community, and so again I say that Nigel did me a great favour in naming the volume for me. I think that, notwithstanding what I feel are the definitional imperfections of the term 'arms control law' for expressing this scope, the book will be better served by this title than it would have been by the title 'Nonproliferation Law' because it will be more easily understood by readers at first glance. Then, hopefully, in reading this introduction the reader will find the requisite refinement of the scope of this volume's treatment in order to understand and appreciate the materials that will be presented herein.

Subject of the Volume

With all of this being said about the title of this volume and the descriptive scope of the three competing terms that float around in this area, let me move on to discussing the discrete subject matter of this volume and the materials it contains.

My concept for this volume was to select some of the very best scholarship, by a range of scholars working both inside and outside of academia, to provide readers with an introduction to the full scope of writing about international law relevant to WMD proliferation. This was actually something of a challenge, because the best scholarship on international legal issues related to WMD proliferation is spread out over a wider range of publication outlets than is the case with most other substantive areas of international legal scholarship. Also, the best scholarship in this area is not written exclusively by academic lawyers. Rather, in addition to more traditional academics like myself, there are many leading international legal scholars in this area (for example, George Bunn, Jack Beard, Dieter Fleck, Mohamed Shaker) whose careers were spent largely in government service, and whose writings appear not only in traditional law journals but also in the journals of other academic disciplines, like *The Nonproliferation Review*, or in professional publications like *Arms Control Today*. Thus, to get a full picture of the best international legal scholarship which has been and which is being written on nonproliferation issues, I have tried to cast a wide net for both authors and publication sources.

In terms of the scope of issues covered in this volume, I have tried to present writing on the full range of normative sources regulating the technology areas of nuclear, chemical and biological weapons, as well as delivery vehicles (that is, missiles). Thus, in each technology area I have presented writing on the fundamental multilateral nonproliferation treaties underpinning each normative regime. These again include the NPT, the CWC and the BWC. I have additionally including writing on the monitoring and verification treaties and related organizations which seek to implement the provisions of these cornerstone nonproliferation treaties. These include the International Atomic Energy Agency (IAEA) safeguards agreements, and the Organization for the Prohibition of Chemical Weapons (OPCW). To complete the picture of the normative regimes regulating WMD proliferation, I have also included writing on the multilateral export control regimes whose purpose is to harmonize among supplier states those provisions of their domestic law related to controlling exports of WMD-related materials and technologies. These include the Nuclear Suppliers Group, the Australia Group and the Missile Technology Control Regime. It is vital to understand that all of these normative sources *taken together* comprise the international normative regime for regulating proliferation of WMD. They should be viewed together, and not in isolation, as they are all interdependent normative sources that each play a particular and necessary role in the overall nonproliferation normative regime.

Nonproliferation as a Normative System

With this holistic view of the normative sources in mind, in the first part of the volume I have first presented two essays discussing the nonproliferation treaties and regimes system as a whole, from a systemic perspective. The first essay is by David Koplow, 'The Jurisprudence of Non-Proliferation: Taking International Law Seriously' (Chapter 1), in which he takes on the popular perception that there is in fact no international law to be found in an area of such national security sensitivity as WMD nonproliferation. He argues convincingly that law has played and continues to play an important role in this area of international relations. The second essay in this part is by David Fidler, 'International Law and Weapons of Mass Destruction: End of the Arms Control Approach?' (Chapter 2). Fidler's essay gives a very valuable overview of the legal sources comprising the nonproliferation treaties and regimes system, as well as a discussion of important political and legal trends which continue to shape the way the international community confronts the challenge of WMD proliferation.

Nuclear Weapons

With these system-perspective discussions as an introduction to the sources of law related to WMD nonproliferation, and to the integrated normative regime they comprise, the following parts proceed to a more discrete consideration of each WMD technology area in turn. The first technology area to be addressed is nuclear weapons. Nuclear weapons are the only uncontroversially designated weapons of mass destruction. The incomparable physical destructive power of nuclear fission and fusion weapons unquestionably demands such a separate classification from any other weapon conventionally used by the world's militaries. The effects of a high-yield nuclear weapon detonation, including the massive destructive force of the initial blast, thermal radiation and electromagnetic pulse, followed by the short-, medium- and long-term effects of residual nuclear radiation on an area extending up to hundreds of miles from the epicentre of the detonation, are simply unmatched in their effects upon physical structures and upon human, animal and plant life within the affected area.

The first essay in this part is a classic *Yale Law Journal* essay by Mason Willrich from 1968, 'The Treaty on Non-Proliferation of Nuclear Weapons: Nuclear Technology Confronts World Politics' (Chapter 3). Willrich was among the first to publish serious and sustained legal interpretive treatment of the Nuclear Nonproliferation Treaty. In this essay, we see some of the earliest thinking about the scope and meaning of the provisions of the NPT, and about the nuclear nonproliferation normative system which the newly established treaty had put into place. It is a long essay, but it is a classic and well worth the time spent in reading it. The second essay is something of a juxtaposition with Willrich's essay, as it represents some of the most current legal thinking about the NPT, both at present and for the future. John Simpson's essay, 'The Future of the NPT' (Chapter 4), represents the culmination of his professional life's study of the NPT, and his educated thoughts about the future of the treaty system.

The rest of the essays in the nuclear weapons part are more targeted treatments of discrete aspects of the legal and institutional structure of the nuclear nonproliferation normative regime. George Bunn and Roland Timerbaev's essay, 'Nuclear Disarmament: How Much Have the Five Nuclear Powers Promised in the Non-Proliferation Treaty?' (Chapter 5), is an extremely important examination – written by two men who were directly involved in the negotiation of the NPT – of the legal scope and meaning of Article VI of the NPT, which covers nuclear disarmament. Laura Rockwood's essay, 'The IAEA Safeguards System' (Chapter 6), is a masterful treatment of the IAEA safeguards system – and Laura should know, as she heads the section of the IAEA's Office of Legal Affairs charged with safeguards. The next essay is one of my early publications on the Nuclear Suppliers Group (NSG), 'The Nuclear Suppliers Group: History and Functioning' (Chapter 7). I included it here not so much for its masterful analysis – this essay was not really an analytical essay as much as it was a product of a serious study I had just completed of the primary documents of the NSG. My hope in this essay was to give an accurate and detailed accounting of the NSG's history and functioning, as few if any published works had attempted to do so.

The next two essays in this part address the establishment of, often regional, nuclear weapon free zones, which is a topic of growing importance in nonproliferation law. Jozef Goldblat's 'Nuclear-Weapon-Free Zones: A History and Assessment' (Chapter 8) and Marco Roscini's 'Something Old, Something New: The 2006 Semipalatinsk Treaty on a Nuclear Weapon-Free Zone in Central Asia' (Chapter 9), together provide a review and assessment of existing nuclear weapon free zones.

These are followed by an excellent essay by Masahiko Asada, 'Arms Control Law in Crisis? A Study of the North Korean Nuclear Issue' (Chapter 10), in which he considers the legal questions surrounding North Korea's purported withdrawal from the NPT. The final essay in the nuclear weapons part, 'Why Less Is More: Law and Policy Considerations on the Iranian Nuclear Issue' (Chapter 11), is another of my essays, this time a very recent short essay in which I attempt to address both law and policy questions surrounding the Iranian nuclear crisis.

Chemical and Biological Weapons

In the third part I have chosen to present writing on both chemical and biological weapons. There are four reasons for this joined-up approach. The first is the profound historical and documentary links between the regulation through international law of biological weapons and chemical weapons. Both legal regimes are direct outgrowths of the same programme of work that began in the late 1960s, the CWC simply taking longer to achieve realization than the BWC due to Cold War politics and tensions. Their legal foundations as well are directly linked to the same legal progenitor – the 1925 Geneva Protocol. The second reason for a joined-up analysis of the BWC and the CWC regimes is that both areas of regulation enjoy a similar, peculiar normative and moral support for their prohibitive efforts. This support stems from a strong historical aversion in international society to the use of chemical and biological weapons, which has translated into a strong communal norm that such use is, in a word, taboo. This peculiar yet pervasive taboo regarding chemical and biological weapons is the single most significant reason for the successes achieved in implementation of both the BWC and CWC. The third reason for joint analysis of the BWC and CWC regimes is the decreasingly clear line separating biological weapons and chemical weapons. The fields of chemistry and biology are converging, as evident in the recent rise to prominence of the field of molecular biology, and this convergence has blurred whatever clear distinctions were in the past perceived to exist between biological and chemical weaponizable materials. Fourth and finally, from an institutional/regime perspective, due to the coverage of the Australia Group control lists of both chemical and biological materials and dual-use technologies, there is parsimony to be found in addressing both regimes within the scope of one part.

Julian Robinson's essay, 'Chemical and Biological Weapons' (Chapter 12), leads off this part with an excellent overview examination of the area of chemical and biological weapons, with profound insights into how we should think about proliferation in this context. The second essay, 'The Organization for the Prohibition of Chemical Weapons: Moving Closer towards an International Arms Control Organization? A Quantum Leap in the Institutional Law of Arms Control' (Chapter 13), is a masterful and comprehensive overview by Eric Myjer of the key provisions of the CWC, as well as the role of the OPCW. With Jack Beard's essay, 'The Shortcomings of Indeterminacy in Arms Control Regimes: The Case of the Biological Weapons Convention' (Chapter 14), we move to a targeted consideration of the biological weapons legal regime, with a focus on the relative indeterminacy of the legal provisions of the regime – this a direct result of the unfortunate history of failed attempts to adopt an additional protocol to the BWC on monitoring and verification.

As with the nuclear weapons part, after addressing the fundamental legal sources and institutions, the part on chemical and biological weapons at this point proceeds with a consideration of other aspects of the legal and institutional structure of the CBW normative regime. In this part, Alexander Kelle's essay, 'CBW Export Controls: Towards Regime Integration?' (Chapter 15), provides a very insightful analysis of the distinction and overlap in roles as between the Australia Group and the OPCW in the area of chemical weapons export controls.

Missiles

The fourth part moves away from weapons technologies themselves to provide two readings on weapons delivery platforms, focusing on missiles. Notwithstanding the importance of missile technologies, and their close relationship with WMD technologies, there is currently no multilateral treaty regulating possession, development or trade in missile technologies. This area of technology has always bedevilled and resisted efforts of formal multilateral normative regulation due largely to the fact that missile technologies are by far the most dual-use in character among all WMD-related technologies. Missile components have many legitimate civilian uses quite apart from their military uses, many of which are themselves widely considered to be legitimate. These include, most importantly, use in peaceful space exploration and development. To add to the difficulty, there is virtually no means available to distinguish between a civilian space missile programme and a military missile programme up until the very late stages of its development. Thus normative progression in this area has been effectively stalled over difficulties in addressing the specific technologies involved by means of formally binding instruments, due to the inability of such an instrument to distinguish effectively between legitimate materials and technologies and those which should be subject to regulation in this rapidly changing technological landscape.

However, the Missile Technology Control Regime (MTCR) was founded as a non-binding political arrangement in 1987 for the purpose of controlling the proliferation of rocket and unmanned air vehicle systems capable of delivering WMD, and their associated materials and technology. Its membership currently stands at 34 countries, which use the MTCR as a forum for co-ordination of export control measures specifically related to the two categories of missile-related items contained in the MTCR Annex. Its intended goal as a concept was to restrict exports of these sensitive items, and therefore inhibit their proliferation outside the boundaries of MTCR membership. The Hague Code of Conduct Against Ballistic Missile Proliferation was additionally agreed in 2002 as a non-binding arrangement among its original 93 (now 124) declarants, and as a supplement to the supply-side controls of the MTCR. Scott Jones reviews the MTCR and the Hague Code, and discusses the future of the missile nonproliferation normative regime in the first essay in this part, 'Emptying the Haunted Air: The Current and Future Missile Control Regime' (Chapter 16).

The second essay in this part by Rein Müllerson, 'The ABM Treaty: Changed Circumstances, Extraordinary Events, Supreme Interests and International Law' (Chapter 17), considers one of the few missile-related treaties that have come into being. Though not a multilateral treaty, but rather a bilateral treaty between the United States and the Soviet Union (and later Russia), the ABM Treaty played an important role in regulating anti-missile defence systems until the USA unilaterally withdrew from the Treaty in 2002.

The UN Security Council and Nonproliferation Law

The fifth part of this volume breaks from the consideration of the primary sources of WMD nonproliferation law, in order to consider closely related questions of the role, authority and track record of the UN Security Council in monitoring, implementing and enforcing compliance with these primary sources of nonproliferation law. The Security Council has increasingly played such a role since the end of the Cold War, beginning dramatically with the Council's actions surrounding the first Gulf War in 1990–91. In the past 20 years the Council has addressed WMD proliferation concerns in Iraq, Iran, North Korea, Libya, Pakistan and India.

The first essay in the part by Dieter Fleck, 'Developments of the Law of Arms Control as a Result of the Iraq-Kuwait Conflict' (Chapter 18), reviews the Council's actions surrounding the first Gulf War and continuing on the subject of Iraq through the decade of the 1990s. The second essay written by myself, 'Nuclear Non-Proliferation and the UN Security Council in a Multipolar World: Can International Law Protect States from the Security Council?' (Chapter 19), considers the history of Security Council action over the past 20 years more broadly, and questions whether the Council's manifested understanding of its authority to act should be a cause for concern at a fundamental level for the international legal system.

Conclusion

I hope that through the readings selected for inclusion in this volume, readers will become more aware of the existing depth of scholarly writing on issues of WMD nonproliferation law. I hope further that this realization will contribute to a greater acceptance of the importance of legal analysis, and the legitimacy and influence of legal norms, in situations of international relations in which WMD proliferation issues are in play. As in other areas of international interaction, international law relating to WMD proliferation can, if sincerely respected and complied with by all sides, contribute to transparency and information sharing between states, predictability of behaviour and trust among nations rooted in mutual rational expectations of reciprocity. International law is no panacea for the troubles states face in their relations with other states. But it is a tool which, if used by all sides in good faith, can help states to accept and live with their differences and co-exist peacefully.

Selected Bibliography

Den Dekker, Guido (2001), *The Law of Arms Control: International Supervision and Enforcement*, Leiden: Martinus Nijhoff.

Goldblat, Jozef (ed.) (2000), *Nuclear Disarmament: Obstacles to Banishing the Bomb*, London: I.B. Tauris Publishing.

Goldblat, Jozef (2002), *Arms Control: The New Guide to Negotiations and Agreements*, London, Thousand Oaks, CA and New Delhi: Sage Publishing.

Joyner, Daniel H. (2009), *International Law and the Proliferation of Weapons of Mass Destruction*, New York: Oxford University Press.

Joyner, Daniel H. (2011), *Interpreting the Nuclear Nonproliferation Treaty*, New York: Oxford University Press.

Krutzsch, Walter and Trapp, Ralf (1994), *A Commentary on the Chemical Weapons Convention*, Leiden: Martinus Nijhoff.

Myjer, E.P.J. (ed.) (2001), *Issues of Arms Control and the Chemical Weapons Convention: Obligations Inter Se and Supervisory Mechanisms*, Leiden: Brill.

Sands, Philippe and Boisson de Chazournes, Laurence (eds) (1999), *International Law, the International Court of Justice and Nuclear Weapons*, Cambridge: Cambridge University Press.

Shaker, Mohamed (1980), *The Nuclear Nonproliferation Treaty: Origin and Implementation 1959–1979*, New York: Oceana Publishing.

Willrich, Mason (1969), *Nonproliferation Treaty: Framework for Nuclear Arms Control*, Charlottesville, VA: Michie Publishing.

Part I
Nonproliferation as a
Normative System

[1]

THE JURISPRUDENCE OF NON-PROLIFERATION: Taking International Law Seriously

by David A. Koplow[*]

[*]Professor of Law, Georgetown University Law Center. The author thanks Burns H. Weston and Jonathan Dean for their comments on an earlier draft of this article.

358   *TRANSNATIONAL LAW & CONTEMPORARY PROBLEMS*   [Vol. 2: 357

I. INTRODUCTION

Skeptical people often make the mistake of thinking that international affairs in general, and arms control matters in particular, are solely questions of policy, not law. They assert that the great public issues of the day are considered and resolved entirely on high political grounds, with national leaders acting in calculated pursuit of raw national interests—and law is added, if at all, as an afterthought, a makeweight in formal deliberations, or a post hoc "cover" for actions truly undertaken for other reasons.

This colloquial perspective neglects a host of compelling questions—including the conundrum of whether there can be, at core, any meaningful distinction between the notions of "law," "policy," "morality," and the like[1]—but as with all good public myths, it contains a grain of truth. Too many crucial international decisions are still undertaken with insufficient attention to the dictates of binding international obligations; too many wanton violations of international order and justice survive unpunished; and too many national leaders behave with unwarranted ignorance of the long-term implications of their lawless behaviors.

But international law is more than just an ephemeral debating point. In disarmament, as in other salient aspects of international life, law has meaning and impact. It guides behaviors, shapes expectations, undergirds notions of appropriateness and legitimacy, and, in the extreme, provides at least an imperfect collective format for redress of violations and other grievances. In the area of arms non-proliferation, in particular, law can be one of the sinews that binds the community of nations, contributing valuably to the overall effort to retard the spread of dangerous weaponry.

This essay is about the power of the international law of non-proliferation—its mounting power in the world today and its properly augmented power in an enlightened future. The article focuses on three primary areas in which international law may play a greater role than is commonly appreciated in affecting the behavior of potential proliferators, their suppliers, and their resolute opponents. The three topics—areas in which the essay pleads for law to be taken even more seriously, and by a wider audience of governments and the international public—are: (a) treaties (especially the provisions of those treaties that commit the parties to pursue further incremental measures of disarmament); (b)

---

1. *See, e.g.,* W. Michael Reisman, *Law from the Policy Perspective, in* INTERNATIONAL LAW ESSAYS: A SUPPLEMENT TO INTERNATIONAL LAW IN CONTEMPORARY PERSPECTIVE 1 (Myres McDougal & W. Michael Reisman eds., 1981).

customary international law (especially those aspects of behavior-based jurisprudence which provide unwritten, but nevertheless binding, constraints upon the preparation for and conduct of state violence); and (c) disarmament institutions (especially those novel multilateral organizations that have recently sprung up to play a variety of fact-finding, confidence-building, and dispute-resolution functions).

In all of this, the core notion is the suggestion that international law works, and that it would work even better if more people would notice it and come to understand how lawfulness advances their own self-interest. Louis Henkin's observation that "almost all nations observe almost all principles of international law and almost all of their obligations almost all of the time"[2] is still true today (and parenthetically is also about as strong a statement as one could realistically support for compliance with most domestic American legal standards). As Burns Weston has noted, every day vehicles ply the highways and the oceans in international commerce, electronic impulses pierce the ether in international communications, and capital surges to exploit new opportunities in international finance.[3] Law alone can hardly claim all the credit for this commercial symbiosis, but it does help shape and sustain the framework of people and institutions that makes it all feasible. The international law of non-proliferation can and should now aspire to similar coverage and impact in safeguarding the modern world.

People around the planet already act as if they believe international law matters. States generally try to position themselves on the high side of a jurisprudential controversy, offering rhetorical justifications that can serve to legitimate their arguments—and sometimes they actually change their policies in order to conform to the dictates of the international community. In the midst of the confrontation with Iraq, for example, the Bush administration regularly cited international law as a primary explanation for American participation:[4] one of the principal reasons why we were

---

2. LOUIS HENKIN, HOW NATIONS BEHAVE 47 (2d ed. 1979).

3. Burns H. Weston, *Law and Alternative Security: Toward a Just World Peace, in* ALTERNATIVE SECURITY: LIVING WITHOUT NUCLEAR DETERRENCE 78, 80 (Burns H. Weston ed., 1990).

4. In press conferences and speeches, President Bush frequently invoked notions of international law to condemn the Iraqi aggression and explain the American and coalition responses. *See Transcript of News Session by Bush and 2 Officials on Mideast,* N.Y. TIMES, Aug. 23, 1990, at A16; *Mideast Tensions: Excerpts From Bush's Remarks on His Order to Enlarge U.S. Gulf Force,* N.Y. TIMES, Nov. 9, 1990, at A12; Exchange With Reporters on the Persian Gulf Crisis, 26 WKLY. COMP. PRES. DOC. 1709, 1710 (1990); The President's News Conference, 26 WKLY. COMP. PRES. DOC. 1257, 1257-1258 (1990).

engaged in hostilities was to uphold the rule of law enshrined in the Charter of the United Nations.[5] The Bush administration seems generally to have attempted—albeit, with incomplete success[6]—to initiate and conduct those hostilities in conformity with relevant international law strictures;[7] at least the government *said* that pursuit of a "new world order," based upon newfound respect for international law, was an important consideration.[8]

Today, the world has a new opportunity to reconfigure, or at least to reconceptualize, global politics, affording us a second chance to avoid repeating—in a new, even more hazardous milieu—some of the security errors of previous generations. During the depths of the Cold War, the United States routinely invoked legal trappings and vocabulary in grappling with the Soviet Union, but even the protagonists never took this assertion of international law quite seriously. For example, American leaders in the early 1980s began issuing annual "compliance reports,"[9] which detailed allegations of perfidious Soviet behavior relative to sequential arms control accords, and they routinely averred that unresolved violations of these treaties were an exceptionally grave matter, calling into

---

5. U.N. CHARTER, June 26, 1945, 59 Stat. 1031. Of course, the U.S. government was not nearly so solicitous of U.N. opinion in previous, less globally popular military incursions, such as the invasions of Panama or Grenada. Even there, however, American diplomats attempted to argue that the actions were justified under various doctrines permitting the unilateral use of force—seeking to shelter the United States actions under the rubric of legality. Ved P. Nanda, *The Validity of United States Intervention in Panama under International Law*, 84 AM. J. INT'L L. 494 (1990); Stuart Taylor, Jr., *Legal Basis for Invasion*, N.Y. TIMES, Oct. 27, 1983, at A22.

6. Richard Homan, *Report Says U.S.-Led Air Campaign Against Iraq Violated "Laws of War,"* WASH. POST, Nov. 17, 1991, at A37; Patrick J. Sloyan, *Army Said to Plow Under Possibly Thousands of Iraqi Soldiers in Trenches*, WASH. POST, Sept. 12, 1991, at A9.

7. Some have argued that the initiation of the sanctions and the fighting against Iraq did not conform properly to United Nations standards, as the United States manipulated the proceedings, merely going through the motions of Security Council consideration while threatening unilateral action if the coalition members did not acquiesce. Burns H. Weston, *Security Council Resolution 678 and Persian Gulf Decision-Making: Precarious Legitimacy*, 85 AM. J. INT'L L. 516 (1991).

8. *Confrontation in the Gulf: Transcript of President's address to joint session of Congress, reprinted in* N.Y. TIMES, Sept. 12, 1990, at A20 (describing the objective of a "new world order" and asserting "today that new world is struggling to be born. A world quite different from the one we've known. A world where the rule of law supplants the rule of the jungle.... America and the world must support the rule of law. And we will.").

9. *See, e.g.*, U.S. DEP'T. ST. SPECIAL REPORT NO. 122, *Soviet Noncompliance With Arms Control Agreements*, Feb. 1, 1985. This type of compliance report has now become an annual event, mandated by statute.

question Soviet good faith and jeopardizing prospects for success on a wide range of collaborative efforts.[10] At the same time, however, it was abundantly clear that these quasi-legal documents were entirely artificial. They were in no way an attempt to fashion workable, mutually-acceptable solutions; instead, they were part of a deliberate effort to isolate and denigrate the Soviet Union, using treaty law as a handy club with which to batter the "evil empire."[11]

Similar tactics today would have even less productive consequences. If Iraq is to be brought back into the community of nations, and if repetition of its disastrous aggression is to be avoided, law will have to play a key role in creating and sustaining a disarmament and inspection regime.[12] If nuclear confrontation is to be avoided on the Korean peninsula,[13] on the Indian subcontinent,[14] or in Latin America,[15] legal documents and processes must be viable. If chemical weapons are to be truly eradicated from the earth, a strict and manageable compliance mechanism will have to arise.[16] Of course politics will play a leading role in all this, but law, too, has a function—a function too often ignored.

---

10. *Id.* at 2.

11. *See Analysis of the President's Report on Soviet Noncompliance With Arms Control Agreements*, 17 ARMS CONTROL TODAY 1A (1987); Stuart D. Goldman, *Verification and Compliance: Soviet Compliance With Arms Control Agreements,* CONGRESSIONAL RESEARCH SERVICE ISSUE BRIEF, June 9, 1989 (arguing that the administration's compliance reports were consistently overstated or one-sided). Taking international law seriously does, of course, include careful monitoring of arms control agreements, and faithful adherance by all parties is key. If the United States was truly interested in resolving the disputes, various diplomatic approaches might have been attempted; however, this was manifestly not what the Administration pursued.

12. *See* George Leopold, *U.N. Inspections Lift Verification Role*, DEF. NEWS, May 4-10, 1992, at 9-10 (intrusive inspections are necessary to root out Iraqi weapons of mass destruction).

13. *See* David E. Sanger, *North Korea Reveals Nuclear Sites to Atomic Agency*, N.Y. TIMES, May 7, 1992, at A8 (national reports and international inspections may unwrap mystery surrounding North Korean nuclear weapons programs).

14. *See* Sanjoy Hazarika, *Moscow Affirms Sale of Technology to India*, N.Y. TIMES, May 7, 1992, at A7 (transfers of weapons-related technology threaten to exacerbate India-Pakistan tensions and weapons competition).

15. *See* Gary Marx, *S. American Nuclear Threat Fades*, CHI. TRIB., May 3, 1992, at C21 (Argentina and Brazil have signed treaties to terminate their incipient nuclear arms race).

16. *See* Lee Feinstein, *Australia Offers New Draft Treaty at Chemical Weapons Negotiations*, 22 ARMS CONTROL TODAY 20 (1992) (new verification proposals might help permit conclusion of a chemical weapons ban).

II. TAKING DISARMAMENT TREATIES SERIOUSLY

The first step in elevating international law is to place greater emphasis upon solemn treaty commitments. Disarmament agreements are the clearest, most reliable and visible form of state assent to the creation of a safer world. Their words should be scrutinized with care, and their obligations should be enforced, not casually dismissed as merely vague or aspirational.

Obviously, the primary effect of most disarmament accords lies in the substantive regulation of weaponry.[17] Specified categories of arms may be banned outright[18] or, more frequently, limited in number,[19] and their deployment[20] or use[21] may be circumscribed. Verification arrangements in support of these substantive bans often consume a disproportionate share of the negotiators' time and text,[22]

---

17. Some agreements are designed as "confidence-building measures," enhancing the "transparency" of countries' military structures (via devices such as notifications of maneuvers or invitations for inspection) and easing the fears about a possible surprise attack, even without reducing the sides' military forces. *See, e.g.,* Document of the Stockholm Conference on Confidence- and Security-Building Measures and Disarmament in Europe, Sept. 19, 1986, *reprinted in* UNITED STATES ARMS CONTROL AND DISARMAMENT AGENCY, ARMS CONTROL AND DISARMAMENT AGREEMENTS: TEXTS AND HISTORIES OF THE NEGOTIATIONS 319, 323 (1990) [hereinafter ACDA TREATY BOOK]; Treaty on Open Skies, Mar. 24, 1992 (on file with *Transnational Law & Contemporary Problems*) [hereinafter Open Skies Treaty].

18. *See, e.g.,* Convention on the Prohibition of the Development, Production and Stockpiling of Bacteriological (Biological) and Toxin Weapons and on Their Destruction, Apr. 10, 1972, 26 U.S.T. 583 [hereinafter Biological Weapons Convention or BWC] (prohibits virtually all offensive activity regarding germ warfare).

19. *See, e.g.,* Treaty on the Limitation of Strategic Offensive Arms, June 18, 1979, U.S.-U.S.S.R., 18 I.L.M. 1112 [hereinafter SALT II Treaty] (not in force) (under which each side would have been permitted to retain a fixed number of nuclear weapons in several categories, reducing their total armaments).

20. *See, e.g.,* Treaty on the Limitation of Anti-Ballistic Missile Systems, May 26, 1972, U.S.-U.S.S.R., 23 U.S.T. 3435 [hereinafter ABM Treaty] (permitted each side no more than two anti-ballistic missile sites, each of which could include no more than 100 interceptor missiles).

21. *See, e.g.,* Protocol for the Prohibition of the Use in War of Asphyxiating, Poisonous or Other Gases, and of Bacteriological Methods of Warfare, June 17, 1925, 26 U.S.T. 571 [hereinafter Geneva Protocol] (prohibits the use in war of chemical weaponry).

22. *See, e.g.,* Treaty on the Reduction and Limitation of Strategic Offensive Arms, U.S.-U.S.S.R., July 31, 1991 [hereinafter START Treaty] (not in force) (where the substantive arms control provisions are stated succinctly, but where the associated inspection provisions, dismantling arrangements, data accounting procedures, and the like required great elaboration).

but the underlying obligations mandating arms limitation constitute the main rationale for the agreement and the principal advantage for global security.

In addition to this immediate weapons limitation impact, however, several modern arms control accords have also come to fulfill an important subsidiary role, worthy of greater attention. These treaties deliberately contribute to the long-term growth of international security by helping to establish and entrench "the arms control process," defined as a regularized, ongoing phenomenon through which the major military powers commit themselves to the institutionalization of disarmament proceedings, conveying reciprocal promises to pursue even further measures of weapons regulation over time. Although little noticed, these commitments already have played a significant role in generating additional negotiations, in driving the parties to further diplomatic exchanges, and in promoting a more constructive, amicable "detente" relationship across a broad range of issues.[23]

Four examples help illustrate the pattern of these treaty commitments and the role they play in shaping international diplomacy. Each merits review.

A. Nuclear Testing

Most leading states of the world have long adhered to the view that a comprehensive test ban treaty (CTBT) would be enormously valuable in regulating the proliferation of nuclear arms and in checking the superpowers' "qualitative" arms race.[24] Nevertheless, it has so far proven possible to approach this ultimate goal only incrementally, in a sequence of step-by-step advances, each imposing only partial constraints upon nuclear testing.

---

23. On the other hand, some observers argued that throughout the Cold War period, the United States and Soviet Union cynically used these partial measures of arms control to protect their planned weapons programs, to evade real efforts at disarmament, and to perpetuate their shared global hegemony. ALVA MYRDAL, THE GAME OF DISARMAMENT: HOW THE UNITED STATES AND RUSSIA RUN THE ARMS RACE xi-xxiv (rev. ed., 1982).

24. PHILIP G. SCHRAG, GLOBAL ACTION: NUCLEAR TEST BAN DIPLOMACY AT THE END OF THE COLD WAR 7-31 (1992); INTERNATIONAL FOUNDATION, TOWARD A COMPREHENSIVE NUCLEAR WARHEAD TEST BAN 3-11 (1991). Proponents assert that a CTBT would promote security in two ways: by inhibiting additional states who might otherwise attempt to develop nuclear weapons (a country might not need explosive tests in order to develop a crude fission "atomic" bomb, but would require testing to be confident about any more sophisticated weapons such as a fusion "hydrogen" bomb); and by complicating any efforts by the states that already possess nuclear weapons to develop additional, more advanced types of devices (the "qualitative" arms race).

The Limited Test Ban Treaty (LTBT) of 1963[25] was the first such step, confining nuclear explosions to deep underground locations, where the radioactivity and other effects would not disturb the biosphere.[26] Dissatisfied with their inability to get closer to a CTBT, the parties declared in the LTBT preamble that they were "[s]eeking to achieve the discontinuance of all test explosions of nuclear weapons for all time, determined to continue negotiations to this end, and desiring to put an end to the contamination of man's environment by radioactive substances."[27]

In addition, in article I of the LTBT, immediately after stating the substantive bans against testing in the atmosphere, in outer space or under water, the parties stated,

> It is understood in this connection that the provisions of this subparagraph are without prejudice to the conclusion of a treaty resulting in the permanent banning of all nuclear test explosions, including all such explosions underground, the conclusion of which, as the Parties have stated in the Preamble to this Treaty, they seek to achieve.[28]

The next contribution to this incremental progression was the 1974 Threshold Test Ban Treaty (TTBT),[29] which regulated the size of underground nuclear explosions, confining each test to no greater than the equivalent of 150 kilotons of TNT.[30] There the parties reaffirmed the commitment to pursue a CTBT, again using both the

---

25. Treaty Banning Nuclear Weapon Tests in the Atmosphere, in Outer Space and Under Water, Aug. 5, 1963, 14 U.S.T. 1313 [hereinafter Limited Test Ban Treaty or LTBT].

26. The United States and the Soviet Union negotiated toward a CTBT over a period of several years, but were unable to fashion a mutually-satisfactory inspection regime that would adequately verify compliance with a complete halt to testing. Therefore they settled for a partial accord which would eliminate testing in the atmosphere, in outer space, and under water, where the existing verification capabilities were deemed sufficient. *See* ACDA TREATY BOOK, *supra* note 17, at 37-44; SCHRAG, *supra* note 24, at 7-19.

27. LTBT, *supra* note 25, pmbl., para. 3.

28. *Id.* art. I.1(b).

29. Treaty on the Limitation of Underground Nuclear Weapon Tests, July 3, 1974, U.S.-U.S.S.R., 13 I.L.M. 907 [hereinafter Threshold Test Ban Treaty or TTBT].

30. The TTBT prohibits the full testing of nuclear weapons with very high yields, preventing some possible twists in the strategic nuclear arms race. Many observers, however, contended that the 150 kiloton ceiling (roughly 10 times the size of the Hiroshima bomb) is so high that the superpowers are not, as a practical matter, restrained from doing anything that they would otherwise elect to do. ACDA TREATY BOOK, *supra* note 17, at 184-86; SCHRAG, *supra* note 24, at 19-23.

preamble[31] and article I[32] to express their determination to continue their negotiations toward that end.

Since then, the United States and the former Soviet Union have negotiated additional accords: a 1976 Peaceful Nuclear Explosions Treaty (PNET),[33] designed to apply restrictions similar to the TTBT in the case of nuclear explosions other than weapons tests;[34] a 1990 protocol inserting additional verification arrangements into the TTBT;[35] and a companion 1990 protocol providing parallel inspection procedures for the PNET.[36]

Although each of these treaties seemed to elicit the next step in the progression, no true comprehensive nuclear test ban agreement has yet been reached, and no bilateral or multilateral negotiations toward such a CTBT currently are underway.[37] The Reagan administration, after long resisting meaningful progress toward a test ban treaty, ultimately reaffirmed CTBT as an eventual goal of the United States. The Bush administration, however, has not made good on the pledge to proceed with negotiations toward that end.[38]

---

31. TTBT, *supra* note 29, pmbl, para. 3. ("Recalling the determination expressed by the Parties to the 1963 Treaty Banning Nuclear Weapon Tests in the Atmosphere, in Outer Space and Under Water in its Preamble to seek to achieve the discontinuance of all test explosions of nuclear weapons for all time, and to continue negotiations to this end."). *Id.*

32. *Id.* art. I.3 ("The Parties shall continue their negotiations with a view toward achieving a solution to the problem of the cessation of all underground nuclear weapon tests.")

33. Treaty on Underground Nuclear Explosions for Peaceful Purposes, May 28, 1976, U.S.-U.S.S.R., 15 I.L.M. 894 [hereinafter Peaceful Nuclear Explosions Treaty or PNET]. The TTBT and PNET did not enter into force until 1990.

34. The PNET was a companion to the TTBT—neither could enter into force without the other—in order to prevent a party from circumventing the TTBT's limitations on weapons tests through the guise of a "peaceful" nuclear explosion, allegedly undertaken for mining or civil engineering purposes. ACDA TREATY BOOK, *supra* note 17, at 191-93; SCHRAG, *supra* note 24, at 19-23.

35. Protocol to the Threshold Test Ban Treaty on the Limitation of Underground Nuclear Weapon Tests, June 1, 1990, U.S.-U.S.S.R., 29 I.L.M. 969 [hereinafter TTBT Protocol].

36. Protocol to the Threshold Test Ban Treaty on Underground Nuclear Explosions for Peaceful Purposes, June 1, 1990, U.S.-U.S.S.R., 29 I.L.M. 1025.

37. There were negotiations toward a CTBT during the Carter Administration, and substantial areas of agreement were reached, but the parties were unable to conclude a treaty. SCHRAG, *supra* note 24, at 23-27.

38. *Id.* at 83, 187-88; R. Jeffrey Smith, *Breaking Pledge, U.S. to Defer Underground Nuclear Test Talks*, WASH. POST, Jan. 24, 1990, at A24 [hereinafter *Breaking Pledge*]. Recently, there have been indications that the Bush Administration would be willing to be somewhat flexible on test ban questions, and some additional limitations—but no

What has been the consequence of this pattern of actions? The world—led largely by the United States—has undertaken a series of steps edging part way down the test ban path, and securing widespread adherance. On the other hand, the world—again, largely at the behest of the United States—has refrained from concluding a CTBT, stopping with, at best, a miserly approach to the legal obligations for continuing negotiations as spelled out in the earlier documents. At the same time, the capacity to conduct nuclear weapons test explosions has proliferated (half a dozen additional states have *de facto* joined the "nuclear club" since 1963, and others are working vigorously in that direction)[39] and the superpowers' arms race continued (at least until very recently) with undiminished vigor.[40]

It is, of course, impossible to calculate what the world would have been like had the community been able to secure a CTBT in conformity with the pre-existing commitments at an earlier date. Certainly, at least some weapons programs in the superpower countries and elsewhere, would have been choked off; others might have found a new way to flourish. But it is increasingly clear, as noted below, that the international political and legal consequences of the United States' ongoing adamant refusal to continue the accretion of testing limitations, called for in the earlier treaties, could soon prove hazardous for the entire global non-proliferation regime, as well as for the system of international law more generally.

B. Chemical and Biological Weapons

The second illustration of an arms control treaty mandating follow-on negotiations toward a more complete, ambitious or significant successor is the 1972 Biological Weapons Convention (BWC).[41] There, the negotiating parties were building upon an international diplomatic history that had, at times, treated both chemical and biological weapons as linked parts of a whole, so that

---

international negotiations—may yet emerge. R. Jeffrey Smith, *Administration Considers Limiting Nuclear Tests; Options Prepared for Bush as Summit Nears*, WASH. POST, May 25, 1992, at A1.

39. LEONARD SPECTOR, THE UNDECLARED BOMB 3-22 (1988) (surveying nuclear weapons-related activities in several developing countries).

40. *See generally* RUTH SIVARD, WORLD MILITARY AND SOCIAL EXPENDITURES 1991; UNITED STATES ARMS CONTROL AND DISARMAMENT AGENCY, WORLD MILITARY EXPENDITURES AND ARMS TRANSFERS 1990 (1991) (surveying global military spending).

41. BWC, *supra* note 18.

any disarmament accord should deal with both simultaneously.[42] At other times, however, the relevant states had concluded that the overall problem should be fractured, to permit immediate progress on biological weapons (which were seen as having little military utility, and were therefore relatively easy for the partisans to surrender),[43] while deferring work on chemical weapons (which, in addition to possessing potential military value, relied upon precursor substances widely used in the civilian chemical industry and therefore posing severe verification hurdles).[44]

Eventually, the treaty drafters decided to pursue the bifurcated approach, drafting a BW-only treaty, but including in it a commitment to attack resolutely the other half of the problem, too.[45] Therefore, in article IX, BWC parties undertook "to continue negotiations in good faith with a view to reaching early agreement on effective measures for the prohibition" of chemical weapons.[46] Over the intervening two decades, negotiations toward a CW accord have proceeded fitfully in a variety of bilateral and multilateral fora, and it now appears that the long-awaited document has finally emerged.[47] This Chemical Weapons Convention thus satisfies the aspirations and obligations originally expressed (and legally adopted) in 1972.

The two decades of delay, however, have carried a substantial price. Imperfect compliance with the legal obligations has kept the door open for additional countries to develop and to apply chemical

---

42. ACDA TREATY BOOK, *supra* note 17, at 129-30. Biological and chemical weapons have been closely linked in the public mind, and the 1925 Geneva Protocol dealt with both categories of weapons. Geneva Protocol, *supra* note 21.

43. In 1969—three years prior to the conclusion of the BWC—President Richard Nixon unilaterally renounced all methods of biological warfare for the United States and ordered the dismantling of all offensive BW capabilities, independent of any reciprocal actions by other countries. ACDA TREATY BOOK, *supra* note 17, at 130.

44. *See* VERIFICATION OF DUAL-USE CHEMICALS UNDER THE CHEMICAL WEAPONS CONVENTION: THE CASE OF THIODIGLYCOL *passim* (S. Lundin ed., 1991) (many of the chemicals that could be used to produce lethal weaponry are simultaneously essential to a range of applications such as plastics, paints, fertilizers, and the like, so any effort to ban the weaponry also threatens to inhibit valuable commerce).

45. ACDA TREATY BOOK, *supra* note 17, at 130-31.

46. BWC, *supra* note 18, art. IX.

47. Will Carpenter, *Completing the Chemical Weapons Convention: An Industry View*, CHEMICAL WEAPONS CONVENTION BULL., Mar. 1992, at 1; Raff Trapp, *Into the "End Game,"* CHEMICAL WEAPONS CONVENTION BULL., Mar. 1992, at 21. The Chemical Weapons Convention will be a comprehensive global ban on the production, deployment and use of lethal chemical weapons in international hostilities. Treaty negotiations have recently produced a final text, which was opened for signature in early 1993.

weapons in combat, and experts now estimate that as many as twenty states have deployed or pursued undeclared CW arsenals.[48] The longstanding taboo against the use of CW has at least partially eroded, and people died on both sides from exposure to chemical ordnance during the Iran-Iraq war.[49] There is, of course, no way of knowing how world events would have unfolded had the 1972 BWC pledge been redeemed earlier, but the negotiators at that time thought it was important, and hoped that a prompt CW agreement could help forestall this type of calamity. The resulting losses for United States security—manifested most recently in the discovery of a massive Iraqi chemical weapons industry[50]—might therefore have been avoided.

C. Strategic Nuclear Weapons

The third example concerns strategic nuclear weaponry. Here, too, the evolutionary progression has taken the form of a series of partial, incomplete accords, each of which consciously pointed the way for its successor. In the SALT I negotiations, for example, the United States and the Soviet Union emplaced a pathbreaking set of constraints upon both offensive and defensive weaponry, and explicitly committed themselves "to continue active negotiations" on deeper reductions.[51] In fact, the United States declared that if those further reductions were not promptly forthcoming, such a failure might jeopardize American willingness to continue adherence with even the first phase of the controls.[52]

The next round of those negotiations, therefore, produced the 1979 SALT II treaty.[53] The most massive and detailed agreement negotiated to that time, SALT II incorporated a delicate balancing of asymmetric reductions and limitations upon the United States and the Soviet Union.[54] Some weapons were to be drawn down immediately, others were permitted over a longer period of time, and

---

48. GORDON BURCK & CHARLES FLOWERREE, INTERNATIONAL HANDBOOK ON CHEMICAL WEAPONS PROLIFERATION xx-xxi (1991).

49. *Id.* at 85-137.

50. *Id.* at 35-84.

51. ABM Treaty, *supra* note 20, art. XI; Interim Agreement on Certain Measures With Respect to the Limitation of Strategic Offensive Arms, May 26, 1972, U.S.-U.S.S.R., 23 U.S.T. 3462, art. VII [hereinafter SALT I Interim Agreement].

52. ABM Treaty, *supra* note 20, Unilateral Statement A; SALT I Interim Agreement, *supra* note 51, Unilateral Statement A.

53. SALT II Treaty, *supra* note 19.

54. ACDA TREATY BOOK, *supra* note 17, at 261-66.

still others were deferred to subsequent deliberations.[55] Consequently, the parties included in the package of treaty documents a "Joint Statement of Principles and Guidelines for Subsequent Negotiations on the Limitation of Strategic Arms."[56] The Joint Statement incorporated some rather general principles, such as "equality and equal security"[57] and "cooperative measures" of verification.[58] However, there was also language clearly laying down markers that some of the more problematic issues (such as cruise missiles) that had been incompletely resolved in SALT II would have to be dealt with more definitively in the next round of talks.[59]

Although the SALT II Treaty never entered into force,[60] subsequent negotiations, under the rubric of START,[61] did proceed, and did, *mutatis mutandis*, deal with the points indicated in the Joint Statement of Principles. Deeper cuts in offensive arms, together with coverage of the wider range of weapons types—all circumscribed by an intrusive verification apparatus—were written into the successor agreement, just as SALT II had forecast and required.[62]

The commitment to negotiate additional treaties and deeper reductions in strategic offensive arms has therefore been honored, but only slowly and incompletely. In the meantime, however, the United States and the Soviet Union both squandered their national resources on billions of dollars worth of arms race gadgets, they imperiled the planet with the threat of massive "overkill," and they perpetuated a system of "mutual assured destruction" which

---

55. During the initial period of the treaty, each side was permitted a total of 2400 strategic weapons, and the ceiling was to be lowered to 2250 within three years. SALT II Treaty, supra note 19, arts. III.1 and III.2.

56. SALT II Treaty, *supra* note 19, Joint Statement of Principles [hereinafter JSP].

57. *Id.* first para.

58. *Id.* second para.

59. *Id.* third para. This provision directed attention at the Protocol to the treaty, in which the parties constructed an interim regime to regulate cruise missiles and mobile ICBMs, pending a more comprehensive successor agreement.

60. After the SALT II Treaty was signed and submitted to the Senate, and while the advice and consent process was pending, the Soviet Union invaded Afghanistan. President Carter then asked that the Senate defer its consideration of the treaty. He and President Reagan both issued statements of intention to abide by the unratified document so long as the Soviet Union reciprocated. In 1986, President Reagan declared that the Soviets had not honored their commitment, and he abrogated American compliance. ACDA TREATY BOOK, *supra* note 17, at 263.

61. START Treaty, *supra* note 22.

62. *Id.* art. II.

contributed to the "psychic numbing" of their citizenry.[63] Greater fidelity to their legal obligations—and better appreciation for the strategic and economic realities underpinning them—might have resulted in a shorter, safer, and more prosperous cold war era on all sides.

D. Nuclear Non-Proliferation

The final, and most important, example of legally-compelled incremental progress in arms control comes from article VI of the 1968 Nuclear Non-Proliferation Treaty.[64] This document, widely regarded as the keystone of the global effort to prohibit the further spread of nuclear weapons capability,[65] embraces a complex set of tradeoffs in pursuit of security and economic growth. The non-nuclear-weapons states (NNWS) pledge never to develop or acquire nuclear weapons[66] and to accept international inspections to verify compliance with that ban.[67] The nuclear-weapons states (NWS) conversely promise to refrain from assisting other states in procuring nuclear weapons,[68] to share the peaceful and civilian benefits of nuclear power,[69] and—most importantly in this context—to arrest their own pursuit of nuclear arms:

> Each of the Parties to the Treaty undertakes to pursue negotiations in good faith on effective measures relating to cessation of the nuclear arms race at an early date and to nuclear disarmament, and on a treaty on general and

---

63. Mutual Assured Destruction (MAD) is the doctrine positing that security in the nuclear age is achieved when each side is confident that it possesses sufficient retaliatory capability to deliver a devastating blow to its opponent, even after absorbing an all-out surprise first attack. Under this premise, each side's civilian population is essentially hostage to the other's nuclear prowess, a condition of reciprocal vulnerability that has strong negative consequences for national mental health and psychic well-being. *See* Spurgeon M. Keeny, Jr. & Wolfgang K. H. Panofsky, *MAD Versus NUTS: Can Doctrine or Weaponry Remedy the Mutual Hostage Relationship of the Superpowers*, 60 FOREIGN AFF. 287 (1981); ROBERT J. LIFTON & RICHARD FALK, INDEFENSIBLE WEAPONS: THE POLITICAL AND PSYCHOLOGICAL CASE AGAINST NUCLEARISM 177-89 (1982).

64. Treaty on the Non-Proliferation of Nuclear Weapons, July 1, 1968, 21 U.S.T. 483 [hereinafter NPT].

65. Mohamed Shaker, *The Nonproliferation Treaty Regime*, *in* BEYOND 1995: THE FUTURE OF THE NPT REGIME 7 (Joseph Pilat & Robert Pendley eds., 1990).

66. NPT, *supra* note 64, art. II.

67. *Id.* art. III.

68. *Id.* art. I.

69. *Id.* arts. IV and V.

complete disarmament under strict and effective international control.[70]

Compliance with article VI has recently become controversial because at least some leading NNWS have adopted the view that behind the rather generic language of the treaty lies a deeper understanding that a comprehensive nuclear test ban treaty, in particular, is mandated.[71] That is, some partisans have asserted that despite the raft of monumental arms control accords in recent years (limiting in dramatic fashion intermediate range weapons, strategic arms, conventional forces in Europe, etc.), article VI will not be satisfied until the superpowers conclude a CTBT.[72]

However, the United States has refused for a decade to negotiate toward, or even talk constructively about, a CTBT. American leaders have denied that article VI really targeted a CTBT in any special way, and have asserted that further restrictions upon testing are not in the national interest as long as the country depends upon nuclear weapons as a bulwark of deterrence.[73]

This issue will be joined in stark form in the coming months because the NPT also includes a novel "renewal" article, mandating that after the treaty has been in force for twenty-five years (i.e., in 1995), a conference of parties will be convened to decide the future of the treaty regime. If many NNWS states are dissatisfied with the record of United States (and other) compliance with article VI—especially regarding the failure to produce, or even pursue, a CTBT—then a consensual extension of the NPT could be in doubt. The international community will therefore be plunged into a debate about the content of article VI: what types of disarmament measures does it really require, and what is the nature of "good faith" in such negotiations?

The point illustrated by these four examples, is that international law plays a role in influencing state behaviors, and, more importantly, that it should play an even bigger role. These treaty

---

70. *Id.* art. VI.

71. *See* Darryl Howlett & John Simpson, *The NPT and the CTBT: An Inextricable Relationship?*, Programme for Promoting Nuclear Non-Proliferation, Issue Review No. 1, Mar. 1992, at 6.

72. Under the NPT, a "review conference" convenes every five years to assess the operation of the treaty. Two of the previous four such meetings have ended in disarray, with the participants unable to reach consensus upon any type of joint concluding statement. The primary reason for this anomie has been the ongoing dispute about CTBT, with some NNWS asserting that a test ban treaty is an essential component for satisfaction of article VI, and with the United States insisting otherwise. SCHRAG, *supra* note 24, at 127-31; Howlett & Simpson, *supra* note 71, at 6.

73. SCHRAG, *supra* note 24, at 83, 187-88; *Breaking Pledge, supra* note 38, at 24.

commitments to pursue additional measures of arms control—and others could easily be added to the list of illustrations[74]—are more than hortatory. Even if imprecisely articulated or cast in rather general, long-term vocabulary, they are part of binding international law, and ought to be taken seriously. No one could prove that the mandate for follow-on negotiations *caused* the subsequent treaties identified above—in each instance, multiple factors were at play in eliciting that progress. But international lawyers should not overlook those treaty provisions, either—we should highlight them, underscore their importance, and stress that they are binding obligations that a law-abiding society ought to respect.

The BWC promise to conclude a chemical weapons accord should have been honored far sooner—the world should not have had to wait twenty years for the next meaningful step. The LTBT and TTBT obligations to work toward a CTBT should not be dismissed as merely aspirational—they have the force of law. The NPT article VI language also has some teeth: a requirement to negotiate "in good faith" may be vague, but it is not meaningless. Where a country simply changes its mind about the feasiblity or wisdom of a treaty commitment—even if a major power such as the United States reverses itself on strategic doctrine—the treaty obligation still stands, and should not be blithely evaded.

Thus the United States has, through these various arms control agreements, voluntarily assumed a set of binding obligations under international law to pursue further measures of weapons regulation. Perhaps, in some instances, these undertakings were accepted casually or cavalierly, not quite comprehending the eventual import of the clauses. Perhaps the treaty drafters could have exercised greater precision and clarity, implanting precise timetables and specifying the contents of the future accords. Perhaps the strategic situation has changed in key ways, and new military and foreign policy approaches should now be adopted in the new milieu. But the fundamental international law principle of *pacta sunt servanda* remains, and the United States and others have accumulated a record of, at best, partial and tardy compliance with these commitments. Doing more than this is now required not merely by considerations of policy and strategy, but by law.

Taking law seriously means, first of all, taking treaty obligations seriously. Treaties are the "coin of the realm" in international

---

74. Other arms control treaties, too, have mandated or otherwise elicited follow-on negotiations. *See, e.g.,* Treaty on the Prohibition of the Emplacement of Nuclear Weapons and Other Weapons of Mass Destruction on the Seabed and the Ocean Floor and in the Subsoil Thereof, Feb. 11, 1971, art V, 23 U.S.T. 701; Treaty on Conventional Armed Forces in Europe, Nov. 19, 1990, art. XVIII, 30 I.L.M. 1 [hereinafter CFE Treaty].

affairs, and the international community must sustain them and execute them in good faith, even if that might occasionally prove disadvantageous in the short term. The United States, in particular, has the biggest stake in the sound maintenance of treaty law: as the most frequent instigator and participant in major treaty negotiations across a broad range of issues, the United States has the most to lose if this form of international communication and commitment is debased. More than most other countries, the United States benefits when the community underscores its commitment to international agreements; violating a treaty, discrediting it as vague or precatory, or seeking to evade its impact through exploitation of alleged loopholes would be foolishly shortsighted for our non-proliferation concerns and for a wide range of other issues.

III. TAKING CUSTOMARY INTERNATIONAL LAW SERIOUSLY

The second major source of international law is custom, focusing upon repeated, notorious state behavior, driven by a sense of obligation and accepted as legitimate by other participants in the community of nations.[75] Although the centuries-old tradition of primary reliance upon custom has been somewhat eclipsed in the modern era by the rise of treaties,[76] custom retains its vitality as a source of law, and may even be primed for something of a resurgence.[77]

Regarding chemical weapons, for example, customary international law still could be a major lawmaking process. The 1925 Geneva Protocol[78] expressed certain prohibitions upon the use of chemical weapons in warfare,[79] but various limitations in that

---

75. RESTATEMENT (THIRD) OF THE FOREIGN RELATIONS LAW OF THE UNITED STATES § 102(2) and cmt. b (1986) [hereinafter RESTATEMENT].

76. The existence, content, and binding character of a norm of customary international law may be difficult to establish. Treaties, in contrast, usually offer clearer, more accessible evidence, and have often been used to codify or develop the customary standards. *Id.* § 102(3) and cmt. i.

77. Controversy has arisen regarding the application of customary international law in domestic disputes by courts of the United States. *See* Philip Trimble, *A Revisionist View of Customary International Law*, 33 UCLA L. REV. 665 (1986). There is, however, little question regarding the continuing binding effect of custom as a matter of international law. *See* RESTATEMENT, *supra* note 75, §111.

78. Geneva Protocol, *supra* note 21.

79. *Id.* first declaration. The Geneva Protocol outlawed only the use of chemical weapons in international combat, and did not proscribe the development, production, or deployment of chemical munitions.

374   *TRANSNATIONAL LAW & CONTEMPORARY PROBLEMS*   [Vol. 2: 357

instrument[80] (including many parties' entry of relatively restrictive reservations)[81] confine its direct impact. Customary international law, in contrast, can provide a more comprehensive, global proscription. A careful analysis of the pattern of state practice (including reactions to the occasional departures from that pattern) helps substantiate the view that first use of lethal chemical agents in international combat is already *per se* illegal under customary international law.[82] If states and other actors in the international scene would pay greater attention to evolving custom, they would realize that the network of law impinging upon chemical warfare is greater than merely the content of treaties.[83] Even a completed Chemical Weapons Convention will be directly binding only upon those states that voluntarily adopt it and become parties to it, but the overarching customary international law proscription against CW may simultaneously obligate the entire community of nations, affecting even the most recalcitrant treaty holdouts.[84]

In the same vein, there is a significant argument that longstanding customary international law also has something to say

---

80. By its terms, the Geneva Protocol applied only to uses of chemical weapons against other parties to the treaty. There was a sustained controversy about the treaty's coverage of non-lethal chemical agents such as riot-control substances and herbicides. ACDA TREATY BOOK, *supra* note 17, at 10-14.

81. Many parties to the Geneva Protocol formally reserved the right to retaliate against an enemy's use of chemical weapons, effectively converting the Geneva Protocol into a no-first-use pledge. ACDA TREATY BOOK, *supra* note 17, at 10.

82. *See* David Koplow, *Long Arms and Chemical Arms: Extraterritoriality and the Draft Chemical Weapons Convention*, 15 YALE J. INT'L L. 1, 19-20 (1990); Elizabeth A. Smith, *International Regulation of Chemical and Biological Weapons: "Yellow Rain" and Arms Control*, 1984 U. ILL. L. REV. 1011, 1048.

83. It could also be argued that the first use of lethal chemical weapons in international combat (or other particularly egregious weapons applications) would be a violation of *jus cogens*, a peremptory norm of international law from which no derogation is permitted. Such a norm supersedes even contrary principles of custom or treaty, and is recognized as a valid source of international law. However, the notion of *jus cogens* has proven ephemeral in practice, a claim asserting *jus cogens* is difficult to substantiate, and no cases have been decided upon that basis. RESTATEMENT, *supra* note 75, §102, cmt. k and reporters' note 6.

84. A state that consistently expresses its opposition to an emerging norm of customary international law may be exempt from its application. By overtly withholding its consent from the initiation of a putative rule of customary law, the objecting state may permanently escape coverage of the rule. RESTATEMENT, *supra* note 75, at § 102, cmt. d. However, no state has consistently objected to the customary prohibitions against chemical warfare, so none would be exempt from the international rules.

about the legality of nuclear weapons.[85] Traditional norms of the international law of war—such as recognition of the distinctions between civilians and soldiers, or between belligerent states and neutrals[86]—require a degree of finesse and precision in the application of force in hostilities, and it is plausible to assert that nuclear weapons inherently ignore these subtleties. Similarly, the well-accepted notion of "proportionality" as a criterion for the legality of force[87] (in the exercise of legitimate self-defense, a state may do "nothing unreasonable or excessive")[88] may automatically exclude weapons of such massive destruction in many circumstances.

This is not the place to rehearse the arguments about the legality *vel non* of nuclear weapons, or to attempt to fashion more refined contentions differentiating "first strike weapons" from others that might be said to play a lawful role in deterrence or defense. But it is a suitable occasion to assert that law should be relevant to these types of discussions. In determining whether to deploy the MX "Peacekeeper" missile, for example, the United States should have considered more fully the possible restraint that customary international law might impose. In determining whether to recognize former Soviet republics that have not yet rid themselves of offensive nuclear weapons, the world should weigh more heavily the impact of binding custom in arms control. In determining how to react to covert attempts to supply chemical weapons-related equipment, materials or technology to Libya or other "rogue" states, the community of nations should focus more on the relevant legal dimensions, not solely on the politics or the economics of the transactions.

Customary international law could become an even more substantial force in disarmament proceedings in the future for three reasons. First, we are in an era where at least some disarmament proposals have progressed with breakneck speed, outstripping the negotiators' abilities to craft suitable written treaties. Consequently,

---

85. *See* FRANCIS A. BOYLE ET AL., IN RE: MORE THAN 50,000 NUCLEAR WEAPONS: ANALYSES OF THE ILLEGALITY OF NUCLEAR WEAPONS UNDER INTERNATIONAL LAW *passim* (1991).

86. STATEMENT ON THE ILLEGALITY OF NUCLEAR WARFARE (C. David Birman ed., 1990) (modern rules of warfare outlaw weapons or tactics that do not discriminate between combatants and noncombatants, and between belligerent and neutral countries).

87. *Destruction of the "Caroline,"* 2 MOORE, A DIGEST OF INTERNATIONAL LAW 409-414 (1906), *reprinted in* BARRY E. CARTER & PHILIP R. TRIMBLE, INTERNATIONAL LAW 1221-23 (1991).

88. Letter from Secretary of State Daniel Webster, regarding the destruction of the "Caroline," CARTER & TRIMBLE, *supra* note 87, at 1223.

we see much greater reliance upon the exchange of "parallel unilateral statements of intention" and "politically binding commitments," through which the parties align their respective behaviors even before they are able to reduce their mutual understanding to satisfactory legal text.[89] In this environment, state practice, and the words that accompany the nuanced behavior, are of growing salience and importance. At least as a temporary measure, state behavior—the genesis of customary international law—may play an increasingly vital role in international affairs. As patterns of disarmament practice endure and spread, they "harden" over time, generating expectations, reliance, and a sense of legitimacy that eventually accretes into law.[90]

Second, the modern era has witnessed a stunningly rapid creation of new states, as former communist empires in the Soviet Union and Yugoslavia undergo a long-delayed fission reaction. Pursuant to standard understandings, a newly emerging state generally must take the existing content of customary international law as given; even if it dislikes some of the rules, and even if it had no opportunity to participate independently in the process of creating those proscriptions, it is too late to dissent and effectively "opt out."[91] Therefore, while these new participants on the world scene do have some high degree of autonomy and flexibility in determining which *treaties* to accept and which to avoid,[92] they cannot easily reject the content and coverage of contemporary customary international law. The more that important arms limitation understandings are poured into the framework of international law adopted as custom,

---

89. For example, in October 1991 and January 1992, Presidents Bush, Gorbachev, and Yeltsin issued dramatic statements containing not only proposals for negotiations toward future deep cuts in nuclear weaponry but also immediate, unilateral reductions that might prompt reciprocal restraint even before any treaty was concluded. R. Jeffrey Smith, *Bush, Yeltsin Add Momentum To Cuts in Atomic Stockpiles*, WASH. POST, Jan. 30, 1992, at A18; Serge Schmemann, *Gorbachev Matches U.S. on Nuclear Cuts and Goes Further on Strategic Warheads*, N.Y. TIMES, Oct. 6, 1991, at 1.

90. For example, the Conference on Confidence- and Security-Building Measures and Disarmament in Europe developed in the "Stockholm Document," a package of measures (advance notification of military maneuvers, invitation of foreign observers, etc.) designed to reduce fears about a surprise attack. ACDA TREATY BOOK, *supra* note 17, at 319-22. Initially, these measures were only "politically binding," but their success, and the vigor with which the participants exercised them, contributed to the subsequent efforts to elaborate similar confidence-building provisions in the CFE Treaty and the Open Skies Treaty. CFE Treaty, *supra* note 74; Open Skies Treaty, *supra* note 17.

91. RESTATEMENT, *supra* note 75, §102, reporters' note 2.

92. John B. Rhinelander & George B. Bunn, *Who's Bound by the Former Soviet Union's Arms Control Treaties?*, 21 ARMS CONTROL TODAY 3 (1991).

the more completely the legal network will automatically embrace these new, inexperienced entries.[93]

Third, there is in modern state practice something of a trend toward regionalism, as particular corners of the globe are indentified as having unique problems and special opportunities. Proposals abound for creating a local "weapons free zone" or a "zone of peace" of various sorts,[94] and some successes have already been achieved.[95] Regional custom may be easier to contemplate, too, as like-minded states, sharing a common location, history, and appreciation of the security situation, can align their behaviors more readily.[96] True global consensus is often elusive, but collaboration among a smaller group may provide a more feasible opportunity for law to advance. For example, future efforts, sustained by custom, may be able to preclude the introduction of selected types of advanced weapons into a particular region, even in the absence of the specificity, mutuality, and verifiability required to craft a treaty.[97]

The point is not that customary international law can solve all the problems of weapons proliferation, but that it can play a role, and that it could play an even greater role if the people involved would simply notice the muse of jurisprudence, recognize the extent to which it promotes the values of stability and peace, and embrace it with greater regularity and fortitude. Even without treaties, customary behavior can have an impact in confining and moderating states—it has done so in the past, and it may prove even more powerful in the future. Each of the world's current troublespots presents its own thicket of dificulties, so it may prove

---

93. *See* Julie Dahlitz, *The Role of Customary Law in Arms Limitation*, *in* THE INTERNATIONAL LAW OF ARMS CONTROL AND DISARMAMENT 157-78 (Julie Dahlitz & Detlev Dicke eds., 1991).

94. *See, e.g.*, Félix Calderon, *Security and Arms Limitation in Latin America and the Caribbean*, *infra* this volume; *see also* entries for proposals such as Nordic Nuclear-Weapon-Free Zone, Mediterranean Zone of Peace, and Indian Ocean as a Zone of Peace, 11 ARMS CONTROL REP. 100.1 (1990).

95. *See* Antarctic Treaty, Dec. 1, 1959, 12 U.S.T. 794 (demilitarizing Antarctica); Treaty for the Prohibition of Nuclear Weapons in Latin America, Feb. 14, 1967, 634 U.N.T.S. 281 [hereinafter Treaty of Tlatelolco] (creating a nuclear-weapons-free zone for Latin America).

96. *See* RESTATEMENT, *supra* note 75, §102, cmt. e (describing the evolution of regional or special customary international law).

97. See R. Jeffrey Smith, *State Department Meeting on Mideast Arms Control Opens Without Rancor*, WASH. POST, May 12, 1992, at A12 (efforts to develop at least a partial solution to a regional arms race, even while no comprehensive settlement is yet in sight); Knut Ipsen, *Explicit Methods of Arms Control Treaty Evolution*, *in* THE INTERNATIONAL LAW OF ARMS CONTROL AND DISARMAMENT 75-93 (Julie Dahlitz & Detlev Dicke eds., 1991) (noting regional approaches to arms control).

futile to attempt to resolve all of them through some grand, generally-applicable strategy; but an *ad hoc* approach, treating each case as unique and relying upon step-by-step lawmaking through the accretion of state practice, may offer more promise.

IV. TAKING DISARMAMENT INSTITUTIONS SERIOUSLY

One of the most dramatic changes in modern arms control agreements has been the extent to which they have spawned new, permanent, specialized institutions[98] designed to implement the treaties, consider improvements to them, and resolve disputes arising under them—the creation of a sort of "peace-industrial complex."

The 1972 SALT I negotiations were the progenitor of this tradition, as the ABM Treaty called for the creation of a Standing Consultative Commission (SCC) through which the parties could regularly communicate in their effort to sustain and improve the treaty regime.[99]   When the Reagan administration, which had roundly criticized the SCC as ineffective, concluded the 1987 INF Treaty, it recognized that a similar institution would be valuable, but felt constrained not to cede greater authority to the disfavored SCC. So the INF Treaty instead created a clone, the Special Verification Commission, with a substantially similar mandate.[100]

Other arms control agreements have also regularly established their own standing bodies,[101] almost as a matter of course in the search for permanence and prestige:

---

98. Arms control and other treaties have long called for periodic review conferences, ongoing consultations, and other episodic meetings of the parties. *See, e.g.,* Convention on the Prohibition of Military or Any Other Hostile Use of Environmental Modification Techniques, May 18, 1977, 31 U.S.T. 333, 16 I.L.M. 88, art. V; Antarctic Treaty, *supra* note 95, art. IX.

99. ABM Treaty, *supra* note 20, art. XIII.

100. Treaty on the Elimination of Their Intermediate-Range and Shorter-Range Missiles, Dec. 8, 1987, U.S.-U.S.S.R., 27 I.L.M. 90, art. XIII.

101. The Conference on Disarmament, a Geneva-based affiliate of the United Nations, has become the primary multilateral body for negotiating new arms control agreements. It and its predecessor organizations assisted in the elaboration of many of the treaty texts noted in this Article. In contrast, the implementation bodies considered in this section are those that have been established by the various treaties to operate and improve the applicable regime.

- 1976 Peaceful Nuclear Explosions Treaty: Joint Consultative Commission;[102]
- 1990 TTBT Protocol: Bilateral Consultative Commission;[103]
- 1990 Conventional Forces in Europe Treaty: Joint Consultative Group;[104]
- 1991 START Treaty: Joint Compliance and Inspection Commission;[105]
- 1992 Open Skies Treaty: Open Skies Consultative Commission;[106] and
- Forthcoming Chemical Weapons Convention: Organization for the Prohibition of Chemical Weapons.[107]

These organizations fulfill a variety of crucial roles. They serve as the primary mechanism for exchanging information between the parties, including notifications of routine weapons actions (dismantlings, etc.) required by the treaty. They oversee the on-site inspection process and the destruction of excess weapons and facilities. They perform the "risk reduction" and "crisis management" functions in various ways. They consider compliance questions, exchanging inquiries and responses. They resolve disputes—not in the sense of some independent, neutral adjudicator, but more as a forum for ongoing negotiations and deliberations.[108] They serve as the venue through which parties may undertake periodic reviews as required by the treaty. They negotiate follow-on accords or implementing arrangements needed to flesh out the day-to-day mechanics of the treaty.

The Board of Governors of the International Atomic Energy Agency (IAEA), operating as an institutional arm of the NPT,

---

102. PNET, *supra* note 33, art. V.

103. 1990 TTBT Protocol, *supra* note 35, § XI.

104. CFE Treaty, *supra* note 74, art. XVI.

105. START Treaty, *supra* note 22, art. XV and Protocol on the Joint Compliance and Inspection Commission.

106. Open Skies Treaty, *supra* note 17, art. X and Annex L.

107. *Report of the Ad Hoc Committee on Chemical Weapons to the Conference on Disarmament*, CD/1108, August 27, 1991, app. I, art. VIII (current "rolling text" of draft chemical weapons convention now being finalized).

108. *Cf.* Phillip R. Trimble, *Beyond Verification: The Next Step in Arms Control*, 102 HARV. L. REV. 885, 897 (1989) (proposing the establishment of a neutral, independent international dispute resolution mechanism for arbitrating arms control controversies).

deserves special consideration here. Although its verification procedures are not above reproach,[109] the IAEA may yet be the prototype of a true international institution, promulgating rules that are accepted as obligatory *per se*. In disseminating instructions to member states regarding reporting and inspection procedures, the IAEA has begun to assume a power to interpret treaties and issue implementing directives, any violation of which would be akin to a violation of the treaty itself.[110] An "international administrative law," replete with some form of notice-and-comment rulemaking procedures, may yet arise from such humble beginnings.

In all of this, the various implementing institutions create and apply international law, and they do so in a wholly constructive and meaningful fashion. They serve as the bricks and mortar of the international law of arms control, and they help nudge the community toward greater reliance upon peaceful, negotiated settlement of problems that too often in the past exploded into something hostile. Again, greater adherence to these organizations, devoting still more care to their use and devolving greater authority upon them, would have a salutory effect upon the international system. These institutions have often been overlooked in the clutter of international traffic—in their quest for businesslike privacy conducive to getting the job done, they have slipped largely below public consciousness, and the world has not fully appreciated their contributions.

To date, the arms control negotiating states have been hesitant about generating truly powerful global security organizations. Despite recurrent plausible proposals, there is no public international verification institute, equipped with its own state-of-the-art satellites; there is no generic international inspection agency, capable of mounting immediate on-site visits across a spectrum of arms issues; and there is no standing global police force, adjudicatory body, or criminal court that could readily redress violations of the international law of arms control.

None of the existing arms control organizations come close to possessing that degree of authority or perspective—none could accomplish much on its own. All of the current generation of institutions are but creatures of their respective national

---

109. The IAEA's safeguards regime has steadily improved over the years, but questions remain regarding the system's capacity for timely detection of attempts to divert nuclear materials from civilian to weapons applications. LAWRENCE SCHEINMAN, THE INTERNATIONAL ATOMIC ENERGY AGENCY AND WORLD NUCLEAR ORDER 225-41 (1987).

110. *See* Jon Wolfsthal, *IAEA to Implement "Suspect Site"'"Inspection Powers*, 22 ARMS CONTROL TODAY 27 (1992).

governments, responsive to diverse political currents and national control. But they do at least start the process of institutionalizing arms control, making it a somewhat more predictable, routine part of international law, less dependent upon episodic "spectactular events" and less vulnerable to sudden perturbations.

V. CONCLUSION

Another common security misperception, comparable to the mistake noted at the outset of this essay, is that the United States is, in 1992, well positioned to assert a new kind of unilateral, self-interested military, economic, and social leadership in the world. As the sole remaining military superpower, America could perhaps "throw its weight around," insisting upon reconfiguring international affairs in a manner more conducive to pursuit of our immediate commercial and other interests.[111] No other country would be able to out-muscle the United States, so a partial return to a Hobbesian state of international nature might seem to work to the advantage of the strongest, most determined player.[112]

This perspective, however, is fundamentally misguided. In fact, the true comparative advantage for the United States, the area in which we are most able to "play to our strengths," is precisely the opposite. Even though the United States is now the planet's dominant military power, our physical safety is far from guaranteed, and we remain susceptible to a host of nuclear, chemical, biological, and other attacks against which there is no adequate defense. In the modern era of proliferating weapons of mass destruction, all states share a common, inescapable vulnerability, and traditional notions of rational deterrence become less compelling.[113]

---

111. *See* Patrick E. Tyler, *U.S. Strategy Plan Calls for Insuring No Rivals Develop*, N.Y. TIMES, Mar. 7, 1992, at 1 (new Department of Defense policy statement advocates measures to promote a world dominated by United States as sole military superpower).

112. Ironically, the converse of this premise supports intensified interest in multilateral disarmament, too. That is, one might start with the proposition that domestic political and economic constraints will prevent the United States from pursuing global military hegemony in the years ahead. In that situation, it would be clearly advantageous to keep other states under controls, too, so that unilateral disarmament does not undermine American security. *See* James Chace, *The Pentagon's Superpower Fantasy*, N.Y. TIMES, Mar. 16, 1992, at A17.

113. *See* Burns H. Weston, *The Logic and Utility of a Lawful United States Foreign Policy*, 1 TRANSNAT'L L. & CONTEMP. PROBS. 1 (1991) (articulating the rationale for

America's real comparative advantage, in fact, lies with invocation of law. We are the foremost maker of, and the foremost beneficiary of, international law. We depend upon treaties, custom, and international institutions more than any other country, and we have the most to lose if these phenomena are undercut. We certainly have more lawyers than any other society, and a greater familiarity with the style and nuance of legal proceedings; if the world would turn to judicial proceedings as the forum of choice for resolution of conflict, it would promote our greatest relative assets. Our economic prosperity, as well as our sheer physical safety, depend more than ever upon the active cooperation of other states; the most effective way to derive a mutually satisfactory, durable, and wise accomodation of interests is for the United States to take the lead in respecting and promoting international law.

Why, then, hasn't this happened? Why does the United States not automatically adhere to international legal constraints with zeal and rigor? Why do leaders persist in cynical, self-defeating behaviors, failing to appreciate the better strategy? It is not simply selfishness—this essay advocates following international law precisely because it is in the selfish United States interest to do so. My argument has proceeded from the basis of pragmatic appraisal of national interests, not international charity.

The difficulty, I suggest, lies in the endemic inability or unwillingness to look at the long term—to build a durable, predictable structure enabling prudent, sustainable growth. It is ignorance, not necessarily malevolence, that diverts us from appreciation of our real interests. Political leaders, geared to the timing of the next election cycle, calculate benefits for the short term only, eschewing attention to true, enduring national values. Just as society is only now beginning to appreciate the dynamics of global environmentalism, similar principles ought to apply in the international law of disarmament: crude, one-sided exploitation cannot persist forever. In the long term we need to sustain our international relations with dignity and husband our collective resources with intelligence.

Sometimes, this strategy of taking law seriously will appear to work to the short-run disadvantage of the United States, in foregoing a material benefit that could be seized or retained through the threat or use of brute force. There are many excesses that the United States probably could "get away with," at least in the immediate term,

---

consistent United States adherence to international law); Thomas M. Franck, *Taking Treaties Seriously*, 82 AM. J. INT'L L. 67 (1988) (arguing for adherence to treaties as promoting national interests).

because no one, these days, is able to enforce many unwanted actions upon the unwilling behemoth.

But in the long term such a strategy would be as unwise as it is unjust. In the long term, the enlightened United States self interest supports international law, builds it up as a meaningful factor in global interaction, and submits willingly to it as a model for other states to imitate. This is the more reliable mechanism for pursuing national security in the modern era: working through international law. This is the sound investment strategy: adhering to international law not out of charity, but out of a pragmatic sense of our more durable gains. In seeking to retard the proliferation of weaponry, in disarmament matters more generally, and in other international law topics across the board, the United States—and the other players in the world community—need to learn to take international law truly seriously.

[2]

INTERNATIONAL LAW AND WEAPONS OF MASS DESTRUCTION: END OF THE ARMS CONTROL APPROACH?

DAVID P. FIDLER*

I. INTRODUCTION

The threat posed by weapons of mass destruction (WMD) has become one of the most important, if not the most important, issue on security and foreign policy agendas at the beginning of the twenty-first century. Iraq's alleged pursuit and possession of WMD dominated the international security agenda from President Bush's speech to the United Nations (UN) General Assembly in September 2002,[1] through UN Security Council Resolution 1441 providing Iraq one last opportunity to comply with previous Security Council Resolutions,[2] and culminating in the U.S. and British invasion of Iraq in March 2003. Through the Bush Doctrine,[3] the world's leading political and military power has made WMD a centerpiece of a new strategic doctrine designed to guide the assessment of national security threats and

* Professor of Law and Ira C. Batman Faculty Fellow, Indiana University School of Law–Bloomington. An earlier version of this article was delivered at a conference in London on December 10, 2002, on Weapons of Mass Destruction and International Law sponsored by the British Institute of International and Comparative Law and the Center on Law, Ethics, and National Security at the Duke University School of Law. The author thanks Scott Silliman and Michael Byers of the Duke University School of Law for inviting him to participate in the conference. The author also thanks David Wilford for his assistance in the research that went into the preparation of this article.

1. *See* George W. Bush, Address to the United Nations General Assembly in New York City, 38 WEEKLY COMP. PRES. DOC. 1529, 1530–32 (Sept. 12, 2002), *available at* http://www.whitehouse.gov/news/releases/2002/09/20020912-1.html (last visited Oct. 19, 2003).

2. *See* S.C. Res. 1441, U.N. SCOR, 58th Sess., 4644th mtg. at 3, U.N. Doc. S/Res/1441 (2002).

3. The Bush Doctrine, previously referred to as the "axis of evil," was first enunciated by President Bush during his State of the Union Address in January 2002. *See* George W. Bush, Address Before a Joint Session of Congress on the State of the Union, 38 WEEKLY COMP. PRES. DOC. 133, 135 (Jan. 29, 2002), *available at* http://www.whitehouse.gov/news/releases/2002/01/20020129-11.html (last visited Oct. 3, 2003) ("States like these and their terrorist allies constitute an axis of evil, arming to threaten the peace of the world. . . . I will not wait on events while dangers gather. I will not stand by as peril draws closer and closer.") [hereinafter State of the Union Address].

the application of U.S. power.[4] As illustrated by the Bush Doctrine, the WMD threat includes possession of these weapons by not only states but also terrorist groups, leading to fears about the rise of catastrophic terrorism[5]—fears exacerbated by the historic terrorist attacks against the United States on September 11, 2001. The U.S.-led military action against Iraq represented the application of the Bush Doctrine against the WMD-centered "axis of evil." Significant security concerns about WMD have also developed and grown more alarming with regard to North Korea's nuclear weapons capability[6] and Iran's possible nuclear weapons program.[7]

These recent developments involving the threat posed by WMD reflect a trend in the security area stretching back more than a decade. The end of the Cold War sparked a host of concerns regarding WMD in the hands of rogue states and terrorists, forcing policy makers, scholars, and pundits to assess the seriousness of the WMD threat and construct responses designed to address it.[8] The Bush Doctrine and the war against Iraq are the latest, and the most dramatic, policy moves by the United States to address the perceived WMD peril.

The rise in the prominence of WMD on security and foreign policy agendas in the 1990s and early 2000s raises questions about the role of international law in this area. International law has a long relationship with efforts to control WMD that began as early as the late

---

4. *See* WHITE HOUSE, NATIONAL SECURITY STRATEGY OF THE UNITED STATES 14 (2002) ("We must be prepared to stop rogue states and their terrorist clients before they are able to threaten or use weapons of mass destruction against the United States and our allies and friends.") [hereinafter NATIONAL SECURITY STRATEGY]; *see also* WHITE HOUSE, NATIONAL STRATEGY TO COMBAT WEAPONS OF MASS DESTRUCTION 1 (2002) ("Weapons of mass destruction (WMD)—nuclear, biological, and chemical—in the possession of hostile states and terrorists represent one of the greatest security challenges facing the United States.") [hereinafter WEAPONS OF MASS DESTRUCTION].

5. NATIONAL SECURITY STRATEGY, *supra* note 4, at 6 ("Our immediate focus will be those terrorist organizations of global reach and any terrorist group or state sponsor of terrorism which attempts to gain or use weapons of mass destruction (WMD) or their precursors;"); WHITE HOUSE, NATIONAL STRATEGY FOR COMBATING TERRORISM 9 (2003) ("Weapons of mass destruction pose a direct and serious threat to the United States and the entire international community. The probability of a terrorist organization using a chemical, biological, radiological, or nuclear weapon ... has increased significantly during the past decade.") [hereinafter COMBATING TERRORISM].

6. *See generally* Nuclear Threat Initiative, *North Korea Nuclear Program Overview: History and Status*, *at* http://www.nti.org/db/profiles/dprk/nuc/cap/NKN_OGO.html (last visited Dec. 1, 2003).

7. *See generally* Nuclear Threat Initiative, *Iran Profile*, *at* http://www.nti.org/e_research/profiles/Iran/index.html (last visited Dec. 1, 2003).

8. *See, e.g.*, RICHARD A. FALKENRATH ET AL., AMERICA'S ACHILLES' HEEL: NUCLEAR, BIOLOGICAL, AND CHEMICAL TERRORISM AND COVERT ATTACK (1998).

nineteenth century with the development of treaty prohibitions on the use of poisonous gas in warfare.[9] As the International Court of Justice's *Advisory Opinion on the Legality of the Threat or Use of Nuclear Weapons* illustrates,[10] three bodies of international law regulate WMD: arms control treaties, international law on the use of force, and international humanitarian law. Historically, the most prominent and direct use of international law in connection with WMD was through arms control treaties—international agreements designed to prohibit or limit the development, possession, and use of nuclear, chemical, and biological weapons by states.[11] As Table 1 shows, only arms control treaties specifically address the development and use of WMD. Through such treaties, states and international organizations crafted a body of international law dealing directly with the control of WMD.

Table 1.

International Law's Application to the Development and Use of Weapons of Mass Destruction

Area of International Law	Development of WMD	Use of WMD
International law on the use of force	Addresses the threat or use of force, not the development of weapons	Establishes legal justifications for the resort to force, not rules on what weapons states may use
International humanitarian law	Does not directly regulate the development of weapons	Disciplines generally the kinds of weapons that can be used in armed conflict (e.g., no use of weapons that cause superfluous injury or unnecessary suffering)
Arms control treaties	Specifically regulate the development of WMD	Prohibit the use of chemical and biological weapons

---

9. Declaration Concerning the Prohibition of the Use of Projectiles Diffusing Asphyxiating Gases, July 29, 1899, *reprinted in* A MANUAL ON INTERNATIONAL HUMANITARIAN LAW AND ARMS CONTROL AGREEMENTS 99 (M. Cherif Bassiouni ed., 2000) [hereinafter Hague Declaration].

10. Advisory Opinion on the Legality of the Threat or Use of Nuclear Weapons, 1996 I.C.J. 226, 244–47, 247–53, 256–60 (July 8) (analyzing international law on the use of force, relevant arms control treaties, and analyzing humanitarian law).

11. *See, e.g.*, Hague Declaration, *supra* note 9; Protocol for the Prohibition of the Use in War of Asphyxiating, Poisonous or Other Gases, and of Bacteriological Methods of Warfare, June 17, 1925, 26 U.S.T. 571, 94 L.N.T.S. 65 [hereinafter Geneva Protocol].

42   DUKE JOURNAL OF COMPARATIVE & INTERNATIONAL LAW   [Vol 14:39

This body of international law reflects the "arms control approach" to WMD—formal agreements among states to regulate the use and development of WMD. According to Kellman, the arms control approach comprises "measures to cope with a dangerous threat to international security: vertical and horizontal weapons proliferation among national militaries, with concomitant acceleration of both the likelihood that war among nations will erupt and that, if and when war does break out, the consequences will be catastrophic."[12] The arms control approach had origins in international humanitarian law's prohibition of the use of weapons that cause superfluous injury or unnecessary suffering,[13] but the approach created an area of international law distinct from the laws of war because it developed a body of rules that applied prior to the outbreak of armed conflict.

The growth of concerns about WMD proliferation and their possible use by states and non-state actors has put the arms control approach to WMD under intense scrutiny, producing controversy about what arms control treaties on WMD contribute to national security and international peace. Bitter international controversies about the effectiveness of UN WMD inspections in Iraq and the legitimacy of preemptive self-defense against states that possess or pursue WMD suggest that the arms control approach has failed to provide an effective strategy for dealing with the contemporary WMD threat.[14]

The problems confronting the arms control approach to WMD are more extensive than references to controversies about UN inspections and preemptive self-defense indicate. Skepticism and opposition have dogged the arms control approach during its history because many experts expressed doubts about the efficacy of this strategy in controlling threats to security in international politics.[15]

---

12. Barry Kellman, *An International Criminal Law Approach to Bioterrorism*, 25 HARV. J. L. & PUB. POL'Y 721, 724 (2002).

13. The Hague Declaration states that its prohibition of the diffusion of asphyxiating gases was "inspired by the sentiments which found expression in the Declaration of St. Petersburg of . . . 1868." Hague Declaration, *supra* note 9, at 99. Under the St. Petersburg Declaration, states parties renounced the use in war of explosive projectiles weighing less than 400 grams under the principle that the use of "arms which uselessly aggravate the sufferings of disabled men, or render their death inevitable . . . would . . . be contrary to the laws of humanity." Declaration Renouncing the Use, in Time of War, of Explosive Projectiles Under 400 Grammes Weight, Dec. 11, 1868, *reprinted in* A MANUAL ON INTERNATIONAL HUMANITARIAN LAW AND ARMS CONTROL AGREEMENTS, *supra* note 9, at 85, 85–86.

14. For analyses of the international legal implications of the use of force against Iraq, see *Agora: Future Implications of the Iraq Conflict*, 97 AM. J. INT'L L. 553 (2003).

15. *See, e.g.*, MALCOM WALLOP & ANGELO M. CODEVILLA, THE ARMS CONTROL DELUSION (1987). The arms control approach has been criticized on other grounds as well.

This article explores the controversy about the role of arms control treaties on WMD in the new security and foreign policy environment of the early twenty-first century. After presenting an analytical framework for evaluating the threat of WMD, I argue that recent developments demonstrate that we are witnessing the end of the arms control approach to the WMD problem. By the end of the arms control approach, I mean that (1) the traditional reliance on arms control treaties as a response to WMD threats is proving inadequate and (2) policy-makers are increasingly turning away from this traditional approach in crafting responses to the WMD threat.

The end of the arms control approach does not mean the end of arms control, because the relevant treaties remain part of the process of addressing the WMD threat. These treaties no longer represent, however, the dominant policy and legal approach to WMD. At the heart of this argument is the assertion that underlying political, technological, and social realities have changed so significantly that the traditional arms control approach to WMD no longer holds center stage politically or legally.

II. THE THREAT FROM WEAPONS OF MASS DESTRUCTION: AN ANALYTICAL FRAMEWORK

A. The Analytical Framework: Interdependent WMD Risk Factors

The increased attention WMD have received in the 1990s and early 2000s in policy circles prompts the question why WMD have become significant security and foreign policy concerns. Answering this question requires understanding WMD risk factors and how perceptions about these risk factors have changed in recent years. Constructing an analytical framework for assessing the gravity of the WMD threat is difficult for many reasons, including the tendency to

---

See, e.g., Richard A. Falk, *Nuclear Weapons, International Law and the World Court: A Historic Encounter,* 91 AM. J. INT'L L. 64, 65 (1997) (criticizing reliance on the arms control approach in the context of nuclear weapons as leading "to a repudiation of general and complete disarmament as a policy goal, and an unwillingness to submit or consider nuclear disarmament proposals as a basis for international negotiations"). Other experts have argued that the arms control approach is not appropriate for certain kinds of new weapons technologies. *See, e.g.,* Kellman, *supra* note 12, at 729 (arguing that the problem of bioterrorism "does not lend itself to an arms control approach"); Greg Rattray, *The Emerging Global Information Infrastructure and National Security,* FLETCHER F. WORLD AFF., Summer/Fall 1997, at 81, 90 (1997) (arguing that the arms control approaches developed during the Cold War "will not work in controlling the tools necessary for strategic information attacks").

44   DUKE JOURNAL OF COMPARATIVE & INTERNATIONAL LAW   [Vol 14:39

lump together nuclear, chemical, and biological weapons—distinct technologies that pose dramatically different kinds of policy challenges—under the single moniker "weapons of mass destruction." Even with limitations, however, an analytical framework provides insight into the nature of the threat and the various policy responses attempted or proposed.

The nature of the WMD threat reflects the interdependence of three basic risk factors: (1) political and military motivations of actors for developing or using WMD; (2) the technological feasibility of developing or using WMD; and (3) the vulnerabilities WMD development or use creates for societies. The following paragraphs further elaborate on each of these risk factors and their interdependence. Figure 1 below summarizes this interplay.

The WMD Threat:
An Analytical Framework

1.   *Political and Military Motivations.* Understanding the WMD threat involves comprehending why actors may or may not see WMD as politically or militarily useful. During the Cold War, the great powers believed that nuclear weapons had great political and military utility.[16] The two superpowers, the United States and the Soviet Un-

---

16. *See generally* Lawrence Freedman, *The First Two Generations of Nuclear Strategists, in* MAKERS OF MODERN STRATEGY: FROM MACHIAVELLI TO THE NUCLEAR AGE 735 (Peter Pa-

ion, diverged, however, in the early 1970s on the military utility of biological weapons because the United States terminated its offensive program while the Soviets accelerated theirs.[17] These two examples demonstrate why the political and military motivations of actors in international relations are critical to gauging the WMD threat.

The analytical framework presented in this article incorporates both state and non-state actors when considering political/military motivations for developing or using WMD. As illustrated by Bush administration policy, fears about WMD today involve both states and terrorist groups.[18] The analytical framework is not, therefore, state-centric because it applies to motivations that terrorist groups might have in developing or using WMD. The United States' *National Strategy for Combating Terrorism* argues that "[m]otivated by extreme, even apocalyptic ideologies, some terrorists' ambitions to inflict mayhem seem unlimited."[19] It further cites Osama bin Laden's proclamation that "acquisition of WMD [was] a 'religious duty.'"[20] One of the significant shifts, discussed later in the article, that contributes to the weakening of the arms control approach is, in fact, the perceived rise in the possibility of "catastrophic terrorism"—terrorism involving WMD.[21]

Political and military perspectives on the utility of any weapon are, of course, influenced by many factors—the structure and dynamics of the international political system, domestic regime types, psychology of individual leaders, state of weapons technologies, and rules of international law. Particularly important to this article's analysis are the changes witnessed in the structure of the international system as it moved from the Cold War to the post–Cold War period.[22]

---

ret et al. eds., 1986) (noting that since 1945 "tens of thousands [of nuclear weapons] have been accumulated by the major powers and their destructiveness and sophistication increased immensely").

17. *See* George W. Christopher et al., *Biological Warfare: A Historical Perspective*, 278 JAMA 412, 415–16 (1997).

18. *See* WEAPONS OF MASS DESTRUCTION, *supra* note 4, at 1 ("We will not permit the world's most dangerous regimes and terrorists to threaten us with the world's most destructive weapons."); *see also* State of the Union Address, *supra* note 3, at 135 ("By seeking weapons of mass destruction, these regimes pose a grave and growing danger. They could provide these arms to terrorists, giving them the means to match their hatred. They could attack our allies or attempt to blackmail the United States. In any of these cases, the price of indifference would be catastrophic.").

19. COMBATING TERRORISM, *supra* note 5, at 10.

20. *Id.*

21. *See infra* Part III.A.

22. *See infra* Part II.B.

46   DUKE JOURNAL OF COMPARATIVE & INTERNATIONAL LAW   [Vol 14:39

The most important changes for purposes of this article are the collapse of the bipolar, nuclearized international system and the development of a new system marked by both a single hegemonic actor and the rising strategic threat posed by terrorist organizations of global scope.

    2. *Technological Feasibility.* The second important WMD risk factor in the analytical framework is technological feasibility. This risk factor focuses on how technologically difficult WMD are to develop or use. Of the WMD, nuclear weapons are more technologically challenging to develop than chemical or biological weapons.[23] Whether the technological feasibility of a particular WMD is difficult or easy affects the assessment of the threat posed by such WMD.[24] The Bush administration declared in its *National Strategy for Homeland Security* that "[t]he knowledge, technology, and materials needed to build weapons of mass destruction are spreading. These capabilities have never been more accessible and the trends are not in our favor."[25] The U.S. *National Strategy for Combating Terrorism* asserted that "[t]he availability of critical technologies, the willingness of some scientists and others to cooperate with terrorists, and the ease of intercontinental transportation enable terrorist organizations to more easily acquire, manufacture, deploy, and initiate a WMD attack either on U.S. soil or abroad."[26] The perception that WMD development is now technologically feasible for states as well as terrorist groups contributes significantly to security and foreign policy concerns about WMD. For example, the fear that terrorist groups may

---

    23. *See* ADVISORY PANEL TO ASSESS DOMESTIC RESPONSE CAPABILITIES FOR TERRORISM INVOLVING WEAPONS OF MASS DESTRUCTION, RAND CORPORATION, FIRST ANNUAL REPORT TO THE PRESIDENT AND THE CONGRESS: I. ASSESSING THE THREAT 21 (1999), http://www.rand.org/nsrd/terrpanel/terror.pdf (last visited Nov. 11, 2003) [hereinafter ASSESSING THE THREAT] (arguing that "[d]eveloping a nuclear weapon requires even greater skills, financial resources, and infrastructure" than chemical or biological weapons).

    24. For example, in assessing the plausibility of nuclear terrorism, Jenkins argued that "the notion that some group outside of government programs can design and build a crude nuclear bomb is certainly more plausible now than it was 30 or 40 years ago. At that time, the secrets of nuclear fission were closely guarded. However, much of the requisite technical knowledge has since gradually come into the public domain." Brian M. Jenkins, *Is Nuclear Terrorism Plausible?, in* NUCLEAR TERRORISM: DEFINING THE THREAT 25, 27 (Paul Leventhal & Yonah Alexander eds., 1986).

    25. WHITE HOUSE, NATIONAL STRATEGY FOR HOMELAND SECURITY 9 (2002) [hereinafter HOMELAND SECURITY].

    26. COMBATING TERRORISM, *supra* note 5, at 9–10.

develop and use WMD capabilities significantly affects U.S. policy on national security,[27] WMD,[28] and homeland security.[29]

3. *Social Vulnerability.* The third important WMD risk factor in the analytical framework is the level of vulnerability societies face when confronted with potential or actual WMD use. Countries that are highly vulnerable to WMD attack will factor such vulnerability into their perceptions of the seriousness of the WMD threat. The attention paid to U.S. vulnerability to terrorist WMD attacks in the development of homeland security policy illustrates the importance of social vulnerability as a WMD risk factor.[30] Conversely, countries not highly vulnerable are unlikely to weigh WMD threats as seriously. Social vulnerability to WMD use is itself a multi-factored category. Key factors include the status of a country in international politics (e.g., great power versus least developed country) and the nature of its government and society (e.g., open versus closed societies). Its "lone superpower" position and its open, affluent society combine to heighten perceptions about the vulnerability of the United States to WMD attack.[31]

4. *Interdependence Among the Risk Factors.* The analytical framework stresses the interdependence among the three risk factors. None of the risk factors by itself adequately conveys the scope of the WMD threat. The technological feasibility of a weapon influences an actor's perception of that weapon's political or military utility. Similarly, strong political motivations to develop a weapon may stimulate efforts to overcome technological development challenges the weapon presents. The technological ease with which a chemical or biological weapon may be developed and deployed affects how a

27. *See* NATIONAL SECURITY STRATEGY, *supra* note 4, at 6 (noting that "[o]ur immediate focus will be those terrorist organizations of global reach and any terrorist . . . which attempts to gain or use weapons of mass destruction (WMD) or their precursors").

28. *See* WEAPONS OF MASS DESTRUCTION, *supra* note 4, at 1 (observing that "terrorist groups are seeking to acquire WMD with the stated purpose of killing large numbers of our people and those of friends and allies").

29. HOMELAND SECURITY, *supra* note 25, at 2 (noting that, in connection with homeland security's objective of defending against terrorism, the United States places special emphasis on "preventing, protecting against, and preparing for catastrophic threats," the greatest risks of which come from, among others, WMD).

30. *See id.* at 9 (analyzing U.S. vulnerability to WMD terrorism).

31. See *id.* at 7–10 for discussion of U.S. vulnerability to terrorist attack, including attacks using WMD.

country views its social vulnerability to the use of such weapon.[32] High social vulnerability to the use of such weapon and high social vulnerability of an enemy country may stimulate political and military interest in WMD or accentuate the attractiveness of certain WMD technologies. The interdependence among the risk factors does not, however, mean that each factor is equally important in every situation involving WMD. Rather, the interdependence suggests that each risk factor should be considered in assessing the scope of the threat posed by a specific WMD.

B.   The Analytical Framework Applied

Applying the analytical framework described in Section II.A helps give it more specificity and explanatory power. In this section, I use the analytical framework to assess the development of the arms control approach to WMD during the pre–Cold War period and the Cold War. My main objective is not to provide a comprehensive history of the negotiation and adoption of arms control treaties on WMD prior to the end of the Cold War; rather, I employ the analytical framework to sketch why the arms control approach dominated international law on WMD in these historical periods.

1.   *Pre–Cold War Arms Control on Weapons of Mass Destruction.* As the Introduction indicated, states began applying international law directly to what we now call "weapons of mass destruction" as early as the late nineteenth century. In the Hague Declaration Concerning the Prohibition of the Use of Projectiles Diffusing Asphyxiating Gases of 1899 (Hague Declaration), the contracting parties agreed "to abstain from the use of projectiles the sole object of which is the diffusion of asphyxiating or deleterious gases."[33] A prohibition on Germany's use and possession of chemical weapons appeared in

---

32. *See* ASSESSING THE THREAT, *supra* note 23, at 19 (noting the "comparative ease" with which low-level chemical and biological attacks could be orchestrated). For an analysis of the differences between making nuclear and biological weapons, see Jonathan B. Tucker, *Preventing the Misuse of Pathogens: The Need for Global Biosecurity Standards*, ARMS CONTROL TODAY, June 2003, *at* http://www.armscontrol.org/act/2003_06/tucker_june03.asp (last visited Nov. 10, 2003). Although easier to develop than nuclear weapons, making chemical and biological weapons confronts serious difficulties. As the National Commission on Terrorism argued, "[w]hile lethal chemicals are easy to come by, getting large quantities and weaponizing them is difficult, and only nation states have succeeded in doing so." NATIONAL COMMISSION ON TERRORISM, COUNTERING THE CHANGING THREAT OF INTERNATIONAL TERRORISM 4 (2000), http://w3.access.gpo.gov/nct/ (last visited Nov. 11, 2003).

33. Hague Declaration, *supra* note 9, at 99.

the Treaty of Versailles of 1919,[34] and a prohibition on the use of chemical weapons appeared in the Treaty in Relation to the Use of Submarines and Noxious Gases in Warfare of 1922,[35] which never entered into force.[36] States reaffirmed the Hague Declaration's prohibition on the use of chemical weapons and expanded the prohibition to include bacteriological methods of warfare in the Geneva Protocol for the Prohibition of the Use in War of Asphyxiating, Poisonous or Other Gases, and of Bacteriological Methods of Warfare of 1925 (Geneva Protocol).[37]

Both the Hague Declaration and Geneva Protocol were, however, limited arms control agreements. First, neither instrument regulated the ability of a state to develop and stockpile chemical or biological weapons—the agreements were limited to prohibitions on the use of such weapons.[38] Second, the prohibition on use in both agree-

---

34. Treaty of Peace with Germany (Treaty of Versailles), June 28, 1919, art. 171, 2 Bevans 43, 119 ("The use of asphyxiating, poisonous or other gases and all analogous liquids, materials or devices being prohibited, their manufacture and importation are strictly forbidden in Germany. The same applies to materials specially intended for the manufacture, storage and use of the said products or devices.").

35. Treaty Relating to the Use of Submarines and Noxious Gases in Warfare, Feb. 6, 1922, art. 5, S. EXEC. DOC. NO. 67-2, 1922 FOREIGN REL. (1) 267, *reprinted in* 16 AM. J. INT'L L. 57 (Supp. 1922), *and in* A MANUAL ON INTERNATIONAL HUMANITARIAN LAW AND ARMS CONTROL AGREEMENTS, *supra* note 9, at 149 ("The use in war of asphyxiating, poisonous or other gases, and all analogous liquids, materials or devices, having been justly condemned by the general opinion of the civilized world and a prohibition on such use having been declared in treaties to which a majority of the civilized Powers are parties, [t]he Signatory Powers, to the end that this prohibition shall be universally accepted as part of international law binding alike the conscience and practice of nations, declare their assent to such prohibition, agree to be bound thereby as between themselves and invite all other civilized nations to adhere thereto.").

36. *See* A MANUAL ON INTERNATIONAL HUMANITARIAN LAW AND ARMS CONTROL AGREEMENTS, *supra* note 9, at 149.

37. *See* Geneva Protocol, *supra* note 11, 26 U.S.T. at 575, 94 L.N.T.S. at 69 ("That the High Contracting Parties . . . accept this prohibition [on the use in war of asphyxiating, poisonous or other gases, and of all analogous liquids, materials, and devices], agree to extend this prohibition to the use of bacteriological methods of warfare and agree to be bound as between themselves according to the terms of this declaration.").

38. *See generally* Hague Declaration, *supra* note 9 ("The Contracting Parties agree to abstain from the *use* of projectiles the sole object of which is the diffusion of asphyxiating or deleterious gases.") (emphasis added); Geneva Protocol, *supra* note 11, 26 U.S.T. at 575, 94 L.N.T.S. at 69 ("The High Contracting Parties . . . accept this prohibition [on the *use* in war of asphyxiating, poisonous or other gases and] agree to extend this prohibition to the *use* of bacteriological methods of warfare") (emphasis added). *See also* R.R. Baxter & Thomas Buergenthal, *Legal Aspects of the Geneva Protocol of 1925*, 64 AM. J. INT'L L. 853, 855 (1970) ("[The Geneva Protocol] does not prohibit the production, acquisition, or stockpiling of [chemical and biological] weapons . . . . This means, among other things, that the testing of these weapons is not proscribed by the Geneva Protocol; the same is true of the manufacture of equipment capable of dispersing them.").

ments was not absolute. The Hague Declaration's ban on the use of chemical weapons applied only in the case of war between contracting parties.[39] The ban was not binding if a non-contracting party joined the conflict as a belligerent.[40] Similarly, the Geneva Protocol's ban applied only in armed conflict between states parties.[41] In addition, many states parties made reservations declaring that they would not be bound by the prohibition in the event that another state party violated the ban during armed conflict.[42] The Geneva Protocol contained, in effect, a prohibition on the first-use of chemical and biological weapons.[43]

Despite this, the adoption of these two international agreements on chemical and biological weapons indicates that states during this era were sufficiently concerned about the use of such weapons in armed conflict. The analytical framework described in Section II.A helps explain the dynamic captured in these international legal documents. The prohibitions on use in both the Hague Declaration and the Geneva Protocol signal that political/military motivations and technological feasibility were sufficiently high to warrant concern about the deployment of chemical and biological weapons in armed conflict.

At the time, the technological feasibility of chemical weapons was more pronounced than that of biological weapons—as illustrated by the extensive use of chemical weapons in World War I[44]—and the legal documents reflect that reality. Still, the state parties to the Geneva Protocol were concerned enough about the potential develop-

---

39. Hague Declaration, *supra* note 9 ("The present Declaration is only binding on the Contracting Powers in the case of a war between two or more of them.").

40. *Id.* ("It shall cease to be binding from the time when, in a war between the Contracting Powers, one of the belligerents shall be joined by a non-Contracting Power.").

41. *See* Geneva Protocol, *supra* note 11, 26 U.S.T. at 575, 94 L.N.T.S. at 69 ("[T]he High Contracting Parties . . . agree to bound as between themselves according to the terms of this declaration."). In addition, a number of states parties made reservations providing that the Geneva Protocol was binding on the reserving state only with respect to other states parties. *See* DOCUMENTS ON THE LAWS OF WAR 144–46 (Adam Roberts & Richard Guelff eds., 2d ed. rev. 1989) (listing reservations of states parties to the Geneva Protocol).

42. For example, the reservation of France provides: "The said Protocol shall *ipso facto* cease to be binding on the Government of the French Republic in regard to any enemy State whose armed forces or whose Allies fail to respect the prohibitions laid down in the Protocol." DOCUMENTS ON THE LAWS OF WAR, *supra* note 41, at 145.

43. DOCUMENTS ON THE LAWS OF WAR, *supra* note 41, at 138 (noting that the Geneva Protocol "is regarded . . . as containing not an absolute prohibition on the use of such weapons, but only an agreement not to use such weapons first").

44. HEDLEY BULL, THE CONTROL OF THE ARMS RACE 124 (2d ed. 1965) (describing the use of chemical weapons in World War I).

ment of biological weapons to prohibit their first-use before the technological feasibility of such weapons had been clearly demonstrated.[45] The use of chemical weapons during World War I demonstrated that political and military leaders had sufficient motivations to develop, deploy, and use chemical weapons on a large scale.

Cutting against these motivations was the principle of the laws of war forbidding the use of weapons that caused superfluous injury or unnecessary suffering.[46] This principle connected to the realization that both armed forces and civilian societies were vulnerable to chemical and biological weapon attacks.

The carnage from chemical weapons on the battlefields of World War I demonstrated the military threat posed by these weapons. Additionally, the development of long-range bombardment technologies, such as long-range artillery and air power, rendered civilian populations increasingly vulnerable to the use of chemical and biological weapons as they continued to develop technologically. One of the leading air-power theorists of the interwar period, Guilio Douhet, based his theory of aggressive air warfare on the assumption that "attacks against population and industrial centers would employ three types of bombs—explosive, incendiary, and poison gas . . . ."[47] As Bull noted, "[t]he belief that gas bombs would be a major element in aerial attacks on cities underlay the movement for the prohibition of chemical warfare [during the interwar period]. It had a primacy in popular imagination as an agent of mass destruction and a product of perverted science . . . ."[48]

In the period prior to World War II, all three WMD risk factors were significantly high, which helps explain why states began to use arms control agreements to address the threat posed by chemical and biological weapons. The analytical framework also helps us understand the substantive nature of the international legal rules developed on chemical and biological weapons. As indicated above,[49] the prohi-

---

45. Although the use of disease as a weapon of warfare has a long history, systematic efforts by states to develop biological weapons capabilities only began in the 1930s. *See id.* at 127.

46. *See* M. Cherif Bassiouni, *Evolution of International Humanitarian Law and Arms Control Agreements, in* A MANUAL ON INTERNATIONAL HUMANITARIAN LAW AND ARMS CONTROL AGREEMENTS, *supra* note 9, at 1, 21–31 (discussing the prohibition in international humanitarian law against weapons that cause unnecessary pain and suffering).

47. David MacIsaac, *Voices from the Central Blue: The Air Power Theorists, in* THE MAKERS OF MODERN STRATEGY FROM MACHIAVELLI TO THE NUCLEAR AGE, *supra* note 16, at 624, 630.

48. BULL, *supra* note 44, at 124.

49. *See supra* notes 38–43 and accompanying text.

52   DUKE JOURNAL OF COMPARATIVE & INTERNATIONAL LAW   [Vol 14:39

bitions on use were limited to the first-use of chemical and biological weapons—and the agreements did not address development, possession, stockpiling, transfer, and deployment of such weapons. States could, thus, legally develop, possess, stockpile, transfer, and deploy chemical and biological weapons because the arms control agreements did not limit their rights in those contexts. Such stockpiles of chemical and biological weapons served as a deterrent against any state's desire to use chemical and biological weapons first in armed conflict. Under these rules, an illegal first-use of chemical or biological weapons could be met legally with response in kind.

In terms of the analytical framework, political/military motivations, technological feasibility, and social vulnerability to chemical or biological attack were sufficiently high for states to be unwilling to rely solely on treaties to protect themselves from attack. In essence, the Hague Declaration and the Geneva Protocol lacked "teeth,"[50] which were provided instead by the policy of deterrence. Deterrence proves successful, however, only when states possess an actual capacity to respond in kind—hence the need to leave development, possession, stockpiling, transfer, and deployment unregulated under international law.

Overall, certain characteristics mark the arms control approach found in the Hague Declaration and Geneva Protocol. First, the approach is state-centric because the international legal instruments address only state behavior. These agreements are not concerned with the possible development and use of chemical or biological weapons by non-state actors, such as terrorist groups. Second, the dynamics of the approach reflect a high level of uncertainty and mistrust among states because they embody only a first-use prohibition and rely on deterrence to control use of chemical and biological weapons. These dynamics reflect the importance that states have placed on military power in international politics.

Third, the reliance on deterrence to uphold the prohibition on use contradicted the international legal norm against using weapons that caused superfluous injury or unnecessary suffering. The bans on chemical and biological weapons found in the Hague Declaration and the Geneva Protocol flowed from the acceptance that these weapons caused superfluous injury or unnecessary suffering in violation of the

---

50. Neither the Hague Declaration nor the Geneva Protocol had any provisions for the enforcement of the prohibitions they contained.

laws of war;[51] yet, states parties to these documents specifically reserved the right to use such weapons in response to a prior illegal use
by another state. The deterrence strategy would not be credible if
states parties threatened to use chemical or biological weapons and
were also genuinely committed to complying with the prohibition on
the use of such weapons in the laws of war.

Fourth, the arms control approach in this period contained a hierarchy in which states viewed chemical weapons as a greater threat
than biological weapons, largely because of the more advanced state
of chemical weapons technologies. As noted above, the development
and use of chemical weapons were more advanced than biological
weapons during this period, illustrated by the Hague Declaration's
prohibition of asphyxiating gases in 1899 and the horrors of chemical
warfare during World War I.

2. *Cold War Arms Control and Weapons of Mass Destruction.*
The arms control approach developed in the pre–Cold War period
represents the first, rather limited, attempt to regulate WMD through
international law in the context of the anarchical politics of the international system. Although the subject of international legal control,
the development and use of chemical and biological weapons during
this period were not central to the dynamics of international politics.
During the Cold War period, the arms control approach to WMD expanded significantly and became an integral feature of the structure
and dynamics of international relations. Key to the growth in the importance of WMD arms control was the development of nuclear
weapons, a new technology with far more destructive power than either chemical or biological weapons.

A comprehensive summary of the arms control experience of the
Cold War period is beyond the scope of this article. Instead, I look at
the arms control approach through the tripartite analytical framework
presented above to understand the basic dynamics of WMD control
in this period. The lion's share of international law relating to WMD
developed in this period addressed nuclear weapons. The arms control approach to chemical weapons remained essentially unchanged,

---

51. Hague Declaration, *supra* note 9, at 99 (stating that the signatory powers were inspired
by the sentiments in the Declaration of St. Petersburg of 1868 on limiting the use of weapons
that aggravate the suffering of combatants); Geneva Protocol, *supra* note 11, 26 U.S.T. at 575,
94 L.N.T.S. at 67 (noting the condemnation of the use of asphyxiating, poisonous, or other gases
"by the general opinion of the civilized world"). *See also* BULL, *supra* note 44, at 129 (arguing
that "[t]he view that *chemical* and *biological* weapons are uniquely immoral is deeply en-
trenched in the folklore of international society").

54   DUKE JOURNAL OF COMPARATIVE & INTERNATIONAL LAW   [Vol 14:39

as no new treaties on such weapons were concluded prior to the end of the Cold War. However, the arms control approach to biological weapons underwent an international legal revolution during this period.[52]

Generally speaking, arms control relating to nuclear weapons during the Cold War had two basic objectives: (1) stabilizing nuclear deterrence between the United States and the Soviet Union and (2) limiting the proliferation of nuclear weapons in the international system to prevent such proliferation from causing instability and conflict among states. Many treaties designed to advance these two objectives appeared during the Cold War, vastly increasing the body of international law directly on WMD. Table 2 provides an overview of key Cold War arms control agreements.

Table 2.
Cold War Arms Control Agreements on Nuclear Weapons

Deterrence Stabilization	Limitation on Proliferation
Nuclear Arms Control Treaties between the United States and Soviet Union	Arms Control Treaties on Proliferation of Nuclear Weapons
Treaty Banning Nuclear Weapons Tests in the Atmosphere, in Outer Space and Under Water (1963)[53]	Treaty on Principles Governing the Activities of States in the Exploration of Outer Space, Including the Moon and Other Celestial Bodies (1967)[58]
Treaty between the United States and Soviet Union on the Limitation of Anti-Ballistic Missile Systems (1972)[54]	Treaty for the Prohibition of Nuclear Weapons in Latin America (Treaty of Tlatelolco) (1968)[59]
Treaty between the United States and the Soviet Union on the Limitation of Strategic Offensive Arms (SALT II)(1979)[55]	Treaty on the Non-Proliferation of Nuclear Weapons (1968)[60]

---

52. *See infra* notes 76–82 and accompanying text.

53. Treaty Banning Nuclear Weapons Tests in the Atmosphere, in Outer Space and Under Water, Aug. 5, 1963, U.S.-U.S.S.R., 14 U.S.T. 1313. The United Kingdom is also a party to this treaty.

54. Treaty on the Limitation of Anti–Ballistic Missile Systems, May 26, 1972, U.S.-U.S.S.R., 23 U.S.T. 3435 [hereinafter ABM Treaty].

55. Treaty on the Limitation of Strategic Offensive Arms (SALT II), June 18, 1979, U.S.-U.S.S.R., S. EXEC. DOC. Y, 96-1 (1979), *available at* http://www.state.gov/www/global/

Treaty between the United States and the Soviet Union on Elimination of their Intermediate-Range and Shorter-Range Missiles (1987)[56]	Treaty on the Prohibition of the Emplacement of Nuclear Weapons and Other Weapons of Mass Destruction on the Sea-Bed and the Ocean Floor and in the Subsoil Thereof (1971)[61]
Treaty between the United States and the Soviet Union on the Limitation of Underground Nuclear Weapons Tests (1990)[57]	Agreement Governing the Activities of States on the Moon and Other Celestial Bodies (1979)[62] South Pacific Nuclear-Free Zone Treaty (1985)[63] African Nuclear-Weapon-Free Zone Treaty (Treaty of Pelindaba) (1996)[64]

arms/treaties/salt2-2.html (last visited Dec. 1, 2003); *see also* Annex: Detailed Analysis of SALT II Provisions, 18 I.L.M. 1122. SALT II never actually entered into force through ratification.

56. Treaty between the United States of America and the Union of Soviet Socialist Republics on the Elimination of their Intermediate-Range and Shorter-Range Missiles, Dec. 8, 1987, U.S.-U.S.S.R., S. TREATY DOC. 100-11 (1987), *reprinted in* 27 I.L.M. 90 (entered into force June 1, 1988).

57. Treaty between the United States and the Union of Soviet Socialist Republics on the Limitation of Underground Nuclear Weapons Tests, July 3, 1974, U.S.-U.S.S.R., S. Exec. Doc. No. 94-2 (1975), *reprinted in* 13 I.L.M. 906 (entered into force Dec. 11, 1990).

58. Treaty on Principles Governing the Activities of States in the Exploration and Use of Outer Space, Including the Moon and Other Celestial Bodies, Jan. 27, 1967, 18 U.S.T. 2410, 610 U.N.T.S. 205.

59. Treaty for the Prohibition of Nuclear Weapons in Latin America, with Annexed Additional Protocols (I and II), Feb. 14, 1967, 22 U.S.T. 762, 634 U.N.T.S. 281 (entered into force Apr. 22, 1968) [hereinafter Treaty of Tlatelolco]; Additional Protocol I to the Treaty of Tlatelolco, Feb. 14, 1967, 22 U.S.T. 786, 634 U.N.T.S. 360 (entered into force Dec. 11, 1969); Additional Protocol II to the Treaty of Tlatelolco, Feb. 14, 1967, 22 U.S.T. 754, 634 U.N.T.S. 364 (entered into force Dec. 11, 1969).

60. Treaty on the Non-Proliferation of Nuclear Weapons, *opened for signature* July 1, 1968, 21 U.S.T. 483, 729 U.N.T.S. 161 (entered into force Mar. 5, 1970) [hereinafter Nuclear Non-Proliferation Treaty].

61. Treaty on the Prohibition of the Emplacement of Nuclear Weapons and Other Weapons of Mass Destruction on the Sea-Bed and the Ocean Floor and in the Subsoil Thereof, Feb. 11, 1971, 23 U.S.T. 701, 955 U.N.T.S. 115 (entered into force May 18, 1972).

62. Agreement Governing the Activities of States on the Moon and Other Celestial Bodies, Dec. 5, 1979, 1363 U.N.T.S. 3, *reprinted in* 18 I.L.M. 1434.

63. South Pacific Nuclear-Free Zone Treaty, *opened for signature* Aug. 6, 1985, 1445 U.N.T.S. 177, 24 I.L.M. 1440 (entered into force Dec. 11, 1986).

64. African Nuclear-Weapon-Free Zone Treaty, *opened for signature* Apr. 11, 1996, 35 I.L.M. 698.

56   DUKE JOURNAL OF COMPARATIVE & INTERNATIONAL LAW   [Vol 14:39

Nuclear deterrence became a central feature of international relations in the Cold War period.[65] The bipolar international system, dominated by two ideologically opposed superpowers, created significant political/military motivations for the United States and the Soviet Union to develop, stockpile, and threaten to use nuclear weapons. Technological developments on nuclear weapons (e.g., multiple independently targeted re-entry vehicles (MIRVs)) reinforced these motivations[66] but also provided incentives for the two countries to try, through arms control treaties, to stabilize the effect of offensive and defensive technological advancements on nuclear deterrence.[67] One such stabilization effort—the Treaty on the Limitation of Anti-Ballistic Missile Systems of 1972 (ABM Treaty)—restricted the development of anti-ballistic missile defenses in order to strengthen nuclear deterrence by increasing each superpower's vulnerability to nuclear attack.[68]

The non-proliferation efforts undertaken through arms control treaties, such as the Nuclear Non-Proliferation Treaty,[69] represented the recognition that more and more countries were acquiring the technological means (e.g., through civilian and military nuclear programs) needed to develop nuclear weapons and that the proliferation of nuclear weapons in the international system would be destabilizing.[70] Experience managing the U.S.-Soviet nuclear threats provided motivation for many states' desire to prevent the spread of such problems throughout the international system. Proliferation would merely exacerbate countries' sense of vulnerability to nuclear blackmail or attack, producing an increasing spiral of proliferation and nuclear stalemates throughout the world. One nuclearized "security dilemma" was seen as sufficient.[71] In addition, nuclear weapons prolif-

---

65. For an overview, see Freedman, *supra* note 16, at 735–78.

66. *See id.* at 774 ("Developments in weapons technology also encouraged the view that more sophisticated nuclear tactics were becoming possible.").

67. *See id.* (arguing that arms control in the 1970s "was bound up with establishing parity between the two superpowers").

68. *See generally* ABM Treaty, *supra* note 54.

69. Nuclear Non-Proliferation Treaty, *supra* note 60.

70. Darryl Howlett, *Nuclear Proliferation, in* THE GLOBALIZATION OF WORLD POLITICS: AN INTRODUCTION TO INTERNATIONAL RELATIONS 415, 431 (John Baylis & Steve Smith eds., 2d ed. 2001) (noting that "[b]etween 1958 and 1968 there was a greater focus on the dangers posed by additional states acquiring nuclear weapons").

71. A debate emerged in the 1980s about whether nuclear proliferation was good or bad. Kenneth Waltz began the debate when he argued in 1981 that more nuclear weapons may be better for international stability and security. *See* KENNETH N. WALTZ, THE SPREAD OF NUCLEAR WEAPONS: MORE MAY BE BETTER (Int'l Institute for Strategic Stud., Adelphi Paper

eration did not serve the national security interests of either of the two superpowers engaged in their titanic bipolar standoff—to the contrary these national security interests were the impetus behind the creation of political and structural restraints on nuclear proliferation.[72]

Although the arms control approach to nuclear weapons did not involve an express first-use prohibition, it mirrored structural and substantive features seen in the arms control approach of the pre–Cold War period. Structurally, the approach in both historical contexts focused on states and their systemic interactions. Like the Hague Declaration and the Geneva Protocol, the nuclear arms control treaties of the Cold War period do not address non-state actors and the potential for nuclear terrorism.[73]

Substantively, the arms control approach in both periods relied on deterrence to prevent the use of WMD. In essence, deterrence is a self-help strategy that depends on the credibility of the threat to use WMD, which itself requires WMD capabilities and stockpiles. In the nuclear weapons context, deterrence was a more complicated strategy, as illustrated by the unique challenges posed to the United States and the Soviet Union from advancing technological capabilities in

---

No. 171, 1981). The subsequent debate over the effect of nuclear proliferation is discussed in THE SPREAD OF NUCLEAR WEAPONS: A DEBATE (Scott D. Sagan & Kenneth N. Waltz eds., 1995).

72. *See* MCGEORGE BUNDY, DANGER AND SURVIVAL: CHOICES ABOUT THE BOMB IN THE FIRST FIFTY YEARS 513–14 (1988) (arguing that decisions not to develop nuclear weapons in West Germany, Japan, and communist states in Eastern Europe resulted from external pressure from the superpowers).

73. Concerns about nuclear terrorism existed during the Cold War. Leventhal and Alexander considered the issue in 1986:

But is nuclear terrorism plausible? There is no consensus on this issue. Some observers see nuclear terrorism as implausible, others see it as possible but not imminent and others are convinced it is inevitable .... It is generally acknowledged that terrorists thus far have been constrained either by a lack of capability, a lack of motivation, or a combination of the two. The key issue is whether these technological and self-imposed constraints are eroding as a result of technological and political developments.

Paul Leventhal & Yonah Alexander, *Introduction, in* NUCLEAR TERRORISM: DEFINING THE THREAT, *supra* note 24, at 2. The danger of the malevolent appropriation of nuclear materials was recognized in 1979 when the Convention on the Physical Protection of Nuclear Material was opened for signature. *See* Convention on the Physical Protection of Nuclear Material, *opened for signature* Mar. 3, 1980, S. TREATY DOC. NO. 96-43 (1980), 1456 U.N.T.S. 101, *reprinted in* 18 I.L.M. 1419. The preamble of this treaty expressed the desire of the states parties "to avert the potential dangers posed by the unlawful taking and use of nuclear material" and their conviction that "offences relating to nuclear material are a matter of grave concern and that there is an urgent need to adopt appropriate and effective measures to ensure the prevention, detection and punishment of such offences." *Id.* pmbl.

both defensive and offensive weapons systems.[74] To be effective, deterrence stability ironically required increasing social vulnerability in the face of the developing nuclear threat, as seen in the ABM Treaty.[75]

The Cold War period also witnessed a major development in arms control in connection with biological weapons. The Convention on the Prohibition of the Development, Production and Stockpiling of Bacteriological (Biological) and Toxin Weapons and on Their Destruction of 1972 (BWC) supplemented the use prohibition in the Geneva Protocol by banning the development, production, and stockpiling, acquisition, or retention of biological weapons.[76] In short, states joining the BWC agreed to disarm themselves, at least in the context of biological weapons. The BWC represented a dramatic break with the arms control approach for biological weapons that had existed from the adoption of the Geneva Protocol. In the BWC, disarmament replaced a first-use prohibition backed by deterrence. BWC States Parties did not reserve the right to develop, produce, stockpile, or use biological weapons in any circumstances, effectively eliminating deterrence as a strategy for biological weapons arms control.

Between 1925 and 1972, the technological feasibility of biological weapons improved because of scientific progress in understanding pathogenic microbes[77] and efforts made by governmental biological weapons programs.[78] The growing technological feasibility of biological weapons increased societal vulnerabilities to bioweapons attacks because civilian biodefense did not effectively advance during the

---

74. *See* BUNDY, *supra* note 72, at 549–52 (discussing problems posed by defensive anti-ballistic missile technologies and offensive technological developments (e.g., MIRVs)).

75. *See id.* at 549–50 (discussing development of U.S. and Soviet positions on restricting anti-ballistic missile defenses, which included the argument that "[d]efensive deployments were bound to stimulate ever larger and more sophisticated offensive systems on both sides").

76. Convention on the Prohibition of the Development, Production and Stockpiling of Bacteriological (Biological) and Toxin Weapons and on Their Destruction, Apr. 10, 1972, art.1, 26 U.S.T. 583, 587, 1015 U.N.T.S. 163, 166 [hereinafter BWC].

77. LAURIE GARRETT, THE COMING PLAGUE: NEWLY EMERGING DISEASES IN A WORLD OUT OF BALANCE 30 (1994) (noting that during the 1950s and 1960s "[n]early every week the medical establishment declared another 'miracle breakthrough' in humanity's war with infectious disease").

78. For example, the development of U.S. efforts to develop biological weapons is detailed in EDWARD REGIS, THE BIOLOGY OF DOOM: THE HISTORY OF AMERICA'S SECRET GERM WARFARE PROJECT (1999) and JUDITH MILLER ET AL., GERMS: BIOLOGICAL WEAPONS AND AMERICA'S SECRET WAR 34–97 (2001).

Cold War.[79] The combination of increased technological feasibility and social vulnerability suggests that the threat of biological weapons was growing prior to the adoption of the BWC, which would tend to lead states to respond with further reliance on deterrence.

The key variable explaining the adoption of the BWC was the United States' conclusion, after an extensive review, that biological weapons had little, if any, military or political utility, even as a deterrent to other states' biological weapons capabilities.[80] Unilaterally, the United States terminated its offensive biological weapons program.[81] In essence, the United States concluded that possession of biological weapons by other states, including adversaries, did not pose a significant threat to U.S. national security and should be addressed through means other than an offensive biological weapons capability.

This change in political/military motivations in the United States converged with the notion, already present as early as 1925, that the use of biological weapons was "repugnant to the conscience of mankind"[82] to produce the WMD arms control breakthrough of the BWC. The breakthrough was substantive in moving the arms control strategy on biological weapons from deterrence to disarmament. Structurally, however, the focus remained state-centric because the BWC was limited state biological weapons programs.

The objective of chemical weapons disarmament also arose during the Cold War. The Preamble to the BWC stated, for example, that the BWC States Parties were "[c]onvinced of the importance and urgency of eliminating from the arsenals of States, through effective measures, such dangerous weapons of mass destruction as those using chemical or bacteriological (biological) agents."[83] Despite the hope in disarmament quarters that the development and possession of chemical weapons would be banned in the same way as biological weapons,

---

79. For background on early biodefense efforts stimulated by fears of Soviet biological weapons, see generally Elizabeth Fee & Theodore M. Brown, *Preemptive Biopreparedness: Can We Learn Anything from History?*, 91 AM. J. PUB. HEALTH 721 (2001). William Foege argued that the expansion and development of what became the U.S. Centers for Disease Control and Prevention began in 1946 "with the desire to improve U.S. military security." William Foege, *Memorandum to the President: Global Health and U.S. National Interests*, in BIOLOGICAL SECURITY & PUBLIC HEALTH: IN SEARCH OF A GLOBAL TREATMENT: A REPORT FROM THE ASPEN STRATEGY GROUP 17, 18 (Kurt M. Campbell & Philip Zelikow eds., 2003).

80. On the U.S. renunciation of its offensive biological weapons capability, see generally Jonathan B. Tucker, *A Farewell to Germs: The U.S. Renunciation of Biological and Toxin Warfare*, INT'L SECURITY, Summer 2002, at 107.

81. *Id.* at 107.

82. BWC, *supra* note 76, pmbl., 26 U.S.T. at 586, 1015 U.N.T.S. at 166.

83. *Id.*

this arms control breakthrough did not occur until after the end of the Cold War in the form of the Convention on the Prohibition of the Development, Production, Stockpiling, and Use of Chemical Weapons and on Their Destruction of 1993 (CWC).[84]

Like the BWC, the CWC seeks disarmament by banning an entire class of WMD.[85] The twenty-one year gap between the adoption of the BWC and the CWC suggests that states possessing chemical-weapons capabilities perceived that the political/military utility of chemical weapons was not as easily discounted as that of biological weapons. In addition, the critical diplomatic breakthrough following the end of the Cold War reinforced the notion that political/military motivations for developing and possessing chemical weapons remained sufficiently strong under the structure and dynamics of the Cold War international system.

III. END OF THE ARMS CONTROL APPROACH? POST–COLD WAR CHALLENGES TO THE ARMS CONTROL APPROACH TO WEAPONS OF MASS DESTRUCTION

The trajectory of the arms control approach on WMD in the early years of the post–Cold War period seemed promising. Biological weapons were already outlawed by the BWC. The CWC had been concluded successfully in 1993. The political and military strain of nuclear deterrence eased substantially with the end of superpower hostilities, as evidenced by the conclusion of the Strategic Arms Reduction Treaty of 1991 (START I)[86] and the Strategic Arms Reduction Treaty of 1993 (START II).[87]

Despite its promising post–Cold War start, the arms control approach could not sustain momentum over the following decade. Instead of receding under the influence of arms control agreements, the WMD threat has grown exponentially during the post–Cold War pe-

---

84. Convention on the Prohibition of the Development, Production, Stockpiling, and Use of Chemical Weapons and on Their Destruction, Jan. 13, 1993, 32 I.L.M. 800 [hereinafter CWC].

85. *See id.* art. I, 32 I.L.M at 804.

86. Treaty on the Reduction and Limitation of Strategic Offensive Arms (START I), July 31, 1991, U.S.-U.S.S.R., S. Treaty Doc. No. 102-20 (1991), *reprinted in* [1991] 16 U.N. Disarmament Y.B. app. II.

87. Treaty on Further Reduction and Limitation of Strategic Offensive Arms (START II), Jan. 3, 1993, U.S.-U.S.S.R., S. Treaty Doc. No. 103-1 (1993).

riod.[88] This growth in the WMD threat has led to questions about the utility of the arms control approach in addressing the problem. In this part, I analyze the post–Cold War challenges to the arms control approach to WMD by focusing on radical developments affecting the risk factors of the WMD threat: political/military motivations; technological feasibility; and social vulnerability.

A. Political Revolution, Proliferation Nightmare

The post–Cold War period has seen a political revolution in world politics that has brought to light a WMD "proliferation epidemic." The political revolution has two features—as the end of the Cold War brought the bipolar, superpower international system to an end, the threat from terrorism—especially terrorism involving WMD—began to loom larger in this new world order.[89] Each of these developments fed into perceptions about the growing threat of WMD.

As indicated above, the global superpower rivalry and its attendant strategy of nuclear deterrence dominated the Cold War international system.[90] This system had a WMD logic focused on nuclear weapons, stabilization of nuclear deterrence between the United States and the Soviet Union, and non-proliferation of nuclear weapons. While chemical and biological weapons were clearly sideshows in the structure and dynamics of the Cold War international system, the end of the Cold War saw this WMD logic evaporate.

First, WMD policy was no longer dominated by stabilizing nuclear deterrence between two superpowers. The primary fear of the United States was no longer attack by an ideologically hostile nuclear adversary, but rather that the former adversary's nuclear arsenal would fall into the clutches of potential state and non-state prolifera-

---

88. ASSESSING THE THREAT, *supra* note 23, at 7 ("Since the end of the Cold War, and especially in the wake of the New York and Oklahoma City bombings and Aum Shinrikyo attacks in Japan . . . there has been a dramatic shift in the perceived threat of CBRN [chemical, biological, radiological, and nuclear] terrorism."); WEAPONS OF MASS DESTRUCTION, *supra* note 4, at 1 (noting in December 2002 that WMD represent one of the greatest security challenges confronting the United States); COMBATING TERRORISM, *supra* note 5, at 9 (arguing in February 2003 that "[t]he probability of a terrorist organization using a chemical, biological, radiological, or nuclear weapon . . . has increased significantly during the last decade").

89. *See, e.g.*, Ashton Carter et al., *Catastrophic Terrorism: Tackling the New Danger*, FOREIGN AFF., Nov./Dec. 1998, at 80 (analyzing the new threats perceived to be growing from terrorism conducted using WMD).

90. *See supra* Part II.B.2.

62   DUKE JOURNAL OF COMPARATIVE & INTERNATIONAL LAW   [Vol 14:39

tors.[91]   As stated earlier, the arms control approach supported the
state-focused, rigid nuclear bipolarity of the Cold War by helping stabilize deterrence.[92] The utility of this approach dissipated as the international system moved into a fluid scenario of multipolar nuclear
proliferation in which non-state actors played an increasingly visible
role.

Proliferation fears overshadowed the revolution in nuclear strategy completed by the United States' withdrawal from the ABM
Treaty[93] and the signing of the Strategic Offensive Reductions Treaty
(Moscow Treaty) between the United States and the Russian Federation.[94] While the old bipolar order was characterized by structural
and political constraints imposed by the superpowers on other states
interested in developing nuclear weapons, the post–Cold War period
has seen these constraints disappear, with at least three countries—
India,[95] Pakistan,[96] and North Korea[97]—openly demonstrating and/or

---

91. Michael Jasinski, *Nonproliferation Assistance to Russia and the New Independent States*,
Nuclear Threat Initiative (Aug. 2001, updated Aug. 2002), *at* http://www.nti.org/e_research/
e3_4b.html (last visited Oct. 21, 2003) ("As the political and economic situation in the Soviet
Union deteriorated in the late 1980s, fears arose that the Soviet government might not be able
to adequately safeguard its weapons of mass destruction (WMD) arsenals, nor the associated
materials and know-how. These fears were intensified by the final break-up of the Soviet Union
in December 1991, which left nuclear weapons on the territories of four states, and components
of the Soviet military-industrial complex scattered across the territories of the Newly
Independent States (NIS). In the ensuing turmoil, the potential for the loss of weapons, theft of
nuclear material, or the emigration of weapons scientists to 'rogue states' posed a new and
unprecedented proliferation threat.").

92. HANS MORGENTHAU, POLITICS AMONG NATIONS 415 (5th ed. rev. 1978) (arguing that
"the United States and the Soviet Union have a common interest in stabilizing the nuclear arms
race by regulating it" through arms control).

93. White House, *ABM Treaty Fact Sheet* (Dec. 13, 2001), *at* http://www.whitehouse.gov/
news/releases/2001/12/20011213-2.html (last visited Oct. 4, 2003) ("Given the emergence of . . .
new threats to our national security and the imperative of defending against them, the United
States is today providing formal notification of its withdrawal from the ABM treaty.").

94. Treaty on Strategic Offensive Reductions, May 24, 2002, U.S.-Russ., S. TREATY DOC.
NO. 107-8 (2002).

95. Nuclear Threat Initiative, *India Profile*, *at* http://www.nti.org/e_research/profiles/
India/index.html (last visited Oct. 4, 2003) ("According to Indian government sources, India is
capable of building a range of nuclear weapon systems ranging from low yields to 200 kilotons,
involving fission, boosted-fission, and two-stage thermonuclear designs.") (ellipsis and quotation
marks omitted).

96. Nuclear Threat Initiative, *Pakistan Overview*, *at* http://www.nti.org/e_research/e1_
pakistan_1.html (last visited Oct. 4, 2003) ("In 1998, Pakistan commissioned the Khushab research reactor, which is capable of yielding 10–15 kg of weapons-grade plutonium annually.").

97. Nuclear Threat Initiative, *North Korea Profile*, *at* http://www.nti.org/e_research/
profiles/NK/index.html (last visited Oct. 4, 2003) ("In mid-2002, U.S. intelligence discovered
that North Korea had been receiving materials from Pakistan for a highly enriched uranium

declaring their nuclear capabilities. The proliferation of nuclear weapons to these states focused attention on the weaknesses of the Nuclear Non-Proliferation Treaty (NPT).[98] Neither India nor Pakistan ever signed this agreement,[99] and, although North Korea is a NPT state party, it violated the rules stipulated therein before announcing its formal decision to renounce the treaty.[100] The proliferation nightmare continued as experts believed that other countries, including Iran,[101] Iraq,[102] and Libya,[103] were actively seeking to join the nuclear club. The rejection by the United States of the Comprehensive Nuclear Test-Ban Treaty[104] only added to concerns that state proliferation of nuclear weapons would continue.[105]

Proliferation fears also came to haunt the arms control approach on biological and chemical weapons in the post–Cold War period. The early 1990s witnessed revelations about the size and scale of biological and chemical weapons programs in the former Soviet Union[106] and Iraq.[107] Both states were parties to the BWC yet violated its prohibitions on a massive scale.[108] These revelations also exposed the fact

---

production facility. . . . On 10 January 2003, North Korea declared its withdrawal from the NPT.").

98. Treaty on the Non-proliferation of Nuclear Weapons, July 1, 1968, 21 U.S.T. 483, 729 U.N.T.S. 161 (entered into force Mar. 5, 1970) [hereinafter NPT].

99. Nuclear Threat Initiative, *India Profile, supra* note 95; Nuclear Threat Initiative, *Pakistan Overview, supra* note 96.

100. Nuclear Threat Initiative, *North Korean Nuclear Program Overview: History and Status, supra* note 6.

101. Nuclear Threat Initiative, *Iran Profile, at* http://www.nti.org/e_research/profiles/Iran/index.html (last visited Oct. 4, 2003).

102. Nuclear Threat Initiative, *Iraq Profile, at* http://www.nti.org/e_research/profiles/iraq/index.html (last visited Oct. 4, 2003).

103. Nuclear Threat Initiative, *Libya Profile, at* http://www.nti.org/e_research/profiles/libya/index.html (last visited Oct. 4, 2003) ("There remain, however, continuing allegations that Libya is indeed pursuing a nuclear weapon capability.").

104. Comprehensive Nuclear Test-Ban Treaty, Sept. 24, 1996, S. TREATY DOC. NO. 105-28, 35 I.L.M. 1439.

105. *See, e.g.*, Daryl Kimball, *What Went Wrong: Repairing the Damage to the CTBT*, ARMS CONTROL TODAY, Dec. 1999, at 3, *available at* www.armscontrol.org/act/1999_12/dkde99.asp (last visited Dec. 1, 2003) (describing the events leading up to the U.S. Senate's rejection of the Comprehensive Nuclear Test Ban Treaty and suggesting a deleterious impact on U.S. security interests).

106. *See* MILLER ET AL., *supra* note 78, at 165–82 (discussing former Soviet Union's biological weapons program).

107. *See generally* Raymond A. Zilinskas, *Iraq's Biological Weapons: The Past as Future?*, 278 JAMA 418 (1997) (analyzing the status of Iraq's WMD programs).

108. MILLER ET AL., *supra* note 78, at 167 (noting that the massive Soviet biological weapons program was created one year after the Soviet Union became a party to the Biological Weapons Convention of 1972); John R. Bolton, Under Secretary for Arms Control and Interna-

64   DUKE JOURNAL OF COMPARATIVE & INTERNATIONAL LAW   [Vol 14:39

that the Soviet Union's perspective on the political/military utility of biological weapons ran counter to the conclusion the United States had reached in the late 1960s. Similarly, Iraq had been pursuing a biological weapons program for strategic or tactical reasons, again suggesting that some regimes saw value in developing and retaining an offensive biological weapons program. Such proliferation of biological weapons by states underscored the weaknesses of the BWC, especially the lack of any compliance or enforcement machinery to back up its prohibitions.[109]

Second, the arms control approach's state-centric focus began to look increasingly anachronistic as experts began to discuss more urgently the threat of WMD terrorism.[110] From 1899 until the end of the Cold War, WMD policy concentrated almost exclusively on WMD in the hands of states operating under the influence of the anarchical structure and dynamics of the international system. None of the WMD arms control agreements reviewed above mentioned, let alone addressed, the perceived threat of "catastrophic terrorism"— terrorism involving WMD, primarily carried out by non-state actors.[111] State proliferation of WMD capabilities produced a radically new environment affecting political/military motivations for pursuing WMD, but the worries about catastrophic terrorism meant that policy makers also had to assess the political/military motivations of terrorist groups in connection with WMD. Terrorist experts argued that terrorism itself was evolving into forms attracted to tactics and strategies designed to destroy and kill on a large scale.[112] Large-scale terrorist attacks and attempted attacks in the 1990s and early 2000s, capped by

---

tional Security, Remarks to the Fifth Biological Weapons Convention RevCon Meeting, Geneva, Switzerland (Nov. 19, 2001), *at* http://www.state.gov/t/us/rm/janjuly/6231.htm (last visited Nov. 10, 2003) ("After signing the BWC in 1972, Iraq developed, produced, and stockpiled biological warfare agents and weapons, and continued this activity even after ratifying the BWC in 1991. Despite the obligation to fully disclose and destroy its BW [biological weapons] program which the UN Security Council required to conclude the Gulf War, Iraq denied having a BW program and pursued a policy of obstruction, denial and evasion to conceal its program.").

109. This weakness in the BWC led to negotiations in the 1990s on a verification protocol to the BWC. *See* Christopher et al., *supra* note 17, at 415–17.

110. *See, e.g.*, FALKENRATH ET AL., *supra* note 8; TOXIC TERROR: ASSESSING TERRORIST USE OF CHEMICAL AND BIOLOGICAL WEAPONS (Jonathan B. Tucker ed., 2000); Carter et al., *supra* note 89.

111. *See* Carter et al., *supra* note 89, at 80 (analyzing the threat of catastrophic terrorism).

112. On the new terrorism, see generally IAN O. LESSER ET AL., COUNTERING THE NEW TERRORISM (1999).

the events of September 11, 2001, clearly indicated that the nature of terrorism was changing—and becoming more dangerous.[113]

The WMD proliferation epidemic, both real and feared, posed an even greater crisis when policymakers considered the merging of the two proliferation vectors—certain states pursuing WMD capabilities have a history of supporting international terrorism,[114] which raised the specter of a synergy between state and non-state WMD proliferation. These fears coalesced in the Bush Doctrine's declaration that the United States would confront national security threats from repressive regimes that pursued WMD as well as those that supported international terrorism.[115]

As a result, the dominant structure of the arms control approach in the pre–Cold War and Cold War periods—agreements among the great powers backed by a strategy of deterrence—no longer seemed as relevant. The repressive regimes targeted by the Bush Doctrine (e.g., Iraq, Iran, and North Korea) are not great powers in the classical sense, and many of them either had not signed the relevant arms control treaties or had violated them. At the same time, the threat of WMD terrorism also served to dilute the significance of arms control treaties because such treaties address state rather than non-state behavior. U.S. political, economic, and military supremacy in the international system does not appear to have had sufficient deterrent effect on either state or terrorist proliferation in WMD.

B. Technological Transformations, Dual-Use Dilemmas

Post–Cold War developments signal a technological transformation that increases the feasibility of WMD development for both states and terrorist groups. In the post–Cold War period, the technological difficulties of developing WMD are diminishing as relevant technologies advance and expertise with such technologies diffuses

---

113. *See* ASSESSING THE THREAT, *supra* note 23, at vi ("As we stand on the threshold of the twenty-first century, the stark reality is that the face and character of terrorism are changing . . ."); NATIONAL COMMISSION ON TERRORISM, *supra* note 32, at 1 ("The terrorist threat is changing in ways that make it more dangerous and difficult to counter.").

114. *See* U.S. DEP'T OF STATE, PATTERNS OF GLOBAL TERRORISM 2001 63–68 (2002), *at* http://www.state.gov/s/ct/rls/pgtrpt/2001/pdf (last visited Dec. 15, 2003) (analyzing state sponsors of international terrorism including Iran, Iraq, North Korea, and Libya).

115. State of the Union Address, *supra* note 3, at 135 ("The United States of America will not permit the world's most dangerous regimes to threaten us with the world's most destructive weapons.").

throughout the world.[116] These technological transformations, simply put, make development and use of WMD easier than was historically possible. Biological weapons have perhaps featured the most frequently in this discourse because of the rapid developments in genomics and biotechnology taking place in science and private industry today.[117]

A central tension that these technological transformations highlight is the dual-use dilemma that confronts each WMD technology. Nuclear, chemical, and biological weapons often depend on skills, information, equipment, and access to precursor materials (e.g., biological agents, chemicals, uranium) that are widely available and used for peaceful, civilian purposes. Striking a balance between encouraging the use and dissemination of such technologies and the know-how to apply them for peaceful purposes while at the same time regulating WMD development has proven difficult both within and outside the purview of WMD arms control treaties.[118]

The dual-use nature of technologies used for WMD also complicates efforts to strengthen arms control regimes through international verification mechanisms. The NPT incorporates safeguard rules and verification procedures from the International Atomic Energy Agency to facilitate peaceful development of nuclear energy and to prevent diversion of technology for building nuclear weapons.[119] Meanwhile, the CWC has a complex international verification system operated by the Organization for the Prohibition of Chemical Weapons that tries to separate the peaceful from the malevolent in terms of

---

116. *See, e.g.*, HOMELAND SECURITY, *supra* note 25, at 9 (noting that the knowledge, technology, and materials required for building WMD are spreading and have never before been more accessible).

117. *See* Carter et al., *supra* note 89, at 81 (arguing that "the combination of new technology and lethal force has made biological weapons at least as deadly as chemical and nuclear alternatives").

118. The problem of the dual-use nature of WMD technologies is apparent in the BWC, CWC, and NPT. Each of these treaty regimes prohibits relevant technologies from being used to produce weapons but allows the same technologies to be employed for peaceful purposes. Article I, paragraph 1 of the BWC prohibits, for example, the development, production, stockpiling, acquisition or retention of microbial or other biological agents of types and quantities that have no justification for prophylactic, protective, or other peaceful purposes. BWC, *supra* note 76, art. I, para. 1, 1015 U.N.T.S at 166. Similar provisions appear in the CWC and NPT. See CWC, *supra* note 84, art. II, paras. 1, 9, 32 I.L.M. at 804–06 (defining chemical weapons as toxic chemicals except where intended for purposes not prohibited under the Convention and defining "purposes not prohibited under the Convention" respectively); NPT, *supra* note 98, art. IV, 729 U.N.T.S. at 172–73 (stating that nothing in the treaty shall affect the inalienable right of states parties to develop nuclear energy for peaceful purposes).

119. *See* Nuclear Non-Proliferation Treaty, *supra* note 60, art. III, 729 U.N.T.S. at 172.

chemical technologies and substances.[120] Extensive, but ultimately unsuccessful, efforts were made to negotiate a protocol to the BWC that would have added an international verification regime for biological weapons modeled on the CWC system.[121] The known and feared WMD proliferation among states and non-state actors in the post–Cold War period also raises skepticism about the effectiveness of arms control treaties in preventing proliferation. The Bush administration's *National Strategy to Combat Weapons of Mass Destruction* highlights "counterproliferation" actions that the United States can unilaterally take to address the fact that "[t]he possession and increased likelihood of use of WMD by hostile states and terrorists are realities of the contemporary security environment."[122]

The analytical framework used in this article also reminds us that the more fluid and uncertain nature of political/military motivations on WMD and the heightened technological feasibility of developing WMD are interdependent.[123] Each feeds and reinforces the other. President Bush stressed this dynamic when he argued that "[t]he gravest danger our Nation faces lies at the crossroads of radicalism and technology."[124] This argument identifies the interdependence between political/military motivations and technological feasibility in assessing the WMD threat.

This interdependent dynamic between political/military motivations and technological feasibility creates enormous problems for the arms control approach because the dynamic (1) makes it easier for states to proliferate in violation of their arms control obligations under treaties or customary international law; and (2) bypasses arms control agreements entirely in the case of terrorist organizations.

---

120. *See generally* CWC, *supra* note 84, Annex on Implementation and Verification, 32 I.L.M. at 824 (establishing system of implementation and verification to ensure use of toxic chemicals is for purposes not prohibited under the CWC).

121. *See, e.g.*, Rebecca Whitehair & Seth Brugger, *BWC Protocol Talks in Geneva Collapse Following U.S. Rejection*, ARMS CONTROL TODAY, Sept. 2001, at 26, *available at* http://www.armscontrol.org/act/2001_09/bwcsept01.asp (last visited Nov. 15, 2003).

122. WEAPONS OF MASS DESTRUCTION, *supra* note 4, at 2. For a critique of the Bush administration's emphasis on counterproliferation, see John M. Spratt, Jr., *Stopping a Dangerous Drift in U.S. Arms Control Policy*, ARMS CONTROL TODAY, Mar. 2003, at 3, 3–4, *available at* http://www.armscontrol.org/act/2003_03/spratt_mar03.asp (last visited Nov. 15, 2003).

123. *See supra* Part II.A.4.

124. NATIONAL SECURITY STRATEGY, *supra* note 4, at v.

68   DUKE JOURNAL OF COMPARATIVE & INTERNATIONAL LAW   [Vol 14:39

C. Vulnerability Crisis, Preparedness Challenge

The post–Cold War period has also seen developments that connect to the social vulnerability risk factor of the analytical framework. The most important development in this regard has been the heightened awareness in many countries—especially the United States—of the extent of their societies' vulnerability to WMD attack, particularly to catastrophic terrorism.[125] Historically, WMD policy, as illustrated by the arms control approach, did not address directly the vulnerability that societies face from use of WMD. The main strategy of states has been to deter the use of WMD by other states, which allowed governments to avoid focusing much attention and resources on preparing to manage the consequences of WMD attacks. None of the arms control treaties mentioned above address the challenge of domestic preparedness for WMD consequence management following WMD events.[126]

Concerns about a proliferation epidemic, especially in regard to fears about catastrophic terrorism, combined with the perceived technological feasibility of WMD development, focused governments' attention increasingly on the social vulnerability risk factor. Indeed, the interdependence of all three risk factors becomes very transparent at this stage in the analysis. The perpetration of biological terrorism in the United States in the fall of 2001 only accelerated political attention and economic resources in the direction of domestic preparedness for WMD events.[127] Efforts in the United States on national missile defense,[128] biodefense,[129] and homeland security[130] reveal

---

125. Carter et al., *supra* note 89, at 81 (arguing that, in the face of WMD, "society is more vulnerable"); HOMELAND SECURITY, *supra* note 25, at 7 ("Our population and way of life are the source of our Nation's great strength, but also a source of inherent vulnerability.").

126. During the Cold War, countries did implement civil defense strategies; but these strategies tended not to be accorded the same priority as arms control in connection with policies on WMD. For analysis on civil defense during the Cold War, see generally ANDREW D. GROSSMAN, NEITHER DEAD NOR RED: CIVILIAN DEFENSE AND AMERICAN POLITICAL DEVELOPMENT DURING THE EARLY COLD WAR (2001); LAURA MCENANEY, CIVIL DEFENSE BEGINS AT HOME: MILITARIZATION MEETS EVERYDAY LIFE IN THE FIFTIES (2000); GUY OAKES, THE IMAGINARY WAR: CIVIL DEFENSE AND AMERICAN COLD WAR CULTURE (1994); LAWRENCE J. VALE, THE LIMITS OF CIVIL DEFENCE IN THE USA, SWITZERLAND, BRITAIN, AND THE SOVIET UNION: THE EVOLUTION OF POLICIES SINCE 1945 (1987).

127. See, e.g., HOMELAND SECURITY, *supra* note 25, at 41 ("We must prepare to minimize the damage and recover from any future terrorist attacks that may occur despite our best efforts at prevention.").

128. See, e.g., U.S. Dep't of State, Bureau of Arms Control, *Fact Sheet, Missile Defense and Deterrence* (Sept. 1, 2001), *at* http://www.state.gov/t/ac/rls/fs/2001/4891.htm (last visited Oct. 4, 2003).

a sea change in political attitudes with relation to addressing social vulnerability as a risk factor in the WMD calculus.

This sea change contributes to the challenges faced by the arms control approach to WMD. Supporters of arms control agreements acknowledge that these instruments do little, if anything, about domestic preparedness for WMD consequence management. Opponents go farther, laying blame for the lack of domestic preparedness at the feet of the arms control approach. One such critic fulminated:

> The growing evidence that the U.S. disarmed, while nations that might use chemical or biological weapons against us did not, was only one of the dangerous absurdities of the arms control delusion. The expectation that such weapons had been dealt with through these bans contributed to the belief that we need not worry about protecting against such scourges. Our vulnerability to incalculably destructive smallpox is a manifestation of the sorry state of American preparedness.[131]

D. End of the Arms Control Approach to Weapons of Mass Destruction

The political revolutions, technological transformations, and vulnerability crises reviewed above have brought an end to relying predominantly on the arms control approach to address the WMD threat. This argument does not mean that the arms control approach and the WMD treaties it has generated have become unimportant or worthless.[132] However, post–Cold War developments in all the WMD risk factors render the arms control approach inadequate to effectively address the contemporary WMD threat. Since 1899, the dominant international legal strategy on WMD has been the negotiation of arms control treaties that ban or regulate the use and development of WMD by states. There is growing awareness, even among its most ardent supporters, that the arms control approach faces challenges on

---

129. *See, e.g.*, Press Release, White House, President Details Project BioShield (Feb. 3, 2003), *at* http://www.whitehouse.gov/news/releases/2003/02/20030203.html (last visited Oct. 4, 2003).

130. *See, e.g.*, HOMELAND SECURITY, *supra* note 25, at 2 ("Homeland security involves a systematic, comprehensive, and strategic effort to reduce America's vulnerability to terrorist attack."); MICHAEL E. O'HANLON ET AL., PROTECTING THE AMERICAN HOMELAND: A PRELIMINARY ANALYSIS (2002) (analyzing the development of homeland security strategy in the United States).

131. Frank J. Gaffney, Jr., *Delusions of Arms Control*, L.A. TIMES, Nov. 20, 2002, at B13.

132. The Bush administration stresses, for example, that multilateral regimes for arms control and nonproliferation remain important elements of the overall strategy against WMD. *See* WEAPONS OF MASS DESTRUCTION, *supra* note 4, at 4.

the political, technological, and social vulnerability fronts that cannot be adequately addressed without use of other policy and legal strategies. This awareness means that we are witnessing, and shall continue to see, a diversification in how states, international organizations, and non-governmental organizations seek to use international law to deal with the WMD threat. The next part of the article explores this international legal diversification.

IV. INTERNATIONAL LAW IN THE NEW WMD ENVIRONMENT

The diversification of international legal strategies is closely linked to policies designed to address the three WMD risk factors in the analytical framework. I organize the analysis of international law's role in the new WMD environment by using the three risk factors from the analytical framework. The reader should remember that each new international legal strategy discussed connects to the interdependence of the risk factors. In other words, a legal strategy designed to reduce political/military motivations for developing or using WMD also affects, and is affected by, the strategies aimed at addressing problems associated with the technological feasibility and social vulnerability risk factors.

The diversification of international law's role in WMD matters analyzed below does not, however, represent a coherent "grand strategy" for WMD. These international legal developments have not coalesced into any discernable or integrated approach to the growing WMD threat. Further, some of the developments are intensely controversial; and others may never become subjects of diplomatic activity.

A. Political/Military Motivations

International legal diversification appears most clearly in connection with efforts to affect political/military motivations toward WMD development and use. The arms control approach on chemical and biological weapons in the post–Cold War period relied on a first-use prohibition backed by deterrence,[133] a policy that addressed political/military motivations for use but did little to address concerns about technological developments and social vulnerabilities. The arms control approach on nuclear weapons in the Cold War period

---

133. *See supra* notes 33–43 and accompanying text.

similarly centered on deterring political/military motivations on use.[134] This strategy involved increasing the mutual vulnerabilities of the superpowers to nuclear attack through the ABM Treaty and some efforts to limit the destabilizing effects of new offensive nuclear weapons technologies (e.g., the SALT treaties). The bans on the development and use of chemical and biological weapons rested on the assumption that political/military interest in these weapons by states would not be strong and, to the extent it remained, could be managed through arms control methods other than deterrence (e.g., prohibition and verification).

The international legal developments that connect to the political/military motivations risk factor utilize deterrence as the major strategic concept, supported by international legal principles and approaches outside the traditional arms control approach to WMD. These developments reflect a belief that the arms control approach has not adequately managed the political/military motivations that state and non-state actors have for developing and using WMD.

1. *Deterrence of State Actors: Exercising the Right of Self-Defense.* The problem of WMD proliferation among states in the post–Cold War period has raised the policy question of how to decrease state interest in WMD. The most powerful move in this regard has been away from the arms control approach toward policies and arguments supporting a more robust exercise of the right of self-defense under international law. The U.S. termination of the ABM Treaty paved the way for the United States to move ahead with plans for national missile defense.[135] This policy shift is grounded in a state's sovereign right to protect its territory and people from external attack, a right recognized by international law.[136] The policy shift also indicated that the United States does not believe that it can adequately deter potential adversaries only through WMD arms control but needs to adopt stronger measures against state actors.

---

134. *See supra* notes 53–73 and accompanying text.

135. John R. Bolton, Missile Defense in a New Strategic Environment: Policy, Architecture, and International Industrial Cooperation after the ABM Treaty, Remarks to the Fourth RUSI Missile Defense Conference (Nov. 18, 2002), *at* http://www.state.gov/t/us/rm/15224.htm (last visited Oct. 4, 2003) ("In the context of our new strategic relationship with Russia, the demise of the ABM Treaty has not brought about the dire consequences predicted by many pundits; quite the contrary. The Treaty's demise instead has been liberating. It has freed us to explore the full range of technologies and architectures to defend against an increasing ballistic missile threat.").

136. U.N. CHARTER art. 51 ("Nothing in the present Charter shall impair the inherent right of individual or collective self-defense if an armed attack occurs against a Member of the United Nations . . . .").

The second development in the area of the right to self-defense and WMD has been the efforts made by the United States to argue that customary international law on self-defense provides a legitimate justification for preemptive military action against hostile countries possessing or developing WMD.[137] Such arguments were alive before September 11, 2001,[138] but became more prominent and influential after the attacks on the World Trade Center and the Pentagon.[139] The U.S. position on its use of force against Iraq in March 2003 was partly based on updating the customary doctrine of anticipatory self-defense for the threat posed by state adversaries possessing or pursuing WMD.[140] Even though the United States also defended military action against Iraq on the basis of upholding UN Security Council resolutions on Iraqi WMD disarmament,[141] the war against Iraq revealed the United States' desire to deploy a doctrine of preemptive self-

---

137. *See* NATIONAL SECURITY STRATEGY, *supra* note 4, at 15 ("We must adapt the concept of imminent threat to the capabilities and objectives of today's adversaries. Rogue states and terrorists do not seek to attack us using conventional means. . . . Instead, they rely on acts of terror and, potentially, the use of weapons of mass destruction—weapons that can be easily concealed, delivered covertly, and used without warning.").

138. *See, e.g.,* Guy B. Roberts, *The Counterproliferation Self-help Paradigm: A Legal Regime for Enforcing the Norm Prohibiting the Proliferation of Weapons of Mass Destruction,* 27 DENVER J. INT'L L. & POL'Y 483 (1999) (proposing a "counterproliferation self-help paradigm" to clarify when and how using force in response to the proliferation of WMD is justified).

139. *See, e.g.,* John C. Yoo, *International Law and the War in Iraq,* 97 AM. J. INT'L L. 563, 565 (2003) ("The attacks on the World Trade Center and the Pentagon, carried out by Al Qaeda operatives trained and led from their bases in Afghanistan, demonstrated the threat posed by terrorists who could seek safe haven in rogue nations with potential access to WMD.").

140. *See* NATIONAL SECURITY STRATEGY, *supra* note 4, at 15 ("The United States has long maintained the option of preemptive actions to counter a sufficient threat to our national security. The greater the threat, the greater the risk of inaction—and the more compelling the case for taking anticipatory action to defend ourselves, even if uncertainty remains as to the time and place of the enemy's attack."); Press Release, White House, President George Bush Discusses Iraq in National Press Conference, 39 WEEKLY COMP. PRES. DOC. 295, 296 (Mar. 6, 2003), *available at* http://www.whitehouse.gov/news/releases/2003/03/20030306-8.html (last visited Oct. 21, 2003) ("Saddam Hussein has a long history of reckless aggression and terrible crimes. He possesses weapons of terror. He provides funding and training and safe haven to terrorists— terrorists who would willingly use weapons of mass destruction against America and other peace-loving countries. Saddam Hussein and his weapons are a direct threat to this country, to our people, and to all free people. If the world fails to confront the threat posed by the Iraqi regime, refusing to use force, even as a last resort, free nations would assume immense and unacceptable risks. The attacks of September the 11th, 2001, showed what the enemies of America did with four airplanes. We will not wait to see what terrorists or terrorist states could do with weapons of mass destruction. We are determined to confront threats wherever they arise. I will not leave the American people at the mercy of the Iraqi dictator and his weapons.").

141. Sean D. Murphy, *Use of Military Force to Disarm Iraq,* 97 AM. J. INT'L L. 419, 427–28 (2003).

defense that would deter states from pursuing WMD and provide the United States with a course of action if deterrence failed.

The U.S. stance on preemptive self-defense under customary international law is not universally shared.[142] Australian, Spanish, and British support for military action against Iraq was premised not on an updated doctrine of self-defense under customary international law but only on the enforcement of UN Security Council Resolutions on Iraqi disarmament stretching back to 1991.[143] But the still ongoing debate about the U.S. position on preemptive self-defense in connection with WMD threats and its impact on the international law on the use of force[144] illustrates that policy and international legal thinking on WMD have moved beyond the arms control approach. Further evidence of this transition away from the arms control approach can be found in policy debates about preemptive military strikes against North Korean nuclear facilities.[145]

The third development in the self-defense context concerns the use of force in self-defense against states that harbor terrorists who might be planning or who have committed acts of violence against another state. Countries, including the United States, have long argued that state-sponsored terrorism triggers the right to respond with force in self-defense.[146] In the aftermath of the September 11, 2001 violence, the international community recognized that the United

---

142. *See, e.g.*, Michael White & Patrick Wintour, *No Case for Iraq Attack Say Lawyers*, GUARDIAN, Mar. 7, 2003, at P1 ("Tony Blair last night faced fresh pressure to abandon the threat of war against Iraq when 16 eminent academic lawyers warned him that the White House doctrine of 'pre-emptive self-defence' has no justification under international law.").

143. Murphy, *supra* note 141, at 427.

144. See, e.g., Michael J. Glennon, *Why the Security Council Failed*, FOREIGN AFF., May/June 2003, at 16 (arguing that attempts to impose binding international legal obligations on the use of force by states through the UN Charter has failed). Responses to Mr. Glennon's article were published in a section of a later issue of Foreign Affairs, entitled *Staying Alive: The Rumors of the UN's Death Have Been Exaggerated. See* Edward C. Luck, *The End of an Illusion*, FOREIGN AFF., March/Apr. 2003, at 201 (criticizing Glennon for arguing that the Security Council is finished); Anne-Marie Slaughter, *Misreading the Record*, FOREIGN AFF., Mar./Apr. 2003, at 202 (attacking Glennon's argument that the Security Council has failed).

145. A discussion of the pros and cons of preemptive military attacks against North Korea's nuclear weapons capabilities are contained in Nuclear Threat Initiative, *Option 4: Pre-emptive Strikes Against North Korean Nuclear Facilities, at* http://www.nti/org/f_wmd411/f2d1_4.html (last visited Oct. 21, 2003).

146. President Ronald Reagan, Address to the Nation on the United States Air Strike Against Libya, 1 PUB. PAPERS 468, 468–69 (Apr. 14, 1986) (justifying U.S. military action against Libya for its acts of state-sponsored terrorism against the United States under the right to self-defense in international law); *see also* Gregory Francis Intoccia, *American Bombing of Libya: An International Legal Analysis,* 19 CASE W. RES. J. INT'L L. 177 (1987) (analyzing the international legality of the U.S. bombing of Libya in 1986).

States could legally use force in self-defense against Afghanistan because it was harboring the terrorist groups responsible for the attacks.[147] With support from allies, the United States destroyed the Taliban government in Afghanistan through military force. These events signaled that the right to use force in self-defense under international law could be used against states harboring terrorist groups that were planning or that had committed acts of violence. Such an interpretation of the right to self-defense should act as a deterrent for states in connection with the activities of terrorist groups. The U.S. position on preemptive self-defense links with the "harboring" doctrine in an attempt to increase deterrence for state actors in the context of WMD development and possession.

2. *Deterrence of Non-State Actors.* Part of the political revolution that created the current concerns about WMD involves the rise of terrorism as a factor in WMD policy. The arms control approach did not address the political/military motivations that terrorist groups might have to develop or use WMD, nor is this international legal mechanism well suited for such purposes. New strategies to increase deterrence against WMD terrorism involve (1) militarization of counter-terrorism efforts and (2) the law enforcement approach of creating criminal offenses and crafting a system for attribution of—and retribution against—perpetrators.

In the war on terrorism sparked by the violence of September 11, 2001, the United States has staked out the position that individuals suspected of being involved in international terrorist activity can be captured and detained as "enemy combatants" who are not entitled to the protections of either international humanitarian law or national

---

147. For analysis of the impact of the September 11, 2001 violence on the international law on the use of force, see generally Antonio Cassese, *Terrorism is Also Disrupting Some Crucial Legal Categories of International Law*, 12 EUR. J. INT'L L. 993 (2001); Jonathan I. Charney, *The Use of Force Against Terrorism and International Law*, 95 AM. J. INT'L L. 835 (2001); Thomas M. Franck, *Terrorism and the Right of Self-Defense*, 95 AM. J. INT'L L. 839 (2001); Yutaka Arai-Takahashi, *Shifting Boundaries of the Right of Self-Defence—Appraising the Impact of the September 11 Attacks on Jus Ad Bellum*, 36 INT'L LAW. 1081 (2002); Michael Byers, *Terrorism, the Use of Force and International Law after 11 September*, 51 INT'L & COMP. L.Q. 401 (2002); Mark A. Drumbl, *Victimhood in Our Neighborhood: Terrorist Crime, Taliban Guilt, and the Asymmetries of the International Legal Order*, 81 N.C. L. REV. 1 (2002); Michael J. Glennon, *The Fog of Law: Self-Defense, Inherence, and Incoherence in Article 51 of the United Nations Charter*, 25 HARV. J.L. & PUB. POL'Y 539 (2002); Sean D. Murphy, *Terrorism and the Concept of "Armed Attack" in Article 51 of the U.N. Charter*, 43 HARV. INT'L L.J. 41 (2002); Steven R. Ratner, *Jus Ad Bellum and Jus in Bello After September 11*, 96 AM. J. INT'L L. 905 (2002).

criminal and constitutional law.[148] In November 2001, President Bush established military tribunals to try individuals suspected of terrorist activity who are not U.S. citizens.[149] This military order caused controversy in international legal circles.[150] The Bush administration has also labeled U.S. citizens suspected of international terrorist activity as enemy combatants not entitled to the traditional protections of the U.S. Constitution.[151] One of these U.S. citizens, Jose Padilla, was alleged to have been involved in a plot to detonate a radiological device in the United States.[152]

These moves by the Bush administration represent a militarization of counter-terrorism in response to the growing global scale and danger posed by international terrorist groups, especially those interested in WMD.[153] Behind this policy is the belief that terrorist organizations of global reach can no longer be handled in the traditional manner[154] through civilian law enforcement resources and national criminal law.[155] The utilization of military power in counter-terrorism,

---

148. For discussion of this development, see CURTIS A. BRADLEY & JACK L. GOLDSMITH, FOREIGN RELATIONS LAW: CASES AND MATERIALS 267–73 (2003).

149. Military Order, Detention, Treatment and Trial of Certain Non-Citizens in the War Against Terrorism, § 4, 66 Fed. Reg. 57,833, 57,834 (2001).

150. *See, e.g.,* Kenneth Anderson, *What to Do with Bin Laden and Al Qaeda Terrorists?: A Qualified Defense of Military Commissions and United States Policy on Detainees at Guantanamo Bay Naval Base,* 25 HARV. J.L. & PUB. POL'Y 591, 592 (2002); Harold Hongju Koh, *The Case Against Military Commissions,* 96 AM. J. INT'L L. 337 (2002); Daryl A. Mundis, *The Use of Military Commissions to Prosecute Individuals Accused of Terrorist Acts,* 96 AM. J. INT'L L. 320, 324–25 (2002); Diane F. Orentlicher & Robert Kogod Goldman, *When Justice Goes to War: Prosecuting Terrorists Before Military Commissions,* 25 HARV. J.L. & PUB. POL'Y 653, 659–63 (2002).

151. *See, e.g.,* Hamdi v. Rumsfeld, 316 F.3d 450 (4th Cir. 2003); Padilla *ex rel.* Newman v. Bush, 233 F. Supp. 2d 564 (S.D.N.Y. 2002).

152. *Padilla ex rel. Newman,* 233 F. Supp. 2d at 572–73.

153. *See* COMBATING TERRORISM, *supra* note 5, at 15 ("Preventing terrorist groups from gaining access to technology, particularly that which supports WMD, will be one of our highest priorities.").

154. Walter Gary Sharp, Sr., *The Use of Armed Force Against Terrorism: American Hegemony or Impotence?,* 1 CHI. J. INT'L L. 37, 39 (2000) (observing that "the international community has taken a piecemeal approach and addressed the problem of international terrorism by identifying particular criminal acts inherently terrorist in nature to be prevented and punished by domestic law. The result has been the adoption of a number of global treaties, regional conventions, and bilateral agreements which are relevant to the suppression of international terrorism, and corresponding domestic laws which implement those arrangements.").

155. Abraham D. Sofaer, *Playing Games with Terrorists,* 36 NEW ENG. L. REV. 903, 903 (2002) ("For many years, between 1988 and September 11, 2001, presidents denounced terrorist attacks on Americans and promised to 'pursue' attackers until they were 'brought to justice.' These turned out to be empty words. Rather than use the military to put an end to the groups we knew were responsible, presidents used the FBI to investigate, to develop evidence, and then to pursue through the criminal process those low-level operatives that we were fortunate

under robust notions of the right to use force in self-defense,[156] is part of the Bush administration's strategy to contain and then roll-back terrorism so that eventually it will again be a problem manageable in the traditional domain of law enforcement.[157] The militarization of counter-terrorism has brought areas of international law into WMD policy that previously were not an issue, such as the treatment of enemy combatants under international humanitarian law.

Although the traditional law enforcement approach to terrorism is, in the opinion of the United States, inadequate, it has not been abandoned in the development of strategies to counter WMD. Rather, the law enforcement approach to WMD terrorism builds on a body of international law on terrorism crafted over the course of thirty years.[158] Antiterrorism treaties did not specifically begin to incorporate WMD terrorism until the 1990s, which reflects the growth of concern about the possibility of catastrophic terrorism. In 1998, WMD terrorism featured in the adoption of the UN Convention on the Suppression of Terrorist Bombings[159] and the proposed draft UN Convention for the Suppression of Acts of Nuclear Terrorism.[160]

The UN Convention on the Suppression of Terrorist Bombings broadly defines "explosive or other lethal device" to include "[a] weapon or device that is designed, or has the capability, to cause death, serious bodily injury or substantial material damage through the release, dissemination or impact of toxic chemicals, biological agents or toxins or similar substances or radiation or radioactive material."[161] This convention then follows the standard law enforcement approach found in previous antiterrorism treaties: states parties criminalize certain offenses,[162] take jurisdiction over the commission

---

enough to arrest. This policy of dealing with the terrorist threat allowed Osama bin Laden and his leadership, and the Taliban Government that gave them sanctuary, time to plan, prepare, and implement new attacks of increasing seriousness, with impunity.").

156. *See supra* notes 137–145 and accompanying text.

157. *See* COMBATING TERRORISM, *supra* note 5, at 2.

158. *See generally* TERRORISM AND INTERNATIONAL LAW (Rosalyn Higgins & Maurice Flory eds., 1997). For treaties on international terrorism, see INTERNATIONAL TERRORISM: MULTILATERAL CONVENTIONS (1937–2001) (M. Cherif Bassiouni ed., 2001).

159. *International Convention for the Suppression of Terrorist Bombings*, G.A. Res. 52/164, U.N. GAOR, 52d Sess., 72d mtg., U.N. Doc. A/RES/52/164 (1997).

160. *Draft International Convention for the Suppression of Acts of Nuclear Terrorism*, U.N. GAOR 6th Comm., 53d Sess., Annex 1, Agenda Item 155, at 4, U.N. Doc. A/C.6/53/L.4 (1998).

161. United Nations International Convention for the Suppression of Terrorist Bombings, *supra* note 159, art. 1.3(b).

162. *Id.* arts. 2, 4.

of such acts,[163] agree to prosecute or extradite alleged perpetrators,[164] and participate in law enforcement cooperation and assistance.[165] The objective is to increase the potential that terrorist acts will be punished and thus deter terrorist activity.

A second development involving the law enforcement approach is the U.S. policy of building on existing counter-terrorism treaties to create "new, strict standards for all states to meet in the global war against terrorism."[166] The United States points to UN Security Council Resolution 1373 of September 28, 2001, as creating international legal obligations on all UN members in connection with the global fight against terrorism.[167] Enacted pursuant to Chapter VII of the UN Charter, UN Security Council Resolution 1373 contains numerous obligations on UN member states relating to combating terrorism.[168] Experts on national security and arms control referred to Resolution 1373 as making "instant global law" that will be monitored by a Committee Concerning Counter-Terrorism.[169] By combining the standards that exist in counter-terrorism treaties and the duties contained in UN Security Council Resolution 1373, the United States hopes to establish a baseline level of international legal responsibility for states in the fight against terrorism.[170]

A third development involving the law enforcement approach involves proposals to criminalize the development, possession, and use of biological and chemical weapons. The most well-known proposal in this area is the Harvard/Sussex Draft Convention on the Prevention and Punishment of the Crime of Developing, Producing, Acquiring, Stockpiling, Retaining, Transferring or Using Biological or Chemical Weapons.[171] This proposal seeks to make developing, pro-

---

163. *Id.* art. 6.

164. *Id.* art. 8.

165. *Id.* art. 10.

166. COMBATING TERRORISM, *supra* note 5, at 18.

167. *Id.*

168. *See* S.C. Res. 1373, U.N. SCOR, 58th Sess., 4385th mtg., U.N. Doc. S/RES/1373 (2001); COMBATING TERRORISM, *supra* note 5, at 18–19 ("The resolution calls upon all member states to cooperate to prevent terrorist attacks through a spectrum of activities, including suppression and freezing terrorist financing, prohibiting their nationals from financially supporting terrorists, denying safe haven, and taking steps to prevent the movement of terrorists.").

169. John R. Burroughs et al., *Arms Control and National Security*, 36 INT'L LAW. 471, 487 (2002).

170. COMBATING TERRORISM, *supra* note 5, at 18–19.

171. Matthew Meselson & Julian Robinson, Harvard/Sussex Program on CBW Armament and Arms Limitation, *Draft Convention on the Prevention and Punishment of the Crime of Developing, Producing, Acquiring, Stockpiling, Retaining, Transferring or using Biological or*

ducing, acquiring, stockpiling, retaining, or transferring any chemical or biological weapon a criminal offense.[172] The draft convention then requires states parties to take jurisdiction over such offenses,[173] either prosecute or extradite people alleged to have committed such crimes,[174] and engage in law enforcement cooperation and assistance.[175] This proposal seeks to transform the ban on chemical and biological weapons applicable to governments into a criminal process that seeks to deter and punish individuals who participate in chemical or biological weaponeering. Such a criminal process would apply to individuals who are government officials or terrorists.[176] Targeting individuals in the manner the Harvard/Sussex proposal envisions reveals the differences between the law enforcement approach and the traditional arms control approach.

Barry Kellman has also prominently advocated using an international criminal law approach to address the threat of bioterrorism. Kellman argues that, although the arms control approach and an approach based on criminal law enforcement are not inherently contradictory or mutually exclusive, their paths diverge substantially.[177] Kellman asserts that the problem of bioterrorism "shares more characteristics with illicit smuggling operations than with state weapons development programs," meaning that "anti-bioterrorism efforts should be directed at denying necessary materials and equipment to bioterrorists and at interdicting their networks before there is an attack."[178] Kellman's international criminal law approach to bioterrorism contains four categories of initiatives:

> (1) criminalization of both the use of biological agents and unauthorized possession of pathogenic agents; (2) regulation of possession and transfer of pathogenic agents, including oversight of basic bio-research and tracking of sophisticated weaponization equipment; (3) anti-smuggling initiatives, including authority to undertake investigations; and (4) empowerment of an institution capable of directing the entire set of efforts.[179]

Chemical Weapons (Nov. 1, 2001), *at* http://fas-www.harvard.edu/~hsp/crim01.pdf (last visited Oct. 21, 2003).

172. *See id.* art. I.

173. *See id.* art. V.

174. *See id.* art. VII.

175. *See id.* art. IX.

176. *See id.* art. I, para. 1 (stating that *"any person* commits an offence" who engages in activity prohibited by the Convention) (emphasis added).

177. Kellman, *supra* note 12, at 721–22.

178. *Id.* at 730.

179. *Id.*

B. Technological Feasibility

The perceived increase in the technological feasibility of WMD development has contributed to the growth of concerns about WMD proliferation by state and non-state actors.[180] The arms control approach to nuclear weapons included limitations on the superpowers developing defensive anti-ballistic missile technologies[181] and controls on the deployment of certain offensive nuclear weapons technologies.[182] The bans on biological and chemical weapons rested on the assumption that governments would not turn to these WMD even though science made such weapons easier to develop and deploy. The technological feasibility risk factor has become more important in WMD policy because of the fluidity and uncertainty of WMD politics after the end of the Cold War and the rise of "new terrorism."

The most prominent response developed to address the growing technological feasibility risk involves national efforts to tighten controls on access to and transfer of matériel necessary to make WMD.[183] Existing examples of this policy response do not involve the direct use of international law, such as the negotiation of treaties. The United States has, for example, worked bilaterally with Russia to secure former Soviet nuclear, chemical, and biological weapons facilities to ensure that Soviet WMD technologies do not proliferate.[184] The Group of Eight Global Partnership Against the Spread of Weapons and Materials of Mass Destruction, established in June 2002, seeks to enhance the security of WMD technologies in the former Soviet Union through securing WMD matériel, employing former Soviet weaponeers, enhancing export controls, and strengthening border security.[185]

---

180. *See supra* notes 116–124 and accompanying text.

181. *See, e.g.*, ABM Treaty, *supra* note 54.

182. *See, e.g.*, SALT II, *supra* note 55.

183. *See, e.g.*, Uniting and Strengthening America by Providing Appropriate Tools Required to Intercept and Obstruct Terrorism (USA PATRIOT) Act of 2001, Pub. L. 107-56, 115 Stat. 272 (2001); Public Health Security and Bioterrorism Preparedness and Response Act of 2002, Pub. L. 107-188, 116 Stat. 594, Title II.

184. *See* Jasinski, *supra* note 91.

185. *See generally* Press Release, White House, Fact Sheet: G-8 Summit—Preventing the Proliferation of Weapons of Mass Destruction (June 27, 2002), *at* http://www.whitehouse.gov/news/releases/2002/06/20020627-7.html (last visited Oct. 21, 2003); *see also* ROBERT J. EINHORN & MICHÈLE A. FLOURNOY, CENTER FOR STRATEGIC & INTERNATIONAL STUDIES (CSIS), PROTECTING AGAINST THE SPREAD OF NUCLEAR, BIOLOGICAL, AND CHEMICAL WEAPONS: AN ACTION AGENDA FOR THE GLOBAL PARTNERSHIP (2003) (making recommendations to take the Group of Eight Global Partnership Against Weapons and Materials of Mass Destruction from financial commitments to implementation of projects).

The members of the Australia Group have tightened export control measures on items that could be used to produce WMD.[186]

The United States and other countries have undertaken to strengthen their national laws on security of WMD items, such as biological agents.[187] These policy initiatives connect with international law through proposals made by governments and non-governmental experts for international legal action on biosecurity. As alternatives to the rejected Protocol to the BWC, the Bush administration advocated that BWC States Parties should (1) establish sound national oversight mechanisms for the security and genetic engineering of pathogenic organisms; (2) devise a solid framework for bioscientists in the form of a code of ethical conduct that would have universal recognition; and (3) promote responsible conduct in the study, use, modification, and shipment of pathogenic organisms.[188] The British government connected these ideas to international law by proposing a Convention on Physical Protection of Dangerous Pathogens.[189] Non-governmental experts also called for a Biosecurity Convention to improve the safety and security of pathogenic microbes in the face of WMD proliferation and terrorism.[190] Steinbruner and Harris have argued for an international oversight arrangement to ensure that advanced biological research does not contribute intentionally or unintentionally to the development of dangerous pathogens.[191]

Although the likelihood of a new biosecurity treaty or other new international legal arrangements is uncertain, international cooperation on biosecurity as part of the future BWC process was an outcome

---

186. *See* U.S. Dep't of State, *Fact Sheet: U.S. Efforts to Combat the Biological Weapons Threat*, Nov. 14, 2002, *at* http://www.state.gov/t/ac/rls/fs/15150.htm (last visited Nov. 15, 2003).

187. *See id.*

188. *See* Press Release, U.S. Dep't of State, President's Statement on Biological Weapons: Strengthening the International Regime against Biological Weapons (Nov. 1, 2001), *at* http://www.state.gov/t/ac/rls/rm/2001/7907.htm (last visited Oct. 5, 2003).

189. *See* SECRETARY OF STATE FOR FOREIGN AND COMMONWEALTH AFFAIRS, STRENGTHENING THE BIOLOGICAL AND TOXIN WEAPONS CONVENTION: COUNTERING THE THREAT FROM BIOLOGICAL WEAPONS, Apr. 2002, at 3, *at* http://www.bradford.ac.uk/acad/sbtwc/other/fcobw.pdf (last visited Nov. 15, 2003).

190. *See* Jonathan B. Tucker & Raymond A. Zilinskas, *Assessing U.S. Proposals to Strengthen the Biological Weapons Convention*, ARMS CONTROL TODAY, Apr. 2002, at 10, 11, *available at* http://www.armscontrol.org/act/2002_04/tuczilapril02.asp (arguing that "the United States should propose that the UN General Assembly adopt a 'Biosecurity Convention' requiring countries to follow uniform guidelines for who is given access to dangerous pathogens, as well as universal standards of physical security for those institutions authorized to work with them").

191. *See generally* John D. Steinbruner & Elisa D. Harris, *Controlling Dangerous Pathogens*, ISSUES SCI. & TECH., Spring 2003, at 47.

of the Fifth Review Conference in November 2002.[192] In August 2003, BWC States Parties discussed national mechanisms to strengthen security and oversight of pathogenic agents to prevent them from falling into the wrong hands.[193] In this respect, BWC States Parties are adapting the arms control approach for the new political and technological realities of biological weapons. As the United Nations indicated in a press release before the Fifth BWC Review Conference, the BWC process has to recognize the "rapid progress being made in the bio-sciences, progress which as well as developing important benefits also makes it potentially easier to develop biological weapons."[194] Whether international cooperation on biosecurity through the BWC process agreed upon at the Fifth Review Conference leads to new treaty law remains to be seen.

C. Social Vulnerability

As analyzed in Part III, the growing awareness of the social vulnerability to WMD attacks has contributed to mounting concerns about WMD proliferation. The arms control approach contains little, if anything, that addresses the social vulnerability risk factor. Historically, addressing such vulnerability has remained predominantly at the national level, as illustrated by various national civil defense programs created to deal with the effects of nuclear attack.[195] Contemporary policy appears to be following the same pattern because national policy and law dominate the growing movement toward domestic preparedness for WMD attacks. The United States is, for example, mounting a significant homeland security effort that includes large-

---

192. On the Fifth Review Conference, see Marie Isabelle Chevrier, *Waiting for Godot or Saving the Show? The BWC Review Conference Reaches Modest Agreement*, DISARMAMENT DIPLOMACY, Dec. 2002–Jan. 2003, at 11, *available at* http://www.acronym.org.uk/dd/dd68/68bwc.htm (last visited Nov. 10, 2003); Graham S. Pearson, *Report from Geneva: The Biological and Toxin Weapons Convention Review Conference*, CBW CONVENTIONS BULLETIN, No. 58, Dec. 2002, at 19, http://fas-www.harvard.edu/~hsp/bulletin/cbwcb58.pdf (last visited Nov. 10, 2003).

193. *See* Report of the Meeting of Experts (Part I), Fifth Review Conference of the States Parties of the BWC, BWC/CONF. Doc. BWC/MSP.2003/MX/4 (Part I) (Sept. 18, 2003), *available at* http://www.opbw.org/new_process/mx4_I.pdf (last visited Nov. 15, 2003) (reporting on the Meeting of Experts held from Aug. 18–29, 2003, on consideration of the adoption of necessary national measures to implement BWC prohibitions).

194. Press Release, United Nations, Fifth Review Conference of Biological Weapons Convention to Resume in Geneva from 11–22 November (Nov. 6, 2002), U.N. Doc. DC/2847, *at* www.un.org/news/Press/docs/2002/dc2847.doc.htm (last visited Oct. 21, 2003).

195. *See supra* note 126.

scale efforts to prepare the United States homeland for WMD terrorism.[196]

International cooperation on reducing social vulnerabilities is, however, emerging. The United States is proposing to support the strengthening of the international community's capacity for WMD defense and preparedness by improving mechanisms for early detection, diagnosis, and the mitigation of health threats posed by chemical and biological terrorism.[197] Multilateral forums in which preparedness for chemical and biological terrorism has been discussed include, for example, NATO, the World Health Organization, the Ottawa Group, the World Customs Organization, and the International Maritime Organization.[198] Some of the ideas discussed in these groups, such as the creation of a global smallpox vaccine reserve[199] and regulations to enhance ship and port security against possible WMD terrorism,[200] may require formal international legal activities, leading to the crafting of new international law specially directed toward reducing social vulnerability to WMD attacks. Such international legal developments would be further evidence that international policy and law on WMD have moved beyond the arms control approach.

D. From the Arms Control Approach to a Trifurcated Strategy

The international legal developments, proposals, and ideas analyzed above suggest that WMD policy is moving from a dominant role for the arms control approach to a three-part strategy. Figure 2 provides an overview of this trifurcated strategy. The first part involves international law that addresses WMD threats presented by states. This "international security" framework includes not only the arms control treaties but also the moves to draw on the right of self-defense to address WMD threats from state actors.

The second part comprises international law that attempts to address WMD threats posed by non-state actors, namely terrorists. This "global security" framework is integrated into the anti-WMD effort the law enforcement model developed in antiterrorism treaties. Multilateral antiterrorism treaties, specifically including WMD threats and bilateral extradition treaties, form the heart of this

---

196. *See* HOMELAND SECURITY, *supra* note 25, at 41–45.

197. *See* U.S. Dep't of State, *Fact Sheet: U.S. Efforts to Combat the Biological Weapons Threat, supra* note 186.

198. *See id.*

199. *See id.*

200. *See id.*

framework. The "global security" framework also includes efforts to use international law to improve the safety and security of WMD agents and equipment to ensure that state or non-state proliferators do not gain access to them. Finally, the framework incorporates military responses to terrorist threats.

The third part of the trifurcated strategy focuses on domestic defense against and preparedness for WMD events. This "homeland security" framework is taking shape through international cooperative efforts on improving domestic readiness for WMD attacks against vulnerable societies. Whether the source of such attacks is a state or non-state actor is less relevant in this framework than preparing societies for the consequences of WMD events. International law in the homeland security framework is less developed than the other two pieces of the trifurcated strategy, but developments indicate that this area may be one of growth in the future.

From the Arms Control Approach to a Trifurcated Strategy

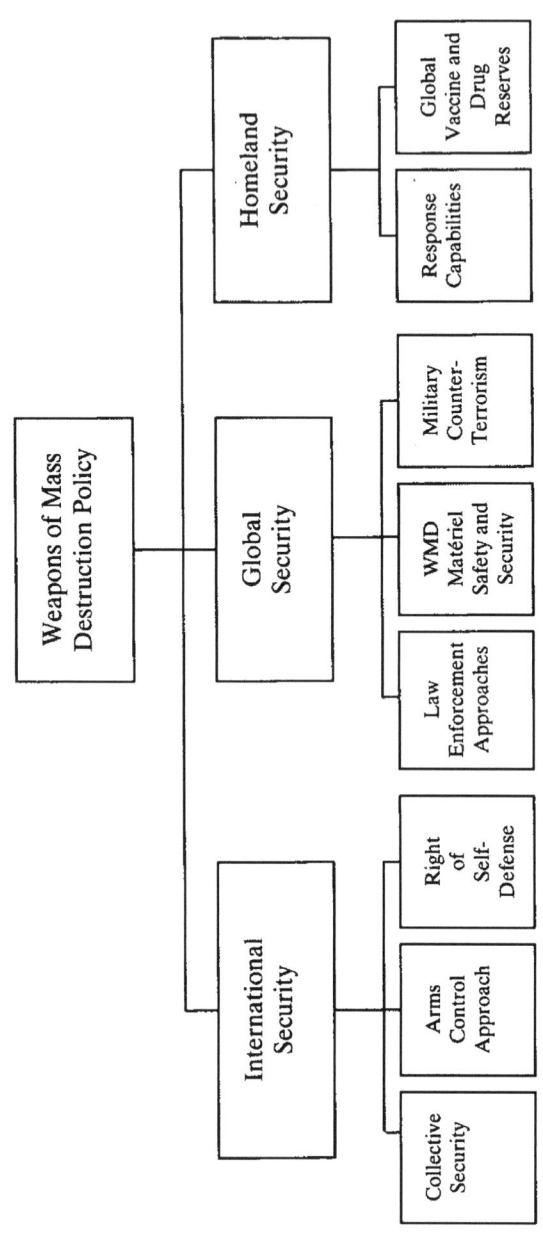

V. CONCLUSION: THE END OF THE ARMS CONTROL APPROACH AND ITS IMPLICATIONS FOR INTERNATIONAL LAW ON WEAPONS OF MASS DESTRUCTION

The end of the arms control approach as the leading international legal strategy against WMD carries deeper implications for international law than the process of diversification and the trifurcated strategy reviewed in Part IV. One such implication involves questions about the future of the arms control approach. The focus in the context of nuclear weapons has shifted from the stabilization of bipolar deterrence to the problem of multipolar proliferation of nuclear weapons technologies and ambitions among states and non-state actors. The proliferation concern has exposed the two basic weaknesses of the Nuclear Non-Proliferation Treaty: (1) state proliferators either are not bound by the treaty or they violate it without fear of sanction under the treaty regime; and (2) the treaty does not directly address the threat of nuclear terrorism carried out by non-state actors.

The continuing crisis over North Korea's pursuit of nuclear weapons reflects well the argument that the arms control approach's dominance in WMD policy is over. Neither the NPT nor the 1994 Agreed Framework[201] between the United States and North Korea has deterred Pyongyang from pursuing a nuclear weapons capability. The United States was on the brink of war with North Korea in 1994 over Pyongyang's push for nuclear weapons,[202] and it is not yet clear how the current crisis will be resolved—through multilateral diplomacy or preemptive military action by the United States.

In August 2003, North Korea agreed to participate in multilateral talks with the United States, China, Japan, South Korea, and Russia.[203] Prior to the talks, China was not holding out much hope for significant progress,[204] leaving the option of preemptive military action

---

201. Under the Agreed Framework concluded in October 1994, "North Korea agreed to shut down its plutonium-based nuclear reactor and related facilities, and the United States agreed to provide two proliferation-resistant reactors and supply North Korea with heating oil while the reactors were under construction." *Nuclear Weapons on the Korean Peninsula*, ARMS CONTROL TODAY, May 2003, at 3, *available at* http://www.armscontrol.org/act/2003_05/nkoreaintro_may03.asp (last visited Nov. 15, 2003).

202. *See* James T. Laney & Jason T. Shaplen, *How to Deal with North Korea*, FOREIGN AFF., Mar./Apr. 2003, at 16, 23 (2003).

203. *Let's All Six of Us Talk About It*, ECONOMIST, Aug. 9, 2003, at 33, *available at* 2003 WL 58583522.

204. *See id.*

86   DUKE JOURNAL OF COMPARATIVE & INTERNATIONAL LAW   [Vol 14:39

on the table.[205] According to the U.S. State Department, these multi-lateral talks did not go well.[206] In October 2003, North Korea agreed to return to the negotiating table two weeks after President Bush indicated a willingness to "extend a written, multilateral security agreement to North Korea in exchange for a complete dismantling of its nuclear weapons program."[207] The same volatile mixture of multi-lateral approaches and potential military action has characterized the crisis over Iran's alleged pursuit of nuclear weapons.[208]

Concerns about the future of the arms control approach in the context of chemical and biological weapons also abound. Although the CWC regime is functioning, many problems—including a lack of resources, failure of CWC States Parties to comply, and leadership controversies—cloud the implementation of the CWC's prohibitions and verification system.[209] New threats to the CWC's main normative objective of banning chemical weapons have appeared in the form of so-called "non-lethal" chemical weapons.[210] The first few years of the CWC's implementation have not sufficiently alleviated concerns about the proliferation of chemical weapons among states and non-

---

205. *North Korea Capitulates: Hardline Pressure Works*, FAR E. ECON. REV., Aug. 14, 2003, at 6, *available at* 2003 WL-FEER 59146994 (noting the U.S. position that it would not let the nuclear situation in North Korea stand, indicating "a willingness to make military strikes just short of outright war").

206. See John R. Bolton, Under Secretary for Arms Control and International Security, Remarks to the Bruges Group, London, United Kingdom (Oct. 30, 2003), at http://www.state.gov/t/us/rm/25752.htm (last visited Nov. 10, 2003) ("During the August six-party talks in Beijing, the United States, China, Russia, Japan, and South Korea emphasized that the Korean Peninsula must be free of nuclear weapons. North Korea further isolated itself by threatening provocative actions such as nuclear tests—adding to threats it made in April that it might build more nuclear weapons and perhaps even transfer nuclear material or weapons to third parties.").

207. See Anthony Faiola, *N. Korea Agrees to Resume Nuclear Talks; U.S. Reacts Coolly to Demand for 'Simultaneous Actions'*, WASH. POST, Oct. 31, 2003, at A18.

208. See Douglas Frantz, *Iran Closes in on Ability to Build a Nuclear Bomb*, L.A. TIMES, Aug. 4, 2003, at A1. In late October 2003, Iran reached an agreement with France, Germany, and the United Kingdom to stop enriching uranium and to provide documents to the International Atomic Energy Agency, thus easing tensions over U.S. allegations that Iran is secretly developing nuclear weapons. See Joby Warrick, *Iran Still Has Nuclear Deadline, U.S. Says*, WASH. POST, Oct. 23, 2003, at A18.

209. On the challenges facing the CWC, see Ian R. Kenyon, *The Chemical Weapons Convention and the OPCW: The Challenges of the 21st Century*, CBW CONVENTIONS BULLETIN, No. 56, June 2002, at 1, http://www.fas.harvard.edu/~hsp/bulletin/cbwcb56.pdf (last visited Nov. 10, 2003).

210. *See, e.g.*, WORKING GROUP ON BIOLOGICAL WEAPONS, FEDERATION OF AMERICAN SCIENTISTS, NON-LETHAL CHEMICAL AND BIOLOGICAL WEAPONS (Nov. 2002), http://www. fas.org/bwc/papers/nonlethalCBW.pdf (last visited Nov. 10, 2003).

state actors, forcing the development of new policies and legal strategies on chemical weapons and chemical terrorism.

The arms control approach also suffered a beating in the context of the BWC, in the form of the United States' rejection in 2001 of a verification protocol that had been years in the making.[211] The death of the verification protocol left the arms control approach with only a weak treaty to confront perhaps the most difficult WMD proliferation and terrorism challenge.[212] Although the BWC Fifth Review Conference did not end in disaster,[213] the arms control approach on biological weapons remains in serious trouble.

The political, technological, and vulnerability challenges to the arms control approach have created a crisis of confidence in its utility. The arms control approach and the treaties it has generated remain necessary but are no longer sufficient (or even in some respects relevant) to address the threat currently posed by WMD proliferation and terrorism. Arms control supporters favor new international legal strategies and global civil society action to address the political, technological, and vulnerability problems that WMD create today. Arms control skeptics see the crisis of confidence in the arms control approach as evidence that the approach itself is a flawed sideshow, at best, and a dangerous delusion, at worst.

Beneath the controversy surrounding the arms control approach to WMD stirs a larger debate about the role of international law in world politics. Does the end of the arms control approach signal a loss of faith in the utility of international law in international politics? Is the diversification of international legal strategies and ideas on dealing with WMD merely, to paraphrase Bull, "anything more than [a] heightened protest against the facts of international politics?"[214] This international legal debate has an analogue in international relations theory in disagreements between realists and institutionalists about the contributions institutions and regimes, such as arms control treaties, make to national security and the prevention of conflict.[215]

---

211. *See* Whitehair & Brugger, *supra* note 121.

212. Burroughs et al., *supra* note 169, at 505 ("The utter breakdown of the Biological Weapons Convention does not bode well for international controls over these weapons.").

213. *See* Chevrier, *supra* note 192; Pearson, *supra* note 192, at 19.

214. HEDLEY BULL, THE ANARCHICAL SOCIETY: A STUDY OF ORDER IN WORLD POLITICS 151 (1977).

215. *See* John J. Mearsheimer, *The False Promise of International Institutions*, INT'L SECURITY, Vol. 19, No. 3, Winter 1994–95, at 5, 16 (1994) (arguing that institutionalism pays "little attention to the security realm, where questions about war and peace are of central importance"). *But see* Robert O. Keohane & Lisa L. Martin, *The Promise of Institutionalist The-*

88   DUKE JOURNAL OF COMPARATIVE & INTERNATIONAL LAW   [Vol 14:39

Pursuing these larger theoretical controversies in international law and international relations is beyond the scope of this article, but I mention them because the political, technological, and vulnerability challenges currently undermining the arms control approach connect to deeper concerns about the nature of international politics and international law's role therein. On the one hand, the emerging trifurcated strategy suggests that international law's role in the effort to control WMD remains critical, even with the end of the arms control approach. On the other hand, the same strategy perhaps indicates that the WMD threat may be pushing past the point at which states, international organizations, and non-governmental actors can effectively use international law to deter, defend, or disarm. The need for international law in the WMD context may be higher now than in previous historical periods. The dangers and uncertainties confronting the use of international law in this new WMD environment may also be historically unprecedented, casting ominous shadows over international legal endeavors against WMD for the foreseeable future.

---

ory, INT'L SECURITY, Vol. 20, No. 1, Summer 1995, at 39, 43 (1995) (arguing that institutionalist theory is relevant to the study of security affairs).

Part II
Nuclear Weapons

[3]

The Treaty on Non-Proliferation of Nuclear Weapons: Nuclear Technology Confronts World Politics

Mason Willrich†

I ask you to stop and think for a moment what it would mean to
have nuclear weapons in so many hands, in the hands of countries
large and small, stable and unstable, responsible and irresponsible,
scattered throughout the world.[1]

President John F. Kennedy

From the dawn of the nuclear era, the problem of nuclear weapons
proliferation has confronted the nations of the world. Since 1945,
despite continuing efforts to prevent further proliferation, there has
been a five-fold increase in the number of nations having nuclear
weapons of their own. At last, after long and arduous negotiations, the
United States and the Soviet Union have reached agreement on a
"Treaty on the Non-Proliferation of Nuclear Weapons."[2] This Treaty
represents "the maximum area of agreement now obtainable."[3] It has

† Professor of Law and Director, Center for the Study of Science, Technology and
Public Policy, University of Virginia; formerly Assistant General Counsel, United States
Arms Control and Disarmament Agency, and member, United States Delegation to the
Eighteen Nation Disarmament Committee. B.A. 1954, Yale University; J.D. 1960, Uni-
versity of California (Berkeley).

The writer wishes to acknowledge the benefits he has received from discussions with
members of a panel on Nuclear Energy and World Order—sponsored by the American
Society of International Law—which he served as *rapporteur*.

1. A Step Toward Peace: Report to the People on the Nuclear Test Ban Treaty,
DOCUMENTS ON DISARMAMENT, 1963, at 250 (U.S. Arms Control & Disarmament Agency Pub.
No. 24, 1964).

2. The complete Treaty did not emerge until June 10, 1968. U.N. General Assembly,
A/RES/2373(xxii), Annex, U.N. Doc. A/7016/Add.1, Annex, June 10, 1968.

3. Statement of United States Representative to the Eighteen Nation Disarmament
Committee (ENDC). Eighteen Nation Disarmament Conference Procès Verbale 378
(prov.), at 23 [hereinafter cited as ENDC/PV].

The Yale Law Journal   Vol. 77: 1447, 1968

been widely discussed in the Eighteen Nation Disarmament Committee in Geneva,[4] the NATO Council in Brussels,[5] and the United Nations

Agreement was first reached between the United States and the Soviet Union on a draft Treaty on August 24, 1967, at the Eighteen Nation Disarmament Committee. The draft was complete in all major respects except for Article III, dealing with safeguards on peaceful nuclear activities. The Soviet Union insisted at that time, perhaps in a peculiar application of a principal of separate *and* equal, on tabling identical drafts rather than one agreed draft. For the treaty draft of August 24, 1967, see DOCUMENTS ON DISARMAMENT, 1967, at 338 (U.S. Arms Control & Disarmament Agency Pub. No. 46, 1968) [hereinafter cited as DOCUMENTS ON DISARMAMENT, 1967]. Speeches by United States and Soviet Union Representatives to the ENDC at the time of tabling are reprinted in *id.* 342, 347.

A second set of identical drafts was tabled by the United States and the Soviet Union at the ENDC on January 18, 1968. For text see ENDC/192/Rev.1. For the United States and Soviet Union tabling speeches, see ENDC/PV.357. The January 18, 1968, draft included Article III and also incorporated as amendments certain suggestions of other delegations to the ENDC made during intervening discussion of the August 24, 1967, draft.

A third agreed draft was presented by the United States and the Soviet Union to the ENDC on March 11, 1968, which incorporated certain minor changes in light of discussions since the second draft had been tabled. ENDC/225, Annex A. For the United States and Soviet Union tabling speeches, see ENDC/PV.376. Article IX, paragraph 2, in which the names of Depositary Governments were to be specified, was still blank. Previously, on March 7, 1968, the United States, the Soviet Union, and the United Kingdom had presented to the ENDC a draft resolution of the United Nations Security Council on security assurances to non-nuclear-weapon states. ENDC/225, Annex B. For tabling speeches of the United States, the Soviet Union, and the United Kingdom, see ENDC/PV.375. The March 11, 1968, draft Treaty and March 7, 1968, draft Security Council resolution were submitted by the ENDC in its report to the United Nations General Assembly on March 14, 1968, and, thereafter, were discussed primarily in the First Committee (Political and Security) of the resumed 22d Session of the General Assembly, which convened on April 26, 1968. In light of these discussions, on May 31, 1968, certain changes were agreed to by the United States and the Soviet Union and incorporated into the June 10, 1968, Treaty text.

Most of the public documents dealing with non-proliferation and the Treaty are collected in DOCUMENTS ON DISARMAMENT, a series compiled and issued annually by the United States Arms Control and Disarmament Agency. An excellent historical account of the Non-Proliferation Treaty, issued under the auspices of the U.S. Arms Control and Disarmament Agency is LAMBERT, EFFORTS TO PREVENT THE SPREAD OF NUCLEAR WEAPONS (1968). The story of post-World War II arms control negotiations in general, up to 1961, is authoritatively and readably told in B. BECHHOEFER, POSTWAR NEGOTIATIONS FOR ARMS CONTROL (1961). *See also* KLEIN, L'ENTREPRISE DU DÉSARMEMENT DEPUIS 1945 (1964); OFFICE OF PUBLIC INFORMATION, THE UNITED NATIONS AND DISARMAMENT 1945-1965 (United Nations, no date).

4.   The ENDC was established by agreement between the United States and the Soviet Union and endorsed unanimously by the U.N. General Assembly on December 20, 1961. 16 U.N. GAOR 1129, A/RES/1722(xvi), Jan. 3, 1962; DOCUMENTS ON DISARMAMENT, 1961, at 741 (U.S. Arms Control & Disarmament Agency, Pub. No. 5, 1961). The Committee is composed of five NATO members: Canada, France, Italy, the United Kingdom, and the United States; five Warsaw Pact members: Bulgaria, Czechoslovakia, Poland, Rumania, and the Soviet Union; and eight non-aligned nations: Brazil, Burma, Ethiopia, India, Mexico, Nigeria, Sweden, and the United Arab Republic. France has never taken part in the meetings. The United States and the Soviet Union serve as permanent co-chairmen. The Committee first convened on March 14, 1962. The basis for discussion was a United States-Soviet Union "Agreed Statement of Principles" for future multilateral negotiations on disarmament. Paragraph 8 of the Joint Statement stated in part: "States participating in the negotiations should seek to achieve and implement the widest possible agreement at the earliest possible date." Under the rubric of this paragraph, a Committee of the Whole was established (since discontinued) to discuss so-called "collateral measures." The Committee of the Whole agreed on May 25, 1962, to begin "concurrent" discussions on two proposals. The United States' item was reduction of the risk of war by accident, miscalculation, or failure of communications; the Soviet Union's item was non-proliferation of nuclear weapons, which at the time meant little more than an excuse for propaganda attacks against West Germany. DOCUMENTS ON DISARMAMENT, 1963, at 544 (U.S. Arms

Nuclear Weapons

General Assembly in New York. Moreover, on June 12, 1968, the Treaty was commended in a resolution of the United Nations General Assembly—adopted by a vote of 95 in favor, 4 against and 21 abstaining[6] —and on June 19, 1968, in conjunction with the Treaty, a resolution on "security assurances" was adopted by the Security Council.[7] Now each nation must decide whether or not to become a party.[8]

A goal of overriding importance in the nuclear era is the avoidance of nuclear war.[9] A flat prohibition on the further spread of nuclear

Control & Disarmament Agency Pub. No. 24, 1964). As of March 14, 1968, when it adjourned for discussion of the Non-Proliferation Treaty in the General Assembly, the ENDC had held 379 plenary meetings divided into 13 sessions. Much in addition to non-proliferation has been discussed, but the Non-Proliferation Treaty is clearly the Committee's major accomplishment to date.

5. An account of NATO consultations regarding the Non-Proliferation Treaty is contained in *Hearings on Arms Control and Disarmament Act Amendments, 1968, Before the House Comm. on Foreign Affairs*, 90th Cong., 2d Sess. 29-30 (1968).

6. For text see A/RES/2373(xxii), U.N. Doc. A/7016/Add.1, at 5, June 10, 1968. Four members were absent at the vote. Those against were Albania, Cuba, Tanzania and Zambia. Among the abstentions were Argentina, Brazil, France, India and Spain. The first three operative paragraphs of the resolution are:

"1. *Commends* the Treaty on the Non-Proliferation of Nuclear Weapons, the text of which is annexed to the present resolution;

"2. *Requests* the Depositary Governments to open the Treaty for signature and ratification at the earliest possible date;

"3. *Expresses the hope* for the widest possible adherence to the Treaty by both nuclear-weapon and non-nuclear-weapon States . . . ."

In a previous resolution of November 19, 1965, the General Assembly had urged "the early conclusion" of a non-proliferation treaty which should "be void of loop-holes" and should "embody an acceptable balance of mutual responsibilities and obligations of the nuclear and non-nuclear Powers." A/RES/2028(xx), Nov. 23, 1965; DOCUMENTS ON DISARMAMENT, 1965, at 532 (U.S. Arms Control & Disarmament Agency Pub. No. 34, 1966) [hereinafter cited as DOCUMENTS ON DISARMAMENT, 1965]. At the resumed 22d Session of the General Assembly, the Treaty was criticized by many non-nuclear-weapon states mainly because it violated, in their view, the principle of "balance" of obligation of non-nuclear and nuclear states.

7. The vote was 10 in favor, 0 against and 5 abstentions. Among the abstentions were France and Pakistan. S/RES/255, June 19, 1968. For text of operative paragraphs see note 154 *infra*.

8. On May 17, 1966, the Senate approved without a dissenting vote a resolution sponsored by Senator Pastore, Chairman of the Joint Committee on Atomic Energy, which recognizes that "the spread of nuclear weapons constitutes a grave threat to the security and peace of all nations," and commends "the President's serious and urgent efforts to negotiate international agreements limiting the spread of nuclear weapons and supports the principle of additional efforts . . . for the solution of nuclear proliferation problems." S. Res. 179, 89th Cong., 2d Sess. (1966). For hearings on this Resolution see *Hearings on Nonproliferation of Nuclear Weapons Before the Joint Comm. on Atomic Energy*, 89th Cong., 2d Sess. (1966).

A conference of non-nuclear-weapon states, not limited to U.N. members, is scheduled to be held in Geneva, August 29—September 28, 1968, pursuant to General Assembly resolution. A/RES/2346(xxii), Jan. 5, 1968. Topics on the agenda will include: (1) methods of assuring the security of non-nuclear-weapon states, (2) implications of the production and acquisition of nuclear weapons by non-nuclear-weapon states, (3) prevention of proliferation through cooperation among non-nuclear-weapon states, (4) programs for the peaceful uses of nuclear energy, and (5) implementation of conference decisions.

9. For a dispassionate and revealing assessment of the effects of a variety of possible uses of nuclear weapons, including a summary of the effects of the Hiroshima and Nagasaki drops, see Report of the Secretary-General, *infra* note 14, at 6-28. The classic work in the field is THE EFFECTS OF NUCLEAR WEAPONS (Glasstone ed. 1962), issued jointly by the AEC and the Department of Defense.

The Yale Law Journal   Vol. 77: 1447, 1968

weapons to additional states seems justified as the preferred policy when it is weighed against other alternatives in relation to this goal. Moreover, even though non-proliferation itself is not likely to reduce the present risk of nuclear war, a general non-proliferation policy may be justified as perhaps the only means of buying the time needed to take further steps which might lead to a significant reduction in that risk.[10]

The principal aim of the Non-Proliferation Treaty is to prevent the present five nuclear-weapon states[11] from increasing to ten or fifteen in the future.[12] At the same time, the Treaty is intended to permit, indeed to accelerate, the future development and spread of peaceful uses of nuclear energy throughout the world.

---

10. It is often asserted that non-proliferation policy should be viewed as a means to the end of disarmament: *e.g.*, "A treaty on non-proliferation of nuclear weapons is not an end in itself but only a means to an end. That end is the achievement of General and Complete Disarmament, and, more particularly, nuclear disarmament." Eight Nation Joint Memorandum Submitted to the ENDC, Sept. 15, 1965, ENDC/158; DOCUMENTS ON DISARMAMENT, 1965, at 424. While non-proliferation policy is related to disarmament policy, both nuclear and conventional, all such policies should be evaluated in terms of their effect on the likelihood of use of force, especially nuclear force. A disarmament scheme which increased the likelihood of nuclear war would not be good policy. For a statement of the reasons why the further spread of nuclear weapons "increases the danger of nuclear war and diminishes the security of all nations," see testimony of Secretary of State Rusk in *Hearings on Nonproliferation of Nuclear Weapons Before the Joint Comm. on Atomic Energy*, 89th Cong., 2d Sess. 3, 4 (1966). For a statement *contra* which concludes that: "a policy of vigorously pursuing a [non-proliferation] treaty over the reservations of a number of allies and friendly neutrals may represent a mistaken notion of the [U.S.] national interest," see testimony of Dr. James McBride, *Hearings on Arms Control and Disarmament Act Amendments, 1968, Before the House Comm. on Foreign Affairs*, 90th Cong., 2d Sess. 37, 40 (1968).

The other basic relationship against which non-proliferation policy must be evaluated, however, is that between proliferation and economic development. The costs of various kinds of nuclear weapons capabilities can be determined with a fair degree of accuracy. *See, e.g.*, Report of the Secretary-General, *infra* note 14, at 29-41. The interaction between achievement of a nuclear weapons capability, or an attempt to achieve such a capability, and the process of economic development in a particular state is, however, much more difficult to judge.

11. Paragraph 3 of Article IX of the Treaty defines "nuclear-weapon State" as "one which has manufactured and exploded a nuclear weapon or other nuclear explosive device prior to January 1, 1967." All other states would presumably fall into the category of "non-nuclear weapon States," an undefined term used throughout the treaty. These terms were introduced by the United States in amendments to its draft treaty proposals on March 22, 1966, in order to "help stop the talk of a 'nuclear club.'" DOCUMENTS ON DISARMAMENT, 1966, at 164 (U.S. Arms Control & Disarmament Agency Pub. No. 43, 1967) [hereinafter cited as DOCUMENTS ON DISARMAMENT, 1966]. Certain nations possessing substantial civil nuclear industries which had chosen not to acquire nuclear weapons, such as India, had objected to being relegated to a status of "non-nuclear States" under the prior United States draft Treaty proposals of August 17, 1965. DOCUMENTS ON DISARMAMENT, 1965, at 348.

12. The identity and number of non-nuclear-weapon states which could probably develop a nuclear weapons capability vary widely depending on the time frame and also the particular perspective of the compiler. Official governmental sources are understandably reluctant to publish their intelligence estimates covering this subject. Nevertheless, there is a group of states which appear at the top of most lists. It has been recently estimated that the following seven non-nuclear-weapon states could produce a nuclear weapon in less than two years: Canada, India, Israel, Japan, Sweden, Switzerland, and West Germany. UNITED NATIONS ASSOCIATION OF THE UNITED STATES OF AMERICA, NATIONAL POLICY PANEL, STOPPING THE SPREAD OF NUCLEAR WEAPONS (1967).

Nuclear Weapons

The range of activities at which non-proliferation policy is aimed has a large political and military, and a growing economic, content. But at the core of nuclear activities is science and technology. Science discovered the energy latent in the nucleus of the atom. With technology that energy has been unleashed. The technological opportunities present in nuclear energy are now being exploited on an increasing scale to achieve a growing variety of human goals throughout the world.

From a global perspective, the processes of research, development and innovation focused on nuclear energy are taking place within and among certain states in a nation-state system. Although one global framework for voluntary cooperation in the peaceful uses of nuclear energy exists and several structures for regional coordination of peaceful and military nuclear activities are established, states remain the primary actors.[13] The development and exploitation of nuclear energy has occurred, and will probably continue to occur, in a predominantly decentralized and competitive world context. Viewed from this perspective, non-proliferation policy seeks to stop diffusion of the science and technology of nuclear weapons across international boundaries and to prevent scientific and technological activities pertaining to nuclear weapons from taking place within any state except the five existing nuclear-weapon states.

The feasibility of such a policy may be questioned. Is an international policy feasible which seeks to prevent only a narrow band of activity pertaining to nuclear weapons within a broad spectrum of activity pertaining to nuclear energy generally? Is such a policy feasible

---

13. The global framework for peaceful nuclear cooperation is the International Atomic Energy Agency, headquartered in Vienna (IAEA). The objectives of the IAEA are to "accelerate and enlarge the contribution of atomic energy to peace . . . throughout the world," and to "ensure, so far as it is able, that assistance provided by it or at its request or under its supervision or control is not used in such a way as to further any military purpose." I.A.E.A. STAT. art. II, *opened for signature* Oct. 26, 1956, [1957] 1 U.S.T. 1093, T.I.A.S. No. 3873, 276 U.N.T.S. 3. For the history, see Bechhoefer, *Negotiating the Statute of the International Atomic Energy Agency*, 13 INT'L ORG. 38 (1959); Stoessinger, *Atoms for Peace: The International Atomic Energy Agency*, in COMMISSION TO STUDY THE ORGANIZATION OF PEACE, ORGANIZING PEACE IN THE NUCLEAR AGE 117 (1959).

The principal regional structure is the European Atomic Energy Community (Euratom), whose aim is "the creation of conditions necessary for the speedy establishment and growth of nuclear industries" in its member states. Treaty Establishing the European Atomic Energy Community (EURATOM), Mar. 25, 1957, art. I, 298 U.N.T.S. 167. For a recent excellent appraisal of Euratom, see Scheinman, *Euratom: Nuclear Integration in Europe*, INT'L CONCIL., May, 1967.

On the military side, efforts to achieve nuclear cooperation as a part of collective defense arrangements, especially within NATO, have created intense arguments and have been a prime source of conflict in the Non-Proliferation Treaty negotiations. These efforts, therefore, will be discussed in some detail below. But any treaty commitment to "act to meet the common danger" in the event of an "armed attack" against any party to the treaty— the common formula for multilateral and bilateral mutual defense treaties to which the United States is a party—has a nuclear aspect.

even though the technology which underlies nuclear weapons production overlaps to a great extent that which applies to peaceful nuclear
activities? Moreover, can a policy to prevent nuclear weapons proliferation be effective without structural change in an international
system in which nation-states are the dominant actors? For these fundamental issues the Non-Proliferation Treaty will provide the acid test.

The purposes of this article are to analyze the Treaty and assess its
potential. First, the technological prerequisites for a nuclear capability,
and, second, the global distribution of these prerequisites are outlined. Next, the existing international legal framework affecting non-
proliferation is described. Thereafter, the Treaty is analyzed in some
detail, primarily in terms of the various interpretations that may
govern its application to specific problems which will be encountered
by the parties as it is implemented. Lastly, the major implications of the
Treaty for the future are assessed.

I. Nuclear Capabilities: The Technological Base

A nuclear weapons capability consists of a stockpile of nuclear
weapons and an effective means of delivery. The Non-Proliferation
Treaty places restraints, however, only on the warhead aspect of
nuclear weapons capabilities. Therefore, we will limit our analysis to
this aspect.

An essential ingredient of any nuclear capability, whether for warlike or peaceful purposes, is fissionable material.[14] The two fissionable
materials of primary interest are uranium-235 and plutonium-239.
The former is the only fissionable material known to occur in nature.

Uranium-235 usable in nuclear weapons can be obtained from natural
uranium by an "enrichment" process in which the proportion of
uranium-235 atoms is increased from 0.7 per cent, as it occurs in nature,
to 90-95 per cent. The enrichment process most widely used, gaseous
diffusion, requires extremely large plants and complex technology. A
single plant of economic size has been estimated to cost upwards of $750

---

14. An important and recent source of expert estimates concerning nuclear weapons
technology is contained in Report of the Secretary-General on the Effects of the Possible
Use of Nuclear Weapons and on the Security and Economic Implications for States of the
Acquisition and Further Development of These Weapons, United Nations General
Assembly, U.N. Doc. A/6858, Oct. 10, 1967; Documents on Disarmament, 1967, at 476. The
report is particularly useful in presenting the elements that comprise a nuclear weapons
capability and the cost estimates, including both warheads and delivery systems, of a range
of possible nuclear weapons capabilities.

Nuclear Weapons

million to build and $500-600 million per year to operate.[15] In addition
to cost and engineering difficulties, information relating to processes
for the separation of uranium isotopes is highly classified within various
national programs.[16]

It is considerably easier to produce plutonium usable in nuclear
weapons than enriched uranium. Uranium-238, the remaining 99.3
per cent of natural uranium, can be converted into plutonium-239 by
subjecting it to a neutron flux in a nuclear reactor fueled with either
natural uranium or uranium that is only 3-5 per cent enriched.[17] In

15. Report of the Secretary-General, *supra* note 14, Annex IV, at 1. The United States
has built three gaseous diffusion plants. The first cost $1 billion and the next two cost a
total of $1.3 billion to build.

16. As the need for additional uranium enrichment plant capacity approaches, pressure
will increase to loosen information controls, at least to the extent of permitting broader
access to classified information. *See, e.g.,* ATOMIC INDUSTRIAL FORUM, REPORT OF THE STUDY
COMMITTEE ON PRIVATE OWNERSHIP AND OPERATION OF URANIUM ENRICHMENT FACILITIES
(1968).

It is possible that the cost barrier to enriched uranium will be lowered in the future if
the gas centrifuge process, an alternate method of separating isotopes of the same elements
which does not require such large-scale and costly facilities, is demonstrated to be economically feasible. A plant capable of producing 50 kilograms of 90 per cent enriched
uranium-235 per year has been estimated to cost $130 million to build and $13
million per year to operate. Report of the Secretary-General, *supra* note 14, Annex IV, at
2. Since large-scale facilities are not required for the centrifuge process, a nuclear weapons
production capability would be easier to conceal as well as being cheaper. Therefore, wide
dissemination of gas centrifuge technology could contribute to nuclear weapons proliferation.

On March 21, 1967, the AEC summarily announced that "national security interests
would best be served if privately sponsored work on the gas centrifuge process for separation of isotopes were discontinued." U.S.A.E.C. Release No. K-70, Mar. 21, 1967, [1962-67
Transfer Binder] CCH ATOM. EN. L. REP. ¶ 10,376, at 16,595. Gas centrifuge work is
the sole business of Electro-Nucleonics, Inc., and as a result of the AEC decision, the SEC
suspended over-the-counter trading in the company's stock. Wall Street Journal, Mar. 23,
1967, at 10, col. 2. Since that time, certain private firms affected by the AEC decision,
including Electro-Nucleonics, have signed contracts with the AEC under which their
research and development work in this field will be continued on a classified basis.
U.S.A.E.C. Press Release No. K-163, June 29, 1967, 2 CCH ATOM. EN. L. REP. ¶ 10,061,
at 16,109.

17. The slightly enriched uranium used as fuel for nuclear power reactors cannot be
used in a nuclear weapon without substantial further enrichment. In evaluating natural
uranium and slightly enriched uranium as potential fuels for a planned nuclear power
reactor, a series of complex technological, economic, political and security comparisons
must be made. On economic grounds alone, enriched reactor technology has the edge
in most cases. Virtually all nuclear power reactors built and planned in the United States
and a large majority in the Soviet Union use enriched fuel. Of the total nuclear power
capacity outside both the United States and the communist bloc by 1980, about 30 per
cent is forecast to be in natural uranium reactors and about 70 per cent in enriched
uranium reactors. ARTHUR D. LITTLE, INC., THE GROWTH OF FOREIGN NUCLEAR POWER
(1966).

If a state uses nuclear power and lacks its own uranium reserves, it must rely on
foreign fuel supplies. If a state uses enriched reactor technology and lacks an isotope
separation plant, although it has its own uranium deposits, it must rely on foreign sources
of enrichment services. The United States, with a large stake in a future share of the
world's nuclear power industry, has given repeated assurances of the availability of United
States enrichment services on a long-term, non-discriminatory basis at attractive and
stable prices. This "toll enrichment" policy is intended not only to assist in the export
of United States enriched reactor technology, but also to minimize incentives for construction of additional uranium isotope separation plants outside the United States. For a

The Yale Law Journal   Vol. 77: 1447, 1968

addition to a reactor, several other specialized facilities are required to
carry out all the operations necessary to obtain usable plutonium. Of
major importance are a facility to fabricate fuel elements for nuclear reactors and a plant to separate by chemical methods the plutonium
produced in irradiated fuel elements from depleted uranium and certain radioactive waste materials. Plutonium technology is unclassified,
well-understood, and already widely diffused.[18] Moreover, the aggregate capital cost of the facilities required for production of militarily
substantial amounts of plutonium is well under $100 million, and
operating costs can be reduced below $10 million per year.[19] Once
fissionable material is in hand, manufacture of crude fission weapons
that work should no longer be considered a particularly demanding or
costly task, although weapons design information is cloaked in secrecy.[20]

more extensive discussion of the political factors in the choice between natural and
enriched uranium technology, see Willrich, *International Control of Civil Nuclear Power*,
BULL. ATOM. SCI., Mar. 1967, at 31, 33.

18. The United States played a leading role in the diffusion process beginning with
President Eisenhower's famous "Atoms for Peace" address to the U.N. General Assembly,
which included a plan to "encourage worldwide investigation into the most effective
peacetime uses of fissionable material." 1 DOCUMENTS ON DISARMAMENT, 1945-1959, at 393,
400 (U.S. Dep't of State Pub. No. 7008, 1960).
The Atomic Energy Act of 1946, then in effect, prohibited "exchange of information
with other nations with respect to the use of atomic energy for industrial purposes." Act
of Aug. 1, 1946, ch. 724, § 10(a)(2), 60 Stat. 755, 766. Following the "Atoms for Peace"
speech, Congress enacted the Atomic Energy Act of 1954, which provided: "The dissemination of scientific and technical information relating to atomic energy should be permitted
and encouraged so as to provide that free interchange of ideas and criticism which is
essential to scientific and industrial progress . . . ." Atomic Energy Act of 1954, 42 U.S.C.
§ 2161(b). The Act also established a scheme for declassification of restricted data from
time to time by the AEC. *Id.* § 2162. The First United Nations Conference on Peaceful
Uses of Atomic Energy, held in Geneva during 1955, resulted in the declassification and
subsequent diffusion of large amounts of information primarily concerning reactor
technology. Thereafter, on December 12, 1956, the United States, the United Kingdom,
and Canada took joint action to revise their information policies to declassify information
relating to "all phases of nuclear power from ore recovery and fabrication of fuel elements
to the design and operation of plants for the chemical recycling of spent fuel elements
from civilian reactors." Statement of Lewis L. Strauss, Chairman, U.S. Atomic Energy
Commission, on the Reciprocal Tripartite Declassification Guide, CCH ATOM. EN. L.
REP. ¶ 5056, at 11,088. Two further United Nations Conferences on the Peaceful Uses of
Atomic Energy have been held in Geneva in 1958 and 1964. The IAEA annually sponsors
between 10 and 15 scientific and technical conferences and symposia involving the most effective
participants from upwards of 50 countries. Annual Report of the Board of Governors to
the General Conference, 1 July 1966—30 June 1967, I.A.E.A. Doc. GC/(xi)/355, at 26.

19. Total costs and costs per unit will vary with the size. It is estimated that 8 kilograms
of 95 per cent plutonium-239 would be required to manufacture one nuclear warhead with
a yield of about 20 kilotons (equivalent to the bomb used on Nagasaki). The estimated
costs of an integrated production complex for 8 kilograms, or 1 bomb, per year are $22
million for construction and $4.8 million annually for operation; comparable costs for
160 kilograms, or 20 bombs, per year are $87 million for construction and $9.5 million
annually for operation. As the scale of operation increases there is a dramatic decrease in
the cost per kilogram: from $0.9 million per kilogram to $0.12 million per kilogram of
plutonium for the two previous examples. Report of the Secretary-General, *supra* note
14, Annex IV, at 3-7.

20. A weapons fabrication and assembly plant which can manufacture ten fission
warheads per year has been estimated to cost only $8 million to construct and $1 million

1454

Nuclear Weapons

The technology involved in the major peaceful uses of nuclear energy is basically the same as that required to produce plutonium for nuclear weapons. The facilities and materials required for a civil nuclear power program consist of nuclear reactors, which use natural or enriched uranium as fuel and produce large amounts of plutonium, fuel fabrication plants and chemical separation plants. Thus, the increasing use of nuclear energy to generate electric power will greatly complicate the task of preventing nuclear weapons proliferation.

A variety of possible peaceful applications for nuclear explosives have also been suggested. These include nuclear excavation of canals, harbors and rail cuts, and underground natural resource development projects, such as nuclear stimulation of natural gas production and the recovery of oil from shale. Such "Plowshare" applications require the development of "clean" thermonuclear explosives.[21] But "[a] device which moves a million tons of earth to dig a canal or create an oil deposit can just as easily pulverize a city of a million people."[22] Therefore, the development of "Plowshare" devices must be restrained in the Non-Proliferation Treaty.

II. Distribution of Nuclear Capabilities

Outside the Communist states, roughly 80 per cent of the known reserves of uranium are located in three countries, the United States, Canada and South Africa.[23] Within Western Europe, France has de-

per year to operate. Report of the Secretary-General, *supra* note 14, Annex IV, at 8. The successful development of a thermonuclear (fusion) device, however, still represents a significant technological achievement. For one thing, enriched uranium is the preferred material for a fission "trigger."

Thorium-232 is the only other important "fertile" material (*i.e.*, material which can be transformed into fissionable material) that occurs in nature, in addition to uranium-238. Upon neutron capture, thorium-232 will convert into uranium-233, another synthetic fissionable material similar to plutonium in its nuclear properties. Therefore, the possibility exists of a thorium-232/uranium-233 fuel cycle which would parallel the uranium-238/plutonium-239 fuel cycle. In either case a fissionable material is needed to begin with. Thorium technology is still in the development stage. Only very small quantities of uranium-233 have been produced, and no nuclear weapons are known to have been constructed using this material.

21. For a simple and general explanation, see Gerber, Hamburger & Hull, Plowshare (U.S.A.E.C. Div. of Technical Information 1966). For a mine of information some of which is now out of date, see *Hearings on Peaceful Applications of Nuclear Explosives—Plowshare—Before the Joint Comm. on Atomic Energy*, 89th Cong., 1st Sess. (1965). A recent critical assessment is found in Inglis & Sandler, *Prospects and Problems: The Nonmilitary Uses of Nuclear Explosives*, BULL. ATOM. SCI., Dec. 1967, at 46.

22. Statement of United Kingdom Representative to the ENDC, Feb. 23, 1967, ENDC/PV.288, at 7.

23. ORGANIZATION FOR ECONOMIC DEVELOPMENT/EUROPEAN NUCLEAR ENERGY AGENCY, WORLD URANIUM AND THORIUM RESOURCES (1965). Of course, reserves must be placed in various price ranges based on costs of recovery. The figure quoted is an approximation at the $5-10 per pound range.

The Yale Law Journal   Vol. 77: 1447, 1968

posits that are sufficient for its own weapons program, but probably insufficient for its civil nuclear power needs as well. In addition, Sweden Australia, Argentina, and a few African states have significant uranium reserves.[24] Of the Communist states, both the Soviet Union and China[25] are believed to have uranium reserves which are adequate for their own military and civil power needs. Within Eastern Europe, the largest uranium deposits are located in East Germany and smaller deposits in Czechoslovakia.

Facilities for enriching uranium are presently located in each of the five nuclear-weapon states. Such facilities are not known to have been built in any non-nuclear-weapon state. With respect to plutonium technology, in addition to over 300 small research reactors located throughout the world,[26] large power reactors with an output above 100 megawatts (electric) are in operation or under construction in all nuclear-weapon states except possibly China and a lengthening list of non-nuclear-weapon states, including Belgium, Canada, Czechoslovakia, West Germany, East Germany, India, Italy, Japan, Netherlands, Pakistan, Spain, Sweden, and Switzerland. The list of states planning to begin construction of nuclear power reactors in the near future is considerably longer.[27] Thus, it is clear that the spread of nuclear power and plutonium production capacity is not confined to particular geographic regions, or to specific political or ideological persuasions, or to countries advanced in economic development.

Fuel fabrication plants to supply the input and chemical separation

24. Gabon has significant uranium deposits which are presently exported to France. Thus far, Gabon has closely followed the French lead in the General Assembly concerning non-proliferation.

25. Terminology is difficult concerning China. Unless otherwise indicated, "China" hereafter in this article refers to the People's Republic of China. No political judgment concerning China policy is intended by this terminology.

26. Plutonium production is nominal in most research reactors, but can be significant in certain test facilities. Nevertheless, it should be recognized that such reactors are essential facilities for the education and training of the manpower required for a state to translate nuclear ambitions into capabilities.

27. *Power Reactors the World Around*, NUCLEONICS, Aug. 1966, at 94. Less than 10 kilograms of plutonium is needed for a bomb which will destroy a medium-sized city. One recent estimate of the aggregate plutonium production capacity represented by these civil nuclear power programs is 8,000 kilograms per year by 1970 and 50,000-70,000 kilograms annually by 1980. WASHINGTON CENTER OF FOREIGN POLICY RESEARCH, REPORT ON INTERNATIONAL ORGANIZATIONAL ARRANGEMENTS FOR THE UNITED STATES PROPOSAL FOR A VERIFIED AGREEMENT TO HALT PRODUCTION OF FISSIONABLE MATERIALS FOR WEAPONS PURPOSES 90 (1966). The corresponding estimated amounts of plutonium accumulated in the world as a result of this production are 28,000 kilograms by 1970 and 300,000-450,000 kilograms by 1980. Another estimate shows that by 1974, plutonium will be produced in the world at an annual rate of 36,700 kilograms, 9,500 kilograms of which will be produced in non-nuclear-weapon states. The cumulative totals for the world, by this estimate, are 127,100 kilograms, of which 28,300 kilograms will be located in non-nuclear-weapon states. Taylor, *The Rapid Growth of Nuclear Technology—Implications for Nuclear Safeguards*, INT'L RESEARCH & TECHNOLOGY J., Jan. 1, 1968, at 8.

Nuclear Weapons

plants to process the output of nuclear reactors have not yet been as widely dispersed throughout the world as the reactors themselves. Since nuclear fuels are readily available in international commerce, the lag is due primarily to the absence of an economic justification for a complete uranium-plutonium fuel cycle within one state unless that state's civil nuclear power program exceeds a minimum size. All the nuclear-weapon states, of course, already possess their own fuel fabrication and chemical separation plants. Chemical separation plants capable of processing industrial quantities of irradiated nuclear fuels are also located in Belgium and India, and construction is planned for the near future in West Germany, Japan and Sweden. Wherever a separation plant is located militarily significant quantities of plutonium will be found in a chemically pure form.[28]

The present distribution of raw materials and production capabilities for obtaining fissionable materials demonstrates that the United States and the Soviet Union are the only nuclear-weapon states with large and self-sufficient military and civil nuclear programs. The United Kingdom lacks its own uranium, and France lacks adequate indigenous uranium to supply both its civil and military needs. China, which probably has sufficient uranium to service both a military and a civil program has thus far focused its limited scientific and technical resources on the acquisition of a nuclear weapons capability.

Canada is the only non-nuclear-weapon state which possesses both large uranium deposits and a strong base in nuclear technology. West Germany and Japan are making bids for leadership in peaceful nuclear technology, in each case backed by a broad industrial capability and a

---

28. To prevent the creation of complete nuclear fuel cycles within non-nuclear weapons states, it has been suggested that an international agency be established which would own all nuclear fuel from the start. It would lease fuel for reactors, but would own and operate the processing facilities, and, in particular, the chemical separation plants used. All plutonium produced in power reactors would, thus, be under international ownership and control. Beaton, *Nuclear Fuel-for-All*, 45 FOREIGN AFFAIRS 662, 667 (1967). The European Company for the Chemical Processing of Irradiated Fuels (EUROCHEMIC) is an interesting example of international cooperation in this field. The Statute of EUROCHEMIC establishes a joint stock company. The stock is held by twelve governments or governmental authorities. The plant is located at Mol, Belgium. For the statute see *Multilateral Agreements*, 1 I.A.E.A. LEGAL SERIES 220 (1959).

Nevertheless, the general tendency for states to place a high value on resource self-sufficiency would seem irresistible, and the suggestion, therefore, impractical. Moreover, the United States supply policy now encourages self-sufficiency. Prior to legislation requiring private ownership of fissionable material, the AEC could insert plutonium buy-back provisions in its agreements for cooperation with other countries. Under the present legislation, the AEC is not permitted to buy back plutonium that is produced in fuel that has been "toll" enriched. AMENDING THE ATOMIC ENERGY ACT OF 1954 TO PROVIDE FOR PRIVATE OWNERSHIP OF SPECIAL NUCLEAR MATERIALS, H.R. REP. NO. 1702, 88th Cong., 2d Sess. 2 (1964).

The Yale Law Journal   Vol. 77: 1447, 1968

firm political commitment;[29] India is embarked on a civil nuclear power program of substantial size; and Israel, which has developed a strong scientific and technical base, is now considering a variety of power applications; but each of these non-nuclear-weapon states lacks a uranium supply of its own. South Africa's large uranium reserves make it a major power to be dealt with in the non-proliferation context, but its nuclear power program is not far advanced. Thus, many more nations, in addition to the present five nuclear-weapon states, could easily acquire nuclear weapons in the future.[30] Yet relatively few could do so exclusively out of their own resources, at least not without substantial cutbacks in their civil nuclear power plans.

III. Non-Proliferation: The Existing Legal Framework

The Non-Proliferation Treaty would be a major step toward nuclear arms control, but it would not be the first. The Antarctic Treaty, concluded in 1959, dedicated the South polar region to exclusively peaceful purposes and prohibited "any measures of a military nature," including "the testing of any type of weapons."[31] In contrast to the strategic nuclear hub in the Artic, Antarctica became the first nuclear-free zone.

During the Cuban missile crisis in October 1962, the United States

29. A comprehensive description of Japan's program is contained in Gilinsky & Langer, The Japanese Civilian Nuclear Program, RAND Memorandum RM-5366-PR (Aug. 1967). A long-range program submitted by the Japanese Atomic Energy Commission to its government in 1967 recommends that Japan import foreign reactor technology that is already developed and concentrate its own resources in the development of breeder technology. If successful, such a "leap-frog" strategy could put Japan in the front rank of nuclear technology after a period of heavy dependence on foreign technology. See id. 38.

30. See note 12 supra. Here it is important to distinguish the costs of nuclear weapons, which are relatively cheap, and the total program costs for a nuclear deterrent force, including the delivery systems, which are generally expensive. It has been estimated that to acquire in 10 years time a modest nuclear capability of 30-50 jet bombers and 50 medium-range missiles in soft emplacements armed with 100 plutonium warheads of 20 kilotons each would cost approximately $15 million per year for warheads and $155 million per year for delivery systems, for a total 10-year program cost of $1.7 billion. A small, high-quality nuclear force composed of 10-15 bombers, 100 intermediate range missiles and 2 missile launching submarines, each equipped with thermonuclear warheads, would cost $560 million per year, for a total 10-year program cost of $5.6 billion. Report of Secretary-General, supra note 14, at 36; id., Annex IV, at 6.

31. The Antarctic Treaty, art. I, para. 1, [1961] 1 U.S.T. 794, 795, T.I.A.S. No. 4780, 402 U.N.T.S. 71, 72. The parties are Argentina, Australia, Belgium, Chile, Czechoslovakia, Denmark, France, Japan, New Zealand, Norway, Poland, the Republic of South Africa, the Soviet Union, the United Kingdom, and the United States. This Treaty was the first arms control arrangement to include both East and West. In 1954 West Germany undertook "not to manufacture in its territory any atomic weapons" as a part of the arrangements for its accession to NATO. Neither the Soviet Union nor the United States are parties to the specific agreements which incorporate the West German renunciation. There are complex arguments pro and con, concerning the continued legal efficacy of the West German pledge. See Willrich, West Germany's Pledge Not to Manufacture Nuclear Weapons, 7 VA. J. INT'L L. 91-100 (1966).

1458

Nuclear Weapons

and the Soviet Union saw clearly that avoidance of nuclear war between them was a rule of necessity on which their mutual survival depended. The Limited Nuclear Test Ban Treaty followed in 1963. This Treaty, now in force among over ninety parties, prohibits nuclear test explosions in the atmosphere, outer space and underwater.[32] The ban is incomplete since it does not prohibit explosions underground as long as the radioactive debris is contained within the territory of the state where the test is conducted. Nevertheless, the Treaty halted the race between the United States and the Soviet Union for ever increasing explosive yields in the 100 megaton range and above,[33] and substantially reduced radioactive contamination of the atmosphere. Moreover, by confining permissible nuclear tests of any party to the costly and time-consuming underground environment, the Limited Nuclear Test Ban Treaty may retard the pace of nuclear weapons proliferation, at least in the absence of a more effective legal barrier.[34]

Since the Limited Nuclear Test Ban Treaty, two additions have been made to the legal structure of nuclear arms control. In 1967 the Treaty for the Prohibition of Nuclear Weapons in Latin America was completed, and it has since been signed by twenty-one states of that region.[35]

32. [1963] 2 U.S.T. 1313, T.I.A.S. No. 5433, 480 U.N.T.S. 43 (1963).
33. The maximum yield of a nuclear explosion that can be contained underground will vary substantially with the depth of burial and surrounding geology. At the Foreign Relations Committee hearings on the Limited Nuclear Test Ban Treaty most experts agreed that "with the passage of time tests of up to 1 megaton would be possible underground." Testimony of Secretary of Defense McNamara, *Hearings on the Nuclear Test Ban Treaty Before the Senate Comm. on Foreign Relations*, 88th Cong., 1st Sess. 126 (1963). "From tests at yields of up to 1 megaton some improvement in high-yield weapons design could be achieved and . . . new warheads—for example, a 35 megaton warhead for our Titan II—could be developed and stockpiled with confidence that they would work." *Id.* 101. Prior to the Limited Nuclear Test Ban Treaty the United States had already emphasized the acquisition of large numbers of invulnerable delivery systems carrying a warhead in the one megaton range. The Soviet Union had tested a device of 60 megatons which could have been scaled up to 100 megatons for aircraft delivery. The significance of very high yield nuclear weapons has been the subject of continuing debate which the Nuclear Test Ban Treaty has by no means ended. Secretary of Defense McNamara has discounted in advance the significance of any "megatonnage gap" between the Soviet Union and the United States. "Far more important is the surviving number of separately targetable, serviceable, accurate, reliable warheads." In these terms, Secretary McNamara has concluded: "our strategic forces are superior to those of the Soviet Union. But I must caution that in terms of national security, such 'superiority' is of little significance." Statement by Secretary of Defense Robert S. McNamara before the Senate Armed Services Committee on the Fiscal Year 1969-73 Defense Program and the 1969 Defense Budget 52 (1968).
34. President Kennedy clearly viewed the Treaty as "the opening wedge" in a campaign to persuade other countries not to acquire nuclear weapons. Radio-Television Address by President Kennedy, July 26, 1963, Documents on Disarmament, 1963, at 250, 255 (U.S. Arms Control & Disarmament Agency, Pub. No. 24, 1964).
35. This Treaty is referred to as the Treaty of Tlatelolco. An English version of the text is found in Documents on Disarmament, 1967, at 69. In addition to signing, Mexico and El Salvador have ratified the Treaty, and also have waived the conditions for entry into force contained in Article 28, paragraph 1, among them two conditions particularly

The Yale Law Journal   Vol. 77: 1447, 1968

When the Treaty enters into force the Latin American States will have applied to themselves a substantially broader concept of non-proliferation than is embodied in the Non-Proliferation Treaty.[36] Also in 1967 the Outer Space Treaty was completed and entered into force.[37] Under this Treaty the parties, and in particular the United States and the Soviet Union as the major space powers, pledged not to place nuclear weapons "in orbit around the Earth," to "install" them "on celestial bodies," or to "station" them in outer space.[38]

"Safeguards" is the concept which has been developed to provide assurance that the materials and equipment used in peaceful nuclear activities are not diverted to use in nuclear weapons programs. Safeguards consist of a system of international accountability applied to the nuclear materials used, produced and processed in a peaceful nuclear activity in a state. The system includes reports to an external authority and physical inspection by that authority to verify the accuracy of the

---

impossible to fulfill: ratification by all Latin American states, including Cuba, and ratification of Protocol II by all nuclear-weapon states, including China. Brazil has signed and ratified the Treaty without waiving any conditions for entry into force.

On April 1, 1968, the United States signed Protocol II to the Treaty. Article 3 of Protocol II contains an undertaking "not to use or threaten to use nuclear weapons against the Contracting Parties . . . ." In signing the Protocol the United States stated that "each of the Contracting Parties retains exclusive power and legal competence, unaffected by the terms of the Treaty, to grant or deny non-Contracting Parties transit and transport privileges;" and that "an armed attack by a Contracting Party in which it was assisted by a nuclear-weapon State, would be incompatible with the Contracting Party's corresponding obligations under Article 1 of the Treaty." Thus, the United States has preserved its right to transport nuclear weapons through the Panama Canal, and has narrowed the scope of its commitment not to use nuclear weapons to circumstances where no other nuclear-weapon state is involved. For a discussion of the Treaty by a man instrumental in the negotiations, see G. Robles, The Denuclearization of Latin America (1967).

36. In addition to prohibiting the acquisition of nuclear weapons by the parties, Article 1(1)(b) of the Treaty of Tlatelolco prohibits "The receipt, storage, installation, deployment and any form of possession of any nuclear weapons, directly or indirectly, by the Parties themselves, by anyone on their behalf or in any other way." Under the Treaty, therefore, the parties could not permit nuclear-weapon states to deploy nuclear weapons on their territories establishing a nuclear free zone in Latin America. Black Africa has also moved in this direction. On July 21, 1964, at an Organization of African Unity Summit Conference, the heads of government declared: "we are ready to undertake, through an international agreement to be concluded under United Nations auspices, not to manufacture or control atomic weapons." Documents on Disarmament, 1964, at 294 (U.S. Arms Control & Disarmament Agency Pub. No. 27, 1965).

37. For text see 55 Dep't State Bull. 953 (1966).

38. *Id.* The question has arisen whether deployment by the Soviet Union of a Fractional Orbital Bombardment System (FOBS) would violate the Outer Space Treaty. The question was quickly dismissed. For one thing, the FOBS would be launched in an operational mode only in time of war. Moreover, the vehicle launched in a FOBS mode is fired into very low orbit about 100 miles above the earth and at a given point in time rockets are fired to bring the vehicle out of orbit. The vehicle is not intended to orbit completely "around the earth." An ICBM normally does not go into orbit, but rather follows a ballistic trajectory with a typical apogee of 500-800 miles. Although a FOBS has the potential to place a nuclear weapon "in orbit around the earth," so does an ICBM. For these reasons the deployment of a FOBS should not violate the Outer Space Treaty.

Nuclear Weapons

reports. The external authority which administers safeguards can be an international or regional organization or another state which has supplied assistance to the activity. Various systems for international safeguards exist. The two principal international systems are administered by the European Atomic Energy Community (Euratom), which covers all civil nuclear activities on the territories of France, West Germany, Italy, Belgium, the Netherlands, and Luxembourg, and the International Atomic Energy Agency (IAEA), which is organized on a worldwide basis and presently has 98 members.[39]

In 1962 the United States adopted a policy of transfering to the IAEA the responsibility for administration of safeguards with respect to its bilateral agreements for cooperation with countries outside Euratom, as these agreements were renewed. This policy and parallel efforts by Britain and Canada have been largely responsible for the recent marked expansion of the applicability of the IAEA's system. As of June 30, 1967, the Agency had signed 34 safeguards agreements with 27 member states covering 61 reactors.[40]

The safeguards responsibilities of Euratom have also increased substantially. For instance, over 70 per cent of the total amount of nuclear materials the United States has supplied to foreign countries is subject to Euratom safeguards. Although the Soviet Union has refused to accept safeguards on any of its own peaceful nuclear activities, since 1963 it has given strong support to the development and application of safeguards by the IAEA.

The four treaties described above and the expanded role of international safeguards represent some progress in the construction of legal barriers to prevent further nuclear weapons proliferation. Nevertheless, the buildup of nuclear armaments in nuclear-weapon states continues and takes on new dimensions which threaten the security of non-nuclear-weapon states. Moreover, the spread of civil nuclear power in a

---

39. For legal analyses, see Szasz, *The Law of International Atomic Energy Agency Safeguards*, 3 Rev. Belge de Droit Int'l 196 (1967) (a useful bibliography is set forth in Annex B); Willrich, *Safeguarding Atoms for Peace*, 60 Am. J. Int'l L. 34 (1966); Gorove, *The First Multinational Atomic Inspection and Control System at Work: Euratom's Experience*, 18 Stan. L. Rev. 160 (1965). For a political-technological analysis, see Willrich, *International Control for Civil Nuclear Power*, 23 Bull. Atom. Sci. (March 1967). For a discussion from the United States point of view, see Hall, *Atoms for Peace or War*, 43 Foreign Affairs 602 (1965).

40. Only four of the reactors are power reactors, located in the United States, the United Kingdom, Spain and Japan. The majority are small research reactors. In addition, the United States has opened a chemical processing plant to IAEA inspection while the plant is engaged in reprocessing fuel from the power reactor in the United States which is subject to IAEA safeguards. Annual Report of the Board of Governors to the General Conference, 1 July 1966—30 June 1967, I.A.E.A. Doc. GC/(xi)/355.

The Yale Law Journal   Vol. 77: 1447, 1968

commercially competitive global environment continually threatens to outrun the willingness of the states concerned to accept safeguards and open their peaceful nuclear activities to international inspection. Clearly, a comprehensive legal framework is needed to achieve the goal of non-proliferation policy on a worldwide scale.

IV. The Non-Proliferation Treaty

To prevent nuclear weapons proliferation, the Treaty[41] establishes the following legal framework: nuclear-weapon states undertake not to transfer nuclear weapons, or to assist non-nuclear-weapon states to acquire such weapons (Article I); non-nuclear-weapon states undertake not to manufacture or otherwise acquire nuclear weapons (Article II); non-nuclear-weapon states agree to accept safeguards on their peaceful nuclear activities (Article III); all parties are guaranteed the right to exploit the peaceful uses of nuclear energy (Article IV); an obligation and procedure for international sharing of any potential benefits from peaceful applications of nuclear explosions is established (Article V). The Treaty enters into force once the Soviet Union, the United Kingdom, the United States, and forty other signatory states have ratified it (Article IX), and may be amended by a majority of the parties, including all nuclear-weapon parties and parties which are members of the IAEA Board of Governors (Article VIII). The Treaty has an initial duration of twenty-five years, but any party may withdraw if it decides that "extraordinary events" have jeopardized its "supreme interests" (Article X). In addition, parties to the Treaty undertake to pursue further nuclear arms control negotiations "in good faith" (Article VI), and groups of states may establish regional nuclear-free zones apart from the Treaty (Article VII).[42]

---

41. The Treaty consists of a preamble and eleven articles. The eleventh Article deals with languages. Discussion of the Treaty's preamble will generally be relegated to appropriate places in the footnotes.

42. The draft Treaty of August 24, 1967, included what is now Article VII as the last paragraph in the preamble. ENDC/192, ENDC/193; DOCUMENTS ON DISARMAMENT, 1967, at 338. In the discussion of the August 24, 1967, draft, Mexico proposed a transfer of this provision from the preamble to the body of the Treaty, considering it an "authentic legal provision." ENDC/PV. 331, at 8-9. This was subsequently done by the superpowers in the revised draft Treaty of January 18, 1968. ENDC/192/Rev.1, ENDC/193/Rev.1. During discussion of the latter draft, Brazil proposed that Article VII be amended so that nothing in the Non-Proliferation Treaty would be interpreted "as affecting, in any way, the rights or obligations of signatory States under regional Treaties on the proscription of nuclear weapons . . . consistent with the objectives of this Treaty." ENDC/201/ Rev.2. Had Brazil's amendment been accepted, difficult problems of priority between the Non-Proliferation Treaty and the Treaty of Tlatelolco could have arisen, especially in light of Brazil's apparent continued insistence on an interpretation of the latter as not precluding its right to develop peaceful nuclear explosives.

Nuclear Weapons

A. *Non-Transfer and Non-Acquisition*

The obligation of nuclear-weapon states under Article I[43] generally complements the obligation of non-nuclear-weapon states under Article II:[44] the Treaty prohibits transfer by nuclear-weapon states on the one hand, and receipt by non-nuclear-weapon states on the other, of "nuclear weapons," "other nuclear explosive devices," and "control" over such weapons or devices. Since none of these terms is explicitly defined, the scope of the Treaty will largely depend on how each is interpreted.

A number of questions arise in defining "nuclear weapon."[45] Obviously, the nuclear warhead on the tip of an ICBM and the nuclear bomb carried in a strategic bomber are nuclear weapons. But does "nuclear weapon" include the delivery system as well as the warhead? What about nuclear reactors used as power plants for Polaris sub-

---

43. "Each nuclear-weapon State Party to the Treaty undertakes not to transfer to any recipient whatsover nuclear weapons or other nuclear explosive devices or control over such weapons or explosive devices directly, or indirectly; and not in any way to assist, encourage, or induce any non-nuclear-weapon State to manufacture or otherwise acquire nuclear weapons or other nuclear explosive devices, or control over such weapons or explosive devices." Art. I.

44. "Each non-nuclear-weapon State Party to the Treaty undertakes not to receive the transfer from any transferor whatsoever of nuclear weapons or other nuclear explosive devices or of control over such weapons or explosive devices directly, or indirectly; not to manufacture or otherwise acquire nuclear weapons or other nuclear explosive devices; and not to seek or receive any assistance in the manufacture of nuclear weapons or other nuclear explosive devices." Art. II.

45. In 1966 the United States was "convinced of the need for such a definition," but apparently changed its mind because no definition appeared in the agreed draft of August 24, 1967. DOCUMENTS ON DISARMAMENT, 1967, at 167. United States amendments to Article IV of the earlier United States draft Treaty submitted on March 21, 1966, included among other defined terms a reference to "nuclear weapons" followed by a blank. DOCUMENTS ON DISARMAMENT, 1966, at 160. Article 5 of the Treaty of Tlatelolco defines "nuclear weapon" as "any device which is capable of releasing nuclear energy in an uncontrolled manner and which has a group of characteristics that are appropriate for warlike purposes. An instrument that may be used for the transport or propulsion of the device is not included in this definition if it is separable from the device and not an individual part thereof." DOCUMENTS ON DISARMAMENT, 1967, at 72. Much of this language seems to have been derived from the United States Atomic Energy Act of 1954, which defines "atomic weapon" as "any device utilizing atomic energy, exclusive of the means for transporting or propelling the device (where such means is a separable and divisible part of the device) the principal purpose of which is for use as, or development of, a weapon, a weapon prototype, or a weapon test device." Atomic Energy Act of 1954, *as amended*, § 11(d), 42 U.S.C. § 2014(d) (1964). Thus the definitions in both the Treaty of Tlatelolco and the United States legislation expressly exclude nuclear delivery and propulsion systems. One important difference in the definitions is that the United States legislation includes a subjective element of purpose while the Latin American definition is more objective and not dependent on the intended purpose for which the device will be used, as long as it possesses a "group of characteristics" which make it "appropriate" for use as a nuclear weapon. Hence Plowshare devices would seem to be excluded from the definition of nuclear weapon under United States law, but included in the Treaty of Tlatelolco.

We may speculate why a definition was omitted from the Non-Proliferation Treaty. A definition similar to the Treaty of Tlatelolco would perhaps have highlighted the Soviet Union's concession to the status quo regarding the United States' arrangements within NATO. It might also have accentuated the exclusion of non-weapons military cooperation from the prohibitions of the Treaty.

The Yale Law Journal   Vol. 77: 1447, 1968

marines or surface warships? The drafters clearly intended to exclude
nuclear delivery and military propulsion systems from the term "nuclear
weapon" and to limit this term to only one aspect of a nuclear weapons
capability, namely the warhead or bomb.[46]

Articles I and II also prohibit the transfer and receipt of "other
nuclear explosive devices." This phrase is primarily intended to cover
nuclear explosives of potential use in peaceful applications—so-called
"Plowshare" devices.[47] These devices are indistinguishable on technical
grounds from nuclear weapons. Moreover, the production of such devices requires a technology "even more sophisticated" than that required to produce serviceable nuclear weapons. Therefore, if the Non-
Proliferation Treaty is to prevent nuclear weapons proliferation, it must
prohibit transfer and acquisition of nuclear explosive devices for peaceful applications on the same terms as nuclear weapons.

Nevertheless, the superpower duopoly which the Non-Proliferation
Treaty would preserve with respect to acquisition of this aspect of
peaceful nuclear technology is bitter medicine for certain non-nuclear-
weapon states. Brazil is a leading critic of any such restriction which
could create, in its view, "an irreparable relationship of dependence"
and prevent the "technological leap that full utilization of nuclear
energy for peaceful purposes can provide" to a developing country.[48]

---

46. On March 14, 1968, the State Department issued a press release which stated:
"For purposes of the treaty a nuclear powered submarine is not, in itself 'a weapon.'
The treaty does not deal with such military applications of nuclear energy as nuclear
propulsion of warships. Therefore, nothing in the treaty would prohibit the provision
of nuclear fuel for this purpose . . . ." Statement by State Department Spokesman Robert
McCloskey, Mar. 14, 1968 (unpublished).
It is clear, however, that the Non-Proliferation Treaty makes no distinction between
offensive nuclear warheads and nuclear warheads associated with ballistic missile defense
systems. The prohibitions on transfer and acquisition under Articles I and II apply
equally to both. This is important because several of the Treaty's critics have suggested
that ballistic missile defense systems be transferred to United State allies, and one noted
authority has stated that "methods have been developed so that defensive nuclear explosives can be used for ballistic missile defense and for that purpose alone." Statement
by Dr. Edward Teller, *Hearings on Arms Control and Disarmament Act Amendments,
1968, Before the House Comm. on Foreign Affairs*, 90th Cong., 2d Sess. 245, 246-47 (1968).
For the Executive Branch reply, see *id.* at 184-85.
47. Statement by United States Representative to ENDC, June 8, 1967, ENDC/PV.303,
at 4-11; DOCUMENTS ON DISARMAMENT, 1967, at 252, 253.
48. Statement by Representative of Brazil to ENDC, May 18, 1967, ENDC/PV.297, at
14-17; DOCUMENTS ON DISARMAMENT, 1967, at 225, 226. Under the Treaty of Tlatelolco
Brazil has agreed (subject to conditions virtually impossible to fulfill) to commit itself
not to acquire nuclear weapons. But it has thus far steadfastly refused to "waive the
right . . . to manufacture or receive nuclear explosives that will enable us to perform
great engineering works." *Id.* Brazil maintains that the Treaty of Tlatelolco "draws a
clear cut distinction between peaceful nuclear explosions and explosions for nuclear
weapons purposes." Statement by Representative of Brazil to ENDC, Mar. 14, 1967,
ENDC/PV.293, at 8-18; DOCUMENTS ON DISARMAMENT, 1967, at 135, 140. The United States
and a majority of the Latin American states have taken repeated exception to such an
interpretation. Article 18 of the Treaty of Tlatelolco permits Parties to "carry out ex-

Nuclear Weapons

The United States and Soviet Union have both taken a hard line in reply. The United States has put it bluntly: "Should a State decide that it does not wish to accept a treaty which prohibits the spread of nuclear explosive devices we will have to conclude that it does not wish to accept a treaty which prevents the spread of nuclear weapons."[49]

Finally, Articles I and II prohibit transfer and receipt of "control" over nuclear weapons and explosive devices. The meaning of "control" and the related Soviet concept of "access" were the major language barriers between the United States and the Soviet Union for the five years of negotiations until agreement was reached in 1967 on Articles I and II. At issue was the future role of non-nuclear members of military alliances, especially West Germany, with regard to their own nuclear defense. Throughout the long years of disagreement, the Soviet Union never tired of reiterating that regardless of United States plans for its NATO allies, "the Soviet Union will never agree to West Germany obtaining access to nuclear weapons."[50] The United States was equally adamant that it was "not going to invite the Soviet Union to sit at the NATO table and determine NATO nuclear policy," and that there was no conflict between non-proliferation policy and possible nuclear arrangements proposed for the NATO alliance.[51] The compromise ulti-

plosions of nuclear devices for peaceful purposes—including explosions which involve devices similar to those used in nuclear weapons, provided that they do so in accordance with . . . articles 1 and 5"; however, in light of the definition of nuclear weapons in Article 5, note 45 *supra*, the United States has stated: "We understand the definition contained in Article 5 of the Treaty as necessarily encompassing all nuclear explosive devices. It is our understanding that Articles 1 and 5 restrict accordingly the activities of the Contracting Parties under paragraph 1 of Article 18." Statement Accompanying Signature of the United States of America of Protocol II to the Treaty for the Prohibition of Nuclear Weapons in Latin America, 58 DEP'T STATE BULL. 555, 556 (1968). In simpler terms, the United States has interpreted the Treaty of Tlatelolco "as prohibiting the contracting parties from acquiring or testing nuclear explosive devices for peaceful purposes . . . unless someone can someday invent a nuclear explosive which cannot be used as a nuclear weapon." Statement by United States Representative to ENDC, Mar. 7, 1967, ENDC/PV.291, at 14-16; DOCUMENTS ON DISARMAMENT, 1967, at 126, 127-28. Moreover, in a statement at the signing ceremony of the Treaty of Tlatelolco, Mexico interpreted the Treaty in this respect similarly to the United States' interpretation. Statement by Representative of Mexico to ENDC, Feb. 21, 1967, ENDC/PV.287, at 23-28; DOCUMENTS ON DISARMAMENT, 1967, at 99, 101.

49. Statement by United States Representative to ENDC, June 8, 1967, ENDC/PV.303, at 4-11; DOCUMENTS ON DISARMAMENT, 1967, at 252, 257. The Soviet Union has been just as unflinching. *See, e.g.,* Statement by Soviet Union Representative to ENDC, July 13, 1967, ENDC/PV.313, at 4-8; DOCUMENTS ON DISARMAMENT, 1967, at 298-300. The steps taken in the Treaty to mitigate, or perhaps reverse the discriminatory effects of the potential Plowshare duopoly will be discussed below in connection with other aspects of cooperation in the peaceful uses of nuclear energy. *See* p. 1498 *infra*.

50. Statement by Soviet Union Representative to ENDC, Feb. 17, 1966, ENDC/PV.241, at 24-33; DOCUMENTS ON DISARMAMENT, 1967, at 24, 29. Earlier in the same speech the Soviet Representative had stated that the "ambivalent approach" of the United States to the solution of the problem of non-proliferation was "as plain as a pikestaff" in the United States draft treaty of August 17, 1965. *Id.* 27.

51. *See, e.g.,* News Conference Remarks by Acting Secretary of State Ball, July 6, 1966,

The Yale Law Journal   Vol. 77: 1447, 1968

mately arrived at and embodied in Articles I and II basically reflects the status quo.[52]

In analyzing the existing circumstances in NATO, as well as possible future arrangements, and the impact of the Non-Proliferation Treaty on these circumstances and arrangements, we must distinguish the warhead from the delivery vehicle. At present the United States has deployed some seven thousand nuclear warheads in non-nuclear-weapon states in Western Europe, principally West Germany. All of these weapons are legally owned by the United States and remain in the physical custody of United States armed forces stationed in Europe.[53]

---

55 DEP'T STATE BULL. 122-23 (1966); DOCUMENTS ON DISARMAMENT, 1966, at 406. The remarks by Acting Secretary Ball followed by one day a remark at a news conference by President Johnson: "We hope the Soviet Union will meet us and find an acceptable compromise in language which we can both live with." News Conference Remarks by President Johnson, July 5, 1966, 2 WEEKLY COMPILATION PRESIDENTIAL DOCUMENTS 905; DOCUMENTS ON DISARMAMENT, 1966, at 405. President Johnson's statement signalled to his own State Department, the NATO allies and the Soviet Union a willingness to take a fresh look at the problem of reconciling NATO nuclear arrangements with a non-proliferation treaty.

52. Article I, paragraph 1, of the Soviet draft Treaty proposal of September 24, 1965, would have prohibited the transfer of control over the "emplacement and use" of nuclear weapons to "units of the armed forces of military personnel of States not possessing nuclear weapons even if such units or personnel are under the command of a military alliance." Article I, paragraph 2, would have prohibited nuclear-weapon states from transmitting to non-nuclear-weapon states "any kind of . . . information or documentation which can be employed for purposes of the manufacture *or use* of nuclear weapons." (Emphasis added.) There were corresponding obligations for non-nuclear-weapon states in Article II. U.N. Doc. A/5976, Sept. 24, 1965; DOCUMENTS ON DISARMAMENT, 1965, at 443-44. This language might have been interpreted as excluding non-nuclear-weapon states from any knowledge concerning nuclear strategy or tactics and any voice in nuclear deployment arrangements, even on their own territory. There is no counterpart for this language in the Treaty text finally agreed upon.

53. Section 92 of the Atomic Energy Act of 1954, as amended, provides in part: "It shall be unlawful, except as provided in section 2121 of this title [Atomic Energy Act § 91], for any person to transfer or receive in interstate or foreign commerce, manufacture, produce, transfer, acquire, possess, import, or export any atomic weapon." 42 U.S.C. § 2122 (1964). The exceptions contained in Section 91 permit cooperation with another nation and the transfer to that nation of nuclear materials for use in atomic weapons, non-nuclear parts of atomic weapons, and reactors and reactor fuels for military applications. The President must determine that any such transfer "will promote and will not constitute an unreasonable risk to the common defense and security, while such other nation is participating with the United States pursuant to an international arrangement by substantial and material contributions to the mutual defense and security . . . ." 42 U.S.C. § 2121(c) (1964). In the event of any transfer of nuclear materials for use in an atomic weapons program or of non-nuclear parts of atomic weapons, there is an added requirement that the recipient nation must have already made "substantial progress in the development of atomic weapons," *id.* § 2121(c)(1), which has generally been construed to mean that the recipient must have already acquired nuclear weapons. In no case, however, can the United States transfer to another nation an entire nuclear weapon or the nuclear parts of a nuclear weapon under existing legislation. With respect to the interaction between Section 92 and the Non-Proliferation Treaty a United States spokesman has said that there is "nothing in this treaty that is an inhibition on the United States that we haven't already adopted on a unilateral basis, basis of U.S. law, as far as the substantive inhibitions are concerned. There is a difference between undertaking an international obligation and having a U.S. statute which can be changed by the will of the Congress." Testimony of Adrian S. Fisher, Deputy Director, United States Arms Con-

Nuclear Weapons

The United States has sold to certain NATO allies which are non-nuclear-weapon states large numbers of aircraft and surface-to-surface missiles capable of delivering nuclear weapons. The bulk of these nuclear capable delivery systems has gone to West Germany.[54]

If a major conflict broke out in Europe which required use of nuclear weapons, under present arrangements the United States would respond with its own nuclear equipped forces and would also release nuclear warheads in its custody to its non-nuclear NATO allies for delivery on target by their weapons delivery systems. Release of United States nuclear weapons to non-nuclear NATO allies would be effected through "permissive action links," or the "PAL" system. Any such release of nuclear weapons from United States custody would require a specific Presidential decision at that time, followed by an affirmative physical act: the turn of a key by a member of the United States armed forces.[55]

Would the Non-Proliferation Treaty, and in particular the prohibitions on transfer and receipt of nuclear weapons in Articles I and II, upset these large-scale but delicately balanced nuclear force arrangements already established within NATO? It may be argued that stationing or deployment of nuclear weapons on the territory of a non-nuclear-weapon state does not, of itself, constitute a "transfer" of weapons by the nuclear-weapon state concerned. Moreover, existing

trol and Disarmament Agency, *Hearings on Arms Control and Disarmament Act Amendments, 1968, Before the House Comm. on Foreign Affairs,* 90th Cong., 2d Sess. 70 (1968).

54. The range of the nuclear delivery systems the United States has provided to non-nuclear-weapon NATO allies, however, limits their use to interdiction missions in Eastern Europe and perhaps the western fringe of the Soviet Union.

55. One of the most comprehensive and authoritative unclassified descriptions of existing nuclear arrangements came on September 16, 1964, at the height of the Johnson-Goldwater contest for the Presidency. In an address by President Johnson entitled "Direction and Control of Nuclear Power," which was his response to Senator Goldwater's assertion that authority to use tactical nuclear weapons should be delegated to NATO field commanders, President Johnson stated unequivocally: "The release of nuclear weapons would come by Presidential decision alone." He then went on to explain: "Complex codes and electronic devices prevent any unauthorized action. Every further step along the way from decision to destruction is governed by the two-man rule. Two or more men must act independently and must decide the order has been given. They must independently take action. An elaborate system of checks and counterchecks, procedural and mechanical, guard against any unauthorized nuclear bursts. In addition, since 1961 we have placed permissive-action links on several of our weapons. These are electromechanical locks which must be opened by secret combination before action at all is possible, and we are extending this system. The American people and all the world can rest assured that we have taken every step man can devise to insure that neither a madman nor a malfunction could ever trigger nuclear war." 51 DEP'T STATE BULL. 458-60 (1964); DOCUMENTS ON DISARMAMENT, 1964, at 429, 431 (U.S. Arms Control & Disarmament Agency Pub. No. 27, 1965).

As might be expected, the Soviet Union took a dim view of this technological "fix" adopted by the United States and its non-nuclear NATO allies. It called for an explanation from the U.S. as to "why these locks cannot be opened by evil-doers." Statement by Soviet Union Representative to ENDC, July 21, 1966, ENDC/PV.275, at 20-29; DOCUMENTS ON DISARMAMENT, 1966, at 460, 462-63.

The Yale Law Journal   Vol. 77: 1447, 1968

United States custodial and release arrangements with non-nuclear NATO allies would not constitute a transfer or receipt of "control" of nuclear weapons as long as the affirmative act effecting release of the weapons has not occured.[56] Thus, "control" would seem to mean actual, not potential, control.

---

56. What would be the legal effect under the Non-Proliferation Treaty of a United States release of nuclear weapons to non-nuclear-weapon NATO allies? A Presidential decision to effect such a release would not be made except in what appeared at the time to be an extreme emergency at the brink of nuclear war. It is doubtful, however, that sufficient time exists between actual launch of a Soviet nuclear attack and its impact in Western Europe (about 15 minutes) for receipt of warning, a Presidential decision in Washington, nuclear arming of NATO delivery systems in Europe, and, in the case of aircraft at least, stationing on airborne alert. Therefore, it would be possible, if not probable, for the release of United States nuclear weapons to be effected in certain situations prior to actual launch of a Soviet nuclear attack. In these circumstances, two basic scenarios can be envisioned: (1) a major crisis in Europe in which war was subsequently avoided; and (2) a major crisis which resulted in armed conflict.

If war was subsequently avoided and United States nuclear weapons had been released, both the United States and recipient NATO allies would be vulnerable to being charged with a violation of the Non-Proliferation Treaty (assuming the fact of release became known). Of course, the Soviet Union might have an interest in not pressing the charge.

If war subsequently occurred, the question of the impact of war on the Non-Proliferation Treaty would arise. During Senate Foreign Relations Committee hearings on the Limited Nuclear Test Ban Treaty the question arose as to whether Article I of that Treaty, which banned "any other nuclear explosion" in addition to a "nuclear weapon test explosion" in the atmosphere might ban the use of nuclear weapons in war. Both the United States and the Soviet Union had publicly taken the position that the Treaty did not restrict the use of nuclear weapons in war, but only the peacetime conduct of certain nuclear explosions. The implications of the Treaty itself and the intentions of the drafting parties clearly expressed in the legislative history support this position. The Senate Foreign Relations Committee report concluded: "As a practical matter, it would be inconceivable that the treaty, or any of its provisions, could affect a decision to use nuclear weapons should a situation develop in which the security of the United States or any of its allies appeared to be in jeopardy." SENATE COMM. ON FOREIGN RELATIONS, REPORT ON THE NUCLEAR TEST BAN TREATY, S. EXEC. DOC. No. 3, 88th Cong., 1st Sess. 5 (1963). *See also Hearings on the Nuclear Test Ban Treaty Before the Senate Comm. on Foreign Relations,* 88th Cong., 1st Sess. 76 *et seq.* (1963) (opinion of the Legal Adviser on the meaning of the words "Or Any Other Nuclear Explosion," Aug. 14, 1963); Letter to Senator Fulbright from General Counsel of the Department of Defense concerning use of nuclear weapons in time of war. *Id.* 177-78.

However, the effect of a war involving nuclear weapons on the Non-Proliferation Treaty is not as clear as in the case of the Limited Nuclear Test Ban Treaty. Although the record is unclear, the United States and the Soviet Union may have agreed to interpret the Treaty as being suspended or ended by war. *See* Testimony of Adrian S. Fisher, *Hearings on Arms Control and Disarmament Act Amendments, 1968, Before the House Comm. on Foreign Affairs,* 90th Cong., 2d Sess. 67 (1968). It may be argued that a major purpose of the Treaty is to prevent from arising the circumstances under which United States nuclear weapons must be released. If such circumstances do arise, then the purpose of the Treaty will already have been defeated and the restraints of the Treaty would be suspended. Moreover, a case might be made justifying United States action because of prior violations by another Party, or hostile acts justifying a resort to individual or collective self-defense which would override the Treaty's prohibitions.

An argument can also be made that the Non-Proliferation Treaty should not be suspended in time of war. The first two paragraphs of the Preamble read:

"Considering the devastation that would be visited upon all mankind by a nuclear war and the consequent need to make every effort to avert the danger of such a war and to take measures to safeguard the security of peoples.

"Believing that the proliferation of nuclear weapons would seriously enhance the danger of nuclear war . . . ."

It can be argued that these introductory paragraphs indicate an intention that the Treaty

Nuclear Weapons

How much influence must a nation have over or within the decision-making process concerning the use of nuclear weapons to be deemed to have "control"? Nuclear-weapon states consult with non-nuclear-weapon states within both NATO and the Warsaw Pact. Indeed, consultation would seem to be an essential part of any concept of collective defense. In the course of the consultation process, non-nuclear-weapon states have an opportunity to influence to some extent decisions made concerning use of nuclear weapons in the common defense.[57] It would be difficult to assert, however, that the non-nuclear-weapon states either individually or collectively, would "control" the decision process simply as a result of their participation in consultations.

Planning concerning the deployment and use of nuclear forces has been a central activity of NATO. Participation in detailed planning would accord non-nuclear-weapon states a substantially larger role in the decision-making process than the mere exchange of views which would normally constitute consultation.

In particular, as the United States and certain of its NATO allies gradually backed away from proposals for a multilateral nuclear force (MLF) during 1966 and 1967, the United States came forward with a series of proposals for intensifying consultation and planning concerning nuclear force posture, deployment, strategy and tactics. United States efforts to construct a satisfactory framework for sharing responsibility within NATO for planning and decision-making concerning

---

not be suspended during hostilities, and that it is essential to the achievement of the purposes of the Treaty that it be maintained during future periods of tension and nuclear crises, including an armed conflict.

Finally, it should be noted that there is no express authority in the Atomic Energy Act of 1954 for lifting in time of major crisis or war the prohibitions on transfer of nuclear weapons contained in Section 92. The assumption on which both Congress and the President have clearly operated has been that the President's inherent authority as Commander-in-Chief to effect release of nuclear weapons in wartime remains unimpaired by Section 92. For discussion, see *Hearings on Amending the Atomic Energy Act of 1954 —Exchange of Military Information and Material with Allies—Before the Subcomm. on Agreements for Cooperation of the Joint Comm. on Atomic Energy*, 85th Cong., 2d Sess. 470-74 (1958).

57. In the course of ENDC discussions, Poland attacked the United States draft treaty because it would permit NATO nuclear arrangements which might "increase the influence of a State among its allies." The United States replied: "influence among members of either of the alliances has nothing to do with proliferation and cannot be governed by a treaty." Statement by United States Representative to ENDC, Mar. 3, 1966, ENDC/PV.245, at 25-32; DOCUMENTS ON DISARMAMENT, 1966, at 78, 82-83. Subsequently the United States affirmatively stated the need for consultation: "There must be, in fact, a measure of consultation in any military alliance of sovereign States on the overall strategy or plan of use of all the integrated forces available to the alliance, whether for air defense or other purposes. This consultation must above all seek to achieve an understanding as to the circumstances in which the most devastating of all weapons—that is, nuclear weapons—could be used." Statement by United States Representative to ENDC, Mar. 31, 1966, ENDC/PV.253, at 10-16; DOCUMENTS ON DISARMAMENT, 1966, at 183, 187.

The Yale Law Journal   Vol. 77: 1447, 1968

nuclear defense culminated with the establishment in December 1966 of a Nuclear Defense Affairs Committee and a Nuclear Planning Group. The Committee is open to any NATO nation willing to participate. The Nuclear Planning Group is composed of seven Defense Ministers drawn from the full Committee, with the United States, the United Kingdom, West Germany, and Italy as permanent members, and three other Committee members on a rotating basis.[58] Do the non-nuclear-weapon NATO members which participate in this planning structure have "control" of nuclear weapons?

It may be argued on legal grounds that even joint and detailed planning does not involve a shift in control over an actual decision to use nuclear weapons. Furthermore, the United States has made clear throughout the negotiations its view that a non-proliferation treaty to which it would subscribe must not affect existing consultative and planning arrangements with its NATO allies. The Soviet Union has apparently acquiesced in this view as evidenced by dropping objectionable language in its earlier draft treaty proposals and a subsequent press release.[59]

Thus, we are driven toward an interpretation of "control" which focuses on the actual decision to use nuclear weapons. If a non-nuclear-weapon state could make a *unilateral* and *effective* decision to use nuclear weapons, it would clearly have control—a "finger on the trigger" —whether or not it had physical possession of the weapons. On the other hand, if use of a nuclear weapon by a nuclear-weapon state required concurrence of a non-nuclear-weapon state, then the non-nuclear-weapon state would have control in a negative sense. How-

---

58. A short summary of the various proposals beginning in 1960 to promote integration between nuclear-weapon and non-nuclear-weapon NATO allies is contained in a statement by Secretary Robert McNamara preceding the first meeting of the Nuclear Planning Group which took place in Washington on April 6-7, 1967. 56 DEP'T STATE BULL. 686-87 (1967). Concerning technical arrangements, in 1964 the United States entered into an agreement for cooperation regarding the exchange of military nuclear information with NATO and its members. Agreement Between the Parties to the North Atlantic Treaty for Cooperation Regarding Atomic Information, [1965] 1 U.S.T. 109, T.I.A.S. No. 3768. The agreement, which supersedes an earlier 1955 agreement, provides for exchange of "atomic information" necessary to development of defense plans, training of personnel in the military applications of atomic energy, evaluation of atomic capabilities of potential enemies "and other military applications," and "development of delivery systems compatible with the atomic weapons which they carry." *Id.* art. III. The agreement specifies that there will be "no transfer [by the United States] of atomic weapons, non-nuclear parts of atomic weapons, or non-nuclear parts of atomic weapons systems involving Restricted Data." *Id.* art. IV.

59. For language dropped by the Soviet Union from its draft Treaty proposals, see note 52 *supra.* West German newspapers reported on April 23, 1968, statements by a Soviet Union official that "the so-called McNamara Committee does not deal with questions relating to proliferation of nuclear weapons, and from this viewpoint discussions of questions which do not concern non-proliferation are not a violation of commitments which can be taken or have already been taken by parties to the treaty."

Nuclear Weapons

ever, this kind of decisional control—a "finger on the safety catch"—would seem not to be the kind of control which the Non-Proliferation Treaty is intended to prevent non-nuclear states from acquiring.

Between a finger on the trigger and one on the safety catch, there are a number of intermediate positions. To illustrate three major possibilities, assume that the NATO Nuclear Planning Group, composed of two nuclear-weapon states and five non-nuclear weapon states, is delegated authority to make a binding decision to use nuclear weapons assigned but not transferred to it by the nuclear-weapon states.

One way to make such a decision would be by a simple majority vote. This clearly amounts to a transfer of control in a decisional sense from the nuclear-weapon states to non-nuclear-weapon states and is barred by the Treaty. The result is the same even if a two-thirds, or three-fourths majority were required as long as the majority could be constituted exclusively from non-nuclear-weapon states.

The second possibility is to require a majority vote, which must include the concurring vote of at least one nuclear-weapon state, for decision by the Group to use any of the nuclear weapons assigned to it. This is also prohibited since a nuclear-weapon state is barred by the Treaty from transferring control "to any recipient whatsoever." This language would bar an arrangement under which a majority of the Group could decide to use nuclear weapons in the physical possession of the United States upon the vote of a majority, including the United States *or* the United Kingdom.

The third possibility is to require a majority which must include the concurring votes of both the United Kingdom *and* the United States. Does retention of a veto over use by every nuclear-weapon state participating take such an arrangement outside the reach of the Non-Proliferation Treaty's prohibitions? In one sense, as long as a nuclear-weapon state retained a veto over the decision to use any nuclear weapons it had assigned, control would not have passed to any other state or states. If a multilateral decision framework as such is deemed a "recipient" of control, then it would seem to be ruled out by the Treaty. However, if such a framework is deemed to have no organic existence apart from its members, then it may be argued that retention of a veto by each participating nuclear-weapon state is effective to preclude a "transfer" of "control" to a "recipient." Control would not pass in these circumstances because there is, alternatively, either no transfer or no recipient.[60]

60. Such an argument is supported by analogy to the authority of the United Nations Security Council. Nuclear-weapon states are members of the Security Council. In theory,

The Yale Law Journal   Vol. 77: 1447, 1968

Each of the three possibilities discussed above reflects positions taken by the United States during succeeding stages of the Non-Proliferation Treaty negotiations. These efforts to preserve some possibility for joint decision-making concerning the use of nuclear weapons were mounted primarily to keep open an MLF option and other possible "hardware" solutions to the problem of sharing nuclear defense within NATO. These "hardware" solutions would have involved the "transfer" of nuclear weapons to a group or association of NATO allies composed of both nuclear-weapon and non-nuclear-weapon states. "Control" over use of nuclear weapons would have been subject, at least at the outset, to a United States veto.[61]

the Charter could provide a legal basis for a decision by the Council ordering the nuclear-weapon permanent members to use nuclear weapons in their custody as part of its authority to use force. Although such a decision may seem beyond the realm of political reality, it is precisely the possibility that such a decision may be made which provides whatever "muscle" there is in the proposed Security Council resolution on security assurances which would be adopted in conjunction with the Non-Proliferation Treaty. *See* discussion at pp. 1512-13 & note 54 *infra*. Of course, it is arguable that a distinction should be drawn between the Security Council and a group within a military alliance.

61. During the 1963-1965 period (before any draft non-proliferation treaty was tabled) under the United States MLF proposal, "firing of the missiles in wartime would be by decision of an agreed number of participants including the United States." However, "in the longer term . . . evolution toward European control as Europe marches toward unity is by no means excluded." Address by Gerald C. Smith, Special Adviser to the Secretary of State, before the United States Naval Academy Foreign Affairs Conference, Dep't of State Release No. 178, Apr. 22, 1964, at 5. This address is one of the fullest official public descriptions of the United States proposal for an MLF. While under the proposal the United States would retain a veto at the outset, it could have been relinquished. Moreover, the recipient of control of the nuclear force might have been an entity composed entirely of non-nuclear-weapon NATO allies. The United States draft non-proliferation treaty of August 17, 1965, retreated somewhat from this position. Article I, paragraph 1, read as follows: "Each of the nuclear States Party to this Treaty undertakes not to transfer any nuclear weapons into the national control of any non-nuclear State, either directly, or indirectly through a military alliance, and each undertakes not to take any other action which would cause an increase in the total number of States and other organizations having independent power to use nuclear weapons." ENDC/162, Aug. 17, 1965; DOCUMENTS ON DISARMAMENT, 1965, at 347. As the United States conceded, this formulation might have been interpreted "to permit the creation of a new nuclear entity composed entirely of non-nuclear-weapon states, in the event that a pre-existing nuclear-weapon state had previously unilaterally disarmed itself of nuclear weapons." Statement by United States Representative to ENDC, Mar. 22, 1966, ENDC/PV.250, at 4-12; DOCUMENTS ON DISARMAMENT, 1966, at 160, 164. The United States draft treaty of August 17, 1965, might also have been interpreted as permitting the creation of a multilateral nuclear force to which a nuclear-weapon state had assigned its entire nuclear force and in which a decision to use nuclear weapons could have been taken by a majority vote. On March 22, 1966, the United States amended its proposed Article I to read: "Each of the nuclear-weapon States party to this treaty undertakes: 1. Not to transfer nuclear weapons into the national control of any non-nuclear-weapon State, or into the control of any association of non-nuclear-weapon States." The word "control" was defined in Article IV to mean "right or ability to fire nuclear weapons without the concurrent decision of an existing nuclear-weapon State." In addition, Article I, paragraph 3, obligated the nuclear-weapon states "[n]ot to take any other action which would cause an increase in the total number of States and associations of States having control of nuclear weapons." ENDC/152/Add. 1, Mar. 21, 1966; DOCUMENTS ON DISARMAMENT, 1966, at 159. Under this formulation an MLF in which the United States retained its veto would have been permitted. An MLF in which more than one nuclear-weapon state participated,

Nuclear Weapons

The Soviet Union attacked all such schemes as involving proliferation because nuclear weapons would be transferred to the group of states, and, thus, indirectly to the participants in the group. The United States contended there would be no proliferation since there would be no transfer of control over a decision to use nuclear weapons. Moreover, because of the permissive action link system, participants in an MLF would lack not only the right but the ability to fire nuclear weapons. The Soviet Union replied with a series of questions:

> We might, for example, ask what the situation would be if the partners of the United States in NATO were to reject the legality of the United States veto at a decisive or crucial moment? What would happen if the partners of the United States in NATO were to find means of opening the lock on nuclear weapons in circumvention of the United States veto? Who would inherit the United States right of veto if NATO ceased to exist? . . . Can it be seriously suggested that a vital multilateral international agreement, to which according to our calculations many States, probably even more than a hundred, could become parties, should be based on the unilateral right of veto of one of the parties to this agreement, the United States? . . . [N]either the Soviet Union nor the many other States . . . can base their security on the United States right of veto on decisions within NATO relating to the use of nuclear weapons.[62]

There the matter stood, with the United States focusing on "control" and no transfer of control and the Soviet Union emphasizing a vague concept of "access" and simply no transfer, until the United States, for a variety of reasons, gave up all efforts to create a multilateral nuclear force within NATO.[63] Although the public record is not clear on this point, it is reasonable to conclude that the Non-Proliferation Treaty

---

and which permitted nuclear weapons to be fired with the concurrence of either nuclear-weapon state, but not both, would also have been possible. As a practical matter, however, the United States does not seem to have seriously contemplated any such possibility. Shortly before the United States treaty amendments were tabled, on February 23, 1966, Secretary of State Rusk had stated: "We would have to insist . . . that the United States be a party to a decision to use nuclear weapons. Because the vast arsenals of the United States are so heavily involved in that decision, we must be present for that decision and must ourselves agree to the decision taken." *Hearings on Nonproliferation of Nuclear Weapons Before the Joint Comm. on Atomic Energy,* 89th Cong., 2d Sess. 20 (1966). Moreover, the United States could not relinquish its veto without an amendment to existing United States law. *Id.*

62. Statement by Soviet Union Representative to ENDC, Apr. 5, 1966, ENDC/PV.255, at 16-25; DOCUMENTS ON DISARMAMENT, 1966, at 199, 202-03.

63. For a dialogue which reveals some of the thinking behind the United States move, see Testimony of Adrian S. Fisher, Deputy Director, United States Arms Control and Disarmament Agency, *Hearings on Arms Control and Disarmament Act Amendments, 1968, Before the House Comm. on Foreign Affairs,* 90th Cong., 2d Sess. 200 (1968).

does not necessarily rule out a multilateral decision process which may authorize use of nuclear weapons if each participating nuclear-weapon state retains its individual veto and no nuclear hardware is transferred to the group. Indeed, the net effect of such an arrangement would be more fingers on the nuclear safety catch, but no more on the trigger.

Articles I and II are concerned not only with prohibiting the transfer and acquisition of nuclear weapons or of their control, but also with prohibiting the receipt and transfer of nuclear weapons by certain parties. Although this latter prohibition has been adverted to in discussing the issue of "control," two further implications should be analyzed.

First, Article I prohibits the transfer of nuclear weapons "to any recipient whatsoever," to nuclear-weapon as well as non-nuclear-weapon states. For example, the United States could not, under the Treaty, supply nuclear warheads to the United Kingdom for the Polaris missiles which the United Kingdom will obtain from the United States.[64] Similarly, Article II prohibits the receipt of nuclear weapons by a non-nuclear-weapon state "from any transferor whatsoever." This language is probably intended to make the undertaking coextensive with the non-transfer obligation of the nuclear-weapon states; it also serves to reinforce the conclusion that transfer and receipt through international organizations or multilateral frameworks is not permitted under the Treaty.[65]

Second, whether these restrictions concerning transfer and receipt would operate as an obstacle to Western European unity deserves discussion. For example, would either France or the United Kingdom, or both, be able to weld their nuclear forces into a "United States of Europe" under the Treaty? Although such a possibility is far below the horizon of political reality today, preservation of the option through some form of express "European clause" has been a continuing concern of some of those favoring European integration. Earlier United States proposals for a non-proliferation treaty contained specific language to protect such a possible political evolution.[66] At that time the Soviet

---

64. Under the Nassau agreement the United States and the United Kingdom agreed "that the United States will make available on a continuing basis Polaris missiles (less warheads) for British submarines." Statement on Nuclear Defense Systems, attached to Nassau Communique by President Kennedy and Prime Minister Macmillan, Dec. 21, 1962, 49 Dep't State Bull. 43-45 (1963); Documents on Disarmament, 1962, at 1274, 1276 (U.S. Arms Control & Disarmament Agency Pub. No. 19, 1963).

65. Under Articles I and II, "transfer" and "receive" are also modified by "directly, or indirectly." Although this expression is deeply rooted in the history of the negotiations it now seems merely to add further cement to the interpretation suggested previously concerning nuclear sharing arrangements.

66. *See* analysis, note 61 *supra*.

Nuclear Weapons

Union took a firm stance against any evolution in Western Europe, federated or otherwise, which would multiply the number of states or former states having "access" to nuclear weapons.[67]

Since no comparable language appears in the agreed Treaty text, may such a provision still be implied? It would seem reasonable to make a distinction between the notions of "transfer" and "succession." In the process of political unification a United Western Europe would "inherit" the nuclear weapons of France and/or the United Kingdom without transfer or acquisition.[68]

In addition to the prohibitions against transfer and receipt of nuclear weapons, Articles I and II proscribe a further range of activity which is broad, vague, and in large measure susceptible only of subjective appraisal. A nuclear-weapon state undertakes "not in any way to assist, encourage, or induce" any non-nuclear-weapon state to "manufacture or otherwise acquire" nuclear weapons or "control" over such weapons; a non-nuclear-weapon state undertakes "not to seek or receive any assistance in the manufacture of nuclear weapons."[69]

67. In reference to Article I, paragraph 3, of the United States draft treaty amendments of March 22, 1966, the Soviet Union envisioned the possibility that "one or another nuclear Power will give up the rights to use nuclear weapons in favour of a group of States or in favour of the whole military alliance . . ." and "will thus be transformed into a whole series of nuclear States, and instead of one there may be five, ten, fourteen or fifteen Powers having the right and ability to use nuclear weapons." Statement by Soviet Union Representative to ENDC, June 23, 1966, ENDC/PV.267, 4-13; DOCUMENTS ON DISARMAMENT, 1966, at 359, 361.

68. Foreign Minister Brandt of West Germany has stated that a united Europe "would not automatically become a member of such a treaty. A federal European state would instead inherit what its members possess." Interview with *Die Welt*, Feb. 23, 1967, DOCUMENTS ON DISARMAMENT, 1967, at 92, 93. Italy also has made a distinction between an alliance and a federation which would provide for defense under a unified government and would receive only those nuclear weapons that its original members possessed. Statement by Representative of Italy to ENDC, ENDC/PV.267, at 16-17. The United States based its support for keeping the "European option" open on the ground that "welding of all a nuclear weapon State's nuclear forces into a collective unit could take place only in the event of a very profound change in the political relationships existing between States . . . ," and even if such a change came about the "centres of nuclear power . . . would not be increased . . . ." Statement by United States Representative to ENDC, Mar. 31, 1966, ENDC/PV.253, at 10-16; DOCUMENTS ON DISARMAMENT, 1966, at 183, 185-86.

69. The meaning of "manufacture" which is used in both Articles I and II is extremely important, yet difficult to ascertain. The United States draft treaty of August 17, 1965, had simply prohibited "manufacture" by non-nuclear-weapon states and "assistance to any non-nuclear State in the manufacture of nuclear weapons" by nuclear-weapon states. ENDC/162, Aug. 17, 1965; DOCUMENTS ON DISARMAMENT, 1965, at 347. On the other hand, the Soviet Union draft treaty of September 24, 1965, had included "preparations for the manufacture" of nuclear weapons among the forms of prohibited assistance by nuclear-weapon states and activities prohibited to non-nuclear-weapon states. U.N. Doc. A/5976, Sept. 24, 1965; DOCUMENTS ON DISARMAMENT, 1965, at 443, 444. Sweden addressed the problem fully during the course of the ENDC discussion. Referring to manufacture as "a long ladder with many rungs," the Representative of Sweden contended "the practical question is: on which of these is it reasonable and feasible to introduce international blocking?" *Planning* decisions to undertake research on nuclear weapons and to obtain fissionable material for use in weapons could be described as preparations for manufacture,

The Yale Law Journal   Vol. 77: 1447, 1968

Almost any kind of international nuclear assistance is potentially useful to a nuclear weapons program. Indeed, most nuclear activity is objectively ambiguous. Therefore, if only Articles I and II applied, any nuclear assistance received by a non-nuclear-weapon state could be subjectively appraised as falling within the range of prohibited activity. Fortunately, the application of safeguards to all peaceful nuclear assistance to non-nuclear-weapon states, as required by Article III, provides a way to establish and clarify the peaceful purpose of most international nuclear assistance.[70]

The prohibitions against encouragement and inducement by nuclear-weapon states are even broader and more nebulous than those against assistance, and no other parts of the Treaty would operate to narrow or sharpen the meaning of the terms used.[71] Could China's blandishments to the Afro-Asian nations to follow their example be deemed the kind of encouragement proscribed by the Treaty? Or is something more than

as, of course, could *operational* decisions to build plants and conduct tests. "To prohibit just the final act of 'manufacture' would seem to come late in these long chains of decisions. On the other hand, already to probe the preliminary thinking of politicians and the laboratory research of scientists obviously is as difficult, as it would be considered undesirable intervention. Could a middle link be found on which the prohibitory regulation should most definitely be focused?" Statement by Representative of Sweden to ENDC, Feb. 24, 1966, ENDC/PV.243, at 4-15; DOCUMENTS ON DISARMAMENT, 1966, at 49, 56.

In the March 22, 1966, amendments to its draft Treaty, the United States adopted to some extent the Soviet Union's position concerning preparations for manufacture. Under Article I, as amended, nuclear-weapon states would have undertaken not to provide assistance "in preparations for such manufacture." Under Article II, as amended, non-nuclear-weapon states would have undertaken not to seek or receive assistance "in preparation for such manufacture." However, as distinguished from the Soviet Union's position, there would have been no express prohibition on preparations for the manufacture of nuclear weapons by a non-nuclear-weapon state as long as such activity was carried on without any outside assistance. Articles I and II of the Non-Proliferation Treaty as finally agreed upon do not contain any reference at all to preparations for manufacture, either in relation to prohibited nuclear-weapon state assistance or to prohibited non-nuclear-weapon state activities. In view of this omission together with the historical background, it would appear that at least under Article II of the Treaty non-nuclear-weapon states would remain free to engage in many of those activities on the "long ladder" which stop short of actual manufacture, including perhaps a major portion of nuclear weapons research and development work.

70. Safeguards would not, however, be applicable under Article III to a nuclear weapons research program which did not constitute "manufacture." Moreover, if past IAEA practice is followed in implementing Article III, the specific agreements governing the application of safeguards to peaceful nuclear activities in a non-nuclear-weapon state will provide in general for termination on six months' notice at the option of the state concerned. *See* Szasz, *The Law of International Atomic Energy Agency Safeguards,* REV. BELGE DE DROIT INT'L 196, 219-20 (1967); Willrich, *Safeguarding Atoms for Peace,* 60 AM. J. INT'L LAW 34, 50-51 (1966).

71. The concept of a prohibition on encouragement or inducement to manufacture nuclear weapons has its origin in Article I of the Limited Nuclear Test Ban Treaty, which, in addition to prohibiting nuclear weapon test explosions in the atmosphere, outer space and underwater in paragraph 1, also prohibits any Party from "causing, encouraging, or in any way participating in" a nuclear weapon test explosion conducted by any state in a prohibited environment. Limited Nuclear Test Ban Treaty, art. I, para. 2, [1963] 2 U.S.T. 1313, T.I.A.S. No. 5433, 480 U.N.T.S. 43 (1963).

Nuclear Weapons

words necessary? The range of possible activities by nuclear-weapon states which constitute assistance, encouragement or inducement under the Non-Proliferation Treaty might develop into a fertile field for future legal controversy, if the parties choose to pour the foreign policy process into this form.

There are also some important limitations on the scope of prohibited activity. Although the transfer of nuclear weapons is prohibited "to any recipient whatsoever," including a transfer from one nuclear-weapon state to another, nuclear-weapon states are prohibited from assisting only non-nuclear-weapon states in the manufacture of nuclear weapons. This leaves open the possibility that nuclear-weapon states could "assist" each other in their respective nuclear weapons programs in a variety of ways, short of transfer, without violating the Non-Proliferation Treaty. In particular, the so-called "special relationship" between the United States and the United Kingdom with respect to nuclear weapons cooperation is apparently unimpaired by Article I.[72]

The undertaking by nuclear-weapon states not to assist non-nuclear-weapon states under Article I is universal and applies with equal force to all such states, whether or not they are parties to the Treaty. Indeed, any other result would constitute an inducement to non-nuclear-weapon states not to become parties to the Treaty. Article II, on the other hand, does not on its face prohibit a non-nuclear-weapon state from assisting *any* state in the manufacture of nuclear weapons. Article I does not prohibit a nuclear-weapon state from *receiving* such assistance. Therefore, the Treaty does not limit a nuclear-weapon state's ability to purchase uranium for its weapons program from any foreign supplier. On the other hand, assistance in the manufacture of nuclear weapons may not be given by a non-nuclear-weapon state to another non-nuclear-weapon state if the latter is a party to the Treaty without the recipient being in violation of its obligations under Article II not to seek or receive such assistance. But Article II does not expressly prohibit a non-nuclear-weapon party from giving assistance in the manufacture of nuclear weapons to another non-nuclear-weapon state which is not a party.

It might appear that this loophole in Article II is closed by Article III, since under paragraph 2 all parties undertake not to supply nuclear materials and equipment to non-nuclear-weapon states, whether or not

---

72. The basic United States-United Kingdom agreement for cooperation on the uses of atomic energy for mutual defense purposes entered into force Aug. 4, 1958. [1958] U.S.T. 1028, T.I.A.S. No. 4078, 326 U.N.T.S. 3. It was amended May 7, 1959, [1959] 2 U.S.T. 1274, T.I.A.S. No. 4267, 351 U.N.T.S. 458. For recent criticism of the "special relationship," see G. BALL, THE DISCIPLINE OF POWER 90-117 (1968).

The Yale Law Journal   Vol. 77: 1447, 1968

parties, except under safeguards. But this argument fails because safe-guards under Article III are applicable only to nuclear materials and equipment provided "for peaceful purposes." Therefore, under the Treaty as it stands, there would seem to be no legal obstacle to a non-nuclear-weapon party furnishing material assistance to another non-nuclear-weapon state not a party to the Treaty for a nuclear weapons program. In spite of the plain meaning of the Treaty's language in this regard, both the United States and the Soviet Union have tried to close this loophole by questionable interpretations.[73] Of course, the Treaty could have been amended to cover this problem clearly.[74] But such an amendment might well have resulted in pressure from other nations to have the Treaty bar assistance by non-nuclear-weapon states not only to other non-nuclear-weapon states, but also to the nuclear-weapon states themselves.

The prohibitions contained in Articles I and II of the Non-Proliferation Treaty thus far discussed have been directed at actions between states, including transfer and receipt of nuclear weapons and assistance

---

73. The United States has stated: "It seems clear that a non-nuclear-weapon state which accepts the treaty's restrictions on itself would have no reason to assist another country not accepting the same restrictions to gain advantage from that fact in the field of nuclear-weapon development. If a non-nuclear-weapon party did nevertheless attempt to provide such assistance in the territory of a non-party, the presumption would im-mediately arise that these acts had the purpose of developing nuclear weapons itself, in violation of the treaty." Statement by United States Representative to ENDC, ENDC/PV.370 (prov.), at 52-60. The Soviet Union has stated on the same point: "If a non-nuclear State were to give assistance to another non-nuclear State in producing or acquiring nuclear weapons, in that case, under the provisions of Article II and the preamble to the treaty, it would be viewed as a violation of the treaty." Statement by the Soviet Union Representative to ENDC, ENDC/PV.370 (prov.), at 41-44.

74. On two occasions the United Arab Republic suggested that Article II should be amended to ban assistance by one nuclear-weapon state to another (and also to amend Article I to ban expressly transfer by private organizations and individuals). Statements by Representative of United Arab Republic to ENDC, ENDC/PV.333, at 4ff; ENDC/PV.367 (prov.), at 12-16. Brazil and India supported the U.A.R. with regard to Article II. ENDC/PV.363 (prov.), at 32-35; ENDC/PV.368 (prov.), at 23-25. The United States draft treaty of August 17, 1965, covered the point nicely. Article II, paragraph 2, provided: "Each of the non-nuclear States Party to this Treaty undertakes not to seek or to receive assistance in the manufacture of nuclear weapons, *or itself to grant such assistance.*" ENDC/162, Aug. 17, 1965; DOCUMENTS ON DISARMAMENT, 1965, at 347, 348 (emphasis added). The United States draft Article II as amended on March 22, 1966, also covered the point. ENDC/152/Add. 1, Mar. 22, 1966; DOCUMENTS ON DISARMAMENT, 1966, at 159. The Soviet Union draft treaty of September 24, 1965, was less clear, but Article II, paragraph 1, did prohibit non-nuclear-weapon states from manufacturing nuclear weapons "either inde-pendently or together with other States, in their own territory or in the territory of other States." U.N. Doc. A/5976, Sept. 24, 1965; DOCUMENTS ON DISARMAMENT, 1965, at 443, 444. The reluctance of the superpowers to amend their draft in this respect seems difficult to justify, especially if there was support for such an amendment from the non-nuclear-weapon states, and if there was no latent conflict between the superpowers as to interpreta-tion. With reference to the statements by the United States and Soviet Union, at note 73 *supra*, the United Arab Republic Representative has stated that the fact that these statements were made by the co-Chairmen and co-authors of the Treaty "confers im-portant weight upon them." Statement by Representative of United Arab Republic to ENDC, Feb. 27, 1968, ENDC/PV.370, at 31.

Nuclear Weapons

in the manufacture of such weapons. Of course the gut provision of the Treaty, directed at non-nuclear-weapon states individually, is the undertaking "not to manufacture or otherwise acquire" nuclear weapons or other nuclear explosive devices, even with indigenous resources and without any outside help. In effect, all the measures of nuclear disarmament which the nuclear-weapon states have been unable to agree upon in 23 years of almost uninterrupted negotiation would be applied prospectively to the non-nuclear-weapon states, including a comprehensive ban on all nuclear weapon tests and a halt in production of fissionable materials for use in weapons.[75] Non-nuclear-weapon parties must henceforth be satisfied with pursuing the peaceful uses of nuclear energy.[76]

B. *Peaceful Nuclear Activities*

Since peaceful and warlike uses of nuclear energy spring from the same technology, the provisions of the Non-Proliferation Treaty concerned with peaceful nuclear activities (Articles III, IV, and V) are at least as important in the overall non-proliferation scheme as those focused directly on nuclear weapons. Article III provides for safeguards on peaceful nuclear activities in non-nuclear-weapon states to ensure that nuclear materials used in such activities are not diverted to use in weapons. Articles IV and V contain important undertakings regarding future cooperation in the peaceful uses of nuclear energy. Many of the undertakings concerning cooperation laid on the nuclear-weapon states, some hortatory and some real, have been inserted to reduce the discrimination inherent in asking non-nuclear-weapon states to pledge not to manufacture nuclear weapons, even out of their own resources. Furthermore, the opportunity of receiving expanded nuclear assistance for peaceful purposes provides a carrot for the non-nuclear-weapon states to accept safeguards, while the threat of a refusal of further cooperation unless such safeguards are accepted could be a rather effective stick.

1. *Treaty Safeguards*

The character of existing international safeguards systems has been previously outlined. A major part of the problem with implementing

---

75. In 1955 both the Soviet Union and the United States conceded that, as a technical matter, in view of the amounts of fissionable material that has already been produced, it would be impossible to provide assurance that all stockpiles of nuclear weapons had been eliminated under any practicable verification system. After 1955, therefore, talk of complete nuclear disarmament by the nuclear-weapon states became at most propaganda. For the text of the Soviet statement, see 1 DOCUMENTS ON DISARMAMENT, 1945-1959, at 456, 464-67 (U.S. Dep't of State No. 7008, 1960); and for the United States statement, see *id.* 510-13.

76. But the breadth of the pledge not to manufacture depends on the interpretation of "manufacture." See note 69 *supra.*

The Yale Law Journal   Vol. 77: 1447, 1968

the Non-Proliferation Treaty will be to fit the Treaty safeguards requirements into the framework which already exists.

At the outset, it is important to stake out certain ground which is
beyond the reach of any international inspection requirement under
the Treaty. There is no verification of the undertakings by the parties
under Articles I and II not to transfer or receive nuclear weapons.[77]
Moreover, safeguards are not intended to ensure that a non-nuclear-
weapon state does not establish a secret nuclear weapons program entirely outside and independent of its peaceful nuclear industry. A
system for effective verification of these fundamental obligations would
require access not only to declared peaceful nuclear activities within
states, but also to all areas and activities suspected of being related to a
nuclear weapons program. Such verification would probably be so intrusive and extensive as to render the Non-Proliferation Treaty unacceptable to some nuclear-weapon as well as many non-nuclear-weapon
states.[78]

Finally, safeguards are not required on peaceful nuclear activities
within nuclear-weapon states. A logical reason for this exemption is that
in a nuclear-weapon state verification that the nuclear materials used
in the peaceful program are not diverted to weapons loses its non-proliferation purpose.[79] The political reason for the exemption is that an
international inspection of civil nuclear activities in nuclear-weapon

---

77. Rumania and India questioned the absence of any method of assuring that the
nuclear-weapon states and their non-nuclear-weapon allies were respecting their obligations under Articles I and II. Statement by Representative of Rumania to ENDC, ENDC/
362 (prov.), at 12; Statement by Representative of India to ENDC, ENDC/PV.370 (prov.),
at 17.

78. Article 16 of the Treaty of Tlatelolco, however, provides for "special inspection"
when so requested "by any party which suspects that some activity prohibited by this
Treaty has been carried out or is being carried out . . . ," or when requested "by any
party which has been suspected or charged with having violated the Treaty." The
inspection is to be carried out in such a situation not by the IAEA which has general
safeguards responsibilities with respect to declared peaceful nuclear activities in the
territories of the parties, but by the Council of the Agency for the Prohibition of Nuclear
Weapons in Latin America. The Council is composed of five of the parties, each elected
for a four-year term. Therefore, although the Latin American nuclear free zone concept
includes peremptory inspection for clandestine nuclear weapons facilities, the inspection
agency is regional rather than global in make-up.

79. The logic, however, can be questioned. In the past, much of the plutonium produced in civil nuclear power reactors in the United Kingdom, and probably in the Soviet
Union, has been used in nuclear weapons programs. In the United States one dual
purpose power and plutonium production reactor was specially built at Hanford, Washington. The bulk of the plutonium produced in France's nuclear power reactors is being
used in the French weapons program. For this reason, the French, on doubtful legal
grounds, are believed not to have permitted Euratom inspection of most of their nuclear
power reactors. These circumstances suggest that safeguards on reactors in nuclear-
weapon states could force a clear separation between civil power and military production
facilities and, in some cases, make the production of plutonium for weapons more
expensive for nuclear-weapon states.

Nuclear Weapons

states is not acceptable to the Soviet Union. The absence of any requirement that the nuclear-weapon states accept safeguards on their peaceful
nuclear activities creates another major political discrimination in the
Treaty between nuclear-weapon and non-nuclear-weapon states.[80] Concern has also been expressed that nuclear industries in non-nuclear-
weapon states would risk disclosure of industrial secrets in the international inspection process, while their commercial competitors in
nuclear-weapon states would not.[81] To meet this concern with possible

80. On May 30, 1967, before any superpower-agreed draft had been tabled, Sweden
outlined five possible safeguards systems for a non-proliferation treaty in descending order
of acceptability: (1) Universal and obligatory submission to safeguards of all nuclear
industry of all states and of all transfers of nuclear materials between states. This would
amount to a verified cut-off of further production of fissionable materials for weapons as
well as assurance that civil nuclear industries were not diverted. It would stop vertical
and horizontal proliferation. (2) Compulsory submission to safeguards of all peaceful
nuclear activities of all states, and all transfers between all states. This would provide a
complete stop to horizontal proliferation, including additions from abroad to the weapons
programs of nuclear-weapon states. It would also provide non-discrimination and commercial equity in the peaceful nuclear sector. (3) Compulsory submission to safeguards
of all peaceful nuclear activities in non-nuclear-weapon states and on all transfers between
all states. This would stop horizontal proliferation, but would introduce the possibility of
discrimination in regard to the commercial markets within the nuclear-weapon states
between domestic and foreign suppliers. (4) Application of safeguards to all transfers
between all states. This would be non-discriminatory in a sense, but would favor those
states which were self-sufficient and would be ineffective from the standpoint of insuring
against horizontal proliferation. (5) Application of safeguards to all peaceful nuclear
activities in non-nuclear-weapon states and all transfers to non-nuclear-weapon states.
This would stop horizontal proliferation to non-nuclear-weapon states, but would not
prevent foreign contributions to nuclear weapons programs in nuclear-weapon states. It
would also be commercially discriminatory. Sweden called the fifth alternative "very
unsatisfactory" and "unbalanced in all respects." Statement by Representative of Sweden
to ENDC, May 30, 1967, ENDC/PV.300, at 4-15; DOCUMENTS ON DISARMAMENT, 1967, at 239,
243-45. Nevertheless, the fifth alternative is essentially the alternative adopted in Article
III of the Non-Proliferation Treaty.

81. The IAEA system itself gives broad protection to commercial and industrial secrets. Members of the Agency staff are prohibited from disclosing, except to authorized
Agency officials, commercial secrets "or any other confidential information" coming to
their knowledge by reason of safeguards administration. Specific information relating to
the implementation of safeguards may be given to the Board of Governors and to staff
members "only to the extent necessary for the Agency to fulfill its safeguards responsibilities." Summarized lists of items being safeguarded may be published upon Board
decision, but publication of additional information requires the further consent of all
states "directly concerned." I.A.E.A. INFCIRC/66, at para. 14 (1965).

The fear that implementation of safeguards could result in unwanted disclosure of
valuable industrial secrets is probably derived in large measure from the international
character of the inspectorate. Western and capitalist countries may be concerned that
Agency inspectors who are nationals of Communist states would have little respect for
property rights in information. Moreover, countries engaged in stiff technical competition in developing advanced reactor concepts might well be concerned about inspection
by the national of a competitor, regardless of the economic ideology of his government.

The IAEA system also contains requirements that safeguards be implemented "in a
manner designed to avoid hampering a State's economic or technological development,"
and "in a manner designed to be consistent with prudent management practices required
for the economic and safe conduct of nuclear activities." I.A.E.A. INFCIRC/66, at paras.
9-10 (1965). A more specific provision dealing with a related question states that the
Agency shall not request the state concerned "to stop construction or operation" of any
nuclear facility "except by explicit decision of the Board." *Id.* para. 11. These "safeguards
against safeguards" provided in the IAEA system are echoed in Article III, paragraph 3,

The Yale Law Journal   Vol. 77: 1447, 1968

economic discrimination the United States has declared its intention, when safeguards are applied under the Treaty in non-nuclear-weapon states, to "permit the International Atomic Energy Agency to apply its safeguards to all nuclear activities in the United States—excluding only those with direct national security significance."[82] The United Kingdom has made a parallel policy declaration[83] Thus, argument by the non-nuclear-weapon states that Article III of the Treaty discriminates against them in this way should be primarily directed to the Soviet Union.

In spite of these several limitations on the application of safeguards, Article III would have a broad impact on peaceful nuclear activities within non-nuclear-weapon states, and on international nuclear commerce. Under paragraph 1 of Article III,[84] each non-nuclear-weapon

---

of the Non-Proliferation Treaty, which provides: "The safeguards required by this Article shall be implemented in a manner designed to comply with Article IV of this Treaty, and to avoid hampering the economic or technological development of the parties or international co-operation in the field of peaceful nuclear activities, including the international exchange of nuclear material and equipment for the processing, use or production of nuclear material for peaceful purposes in accordance with the provisions of this Article and the principle of safeguarding set forth in the preamble."

82. Address by President Johnson, Dec. 2, 1967, 57 DEP'T STATE BULL. 862, 863 (1967); DOCUMENTS ON DISARMAMENT, 1967, at 613-15. Previously, the United States attitude had been that "the application of a system of safeguards to all the peaceful activities of existing nuclear-weapon Powers would involve a tremendous strain on the safeguard system. A strict inspection of the peaceful nuclear activities of existing nuclear-weapon Powers when there is no restriction on their increasing their large nuclear stockpiles might well be described as straining at gnats while swallowing camels." Statement by United States Representative to ENDC, July 28, 1966, ENDC/PV.277, at 407; DOCUMENTS ON DISARMAMENT, 1966, at 482, 183-84.

83. For statement by United Kingdom Disarmament Minister Mulley to the House of Commons, Dec. 4, 1967, see ENDC/207, Dec. 5, 1967; DOCUMENTS ON DISARMAMENT, 1967, at 616.

84. "Each non-nuclear-weapon State Party to the Treaty undertakes to accept safeguards, as set forth in an agreement to be negotiated and concluded with the International Atomic Energy Agency in accordance with the Statute of the International Atomic Energy Agency and the Agency's safeguards system, for the exclusive purpose of verification of the fulfillment of its obligations assumed under this Treaty with a view to preventing diversion of nuclear energy from peaceful uses to nuclear weapons or other nuclear explosive devices. Procedures for the safeguards required by this article shall be followed with respect to source or special fissionable material whether it is being produced, processed or used in any principal nuclear facility or is outside any such facility. The safeguards required by this article shall be applied on all source or special fissionable material in all peaceful nuclear activities within the territory of such State, under its jurisdiction, or carried out under its control anywhere." Art. III, para. 1.

The question may be asked whether Article III incorporates by reference the IAEA safeguards system as it would exist when the Treaty enters into force. If such were the case, it might be argued that a Treaty amendment would be required to change the IAEA safeguards system applicable by virtue of Article III. The United States has stated that the Non-Proliferation Treaty should not be interpreted in this way. Statement by United States Representative to ENDC, Jan. 18, 1968, ENDC/PV.357, at 14, 16. The IAEA system itself contains provision for "periodic review in the light of the further experience gained by the Agency as well as of technological developments." I.A.E.A. INFCIRC/66, at para. 8 (1965). The Preamble to the Non-Proliferation Treaty also contains a paragraph: "Expressing their support for research, development and other efforts to further the application, within the framework of the International Atomic Energy

Nuclear Weapons

state undertakes to accept safeguards which would be applied "on all source or special fissionable material in all peaceful nuclear activities" within its territory or under its jurisdiction or control. Hence, safeguards would be applicable to the entire peaceful nuclear industries of all non-nuclear-weapon states which become parties to the Treaty. Widespread adherence to the Non-Proliferation Treaty would, therefore, constitute a major step toward international security regulation of the nuclear phase of the energy economy in many countries of the world, and in Eastern as well as Western Europe.[85]

But the undertaking of the non-nuclear-weapon states under paragraph 1 to accept safeguards is imperfect. Since the "exclusive purpose" of safeguards under Article III is "verification of the fulfillment of [each non-nuclear-weapon state's] obligations assumed under this Treaty with a view to preventing diversion of nuclear energy from peaceful uses to nuclear weapons or other nuclear explosive devices," the Treaty safeguards do not necessarily prohibit diversion to any military purpose aside from nuclear weapons. Under paragraph 2 of Article III, which covers international nuclear transactions, safeguards are not required on imports for a military reactor program in a non-nuclear-weapon state.[86] Unless the safeguards concept is applied more broadly under paragraph 1 than under paragraph 2, therefore, safeguards would not follow nuclear materials transferred by a non-nuclear-weapon state

Agency safeguards system, of the principle of safeguarding effectively the flow of source and special fissionable materials by use of instruments and other techniques at certain strategic points." Under the IAEA safeguards system, however, the specific safeguards agreements would be negotiated with reference to the system as it exists at that time. Further modification in the IAEA system would not affect safeguards agreements already in effect unless so provided in the agreement or consented to by the state concerned. I.A.E.A. INFCIRC/66, at para. 6 (1965). *See also* Statement by United States Representative to ENDC, ENDC/PV.368 (prov.), at 23-26.

85. Although in the past the Communist states have been adamant against arms control inspection, Eastern European states have declared their willingness to accept IAEA safeguards while West European states have been reluctant. At the Tenth General Conference of the IAEA (Sept. 21-28, 1966) East Germany, not an IAEA member, declared its willingness to "accede" to IAEA safeguards on condition that West Germany, an IAEA member, would do likewise. I.A.E.A. Doc. GC(x)/INF/91, Sept. 27, 1966; DOCUMENTS ON DISARMAMENT, 1967, at 640. Poland and Czechoslovakia made similar offers to place their nuclear facilities under IAEA safeguards if West Germany would reciprocate. *Id.* 642-43. West Germany responded that it had expressly renounced production of nuclear weapons in 1954, had already accepted Euratom safeguards on all its nuclear facilities, and would be willing to require IAEA safeguards on all its nuclear exports outside the Euratom area, "provided other supplying countries are willing to impose the same condition." I.A.E.A. Doc. GC(x)/OR.104, at 14; DOCUMENTS ON DISARMAMENT, 1967, at 644.

Participation of East Germany in the Non-Proliferation Treaty will raise some interesting problems. If East Germany joins the Treaty and accepts IAEA safeguards, its claim for membership in the IAEA would be strengthened. If East Germany is admitted to the IAEA it will be the first time that both halves of Germany have been members of the same international organization and the first time East Germany will be a member of a U.N.-related agency.

86. *See* pp. 1489-90 *infra.*

The Yale Law Journal Vol. 77: 1447, 1968

from a civil power reactor to a military propulsion reactor program, for example.[87]

These are intricate but limited problems concerning the purpose of the safeguards. Under the word "verification" is buried the major part of a much larger and more politically charged problem. How should the global IAEA system of safeguards be related to the regional Euratom system within the framework of the Non-Proliferation Treaty?[88] Should "verification" require basically the same arrangements between

---

87. In connection with this problem, the United States has stated: "The present IAEA Statute and safeguards system do not provide for safeguards on military facilities . . . ." Statement by State Department Spokesman Robert McCloskey, Mar. 14, 1968 (unpublished). This statement can support a conclusion that safeguards under Article III do not apply to military non-weapon nuclear programs. However, the statement does not resolve the problem of whether a non-nuclear-weapon state would be free to transfer nuclear materials subject to safeguards into a military nuclear program. The IAEA is authorized to establish and administer safeguards designed to ensure that safeguarded nuclear materials and equipment "are not used in such a way as to further any military purpose." I.A.E.A. STAT. art. III, A, 5. If non-nuclear-weapon states were free at will to terminate a safeguards agreement as to particular nuclear material or a piece of equipment it wished to use for a military purpose, the purpose of IAEA safeguards would seem to be distorted. This potential conflict between the IAEA Statute and Article III of the Non-Proliferation Treaty may be eased somewhat by the limitation in I.A.E.A. STAT. art. II, that the IAEA shall ensure only "so far as it is able" against diversion to "any military purpose." Nevertheless, having accepted safeguards on their peaceful nuclear activities, the non-nuclear-weapon states might find that safeguards obstruct, to some extent, their ability to engage in military non-weapon nuclear programs or nuclear-weapon research programs which are not deemed to be manufacture. Of course, from the standpoint of non-proliferation policy, this seems a desirable effect.

88. Any relationship between Euratom and IAEA will raise a number of legal and political issues. From the Euratom perspective, do the Community and its member states have power under the Euratom Treaty to consent to the application of IAEA safeguards on peaceful nuclear activities with the Community, or would amendment to the Treaty be required? Assuming amendment would not be required, who would have to consent or be a party to an arrangement between Euratom and IAEA or the application of IAEA safeguards within a particular Euratom member state—the state concerned, other member states, the Commission, the Council? In general, there are a variety of legal roadblocks which could be thrown in the way of any arrangement which accorded IAEA a right for its inspectors to enter Euratom territory, even though the particular Euratom member state concerned agreed. Not the least of these is the fact that under Article 86 of the Treaty all fissionable material subject to Euratom safeguards is ipso facto owned by the Community. On the other hand, there appears to be enough flexibility in the constitutional arrangements to permit a variety of relationships such as according IAEA a right to enter Euratom territory as long as no single member state voices strong objection. Whether one Euratom member state could veto arrangements proposed to be concluded with the IAEA which would be applicable only to other consenting member states is problematic.

From the perspective of IAEA, the kind of arrangement with Euratom and/or some of its member states that the Agency could become a party to is limited by its statute. Unlike Euratom, however, the basis for IAEA safeguards jurisdiction is primarily consensual and ad hoc. The Board of Governors of the IAEA will have considerable flexibility in the kind of arrangements which it can properly approve under Article III. The present safeguards system provides that the IAEA will not assume safeguards responsibility for nuclear materials "unless the principles of the safeguards and the procedures to be used are essentially consistent with those set forth in this document." I.A.E.A. INFCIRC/66, at para. 5 (1965). However, the present system also includes provision for transfer of safeguarded nuclear material into a state if it will be subject in the recipient state "to safeguards other than those of the Agency but generally consistent with such safeguards and accepted by the Agency." Id. para 28(d). See also p. 1485-86 & note 90 infra.

Nuclear Weapons

the IAEA and all non-nuclear-weapon parties to the Treaty?[89] If so, the result could be the application of IAEA safeguards in parallel with, if not in lieu of, Euratom safeguards in the territory of non-nuclear-weapon Euratom members which adhered to the Non-Proliferation Treaty. Or, in the case of the five non-nuclear-weapon states whose peaceful nuclear activities are already subject to Euratom's system of safeguards, should "verification" be accomplished by an IAEA decision to accept Euratom safeguards in lieu of those of the Agency?[90] Between these extremes of parallel application of IAEA safeguards in Euratom territory on the one hand, and complete delegation of IAEA responsibilities to Euratom on the other, a range of intermediate possibilities exists.

89. Sweden has called for "the application of *one* system of safeguards to the activities of *all* countries." Statement by Representative of Sweden to ENDC, ENDC/PV.300, at 6-7. The United Arab Republic has similarly stated that a non-proliferation treaty should require "compulsory and uniform application" of IAEA safeguards to all non-nuclear-weapon states. Statement by Representative of United Arab Republic to ENDC, ENDC/ PV.294, at 7. Section 11(E) of the United States Euratom Agreement for Cooperation provides: "In recognition of the importance of the International Atomic Energy Agency, the United States of America and the European Atomic Energy Community will consult with each other from time to time to determine whether there are any areas of responsibility with regards to safeguards and controls and matters relating to health and safety in which the Agency [IAEA] might be asked to assist." In an exchange of correspondence with reference to Section 11(E), the understanding was reached that "in the event of the establishment of an international safeguards and control system by the International Atomic Energy Agency, the United States and Euratom will consult regarding assumption by that agency of the safeguard and control over the fissionable material utilized or produced in implementation of the program contemplated by the Memorandum of Understanding." European Atomic Energy Community, Agreement for Cooperation between the European Atomic Energy Community and the Government of the United States of America and Related Documents, Nov. 8, 1958, at 45-48. The United States has been able to make no tangible progress in implementation of Section 11(E) and the understanding.

Until recently, in addition to the United States-Euratom Agreement for Cooperation, bilateral agreements for cooperation were in effect between the United States and the Euratom member states individually. Although various Euratom members would have preferred that these bilateral agreements continue, the United States adopted a "fold-in" policy of non-renewal upon expiration of their fixed terms, continuing the same nuclear cooperation, however, under the aegis of the overall United States-Euratom agreement. This move was designed to strengthen Euratom at a time when nuclear industries within the member states were tending to become increasingly nationalistic. The trend toward nuclear nationalism has not been substantially affected by the fold-in policy, but by adopting it the United States has given up a series of bilateral agreements. The responsibility for safeguards under these agreements might have been transferred from the AEC to the IAEA in accord with general United States safeguards policy, and by this time the problem of relating IAEA safeguards to peaceful nuclear activities in non-nuclear-weapon Euratom member states might have been largely resolved, at least in principle. The United States, however, did not get its priorities as between promoting European nuclear integration and global non-proliferation readjusted in time.

90. The present IAEA safeguards system would allow for this, upon a decision of the Board of Governors, as to transfers into the Community. The principle might be extended to safeguarding peaceful nuclear activities in a state. *See* Willrich, *Safeguarding Atoms for Peace*, 60 Am. J. Int'l. L. 34, 49-50. Nevertheless, it seems unlikely the Board would ever make such a decision generally to abdicate its responsibilities in relation to Article III of the Non-Proliferation Treaty.

These possibilities will be analyzed in terms of the two basic requirements which both IAEA and Euratom safeguards systems include:
first, that reports which reflect the running inventory of nuclear materials in various declared locations be submitted to an external authority; second, that the external authority have physical access to the
declared locations to check by independent means the accuracy of the
reports. There are many intermediate positions around which a
Euratom-IAEA relationship could be built. With respect to reporting,
declared locations could submit reports directly to the IAEA; they
could submit reports to Euratom for forwarding to the IAEA; or they
could submit reports only to Euratom, and Euratom could compile its
own set of reports for submission to IAEA. All reporting requirements
could be more or less based on the Euratom or on the IAEA system.
With respect to physical access, declared locations could be open to
IAEA inspection as prescribed under the IAEA safeguards system;
they could be open to IAEA inspection on a less frequent basis than
generally prescribed under the IAEA system; they could be open to
IAEA inspection only if reports to the IAEA revealed a discrepancy;
they could be closed to IAEA inspection as such, but IAEA inspectors
could accompany Euratom inspectors on a limited basis; they could be
closed to IAEA inspection, with IAEA inspectors being limited to consultation with Euratom inspectors and review of Euratom inspection
procedures used. With respect to all IAEA access to declared locations,
Euratom might or might not be given advance notice and a right to
accompany IAEA inspectors.[91]

The governments concerned have disclosed little beyond general

---

91. In general, the IAEA system provides for the right of access at all times without
advance notice to reactors capable of producing more than 60 kilograms of plutonium
per year (which includes virtually all power reactors). Chemical processing plants with
an annual throughput exceeding 5 kilograms of plutonium are subject to be "inspected
at all times," and in such plants with a throughput exceeding 60 kilograms "the right
of access at all times would normally be implemented by means of continuous inspection."
See I.A.E.A. INFCIRC/66, at para. 57 (1965); I.A.E.A. Doc. GC(x)/INF/86, Annex, para. 3
& n.2 (1966). Thus, large nuclear facilities under IAEA safeguards are open to inspection
at any time, and resident inspection is a distinct possibility.

IAEA inspectors for a particular state are designated by the Director General from
a panel previously nominated by him and approved by the Board of Governors. In each
case the state concerned must approve the identity of the inspectors designated. I.A.E.A.
Doc. GC(v)/INF/39, Annex, paras. 1-3 (1961); *see* Szasz, *The Law of International Atomic
Energy Agency Safeguards*, 3 REV. BELGE DE DROIT INT'L 196, 224-25 (1967). *See also*
Statement by Department of State, DOCUMENTS ON DISARMAMENT, 1967, at 96, 97. In practice, therefore, a Western state could refuse to admit an IAEA inspector from a Communist state and vice versa. A Western state may also be reluctant to admit an inspector
from another Western state with which it is in commercial competition. If these attitudes
persist under the Non-Proliferation Treaty it would place a very large burden of inspection on neutral and developing states, some of which do not have available personnel
or can ill afford to supply people well qualified to be inspectors.

Nuclear Weapons

positions as to the nature of the IAEA-Euratom arrangement that might emerge under Article III, leaving plenty of room for future conflict. On the one hand, the Soviet Union has characterized Euratom as a "closed organization of West Germany's allies in the military NATO bloc," and Euratom's safeguards as nothing more than self-inspection.[92] Acceptable safeguards, in their view, are those of the IAEA, an organization in which all social and political systems are represented and in which all states can have confidence. On the other hand, Euratom member states have agreed among themselves that any arrangement between the IAEA and Euratom resulting from the Non-Proliferation Treaty "should concern the verification of Euratom control methods and not direct IAEA control."[93] Caught in the middle, the United States has stated that:

> In order to avoid unnecessary duplication, the IAEA should make *appropriate* use of existing records and safeguards, provided that under such mutually-agreed arrangements IAEA can satisfy *itself* that nuclear material is not diverted to nuclear weapons or other nuclear explosive devices.[94] (Emphasis added.)

92. Statement by Representative of Soviet Union to First Committee of the U.N. General Assembly, Oct. 20, 1966, U.N. Doc. A/C.1/PV.1431, at 6-21 (1966); DOCUMENTS ON DISARMAMENT, 1966, at 657, 661. The element of self-inspection, while not a major concern in the present political context in Western Europe, would become increasingly important if progress toward the political integration of Western Europe were achieved. Secretary of State Rusk has also recognized the precedent the relationship of IAEA to Euratom would set for "other parts of the world who might wish to put together a little family group which would inspect itself and deny outside inspection on the grounds that it is up to each regional group to provide its own inspection." Television Interview with Secretary of State Rusk, Feb. 10, 1967, 56 DEP'T STATE BULL. 360 (1967). It is noteworthy in this regard that although the Treaty of Tlatelolco would establish an "Agency for the Prohibition of Nuclear Weapons in Latin America" with certain inspection functions, Article 13 of the Treaty also provides: "Each Contracting Party shall negotiate multilateral or bilateral agreements with the International Atomic Energy Agency for the application of its safeguards to its nuclear activities." Thus, the element of self-inspection will be avoided as to declared facilities in the Latin American nuclear free zone. For the treatment accorded inspection for possible clandestine facilities, see note 78 *supra*.

93. EUROPEAN COMMUNITY, Apr. 1968, at 17. West German Foreign Minister Brandt has stated that the IAEA could be related to Euratom by means of a "verification treaty." He has also said that under a non-proliferation treaty, "[t]he IAEA should be able to convince itself of the effectiveness of the other control systems." Statement by Foreign Minister Brandt to the Bundestag, Apr. 27, 1967, at 1-8; DOCUMENTS ON DISARMAMENT, 1967, at 206, 213. France has remained aloof during the course of discussions in Euratom and will probably not become a party to the Treaty. Even if it did, as a nuclear-weapon state, France would not be required to accept safeguards under Article III. While the objective of Euratom is intended to create one integrated legal and economic community as regards the peaceful uses of nuclear energy among its member states, the results of the Non-Proliferation Treaty will be to apply to peaceful nuclear activities in the five non-nuclear-weapon Euratom members certain measures not applied to similar activities in France.

94. Statement by the United States Representative to ENDC, Jan. 18, 1968, ENDC/PV.357, at 14, 17. Statement of this principal was the *quid* by which the United States was able to obtain the *quo* of Soviet agreement to a text for Article III which had been previously approved by the NATO Council. For a fascinating account of the history by

The Yale Law Journal   Vol. 77: 1447, 1968

With these diverse viewpoints and interests involved, putting together
a combination of reporting and access provisions from the possibilities
outlined, and elaborating these into an overall relationship among
IAEA, Euratom and the non-nuclear-weapon Euratom members will
be a complicated process. However, it will revolve around one central
question. Should the IAEA have access to declared locations within
Euratom territory as a matter of right? Diplomats and their lawyers
will perhaps invent solutions to obscure or gloss over this issue. But it
can be avoided only if the participants in future negotiations agree to
do so.

While paragraph 1 of Article III deals with acceptance of safeguards
on peaceful nuclear activities within non-nuclear-weapon parties, paragraph 2 pertains to international transactions in nuclear materials and

a participant, see Testimony of Adrian S. Fisher, Deputy Director, United States Arms
Control and Disarmament Agency, *Hearings on Arms Control and Disarmament Act
Amendments, 1968, Before the House Comm. on Foreign Affairs*, 90th Cong., 2d Sess.
61-62 (1968). In addition to the principle quoted above, the United States set forth two
other principles as follows:
"There should be safeguards for all non-nuclear-weapon parties of such a nature that
all parties can have confidence in their effectiveness. Therefore safeguards established
by an agreement negotiated and concluded with the IAEA in accordance with the Statute
of the IAEA and the Agency's safeguards system must enable the IAEA to carry out its
responsibility of providing assurance that no diversion is taking place.
"In discharging their obligations under article III, non-nuclear-weapon parties may
negotiate safeguards agreements with the IAEA individually or together with other
parties; and, specifically, an agreement covering such obligations may be entered into
between the IAEA and another international organization the work of which is related
to the IAEA and the membership of which includes the parties concerned."
The United States is well aware of the difference between being convinced of the
effectiveness of another safeguards system, as advocated by Euratom and West Germany
in particular, and being satisfied that nuclear materials subject to another safeguards
system are not being diverted to nuclear weapons, as advocated by the United States,
from its own experience under the United States-Euratom Agreement for Cooperation.
[1958] U.S.T. 1116, T.I.A.S. No. 4091, 335 U.N.T.S. 161 (1958); *as amended*, [1962] 2
U.S.T. 1403, T.I.A.S. No. 5103, 453 U.N.T.S. 390 (1962). Under Section 11(B) Euratom
is given "the responsibility for establishing and implementing a safeguards and control
system" which is "reasonably compatible" with the IAEA system. Section 11(D) provides:
"There will be frequent consultations and exchanges of visits between the parties to
give assurance to both parties that the Euratom safeguards and control system effectively
meets the responsibility and principles stated in B above and that the standards of the
materials accountability systems of the United States and Euratom are kept reasonably
comparable." In an exchange of correspondence on June 18, 1958, the following understanding was reached with reference to Section 11(D): "[T]he consultations and exchanges
of visits agreed upon in the referenced section and the assurance provided for therein
include within those terms permission by each party for the other party to verify, by
mutually approved scientific methods, the effectiveness of the safeguards and control
systems applied to nuclear materials received from the other party or to fissionable
materials derived from these nuclear materials." European Atomic Energy Community,
Agreement for Cooperation between the European Atomic Energy Community and the
Government of the United States of America and Related Documents, Nov. 8, 1958, at
45, 47. In implementing the understanding, the United States AEC has not been accorded
a right of physical access to Euratom facilities, although it has been asserted that such
access is a necessary part of verifying the effectiveness of Euratom safeguards by scientific
methods.

Nuclear Weapons

equipment. Under paragraph 2 of Article III[95] each party to the Treaty, including a nuclear-weapon state, undertakes not to export or provide nuclear material or equipment for peaceful purposes to any non-nuclear-weapon state, whether or not a party, unless the materials or equipment are subject to safeguards. If the importing state is a nuclear-weapon state, however, safeguards are not required.[96]

Safeguards apply only to a transaction "for peaceful purposes." International nuclear transactions entered into expressly for non-weapons military purposes are neither reached by any safeguards requirement under paragraph 2 of Article III, nor prohibited by any other provision of the Treaty. Thus, nuclear materials and equipment could be furnished free and clear of safeguards to a non-nuclear-weapon state

95. "Each State Party to the Treaty undertakes not to provide: (a) source or special fissionable material, or (b) equipment or material especially designed or prepared for the processing, use or production of special fissionable material, to any non-nuclear-weapon State for peaceful purposes, unless the source or special fissionable material shall be subject to the safeguards required by this article." Art. III, para. 2.

96. This exclusion is similar to the exclusion of nuclear-weapon states from the prohibition on receiving and giving assistance in the manufacture of nuclear weapons under Articles I and II. The United States position has not always been that which is embodied in paragraph 2 of Article III. Rather, the United States position on July 28, 1966, was that "in the transfer of such materials and equipment between States for peaceful purposes, all States would be treated alike" as regards safeguards. Statement by United States Representative to ENDC, July 28, 1966, ENDC/PV.277, at 4-7; DOCUMENTS ON DISARMAMENT, 1966, at 482, 485.

On June 3, 1965, the Government of Canada announced that, in the future, export permits covering sales of uranium will be issued only if the unranium is to be used for peaceful purposes, and that an agreement with the government of the importing state to this effect will be required together with "appropriate verification and control." Statement by Foreign Minister Martin in the Parliament of Canada, June 3, 1965. This policy was resisted by some firms within Canada which were seeking to negotiate long-term supply arrangements with France, which refused to accept any safeguards requirement. Under paragraph 2 of Article III, the Canadian Government may in the future be somewhat more hard pressed to refuse to approve a substantial uranium export contract to a nuclear-weapon state for lack of safeguards, especially if another seller such as South Africa is in competition for the business.

Although Article III, paragraph 2, itself permits unsafeguarded exports to nuclear-weapon states, the present IAEA system, in conjunction with Article III, may not permit such unsafeguarded exports to occur. Article III, paragraph 1, of the Non-Proliferation Treaty requires safeguards on "all source or special fissionable material in all peaceful nuclear activities" of a non-nuclear-weapon state. Once IAEA safeguards are applied to particular nuclear material it cannot, in general, be transferred to another state unless safeguards follow the material or an equivalent amount of material has been substituted for that upon which safeguards are to terminate. The IAEA system does not differentiate between nuclear-weapon and non-nuclear-weapon states in this regard as does the Non-Proliferation Treaty.

The possibility of terminating safeguards on material to be transferred to a nuclear-weapon state by substitution by the non-nuclear-weapon state of an equivalent amount of unsafeguarded material would not exist because safeguards would apply to all material in its jurisdiction under paragraph 1 of Article III. The possibility of the nuclear-weapon state providing material to the non-nuclear-weapon state desiring to export to it for purposes of substitution by the non-nuclear-weapon state does not exist because paragraph 2 of Article III requires safeguards on exports to non-nuclear-weapon states. *See* Szasz, *The Law of International Atomic Energy Agency Safeguards*, 3 REV. BELGE DE DROIT INT'L 196, 218 (1967); Willrich, *Safeguarding Atoms for Peace*, 60 AM. J. INT'L L. 34, 48 (1966).

1489

The Yale Law Journal   Vol. 77: 1447, 1968

for use by that state in a naval propulsion reactor program or a reactor for irradiating military equipment.[97]

Excluding exports for military purposes from the safeguards requirements may appear to be a large loophole in Article III. The size of this loophole, however, is reduced by Articles I and II. The exporters, and the importers if parties to the Treaty, would violate their undertakings under Articles I and II if the materials and equipment provided pursuant to a military nuclear agreement were used for nuclear weapons. Moreover, the amounts of nuclear materials used in military programs in non-nuclear-weapon states will probably be very small compared with the amounts involved in their civil power programs. In any case, it would be extremely difficult, if not impossible, to develop and administer a system of international safeguards to verify that nuclear materials used in a classified military program in a non-nuclear-weapon state were not being diverted to a nuclear weapons program. It is doubtful whether the IAEA has the authority under its present statute to involve itself in such an activity. Therefore, it seems reasonable to leave it to the exporter to police transactions of this kind, at least until some experience has been gained with the Treaty in operation.

Finally, Article III applies to transactions in three kinds of subject matter: "source material," "special fissionable material," and "equipment or material especially designed or prepared for the processing, use or production of special fissionable material." It is the "source of special fissionable material" which is actually subject to safeguards. Consistent with the present IAEA and Euratom systems, the Non-Proliferation Treaty safeguards are based on accounting for the nuclear materials as they are used, produced or processed in principal nuclear facilities, and while they may be stored outside such facilities.[98]

The operation of paragraph 2 of Article III can be illustrated by two examples. First, if either natural uranium ("source material") or enriched uranium ("special fissionable material") is provided by a party

97. Statement by State Department Spokesman, Mar. 14, 1968 (unpublished); *see* note 46 *supra*.
98. There are certain exemptions provided in the IAEA safeguards system for militarily insignificant quantities of nuclear materials. Above the exemption limit is a sliding scale of frequency of required reports and inspection up to a certain amount where access at all times must be permitted. There are no such exemptions in the Euratom system. *See* Willrich, *Safeguarding Atoms for Peace*, 60 AM. J. INT'L L. 34, 42 n.28 (1966). Rumania proposed that Article III be amended to provide that safeguards would apply only "to such peaceful nuclear activities of non-nuclear-weapon states as, by their nature and the quantities of source and special fissionable materials which they produce, process or use, may lead to the proliferation of nuclear weapons." ENDC/223/Rev.1, Mar. 8, 1968. The amendment was not accepted.

Nuclear Weapons

to the Treaty to any non-nuclear-weapon state, safeguards would be applied to the material. Safeguards, and associated reporting requirements and inspection rights, would be applied while the material was stockpiled after its arrival in the importing non-nuclear-weapon state, and would follow the material as it progressed through the nuclear fuel cycle in that state. While safeguarded nuclear material was being fabricated into reactor fuel elements, the fabrication plant would be open to inspection. Thereafter, while the fuel elements containing safeguarded nuclear material were being irradiated in a nuclear reactor, international inspectors would have access to that reactor. Moreover, safeguards would automatically attach to every gram of plutonium produced in safeguarded nuclear fuel irradiated in a reactor. When the irradiated fuel elements were removed from the reactor and sent to a processing plant to be chemically dissolved and separated into constituent elements, the plant would be open to inspection. After the depleted nuclear material and produced plutonium emerged from the chemical processing plant, safeguards would continue to apply to all that material wherever it went, at least until it was transferred to a nuclear-weapon state.[99]

Second, suppose that a party to the Treaty provides a civil nuclear power reactor ("equipment . . . especially designed . . . for the . . . use or production of special fissionable material") to a non-nuclear-weapon state.[100] The importing state intends to supply its own nuclear fuel and process the fuel in its own fuel fabrication and chemical separation plants. Safeguards would be applied to fissionable material as it was

---

99. The difficulties which may be encountered if such a transfer is attempted under the existing IAEA system are outlined in note 96 *supra*.

100. Determination of what items of equipment and material are "especially designed or prepared for the processing, use or production of special fissionable material" will be a difficult task. Obviously, the drafters did not intend to require safeguards on all equipment and material flowing into a non-nuclear-weapon state. They clearly intended, however, to require safeguards on something less than an entire reactor or other principal nuclear facility. In many cases, a nuclear project in a particular state will utilize a variety of domestic and foreign manufacturers and suppliers in putting together a nuclear project. A detailed list of equipment and non-nuclear materials which will trigger safeguards has not been incorporated into the IAEA system because the Board of Governors has been unable to agree on the items which should be included. The present test under the IAEA system is whether the nuclear facility involved would be "substantially assisted." This imprecise criterion is applied by the IAEA Board of Governors on a case-by-case basis. *See* Willrich, *Safeguarding Atoms for Peace*, 60 AM. J. INT'L L. 34, 42-43 (1966). The Non-Proliferation Treaty represents an attempt to be somewhat more specific. However, the criteria there established—"especially designed or prepared for"—are perhaps unfortunate in that they seem to depend to some extent on the intent of the exporting or perhaps the importing state. Hopefully, in practice this provision will not cause difficulty, because nuclear projects are generally relatively large scale and each has some rather unique features. Therefore, it would seem that most international nuclear transactions will take place with specific nuclear projects in mind.

1491

The Yale Law Journal   Vol. 77: 1447, 1968

produced in all fuel loadings over the lifetime of the reactor and would follow that produced material throughout the fuel cycle as it was processed and recycled into other reactors. Furthermore, safeguards would be applied to all subsequent generations of fissionable material produced in fuel elements containing previous generations of fissionable material subject to safeguards.

From these two examples it becomes clear that if a non-nuclear-weapon state, even though not a party to the Treaty, were to import nuclear materials or equipment from any party, the potential reach of international safeguards into its civil nuclear industry could be very broad. Even if the state's nuclear imports were small, safeguards could in time creep throughout its civil nuclear industry. If it wishes to avoid the safeguards required by Article III, the non-party, non-nuclear-weapon state would be limited to importing from other non-parties to the Treaty. On the other hand, if such a non-nuclear weapon state decides to accept safeguards in order to import from a party to the Treaty, the importing state would have gone a long way toward accepting one of the most serious restraints in the Non-Proliferation Treaty.[101]

---

101. This may be a useful argument with India. However, nothing in the Treaty prevents a non-nuclear-weapon state which is not a party from importing nuclear materials subject to safeguards for use in its civil nuclear power program, thereby freeing its limited indigenous resources for concentration in a nuclear weapons program. In fact, if India does not become a party to the Treaty, this may be the strategy it will pursue with respect to utilization of its limited uranium resources.

The Indian view of safeguards has been colorfully put:

"Institution of international controls on peaceful reactors and power stations is like an attempt to maintain law and order in a society by placing all its law-abiding citizens in custody while leaving its law-breaking elements free to roam the streets. . . . Reactors engaged in peaceful pursuit, and atomic power stations of the developing countries, do not in themselves pose any threat to the security of the international society. It is the chemical separation plants and the gaseous diffusion plants which produce the fissile material used in bombs; and it is these facilities which need to be controlled in any system of controlled disarmament.

"Here . . . I am referring to international treaties and conventions as distinct from national decision. We in India, for example have with our friends who have assisted us in the past perfectly satisfactory arrangements for safeguards, and we are determined to observe and implement them. But that is entirely different from entering into an international instrument for International Atomic Energy Agency or other international safeguards over the reactors and power stations of the developing countries."

Statement by Representative of India to ENDC, Aug. 12, 1965, ENDC/PV.223, at 5-21; DOCUMENTS ON DISARMAMENT, 1965, at 326, 339. There is superficial logic in the Indian position since plutonium when it is encased in fuel elements lodged in a reactor cannot be used for nuclear weapons. It must first be separated from the depleted uranium and fission products. It is at the chemical separation and fuel fabrication plants that the major opportunities for diversion exist. However, there are good grounds for having safeguards apply to all facilities in the nuclear fuel cycle since this decreases the overall technical uncertainty in the system and forecloses the opportunity of diverting fuel elements from a reactor to a clandestine chemical separation plant. India has already agreed to accept IAEA safeguards, consistent with other treaty terms, on its major power reactor projects assisted by the United States and Canada. *E.g.*, United States-India Agreement for Cooperation, art. VIII, [1963] 2 U.S.T. 1484, T.I.A.S. No. 5446, 488 U.N.T.S. 21.

Nuclear Weapons

Few, if any, non-nuclear-weapon states will have a completely self-sufficient civil nuclear industry, at least in the near future. The safeguards requirements on all peaceful nuclear exports of parties could, therefore, become a powerful inducement to broad adherence to the Non-Proliferation Treaty once the substantial exporters of nuclear materials and equipment become parties. On the other hand, one or a few nuclear exporters which remained outside the Treaty and avoided the requirement of safeguards on their exports would be in a powerful position to spoil the operation of the Treaty in this respect.[102]

2. *Sharing Peaceful Uses*

Paragraph 1 of Article IV[103] sets forth the "inalienable right" of all parties to continue to engage in peaceful nuclear activities under the Treaty, qualified only by the requirement that such activities be conducted in a manner "in conformity with" Articles I and II (pertaining to non-transfer and non-acquisition of nuclear explosives). While preservation of such a right is of cardinal importance to industrially advanced states, the undertakings in the Treaty to share the benefits of peaceful nuclear energy are of particular interest to the developing states.[104]

(a) *Nuclear materials, equipment and information.* Under para-

---

102. It would seem difficult to maintain the Non-Proliferation Treaty in effect for very long if a comparatively few large exporters and some important importers remained outside. If all major exporters joined the Treaty, then all non-nuclear-weapon importers would have to accept safeguards on their imports whether or not they were parties. If some exporters, *e.g.*, France or South Africa, stayed outside the Treaty and exported reactors or uranium to non-nuclear-weapon importers which were not parties to the Treaty, the unsafeguarded nuclear industries in these importing states could in time be perceived as a threat by neighboring non-nuclear-weapon states which had joined the Treaty and accepted safeguards.

In this connection, France's statement that, although it will not sign the Treaty, it "will behave in the future in this field exactly as the States adhering to the treaty" takes on both importance and ambiguity. Statement by Representative of France to U.N. General Assembly, June 12, 1968, U.N. Doc. A/PV.1672 (prov.), at 3, 6. Does this mean France will behave in accordance with Article III, as well as Articles I and II?

103. "Nothing in this Treaty shall be interpreted as affecting the inalienable right of all the Parties to the Treaty to develop research, production and use of nuclear energy for peaceful purposes without discrimination and in conformity with articles I and II of this Treaty." Art. IV, para. 1.

104. West Germany has gone so far as to state that "the future of the Federal Republic of Germany as a modern industrial state depends on this principle." Statement by Foreign Minister Brandt to the Bundestag, Apr. 27, 1967, DOCUMENTS ON DISARMAMENT, 1967, at 211. India has made the same point more colorfully: "[T]he civil nuclear powers can tolerate a nuclear weapons apartheid, but not an atomic apartheid in their economic and peaceful development." Statement by Representative of India to ENDC, May 23, 1967, ENDC/PV.298, at 4-17; DOCUMENTS ON DISARMAMENT, 1967, at 229, 234. At the beginning of the nuclear era, when there was but one nuclear-weapon state, President Truman stated: "No nation could long maintain or morally defend a monopoly of the peaceful benefits of atomic energy." 13 DEP'T STATE BULL. 514 (1945).

The Yale Law Journal   Vol. 77: 1447, 1968

graph 2 of Article IV[105] all parties have the right and undertake "to participate in the fullest possible exchange of equipment, materials and scientific and technological information." An important limitation on the undertaking and the right is that the subject matter of the exchange be "for the peaceful uses of nuclear energy."[106] Moreover, use of the word "exchange" means that the nuclear haves are not obligated to make a gift to the have-nots.

In addition to providing for exchange of peaceful nuclear materials, equipment and information, paragraph 2 of Article IV contains an important general undertaking to "cooperate in contributing" to peaceful nuclear development, "especially in the territories of non-nuclear-weapon States Party to the Treaty, with due consideration for

---

105. "All the Parties to the Treaty undertake to facilitate, and have the right to participate in, the fullest possible exchange of equipment, materials and scientific and technological information for the peaceful uses of nuclear energy. Parties to the Treaty in a position to do so shall also co-operate in contributing alone or together with other States or international organizations to the further development of the applications of nuclear energy for peaceful purposes, especially in the territories of non-nuclear-weapon States Party to the Treaty, with due consideration for the needs of the developing areas of the world." Art. IV, para. 2.
The draft Treaty of March 11, 1968, provided only that all parties "have the right to participate in the fullest possible exchange." ENDC/225, Annex A, Mar. 14, 1968. The undertaking "to facilitate" such exchanges was originally proposed by Nigeria in the First Committee debate and finally incorporated by the United States and the Soviet Union as an amendment on May 31, 1968. "Thus, the right to such sharing is recognized explicitly not only as a right of non-nuclear Powers but also as a commitment to action by nuclear Powers and all others in a position to contribute thereto." Statement by United States Representative to First Committee of U.N. General Assembly, May 31, 1968, U.N. Doc. A/C.1/PV.1577 (prov.), at 77. Furthermore, in the draft Treaty of March 11, 1968, the exchange was limited to "scientific and technological information." In line with its long standing position, *see* note 110 *infra*, Italy took the lead in the First Committee debate in urging that the exchange provision be broadened by specifically including "equipment" and "materials" in addition to information. "This important clarification of article IV of the treaty considerably expands the scope of co-operation in the peaceful uses of nuclear energy which, without any doubt, would correspond to the interests of non-nuclear States." Statement by Soviet Union Representative to First Committee of U.N. General Assembly, May 31, 1968, U.N. Doc. A/C.1/PV.1577 (prov.), at 67.
106. In connection with assurances of their right to participate in the peaceful uses of nuclear energy, various non-nuclear-weapon states raised the question of "spin-off"—benefits that civil nuclear activities in nuclear-weapon states could derive from nuclear weapons programs. West Germany initially expressed particular concern in this regard. Statement by Foreign Minister Brandt to the Bundestag, Feb. 1, 1967, DOCUMENTS ON DISARMAMENT, 1967, at 48, 49. In reply Secretary of State Rusk stated: ". . . [T]he fact is that the non-proliferation treaty has nothing to do whatever with the use of nuclear materials for peaceful purposes, and that includes a wide range of industrial application. The actual industrial spin-off from so-called weaponry, that is, those items which are limited to the gadgetry of weapons, is very small, indeed, infinitesimal. And I think exchanges on the technical level will clarify that point." 58 DEP'T STATE BULL. 320-21 (1968). Nevertheless, to allay concern in this regard, the Preamble of the Non-Proliferation Treaty affirms the principle "that the benefits of peaceful applications of nuclear technology, including any technological by-products which may be derived by nuclear-weapon States from the development of nuclear explosive devices, should be available for peaceful purposes to all Parties to the Treaty, whether nuclear-weapon or non-nuclear-weapon States." The United States has also interpreted the exchange of information provisions in paragraph 2 of Article IV as covering information concerning peaceful applications of nuclear explosions. Statement by United States Representative to ENDC, ENDC/PV.378 (prov.), at 5-11.

Nuclear Weapons

the needs of the developing areas of the world."[107] This particular undertaking exists for "Parties . . . in a position to do so . . . ." Thus paragraph 2 introduces a new category of states, broader than nuclear-weapon states and narrower than non-nuclear-weapon states, which we will call "contributing states."

The contributing states are not specified, nor is any criterion established in the Treaty for identifying them.[108] Will each state make a unilateral determination whether and to what extent it is itself in a position to contribute to development of peaceful nuclear activities in non-nuclear-weapon states? An affirmative answer would seem to pull the teeth from the obligation to cooperate and would also run counter to the express undertaking "to facilitate . . . the fullest possible exchange." On the other hand, should a non-nuclear-weapon state be able to direct a claim for cooperation at a contributing state of its own choice, a claim which the contributing state would have to honor? Would this mean, for example, that the United States or West Germany, in adhering to the Treaty, would become obligated to subsidize the export of its nuclear power reactor technology to any non-nuclear-weapon states which request it? An obligation of such breadth would not seem to be intended. The undertaking under the Treaty is "to *cooperate* in contributing." Such an undertaking is less firm than one simply "to contribute," or "to make available."[109]

---

107. The phrase "with due consideration for the needs of the developing areas of the world" was added to paragraph 2 of Article IV on May 31, 1968, based on a suggestion by Chile. Statement by United States Representative to First Committee of U.N. General Assembly, May 31, 1968, U.N. Doc. A/C.1/PV.1577 (prov.), at 77. Any general assumption that nuclear power will be a boon for the developing countries is, of course, erroneous, especially in view of the large plant size required to achieve the economies of scale.

108. Some guidance might be found in the composition of the IAEA Board of Governors. Under Article VI of the IAEA statute, the outgoing Board of Governors, by majority vote, makes the following designations of membership for the succeeding Board: "The five members most advanced in the technology of atomic energy"; the member most advanced in the technology of atomic energy, including the production of source materials, not represented by the original five in each of the following eight geographic regions: (1) North America, (2) Latin America, (3) Western Europe, (4) Eastern Europe, (5) Africa and the Middle East, (6) South Asia, (7) Southeast Asia and the Pacific, (8) Far East; two members from among Belgium, Czechoslovakia, Poland, and Portugal as producers of source material; and one additional member as a supplier of technical assistance. The General Conference elects the remaining 12 out of a total of 25 members on the basis of "equitable representation." *See also* Willrich, *Safeguarding Atoms for Peace*, 60 AM. J. INT'L L. 34, 39 n.18 (1966).

109. Mexico proposed that the second sentence of Article IV, paragraph 2, be amended to read: "Those parties that are in a position to do so, *have the duty* to contribute, according to their ability, alone or in cooperation with other states or international organizations, to the further development of the production, industries, and other applications of nuclear energy for peaceful purposes specially in the territories of non-nuclear-weapon states." (Emphasis added.) Mexico justified and interpreted its proposal as follows: "We believe that this duty can and should be enunciated as a true legal obligation, although the obligation is imperfect and general and its practical significance will continue to depend ultimately on the will of the nuclear powers. . . . The phrase "according to their

The Yale Law Journal   Vol. 77: 1447, 1968

"Contributing" also raises a problem concerning the basis for co-operation. If contributing means "cost-free" to the recipients, expense to the contributing state could constitute a deterrent to cooperation rather than an incentive. On balance, the most that could probably be inferred from the Treaty is some generosity and perhaps a degree of departure from the normal pursuit of commercial profit in world nuclear trade on the part of the contributing states, especially in relation to developing countries.[110]

Although some doubt surrounds the basis of peaceful nuclear co-operation under paragraph 2 of Article IV, the Treaty clearly permits the parties to any cooperative arrangement to determine whether the channel for cooperation should be "alone or together with other States or international organizations." Such flexibility would seem to have advantages for both the supplier and recipient of peaceful nuclear assistance. There is already a trend, reinforced by Article III, toward organizing the administration of safeguards on a worldwide and centralized basis. There is no parallel trend, however, in the organiza-tion of actual international cooperation in peaceful uses of nuclear energy. Certain recipients of nuclear assistance may prefer to deal directly with the supplier, while others might prefer to have the supply channel run through an international organization such as the IAEA. The IAEA's role as a channel for the supply of nuclear materials and equipment, however, has thus far been limited to small research facilities.[111] The larger, more complex and costly transactions involving

---

ability" refers not only to the parties' financial and technical ability but also to their legal ability, since much of this knowledge is covered by patents owned by private persons." Statement by Representative of Mexico to ENDC, Sept. 17, 1967, ENDC/PV. 331, at 4-11; DOCUMENTS ON DISARMAMENT, 1967, at 395, 397-98.

Canada, a non-nuclear-weapon state which clearly falls into the category of contributing states, expressed concern that the Mexican suggestion might be construed as an unre-stricted obligation to comply with all requests from non-nuclear-weapon states. ENDC/ PV.336, at 6. The United States stated that while it "shares the objectives sought" by Mexico, "the precise terms of the Mexican formulation may in some respects create too sweeping and too general an obligation." Statement by United States Representative to ENDC, Oct. 12, 1967, ENDC/PV.338, at 7-10; DOCUMENTS ON DISARMAMENT, 1967, at 513, 514.

110. Italy proposed, as a measure that could be independent of the Non-Proliferation Treaty: "An agreement under which the nuclear powers would transmit periodically to the non-nuclear-states signatory to the treaty an agreed quantity of the fissile materials they produce . . . . [T]he non-nuclear countries . . . should pay a reduced price com-pared to the market value. Whereas part of this price would go to the nuclear producing powers, the other part could be paid into the United Nations funds for the progress of the developing countries." Statement by Italian Foreign Minister Fanfani to the ENDC, Aug. 1, 1967, ENDC/PV.318, at 6-9; DOCUMENTS ON DISARMAMENT, 1967, at 312, 313.

111. As of June 30, 1967, 13 project agreements were in effect between the IAEA and various countries covering primarily the supply of research reactors. Annual Report of the Board of Governors to the General Conference, 1 July 1966—30 June 1967, I.A.E.A. Doc. GC(xi)/355, at 32.

Nuclear Weapons

civil nuclear power reactors will probably occur in the future, as in the past, largely outside the IAEA framework.[112]

It seems, therefore, that paragraph 2 of Article IV is unlikely to have a major effect on either the volume or pattern of world trade related to the growth and spread of civil nuclear power. This conclusion is contrary to the official wisdom which maintains that the Treaty will provide a favorable basis for the spread of peaceful nuclear technology and implies that without the Treaty the spread might not occur. With or without the Treaty, the Soviet Union will, subject to a few exceptions, probably continue not to cooperate in peaceful nuclear power development outside Eastern Europe, and do so only half-heartedly within the Warsaw Treaty area. On the other hand, it seems inconceivable in view of the economic stakes that the United States would refrain from attempting to maintain a leading role in the future world market for peaceful nuclear technology, whether or not the Treaty enters into force.[113] Moreover, the number of suppliers competing in each sector of the nuclear fuel cycle is increasing rapidly and the ability in such circumstances of the United States—or any other nuclear supplier alone—to influence the nature and rate of nuclear technological innovation by a policy of abstention is swiftly diminishing.[114]

Therefore, whether or not the Treaty enters into force, international nuclear commerce will probably increase dramatically in the coming years, and states "in a position to do so" will facilitate and contribute to peaceful nuclear power development throughout the world primarily because it will be in their economic or political interests to do so. Al-

112. For example, the United States has entered into 13 bilateral agreements for cooperation involving power applications (not all of which have involved actual transfer of power reactors as yet). No power reactors have yet been supplied through the IAEA. U.S.A.E.C., Major Activities in the Atomic Energy Programs, January-December 1967, at 345 (1968).

113. At power costs of 4.5 mills per kilowatt hour (a conservative figure) the value worldwide of the annual production of electricity from nuclear power sources in 1970 is estimated to reach about $1 billion, and in 1975 about $5 billion. Capital costs of the nuclear plants to produce this power will be about $3 billion and $5 billion, respectively. The value of the plutonium produced annually in power reactors has been estimated to reach $0.5 billion by 1975. Taylor, *The Rapid Growth of Nuclear Technology—Implications for Nuclear Safeguards.* INT'L RESEARCH & TECHNOLOGY J., Jan. 1, 1968, at 9.

114. While at the outset nuclear power plants and their initial fuel loadings were sold as a unit under "turnkey" contracts, now there is an increasing trend to shop around for "bits and pieces." The implications are that no single nuclear supplier will be able to control the supply policy of other suppliers, and dependence on imports in sectors of the nuclear fuel cycle where multiple sources of supply exist should not be too risky. The limited sources of enrichment services—primarily the United States—may constitute political incentive in favor of natural uranium reactors, especially in developing states where a civil nuclear power program frequently serves political as well as economic objectives. *See also* Willrich, *International Control of Civil Nuclear Power,* BULL. ATOM. SCI., March 1967, at 31, 35.

1497

though the Treaty may not substantially affect the rate of diffusion of peaceful nuclear technology, it will improve the possibilities for keeping the potential security costs within acceptable limits as the economic benefits of nuclear power come to be widely shared.

(b) *Plowshare projects.* Under the Treaty, the right to develop or otherwise acquire Plowshare explosive devices is excluded from the general "inalienable right" of all non-nuclear-weapon states to develop and use nuclear energy for peaceful purposes under Article IV. To this extent the Treaty would again discriminate against non-nuclear-weapon states with respect to peaceful nuclear activities. In return for renunciation of their rights to develop this aspect of nuclear technology for themselves, however, the non-nuclear-weapon states would receive under Article V[115] important undertakings by the nuclear-weapon states concerning access to any potential Plowshare benefits.

Under Article V, "benefits" from "explosions" would be made available to non-nuclear-weapon states, but not nuclear explosive devices themselves. Articles I and II of the Treaty deal with Plowshare explosive devices as with nuclear weapons and require that the supplier of Plowshare devices retain "control" of them throughout any project until detonation.

The United States and the Soviet Union are likely to be the only two states which will develop and be able to supply Plowshare explosives in the near future. The "appropriate measures" which the two super-

115. "Each Party to the Treaty undertakes to take appropriate measures to ensure that, in accordance with this Treaty, under appropriate international observation and through appropriate international procedures, potential benefits from any peaceful applications of nuclear explosions will be made available to non-nuclear-weapon States Party to the Treaty on a non-discriminatory basis and that the charge to such Parties for the explosive devices used will be as low as possible and exclude any charge for research and development. Non-nuclear-weapon States Party to the Treaty shall be able to obtain such benefits, pursuant to a special international agreement or agreements, through an appropriate international body with adequate representation of non-nuclear-weapon States. Negotiations on this subject shall commence as soon as possible after the Treaty enters into force. Non-nuclear-weapon States Party to the Treaty so desiring may also obtain such benefits pursuant to bilateral agreement." Art. V.
In the agreed draft treaty of August 24, 1967, the Plowshare provision appeared in a much less specific form as a declaration of intention in the Preamble. ENDC/192, ENDC/193; DOCUMENTS ON DISARMAMENT, 1967, at 338-39. The agreed draft treaty of January 18, 1968, contained an Article V in which the parties undertook "to cooperate to insure" that potential Plowshare benefits will be made available. ENDC/192/Rev. 1; ENDC/193/Rev.1. Although this version of Article V was attacked repeatedly at the ENDC by the non-nuclear-weapon states—principally Brazil and India—for a variety of reasons, it was retained intact in the draft treaty of March 11, 1968. After further criticism in the First Committee and concrete suggestions from Mexico, however, the United States and the Soviet Union finally rewrote it and in the process substantially strengthened their supply obligations and clarified the channels through which non-nuclear-weapon states could claim Plowshare benefits. Nevertheless, the changes were apparently insufficient to induce either Brazil or India to change their positions on the Treaty.

Nuclear Weapons

powers will be obligated to undertake to make Plowshare benefits available remain to be spelled out in a "special international agreement or agreements." The potential suppliers of Plowshare explosions will have a large influence over the details of any such agreement. But the principle that non-nuclear-weapon parties to the Treaty "shall be able to obtain such benefits . . . on a non-discriminatory basis" is clearly established.[116] Moreover, the cost to non-nuclear-weapon states of nuclear explosive devices is fixed with some certainty. The charge must be "as low as possible" and must exclude "research and development" costs. Inclusion of an allocable share of the acquisition cost of the thermonuclear weapons technology which underlies Plowshare would, of course, render the whole scheme uneconomic. On the other hand, the charges for nuclear explosives, even though based on production costs alone, will in many cases constitute a relatively small fraction of the total costs of a Plowshare project. Production costs of the nuclear explosives used will be far outweighed by the costs of engineering and safety surveys, drilling emplacement holes, possibly moving local inhabitants, and clean-up operations.[117] Nevertheless, the price established for Plowshare explosions under Article V is in fact favorable to the recipient.

Another aspect of Article V concerns the channels through which Plowshare explosions could be made available. The non-nuclear-weapon states have the option to obtain Plowshare benefits either "through an appropriate international body with adequate representation of non-nuclear weapon States," or on a bilateral basis.[118] The Treaty, however,

116. The United States has stated that Article V "binds the parties clearly and emphatically." Statement by United States Representative to First Committee, May 31, 1968, U.N. Doc. A/C.1/PV.1577 (prov.), at 78. Early in the ENDC discussions of this subject Mexico stated: "[A]lthough the details . . . must be regulated in a separate agreement, the actual right to enjoy the benefits of peaceful explosions must be recognized and enunciated in the non-proliferation treaty itself." Statement by Representative of Mexico to ENDC, Sept. 19, 1967, ENDC/PV.331, at 4-11; Documents on Disarmament, 1967, at 395, 398.

117. The United States has stated it will charge the same price for nuclear explosives to foreign and domestic users. Statement by United States Representative to ENDC/PV. 369 (prov.), at 32-35. The AEC currently projects that charges for nuclear explosives will range from $350,000 for a 10-kiloton yield to $600,000 for a two-megaton yield. The larger the yield the cheaper the cost per unit of energy released. Gerber, Hamburger & Hull, Plowshare 50 (U.S.A.E.C. Div. of Technical Information 1966). Cost estimates for nuclear excavation of a sea-level canal across the Isthmus of Panama show that charges for explosive *and* firing services will amount to roughly 15 per cent of the total project costs. See *Hearings on Peaceful Applications of Nuclear Explosives—Plowshare—Before the Joint Comm. on Atomic Energy,* 89th Cong., 1st Sess. 376 (1965).

118. With bilateral channels of supply open as well as a channel through the international body, the issue has arisen whether the same international supervision should apply to both cases. Sweden argued that an international authority should license each Plowshare project; bilateral arrangements should receive the same treatment as arrangements through the international body; and there should be international supervision of

The Yale Law Journal   Vol. 77: 1447, 1968

contains no guidance for determining the composition of the international body and no indication whether "adequate representation" for the non-nuclear-weapon states would amount to control of the decision-making process in such a body. Moreover, it is not clear which of the two potential Plowshare suppliers would be obligated by an affirmative decision of the international body in a particular case.[119]

Finally under Article V, Plowshare benefits must be made available "under appropriate international observation and through appropriate international procedures." The United States has stated that "procedures for international cooperation . . . should be developed in full consultation with the non-nuclear-weapon States."[120]

peaceful nuclear explosions in nuclear-weapon states to prevent suspicion that such explosions were nuclear weapon tests. Statements by Representative of Sweden to ENDC, ENDC/PV.364 (prov.), at 16-20; ENDC/PV.373 (prov.), at 11-20. As a matter of interpreting Article V, it seems clear that the "appropriate international observation" and "appropriate international procedures" mentioned in the first sentence are intended to apply to whatever benefits from peaceful nuclear explosions are made available, regardless of the channel. Use of the word "appropriate," however, may allow in each case some differentiation in the treatment accorded depending on the channel.

119. The United States has assured the non-nuclear-weapon states that there would be no scarcity of devices once peaceful explosions became practical. Statement by United States Representative to ENDC, ENDC/PV.369 (prov.), at 28ff. Both superpowers might be eager to supply explosions for a particular project in which case the "international body" would have to choose between the two. Or, neither superpower might wish to supply the project, in which case the "international body" would have to choose one that was unwilling, and an element of compulsion would enter into performance of the arrangement. These are the kinds of decisions, however, that international organizations are reluctant to make. Sweden has suggested that Plowshare devices "might be committed to a formal pool for allocation, by this body, to interested customers." Statement by Representative of Sweden to ENDC, June 6, 1967, ENDC/PV.302, at 4-8; DOCUMENTS ON DISARMAMENT, 1967, at 248-49. While prior allocation of Plowshare explosives might ease the decision-making problem, it would not dispose of it. Of course, if there were a willing supplier and a willing receiver, a bilateral arrangement might well suffice.

120. Statement by United States Representative to ENDC, June 8, 1967, ENDC/PV.303, at 4-11; DOCUMENTS ON DISARMAMENT, 1967, at 252, 255. The United States has stated: "The international body might consider such matters as the feasibility of requested projects, priority among such requests, and necessary safety precautions." Statement by United States Representative to ENDC, Mar. 21, 1967, ENDC/PV.295, at 23-26; DOCUMENTS ON DISARMAMENT, 1967, at 172-73. In an effort to minimize the fact that the Non-Proliferation Treaty would exclude non-nuclear-weapon states from a proprietary role in relation to peaceful nuclear explosives, the United States has emphasized the relatively large role the recipient of Plowshare explosions would have with respect to all phases of particular projects other than control over the device, its emplacement and detonation. For example: "The type of international procedures we have in mind would permit countries to perform their own engineering work, utilizing nuclear explosives detonated under the control of a nuclear-weapon state . . . . [N]uclear-weapon states would merely provide nuclear explosive services, and the country in which the project was conducted would be responsible for the remainder of the project, if that was its choice. In essence, this would not be different from a situation in which conventional explosives or other equipment are purchased abroad." Statement by United States Representative to ENDC, June 8, 1967, ENDC/PV.303, at 4-11; DOCUMENTS ON DISARMAMENT, 1967, at 252, 256. The analogy between nuclear explosive services and purchase of conventional explosives abroad should not be accepted uncritically. Given the complexity of the tasks involved, the intimate relationship of the device to other parts of a Plowshare project, the risks of major harm if something goes wrong, and the technical uncertainties involved, both the supplier and the recipient will have a major political stake in any Plowshare application. Success would seem to

Nuclear Weapons

Health and safety aspects of Plowshare projects are one area of international concern which might be subject to appropriate procedures under Article V.[121] For instance, it would be necessary to make careful and objective assessments of fall-out levels anticipated from surface excavation projects. Likewise, underground natural resource development projects close to national borders would need to be monitored since they could contaminate water flowing under the surface into an adjacent state.[122] Should the international procedures include a requirement for review and approval of Plowshare projects on safety grounds? Without such authority, the effectiveness of international safety procedures would be greatly reduced. But the possibility of disapproval of Plowshare projects at the international level on safety grounds might increase the risk that political considerations would enter· into the review process. Should provisions for on-site safety inspection of the Plowshare project be included? Safety review only "on the record" would be likely to be little more than a formality, while international on-site inspection might be a sensitive issue with some states.

The economic feasibility of Plowshare projects proposed by non-nuclear-weapon states, might also be subject to review as a part of the procedures under Article V. An unfavorable international assessment of the economic merits of a project would give Plowshare suppliers a basis for resisting pressures to assist projects of doubtful value. But an international approval of the economic aspects of a particular project would strengthen the claim of a non-nuclear-weapon state to Plowshare benefits.[123]

depend on close international cooperation and a sharing of responsibilities throughout all phases of a project.

121. Some form of international review could have several advantages. First, concern with the health and safety implications of Plowshare will be a major focus of public resistance, both within the recipient state and elsewhere. External review and approval would be perhaps the best way of establishing public confidence in Plowshare. Second, certain non-nuclear-weapon states might view an attempt by Plowshare supplier states to require their own health and safety standards as an obnoxious interference, whereas non-nuclear-weapon states would be more willing to conform to an "impartial" set of standards developed by an international body. Third, from the perspective of the Plowshare supplier states, it would be preferable if each knew that the other was bound by the same technical standards. Finally, in light of the uniqueness of each project it would be preferable to have a central repository of information concerning health and safety experience.

122. Safety issues are likely to be more substantial and certainly more dramatically raised in relation to surface excavation projects than in underground engineering. The presence of unique elements in each Plowshare application coupled with the fact that large scale applications are not likely to be frequent, at least during the initial phases of technological innovation and public acceptance, will make general criteria for determining whether a particular project is "safe" not only difficult to develop, but also of limited utility in concrete cases. Plowshare applications will also raise serious difficulties in allocating the risk of loss and in providing adequate indemnity for loss.

123. If and when we move closer to Plowshare applications, the United States Government may have to make some difficult choices between protecting its own natural re-

The Yale Law Journal   Vol. 77: 1447, 1968

"International observation" and review procedures might be used to ensure that a Plowshare project in a non-nuclear-weapon state did not conceal or serve a military purpose of the supplier, the recipient, or both in collusion.[124] And if the Limited Nuclear Test Ban Treaty is broadened in the future into a comprehensive ban on all nuclear weapon tests, it would become especially important to establish procedures to provide assurance that the supplier nuclear-weapon state does not derive any information from Plowshare projects that would be useful for nuclear weapons development.[125]

Who would be the administering authority for the "international procedures" under Article V? The "international body" that serves as a possible supply channel for Plowshare benefits might also administer the international procedures. Such a body might exist apart from or within the IAEA.[126] The monitoring activities concerning Plowshare projects, however, would be quite different from the IAEA's present responsibilities to foster peaceful nuclear research and power projects and to administer safeguards with respect to these activities. New procedures based on different technical concepts would be required. Although such procedures could be administered within the IAEA framework, a new organizational set-up would probably be needed.[127]

source extraction industries operating in both domestic and foreign markets and its responsibilities to assist non-nuclear-weapon states in their own national development using Plowshare explosions. In this respect, surface excavation projects for harbors, canals, and rail cuts would seem likely to pose fewer conflicts with private United States interests than underground resource development and extraction projects.

124. The Soviet Union has stated that the purpose of international supervision is "to exclude the possibility of using peaceful nuclear explosions as a means for non-nuclear-weapon States to obtain special information necessary for the production of nuclear weapons." Statement by Representative of Soviet Union to First Committee, May 31, 1968, U.N. Doc. A/C.1/PV.1577 (prov.), at 68-70.

125. This is not a current issue since the Limited Nuclear Test Ban Treaty permits underground nuclear weapon tests. If a comprehensive nuclear test ban is ever achieved, however, Plowshare would become the only form of legitimate nuclear explosions. The incentives to use Plowshare for a double purpose in these circumstances would seem to increase. Moreover, the development and applications of surface excavation technology will generate cratering information, some of which might be of use to a military program.

The United States has stated that Article V of the Non-Proliferation Treaty is compatible with a comprehensive test ban. "If under a comprehensive test ban treaty, international approval were needed for the conduct of a nuclear explosion for peaceful purposes, such approval would constitute an 'appropriate international procedure' applicable to services conducted bilaterally or through an appropriate international body." Statement by United States Representative to ENDC, ENDC/PV.369 (prov.), at 28.

126. The United States and others have supported using the IAEA for this purpose. Statement by United States Representative to ENDC, Mar. 21, 1967, ENDC/PV.295, at 23-26; DOCUMENTS ON DISARMAMENT, 1967, at 172, 174.

127. A further issue is the extent to which Plowshare projects in nuclear-weapon states would be subject to the "international procedures" of Article V. Sweden in particular has urged that there be no differentiation between projects in nuclear-weapon and non-nuclear-weapon states in this regard. *See* Statement by Representative of Sweden to ENDC, June 6, 1967, ENDC/PV.302, at 4-8; DOCUMENTS ON DISARMAMENT, 1967, at 248, 251. As to health and safety, and verifying the exclusively peaceful purpose of the project in

Nuclear Weapons

The undertaking to share Plowshare benefits enshrined in Article V amounts to a "carrot" for the non-nuclear-weapon states to chew on. Such states could not develop their own Plowshare devices without incurring the enormous costs of acquiring a capability in nuclear explosive technology on a par with the United States and the Soviet Union. Thus, under the Non-Proliferation Treaty the non-nuclear-weapon states simply concede a Plowshare duopoly which they are incapable of breaking.[128] In return, the United States and the Soviet Union make a major political concession to the concerns of the non-nuclear-weapon states by undertaking a firm legal obligation to share that area of peaceful nuclear technology where the economic uncertainties are largest.[129]

the event of a comprehensive test ban, it would seem that there would be good reason to subject Plowshare projects in the United States and the Soviet Union to the same international procedures applied to projects in non-nuclear-weapon states. There would be little point however, in having an international review of the economic feasibility of projects within the territory of the Plowshare supplier state. In any event, it is doubtful that the Soviet Union will agree to any Plowshare supervision in its territory.

128. The position of the non-nuclear-weapon states in bargaining for an equitable distribution of Plowshare benefits is further strengthened by present restraints imposed on future Plowshare applications by the Limited Nuclear Test Ban Treaty with respect to surface excavation. It is clear that if nuclear surface excavation techniques prove feasible and economical, the Limited Nuclear Test Ban Treaty will have to be amended at least in order for the United States to use nuclear excavation for a sea-level trans-Isthmian canal. Article II of the Limited Nuclear Test Ban Treaty provides for amendments "by a majority . . . of all the parties . . . including the votes of all of the original parties [the United States, the Soviet Union, and the United Kingdom]." Thus, to the extent that Plowshare programs conflict with the Limited Nuclear Test Ban Treaty as it stands, the United States and the Soviet Union each have a veto over the other's program. Moreover, a simple majority of the total number of signatories, which could be constituted entirely of developing and "mini-" states, have a veto over both United States and Soviet programs.

129. "It is a fact that the United States has not yet demonstrated that the technology for any—I repeat, any—specific peaceful application of nuclear explosions is technically and economically feasible. Some private companies in the United States and elsewhere and some foreign governments have evaluated certain applications of nuclear explosions for peaceful purposes and have made assessments that the technology, if successfully developed, would have economic potential in certain applications. Whether those evaluations will be confirmed requires further development, such as additional experiments with nuclear explosives." Statement by United States Representative to ENDC, June 8, 1967, ENDC/PV.303, at 4-11; DOCUMENTS ON DISARMAMENT, 1967, at 252, 257. The Plowshare development which is probably the closest to realization is the use of nuclear explosives to stimulate natural gas production. The United States Bureau of Mines estimates that if nuclear explosions prove successful in stimulating gas production, United States recoverable gas reserves would more than double from under 300 trillion cubic feet to about 600 trillion cubic feet. *Hearings on AEC Authorizing Legislation Fiscal Year 1968 Before the Joint Comm. on Atomic Energy*, 90th Cong., 1st Sess., pt. 3, at 1797 (1967). On December 10, 1967, a nuclear explosion of approximately 26 kilotons yield was detonated by the AEC at a depth of 4240 feet in a natural gas field in New Mexico (Project Gasbuggy sponsored jointly by the AEC and El Paso Natural Gas Company). The purpose of the experiment was to determine to what extent a low permeability natural gas formation can be stimulated by an underground nuclear detonation. *See generally Hearings on AEC Authorizing Legislation Fiscal Year 1969 Before the Joint Comm. on Atomic Energy*, 90th Cong., 2d Sess., pt. 2, at 1915-2022 (1968). Results of the explosion are not yet available.

The Yale Law Journal   Vol. 77: 1447, 1968

C. *Durability*

Issues related to the durability[130] of the Non-Proliferation Treaty magnify the difficulty of predicting the outcome of many of the major problems previously discussed. Yet these issues are among the most important to be considered in determining the scope and effect of the Treaty.

It is by no means certain that the Treaty will ever enter into force, and putting it into effect will probably, in itself, be a time consuming process involving significant political costs. Article IX provides that the Treaty will enter into force upon ratification by the "Depositaries"— the Soviet Union, the United Kingdom and the United States—and forty non-nuclear-weapon states.[131] Thus all five nuclear-weapon states need not become parties for the Treaty to become effective—a necessary provision since France and China have clearly stated they will not adhere to the Treaty.[132] The number forty has no particular magic to it

---

130. I am grateful to the National Policy Panel convened by the United Nations Association of the United States of America for the term "durability" in this connection, although I have grouped procedural issues under it as well as the major substantive problems discussed by the Panel. *See* REPORT OF A NATIONAL POLICY PANEL ESTABLISHED BY THE UNITED NATIONS ASSOCIATION OF THE UNITED STATES OF AMERICA, STOPPING THE SPREAD OF NUCLEAR WEAPONS 26 *et seq.* (1967).

131. Article IX, paragraph 1, of the Treaty provides in part: "This Treaty shall be open to all States for signature." The Limited Nuclear Test Ban Treaty, art. III, para. 1, contains the same provision. There are a number of practical legal problems encountered in giving any treaty potentially global coverage these days. For globally oriented international organizations the usual method is to open the treaty to "all States Members of the United Nations or of any of the specialized agencies." I.A.E.A. STAT. art. XXI, para. A. Under such formulas the Western-oriented halves of divided countries such as Germany, China, Korea and Vietnam have generally been admitted to membership in the U.N. specialized agencies while the Communist halves have been excluded. Neither half of any divided country except Nationalist China is a member of the United Nations itself. For arms control treaties, it is important that status as parties not be denied to entities not recognized as states by all the major powers, and that the challenged status of certain regimes not prevent those regimes from acting as governments of states for purposes of becoming parties. The way around the difficulty, first adopted in the Limited Nuclear Test Ban Treaty and now followed in the Non-Proliferation Treaty, is to make the Treaty open to all states and provide three depositary governments, the United States, the United Kingdom and the Soviet Union. A particular entity unrecognized by one or more of the depositaries can become a party to the Treaty by depositing instruments with that depositary which is friendly to it. Since each depositary keeps its own list, no single agreed list of parties exists. Problems may well arise under the Non-Proliferation Treaty in connection with whether particular entities are entitled to participate in review conferences and whether amendments have received the requisite majority. On the question whether recognition is accorded to an unrecognized regime that subscribes to the Nuclear Test Ban Treaty, see Opinion of the Legal Adviser, Aug. 12, 1963, *Hearings on the Nuclear Test Ban Treaty Before the Senate Comm. on Foreign Relations*, 88th Cong., 1st Sess. 15 (1963).

132. "France, for its part, which will not sign the non-proliferation treaty, will behave in the future in this field exactly as the States adhering to the treaty." Statement by Representative of France to U.N. General Assembly, June 12, 1968, U.N. Doc. A/PV.1672 (prov.) at 6.

China's attitude toward the Treaty is illustrated by their reaction to the draft treaty of August 24, 1967: "Obviously, Washington and Moscow are hoping to use the draft treaty as a means of pushing their criminal activity against communism, against the

Nuclear Weapons

as far as the non-nuclear-weapon states are concerned. It seems to have been selected simply as a substantial number, but one which will permit the Treaty to enter into force without undue delay. Ratification by any forty non-nuclear-weapon states, regardless of their nuclear capabilities, will be sufficient to bring the Treaty into force.

The United States, the Soviet Union and the United Kingdom, after signing the Treaty, can each block entry into force until it is satisfied with the identity as well as numbers of non-nuclear-weapon parties. The Soviet Union may be among the first to sign the Treaty, but might delay ratification until West Germany becomes a party. Moreover, certain non-nuclear-weapon states might make their own signature or ratification contingent on ratification by one or more other states. For example, Israel and the United Arab Republic might await each other's pleasure. Pakistan might wish to follow India.[133] Nothing in the Treaty precludes such procedures.

The Treaty's requirements that non-nuclear-weapon states negotiate with the IAEA and conclude agreements accepting safeguards could also delay its early entry into force. Under paragraph 4 of Article III,[134] negotiations must begin within six months after the Treaty is in force. States which become parties more than six months after the Treaty's effective date, however, must commence negotiation simultaneously with their ratification. Safeguards agreements with the IAEA must become effective within eighteen months after the date of initiation of negotiations, giving original parties as long as two years to negotiate and

people, against revolution and against China, in an attempt to stem the revolutionary tide in the world . . . . But atom bombs, guided missiles and hydrogen bombs were possessed by the Chinese people before their treaty was drawn up. This magnificent achievement of the Chinese people dealt a death-blow to the U.S.-Soviet policy of nuclear monopoly and nuclear blackmail and has encouraged the revolutionary people of the world tremendously. Thus, Washington and Moscow had to come up with the treaty in the hope of using it as a means of agitation against China and to contain socialist China's influence abroad . . . . Obviously, the U.S. imperialists and Soviet revisionists concocted the treaty to put all non-nuclear countries in a subordinate position, that of being 'protectorates,' so that they may maintain their special status as big nuclear powers and remain 'nuclear overlords.' " Chinese Communist Comment, Sept. 3, 1967, PEKING REV., Sept. 8, 1967, at 34; DOCUMENTS ON DISARMAMENT, 1967, at 380, 381.

133. India has stated that its present intention is not to become a party to the Treaty. Statement by Representative of India to First Committee, U.N. Doc. A/C.1/ PV.1567, at 82.

134. "Non-nuclear-weapon States Party to the Treaty shall conclude agreements with the International Atomic Energy Agency to meet the requirements of this article either individually or together with other States in accordance with the Statute of the International Atomic Energy Agency. Negotiation of such agreements shall commence within 180 days from the original entry into force of this Treaty. For States depositing their instruments of ratification or accession after the 180-day period, negotiation of such agreements shall commence not later than the date of such deposit. Such agreements shall enter into force not later than eighteen months after the date of initiation of negotiations." Art. III, para. 4. This paragraph of the Non-Proliferation Treaty is based on Article 13 of the Treaty of Tlatelolco.

The Yale Law Journal   Vol. 77: 1447, 1968

conclude a safeguards agreement with the IAEA. Such agreements can be concluded "either individually or together with other States," so the five Euratom members that are non-nuclear-weapon states can negotiate as a bloc with the IAEA.[135]

What would happen if a non-nuclear-weapon state which had become a party did not conclude an agreement with the IAEA within the prescribed time limits? No provision in the Treaty deals with this question. The recalcitrant state would possibly have breached an important obligation under the Treaty, but it would not automatically cease to be a party. Nor would IAEA safeguards be automatically applied to that state's peaceful nuclear activities.[136]

Even though the deadline for IAEA negotiations may be unenforceable, some non-nuclear-weapon states might prefer to negotiate their safeguards agreements before ratifying the Treaty rather than after: the subject matter involved is complex and technical, and the commitments required are substantial and controversial. If the non-nuclear-weapon states with major civil nuclear industries become reluctant to sign the Treaty until the nature of their agreements with the IAEA becomes more precisely defined, the Treaty's entry into force will be substantially delayed at least as to this most important category of states.

After the Treaty enters into force, paragraph 2 of Article X[137] provides that the initial term will be twenty-five years, subject at that time to two options which are exercisable by a simple majority of the parties:[138] first, the Treaty may be renewed for a fixed period or periods;

---

135. Article III(D) and Article XIV(A) of the IAEA Statute provide ample authority for the IAEA to conclude an agreement with Euratom.

136. Earlier proposals for Article III, which were never officially published, included a clause which required the IAEA system automatically to enter into force at the end of three years if no agreement had been reachd with IAEA in the interim. Euratom member states objected strongly to this "guillotine clause," and it was deleted from the version of Article III which was tabled on January 18, 1968. EUROPEAN COMMUNITY, April 1968, at 17.

137. "Twenty-five years after the entry into force of the Treaty, a Conference shall be convened to decide whether the Treaty shall continue in force indefinitely, or shall be extended for an additional fixed period or periods. This decision shall be taken by a majority of the Parties to the Treaty." Art. X, para. 2.
Article VII of the draft treaty of August 24, 1967, provided for "unlimited duration." ENDC/192; ENDC/193; DOCUMENTS ON DISARMAMENT, 1967, at 338, 341. Italy characterized the provision for unlimited duration in the August 24, 1967, draft as an "iron corset.' Statement by Representative of Italy to ENDC, ENDC/PV.341, at 5-6. The government of Switzerland suggested a treaty for a definite period with a review conference at the end, stating: "The non-nuclear-weapon states certainly cannot take the responsibility of tying their hands indefinitely if the nuclear-weapon states fail to arrive at positive results "in the direction of nuclear disarmament measures." ENDC/204. There has been little objection to the twenty-five year period specified in the draft treaty of January 18, 1968, and subsequent versions. Article IV of the Limited Nuclear Test Ban Treaty specifies "unlimited duration." Article 30 of the Treaty of Tlatelolco specifies that the Treaty shall remain in force "indefinitely."

138. It might be argued that the decision to extend the duration of the Treaty

Nuclear Weapons

second, the Treaty may be continued indefinitely. Once the Treaty enters into force, therefore, a few more than a majority of the non-nuclear-weapon parties can control how long the Treaty will remain in effect after the initial twenty-five year period.

Since some rather severe stresses on the Treaty can be anticipated during its first twenty-five years of operation, it is well that it contains rather liberal provisions for review in the interim.[139] Paragraph 3 of Article VIII[140] contains requirements that five years after entry into force, and at five-year intervals thereafter at the request of a majority of the parties, a conference of the parties "shall be held" in Geneva "to review the operation" of the Treaty "with a view to assuring that the purposes of the Preamble and the provisions of the Treaty are being realized." The Treaty offers no guidance concerning the form of the assurance or what would be the effect of the decision by a majority of the parties at such a conference that certain parts of the Treaty were not working well. Indeed, there is no specific authorization for the five-year review conferences to make any decisions at all. A specific proposal that the review conference adopt "findings" by "a majority of the signatory states present"[141] was not accepted by the drafters. Such a conference would, however, at least offer a forum for any party to propose, discuss and perhaps obtain initial approval of amendments to the Treaty.

Under paragraph 1 of Article VIII,[142] any party is authorized to propose amendments to the Treaty at any time. At the request of one-

constitutes an amendment to the Treaty which could not take effect under paragraph 2 of Article VIII, note 143 *infra*, as to any non-consenting party. However, this would distort paragraph 2 of Article X, which clearly seems intended to place the decision concerning this particular phase of the Treaty in the hands of a majority of the parties and to make that decision effective against all parties.

139.   The nuclear era is barely twenty-five years old. The changes probable in the next twenty-five years due to nuclear research, development and innovation seem at least as great as those which have occurred in the first twenty-five year period. For a stimulating glimpse into the future concerning peaceful uses of nuclear energy, see Weinberg, *The Coming Age of Nuclear Energy*, I.A.E.A. BULL., Dec. 1967, at 11-21.

140.   "Five years after the entry into force of this Treaty, a conference of Parties to the Treaty shall be held in Geneva, Switzerland, in order to review the operation of this Treaty with a view to assuring that the purposes of the Preamble and the provisions of the Treaty are being realized. At intervals of five years thereafter, a majority of the Parties to the Treaty may obtain, by submitting a proposal to this effect to the Depositary Governments, the convening of further conferences with the same objective of reviewing the operation of the Treaty." Art. VIII, para. 3.

141.   Statement by Representative of Nigeria to ENDC, ENDC/PV.371 (prov.), at 17.

142.   "Any Party to the Treaty may propose amendments to this Treaty. The text of any proposed amendment shall be submitted to the Depositary Governments which shall circulate it to all Parties to the Treaty. Thereupon, if requested to do so by one third or more of the Parties to the Treaty, the Depositary Governments shall convene a conference, to which they shall invite all the Parties to the Treaty, to consider such an amendment." Art. VIII, para. 1.

The Yale Law Journal   Vol. 77: 1447, 1968

third of the parties, a conference must be convened to consider the proposed amendment. Any amendment would have to be approved by a majority vote of all parties, including the affirmative votes of all nuclear-weapon parties and all other parties which were members of the IAEA Board of Governors on the date the amendment was circulated. Each amendment would enter into force, assuming the requisite majorities were obtained, only as to those parties that specifically consented by ratifying the amendment. Presumably, the unamended version of the Treaty would remain in force among parties which did not consent and between consenting and non-consenting parties.[143] The requirement that the major nuclear powers, in both military and civil fields, must approve each amendment provides stability to the Treaty and probably eliminates the danger of its being reduced by amendment to a set of conflicting and unworkable obligations.

The analysis of the Non-Proliferation Treaty so far has been primarily directed at provisions intended to prevent the spread of nuclear weapons in the horizontal plane to additional states. But proliferation also has a vertical dimension—the build-up of nuclear armaments within the nuclear-weapon states. These two dimensions are generally perceived as dependent variables in any nuclear security equation.[144] Thus, the

---

143. Article VIII, paragraph 2, provides: "Any amendment to this Treaty must be approved by a majority of the votes of all the Parties to the Treaty, including the votes of all nuclear-weapon States Party to the Treaty and all other Parties which, on the date the amendment is circulated, are members of the Board of Governors of the International Atomic Energy Agency. The amendment shall enter into force for each Party that deposits its instrument of ratification of the amendment upon the deposit of such instruments of ratification by a majority of all the Parties, including the instruments of ratification of all nuclear-weapon States Party to the Treaty and all other Parties which, on the date the amendment is circulated, are members of the Board of Governors of the International Atomic Energy Agency. Thereafter, it shall enter into force for any other Party upon the deposit of its instrument of ratification of the amendment."

Article V, paragraph 2, of the draft treaty of August 24, 1967, had provided that upon obtaining the requisite majorities amendments would enter into force *as to all parties*, whether or not they had consented. Rumania and others criticized this provision, and it was changed in the draft of January 18, 1968. Statement by Representative of Rummania to ENDC, ENDC/PV.348, at 7-8. The Treaty's amendment process is sanctioned and described in Article 36 of the Draft Articles on the Law of Treaties of the International Law Commission. 21 U.N. GAOR, Supp. 9, at 15, U.N. Doc. A/6309/Rev.1 (1966).

Rumania criticized this provision for giving the members of the IAEA Board of Governors a privileged position. Statement by Representative of Rumania to ENDC, ENDC/PV.348, at 7-8. Certainly, the Non-Proliferation Treaty amendment process will add a major new factor to the designation and election of members of the IAEA Board of Governors. It is interesting that *no* member of the IAEA Board has a veto over decisions by the Board concerning peaceful uses of nuclear energy, many affecting the Non-Proliferation Treaty, while *every* member of the IAEA Board that is a party to the Treaty will have a veto over amendments to it circulated at that time.

144. Although the interaction between horizontal and vertical proliferation is recognized, the conclusion is not inevitable that nuclear-weapon states must reduce their nuclear armaments if they expect to prevent further proliferation. Rather than minimizing the gap between nuclear-weapon and non-nuclear-weapon states—a "low posture" —a nuclear-weapon state might choose to widen the gap to make it unbridgeable—a "high

Nuclear Weapons

durability of the Treaty and the underlying policy of preventing further horizontal proliferation will depend, perhaps decisively, on the future success of efforts to control the nuclear arms race among the nuclear-weapon states. Article VI of the Treaty obligates all parties, including the two superpowers, "to pursue negotiations in good faith on effective measures relating to cessation of the nuclear arms race at an early date and to nuclear disarmament . . . ."[145]

Present trends in nuclear weapons capabilities, however, fly in the face of these words on paper.[146] Moreover, nuclear power politics is

posture." For good analysis pro and con of each alternative and a conclusion in favor of a low posture, see Bull, *The Role of Nuclear Powers in the Management of Nuclear Proliferation*, in ARMS CONTROL FOR THE LATE SIXTIES 143 (Dougherty & Lehman ed. 1967).

145. "Each of the Parties to the Treaty undertakes to pursue negotiations in good faith on effective measures relating to cessation of the nuclear arms race at an early date and to nuclear disarmament, and on a Treaty on general and complete disarmament under strict and effective international control." Art. VI.

The undertaking regarding "general and complete disarmament" is propaganda. In addition to these undertakings, the Preamble contains declarations of intention regarding nuclear disarmament, general and complete disarmament, and achievement of "the discontinuance of all test explosions of nuclear weapons for all time." "As has been pointed out by many non-aligned delegations, a non-proliferation treaty must . . . embody an article of solemn obligation under which the state possessing nuclear weapons would negotiate a meaningful programme of reduction of existing stockpiles of weapons and their delivery systems. This provision cannot be merely a pious preambular platitude like the unfulfilled 'determination' in the four-year-old partial test-ban treaty." Statement by Representative of India to ENDC, May 23, 1967, ENDC/PV.298, at 4-17; DOCUMENTS ON DISARMAMENT, 1967, at 229, 238.

From time to time various states proposed the inclusion of references in Article VI to various specific measures of control on vertical proliferation, including a comprehensive nuclear test ban, cut-off of production of fissionable materials for use in weapons, and a freeze on further production of nuclear weapon delivery systems. The United States has stated: "We all know why it would not be feasible to incorporate specific obligations to that end in the treaty itself. The differences that have prevented agreement on these measures have not yet been resolved. Any attempt to incorporate specific nuclear arms limitation obligations in the treaty would inevitably also inject these differences into the consideration of the treaty itself and could only jeopardize its prospects." Statement by United States Representative to ENDC, Aug. 24, 1967, ENDC/PV.325, at 4-11; DOCUMENTS ON DISARMAMENT, 1967, at 342, 346. The Soviet Union Representative to ENDC made a statement to the same effect. ENDC/PV.361 (prov.), at 5-22. Moreover, it has been suggested that the view held by some non-nuclear-weapon states—requiring nuclear disarmament as a *quid pro quo* for accepting the Non-Proliferation Treaty—overlooks the fact that the Treaty is intended to enhance the security of all states, and in particular the non-nuclear-weapon states. *See* Statement by United States Representative to ENDC, ENDC/PV.362 (prov.), at 21-23. In a recent speech, Secretary of State Rusk listed the following as possible next steps: "achieving an understanding with the Soviet Union to halt the strategic missile arms race," including "control of both offensive vehicles and antiballistic missiles;" a cut-off of production of fissionable materials for weapons; and a comprehensive nuclear test ban. Address by Secretary of State Rusk, May 2, 1968, 58 STATE DEP'T BULL. 632, 633-34 (1968).

146. For example, in the United States during the eight years, FY 1962—FY 1969, approximately $78.7 billion will have been spent on strategic nuclear forces. In the last three years the trend is as follows: FY 1967, $6.9 billion; FY 1968, $7.9 billion; FY 1969, $9.6 billion. Statement by Secretary of Defense Robert S. McNamara on the Fiscal Year 1969-73 Defense Program and the 1969 Defense Budget, Table 1, at 214 (1968). In mid-1967 a $100.5 million project to provide additional nuclear weapons production facilities was authorized for the AEC in support of the decision to deploy an anti-ballistic missile defense system. U.S.A.E.C., Major Activities in the Atomic Energy Programs, January-December 1967, at 60 (1968).

The Yale Law Journal   Vol. 77: 1447, 1968

not within the control of the United States and the Soviet Union, individually or collectively. China, in particular, is moving into a position of pivotal importance. On the one hand, China's nuclear weapons program has already triggered a decision to deploy a ballistic missile defense system in the United States and could in the future catalyze a full-scale renewal of the nuclear arms race between the United States and the Soviet Union. On the other hand, China's growing nuclear power will increase the problems for India and Japan in maintaining their own nuclear security.[147] Even if the United States and the Soviet Union play down China's nuclear power and, under the injunction of Article VI, freeze the nuclear arms build-up between themselves, this would not resolve the difficulties of those non-nuclear-weapon states which feel menaced by China.[148]

The withdrawal provision of the Treaty and the security assurances that the United States, the Soviet Union and the United Kingdom have extended to non-nuclear-weapon parties are intended to deal with the potential insecurity of those non-nuclear-weapon states which give up their nuclear weapons options. Paragraph 1 of Article X[149] provides that a party may withdraw from the Treaty if it decides that "extraordinary events, related to the subject matter of this Treaty, have jeopardized the supreme interests of its country." This provision is identical with Article IV of the Limited Nuclear Test Ban Treaty.[150] However, the

---

147. "India's peculiar position with regard to the nonproliferation treaty . . . is that it is a nonaligned country, not in military alliance with any country nor under the nuclear umbrella of any country. Secondly, India is far advanced in nuclear research, and third, it is under the continuing threat and menace of China, which has already become a nuclear power." News Conference Remarks by External Affairs Minister Chagla of India, April 27, 1967, DOCUMENTS ON DISARMAMENT, 1967, at 204.

148. For further analysis see Willrich, *ABM and Arms Control*, 44 INT'L AFFAIRS 228 (1968); Rothstein, *The ABM, Proliferation and International Stability*, 46 FOREIGN AFFAIRS 487 (1968).

149. "Each Party shall in exercising its national sovereignty have the right to withdraw from the Treaty if it decides that extraordinary events, related to the subject matter of this Treaty, have jeopardized the supreme interests of its country. It shall give notice of such withdrawal to all other Parties to the Treaty and to the United Nations Security Council three months in advance. Such notice shall include a statement of the extraordinary events it regards as having jeopardized its supreme interests." Art. X, para. 1.

150. The withdrawal clause in the Non-Proliferatoin Treaty was a United States suggestion. Testimony of Adrian S. Fisher, Deputy Director, United States Arms Control and Disarmament Agency, *Hearings on Arms Control and Disarmament Act Amendments, 1968, Before the House Comm. on Foreign Affairs*, 90th Cong., 2d Sess. 70 (1968).

The notion of an express provision for withdrawal when one's "supreme interests" are jeopardized may well have had its origins in another agreement for quite another purpose. The Nassau agreement provided that certain existing United Kingdom nuclear forces and the United Kingdom Polaris submarine forces to be built with United States assistance "would be assigned as part of a NATO nuclear force and targeted in accordance with NATO plans." "The Prime Minister made it clear that except where Her Majesty's Government may decide that *supreme national interests* are at stake, these British forces will be used for the purposes of international defense of the Western Alliance in all circumstances." (Emphasis added.) Statement on Nuclear Defense Systems, paras. 6, 8, Nassau

Nuclear Weapons

provisions for notice accompanying withdrawal differ by requiring the withdrawing state to give three months' notice to the Security Council, in addition to all other parties, and to identify the events it regards as having jeopardized its supreme interests.[151]

The "extraordinary events" justifying withdrawal must not only be determined by the withdrawing party to have jeopardized its "supreme interests," but must also be "related to the subject matter of this Treaty." Thus, India might be justified in withdrawing from the Treaty on the basis of a nuclear threat from China, while Israel might not be justified in withdrawing on the basis of a growing conventional threat from the Arab states.

The withdrawal clause provides a revolving door in the Non-Proliferation Treaty, a feature that seems to be essential if the Treaty is to be a viable political structure, since it touches vital security interests. If a party believed its security was seriously threatened and it could not withdraw, it would probably either secretly circumvent or openly abrogate the Treaty. In these circumstances, the withdrawal clause serves two important functions. First, by providing a legitimate avenue of escape, it should make it easier for key states such as West Germany, Japan, Sweden, and perhaps India to become parties to the Treaty. Second, it should provide an important channel in which the political process can operate in the event a party should feel its security threatened. Although the withdrawal clause provides a means of escape, in another sense it is legitimate, even desirable, for a non-nuclear-weapon state to view it as a type of nuclear security gurarantee, particularly since the Treaty itself provides no specific guarantee.[152]

Communique by President Kennedy and Prime Minister Macmillan, Dec. 21, 1962, 48 Dep't State Bull. 43-45 (1963); Documents on Disarmament, 1962, at 1274, 1276 (U.S. Arms Control & Disarmament Agency Pub. No. 19, 1963). Article 30, paragraph 1, of the Treaty of Tlatelolco contains a provision analogous to the Non-Proliferation Treaty.

151. Rumania objected to the requirement of submitting a statement to the Security Council concerning the basis for withdrawal, maintaining that the right of withdrawal was within the exclusive competence of every state and no other state or international organization was qualified to discuss it. Statements by Representative of Rumania to ENDC, ENDC/PV. 362 (prov.), at 12; ENDC/PV.376 (prov.), at 22. As discussed *infra*, the procedural requirement—that a statement of justification be submitted to the Securtiy Council—can be made to work in favor of a party considering withdrawal for legitimate security reasons. The Security Council would probably become involved, in any event, if a state sought to withdraw from the Treaty, if not to assist the party considering withdrawal, then to consider sanctioning it for creating a situation endangering the peace.

152. As the Treaty was being drafted and debated, a number of non-nuclear-weapon states proposed that a specific guarantee be included that would protect the non-nuclear-weapon states from nuclear attack or "blackmail" by the nuclear-weapon states. The United States, in particular, resisted the incorporation of any security guarantee into the Treaty, because the issues involved were "too difficult and complicated to be reduced to a treaty provision" and should be dealt with in the context of the United Nations, which had primary responsibility for the maintenance of peace and security. Statement by

The Yale Law Journal   Vol. 77: 1447, 1968

In order to obtain the benefits of the guarantee implicit in the withdrawal clause, a non-nuclear-weapon state would first have to become a party to the Treaty. Once a party, the non-nuclear-weapon state which believed itself threatened by another state's nuclear capabilities or intentions could begin the process of withdrawal, perhaps with a simple statement of its concern rather than a formal notice. If the Treaty was working well, the statement from the threatened non-nuclear-weapon party should generate a prompt response from some or all of the parties to which it was addressed, possibly including one or more of the nuclear-weapon states. If, however, the initial response of the other parties was insufficient to allay the concerns of the threatened non-nuclear-weapon party, it could proceed to give formal notice of its intention to withdraw. Notice as required in the withdrawal process would dramatize the plight of the withdrawing state, and the Security Council would be a suitable forum in which to generate an adequate response.[153]

Outside the Treaty framework but related to it, a resolution on "security assurances," sponsored by the United States, the Soviet Union, and the United Kingdom, has been adopted by the Security Council.[154] This is intended to provide a new basis for responding to acts or threats of "aggression with nuclear weapons" against non-nuclear-

United States Representative to ENDC, ENDC/PV.368 (prov.), at 17. In addition, incorporation of a specific security commitment into the Non-Proliferation Treaty could cause substantial complications for the United States Government in obtaining Senate consent to ratification.

The Soviet Union has declared its willingness "to include in the draft treaty a clause on the prohibition of the use of nuclear weapons against non-nuclear states parties to the Treaty which have no nuclear weapons in their territory." Message from Premier Kosygin to ENDC, Feb. 1, 1966, ENDC/167, Feb. 3, 1967; DOCUMENTS ON DISARMAMENT, 1966, at 9, 11. In this proposal the Soviet Union combined two favorite foreign policy themes. In the first place, the proposal is aimed at West Germany which is a non-nuclear-weapon state that would clearly not qualify for preferred treatment. Second, the proposal plays to "world public opinion" which will support "ban the bomb" resolutions in the U.N. General Assembly and is unsympathetic to United States reluctance in this regard. The concept of an affirmative guarantee of the security of a state against attack should be carefully distinguished from the negative concept of a restraint in the use of a particular weapon.

153. But the process could also lead in a different direction. It might be suggested that one effect of the Treaty would be to make the act of withdrawal by a party in order to acquire nuclear weapons a "situation which might lead to international friction" justifying an investigation by the Security Council under Article 34 of the U.N. Charter. The entire situation might be, thereafter, characterized as a "threat to the peace" under Article 39, justifying the application of appropriate sanctions under Articles 40, 41, and 42. Of course, the target state would not necessarily be the state which had just withdrawn and declared its intention to acquire nuclear weapons, but it could be.

154. The operative paragraphs are:

"[Each Council member] 1. Recognizes that aggression with nuclear weapons or the threat of such aggression against a non-nuclear-weapon state would create a situation in which the Security Council, and above all its nuclear-weapon state permanent members, would have to act immediately in accordance with their obligations under the United Nations Charter;

Nuclear Weapons

weapon parties to the Treaty. Paragraph 2 of the resolution envisages declarations of "intention" in support of the assurances. In conjunction with Security Council action on their proposed resolution, each of the three sponsors has declared: "[A]ggression with nuclear weapons, or the threat of such aggression, against a non-nuclear-weapon state would create a qualitatively new situation . . . ;" and affirmed "its intention, as a permanent member of the United Nations Security Council, to seek immediate Security Council action to provide assistance in accordance with the Charter to any non-nuclear-weapon state party to the Treaty on the Non-Proliferation of Nuclear Weapons that is a victim of an act of aggression or an object of a threat of aggression in which nuclear weapons are used."[155] Will it follow from such a resolution that, as declared by the three proponents, "any state which commits . . . or . . . threatens such aggression, must be aware that its actions are to be countered effectively . . ." ?[156] Would such Security Council action constitute a reliable nuclear security "umbrella" over the non-nuclear-weapon states which become parties to the Non-Proliferation Treaty?[157] Action "through" the Security Council under the assurances resolution will require the support or acquiescence of the other two permanent members of the Security Council, France and Nationalist China. Since Nationalist China is both a non-nuclear-weapon state and a prime target for nuclear threats from Communist China, it will probably support action under the security assurances resolution. It is not so clear where France's interests will lie. But the resolution will give France, which has refused to subscribe to the Non-Proliferation

"2. Welcomes the intention expressed by certain states that they will provide or support immediate assistance, in accordance with the Charter, to any non-nuclear-weapon state party to the Treaty on the Non-Proliferation of Nuclear Weapons that is a victim of an act or an object of a threat of aggression in which nuclear weapons are used;

"3. Reaffirms in particular the inherent right, recognized under Article 51 of the Charter, of individual and collective self-defense if an armed attack occurs against a member of the United Nations, until the Security Council has taken measures necessary to maintain international peace and security." 58 DEP'T STATE BULL. 401-03 (1968) (complete text and U.S. statement).

155. *Id.* 402.

156. *Id.*

157. A United States official has stated that the security assurances resolution "does not involve a new commitment but it is a statement of the ways we would act under the charter of the U.N. and a statement which would be meaningful as far as the nonalined are concerned, if a similar statement was made by the Soviet Union." Testimony of Adrian S. Fisher, Deputy Director, United States Arms Control and Disarmament Agency, *Hearings on Arms Control and Disarmament Act Amendments, 1968, Before the House Comm. on Foreign Affairs,* 90th Cong., 2d Sess. 78 (1968). On October 18, 1964, following China's first nuclear explosion President Johnson stated: "The nations that do not seek national nuclear weapons can be sure that, if they need our strong support against some threat of nuclear blackmail, then they will have it." 50 DEP'T STATE BULL. 610-14 (1964); *see* Willrich, *Guarantees to Non-Nuclear Nations,* 44 FOREIGN AFFAIRS 683 (1966).

The Yale Law Journal   Vol. 77: 1447, 1968

Treaty, a large influence over the effectiveness of the security assurances which are viewed by many non-nuclear-weapon states as a vital, if
not integral, aspect of the Treaty.

A major substantive weakness of the Security Council resolution on
security assurances is that the events which will bring it into operation
are "aggression" or "the threat of aggression" with nuclear weapons
against a non-nuclear-weapon state. Thus, the resolution rests on all the
unresolved problems of defining aggression and identifying the aggressor, and determination of the threshold question whether "aggression with nuclear weapons" has occurred in a particular case will be by
the usual Security Council procedures, including the veto of any one
of the five permanent members.

The thrust of the first two paragraphs of the security assurances resolution is action through the Security Council. Paragraph 3, however,
reaffirms the right to individual or collective self-defense under
Article 51 of the Charter. This reaffirmation may be viewed as serving
two purposes. On the one hand, it seems to offset any suggestion, which
might be inferred from the pledges by the three nuclear-weapon parties
to the Treaty to seek action through the Council, that they had delegated any veto-free power to the Security Council. On the other hand,
the reaffirmation of the rights of individual and collective self-defense
provides a "fall-back" assurance to the non-nuclear-weapon states if
assistance from or through the Security Council is not forthcoming.[158]
Such an affirmation recognizes, but does not seem to add to or detract
from, the credibility of nuclear security guarantees which already exist
in collective security agreements.

The withdrawal clause of the Treaty and the Security Council
security assurances resolution are directed at different kinds of circumstances, but share a common purpose—preserving the Treaty. The
"extraordinary events" which a non-nuclear-weapon state might consider to have "jeopardized the supreme interests of its country," thereby
justifying its withdrawal from the Treaty, might well fall short of what
the Security Council might determine "aggression with nuclear weapons
or the threat of such aggression." Thus, the Treaty's withdrawal clause
coupled with the Security Council resolution on assurances might seem
to provide a gradation of responses applicable to a broad range of
events which, if they occurred, would challenge the continued existence

---

158. Assuming United States-Soviet cooperation, the veto of another Security Council
permananent member or the absence of sufficient time for Security Council action would
not necessarily block coordinated superpower action outside the Security Council on the
basis of the right to collective self-defense.

Nuclear Weapons

of the Treaty. The umbrella of the security assurances resolution, however, extends only to non-nuclear-weapon states which are parties to the Treaty. This limitation is intended to create incentives, first, to adhere to the Treaty and, thereafter, to remain a party. But it will also undercut any assurance effect of the withdrawal clause for non-nuclear-weapon states, since the benefit of the resolution can not be claimed after withdrawal from the Treaty.

What, in practice, might the resolution on security assurances accomplish? The veto which each permanent member possesses limits the possible target of Security Council action to China, and no other potential nuclear aggressor. In this respect, the Security Council may become a principal organ for future collaboration between the United States and the Soviet Union in the containment of China—as long as China is not a member of the United Nations.[159] Such open and institutionalized collaboration seems an important ingredient of any meaningful security assurance to non-aligned non-nuclear-weapon states such as India. It is too early to tell, however, whether the security assurances resolution constitutes a real move by the United States and the Soviet Union towards this kind of cooperation or merely a short-term expedient to obtain subscriptions to the Non-Proliferation Treaty.

V. Assessment

The competitive forces inherent in the existing international system, reinforced by conflicts over basic values among competing states in the system, have greatly accelerated the exploitation of nuclear energy. A series of upward and outward trends are established in both the military and the peaceful nuclear fields. The Non-Proliferation Treaty is an attempt to reverse the military trends, confirm the peaceful trends and establish a barrier between the two. In short, the Treaty is a major attempt to achieve political control on a global scale over the scientific and technological processes by which nuclear energy is exploited.[160]

159. China sees the Non-Proliferation Treaty as just such collusion between the superpowers. *See* note 132 *supra*. United States-Soviet collaboration in this respect will be a mixed blessing, as far as future accommodation with China is concerned, and like so much else in the non-proliferation field, it seems primarily intended to buy a few years time.
160. "This treaty confronts us in this form for the first time with the problem of finding a political solution to the mass of information and knowledge brought to us by science and technics, knowledge which we can no longer remove from our world. This makes the help and the counsel of science indispensable in the political field. But it also raises the problem to a new and somewhat unsure level, that of insuring the primacy of the political. The political requires the helping partnership of the scientific, but the responsibility of the final determination—even in regard to important detailed decisions —cannot be taken away from the political leadership." Statement by Foreign Minister

The Yale Law Journal   Vol. 77: 1447, 1968

The attempt is justified mainly by the increasing probability of nuclear war if nuclear energy continues to be exploited in a largely uncontrolled manner within the present international system.

Each government faced with the issue of whether or not to become a party to the Treaty will strike the balance among nuclear incentives and disincentives for itself, and assess the consequences of the Treaty from its own peculiar perspective. This will be a difficult political task, in particular for such non-nuclear-weapon states as West Germany, Japan, India and Israel, which are faced with major security problems and already possess technological capabilities to seek nuclear solutions. But no decision by any government regarding the Non-Proliferation Treaty can be taken in isolation. As with a decision to acquire nuclear weapons, a decision to accept or reject the Treaty might well have a chain reaction effect. Assessment of the consequences of the Treaty by any particular state, therefore, should be made with the general implications of the Treaty firmly in mind.

The Non-Proliferation Treaty implies that nuclear weapons will remain under the exclusive control of the present five nuclear-weapon states for the indefinite future. The Treaty is intended to prohibit any sixth state from acquiring nuclear weapons and forecloses the possibility of transfering nuclear weapons to multilateral structures, even though no increase would occur in the number of powers in the global system having control of nuclear weapons.

The Non-Proliferation Treaty leaves the freedom of action of nuclear-weapon states relatively untouched. But along with this freedom come serious responsibilities. The nuclear-weapon parties to the Treaty, in particular the United States and the Soviet Union, will have to control their development, procurement and deployment of nuclear armaments if they expect the non-nuclear-weapon parties to continue to abide by their pledge of nuclear weapons abstinence. At the same time, the nuclear-weapon parties will have to make the system of security assurances credible both to the non-nuclear-weapon beneficiaries and to all potential nuclear-weapon aggressors. How the United States and the Soviet Union can resolve the long-term contradiction between simultaneous calls for nuclear disarmament and for effective security assurances against China's growing nuclear threat is by no means clear. What is clear, however, is that the superpowers cannot avoid shared responsibility for effecting such a resolution.

Brandt to the Bundestag, Apr. 27, 1967, News from the German Embassy, May 5, 1967, at 1-8; DOCUMENTS ON DISARMAMENT, 1967, at 206-07.

1516

Nuclear Weapons

Nuclear weapons will remain contained within the existing international structure for only a limited period of time. A question of fundamental importance is whether new solutions embracing necessary structural change can be found or will emerge during the period in which the rule of nuclear weapons containment established by the Treaty lasts. Perhaps the greatest risk related to the Treaty is that the search for new forms will be unsuccessful. Having maintained the status quo against increasing pressures, if the Treaty structure then breaks down, the ensuing instabilities could be more severe and dangerous than if the natural course of nuclear weapons proliferation had not been interrupted. This does not mean that the risks inherent in the Treaty outweigh the risks without the Treaty, but it highlights the need for receptivity to structural innovation in the international system in the critical interim period.

While the Treaty confirms the status quo regarding nuclear weapons, it looks forward to change concerning the peaceful uses of nuclear energy. Under the Treaty, civil nuclear industries throughout the world, except in the Soviet Union, will be open to international inspection. Non-nuclear-weapon states will come to rely mainly on an international system of accountability for assurance against nuclear weapons manufacture in other non-nuclear-weapon states. A new multilateral decision-making framework for peaceful application of nuclear explosives is established.

The provisions concerning the application of safeguards and the range of international nuclear transactions permitted when a nuclear-weapon state is the recipient are, however, more discriminatory than they need be. Civil nuclear industries within states and nuclear commerce between states should be placed on the same footing throughout the world as soon as possible. The exclusions presently in the Treaty with respect to these matters may be justified as expedients to obtain its initial acceptance, but the question whether such exclusions ought to continue should be placed high on the agenda of the first review conference under the Treaty.

We look forward to a world in which plutonium will be available in very large quantities in all industrially advanced states and in many developing states.[161] Safeguards on peaceful nuclear activities will at most serve to flash a red warning light if this material is diverted from

---

161. For an excellent description and analysis, see Gilinsky, Fast Breeder Reactors and the Spread of Plutonium, RAND Memorandum RM-5148-PR (1967).

The Yale Law Journal   Vol. 77: 1447, 1968

peaceful uses.[162] There is nothing that safeguards alone can do to prevent diversion from occurring once a non-nuclear-weapon state decides to embark on a nuclear weapons program. Thus, safeguards are but a part of, not a complete response to, the challenge to the international system presented by continuing peaceful nuclear innovation.[163] Here again, an adequate response to nuclear energy will require further structural innovation in the international political system.[164]

---

162. There is not even a clear red light in the safeguards system. If a state was bent on diverting nuclear material from a safeguarded nuclear facility, the only signal the international inspectorate could count on receiving would be a series of yellow warning lights as a result of statements by the host state that inspection would be inconvenient.

Concerning sanctions, the IAEA Board of Governors has not ventured beyond references to the relevant statutory provisions in its development of a system of Agency safeguards. Article XII, paragraph C, sets forth procedures to be followed in the event of non-compliance. These include: a report by the inspectors to the Director General; the transmittal of the report by the Director General to the Board of Governors; a call upon the state concerned to remedy the situation if non-compliance is found by the Board; a report by the Board to the members of IAEA and to the U.N. Security Council and General Assembly; and the Board's decision to curtail or suspend assistance in event of failure of the state concerned to take "fully corrective action within a reasonable time," or to call for the return of materials and equipment made available. Provision is also made for suspension of the non-complying state from membership in the IAEA. For discussion, see Szasz, *The Law of International Atomic Energy Agency Safeguards*, 3 REV. BELGE DE DROIT INT'L 196, 220-23 (1967).

163. One observer has concluded: "The proposed nonproliferation treaty must be judged primarily for its effect on the growing threat of a worldwide diffusion of plutonium. If it reinforces the false security of the safeguards system by persuading the legalists that no country which has signed is ever capable of building nuclear weapons, it will do a grave disservice to the cause of nonproliferation. . . . [U]nder the placid rule of safeguards as they are now understood, the plutonium will spread far and wide. When the collapse comes, no one will remember how easy it might have been to hold a narrow ring." Beaton, *Nuclear Fuel-For-All*, 45 FOREIGN AFFAIRS 662, 669 (1967). However, holding "a narrow ring" based on international ownership and processing control in addition to safeguards accountability control over plutonium, as Beaton suggests, does not seem to be a solution easily achieved either.

It has also been suggested that detailed studies will reveal that: "There is some optimum way for the elements of nuclear energy systems to be distributed throughout the world. If facilities are collected together into too small a number of "closed fuel cycle" systems, then unattainable surveillance accuracies are likely to be required to detect diversion from a single facility at levels that correspond potentially to many nuclear explosives. At the other extreme, however, nuclear facilities might be so widely dispersed that high surveillance accuracies and effective physical security measures become too costly, and the possibility of open, armed theft of enough material to produce a few nuclear explosives for criminal purposes could become intolerably large." Taylor, *The Rapid Growth of Nuclear Technology-Implication for Nuclear Safeguards*, INT'L RESEARCH & TECHNOLOGY J., Jan. 1, 1968, at 16. The problem with such a suggestion is that economic and political forces will probably cut in a different direction and the result will not approximate the optimum from the safeguards standpoint.

164. As the availability of plutonium increases, the threat will become as much a problem of internal as external security. Recently a United States contractor operating a fuel fabrication plant reported losses in excess of 100 kilograms of uranium-235 over a period of years. Address by John T. Conway, Executive Director, Joint Committee on Atomic Energy, to 7th Annual Meeting, Institute of Nuclear Materials Management, June 14, 1966. This triggered the convening of an outside review panel, the establishment of a new Office of Safeguards and Materials Management within the AEC, A.E.C. Press Release No. K-108, May 3, 1967, and the stationing of a resident AEC inspector at four private facilities in the United States which process significant quantities of fissionable material. A.E.C. Press Release No. K-121, May 12, 1967.

Nuclear Weapons

Einstein once said: "The unleashed power of the atom has changed everything save our modes of thinking, and thus we drift to unparalleled catastrophe." The Non-Proliferation Treaty could give us some additional time to change our modes of thinking.

[4]
The Future of the NPT

John Simpson

Futurology is at best a risky occupation. It usually involves discriminating between those elements of the present (and in some cases the past) which will remain relevant and those which will suddenly or slowly lose salience, as well as identifying new and relevant developments. In the case of the Treaty on the Nonproliferation of Nuclear Weapons (NPT), it is made more difficult because assessments of its future appear to revolve around both the significance of the diplomatic activities associated with it and evolving national and international security threats.

If the starting point for any assessment is to be the past and present, then there can be little doubt that the situation with respect to the proliferation of nuclear weapons today is better than in the 1970s when the NPT came into force. To take just one example, a little-known Hudson Institute study published in 1976 on trends in nuclear proliferation over the period through to 1995 offered a number of proliferation trajectories involving from nine to thirty additional states acquiring nuclear weapons.[1] This did not happen. India and Pakistan declared themselves to be nuclear weapon states (NWS) in 1998; observers confidently claim that Israel has had nuclear weapons for some decades; the Democratic People's Republic of Korea (DPRK) has tested a nuclear device and claims to have a weapon; and Iran is believed by many to have a nuclear weapon program several years away from fruition. All other states which were of proliferation concern in the 1970s (and in several cases are known to have had active nuclear weapon programs) are now nonnuclear weapon state (NNWS) parties to the NPT.

The core issue for the future is thus no longer whether the NPT can be made universal. It is whether the impact on the treaty of the actions of the three states which have never been members, one actual renegade, and one potential renegade can be contained and minimized. At the same time, the treaty has become a victim of both the changed international security environment and its near universality. The threat of nuclear war has been removed from many regions, often accompanied by the creation of nuclear weapon–free zones (NWFZs), thus reducing the apparent and immediate salience of the treaty. The reduction in nuclear stockpiles and 9/11 have stilled the former apocalyptic visions of the end of humankind resulting from interstate and intercontinental nuclear warfare and replaced them by a rise in concerns about individual acts of nuclear terrorism. Thus it is the sense of decreased relevance, if not apathy, toward the NPT which threatens its long-term survival as well as obvious and direct actions by a very few states both inside and outside of the treaty which run counter to its norms.

What Is the NPT?

The Treaty on the Nonproliferation of Nuclear Weapons is just that: *a treaty.* It does not create any administrative structures or integral enforcement mechanisms to support it. Its role is to offer an opportunity for states that do not possess nuclear weapons to make legally binding commitments to remain permanently in that state. They also have to accept International Atomic Energy Agency (IAEA) safeguards over the nuclear materials within their jurisdiction, thus providing assurances to their neighbors that they are not diverting such materials to nondeclared purposes (i.e., nuclear weapons). As no other legal instruments, except those creating regional NWFZ treaties, do this, the NPT is often characterized as the "cornerstone" of the nuclear nonproliferation regime.

This regime is much broader in scope than the NPT and comprises a wide range of legal and political instruments. Its other treaties and arrangements fall into four categories. First there are those treaties which prevent nuclear explosive testing and thus make the development of nuclear weapons by a proliferating state more difficult.[2] Second, there are the NWFZ treaties, which prohibit the development, manufacture, deployment, and stationing of nuclear weapons on the territories of zonal states.[3] Third, there are a series of more informal and exclusive export control guidelines and other arrangements among technology holders aimed at constraining the ability of a proliferating state to make and deliver its own nuclear weapons.[4] Finally, there are the arrangements which together loosely comprise the mechanisms for the global governance of nuclear energy. These center on the IAEA. At their heart is a system to provide assurances that states are not diverting nuclear materials from declared locations. The IAEA also manages mechanisms for monitoring and standard setting in areas such as radiological material and the physical safety and security of nuclear transport and facilities.[5]

Given the wide-ranging and multifaceted nature of the nuclear nonproliferation regime, its relationship to the NPT is both philosophical and practical. The treaty acts as its normative underpinnings and its standard-setting legal instrument. As such it is integral to the regime, as many actions taken through the regime are legitimized by the prohibitions accepted by states through the treaty. In addition, meetings of the NPT parties to review its implementation are arguably the only international forum capable of examining the operations of the regime, identifying its limitations, and discussing methods for strengthening it. Yet many elements of the regime existed prior to the NPT or were not created to implement it. The obvious exception to this is the new form of IAEA safeguards created in 1972 for NNWS party to the NPT.[6]

What then are the core norms on which the NPT is based? What are the rules for international behavior that were negotiated through the text of the treaty? The core norm arises from the proposition that nuclear weapon use is unacceptable to the international community. It followed logically from this that the only future world where nonuse could be guaranteed absolutely was one where nuclear weapons no longer existed. However, when negotiations started in 1966 on the NPT, there was no practical option but to accept that the disarmament of the five existing nuclear weapon states was unlikely in the immediate future. The treaty text was therefore structured around two categories of states with differing commitments: NWS and NNWS. The implicit rules generated by this discriminatory structure were that the NNWS would remain disarmed; no additional states would become NWS; and over an undefined period of time the existing NWS would disarm. Moreover, the armament of others did not justify breaking legal commitments to remain disarmed. Indeed in 1995 the South African government, which in that year played a crucial role in advocating that the NPT should have an indefinite duration, based its position on parallels between human rights norms and nuclear nonproliferation. In both cases, its representatives argued, the absolute norms involved could not be conditioned, time-limited, or bargained over in any way.

A second normative assumption was of a somewhat different nature: that economic development was an "inalienable" right of all states, especially the less well developed ones. It therefore followed that a similar right must exist in the area of peaceful uses of nuclear energy for both parties and nonparties to the treaty. Unfortunately, although technical distinctions could be made between those nuclear materials ideal for making nuclear weapons and those less appropriate for this task, the technology and processes used to produce key weapon materials, namely fuel reprocessing and uranium enrichment, also formed part of peaceful fuel cycles. The NPT solutions were to condition the inalienable rights of those NNWS within the treaty by a voluntary legal commitment not to acquire nuclear weapons, and of those outside by a commitment that all nuclear exports to them from NPT parties should be under IAEA safeguards.[7] A more direct solution was that in 1974 a cartel of existing technology holders was formed, the Nuclear

Suppliers Group (NSG), which agreed informally to deny to other states those capabilities that could be used in weapon production.

Norms represent ideal forms of behavior. Using them as the basis for a treaty runs the risk that when adapting them to existing circumstances, the rules derived from them will contain unanticipated weaknesses. The NPT is no exception, especially as it is a framework treaty. Its most obvious shortcomings are the following:

- the treaty does not allow for the existence of any new NWS;
- there is no specific constraint on one NNWS party assisting another NNWS party to acquire nuclear explosive devices;
- the commitment to disarmament is much more opaque and nonspecific than that relating to nonproliferation (though neither is defined in detail in the treaty);
- the disarmament commitments contain no time frame, and what constitutes progress is also undefined; and
- the boundaries between peaceful and explosive development and use of nuclear energy are also undefined.

These lacunae offer opportunities for political arguments, which in turn reduce the possibilities of sustaining an underlying consensus about the treaty's security value and other virtues. They also form a permanent backdrop to any assessment of the future of the treaty.

Although the treaty text opened its parties to diplomatic frictions, it also resulted in the NPT having an indefinite duration as it offered no means for its members to collectively terminate it. Such an arrangement was discussed during the negotiation of the treaty. What eventually emerged was an arrangement for periodic reviews of the operations of the treaty and a requirement to give three months' notice for the withdrawal of individual states from the treaty.[8] Yet even this latter route is conditioned by the need to specify the "extraordinary events, related to the subject matter of this treaty, [which] have jeopardized the supreme interests of its country." As a consequence, it is difficult to conceive of how the NPT would "collapse" or "implode" in a very visible manner, or how it would ever be removed from the UN list of active treaties, even if some extremely traumatic event were to occur.

Instead, what seems most likely is a path between two extremes. One is that total nuclear disarmament will occur, and it will become universalized, or more probably supplanted by a global nuclear disarmament treaty.[9] The second is that the world will incrementally become a nuclear proliferated one, and the relevance and utility of the norms underlying the treaty and its utility as a yardstick for action will erode, as will the effectiveness of the nuclear nonproliferation regime it underpins.

To explore the drivers which will determine where on a spectrum between these two extremes the future of the NPT will fall, the commitments contained in the NPT and some of the controversies and frictions that have arisen out of the structural weaknesses identified above during its four decades of existence are first examined. The two polar alternatives or "ideal types" of nuclear future and how they might emerge are then discussed. Finally, a view is offered on the characteristics of the development path that now appears most likely.

The Commitments Contained in the NPT

As the basic purpose of the NPT was a discriminatory one—preventing the dissemination and proliferation of nuclear weapons to additional states—it was recognized from the beginning that it was unlikely to be sustained indefinitely unless visible movement occurred toward an end state of nuclear disarmament. As a consequence, the treaty text contained three specific rules:

- the NWS should seek to disarm in the medium to long term (i.e., to give an "unequivocal commitment" to do so)[10];
- all NNWS had the right to engage in the development and use of nuclear energy for peaceful purposes if they accepted IAEA safeguards over all the nuclear materials within their jurisdiction; and
- NWS were prohibited from transferring complete nuclear weapons to any other state, while NNWS were not to attempt to make them or accept assistance from a NWS to do so.

To implement these three rules, the NPT contains a series of legal commitments written in the form of a preamble and eleven short articles. While its structure recognized the existence of NWS, it did not positively legitimize their indefinite existence. However, their numbers were limited legally by defining a NWS in Article IX.3 as "one which has manufactured and exploded a nuclear weapon or other nuclear explosive device prior to 1 January 1967." To have done otherwise would have implied the inevitability of proliferation and undermined any hope of the treaty becoming universal in its membership.

Two types of undertaking were accepted by NWS parties to the treaty. One was not to transfer nuclear weapons or nuclear explosive devices to "any recipient whatsoever," including other NWS and nonstate entities, "directly or indirectly" (Article I). Given its similarity to U.S. domestic legislation, the intention appears to have been that this should be interpreted as covering only complete nuclear weapons, while "indirect" transfer of these weapons meant transfers via third parties.[11] The second type of undertaking was not to "assist, encourage or induce"

50   John Simpson

any NNWS to "manufacture or otherwise acquire" nuclear weapons or explosive devices or acquire "control" over them. However, "assisting" activity remained permissible between NWS (e.g., between the United States and the United Kingdom). Finally, during U.S. legislative hearings on ratification of the treaty, Article I was interpreted by administration officials as permitting NATO states to procure delivery systems intended to carry U.S. nuclear weapons in time of major hostilities, as well as planning for their use, an activity known as "nuclear sharing." The argument was that if such hostilities were to occur, the treaty would no longer be applicable and that it was one where "what was not specifically forbidden was permitted."[12]

Article II prescribed the commitments of NNWS. These parties were not to receive transfers of nuclear weapons or explosive devices from any source; not to seek or receive assistance in manufacturing such weapons or devices; and not to manufacture them indigenously. What the treaty did not specifically address, however, was the case of a NNWS which assisted another NNWS in manufacturing nuclear weapons: at the time it was assumed by most states that this was not possible.

Article III.1 and III.4 committed NNWS parties to accept IAEA "safeguards" and to negotiate and conclude a suitable agreement with the agency to verify "the fulfillment of its obligations assumed under [the NPT] with a view to preventing diversion of nuclear energy from peaceful uses to nuclear weapons or other nuclear explosive devices." The initial safeguards agreement of June 1972 between the IAEA and a state party to the NPT (INFCIRC/153) focused narrowly on diversion of nuclear material from declared facilities and not on the wider task of verifying "the fulfillment of [an NNWS's] obligations under the NPT."

The remaining articles of the treaty applied to all states parties. Article III.2 and III.3 addressed the conditions to be applied by an NPT state party in its nuclear trading activities. The key conditions were that transfers had to be subject to "the safeguards required by this Article" and were to comply with Article IV. Many states believed these safeguards to be NPT or INFCIRC/153 safeguards on all of a state's nuclear materials. A minority held that they should only apply to the artifact or material being transferred. In addition, since 1997 and the advent of the Additional Protocol (AP) to INFCIRC/153 (INFCIRC/540), there have effectively been two versions of NPT safeguards, known as comprehensive (153) and integrated (153 plus 540).

Article IV.1 states that "Nothing in this Treaty shall be interpreted as affecting the inalienable right of all parties to the Treaty to develop research, production and use of nuclear energy for peaceful purposes without discrimination." It then adds the phrase "and in conformity with Articles I and II of this Treaty." This implies that all NNWS parties accept voluntarily that the right is not inalienable nor without discrimination, as it has been conditioned by this last phrase.[13] States parties can therefore refuse to assist others if they believe their assistance with a state's "peaceful" activities would be diverted to military uses.

The final substantive article is Article VI. This commits all parties to "pursue negotiations in good faith on effective measures relating to cessation of the nuclear arms race at an early date and to nuclear disarmament, and on a treaty on general and complete disarmament under strict and effective international control." Three aspects are worthy of note. One is that the article applies to all state parties, not just the NWS. The second is that from the entry into force of the treaty, disagreements have existed over the implications of the positioning of the comma in the sentence, and whether this means that cessation of the nuclear arms race and nuclear disarmament should precede, and be independent of, general and complete disarmament,[14] or occur in parallel to, and be dependent on, it.[15] A third aspect is that in 1996 the commitment to negotiate was interpreted in an advisory opinion of the International Court of Justice (ICJ) as implying that this meant not only engaging in negotiations but also completing them.[16]

Article V, concerning peaceful nuclear explosions, has never been operative. Equally, Article VII is a permissive statement that the treaty does not affect the right of states to make regional NWFZ agreements. The remaining four articles are procedural, though some do have substantive implications.

Article VIII covers two distinct issues. Paragraphs 1 and 2 relate to the procedure for amending the treaty. This has always been regarded as unworkable in practice.[17] Paragraph 3 deals with a completely different issue: the holding of a conference every five years to review the operations of the treaty.[18] Articles IX and XI deal with signature, ratification, deposition, and entry into force. Finally, Article X deals with two separate and distinct issues. Paragraph 1 lays out the process for withdrawal from the treaty, based on the wording found in the PTBT of 1963.[19] Paragraph 2 sets out the process whereby twenty-five years after the entry into force of the treaty (i.e., 1995) a decision could be taken on the further extension of the treaty.[20]

Also noteworthy are several issues not covered by the NPT text. The first is its lack of any mechanism or procedure for addressing noncompliance. It has often been tacitly assumed that for Articles II and III, this will be handled by the UN Security Council (UNSC) via the IAEA safeguards system, the agency's board of governors, and Articles II.B.4 and Article XII of its Statute. Until the early 1990s IAEA safeguards focused narrowly on declared fissile material accountancy and ignored the issue of weaponization. Indeed, the issue of whether it has the authority to address this remains controversial within the Agency, even though this is banned by the NPT.[21] For other articles, there is no specified or obvious route to handle noncompliance.

The second issue is that the treaty has no permanent secretariat or other organizational structure: its only monitoring or deliberating body is a conference of treaty parties to review its operations every five years. The text gives no indication of how these conferences are to be organized and what powers they should have. A third issue is that during the negotiations attempts were made to build into the treaty commitments by the NWS not to use nuclear weapons against NNWS party to the NPT and to assist those who were attacked with such weapons. These commitments were seen as a "halfway house" toward nuclear disarmament. In the end such commitments were omitted from the treaty, though the three depositary states did provide limited commitments of this type through unilateral statements and UNSC resolutions.[22]

Finally, the preamble to the treaty has significance in indicating what the objectives of its architects were. In particular it appears to give priority in disarmament to the "cessation of the nuclear arms race" and the undertaking of "effective measures in the direction of nuclear disarmament." It also recognizes the need to "achieve the discontinuance of all test explosions of nuclear weapons for all time and to continue negotiations to this end." Moreover, it suggests that the "easing of international tension and the strengthening of trust" is necessary in order to pursue a treaty on general and complete disarmament. This process would include measures to halt the manufacturing of nuclear weapons, their stockpiling, and the elimination of nuclear weapons and their means of delivery from national arsenals.

The text of the preamble also has significance in indicating the central role that has been played in discussions at NPT review conferences by the need to achieve a comprehensive test-ban treaty (CTBT) (and the pre-1970 vision that this was the necessary first step toward nuclear disarmament). The preamble also suggests that the end of the nuclear arms race (which in 1968 was clearly interpreted as the U.S.-USSR process of competitive arming) and a process of nuclear disarmament would precede an end state of nuclear disarmament. The latter would encompass manufacture, stocks, and delivery systems and be negotiated in the context of a broader process of WMD and conventional disarmament.

The NPT Review Process as a Guide to the Future of the NPT

The only public forums offering indicators of the successes, failures, and possible futures of the NPT are the NPT review conferences held every five years to assure that "the purposes of the Preamble and the provisions of the Treaty are being realized."[23] However, the way that these conferences have been organized has in itself become an intervening variable for those seeking to use them to make such judgments. The obvious criterion for judging their success, and thus that of the NPT, is a consensus report or Final Document (i.e., one to which no state present objects). Yet this is inherently difficult to achieve: failure is a much more probable outcome. As a result, the strength of any causal link between the visible outcomes of such conferences and the degree of success or failure of the treaty in assuring "the realization of (its) purposes" appears profoundly opaque. This is illustrated by a brief history of these events.

The first NPT review conference in March 1975 divided the articles of the treaty between two main committees for detailed scrutiny. The reports from the committees were to be sent to a drafting committee for consolidation into a single text, called the Final Declaration, to be agreed to by consensus. In practice, consensus through this route proved impossible to achieve, largely because of disagreements over language on a CTBT. The Swedish president of the conference then circulated her own draft and forced it through the final plenary, thus offering the appearance of a successful review.[24]

In 1980 similar disagreements over a CTBT and disarmament occurred, but the Iraqi president was unable to rescue the incomplete report or present an alternative document.[25] In 1985, under an Egyptian president, the structure of the meeting changed, with the number of Main Committees increasing from two to three. This conference did agree to a Final Document by consensus, even though it incorporated differing views in a key passage on a CTBT.[26] In 1990, under a Peruvian president, lack of movement on disarmament and a CTBT could not be circumvented as had happened in 1985, and no Final Declaration emerged.[27]

In 1995, the fifth NPT review conference was merged with the conference "to decide whether the Treaty shall continue in force indefinitely, or shall be extended for an additional fixed period or periods."[28] This choice was narrowed down to an indefinite extension and one for an indefinite number of fixed periods, with the former eventually winning the day. However, a consensus decision on this necessitated the production of three decision documents, followed by the passing of a resolution on the Middle East. The legal implication of this procedure and the linkage, if any, between the three decisions remain open questions.[29] So too does the significance and status of the resolution on the Middle East, without which the consensus decision on the extension might not have been possible politically.[30] This resolution was a procedural first for the NPT review process. It was cosponsored by the United States, and although Israel was not named, the resolution was clearly intended to pressure it to accept IAEA safeguards (and the cosponsorship gave hope to some that the United States would do this).

The 1995 decisions changed the existing NPT review process significantly. The five-yearly conferences were made permanent; ten-day sessions of the Preparatory Committee (PrepCom) of a review conference were to be held in the three years preceding a conference to discuss matters of substance in a systematic manner; and the committee was to make substantive recommendations to its review conference, as well as the more traditional procedural ones.[31] However, the United States was insistent that the annual PrepCom sessions were not meetings of the parties and had no decision-making powers other than to make recommendations to review conferences. The first PrepCom session under the new arrangements was structured similarly to the review conferences, with three sets of "cluster" discussions and an aim of producing some type of rolling text and a compendium of national proposals.[32] These latter exercises collapsed at the end of the 1998 session, and in 1999 no recommendations were sent to the review conference.[33]

The 2000 NPT review conference occurred in what many regarded as a set of very negative internal and external contexts for the treaty: the chances of achieving a consensus outcome appeared near zero. Yet this proved to be the only NPT review conference which produced a genuine "consensus" Final Document out of the work of the main committees. It also appeared to build on, and define in greater detail, the "objectives" set for states parties in 1995. In addition, text was agreed to that removed from the first two annual PrepCom sessions in a cycle the need for a negotiated outcome, with a "factual summary" of the proceedings for transmission to the next session being substituted.[34] As a consequence, the next review cycle started in a relatively harmonious manner.[35] In 2004, however, no substantive recommendations were sent to the review conference, nor was there any agreement on key procedural issues such as its agenda and program of work.

These latter disagreements arose from two interlinked issues: the status and thus significance of the commitments entered into in 1995 and the nonfulfillment of certain of the disarmament pledges made in 2000.[36] The disagreements also raised a more practical question: was the review process "fit for purpose"? Were its specific products supposed to advance those of previous ones in an incremental manner, or was all that could be expected political commitments applicable over the next five years? Some among the NAM (Nonaligned Movement) leadership regarded all future agreements as conditioned by the 1995 extension decision and its linked documents and the 2000 Final Document. In contrast, some of the NWS only accepted that it was the commitments made in 1995 that were indefinite in nature, due to their links to the legally mandated extension decision. Those made in 2000 were seen to have a lesser status, and thus open to change in 2005. The consequence of this and other procedural disagreements was that the conference took more than half of its allotted time to agree on its agenda and program of work, leaving the main committees with no time to complete their tasks—even without the alleged desire of some parties to have a no-consensus outcome.[37]

Outside observers imputed from this situation, and particularly from the lack of a consensus outcome to the conference, that the NPT and the nonproliferation regime were in deep trouble. Indeed some went on to argue that if no Final Document was agreed to at the next review conference in 2010, the demise of the NPT might be at hand. Yet based on its past record and the tasks that have been asked of it, what is usually defined as a "successful" outcome of an NPT review conference is intrinsically unlikely, and the 2000 outcome was probably the result of a unique and unrepeatable set of circumstances.

In the absence of any alternative highly visible internal method of gauging the strength or weakness of the NPT and the nuclear nonproliferation regime, it seems likely the single criterion of the outcome of NPT meetings will continue to be used by the media and those with no direct involvement in the review process as their sole method of evaluating the future of the NPT. Yet while a failure to agree on a Final Document clearly indicates that states parties did not give priority to any common interest in sending a message to the outside world that the "purposes" of the treaty were being assured in 2005, it is at best a problematic indicator of whether international support for the treaty remains strong. But if outcomes of the NPT review process do not offer a clear indicator of the NPT's future, what does?

Alternative Criteria for Assessing the Future of the NPT

Given the opaque and possibly noncausal connections between events in the NPT review process and support for, and engagement with, the treaty, events outside of this process may be where indicators of the NPT's future should be sought, rather than within the treaty's own evaluative mechanism. Four distinct issue areas can be identified here:

- accession of additional states to the treaty, or withdrawal of states from the treaty, and how the treaty mechanisms respond to such withdrawals;
- whether the treaty arrangements can facilitate effective responses to noncompliance with its norms and rules by both member and nonmember states;
- the relevance of the treaty text, and the commitments within it, to evolving perceptions of proliferation threats, particularly after 9/11; and
- explosions of a nuclear weapon or improvised nuclear explosive device.

A. NPT Accessions and Withdrawals

i. Accessions. The NPT is the multilateral arms control treaty with the greatest number of adherents. This has, however, generated perceptions of both strength and weakness. On the one hand, its near universality gives its rules a status similar to customary international law. On the other, the number and significance of recent ratifications or accession can no longer be used as a yardstick of growing support and strength. It is highly unlikely that India, Israel, and Pakistan will join the treaty in the near future. The situation of the remaining possible new entrant, the DPRK, is uncertain. As a consequence, proliferation can now only occur from within the treaty, and logically the only available vector for the treaty appears to be one of it becoming less universal.

When in 1998 first India and then Pakistan engaged in nuclear explosive testing, this resulted in claims that the NPT was no longer relevant, even though both states were not parties to it. In taking this action they destroyed an existing tacit international rule, namely that states outside the treaty would continue to be regarded and treated as NNWS so long as they did not test. This meant that they could evade international sanctions. Before 1993 at least six states fell into this "opaque" category (Argentina, Brazil, India, Israel, Pakistan, and South Africa), but the proliferation situation appeared relatively stable and the NPT effective.

After 1998 this situation changed permanently. The positive impact of the accessions by Argentina, Brazil, and South Africa was overshadowed by the negative effects of the actions of India and Pakistan in testing and declaring themselves to be NWS. There were several reasons for this effect. One was that some foreign ministries had persuaded their governments to agree to become members of the NPT on the grounds that this would prevent further proliferation. A second reason was that the actions of India and Pakistan meant that the text of the NPT could no longer address the situation of these two states. On the one hand, the chances they would enter the NPT as NNWS appeared increasingly remote. On the other, Article IX.3 clearly stated that only states which had exploded a nuclear device prior to the end of 1966 could enter the treaty as NWS. India and Pakistan did not qualify. As in practice the treaty could not be amended, it was impossible for them to engage formally with the NPT in future. Not only did universality of the treaty appear to be out of the question: the consequences of their proliferation could only be handled outside of the treaty context. Thus not only did the NPT appear to have become irrelevant to the situation of these two states, but one of its core rules, nonproliferation, had been ignored by them. Moreover, it had been demonstrated that there existed no treaty mechanism for handling proliferation by nonparties who broke the tacit "nondeclaration" rule.

This situation seems unlikely to improve if states such as the United States, Russia, and China continue to remove nuclear trading constraints imposed on India and Pakistan in 1998 and take actions that gradually recognize their declared nuclear weapon status. The 2005 U.S.-India civil nuclear assistance agreement is a case in point.[38] The situation generates discontent in states within the treaty that see themselves as obtaining no reward for their good behavior, unlike the noncompliant outsiders.

The case of Israel is different, though its effects on the treaty are just as profound. Israel has not declared itself to be a nuclear weapon state and thus does not challenge the basic structure of the NPT. However, the belief among Arab states that Israel has nuclear weapons, and the refusal of the United States to acknowledge this and act on it has both regional and global consequences. The regional consequence is to reduce the relevance and value of the NPT as a nonproliferation mechanism in the eyes of Arab states. It also stimulates them to use the treaty review process as a means of pressuring the United States over Israel's nuclear potential through pressure to implement the 1995 Resolution on the Middle East. The global consequences have been to make the Middle East "regional question" an increasingly significant factor blocking consensus at NPT review conferences. It is a reason also for the Arab states not to engage in chemical and biological disarmament and for internal pressures to arise demanding withdrawal from the NPT.

Overall, the NPT is therefore confronting a structural situation over membership destined to get worse, rather than better, over time. India and Pakistan appear unlikely to roll back their nuclear weapons other than through a global disarmament agreement superseding the NPT. In theory Israel could enter the NPT as a nonnuclear weapon state if it took the route to enter used by South Africa in the early 1990s: disarm first and then accede to the treaty. However, as Israel argues that it will only agree to a regional NWFZ if a political solution is found to the region's frictions, and the Arab states argue equally vehemently that it has to enter a NWFZ before a political solution is possible, its entry appears blocked indefinitely.

ii. Withdrawals. As discussed earlier, while there is no mechanism for collective withdrawal from the NPT, there is one for individual withdrawal. What, then, are the likely forms this would take? It has been suggested that three are available: breaking out, crawling out, and walking out, while the current DPRK case offers a fourth category.[39]

a. Breakouts. In a breakout, a state in good standing has acquired all the necessary capabilities to both make and deliver a nuclear device and has sufficient stockpiled fissile material to move from zero nuclear weapons to tens immediately on reaching the end of its three months' notice period for withdrawal. Having the ability to act in this way has been characterized as being a latent or virtual proliferator. It is unclear how many states are currently in this position. However, advances in the general state of technology, the operation of clandestine state and nonstate procurement networks such as that fashioned by A. Q. Khan, and the projected revival of nuclear power reactor building and operations on a global scale suggest that their numbers will inexorably increase.

Two developments feed into this scenario. The threat of nuclear terrorism is generating a conflict between the commitments contained in the NPT and the knowledge NNWS may regard as essential for creating effective response mechanisms. Where should the line now be drawn between the injunction in Article II to "not otherwise acquire nuclear weapons or other nuclear explosive devices" and such defensive nuclear research? Secondly, many nuclear technologies are inherently dual use in nature, and the inherent technical barriers to nuclear proliferation at the core of the IAEA safeguards mechanisms are degrading. The diffusion of centrifuge enrichment technology for civil purposes is shortening the time between the availability of hard evidence of a state's intention to proliferate and the movement of a proliferating state to an irreversible breakout situation. In some cases, the political "warning time" may now be too short for coercive political (and military?) action to be mobilized to prevent it. Future nonproliferation policies may thus have to be based on noncorroborated intelligence or changes in the rules concerning legitimate and illegitimate fuel cycle activities. This situation is itself closely linked to the second type of withdrawal, crawling out.

b. Crawl-outs. Crawling out implies that states are engaged in a purposeful process to give them an eventual ability to break out from the NPT. The weaponization element of this is likely to be clandestine and difficult to confirm with any certainty due to the dual-use technology involved. Missile or aircraft delivery activities are likely to be more visible but are not subject to international control through an inclusive regime. In addition, nuclear and conventional delivery may be distinguishable only from observation of the flight profiles used in training. Finally, the fissile material needed for weapons might be produced rapidly in bulk by manufacturing safeguarded low-enriched uranium suitable for power reactors and then further enriching it using the same basic technology.

Crawling-out is central to contemporary concerns over Iran's nuclear program. Moreover some in the United States would argue that the situation goes beyond an inability to deal with this specific case. They would argue that what is occurring is "dysfunctional multilateralism."[40] Not only is the NPT unable to prevent proliferation, but it actively assists it by providing a legal umbrella under which proliferators can take shelter while awaiting an opportune moment to proliferate. For over a number of years a "crawl-out state" could position itself to "break out" without being overtly noncompliant with either the NPT or its IAEA safeguards agreements. Only three methods of stopping this from happening appear feasible.

One is to change the rules of global nuclear power activity to ones similar to those envisaged for peaceful nuclear explosives in Article V of the NPT. This would give to a very few states the right to enrich uranium and separate plutonium from used fuel, accompanied by arrangements under which NPT parties would be guaranteed preferential access to nuclear fuel made from these materials. This would alleviate some current proliferation concerns, but it would also create a new form of discrimination and thus be difficult to agree to by consensus.

The second method would be to give the IAEA new powers of intrusive inspection within national territories, including the task of investigating nuclear weaponization in all its aspects. Again this appears unlikely to gain consensus support. Finally there appears to be the option of military action against the key facilities involved once notice of withdrawal from the NPT has been given, something which would be contrary to international law unless the UNSC were to specifically authorize it.

c. Walkouts. In a walkout a state would withdraw from the treaty but would not make any overt attempt to develop a nuclear weapons program. It might be seen symbolically as the ultimate form of protest at the inability of the NPT to address modern proliferation problems. There have been only two cases of walkouts in the history of the NPT—one was that of Taiwan, the province of China which withdrew from the NPT when the PRC took over its seat at the UN. The second was the DPRK, which from 1995 onward ceased to attend NPT meetings on the basis that it had "suspended" its withdrawal from the treaty leading up to the 1994 Framework Agreement and had never returned. Both of these cases were somewhat unique in their circumstances, however.

The type of walkout that might be envisaged is either a tacit or overt one. Tacit walkouts could be defined as situations where states did not participate in any active way in NPT activities. This form of walkout might be evaluated by the number of parties not participating in the NPT review process (although other intervening variables could explain their absence). An overt walkout seems most probable from one of the Arab states as a form of protest against the activities of Israel and the United States. What this might involve is an act of formal withdrawal citing the specific reasons, linked to a request to the IAEA to sustain its NPT safeguards arrangements to provide evidence that it did not intend to acquire nuclear weapons. However, the balance of probability is that few states would act in this way as they would lose the opportunities presented by the NPT review process for direct political action over their concerns.

d. The DPRK case. The activities of the DPRK, and responses to them, have generated a range of negative consequences for the NPT and the nonproliferation regime. It is the only state which has withdrawn from the treaty when in noncompliance; it is also the only one which has then proceeded to explode a nuclear device. It remains to be seen whether this activity was political or security oriented in nature, but it has generated disagreements over whether the DPRK should be treated as a state party in noncompliance with its NPT commitments or a state similar to India and Pakistan which is outside the treaty and has tested.

The situation is further confused by the DPRK not transmitting information on its withdrawal to all the relevant states listed in Article X. Some parties regard it as not having fulfilled the legal conditions for withdrawal and thus remaining a (noncompliant) member of the treaty. Others see it as having been in noncompliance in the past but now being a nonmember. Those taking the latter position appear to have no clear vision of how to respond in the NPT context to the DPRK's actions, other than to negotiate an agreement in the regional six-nation (China, DPRK, Japan, Russia, South Korea, United States) context. In practice, the issue which has driven policies toward the DPRK has been fear of triggering a WMD war on the Korean peninsula rather than any longer-term considerations of the impact of existing and future policies on the nuclear nonproliferation regime and the NPT. Since 1993 this has led negotiations and deal making with the DPRK to take precedence over upholding the NPT rules, first in the shape of the Agreed Framework of October 1994 and more recently the attempts to reach an agreement with the DPRK through the medium of the six-party talks.

It is highly improbable that the eventual outcome of these negotiations will not serve to further reduce the international credibility of the NPT norm and rules. It seems inevitable that it will create new divergences between the overt benefits offered to treaty members and nonmembers. Indeed Iran was not slow to argue in 1994 that even though it was a state in good standing with the NPT, the United States was attempting to prevent it from completing its nuclear power plants while the DPRK was being rewarded for its overt noncompliance with two nuclear reactors and supplies of fuel oil. Now, in similar circumstances, it can again argue that greater rewards are available to the DPRK from leaving the treaty rather than from remaining within it.

e. The Withdrawal Process. The DPRK case has drawn attention to the opaqueness and weaknesses of the existing withdrawal provisions in the treaty. First, Article X.1 allows a state to withdraw by giving three months' notice of its intentions to member states and the UNSC. Second, although the withdrawal clause states that the member has to specify the "extraordinary events" related to the subject matter of the treaty and the "supreme interests" of the withdrawing state that have triggered its action, no process or mechanism is prescribed for questioning such explanations. Indeed the DPRK has never made any attempt to offer a formal explanation on the two occasions it has given notice of withdrawal—and the UNSC has by default acquiesced to this situation.

Moreover, although a withdrawing state has to transmit its notice of withdrawal to all members of the treaty and of the UNSC, the treaty offers no guidance on any responses that might follow. While it is implicit in Article X.1 that the UNSC should act to try to prevent withdrawals, no clear guidance is offered on how this should be done. This was one of the reasons why in the DPRK case, in contrast to that of Iran, action was left to bilateral or six-party negotiations.

A significant number of states have found this situation increasingly unsatisfactory, and the European Union (EU) collectively sought to obtain agreement from the 2005 NPT review conference on a set of guidelines to handle future withdrawal cases.[41] However, Egypt and other states argued this placed additional and unjustified duties on them in the context of the treaty, and no agreement on this course of action was possible. No doubt further attempts will be made to move this matter forward in the 2007–10 review cycle, but it seems likely to continue to generate opposition from NAM states who see themselves as being asked by the developed states to accept added commitments with no apparent reciprocal action in return.

iii. Accessions and Withdrawals: Some Conclusions. If the NPT is to collapse, rather than just degrade in its effectiveness and significance for nuclear nonproliferation, a mass withdrawal of the parties through the Article X.1 route would be required. There are few indications at the moment of this happening. However, in the longer term the only movements related to its universality appear likely to be negative ones: withdrawals and cases of proliferation from within. On the one hand this is an indication of its success in facilitating states accepting its norms and rules. On the other, it suggests that the spotlight will be increasingly focused on the limitations of the NPT and the nuclear nonproliferation regime to address modern proliferation challenges.

One of these limitations is the ability of a state to facilitate proliferation while operating within the NPT and IAEA safeguards contexts or breaching their rules: in short, its dysfunctional multilateralist attributes. Another is its structural inability to address the existence of declared NWS outside the treaty, whose existence impacts negatively on progress in global nuclear disarmament and fulfillment of the treaty's Article VI commitments. It also has a disruptive effect through the "regional issues" such states generate. Finally, problems of recognition hinder effective engagement to persuade the DPRK, India, and Pakistan to accept the NPT rules for technology transfers and thus dissuade them from the types of nuclear-relevant trading activities that have occurred in the past between the DPRK, Pakistan, Iran, and Libya.

One further area of weakness that is now apparent is the lack of clear guidelines for the conditions under which states may withdraw from the treaty. While some want withdrawal to be regarded as unacceptable, others wish it to remain as easy as possible. The latter is in part a product of a move since 1998 from a situation where proliferation was latent and membership of the treaty was moving toward universality to the current situation of almost as many NWS existing outside the treaty as there are within it. In this new postproliferation world, two vectors are discernable: the desire to lock in the accession gains made by the treaty in the past by making withdrawal more difficult and the trend for others to seek to keep options open for the medium term. A similar situation existed in the decade after 1968 as states assessed whether membership of the NPT would gather momentum and nuclear weapon aspirations could safely be abandoned as a result of the belief that it would prove an effective method of preventing proliferation. In the current decade, the tide may again be on the turn, with decreased faith in the treaty leading to a desire on the part of some states to prevent withdrawal becoming more difficult.

B. Noncompliance with the NPT

The issue of noncompliance with the NPT can be approached from either a legal or political perspective. From a legal perspective compliance is an absolute commitment: from a political perspective, equity, reciprocity, and nondiscrimination often color perceptions. Moreover, the commitments in the NPT text differ somewhat in their nature. While Article I, II, and III commitments are absolute, those in Articles IV and VI are more opaque and thus open to different interpretations. While some states view the issue of noncompliance as being almost entirely about the "hard" Article II commitment not to acquire nuclear weapons, others argue that there is a similar commitment contained in Article VI and thus any moves to strengthen noncompliance mechanisms should cover Articles II, IV, and VI equally: nonproliferation, peaceful uses, and disarmament.

i. Article II Noncompliance. Until 1991 and the Iraq case, the issue of dealing with Article II noncompliance was latent. Iraq generated three sets of responses: its nuclear disarmament under far-reaching UNSC resolutions, changes to the scope of IAEA safeguards to facilitate detection of clandestine activities, and the negotiation of the Additional Protocol (AP) to give the agency enhanced investigative powers. This was followed swiftly by the first DPRK crisis. Agreement to implement IAEA safeguards on its territory led to the discovery that its initial declaration was inaccurate. The NPT verification system worked, but the UNSC proved incapable of dealing with the outcome, and the crisis had to be resolved through bilateral negotiations.

One consequence of these two cases was that through to 1991 the NPT Article II rules and norms appeared to have been largely upheld by both participating and nonparticipating states. After that point Iraq's activities demonstrated that sustaining a ban on WMD activities within a sovereign state was going to be extremely difficult. Moreover, even when a disarmament regime was imposed on a state that was more rigorous than the IAEA one, the diverging national interests of the permanent members of the UNSC would make it difficult to enforce. In addition, the rules of procedure of the NPT review system did not debar such a state from participating in decisions and blocking consensus, thus giving it a veto on wording critical of its actions. Indeed the 2000 Final Document was only possible because Iraq and its accusers could read the phrase "the importance of Iraq's full continuous cooperation and compliance with its obligations" as relating to both the past and the future[42]—and the DPRK was absent.

In the period 2002–6 a similar series of contrary trends existed. On the one hand the Iraq issue was resolved by regime change. Arguably this had the positive effect of triggering a decision by Libya to openly declare it had been engaged in nuclear proliferant activities though the A. Q. Khan network and engaging in a process of nuclear and other WMD disarmament.

On the other hand, the DPRK gave notice of its withdrawal from the treaty, reprocessed the fuel rods that had previously been under IAEA observation, and exploded a nuclear device. It was not until February 2007 that the six-party talks led to agreement on a series of step-by-step arrangements holding out some hope of the DPRK retreating to its previous nonnuclear weapon status.

Finally, Iran admitted to a number of clandestine activities dating back to the 1980s. It agreed to freeze its centrifuge enrichment program under arrangements negotiated with France, Germany, and the UK but then reversed that decision. The issue was eventually remitted to the UNSC, which imposed graduated sanctions with time limits for halting its enrichment activities.

All of these cases illuminate the limited ability and willingness of NPT parties to collectively respond to nonproliferation. The treaty has no integral provisions for dealing with noncompliance with Article II. Its review process was not tasked to do this; its text offers no clear or detailed definition of what constitutes noncompliance; and the process of dealing with this issue is external to the treaty. The consequence is that the NPT cannot be directly blamed for the inability of the international community to deal with Article II noncompliance cases, as it offers its parties no means to do so. At the same time it cannot be praised for its handling of those cases where noncompliant behavior has been reversed, except insofar as it has provided a legal basis for action.

ii. Article IV Noncompliance. This article is somewhat contradictory.[43] The consequence is that Iran has argued that the treaty gives it an unrestricted right to the peaceful use of nuclear energy, including enrichment and reprocessing technologies. The United States and many other states have argued that due to the close linkages between civil and military uses of these technologies, their transfer to, and indigenous production in, additional states such as Iran should be discouraged and preferably banned—even though this would be discriminatory.

Until the 1990s, the proliferation of technology was enforced through the informal Nuclear Suppliers Group (NSG). The NSG provided guidelines to adherents on what should and should not be exported. It also required them to exercise "particular caution" (i.e., nontransfer) over the trade in enrichment and reprocessing technology. This system of control was condemned by many NAM states as discriminatory, but justified by exporting states as a means of ensuring that they fulfilled their Article I and II responsibilities. By the mid-1990s, however, the NSG guidelines were being outflanked by the activities of A. Q. Khan's procurement network. Khan's network had been used initially to enable Pakistan to evade the NSG restrictions and was then used to supply enrichment technologies to Libya and Iran on an apparently commercial basis.

One consequence of A. Q. Khan's actions is that export constraints have to be deployed overtly. This has involved instruments such as voluntary freezes of limited duration and UNSC resolutions, as well as making Article IV the subject of considerable public friction and disagreement. Above all, it has changed what was previously a very effective covert method of preventing proliferation of these technologies into a situation where the achievement of this end is now problematic at best, and a near impossibility at worst.

Looking to the future, these issues are likely to become more controversial, rather than less, if global warming and energy shortages lead to a round of ordering of nuclear power plants similar to that which occurred in the first half of the 1970s, a situation which has been described as a "nuclear renaissance." Unless new rules are agreed on that enable this renaissance and national energy security to be based on the offer of "turnkey" contracts to guarantee the supply of fuel and reactors to new entrants and repatriate used fuel, it is difficult to see how a key assumption underpinning the NPT will not become increasingly questioned, namely that civil and military nuclear technologies can be clearly distinguished from each other, and the barriers between them sustained at a high level. Difficulties in sustaining the civil/military distinction may thus degrade belief in the future viability of the NPT norms and rules.

iii. Article VI Noncompliance. Many states parties view the issue of the NWS compliance with Article VI as of equal importance to the nonproliferation and peaceful use pillars of the treaty. Thus in NPT forums, any discussion of noncompliance with the treaty's nonproliferation provisions inevitably opens a discussion on noncompliance with its disarmament ones. At the same time the differing commitments are themselves discriminatory, in that the nonproliferation ones appear absolute, while the disarmament and peaceful uses ones are open to differing interpretations. In the disarmament area, the language addresses negotiations rather than rules and leaves open whether these negotiations are to be about ending the arms race and engaging in nuclear disarmament as isolated acts or as part of negotiations on the 1960s concept of general and complete disarmament. Until 1995, debates in the NPT review process on this issue tended to be accusatory rather than constructive. In 1995 a plan for disarmament action was agreed to, and in 2000 this plan was expanded into the thirteen practical steps. Although some of these steps involved negotiations, many did not, and the listing recognized that disarmament was going to a multifaceted, incremental, and prolonged process and that not all steps were applicable to any individual NWS. However, since not all the steps listed are now possible, it is profoundly unclear how objective judgments should and can be made in the future over compliance or noncompliance with Article VI. Also, it is unclear whether what was agreed to by states was a series of commitments to act or a number of yardsticks to measure progress toward disarmament.

iv. Responses to Noncompliance. The NPT text does not address the issue of how its parties should respond to noncompliance, however defined. In practice, responses have been very ad hoc, with the general rule being that a mixture of sticks and carrots have been employed. The carrots were very noticeable in the Libyan, DPRK, and Iran cases, in the form of economic assistance and a move away from pariah status. In the case of Iraq and Iran, military coercion was also threatened, and in the case of Iraq, it was executed. There seems little likelihood that in future there will be any form of more organized response process. However, responses which involve rewards will tend to lead to questioning by compliant parties if noncompliant behavior is seen to be generating greater rewards than the lesser benefits obtained from compliance.

Some argue that the NPT should have internal provisions to deal with noncompliance. Perceptions of the utility of the treaty are diminished when cases of noncompliance emerge and have to be addressed elsewhere. Evidence for this can be found in the attempts by Canada and other states to fill the "institutional deficit" they believe exists in this area with an executive committee or proposals to summon meetings of the parties to discuss such cases.[44] While it is unclear what advantages in practice such arrangements would have over the UNSC becoming seized of an allegation of noncompliance, the search for new solutions undoubtedly reinforces perceptions of an overall decline in the utility of the treaty. Yet it remains the case that the ability of other international mechanisms to act rests on the NPT's norms and rules.

The debate within NPT forums over what constitutes noncompliance will continue into the future, with every indication that consensus on clear definitions will remain elusive. A particular concern must be that the existing discriminatory mechanisms to deny enrichment and reprocessing technology have now been forced into the open, and it seems likely that proliferation by "crawl-out" will become increasingly difficult to control. Consensus interpretations of the NPT permitting such controls to operate in an overt manner will be difficult, if not impossible, to achieve. Just as worrying are the major difficulties this presents for responding to noncompliance in situations where there is no agreement on what precise actions are to trigger a response, especially if those actions in themselves pose no immediate security threat.

Events and the Relevance of the NPT

One consequence of the post–9/11 international environment for the antiproliferation policies of the United States and its allies has been to radically change the focus of these activities. The issue of nonstate actors stealing weapons, acquiring nuclear materials, and manufacturing nuclear explosive devices is now high on their agenda. Both state and nonstate proliferation activities focus attention on clandestine nuclear procurement networks of the A. Q. Khan type, with the distinction between state and nonstate activities often opaque. In parallel, physical counterproliferation activities not mentioned in the text of the NPT have become more visible and salient: prevention by physical denial is acquiring greater significance in comparison to building international trust to remove the underlying security dilemmas that generate proliferation. Counterproliferation tools and policies now appear to dominate the proliferation scene, with nonproliferation agreements and diplomacy receding into the background.

The impact on the NPT of these changes is difficult to evaluate in any quantitative way, but some indicators of what is occurring can be identified. The most obvious is that while the NPT remains the legal basis for counterproliferation actions and contains the norms which justify them, it was drafted in an age when nonstate nuclear weapon activities were inconceivable. Its focus was, and still is, on interstate activities: it appears to some that it now lacks the flexibility to cover nonstate activities also. One consequence is that almost all the responses to the post–9/11 environment have taken place outside of the ambit of the treaty. This includes the increased authority and status the IAEA has acquired as a flexible global nuclear governance instrument; the UNSC Resolution 1540 mandating effective national nuclear control legislation; the Proliferation Security Initiative (PSI) mechanisms for intercepting clandestine shipments of WMD precursor materials and technology; and homeland security and intelligence exchange arrangements to protect against WMD terrorism.

Moreover, as indicated above, the relevance of the NPT to the three main sets of contemporary state proliferation events—those involving Iraq, Iran, and the DPRK—has been to provide the legal context for action by other mechanisms. States have bypassed the treaty review process in their attempts to deal with these events; hence impressions of its irrelevance have strengthened. At the same time, Iran has used treaty language to defend its own position. Some have therefore seen that the ability for proliferators to defend their actions through the NPT makes it a positive barrier to dealing with the realities of proliferation and thus worse than irrelevant.

Both external changes and its own internal contradictions can thus be seen to have lowered perceptions of the value of the treaty in preventing proliferation. In looking to the future, however, two generic types of proliferation events seem likely to figure large: on the one hand, declaratory statements of nuclear weapon aspirations, possession, and nuclear testing, and, on the other, nuclear weapon use.

A. *Declaratory Statements/Nuclear Testing*

A precedent now exists for assessing the impact of these sets of events on the treaty: the DPRK. In practice, its withdrawal from the NPT in 2003 and its later declaratory statement of nuclear weapon possession had little discernable effect on the operations of the NPT. Two reasons may account for this. One was the lack of consensus over whether this was a case of withdrawal or of noncompliance. The second was that the regional states decided it should be dealt with as a regional security issue through their six-party forum, rather than a proliferation one. In these circumstances, the UNSC and the NPT parties did not wish to complicate matters further by taking actions which might reduce the chances of a favorable settlement. This was especially so as one objective in these negotiations has been to return the DPRK to full membership of the NPT as a NNWS. The opaqueness over its legal status seems destined to continue so long as the regional negotiations move forward.

The DPRK's nuclear test in 2006 had no precedent in NPT history. While doubts persist over its purpose and success, the same constraints on positive action applied as in the case of its withdrawal from the NPT, namely that making it a major NPT issue might complicate a favorable regional settlement. In this, and probably in any similar future situation, the circumstances of the case are likely to dominate over any other consideration, particularly where an ongoing regional process exists through which the nuclear issues can be resolved through wider negotiations.

B. Nuclear Weapon Use/Terrorist Devices

It is now over sixty years since nuclear weapons were used against Japanese cities. A very significant taboo would be broken if nuclear explosives were to be used in the future by either state or nonstate actors. Much would clearly depend on the circumstances of use and its human consequences: use in a barren and unpopulated area or at sea would clearly generate a different response than use against a city. But in general, two possible responses could result from this situation.

One is that nuclear weapon use would in some respects become legitimized, and additional NNWS would start to think seriously about acquiring nuclear weapons if they did not have convincing nuclear security guarantees from NWS. This would result in withdrawals from the NPT and a further degrading of its credibility as a useful international instrument. The second response is that as in 1945–46, it would stimulate concerted international action to move toward a nonnuclear world. This could lead to the NPT being strengthened in its usefulness and eventually being superseded by a disarmament treaty.

Some Overall Conclusions: Two Scenarios

Logically the only way open to the NPT parties to move forward in a visible manner now is through a combination of the NPT becoming universal and all the NWS giving up their weapons. This makes defining what nuclear disarmament means in practice an important precondition of such a scenario, as well as shaping IAEA safeguards arrangements so they link into any future verification regime for such a disarmament treaty. It is difficult to predict the circumstances in which this long-term goal would become a short-range reality, though nuclear use could be one of them.

The more likely scenario, however, is a continuing loss of saliency for the NPT in the eyes of many of its parties, though the underlying norms and overt legal commitments it contains will continue to shape state and coalition actions. There will not be any sudden collapse or mass defection from the treaty. The problem will be that it, and the regime and the UNSC, have shown themselves incapable of dealing with the various forms of noncompliance with, and withdrawal from, the NPT that have been experienced since 1991 and no doubt will recur in the future. In addition, its review process is just that: it has no executive powers and is open to regional and global political gamesmanship. However, its atmospherics will be considerably enhanced if the CTBT were to be brought into force and a fissile material cut-off treaty (FMCT) agreed to.

The NPT will therefore have to live with the paradox generated by events in 1998: that its success in gaining sufficient accessions to have a near universal membership has been eroded by the existence of declared NWS outside of the treaty. It will also have to live with its lack of precision over issues such as peaceful uses, where any changes to fuel-cycle rules will have to be negotiated outside of the treaty. But the NPT will continue to exist because of what it is: a treaty based on generally agreed-on norms and containing rules for international behavior based on those norms. More positively, there is little doubt that the small number of proliferation "states of concern" today present a much more hopeful prospect for the future than the much larger numbers anticipated by the Dunn and Kahn study in 1976.

Notes

1. Lewis Dunn and Herman Kahn, *Trends in Nuclear Proliferation, 1975–1995*, Prepared for U.S. Arms Control and Disarmament Agency by the Hudson Institute, May 15, 1976, http://stinet.dtic.mil/oai/oai?verb=getRecord&metadataPrefix=html&identifier=ADB011707.

2. These are the Partial Test-Ban Treaty (PTBT) of 1963, which limited explosive testing to underground locations, and the Comprehensive Test-Ban Treaty (CTBT) of 1996, which banned all such testing. The former is in force and has 125 parties; the latter is not yet in force, but all its signatories have observed a moratorium on testing since 1996. Its associated international monitoring system, designed to detect global nuclear testing, does exist and, despite its very low yield, detected and verified the DPRK test in 2006.

3. These treaties go beyond the commitments contained in the NPT in that they include both a prohibition on the stationing of other states' nuclear weapons on national territory and the provision to states within the zone of unconditional negative security assurances by the NPT nuclear weapon states. The areas covered by them are Antarctica; Latin America and the Caribbean (Treaty of Tlatelolco); the South Pacific (Treaty of Rarotonga); South East Asia (Treaty of Bangkok); Africa (Treaty of Pelindaba); and Central Asia. Only the first three of these are fully operative. Other areas suggested for NWFZs include the Middle East and the Gulf Region.

4. The export control arrangements include the Nuclear Suppliers Group (NSG); the Missile Technology Control Regime (MTCR); Hague Code of Conduct (HCoC), which covers missile technology; and the Proliferation Security Initiative (PSI), a mechanism facilitating the interception of clandestine transit of proliferation relevant artifacts and materials.

5. Unlike the NPT, the IAEA has both a secretariat and inspectors based in Vienna, as well as an executive arm, its board of governors, whose sanction powers are limited to the

70   *John Simpson*

withdrawal of technical cooperation with a state. If these are judged insufficient, it can report a situation to the UN Security Council (UNSC), which can then use its own powers to act.

6. IAEA safeguards had already been in existence for a decade when the NPT was signed. Its first safeguards system, known as INFCIRC/66, was agreed to in 1965. The NPT system, INFCIRC/153, was not agreed to until 1972.

7. This distinction is based on their isotopic composition. The two materials normally used to make nuclear weapons are uranium or plutonium. They can exist in several forms that differ only in their mass, indicated by a number after their name. The two materials most appropriate for weapons are uranium-235 and plutonium-239.

8 Ben Sanders and George Bunn, "A New View of Review," Programme for Promoting Nuclear Non-proliferation (PPNN), Issue Review, no. 6, September 1996.

9. See Preparatory Committee for the 2010 Review Conference of the Parties to the Treaty on the Non-proliferation of Nuclear Weapons, *Model Nuclear Weapons Convention*, Working Paper submitted by Costa Rica, NPT/CONF.2010/PC.I/WP.17, 1 May 2007, http://www.un.org/NPT2010/offdocs_7_May_onward/NPT_CONF_2010_PC_1_WP_17_E.pdf.

10. The wording is from the Final Document of the 2000 NPT Review Conference.

11 *The Atomic Energy Act of 1954*, August 30, 1954, Public Law 83-703, 68 Stat. 919. The treaty was worded in such a way as to allow continued U.S.-UK collaboration in weapon development by using similar language to that in the U.S. 1958 amendments to its nuclear energy legislation, which prohibited transfer of complete weapons, but not components, materials, and design information.

12. For a detailed discussion to the negotiating background to these issues and the statements in relevant U.S. Senate hearings in 1969, see John Simpson and Jenny Nielsen, *The NPT and Nuclear Sharing*, http://www.mcis.soton.ac.uk.

13. Mohamed I. Shaker, *The Nuclear Non-Proliferation Treaty: Origin and Implementation, 1959–1969*, vol. 1 (London: Oceana, 1980).

14. General and Complete Disarmament was a concept first put forward by the UK in September 1959 at the UN General Assembly and discussed in detail through 1962. Its origins lay in the USSR's perceived preponderance of conventional military armaments in Europe and the belief that U.S. and UK nuclear weapons were offsetting this and thus creating a military balance. Thus any attempt at nuclear disarmament would have to be balanced by a parallel reduction in conventional capabilities. By 1961 a set of guidelines had been agreed to between the U.S. and USSR (the McCloy-Zorin statement), but the parties could not agree on how to implement them, and the exercise eventually produced no concrete results, other than to remain a part of the agenda of successive global disarmament bodies meeting in Geneva. See Jozef Goldblat, *Arms Control: A Guide on Negotiations and Agreements* (London: Sage, published for International Peace Research Institute, Oslo, 1994), 36–38.

15. See Statement by H. E. Mr. François Rivasseau, ambassador, permanent representative of France to the Conference on Disarmament, third session of the Preparatory Committee for the 2005 Review Conference of the Parties to the Treaty on the Non-Proliferation of Nuclear Weapons, cluster I, New York, April 29, 2004.

16. International Court of Justice, *Legality of the Threat or Use of Nuclear Weapons*, advisory opinion, July 8, 1996.

17. While it is feasible that sixty-three states parties could be assembled to trigger an amendment conference, any amendment must then pass over two barriers that appear insuperable. The first is that the amendment must be approved by a majority of the parties to the treaty (i.e., ninety-five states) including the five NWS and all NPT parties that are on the board of the IAEA. If it passes over that barrier, the same conditions apply for its entry into force for those states that have ratified it. In the highly unlikely circumstances where all of these conditions were met, there would then be two treaties extant, the amended and unamended versions, with differing memberships—with those opposed to the amendments in the unamended version of the treaty.

18. See George Bunn and John B. Rhinelander, "NPT Withdrawal: Time for the Security Council to Step In," *Arms Control Today* 35, no. 4 (May 2005): 17–21; and Shaker, *Nuclear Non-Proliferation Treaty*, 885–99.

19. Jenny Nielsen and John Simpson, "The NPT Withdrawal Clause and Its Negotiating History," Mountbatten Centre for International Studies, NPT issue review, July 2004, http://www.mcis.soton.ac.uk/Site_Files/pdf/withdrawal_clause_NPT_nielsen&simpson_2004.pdf.

20. George Bunn, Charles N. van Doren, and David Fischer, "Options and Opportunities: The NPT Extension Conference of 1995," Programme for Promoting Nuclear Non-Proliferation study 2, Mountbatten Centre for International Studies, 1991.

21. James Acton, with Carter Newman, *IAEA Verification of Military Research and Development*, Verification Matters, VERTIC Research Report no. 5, July 2006, http://www.vertic.org/publications/VM5%20(2).pdf.

22. See UN General Assembly resolution 2028 (XX), adopted November 23, 1965, UNSC resolution 255, adopted June 19, 1968, and unilateral statements made in 1978 by the United States and the Soviet Union. For analysis and historical background on security assurances, see George Bunn and Roland M. Timerbaev, "Security Assurances to Non-Nuclear-Weapon States," *Nonproliferation Review* 1, no. 1 (Fall 1993): 11–20; and George Bunn and Roland M. Timerbaev, "Security Assurances to Non-Nuclear-Weapon States: Possible Options for Change," Programme for Promoting Nuclear Non-Proliferation (PPNN) Issue Review no. 7 (September 1996), Mountbatten Centre for International Studies.

23. Article VIII.3.

24. "The Implementation of Agreements Related to Disarmament," in *SIPRI Yearbook 1976: World Armaments and Disarmament* (Cambridge, MA: MIT Press, 1976), 364; and "Appendix 9A: Final Declaration of the Review Conference of the Parties to the Treaty on the Non-Proliferation of Nuclear Weapons, 30 May 1975," in *SIPRI Yearbook 1976*, 403–13.

25. "The Second NPT Review Conference," in *SIPRI Yearbook 1981: World Armaments and Disarmament* (London: Taylor and Francis, 1981), 297–338; and Jozef Goldblat, *Twenty Years of the Non-Proliferation Treaty: Implementation and Prospects* (Oslo: International Peace Research Institute [PRIO], 1990), 50–51.

26. Jozef Goldblat, "The Third Review of the NPT Treaty," in *SIPRI Yearbook 1986: World Armaments and Disarmament* (Oxford: Oxford University Press, 1986), 469–80, and Jozef Goldblat, "Appendix 20A: Final Declaration of the Third Review Conference," in *SIPRI Yearbook 1986: World Armaments and Disarmament*, 481–94.

27. David Fischer and Harald Müller, "The Fourth Review of the Non-Proliferation Treaty," in *SIPRI Yearbook 1991: World Armaments and Disarmament* (Oxford: Oxford University Press, 1991), 555–84, and John Simpson, "The 1990 Review Conference of the Nuclear Non-Proliferation Treaty: Pointer to the Future or Diplomatic Accident," *The Round Table*, no. 318 (April 1991): 139–54.

28. John Simpson, "The Nuclear Non-proliferation Regime after the NPT Review and Extension Conference," in *SIPRI Yearbook 1996: Armaments, Disarmament and International Security* (Oxford University Press: Oxford, 1996), 561–89.

29. In part the uncertainty arises from the procedure used: to agree on the three documents separately, with the extension document last, and then collectively. This process appeared to have been done purposefully to infuse the review conference with both political and legal symbolism, though what it implies remains obscure.

30. NPT/CONF.1995/32/Res.1, May 11, 1995.

31. The wording of paragraph 4 is as follows: "The purpose of the Preparatory Committee meetings would be to consider principles, objectives and ways in order to promote the full implementation of the Treaty, as well as its universality, and to make recommendations thereon to the Review Conference."

32. John Simpson, "The Consequences of the 1997 PrepCom and Their Implications for the Review Process," in *South East Asia: Regional Security and Nuclear Non-Proliferation* (Southampton, UK: Mountbatten Centre for International Studies, Programme for Promoting Nuclear Non-Proliferation, 1997).

33. Tariq Rauf, "The April 1998 NPT PrepCom," *Nonproliferation Review* 5, no. 2 (Winter 1998): 121–31; Tariq Rauf and John Simpson, "The 1999 NPT PrepCom," *Nonproliferation Review* 6, no. 2 (Winter 1999): 121–23; chairman's working paper, NPT/CONF.2000/PC.III/29, May 14, 1999; chairman's revised working paper, NPT/CONF.2000/PC.III/58, May 20, 1999.

34. Rebecca Johnson, "The 2000 NPT Review Conference: A Delicate, Hard-Won Compromise," *Disarmament Diplomacy* 5, no. 46 (May 2000): 4, http://www.acronym.org .uk/dd/dd46/46npt.htm; Tariq Rauf, "An Unequivocal Success? Implications of the NPT Review Conference," *Arms Control Today* 30, no. 6 (July/August 2000): 9–16; Norman A. Wulf, "Observations from the 2000 NPT Review Conference," *Arms Control Today* 30, no. 9 (November 2000): 3–9; John Simpson, "The 2000 NPT Review Conference," *SIPRI Yearbook 2001: Armaments, Disarmament and International Security* (Oxford: Oxford University Press, 2001), 487–502

35. "Interview: Ambassador Salander on the 2002 NPT Preparatory Committee," conducted by William Potter, Mary Beth Nikitin, and Tariq Rauf, *Nonproliferation Review* 9, no. 2 (Summer 2002): 1–14; Rebecca Johnson, "The NPT PrepCom: Papering Over the Cracks?" *Disarmament Diplomacy*, no. 64 (May/June 2002); Tanya Ogilvie-White and John Simpson, "The NPT and Its 2003 PrepCom Session: A Regime in Need of Intensive Care," *Nonproliferation Review* 10, no. 1 (Spring 2003): 40–58.

36. See Rebecca Johnson, "Report on the 2004 NPT PrepCom," *Disarmament Diplomacy*, no. 77 (May/June 2004); John Simpson and Jenny Nielsen, "Fiddling While Rome

Burns? The 2004 Session of the PrepCom for the 2005 Review Conference," *Nonproliferation Review* 11, no. 2 (Summer 2004): 1–26.

37. See Rebecca Johnson, "Politics and Protection: Why the 2005 NPT Review Conference Failed," *Disarmament Diplomacy*, no. 80 (Autumn 2005); John Simpson and Jenny Nielsen, "The 2005 NPT Review Conference: Mission Impossible?" *Nonproliferation Review* 12, no. 2 (Summer 2005): 271–301.

38. White House, "Joint Statement between President George W. Bush and Prime Minister Manmohan Singh," July 18 2005, http://www.whitehouse.gov/news/releases/2005/07/20050718-6.html. For analysis of the implications of the U.S.-India nuclear deal, see David Albright, testimony before the House Committee on International Relations, Hearing on the U.S.-India "Global Partnership" and Its Impact on Non-Proliferation, October 26, 2005, http://www.isis-online.org/publications/southasia/abrighttestimonyoctober262005usindiadeal.pdf; and Fred McGoldrick, Harold Bengelsdorf, and Lawrence Scheinman "The U.S.-India Nuclear Deal: Taking Stock," *Arms Control Today* 35, no. 8 (October 2005): 6–12.

39. I am grateful to Dr Lewis Dunn for suggesting this useful typology during a recent workshop.

40. See John Simpson, "The Nuclear Landscape in 2004: Past, Present and Future," Weapons of Mass Destruction Commission paper no. 3, 2004, 15–16, http://www.wmdcommission.org/files/No3.pdf.

41. See Preparatory Committee for the 2005 Review Conference of the Parties to the Treaty on the Non-proliferation of Nuclear Weapons, *Withdrawal from the Treaty on the Non-proliferation of Nuclear Weapons: European Union Common Approach*, working paper submitted by Luxembourg on behalf of the European Union, NPT/CONF.2005/WP.32, May 10, 2005, http://www.un.org/events/npt2005/working%20papers.html.

42. See Johnson, "2000 NPT Review Conference"; and Rauf, "Unequivocal Success?"

43. For an extended discussion on these issues see Darryl Howlett and John Simpson, "Nuclear Non-proliferation: How to Ensure an Effective Compliance Mechanism," ch. 1 in *Effective Non-proliferation: The European Union and the 2005 NPT Review Conference*, Chaillot Papers, no. 77, European Union Institute for Security Studies, 11–19, April 2005, http://www.iss.europa.eu/index.php?id=143.

44. See Preparatory Committee for the 2005 Review Conference of the Parties to the Treaty on the Non-proliferation of Nuclear Weapons, *Overcoming the Institutional Deficit of the NPT*, working paper submitted by Canada, NPT/CONF.2005/PC.III/WP.1, April 5, 2004, http://www.dfait.gc.ca/arms/2004npt5-en.asp.

[5]

Nuclear Disarmament

How Much Have the Five Nuclear Powers Promised in the Non-Proliferation Treaty?

George Bunn and Roland M. Timerbaev

Introduction

The 1968 Nuclear Non-Proliferation Treaty (NPT) constitutes a bargain between five nuclear-weapon powers (Britain, China, France, Russia and the United States) and 160 other NPT parties that do not have nuclear weapons (See Appendix B for a listing of NPT parties states). The non-nuclear-weapon parties, among other things, agree not to acquire nuclear weapons without insisting that the five give up their weapons—at least for the time being. Instead, under Article VI of the NPT, all parties agree "to pursue negotiations in good faith on effective measures relating to cessation of the nuclear arms race at an early date and to nuclear disarmament, and on a treaty on general and complete disarmament under strict and effective international control."[1] (See Appendix A for a full text of the treaty.)

The purpose of this paper is to consider the meaning of this language. Under what circumstances does Article VI obligate the five NPT nuclear-weapon parties to negotiate toward zero nuclear weapons in national arsenals? Must there *first* be agreement on more measures designed to limit the production and use of nuclear

At the Nuclear Crossroads

weapons, greater reductions in nuclear weapons, fewer international tensions or sharp cuts in conventional arms? Is it sufficient for the present to negotiate toward the lesser goal of Article VI, "cessation of the nuclear arms race"? (Long-sought measures toward that goal are a ban on all nuclear tests, a restraint in the production of fissionable material for nuclear weapons, and a prohibition on the use of nuclear weapons except in response to a nuclear attack.) In an attempt to answer these and related questions, we will look at the text of the NPT, its negotiating history, and the practice of its members in implementing its terms.

The negotiation of the NPT during the mid-1960s was led by the Soviet Union and the United States—then the two "co-chairs" of the multilateral Geneva disarmament conference. The treaty's main purpose was to halt the spread of nuclear weapons to additional countries beyond the five that had tested nuclear weapons by 1967— Britain, China, France, the Soviet Union and the United States.[2] It has been joined by more than 155 non-nuclear-weapon countries having the same goal. But, unwilling to legitimize forever a "discriminatory" world divided between the five that had nuclear weapons and the many that did not, those without nuclear weapons forced a compromise. The compromise limited the NPT to a first term of 25 years; imposed Article VI on the nuclear-weapon parties; required review of the NPT every five years to determine whether this and other obligations were being realized; called for such a review in the same year (1995) that the parties were to decide by majority vote how much longer the treaty should last; and established the right to withdraw from the treaty if "extraordinary events" relating to nuclear non-proliferation jeopardized "the supreme interests" of a party concerned.[3] As described below, the NPT's negotiating history and the practice of the parties in implementing it suggest that a reason for this compromise, from the point of view of the non-nuclear-weapon countries, was to keep pressure on the nuclear-weapon powers to halt the nuclear arms race and to move toward zero nuclear weapons. First, however, let us turn to Article VI itself to look for an answer to the question of *when* negotiation toward *zero* nuclear weapons is required.

12

Nuclear Disarmament

The Meaning of Article VI as Derived from its Text

Article VI itself shows that first priority was to be given to negotiation of measures "relating to cessation of the nuclear arms race." This phrase was followed immediately by "at an early date." In contrast, Article VI's call for negotiations relating to "nuclear disarmament" and on "general and complete disarmament" was not qualified by language suggesting that their achievement was to be given similar urgency. Article VI clearly gave priority to "cessation-of-the-nuclear-arms-race" measures. While not stating that they had to be negotiated first—before nuclear-reductions talks became obligatory—it gave them greater urgency.

When Article VI was negotiated, both American and Soviet plans for "general and complete disarmament" on the Geneva negotiating table called for zero *national* nuclear weapons by the third and last stage of disarmament.[4] This was, however, only to be undertaken in conjunction with world-wide reductions of national armed forces and conventional arms to very low levels. In the U.S. plan, the preconditions for moving to zero included reduced international tension, improved mechanisms for peaceful settlement of international disputes, and a strengthened United Nations peace force.[5]

Did Article VI establish the same linkages and pre-conditions for "nuclear disarmament" as Soviet or U.S. plans did for "general and complete disarmament"? The Article VI obligation to negotiate on measures "*relating* to . . . nuclear disarmament" (emphasis added) could include a variety of measures that would reduce deployed nuclear weapons to levels far short of zero. Did Article VI require negotiation of "nuclear disarmament"—meaning zero national nuclear weapons—without the accompanying drastic reductions in conventional weapons and armed forces contemplated by both the American and Soviet plans for general and complete disarmament? Did the requirement include the reduction in tensions and the strengthened UN, as called for by the American plan?

"Disarmament" can sometimes mean reductions short of zero.[6] However, the ordinary meaning of "nuclear disarmament" clearly *includes* zero even if it also includes reductions short of zero. Therefore, the obligation to negotiate on measures "relating to . . . nuclear disarmament" seems to include, among other things, zero. Thus,

At the Nuclear Crossroads

one meaning of Article VI, probably its plainest, is for eventual negotiations dealing with the elimination of nuclear weapons through either of two routes: (1) toward "nuclear disarmament" without linkages and preconditions, and (2) toward "general and complete disarmament" with them.

The NPT's preamble, however, suggests a different meaning. It contains two relevant provisions, one suggesting the purpose of negotiations relating to "nuclear disarmament," and the other of negotiations—concurrent or sequential—relating to "general and complete disarmament." In the first provision, the parties declare:

> their intention to achieve at the earliest possible date the cessation of the nuclear arms race and to take effective measures *in the direction of* nuclear disarmament . . . . [7]

In the second instance, the parties state their desire:

> to further the easing of international tension and the strengthening of trust between States in order to facilitate the cessation of the manufacture of nuclear weapons, the liquidation of all their existing stockpiles, and the elimination from national arsenals of nuclear weapons and the means of their delivery *pursuant to a treaty* on general and complete disarmament under strict and effective international control . . . . [8]

The contrasting language of these two preambular provisions suggests that Article VI does not require negotiation on proposals calling for zero nuclear weapons except in the context of general and complete disarmament, including the pre-conditions—easing of international tensions and strengthening of trust between states. At the same time, "effective measures *in the direction of nuclear disarmament*" (but presumably short of it) are to be pursued without reference to general and complete disarmament or to such conditions precedent. Therefore, one could argue from the preamble that the achievement of complete nuclear disarmament was only contemplated in the context of general and complete disarmament.

There is thus some conflict between the plain meaning of Article VI itself and the preambular provisions suggesting its purpose. However, the negotiating history of the treaty and the practice of the parties suggest that pursuit of zero was foreseen along two alternative routes: one to "nuclear disarmament" without a requirement of linkages and pre-conditions, and the other to "general and complete disarmament" with linkages and pre-conditions.

14

Nuclear Disarmament

The Meaning of Article VI as Derived from its Negotiating History

In 1962, soon after the adoption of the "Irish resolution" by the UN General Assembly calling for a non-proliferation agreement, the United States met with a group of its NATO allies who were also members of the multilateral Geneva disarmament conference where such an agreement was to be discussed. Two U.S.-proposed options considered at this meeting were declarations by countries having nuclear weapons not to disseminate them to those that did not, and separate declarations by those that did not—not to acquire them. At the meeting, Italy expressed reservations about such declarations unless there were promises from the countries having nuclear weapons to get rid of them eventually.[9] Later in 1962, the Italians acquiesced in a revised U.S. non-dissemination draft for the countries having nuclear weapons. This draft would not have required a non-acquisition promise from countries not having them, and it would have permitted the use of U.S. nuclear weapons by a multilaterally-manned naval force of NATO countries (the so-called MLF) in which Italy could participate.[10] The Soviet Union, however, rejected this draft.[11]

Criticism of a non-proliferation accord that discriminated by permitting some but not others to have nuclear weapons was thus raised originally by a U.S. ally—Italy. Moreover, the Italians seemed to speak for the Germans as well; for Cold War reasons, the Federal Republic of Germany (West Germany) had not at that point been invited to participate in the Geneva disarmament conference.[12] When the Italians later proposed that countries not having nuclear weapons forswear acquiring them in short-term unilateral declarations pending negotiation of additional obligations for those having nuclear weapons (including steps toward nuclear disarmament), German Chancellor Erhard announced that Germany had already signed a non-acquisition declaration and called upon others to follow suit.[13] This Italian-German idea seemed to imply that if they and other countries with the potential to make nuclear weapons renounced them, the nuclear-weapon powers should take steps toward nuclear disarmament.

The measures mentioned most often in the negotiating history are a test ban, cut-off and prohibition on use.

15

At the Nuclear Crossroads

When the focus later shifted to Soviet and U.S. drafts for a non-proliferation treaty of unlimited duration, Germany pointed out that more was needed than such a "limited" NPT:

> It is incumbent on the nuclear-weapon powers to stop the further development of increasingly more dangerous weapons, not to increase existing stocks, including the means of their delivery, to begin reducing them, to stop the production of fissionable material for military purposes, and to aim at a comprehensive test ban. When the nuclear-weapon powers explicitly announce their willingness to take their own steps to restrict and reduce armaments, a limited non-proliferation treaty would be the beginning of international cooperation for a genuine guarantee of peace in the nuclear age .... The execution of the promised disarmament measures [by nuclear-weapon powers] couldbe checked by an international authority at each further stage of disarmament process .... The nuclear-weapon powers are called upon to take the next steps .... [14]

This statement was issued after several years of negotiations had made agreement on an NPT seem possible in the near future. The first public U.S. draft NPT in 1965 had been followed soon by a Soviet counter proposal. Both called for a treaty of unlimited duration that would prohibit those having nuclear weapons from disseminating them to those that did not, and that would prohibit those that did not have nuclear weapons from acquiring them. Neither draft contained any article obligating the countries having nuclear weapons to negotiate an end to the nuclear arms race or to reduce their nuclear arsenals. The major differences concerned how they would deal with existing and planned multilateral arrangements within NATO for control over nuclear weapons that might be used in response to an attack by the Soviet-led Warsaw Pact.[15]

At Geneva, Italy submitted a draft short-term "unilateral-renunciation" declaration for advanced non-nuclear-weapon countries that was essentially a counter proposal to the draft U.S. treaty. In the Italian proposal, the non-nuclear-weapon declarants were to meet just before the end of an initial term of years to review "the progress which has been made toward international agreements to prevent the spread of nuclear weapons, or to halt the nuclear arms race, and to reduce nuclear arsenals." Any decision by these declarants to extend their declarations would be based upon this review—including, clearly, what progress the nuclear-weapon powers had made toward limiting and reducing their nuclear weapons.[16]

16

Nuclear Disarmament

The "Non-Aligned Eight," the non-aligned, non-nuclear-weapon countries represented at the Geneva conference, then made the same point about a non-proliferation treaty:

> A treaty on non-proliferation of nuclear weapons is not an end in itself but only a means to an end. That end is the achievement of *general and complete disarmament, and, more particularly, nuclear disarmament.* The eight delegations are convinced that measures to prohibit the spread of nuclear weapons should, therefore, be *coupled with or followed by tangible steps*, to halt the nuclear arms race and to limit, reduce and eliminate stocks of nuclear weapons and the means of their delivery.[17]

Later in 1965, after negotiations among many delegations, the General Assembly adopted a resolution containing guiding principles for the negotiation of a non-proliferation treaty. Among other things, the resolution said that such a treaty "should embody an acceptable balance of mutual responsibilities and obligations of the nuclear and non-nuclear powers" and that it should be a step towards "general and complete disarmament and, more particularly, nuclear disarmament."[18] Thus, the UN resolution, the non-aligned memorandum, and the Italian proposal all called for progress *toward* "nuclear disarmament" even before the steps and conditions necessary for general and complete disarmament had been achieved.

When the Geneva conference resumed in 1966, the debate centered on how to link a non-proliferation treaty with steps toward nuclear disarmament. The Egyptian delegate proposed that a non-proliferation treaty include a *"legal obligation* to halt the nuclear arms race, limit, reduce and eliminate stocks of nuclear weapons and delivery vehicles, and to that end continue and expedite negotiations in order to reach agreement on concrete measures." With such an obligation, he said, countries not having nuclear weapons could judge "objectively" whether sufficient progress had been made by those having them to satisfy the treaty, and they could withdraw from it if progress was so small as to constitute "non-observance."[19]

The Non-Aligned Eight agreed on a new memorandum listing specific proposals for "tangible steps to halt the nuclear arms race and to limit, reduce and eliminate the stocks of nuclear weapons and the means of their delivery." These included a ban on nuclear testing, an end to the production of fissionable material for weapons, and "a freeze and a gradual reduction of the stocks of nuclear weapons

17

At the Nuclear Crossroads

and the means of their delivery, the banning of the use of nuclear weapons and assurance of the security of non-nuclear-weapon states." The memorandum added: "Such different steps could be embodied in a treaty as part of its provisions or as a declaration of intention."[20]

In 1967, after the Soviet Union and the United States had resolved many of their differences and submitted identical drafts of a treaty, the Mexican delegation proposed the following article as an amendment:

> Each nuclear-weapon State Party to this Treaty undertakes to pursue negotiations in good faith, with all speed and perseverance, to arrive at further agreements regarding the prohibition of nuclear weapon tests, the cessation of the manufacture of nuclear weapons, the liquidation of their existing stockpiles, the elimination from nuclear arsenals of nuclear weapons and the means of their delivery, as well as to reach agreement on a treaty on general and complete disarmament under strict and effective international control.[21]

This language clearly contemplated that negotiations for the elimination of nuclear weapons from national stockpiles could take place outside the context of general and complete disarmament. Brazil, Burma, India, Romania and Switzerland made somewhat similar proposals—that the treaty contain language obligating the nuclear-weapon powers to "adopt," "take," "resolve . . . to undertake," or "undertake . . . to negotiate" specific steps toward nuclear disarmament.[22] None of these proposals mentioned general and complete disarmament.

Even earlier, U.S. allies considering a U.S.-Soviet draft before it was made public at Geneva had expressed interest in linking non-proliferation obligations to new limitations on the nuclear arms race. The Canadian representative had said: "It is neither unnatural nor unreasonable that countries forgoing their option to produce nuclear weapons should wish to ensure that their act of self-denial should in turn lead the nuclear weapon powers to undertake tangible steps to reduce and eliminate their vast stockpiles of nuclear weapons and delivery vehicles."[23] The Japanese foreign minister had

> *One route to "nuclear disarmament" was foreseen without preconditions, and another to "general and complete disarmament" with them.*

Nuclear Disarmament

announced that a treaty prohibiting non-proliferation should "go further to make clear the sincere intention on the part of the the countries which possess nuclear weapons to make efforts toward nuclear disarmament . . . ."[24] The British representative had argued that the treaty's terms "must provide the *means of redress* for the non-nuclear powers if the nuclear states are unreasonably slow in translating their intentions ["to halt and reverse" the nuclear arms race] into action."[25] (The "means of redress" commonly mentioned at the Geneva conference were: [1] withdrawal from the NPT by have-nots; [2] meetings of the parties every five years to review the treaty; and [3] a meeting at the end of its initial term to consider how long to extend it.[26])

The Soviet Union and the United States had no choice but to heed these views if they wanted to secure widespread adherence to a non-proliferation treaty. They revised the Mexican language, deleting references to specific measures and proposing what became the obligation in Article VI to negotiate "in good faith on effective measures relating to the cessation of the nuclear arms race at an early date and to nuclear disarmament, and on a treaty on general and complete disarmament . . . ."[27]

They later revised their draft Treaty to offer a review conference every five years of the treaty's life instead of once at the end of the first five. Also, treaty duration was changed from "unlimited" to an initial term of 25 years at the end of which the parties would review whether the treaty's obligations were being observed and decide how much longer it should last.[28]

For Article VI and other obligations, these arrangements provided something akin to enforcement. The negotiators assumed that the Security Council would deal with treaty violations that constituted a threat to the peace because the UN Charter already gave it that authority.[29] However, the five acknowledged nuclear-weapon powers were each permanent members of the Security Council with veto power. No new authority was provided in the NPT to refer disputes over alleged treaty violations to the Security Council, to World Court adjudication, to mediation, or to arbitration. A dissatisfied party could withdraw from the treaty, but that required a report by it to the Security Council stating that its "supreme interests" had been jeopardized by "extraordinary events related to the subject

At the Nuclear Crossroads

matter of the treaty."[30] Examples could be the development of nuclear explosives by a hostile neighbor or a credible nuclear-weapon threat against its territory or forces by a nuclear-weapon state. From the point of view of the countries not having nuclear weapons, the provisions for conferences to review the implementation of the NPT every five years and to consider its extension after 25 were the most important opportunities available to pressure parties having nuclear weapons to negotiate seriously to limit or eliminate them.

In a statement offering the final NPT text to the General Assembly, the U.S. representative to the United Nations, former U.S. Supreme Court Justice Arthur Goldberg, stated that these added provisions gave Article VI "*further force.*" He added:

> My country believes that the *permanent viability* of this treaty will *depend in large measure on our success in the further negotiations contemplated by Article VI*.... Following the conclusion of this treaty, my government will, in the spirit of Article VI ... pursue further disarmament negotiations with redoubled zeal and hope and with promptness .... [31]

To many, Article VI's "pursue negotiations in good faith" may seem so vague as to be almost meaningless. In other contexts, however, both national and international courts have given it sufficient meaning to make it an enforceable promise where there is a judicial system that has jurisdiction.[32] In the NPT, as we have seen, that was not offered. But, if those not having nuclear weapons were not satisfied that the five were complying with Article VI, their most important remedies beyond criticism were to frustrate agreement at review conferences every five years and to refuse to vote for a long extension for the NPT in 1995. As we shall see, they have already prevented consensus at two of the four review conferences because they thought the nuclear-weapon parties were not living up to their Article VI obligations.

The Practice of the NPT Parties Pursuant to Article VI

The NPT was opened for signature on July 1, 1968. At the signing, President Johnson announced that, consistent with the NPT's purpose of promoting arms control and disarmament, agreement had been reached with the Soviet Union for negotiations on the

20

Nuclear Disarmament

limitation and reduction of strategic ballistic missiles and defenses against them.[33] On the same day, the Soviet government issued a memorandum agreeing to negotiate on strategic delivery vehicles and proposing, in addition, negotiation on a list of eight other arms control measures, including "cessation of production of nuclear weapons and the reduction and elimination of stockpiles"—separately from general and complete disarmament.[34]

Later that summer at the Geneva conference, the Soviet Union, the United States, and the other countries present gave meaning to Article VI by agreeing to an agenda of measures that could be discussed there under a heading taken from Article VI's "effective measures relating to the cessation of the nuclear arms race at an early date and to nuclear disarmament." The agenda *under this heading* included "the cessation of testing, the non-use of nuclear weapons, the cessation of production of fissionable materials for weapons use, the cessation of manufacture of weapons, and reduction and subsequent *elimination* of nuclear stockpiles, nuclear free zones, etc." (emphasis added). The "effective measures . . ." heading was first on the agenda. General and complete disarmament was fourth.[35]

Thus, as interpreted by the Geneva conference that had helped negotiate the NPT, negotiations for elimination of nuclear stockpiles pursuant to Article VI could and should take place either under "nuclear disarmament" without the specified pre-conditions, or under general and complete disarmament with them. During the period

> *In the eyes of the non-nuclear NPT parties, a CTB is the most important measure the nuclear weapon states can adopt.*

when tensions had not yet been eased and trust between states had not been strengthened, the more meaningful of these two routes toward the elimination of all nuclear weapons would clearly be the first.

This assessment has been reflected in the practice of the parties. The U.S. and U.S.S.R. pursued negotiations bilaterally on their nuclear arsenals, eventually reaching extremely important agreements on reductions. General and complete disarmament, although it has been mentioned on the agenda of the Geneva Conference, was not seriously addressed by the nuclear-weapon states in the 26 years since "agenda item 4" was originally adopted. Complaints about this

At the Nuclear Crossroads

lack of action have not been prominent in the four NPT review conferences.

Relying in part upon Article VI, more than 160 countries have so far joined the NPT. Among the few that presented special statements to the depositary governments when they joined, the majority mentioned the importance of achieving agreements pursuant to Article VI.[36] At each of the four NPT review conferences held so far, the slow progress of the nuclear powers in implementing Article VI has gotten the most attention of the delegates. Indeed, the failure to negotiate a comprehensive test ban despite both Article VI and a separate preambular paragraph calling for CTB negotiations has been the single most contentious issue. Two of the four review conferences (in 1980 and 1990) broke up without achieving a consensus on any final declaration on the implementation of the NPT because of disagreement over language relating to the failure to negotiate a comprehensive test ban. (By agreement, decisions at these conferences were by consensus.)

By 1975, the SALT I Interim Agreement and the ABM Treaty had been achieved. But the non-aligned parties nevertheless criticized the Soviet Union and the United States for failure to live up to their part of the NPT bargain and achieve more than this. The conference president summarized their views by saying they "rather impatiently await concrete and binding results of on-going bilateral negotiations, aiming at ending the quantitative and qualitative arms race, and reducing substantially the levels of nuclear armaments . . . . The comprehensive test ban is clearly recognized as a most decisive element in these efforts. Article VI must be implemented in letter and spirit."[37] A compromise final declaration was agreed at the last minute containing recommendations on the test ban, on further steps in the SALT process, and on other nuclear arms control measures.[38]

At the 1980 review conference, the non-aligned NPT members prevented a consensus on a final declaration even though serious U.S.-Soviet-U.K. negotiations on ending nuclear testing had made progress. The conference followed the Soviet invasion of Afghanistan and the sharp Western reaction to that invasion. The non-aligned countries again indicated that the nuclear-weapon parties, through their failure to agree on a comprehensive test ban, on bringing the SALT II treaty into force, and on continuing negotiations to achieve

Nuclear Disarmament

substantial reductions in strategic offensive arms, had not kept their end of the NPT bargain.[39]

At the 1985 review conference, there was little new progress pursuant to Article VI to report, but U.S.-Soviet strategic arms negotiations had just begun in Geneva after a long lapse and a Reagan-Gorbachev summit meeting was imminent. After several years of sharpened East-West hostility, the delegates to the conference were reluctant to criticize such hopeful efforts too severely and thus permitted a consensus on a final declaration.

The 1985 conference declaration is of particular interest here, since the language relating to Article VI reflects agreement by the NPT's parties that zero nuclear weapons were to be pursued, but not solely in the context of general and complete disarmament. The declaration summarized with approval the final report of the 1978 special session of the UN General Assembly dealing with disarmament. That report had noted that progress *toward* general and complete disarmament could be taken by specific steps which should be implemented within a few years. It outlined a "Programme of Action" to accomplish such steps without awaiting agreement on general and complete disarmament. This included "a comprehensive, phased programme with agreed time-frames, whenever feasible, for progressive and balanced reduction of stockpiles of nuclear weapons and their means of delivery, leading to *their ultimate and complete elimination at the earliest possible time*."[40]

To put this in the context of Article VI, the 1985 NPT review conference's final declaration summarized it with approval. NPT parties in 1985 thus agreed that the "phased programme" leading to zero was within the Article VI obligation relating to "nuclear disarmament," not just that relating to general and complete disarmament.[41] The final report also reflected sharp criticism by the non-nuclear-weapon parties of the failure to achieve a nuclear test ban; it also contained this language:

> [T]he Conference noted that certain states Party to the Treaty [understood to mean Britain and the United States], while committed to the goal of an effectively verifiable comprehensive Nuclear Test-Ban Treaty, considered *deep and verifiable reductions in existing arsenals of nuclear weapons* as the highest priority in the process of pursuing the objectives of Article VI.[42]

23

At the Nuclear Crossroads

This clearly implied that deep cuts in nuclear weapons could and should be negotiated outside the context of general and complete disarmament (as was later done in START I and START II).

By the time of the 1990 review conference, there had been successful Reagan-Gorbachev summits, an end to the Cold War, agreement on an Intermediate-Range Nuclear Force (INF) treaty, and progress toward the first START treaty. Both of these treaties were intended to reduce nuclear delivery vehicles, but both had or would have the additional effect of withdrawing nuclear warheads from active deployment. However, in 1990 a consensus final declaration again proved elusive, owing primarily to the failure of the nuclear powers to achieve a test ban. Mexico, the leader of the non-aligned countries, refused to accept a compromise such as that of 1985—a compromise that would have criticized the failure to achieve a test ban pursuant to Article VI, but also would have reflected views of Britain and the United States such as those quoted above.[43]

Conclusions on the Meaning of Article VI

1. Article VI said that measures relating to "cessation of the nuclear arms race at an early date" were to be negotiated when the treaty entered into force (1970). The three such measures most often mentioned in the negotiating history and in the parties' 1968 agreement on an agenda to implement Article VI were a ban on nuclear testing; a cut-off in the production of fissionable materials for nuclear weapons; and a prohibition on the use of nuclear weapons.

After almost 25 years, none of these measures has been achieved in internationally binding form. There exist four-power, reciprocal moratoria on testing (China being the sole holdout), a U.S.-Soviet Threshold Test Ban Treaty, unilateral cut-offs of fissionable-material production for weapons by the United States and soon by Russia, and national declarations promising not to use nuclear weapons on non-nuclear-weapon countries by each of the five prowers—with differences in their coverage.[44] Negotiations for multilateral treaties covering all three measures—to end tests and production of material for weapons and to ban their use with agreed exceptions—are now on the agenda of the Conference on Disarmament (CD) in Geneva. But agreements since 1970 in the "cessation-of-the-nuclear-arms-race" category are quite few.

24

Nuclear Disarmament

The five countries accepted by the NPT as nuclear-weapon states have a clear Article VI obligation to negotiate in good faith on all three of these measures at Geneva. The measures have greater urgency under Article VI than measures relating to "nuclear disarmament"—though they are not required to be completed before an obligation to negotiate toward nuclear disarmament arises.

Three of the five nuclear-weapon powers—Britain, the Soviet Union (now Russia) and the United States—participated in the last serious test ban negotiations ending in 1980. All five are members of the multilateral CD in Geneva, but China and France (also members of the CD) were not obliged to negotiate in good faith on "cessation-of-the-nuclear-arms-race" measures until they joined the NPT in 1992.

Until this year, there had been little recent discussion in the CD about a cut-off in the production of fissile material for nuclear weapons. However, a 1993 UN General Assembly resolution on such a cut-off, new support from the United States, and the joint US-Russian statement of January 14, 1994—in which both powers "expressed their resolve to implement effective measures to limit and reduce nuclear weapons" and announced that "an important contribution to the goal of non-proliferation of nuclear weapons would be made by a verifiable ban on the production of fissile materials for nuclear weapons and by the most rapid conclusion of an international convention to this effect"—may all give impetus to that subject.[45] At the beginning of its 1994 session, the CD appointed a Special Coordinator (a representative of Canada) to consult the other parties on the scope and forum for negotiating "a non-discriminatory, multilateral and internationally and effectively verifiable treaty banning the production of fissile material for nuclear weapons or other nuclear explosive devices."

> *There have been no American or Russian plans to go to zero nuclear weapons. The NPT requires more than this.*

Disagreement over exceptions to an obligation not to use nuclear weapons against non-nuclear-weapon states has prevented agreement on a treaty on the non-use of nuclear weapons at Geneva for years.[46] However, new efforts are likely in view of both the upcoming 1995 NPT review and extension conference and the need of assurances to persuade Ukraine to release the nuclear weapons left

At the Nuclear Crossroads

on its territory when it declared independence.[47] In the January 14,
1994 trilateral statement signed in Moscow by the presidents of Russia, United States, and Ukraine, the first two agreed to give Ukraine
identical security assurances as soon as it accedes to the NPT. Thus
all three measures (CTB, cut-off, and security assurances) will, in all
likelihood, receive new attention during 1994.

2. Of the three "cessation-of-the-nuclear-arms-race" measures, the
comprehensive test ban has always been mentioned as a first-order
priority; recall that it alone is specified in the preamble of the NPT.[48]
At the preceding four NPT review conferences, the failure to achieve
a CTB received the greatest attention and was the reason two of the
four conferences adjourned without agreement on a final declaration. In the eyes of the NPT parties not having nuclear weapons,
there is no question that a CTB is the most important measure
the nuclear-weapon states can adopt in satisfying their Article VI
obligations.

There will be two important differences at the 1995 conference from
past NPT review conferences. The first is that a failure to reach
agreement at the 1995 conference could mean an end to the NPT.
For the first time, the NPT parties not having nuclear weapons will
possess real bargaining leverage vis-à-vis the nuclear powers to push
for a test ban. Realizing their leverage, the non-aligned members of
the Geneva CD issued a statement on December 1, 1993 in which
they demanded achievment of a "final text" of a CTBT during 1994.[49]

The second difference is that the decision on the length of the NPT
extension will be made by majority voting, not by the consensus
procedure of the review conferences. This is especially significant
since the parties will be asked to decide the treaty's term of renewal, not just to comment on the treaty's performance. Moreover,
this important conference decision cannot be blocked by a small
minority as was the case with decisions at past review conferences.

What impact will these changes have on the prospects for achieving
a test ban? NPT parties seeking such a ban would certainly not get
what they want by bringing the NPT to an end. Moreover, all or
most of the developing countries that are among the strongest advocates of a test ban have an interest in continuing the NPT as long
as it is seen as effective in preventing other countries from securing

26

Nuclear Disarmament

nuclear weapons and in promoting trade in nuclear material and equipment under safeguards.[50] But given the failure of the nuclear-weapon countries to achieve a test ban for 25 years, the developing countries may not trust them to agree on a CTB without exerting strong pressure on them to do so.

One developing-country proposal to deal with this dilemma could be to extend the NPT in 1995 for a short period, perhaps two years, in order to provide more time for test ban negotiations, and then to extend it for a longer period if a test ban has been achieved. There are, however, serious doubts about the legality of this proposal, and the result of a two-year extension could well be an end to the NPT in 1997.[51]

A more likely alternative of the non-nuclear parties could be to call for a recess of the 1995 conference, perhaps for six months, with the idea of reconvening it to make the extension decision once a test ban has been achieved.[52] Since the non-aligned countries constitute some two-thirds of the NPT's membership, they have it within their power to precipitate such a recess if they cooperate. Moreover, since preventing proliferation depends so heavily on the consent of all the countries capable of building nuclear weapons, the proponents of a long NPT extension are unlikely to press their proposal to a vote in 1995 unless they have a substantial majority. Having nuclear-capable countries going home mad from the conference and threatening withdrawal from the NPT would be an unhealthy result.[53] Given the interest of almost all the NPT parties in preventing the NPT from lapsing after a short (two years?) extension, a recess of the 1995 conference until a test ban is negotiated seems quite possible if no test ban text has been agreed to by the opening of the conference.[54]

3. Turning to Article VI measures "relating to . . . nuclear disarmament," the Soviet Union and the United States have implemented the INF treaty eliminating their intermediate-range nuclear forces. In the START I and II treaties, Russia and the United States have agreed on deep cuts down to at least 3,500 warheads each in their strategic nuclear forces. By reciprocal action, Russia and the United States have deactivated, withdrawn, or dismantled many nuclear warheads of all ranges, including many not covered by the INF and START treaties. These are major achievements in compliance with

At the Nuclear Crossroads

the obligation of Article VI to negotiate in good faith on measures "relating to . . . nuclear disarmament."

So far, the other three nuclear-weapon parties, Britain, China and France, have not participated in the American-Soviet (now Russian) negotiations to reduce nuclear weapons. China and France did not become obligated to do so until they joined the NPT in 1992, but they will surely need to talk about nuclear reductions with the other nuclear-weapon powers before the 1995 conference opens to demonstrate compliance with Article VI.

Russia and the United States have not yet had any serious negotiations on going below the final START II levels of land-based and sea-based strategic missile warheads—levels *higher* than what existed on both sides in 1970 when the NPT went into effect.[55] Furthermore, except for 30-year old plans for general and complete disarmament and a Gorbachev proposal of 1986 to eliminate nuclear weapons by the year 2000, there have been no specific American or Russian national plans for going to zero—much less talks between the two or among the five toward that end. Article VI clearly requires more than this.

4. The NPT's preambular language dealing with general and complete disarmament suggests that "easing of international tensions and the strengthening of international trust between states" was thought necessary in 1968 to facilitate the "elimination from national arsenals of nuclear weapons and the means of their delivery." Even if these pre-conditions must be met not just for "general and complete disarmament," but also for "nuclear disarmament," the fear of a U.S.-Russian nuclear exchange has receded greatly with the end of the Cold War. That has eased East-West tensions. However, the world remains a dangerous place. Regional conflicts, ethnic violence, nationalistic separatism and civil wars have in fact increased since the Cold War's end. The peaceful world necessary as a prerequisite for deep cuts in conventional armaments has not yet arrived, the UN has not yet shown itself capable enough of handling violent disputes, and general and complete disarmament still does not seem to be realistic.

But the plain meaning of Article VI, its negotiating history, and the parties' practice in implementing it all suggest that these pre-

Nuclear Disarmament

conditions do not need to be satisfied to trigger an obligation to negotiate in good faith toward zero nuclear weapons along the "nuclear disarmament" route. After 25 years and an end to the Cold War, the time has been reached when Article VI requires all five nuclear-weapon states to begin such talks. Article VI does not say whether negotiating toward zero means taking one step downward after another through one negotiation after another, or a "phased programme" involving a package of steps agreed in one long negotiation. At the same time, Article VI does not authorize an avoidance of negotiations by any of the five just because the Americans and Russians have agreed to reduce to 3,500 strategic warheads. Indeed, all five nuclear powers have a present, pressing obligation to begin discussing proposals for moving in the direction of zero along one route or the other. [56]

Notes

1. The full text of Article VI reads:

    Each of the Parties to the Treaty undertakes to pursue negotiations in good faith on effective measures relating to cessation of the nuclear arms race at an early date and to nuclear disarmament, and on a treaty on

At the Nuclear Crossroads

general and complete disarmament under strict and effective international control.

2.   The 1967 date comes from the NPT: Art.IX.3 defines "nuclear-weapon state," for the purposes of the treaty, as one "which has manufactured and exploded a nuclear weapon or other nuclear explosive device prior to January 1, 1967." That included only the five mentioned in the text. The NPT's purpose was to prevent increases in this number if that was possible. The 1961 "Irish resolution," the UN General Assembly resolution that was the origin of the NPT negotiations, sought a treaty in which nuclear-weapon states would promise not to disseminate nuclear weapons or information on their manufacture, and non-nuclear-weapon states "would undertake not to manufacture or otherwise acquire control of such weapons." UNGA Res. 1665 (XVI), Dec. 4, 1961. See G. Bunn, *Arms Control by Committee: Managing Negotiations with the Russians* (Stanford University Press, 1992), pp. 64–66.

3.   See NPT Arts. VI, VII.3 and X.

4.   See, e.g., Soviet Proposal Submitted to the Eighteen-Nation Disarmament Committee: Draft Treaty on General and Complete Disarmament Under Strict International Control, Mar. 15, 1962, ACDA, *Documents on Disarmament, 1962,* pp. 103–127; U.S. Proposal Submitted to the Eighteen-Nation Disarmament Committee: Outline of Basic Provisions of a Treaty on General and Complete Disarmament in a Peaceful World, April 18, 1962, ACDA, *Documents on Disarmament, 1962,* pp. 351–382.

5.   See U.S. proposal, cited above, pp. 352–53, 367–68, 374–75, 380–81.

6.   One meaning for "disarm" is to "reduce armed forces." See *Webster's Ninth New Collegiate Dictionary* (Merriam-Webster, 1986), p. 359.

7.   NPT, 8th preambular paragraph, (emphasis added).

8.   NPT, 11th preambular paragraph, (emphasis added).

9.   Dept. of State Telegram 13195 to NATO capitals, Feb. 28, 1962, National Security Archive (NSA), Nuclear Non-Proliferation Collection.

10.   Dept. of State Telegram 01153 to NATO capitals of Mar. 2, 1962, NSA, NNP Collection.

11.   See George Bunn, *Arms Control by Committee: Managing Negotiations with the Russians* (Stanford University Press, 1992), p. 66.

12.   See George Bunn and Charles N. Van Doren, "Options for Extension of the NPT: the Intention of the Drafters of Article X.2," in Bunn, Fischer and Van Doren, *Options & Opportunities: The NPT Extension Conference of 1995* (Programme for Promoting Nuclear Non-Proliferation, 1991), pp. 3–6.

13.   Bunn and Van Doren, cited above, p. 5.

14.   Memorandum of the Federal Republic of Germany to other governments, April 7, 1967, ACDA, *Documents on Disarmament, 1967,* pp. 179, 180, 182.

15.   ACDA, *International Negotiations on the Treaty on the Non-Proliferation of Nuclear Weapons* (GPO, 1969), pp. 133, 135.

16.   Italian Proposal Submitted to the Eighteen Nation Disarmament

29a

Notes

Committee: Draft of Unilateral Nonacquisition Declaration, September 14, 1965, *Documents on Disarmament, 1965* (1966), p. 411–12.

17. ACDA, *Documents on Disarmament, 1965*, p. 424–25 (emphasis added).

18. UNGA Res. 2028 of Nov. 19, 1965, ACDA, *Documents on Disarmament, 1965*, pp. 532–34.

19. Statement of March 3, 1966, ACDA, *Documents on Disarmament, 1966*, pp. 68, 77 (emphasis added).

20. Memorandum of Aug. 19, 1966, ACDA, *Documents on Disarmament, 1966*, pp. 576–78.

21. Mexican Working Paper of Sept. 19, 1967, ACDA, *Documents on Disarmament, 1967*, pp. 394–95.

22. Brazilian Amendments of October 31, 1967, *Documents on Disarmament, 1967*, p. 546; Statement of the Burmese representative of Oct. 10, 1967, *Documents, 1967*, p. 459, 463; Statement of Indian Delegate of Sept. 28, 1967, *Documents, 1967*, pp. 430, 440; Rumanian Working Paper of October 19, 1967, *Documents, 1967*, pp. 525–26; Swiss Aide-Memoire of Nov. 17, 1967, *Documents, 1967*, pp. 572–574.

23. Statement of Feb. 24, 1967 ENDC/PV.289.

24. Statement to the Diet, Mar. 14, 1967.

25. Statement of Feb. 23, 1967, ENDC/PV.288 (emphasis added).

26. Bunn and Van Doren, cited above, at pp. 5–8.

27. Revised identical American and Soviet NPT drafts of Jan. 18, 1968, in ACDA, *International Negotiation of the Treaty on the Non-Proliferation of Nuclear Weapons* (GPO, 1969), pp. 150, 153–54. The earlier Soviet and U.S. drafts also appear in this book.

28. ACDA, *International Negotiations*, cited above, at pp. 150–59. These changes appeared in drafts of Jan. 18, 1968 and March 11, 1968.

29. U.N. Charter, chap. VII.

30. NPT Art. X.1.

31. Statement of April 26, 1968, ACDA, *Documents on Disarmament, 1968*, p. 230–231 (emphasis added).

32. David A. Koplow, "Passing Good Faith: Has the United States Violated Article VI of the Nuclear Non-Proliferation Treaty?" 1993 *Wis. Law Review*, pp. 301, 367–374.

33. Statement of July 1, 1968, ACDA, *Documents on Disarmament, 1968*, pp. 458–60.

34. Memorandum of July 1, 1968, ACDA, *Documents on Disarmament, 1968*, pp. 466–70.

35. Report to the United Nations and the UN Disarmament Commission of August 28, 1968, ENDC/236, ACDA, *Documents on Disarmament, 1968*, pp. 591, 593.

36. These included Australia, Germany, Japan, Indonesia, Turkey and Yugoslavia.

At the Nuclear Crossroads

37. Warren H. Donnelly & Robert L. Beckman, "Nuclear Non-Proliferation Treaty Conference," reprinted in Environment and Natural Resources Policy Division of the Congressional Research Service, 99th Cong., 1st Sess., *Nuclear Proliferation Factbook*, p. 577, 581 (1985).

38. Final Declaration of the Review Conference of the Parties to the Treaty on the Non-Proliferation of Nuclear Weapons, May 30, 1975, ACDA, *Documents on Disarmament, 1975*, pp. 146, 153–155.

39. Working paper submitted by the Group of 77 non-aligned countries on Aug. 26, 1980. NPT/CONF. II/C.I/2.

40. Final Document of the Tenth Special Session of the General Assembly, June 30, 1978, ACDA, *Documents on Disarmament, 1978*, pp. 411, 420–21 (emphasis added).

41. Final Declaration by the Third Review Conference of the Parties to the Treaty on the Non-Proliferation of Nuclear Weapons, Sept. 21, 1985. ACDA, *Documents on Disarmament, 1985*, pp. 641, 650–56.

42. Mohamed I. Shaker, "The Legacy of the 1985 Nuclear Non-Proliferation Treaty Review Conference: The President's Reflections [Shaker was president of the conference]," in John Simpson, ed., *Nuclear Non-Proliferation: An Agenda for the 1990s* (Cambridge, UK: Cambridge University Press, 1987), pp. 9,10,15 (emphasis added).

43. Charles N. Van Doren and George Bunn, "Progress and Peril at the Fourth NPT Review Conference," *Arms Control Today* (Oct. 1990), p. 89.

44. See George Bunn and Roland Timerbaev, "Security Assurances to Non-Nuclear-Weapon States," *The Nonproliferation Review*, v.1, no.1 (Fall 1993), p. 11.

45. UNGA Res.48/75L (1993); Statement of President Clinton to UNGA, Sept. 27, 1993; White House Fact Sheet on nuclear issues dated Sept. 27, 1993; Joint Statement by the President of the Russian Federation and the President of the United States on the Non-Proliferation of Weapons of Mass Destruction and the Means of their Delivery dated January 14, 1994.

46. For a report showing the current differences of views at the Geneva conference on this subject, see "Report of the Ad Hoc Committee on Effective International Arrangements to Assure Non-Nuclear-Weapon States against the Use or Threat of Use of Nuclear Weapons," Conference on Disarmament, CD/1219, August 25, 1993.

47. See Bunn and Timerbaev, "Security Assurances . . . ," cited above.

48. For an argument that, until the United States agreed to resume negotiations for a comprehensive test ban, it was in violation of Article VI, see Koplow, "Passing Good Faith . . . ," cited above.

49. Doc. CD/1231.

50. See G. Bunn, "The Non-Proliferation Treaty of 1968 and its Extension in 1995," *Nonproliferation Review* (published by the Monterey Institute for International Studies) Winter 1994, v.1, no.2, pp, 51–60.

51. See Bunn and Van Doren, "Options for Extension . . . ," cited above, p. 10.

Notes

52. Cf. William Epstein, "Amendment Conference is Best Way to Achieve Early CTBT & Help NPT," *Disarmament Times* (Dec. 21, 1993), p. 4.

53. See Lewis Dunn, "NPT 1995: Time to Shift Gears," *Arms Control Today* 23 (November 1994), pp. 14–19.

54. For an argument that such a recess would not bring the NPT to an end, see Bunn and Van Doren, "Options for Extension . . . ," cited above, pp. 9–10. For further discussion, see Serge Sur, "The problem of the continuance in force of the NPT after 1995 in the absence of a decision extending the Treaty—UNIDIR/91/52" and the reply from David Fischer, "Postscript-Some Comments on Professor Sur's Note," both in Bunn, Fischer and Van Doren, "Options & Opportunities . . . ," cited above.

55. The total Russian and U.S. land-based and sea-based strategic nuclear missile warheads (not counting gravity bombs or cruise missiles launched from aircraft) will be about 2,200 each if START II is fully implemented. *New York Times*, Dec. 30, 1992, table entitled "Limiting Nuclear Warheads." These were what seemed the most threatening warheads during the mid-1960s when the NPT was negotiated, and are therefore the most important from the viewpoint of Art. VI. At the end of 1969, at the beginning of the SALT negotiations just before the NPT went into effect, the number of Soviet and U.S. strategic missile warheads that both sides assumed would be frozen if SALT produced an immediate freeze was under 2,000, including all those deployed and in the "pipeline." Lawrence D. Weiler, *The Arms Race, Secret Negotiations and Congress* (Occasional Paper No. 12, Stanley Foundation, 1976), p. 16.

56. For non-governmental proposals for drastic reductions in, and elimination of, national nuclear arsenals, see Gerard C. Smith, "Take Nuclear Weapons into Custody," *Bulletin of the Atomic Scientists*, December 1990; Roger D. Speed, "International Control of Nuclear Weapons" (Center for International Security and Arms Control, Stanford University, publication forthcoming in 1994); Joseph Rotblat, Jack Steinberger and Bhalchandra Udgaonkar, eds., *A Nuclear-Weapon-Free World* (Westview Press, 1993); Edward Teller, "Revival of the Baruch Plan," January 1992 (unpublished memorandum); Robert S. McNamara, "The Changing Nature of Global Security and its Impact on South Asia," Address to the Indian Defence Policy Forum, November 20, 1992, A publication of the Washington Council on Non-Proliferation; Andrew J. Goodpaster, *"Further Reins on Nuclear Arms: Next Steps for the Major Nuclear Powers"*, The Atlantic Council, Consultation Paper Series, August 1993; Roland Timerbaev, "Nonproliferation Organizations and Regimes Beyond 1995," (to be published in 1994 in *Beyond 1995?* by the Center for National Security Studies, Los Alamos National Laboratory).

[6]

The IAEA Safeguards System

by Laura Rockwood*

The nuclear non-proliferation regime is a complex of varied and evolving instruments and measures intended to deter and detect the proliferation of nuclear weapons. It includes, *inter alia*, global and regional treaties on non-proliferation, export controls, physical protection, measures designed to track and deter illicit trafficking in nuclear and other radioactive materials, and international verification. Taken together, these instruments and measures, if effectively implemented, create a finely woven fabric which reduces the risk of the proliferation of nuclear weapons through state and non-state actions. The cornerstone of this regime is the safeguards system of the International Atomic Energy Agency (hereinafter the "Agency" or IAEA). This article describes the legal framework of IAEA safeguards and how the system has developed.

A. Legal framework

I. IAEA Statute

The IAEA's safeguards system is grounded in the provisions of the Agency's Statute which entered into force on 29 July 1957. As originally contemplated, the IAEA was to be a sort of broker of controlled nuclear assistance and trade. It was anticipated that the majority of the safeguards arrangements would be a function of the Agency's responsibility under Article II to "ensure, as far as it is able, that assistance provided by or through it, is not used in such a way as to further any

---

*   Section Head, Non-Proliferation and Policy Making Organs, Office of Legal Affairs, International Atomic Energy Agency. The author alone is responsible of the facts and opinions expressed in this article.

military purpose". However, the Statute was drafted in such a way as to permit growth and flexibility in the system.

Article III.A.5 authorises the Agency to establish and administer safeguards designed to ensure that projects in the field of nuclear energy carried out or fostered by the Agency are not used in such a way as to further any military purpose (a requirement with respect to which Article XI.F.4 sets out in more detail: the assistance provided shall not be used in such a way as to further any military purpose, and the project shall be subject to the safeguards provided for in Article XII to the extent the agreement specifies particular controls to be relevant). In addition, Article III.A.5 authorises the IAEA to apply safeguards to any bilateral or multilateral arrangement, at the request of the parties, and to any of the nuclear activities of a state, at that state's request.

Article XII of the Statute sets out the fundamental features of Agency safeguards in three paragraphs:

1.   the rights and responsibilities that the Agency has when carrying out safeguards, to the extent relevant to the specific situation:

   •   to examine the design of specialised equipment and facilities;
   •   to require the maintenance and production of operating records to assist in ensuring accountability for and control of source and special fissionable materials;
   •   to require the submission of reports;
   •   to send into the state inspectors, designated by the Agency after consultation with the state or states concerned, who shall have access at all times to all places and data and to any person who by reason of his occupation deals with materials, equipment or facilities which are required by this Statute to be safeguarded, as necessary to account for nuclear materials and to determine whether there is compliance with the undertaking against use in furtherance of any military purpose and with any other conditions prescribed in the agreement; and
   •   impose certain sanctions.

2.   the requirement that the Agency establish a staff of inspectors, whose general functions are specified in the Statute (including right of access).

3. the steps available to inspectors, by the Director General and by the Board of Governors in the event a state is found to be in violation of its safeguards agreement, including calling upon the state to remedy the non-compliance, reporting such non-compliance to the member states of the Agency, to the Security Council and the General Assembly of the United Nations and imposing certain sanctions.

II. Treaty and supply agreement obligations

1. Assistance provided by the Agency

Article III.A.5 of the Statute contemplates the application of Agency safeguards to assistance provided by the IAEA. As indicated in Article XI.F of the Statute, assistance may be provided to Agency member states by the IAEA in connection with any project for research on, or development or practical application of, atomic energy for peaceful purposes. Assistance provided under such projects can take the form of special fissionable or other material, services, equipment and/or facilities. These projects, which are administered by the IAEA's Department of Technical Co-operation, normally entail the conclusion of two documents: first, a supply agreement between a supplier state, the recipient state and the Agency and secondly, a project agreement between the Agency and the recipient state which, among other provisions, requires the application of Agency safeguards where relevant. That is so, for example, where the project involves the supply of nuclear material or facilities.

2. Multilateral and bilateral treaties

a. The NPT

The first global treaty calling for IAEA safeguards was the Treaty on the Non-Proliferation of Nuclear Weapons (the NPT) which entered into force on 5 March 1970. Article III.1 of the NPT requires each non-nuclear weapon state[1] (NNWS) to accept safeguards, as set forth in an agreement to be concluded with the IAEA in accordance with its Statute, on all source or special fissionable material in all peaceful nuclear activities within its territory, under its jurisdiction or carried out under its control anywhere, for the exclusive purpose of verifying that such material is not diverted to nuclear weapons or other nuclear explosive devices. The safeguards agreements required under

---

1. Article IX.3 of the NPT defines a nuclear-weapon state (NWS) as one which had manufactured and exploded a nuclear weapon or other nuclear explosive device prior to 1 January 1967, of which there are five: China, France, the Soviet Union (now the Russian Federation), the United Kingdom and the United States.

Article III.1 are referred to as "full scope agreements" or, more commonly, "comprehensive safeguards agreements" (CSAs).

In addition, Article III.2 of the NPT requires each state party to the NPT not to provide source or special fissionable material, or equipment or material especially designed or prepared for the processing, use or production of special fissionable material, to a NNWS for peaceful purposes unless the source or special fissionable material is subject to Agency safeguards. There is no corresponding requirement with respect to exports to NWSs.

Negotiation of the NPT resulted in accommodation of a number of states' interest in retaining the right to use nuclear energy for non-explosive military purposes, specifically, nuclear naval propulsion. In addition, the treaty contemplates availability to NNWSs of the potential benefits of peaceful applications of nuclear explosives, although not necessarily access to the nuclear explosive devices themselves or to the relevant technology.

b.   The Tlatelolco Treaty

The first regional treaty on non-proliferation and a nuclear-weapon-free zone was the Treaty for the Prohibition of Nuclear Weapons in Latin America, which was opened for signature in Tlatelolco, Mexico on 14 February 1967, and has entered into force for the states in the zone of application. Article 1 of the treaty requires all parties to use exclusively for peaceful purposes the nuclear material and facilities which are under their jurisdiction and to prohibit and prevent in their respective territories (a) the testing, use, manufacture, production or acquisition by any means whatsoever of any nuclear weapons by the parties themselves directly or indirectly, on behalf of anyone else or in any other way and (b) the receipt, storage, installation, deployment and any form of possession of any nuclear weapons, directly or indirectly, by the parties themselves, by anyone on their behalf or in any other way.

Articles 12-18 of the Tlatelolco Treaty establish a control system for the purpose of verifying compliance with the obligation under the treaty to use nuclear energy exclusively for peaceful purposes. Under that system, a party to the Tlatelolco Treaty is required to conclude multilateral or bilateral agreements with the IAEA for the application of its safeguards to its nuclear activities. Similar to the NPT, the Tlatelolco Treaty also contemplates the possibility of peaceful applications of nuclear explosions conducted by a nuclear-weapon state (NWS). However, unlike the NPT, the Tlatelolco Treaty does not contain a requirement of safeguards as condition of nuclear supply.

There are two additional protocols to the Tlatelolco Treaty. Additional Protocol I of the treaty is open to any state which has territories in the zone of application of the treaty for which it is, *de jure* or *de facto*, internationally responsible (France, the Netherlands, the United Kingdom and the United States) and requires the state to conclude a safeguards agreement with respect to such territories. Additional Protocol II is open to the five NWSs and contains an undertaking not to use or threaten to use nuclear weapons against the parties to the Tlatelolco Treaty (referred to as "negative security assurances").

c. The Rarotonga Treaty

The South Pacific Nuclear Free Zone Treaty (the Rarotonga Treaty) was opened for signature in 1985 and entered into force on 11 December 1986. Article 8 of the treaty, which establishes the control system under the treaty, requires the application to peaceful nuclear activities of safeguards by the IAEA pursuant to an agreement required in connection with the NPT or equivalent in scope. Unlike the NPT and the Tlatelolco Treaty, no nuclear explosives or nuclear explosive devices are permitted within the zone of application of the treaty. With regard to exports, Article 4 of the Rarotonga Treaty requires each party not to provide source or special fissionable material, or equipment or material especially designed or prepared for the processing, use or production of special fissionable material for peaceful purpose to any NNWS unless subject to IAEA safeguards, or to any NWS unless subject to applicable safeguards agreements with the IAEA. Under that same article, each state party also expressly undertakes to support the continued effectiveness of the international non-proliferation system based on the NPT and the IAEA safeguards system.

The Rarotonga Treaty includes three protocols: Protocol 1 is similar to Additional Protocol I of the Tlatelolco Treaty and is open to states with territories for which they are internationally responsible which are situated within the South Pacific nuclear-free zone (France, the United Kingdom and the United States). Protocols 2 and 3 are open to the five NWSs. Protocol 2 contains an undertaking not to use or threaten to use nuclear explosive device against any party to the treaty or any territory within the zone for which it is internationally responsible. Protocol 3 contains an undertaking not to test any nuclear explosive device within the zone.

d. The Bangkok Treaty

The Southeast Asia Nuclear Weapon-Free Zone Treaty (the Bangkok Treaty) was opened for signature by all states in Southeast Asia, namely Brunei Darussalam, Cambodia, Indonesia, Laos, Malaysia, Myanmar, Philippines, Singapore, Thailand and Vietnam, on 15 December 1995, in Bangkok, and entered into force on 27 March 1997. Under this treaty, each state party undertakes to use exclusively for peaceful purposes nuclear material and facilities which are within its territory and areas under its jurisdiction and control and to conclude an agreement with the IAEA for the application of full-scope safeguards to its peaceful nuclear activities. The treaty also prohibits the export of source or special fissionable material, or specially designed or prepared equipment or material, to any NNWS except under a comprehensive safeguards agreement, and to NWSs, in conformity with applicable safeguards agreements with the IAEA. The control system set up under the Bangkok Treaty also has a mechanism permitting a state party to request that a fact-finding mission be sent to another state party in order to clarify and resolve a situation which may be considered ambiguous or which may give rise to doubts about compliance with the provisions of the treaty. The Bangkok Treaty includes a protocol on negative security assurances open to signature by the NWSs.

e.   *The Pelindaba Treaty*

The African Nuclear Weapon-Free Zone Treaty (the Pelindaba Treaty) was opened for signature in Cairo, Egypt, on 11 April 1996. Pursuant to this treaty, each party undertakes not to conduct research on, develop, manufacture stockpile or otherwise acquire, possess or have control over any nuclear explosive device by any means anywhere; not to seek or receive any assistance in the research on, development, manufacture, stockpiling or acquisition or possession of any nuclear explosive device; and not to take any action to assist or encourage the research on, development, manufacture, stockpiling or acquisition or possession on any nuclear explosive device. The parties also undertake to prohibit the stationing of nuclear weapons on their territory and to prohibit the testing of any nuclear explosive devices on their territory. As regards safeguards, each state party undertakes to conduct all activities for the peaceful use of nuclear energy under strict non-proliferation measures to provide assurance of exclusively peaceful uses, to conclude a comprehensive safeguards agreement with the IAEA and not to export source or special fissionable material, specially designed or prepared equipment or material to NNWSs except subject to a comprehensive safeguards agreement. Associated with the treaty are three protocols: Protocol I, which is open to signature by the five NWSs, binds those states not to use or threaten to use a nuclear explosive device against a party to the treaty or in the African nuclear-weapon-free zone; Protocol II, also open to signature by the five NWSs, commits the parties to it not to test or assist or encourage the testing of a nuclear explosive device within the zone; and Protocol III, which is open to all states with territories with respect to which it has *de jure* or *de facto* international responsibility situated in the zone, requires, *inter alia*, the application of safeguards to such territories.

f.   The CANWFZ Treaty

The Central Asian Nuclear-Weapon-Free Zone (CANWFZ) Treaty was signed on 8 September 2006 by Kazakhstan, Kyrgyzstan, Uzbekistan, Tajikistan and Turkmenistan in Semipalatinsk, Kazakhstan. The treaty, which entered into force on 21 March 2009, created the first denuclearised zone in the northern hemisphere and the first bordered by two NWSs. Similar to the other NWFZ treaties, the parties undertake not to conduct research on, develop, manufacture stockpile or otherwise acquire, possess or have control over any nuclear explosive device by any means anywhere; not to seek or receive any assistance in the research on, development, manufacture, stockpiling or acquisition, or possession of any nuclear explosive device; and not to take any action to assist or encourage the research on, development, manufacture, stockpiling or acquisition or possession on any nuclear explosive device. The parties also undertake to prohibit the stationing of nuclear weapons on their territory and to prohibit the testing of any nuclear explosive devices on their territory. As regards safeguards, each state party undertakes to use nuclear material and facilities for exclusively peaceful uses, to conclude with the IAEA, if it has not already done so, a CSA. Significantly, the CANWFZ Treaty also requires each state party to conclude an additional protocol (AP) as well as a CSA (see discussion below) and not to export source, or special fissionable material, specially designed or prepared equipment or material, to a NNWS unless that state has concluded with the IAEA a CSA and an AP. Associated with the treaty is a protocol, open to signature by the five NWSs, containing negative security assurances and an undertaking not to contribute to any act that constitutes a violation of the treaty or the protocol.

g.   The Argentina/Brazil Agreement

The Governments of Argentina and Brazil entered into an agreement in 1990 calling for the establishment of a bilateral inspectorate (ABACC – the Brazilian-Argentine Agency for Accounting and Control of Nuclear Materials) and for the conclusion of a comprehensive agreement with the IAEA for the application of safeguards to all nuclear material in nuclear activities in Argentina and Brazil.

3.   At the request of a state

This provision of the Statute covers agreements between the IAEA and a state concluded at the request of that state, generally because of supply arrangements with other states who insist on safeguards as a condition of supply to provide assurance that nuclear-related trade is not used for military purposes. This provision also serves as the basis for the conclusion and implementation of the so called voluntary offer agreements (VOAs) concluded with the five NWSs.

III.   Basic documents

1.   INFCIRC/66/Rev.2

The first safeguards document (INFCIRC/26) was worked out by interested governments and the Secretariat in 1959 and 1960 and approved by the Board of Governors on 31 January 1961. It contained the principles and procedures for the application of safeguards to small reactors. This document was extended to larger reactors by decision of the Board on 26 February 1964. In 1964 and 1965, a completely revised safeguards document was worked out by a group of government experts and approved by the Board after unanimous concurrence by the General Conference in September 1965 (INFCIRC/66). Annex I to INFCIRC/66, which contains provisions for reprocessing plants, was approved by the Board in 1966, and Annex II, which contains provisions for safeguarded nuclear material in conversion and fuel fabrication plants, was adopted by the Board in 1968. With its two annexes, the safeguards document is now referred to as INFCIRC/66/Rev.2. Its provisions are incorporated by reference in the safeguards agreement.

In June 1961, the Board of Governors adopted a document referred to as the inspectors document [GC(V)/INF/39, Annex], developed with the help of government experts, which covers four different areas of inspection activities, including designation of Agency inspectors, notification of inspections, the conduct of inspection and rights of access and the privileges and immunities of inspectors. This document is also incorporated by reference in INFCIRC/66-type agreements (the comparable provisions in comprehensive safeguards agreements are included in the text of the agreements themselves). Hence, the inspectors document is of relevance only to agreements concluded pursuant to INFCIRC/66/Rev.2.

INFCIRC/66-type safeguards agreements originally included a basic undertaking on the part of the state or states party to the agreement not to use any safeguarded item for any military purpose. As will be discussed below, after 1974, that undertaking was expanded to limit the use of any item safeguarded thereunder to peaceful purposes and to prohibit the use of such items for the manufacture of any nuclear weapon, or to further any other military purpose or for the manufacture of any other nuclear explosive device.

2. INFCIRC/153 (Corr.)

In 1970, the Board of Governors established a Safeguards Committee (Committee 22) to advise it on the contents of safeguards agreements to be concluded between the NNWSs party to the NPT and the IAEA. Participation in the Committee was open to all member states of the Agency and included, in addition to many states party to the NPT, states which were not party, such as France, India and Pakistan. The Safeguards Committee developed a document entitled "The Structure and Content of Agreements between the Agency and States Required in connection with the Treaty on the Non-Proliferation of Nuclear Weapons", which the Board approved in 1972, and requested the Director General to use as the basis for negotiating safeguards agreements under the NPT. The document was published by the Agency as INFCIRC/153 (Corr.).

INFCIRC/153 has also served as a basis for the structure and content of comprehensive safeguards agreements concluded pursuant to the Tlatelolco Treaty and is considered the standard for safeguards agreements under the Rarotonga Treaty, the Pelindaba Treaty and the Bangkok Treaty. In addition, it provided a basis for the negotiation of the first unilateral comprehensive safeguards agreement with Albania, a non-NPT comprehensive agreement with Ukraine,[2] and the quadripartite safeguards agreement concluded with Argentina and Brazil.

The basic undertaking of the state under a CSA tracks the language of the NPT. In such agreements, the state undertakes to accept safeguards on all source or special fissionable material in all peaceful nuclear activities carried out on its territory or subject to its jurisdiction or control anywhere for the exclusive purpose of verifying that such material is not used for nuclear weapons or any other nuclear explosive device.[3] For its part, the IAEA has the right and obligation to ensure that all such material is safeguarded in accordance with the

---

2. Ukraine has since concluded an NPT CSA.

3. It is worth noting that, as under the NPT, while all explosive uses of nuclear material are prohibited under CSAs, not all military uses of nuclear material are prohibited. However, should a CSA state wish to withdraw nuclear material for use in a non-proscribed military activity, such as nuclear propulsion for submarines, the state must first agree with the IAEA on arrangements to ensure that the material is not removed from safeguards only for so long as it is in that use.

agreement, that is to say, to verify that there is no diversion of declared nuclear material to proscribed purposes and that there is no undeclared nuclear material or activity in the state.

Following the end of the cold war, a series of events resulted in a dramatic change in the IAEA's safeguards system. The discovery of a clandestine nuclear weapons programme in Iraq, the continuing difficulty in verifying the initial report of the Democratic People's Republic of Korea (DPRK) upon entry into force of its NPT CSA and the decision of the South African Government to give up its nuclear weapons programme and join the NPT, all played a role in an ambitious effort by IAEA member states and the Secretariat to strengthen the safeguards system.

Motivated by these events, between 1991 and 1993, the Board confirmed the IAEA's authority under CSAs to verify not just the correctness, but the completeness of states' declarations concerning nuclear material and facilities, with a view to ensuring that there is no diversion to proscribed purposes of any nuclear material in the state, whether declared or undeclared. The Board also confirmed the IAEA's right to have early access to design information about nuclear facilities and its continuing right to verify such information. In addition, the Board confirmed the IAEA's authority to use: environmental monitoring, a novel tool developed by the IAEA during its Security Council mandated verification in Iraq for detecting undeclared enrichment and reprocessing activities; satellite imagery and any other information available to it, whether from open sources or national technical means (intelligence information).

In June 1993, the Board of Governors requested the Director General to submit to it concrete proposals for the assessment, development and testing of measures for strengthening safeguards and improving its cost effectiveness. In response to that request, the Secretariat of the IAEA, in December 1993, initiated "Programme 93+2".

Over the course of the following two years, the Secretariat identified a comprehensive set of strengthening and efficiency measures for greater access to information, more extensive physical access to locations and maximisation of the efficiency and cost-effectiveness of the existing system of safeguards under INFCIRC/153 (GOV/2807) and tabled it for the Board's consideration in June 1995.

The measures were divided into two parts: Part 1, consisting of measures which could, in the Secretariat's view, be implemented under existing legal authority; and Part 2, consisting of measures which were believed to require complementary legal authority. The Board took note of the Director General's plan to implement at an early date those measures which fell within existing authority, thus indicating the Board's concurrence with the Secretariat's legal interpretation of the Agency's existing rights of access to information and locations, and urged states party to comprehensive safeguards agreements to co-operate with the Secretariat to facilitate such implementation. The Board also tasked the Secretariat with developing a legal instrument for the implementation of the Part 2 measures.

3.   Model Additional Protocol – INFCIRC/540 (Corr.)

Between June 1995 and June 1996, the Secretariat of the IAEA, in close consultation with member states of the Agency, developed for the Board's consideration a draft model of a protocol additional to safeguards agreements for that complementary authority. That draft served as the basis for the deliberations of Committee 24, the Committee established by the Board of Governors to negotiate and present to it a model protocol. On 15 May 1997, the Board of Governors, in a special session, approved the model for a new legal instrument designed to strengthen the effectiveness and improve the efficiency of the IAEA safeguards system: the Model Protocol Additional to Agreements between States and the IAEA for the Application of Safeguards [INFCIRC/540 (Corr.)].

The text of the model additional protocol consists of a preamble, eighteen articles and two annexes. The language of the preamble reflects the backbone of the negotiations: the need for a balance to be struck between, on the one hand, the desire to strengthen the effectiveness and improve the efficiency of the Agency's safeguards system and, on the other hand, the obligation to keep the frequency and intensity of activities to a minimum consistent with this objective. The measures provided for in the model additional protocol include:

- information about, and inspector access to, all aspects of a state's nuclear fuel cycle, from uranium mines to nuclear waste and any other location where nuclear material intended for non-nuclear uses is present;
- information on, and short-notice inspector access to, all buildings on a nuclear site;
- information about, and inspection mechanisms for, fuel cycle-related research and development;
- information on the manufacture and export of sensitive nuclear-related technologies and inspection mechanisms for manufacturing and import locations;

- the collection of environmental samples beyond declared locations when deemed necessary by the IAEA; and
- administrative arrangements that improve the process of designating inspectors, the issuance of multi-entry visas (necessary for unannounced inspections) and IAEA access to modern means of communications.

Article 1 of the model additional protocol establishes the relationship between an AP and the relevant safeguards agreement. It provides that the agreement and the AP are to be read as a single document with, in cases of conflict, the provisions of the additional protocol prevailing.

An AP, in combination with a state's CSA, provides as complete a picture as practicable of that state's production and holdings of nuclear source material, the activities for further processing of nuclear material (for both nuclear and non-nuclear application), and specified elements of the infrastructure that directly support the state's current or planned nuclear fuel cycle. The increased "complementary access" not only strengthens the IAEA's ability to verify declared nuclear material and activities but helps it provide assurances that undeclared nuclear activities are not concealed within declared nuclear sites or at other locations in the state.

4.   Privileges and Immunities Agreement – INFCIRC/9/Rev. 2

Agency safeguards inspectors are entitled to certain privileges and immunities while carrying out their responsibilities. These are grounded in Article XV.A of the Agency Statute, which provides that the staff of the Agency shall enjoy such privileges and immunities as are necessary in the independent exercise of their functions in connection with the Agency, and are spelled out in the Agreement on the Privileges and Immunities of the Agency (INFCIRC/9/Rev.2). The relevant provisions of this agreement are incorporated by reference into the safeguards agreements. They include immunity from legal process in respect of words spoken or written and all acts performed by an inspector in his or her official capacity, immunity from personal arrest or detention for non-official capacity, immunity from personal arrest or detention for non-official as well as official acts occurring during a mission, inviolability of papers and documents and freedom from seizure of personal baggage.

These privileges and immunities are extended to inspectors not only by the country in which an inspection takes place, but also by those member states through which inspectors are transiting on their way to and from that country. It bears noting that the IAEA has consistently taken the position that the Statute creates an obligation for member states to grant immunities as specifically defined in INFCIRC/9/Rev.2 and that non-acceptance of that agreement does not reduce the obligation of a member state to accord inspectors immunities adequate to enable them to efficiently complete their missions.

IV. Decisions and practices of the IAEA's Board of Governors

The legal framework of IAEA safeguards is formed not only by legal instruments, such as the documents referred to above, but also by the decisions and practices of the IAEA's Board of Governors. Some of the more significant decisions are referred to above. A number of other significant actions taken by the Board in the context of interpretation of the Agency safeguards agreements are described below.

1. Duration and termination of INFCIRC/66 agreements (GOV/1621)

Paragraph 16 of the INFCIRC/66/Rev.2 makes reference to the "desirability" of providing for the continuation of safeguards with respect to produced special fissionable material and to any materials substituted therefor. In 1973, the Board expressed concern about the need for safeguarding such material after the expiry of a safeguards agreement. As a consequence, since 1974, the duration of 66-type agreements has been tied to the actual use in the recipient state of supplied material or items, rather than to fixed periods of time. Under these agreements, safeguards are required to continue on all safeguarded items, including subsequent generations of produced nuclear material derived from safeguarded material or facilities, until safeguards are terminated in accordance with the revisions of INFCIRC/66/Rev.2.

2. Nature of the "no military" use undertaking

As indicated above, the early safeguards agreements concluded in accordance with INFCIRC/66/Rev.2 contained an undertaking by the state not to use safeguarded items for "any military purposes". Following the Indian testing of a so called "peaceful" nuclear explosive device in 1974, the Director General proposed, and the Board accepted, an interpretation of that undertaking precluding the use of safeguarded items for any nuclear explosive device, whether intended for peaceful or non-peaceful ends, owing to the technical impossibility of distinguishing between a nuclear explosive device for peaceful uses and one for military uses. Although a small number of states expressed reservations about this interpretation, all INFCIRC/66/Rev.2 safeguards agreements since 1975 have incorporated a basic undertaking which expressly precludes the use of safeguarded items for the manufacture of any nuclear weapon or to further any other military purpose or for the manufacture of any other nuclear explosive device.

3.   Coverage of transfers of technology, non-nuclear material

Although originally limited in applicability to nuclear material and certain types of nuclear facilities, the scope of INFCIRC/66-type agreements over the years has been expanded with the approval of the Board. These agreements have since included provisions for the safeguarding of such items as non-nuclear materials (e.g. heavy water, zircaloy), non-nuclear facilities (such as heavy water production plants) and transferred technology.

4.   Containment and surveillance

Although originally not expressly included in INFCIRC/66-type safeguards agreements, the Board of Governors has approved specific provisions for the application of containment and surveillance measures, which have routinely been included in the more recent INFCIRC/66-type agreements.

5.   Policy in implementation of financial clauses in safeguards agreements

While all Agency safeguards agreements reflect the basic principle that the expenses of safeguards are to be shared between the Agency and the state concerned, with each party bearing the expenses of carrying out its own responsibilities under the agreement, questions have arisen over the years as to the responsibility for particular expenses associated with certain safeguards activities. In 1990, the Director General presented to the Board a uniform policy with respect to the allocation of such expenses under INFCIRC/66/Rev.2-type agreements and INFCIRC/153 agreements (GOV/INF/577). The Secretariat has, since that time, included in the Subsidiary Arrangements to all Safeguards Agreements the provisions presented to the Board.

6.   Interpretation of provisions related to the early provision of design information

On 26 February 1992, the Board of Governors adopted a recommendation of the Director General related to the early provision of design information (GOV/2554/Att.2/Rev.2). In so doing, the Board interpreted paragraph 42 of INFCIRC/153, which stipulates that such information shall be provided by a state "as early as possible before nuclear material is introduced into a new facility", as requiring the provision of design information as soon as the decision to construct, to authorise construction or to modify a facility has been taken and, on an iterative basis, as the design is developed. The implementation of this interpretation required the modification of, *inter alia*, the standardised Code 3.1 of the General Part of Subsidiary Arrangements, which previously had provided for the submission of information on new facilities only 180 days before the introduction of nuclear material into a new facility. At the direction of the Board, the Secretariat negotiated with states with subsidiary arrangements in force the modification of Code 3.1. As of 2010, all such states have agreed to the modified Code 3.1.[4]

B.   Contents, comparison and implementation of safeguards agreements

The safeguards agreements concluded by the IAEA may be categorised generally as:

- the item-specific agreements concluded in accordance with INFCIRC/66/Rev.2;
- CSAs concluded in accordance with or along the lines of INFCIRC/153 (Corr.); and
- safeguards agreements applicable to all or part of the civil nuclear fuel cycles of NWSs (the so called voluntary offer agreements or "VOAs").

The basic goals of all safeguards agreements are similar: to verify compliance with the undertakings of the states parties not to use safeguarded items for proscribed purposes. Moreover, the basic technical aspects of the implementation of safeguards are applied in all states subject to safeguards. Each agreement provides for Agency review of design information; reporting and record keeping by the state; inspection activities to be carried out by the IAEA, including rights of access and notification of inspections; and provisions related to the exemption and termination of safeguards. To the extent practical and legally permissible, efforts are made to standardise the Agency's safeguards approaches, taking into account technical variations among the states' nuclear programmes.

While INFCIRC/66/Rev.2 identifies the safeguards procedures which are to be implemented under item-specific agreements, its provisions are simply incorporated by reference into the agreements and, while there is some consistency in the format and content of such agreements, there is no "model" INFCIRC/66-type agreement. INFCIRC/153, however, is much more comprehensive, and was intended to serve as guidance to the Secretariat on the

---

4.   However, Iran, which agreed to the modified Code 3.1 in 2003, announced in 2007 that it was suspending its implementation of the modified Code 3.1 and reverting to the previous formulation of that provision.

content and format of CSAs.[5] Hence, agreements concluded pursuant to INFCIRC/66/Rev. 2 reflect a greater degree of variation than do agreements concluded pursuant to INFCIRC/153. The agreements concluded with the NWSs (all of which are party to the NPT) more closely resemble the latter in format, with substantive variations reflecting the more limited scope of the VOAs. This latter category of agreements is often referred to as "voluntary offer agreements", owing to the fact that the NPT does not impose on NWSs a requirement similar to that assumed by NNWSs party to the NPT to conclude safeguards agreements with the IAEA.

Some of the differences between the three types of agreements are outlined below, the most significant of which relate to the scope of the agreements and the basic undertakings of the states thereunder.

I.   *Scope*

Safeguards agreements concluded pursuant to INFCIRC/66/Rev.2 are designed to cover only specified items, such as certain facilities, equipment, nuclear material and non-nuclear material. Therefore, they must describe in detail their scope of application. This is usually done in the provisions concerning basic undertaking provision and the inventory of safeguarded items. Agreements with NNWSs along the lines of INFCIRC/153 cover all source and special fissionable material in all peaceful nuclear activities of the state party. Hence, there is no elaborate provision on the scope of the agreement and/or on the inventory. The scope of the VOAs varies from agreement to agreement. However, while some provide for the application of safeguards to all of the state's civil nuclear activities and others to only some of the state's civil programme, all provide for the selection by the Agency of all, some or none of the facilities from those which is offered by the state concerned for the application of safeguards.

II.   *Basic undertaking*

Safeguards agreements under INFCIRC/66/Rev.2 prohibit the use of safeguarded items in such a way as to further any military purpose (including non-explosive uses, such as nuclear naval propulsion). Agreements with NNWSs party to the NPT prohibit the diversion of nuclear material from peaceful nuclear activities to nuclear weapons or other nuclear explosive devices. There is, however, no prohibition against non-explosive military

---

5.   The standardised model text for such agreements is contained in GOV/INF/276, Annex A (1974).

applications of nuclear material under the NPT. Accordingly, agreements with NNWS parties to the NPT contain provision for the withdrawal from safeguards of nuclear material for use in non-proscribed military nuclear activities (see para. 14 of INFCIRC/153). As regards VOAs, the NWSs' undertaking is limited to a commitment not to use nuclear material for proscribed purposes while it is subject to the agreement, and not to withdraw material or facilities from safeguards except in accordance with the terms of the relevant agreement, which provide in each case for withdrawal at the state's discretion.

III. Subsidiary arrangements

The nature and content of subsidiary arrangements are discussed below under Section E.

IV. Design verification and inspections

All safeguards agreements require states parties to submit to the Agency information on the design of facilities where safeguards are applied. They also provide for Agency access to verify the design information. All of the agreements contemplate a three-tier approach to inspections (as distinguished from design information verification visits), consisting of *ad hoc* inspections (those carried out prior to entry into force of detailed arrangements for routine inspections and those used to verify exports/imports of nuclear material), routine inspections and special inspections.

Safeguards agreements concluded in accordance with INFCIRC/66/Rev.2 incorporate the Agency's statutory right of access to all persons, places and information relevant to the implementation of safeguards. INFCIRC/153 agreements, on the other hand, limit the Agency's access to carry out routine inspections to strategic points identified in the Subsidiary Arrangements (as do the VOAs). However, it should be noted that this limitation does not apply to *ad hoc* inspections, nor does it apply to special inspections.

INFCIRC/66/Rev.2 limits the maximum number of routine inspections annually at nuclear facilities based on the inventory or throughput of nuclear material at the facility in question, while providing for a right of access at all times to facilities with an inventory or annual throughput in excess of 60 effective kilograms of nuclear material. INFCIRC/153, on the other hand, limits the Agency's "inspection effort", permitting the Agency to distribute its inspection activities within categories of facilities in the state, depending on the type and size of facility.

V.   *Privileges and immunities; visas*

As referred to above, each of the safeguards agreements contains a provision obliging the state or states party to extend to IAEA inspectors while on mission certain privileges and immunities. It must be pointed out that these privileges and immunities are granted to inspectors in the interest of the Agency and not for the personal benefit of the inspectors. Therefore, the IAEA has the right and duty to waive immunity in any case where, in the Agency's opinion, the immunity would impede the course of justice and can be waived without prejudice to the interest of the Agency.

Before an inspector begins to travel for the Agency, he or she must apply for a *Laissez-passer* through the Visa Section. Where required by the state concerned, visas must be secured in the *Laissez-passer*, which is honoured by most member states of the IAEA. In an effort to streamline this process, and allow the IAEA to deploy its inspectors more efficiently, the Model Additional Protocol includes a provision which requires that a state which insists on visas (and not all do) grant IAEA inspectors multiple-entry/exit/transit visas for a period of at least one year.

VI.   *Duration*

The duration of INFCIRC/153 agreements is generally linked to the state's adherence to the NPT, to the Tlatelolco Treaty or to other underlying treaties or agreements. There is no provision for the survival of safeguards on produced special fissionable material upon expiry of such an agreement. However, as noted above, more recent safeguards agreements concluded on the basis of INFCIRC/66/Rev.2 include a provision requiring continuation of the agreement until safeguards are terminated in accordance with the provisions of the safeguards document.

VII.   *Safeguards on exports*

INFCIRC/66/Rev.2 contains provisions requiring in general the application of safeguards as a condition of re-transfer of safeguarded items. INFCIRC/153 contains no such condition as it was considered unnecessary in light of the requirement in Article III.2 of the NPT prohibiting the transfer of nuclear material to NNWSs unless the material will be subject to safeguards in that state.[6] However, INFCIRC/153 does contain a provision requiring notification

---

6.   However, a number of CSAs not concluded pursuant to the NPT do contain undertakings by the state(s) concerned to require safeguards on exports of nuclear material (e.g. early CSAs concluded pursuant to the Tlatelolco Treaty).

to the IAEA if safeguards will not be applied in the importing state, a provision included to address the circumstance of transfers to NWSs.

VIII. Disputes resolution

Because safeguards agreements are treaties, the principles of international law, rather than the rules of domestic national law, are used in the interpretation and application of safeguards agreements. While the court systems of most countries are available to resolve differences between private parties to a contract, the International Court of Justice (ICJ) is available to sovereign states to resolve disputes concerning treaties if the requirements of the Statute of the Court are met. The IAEA, however, is not subject to the jurisdiction of national courts, nor under the Statute of the ICJ is it eligible to be a party to an action before that tribunal. Thus, there is no court or established judicial tribunal which has competence to resolve a dispute between the IAEA and a state relating to the interpretation and application of a safeguards agreement.

For this reason, all safeguards agreements contain provision for resolving disputes concerning the interpretation and application of the agreement. Principally, they provide that the parties shall, at the request of either, consult about any question arising out of the interpretation or application of the agreement and that the state has the right to request that any question arising out of the interpretation or application of the agreement be considered by the Board. The agreements also include the possibility of submitting disputes to binding arbitration. Although several versions of these provisions have been developed, they all basically provide for the establishment of an arbitration panel (or arbitral tribunal) composed of one member selected by each of the parties to the dispute, plus one or two members designated by the panel members chosen by the parties to the dispute, plus one or two members designated by the panel members chosen by the parties. The arbitration provisions are designed to ensure that the panel is always composed of either three or five members to avoid the possibility of a tie vote. However, no recourse to arbitration has been made to date in the course of implementing safeguards.

1. Compliance and enforcement

Because a safeguards agreement is a treaty, the responsibility to fulfil the obligations of the agreement rests with the government of the state that is party to the agreement. For example, if the operator of a privately-owned facility subject to safeguards refused to allow IAEA inspectors to conduct a properly scheduled inspection, the IAEA would request the government of the state concerned to take whatever steps were necessary to ensure that Agency inspectors have adequate access to the facility. If the government did not or could not obtain adequate access for the inspectors, then the government, not the operator, would have violated the agreement, unless the failure to do so was excused. It is the government's responsibility to ensure that persons under its jurisdiction or control act in accordance with the treaty obligations assumed by that government.

The information that a safeguards inspector is likely to uncover, however, is such that, rather than demonstrating a clear violation of the agreement it would raise doubts as to whether the state were fulfilling its obligations under the agreement. Regardless of the type of agreement, the IAEA has the right and the duty to try to resolve these doubts through the examination of the information assembled and by obtaining from the state additional information and/or access to additional locations.

If such doubts cannot be resolved to the satisfaction of the Director General, he would, under an INFCIRC/153 agreement, report to the Board of Governors that action by the state concerned is essential and urgent to ensure the verification of non-diversion or report to the Board the Agency's inability to verify that nuclear material required to be safeguarded has not been diverted, or, under an INFCIRC/66/Rev.2 agreement, that the state is in non-compliance with the agreement.

The nature of non-compliance by a state with its safeguards obligations may vary. Non-compliance could derive, for example, from the unaccounted for presence or absence of nuclear material, from misleading and/or falsified records or reports, from the denial of access to Agency inspectors or from the tampering with Agency instruments or seals.

Upon report by the Director General to the Board under an INFCIRC/66 agreement, the Board is to call upon the state concerned to remedy forthwith any non-compliance which the Board finds to have occurred. The Board is also required to report such non-compliance to all members of the IAEA.

Under INFCIRC/153, any actions considered by the Board to be "essential and urgent" are required to be implemented by the state without delay. If the state does not take the required action, the Board may conclude, on the basis of the information reported to it by the Director General, that the IAEA cannot fulfil its obligation under the agreement to verify non-diversion; the Board may also find that the state is in further non-compliance with its safeguards agreement.

Under the Statute of the Agency, failure by a state to take fully corrective action within a reasonable time with respect to non-compliance could subject the state to curtailment or suspension of assistance provided by the Agency or by a member state, to the recall of material and equipment and to the suspension of the privileges and rights of Agency membership. Non-compliance can also be reported to the Security Council and to the General Assembly of the United Nations which may trigger measures by the Security Council within the framework of the United Nations Charter.

Since the inception of safeguards, the IAEA has reported to the Security Council cases of non-compliance by five states: Iraq, Romania, the Democratic People's Republic of Korea, Iran and Libya. In the cases of Romania and Libya, the non-compliance was reported to the Council "for information" in light of the fact that those states had themselves brought their respective non-compliance to the attention of the IAEA.

C.   Protocols to safeguards agreements

A number of protocols to INFCIRC/153 agreements have been concluded by the Agency, including co-operation protocols, suspension protocols, small quantities protocols and additional protocols.

I.   *Co-operation protocols*

Protocols for co-operation and co-ordination with multinational or national inspectorates have been concluded with EURATOM, with ABACC and with Japan. In each case, the IAEA's ability to reach independent conclusions concerning compliance with the agreement is reaffirmed as an indispensable element.

II.   *Suspension protocols*

Paragraph 24 of INFCIRC/153 requires the suspension of the application of safeguards under other agreements with the state or states concerned while a comprehensive safeguards agreement is in force. Accordingly, the IAEA has concluded protocols giving effect to this article ("suspension protocols") in cases where states have had pre-existing safeguards agreements with the Agency. In cases where a state concerned had concluded a trilateral agreement for the application of safeguards (i.e. between that state, the IAEA and another party), the third party to the trilateral agreement is also a party to the suspension protocol.

III.   *Small quantities protocols*

The standardised text for INFCIRC/153 agreements also provides for the conclusion of protocols with states having little or no nuclear material and no nuclear material in facilities (the so-called "Small Quantities Protocols" or "SQPs"). As originally developed, the model for SQPs provided that implementation of most of the provisions of Part II of the CSA be held in abeyance, with the exception of those relating to the starting point of safeguards, subsidiary arrangements, design information and international transfers, until such time as the quantity of nuclear material in the state exceeds certain prescribed limits or the state has nuclear material in a nuclear facility (GOV/INF/276, Annex B).

In 2005, the Board of Governors, acting on the advice of the Director General, decided that the SQP, in its original form, constituted a weakness in the Agency's safeguards system and that although SQPs should remain part of the system, they should be subject to certain modifications in the standard text and a change in the SQP criteria (GOV/INF/276/Mod.1 & Corr.1). Now, in order for a state to qualify for an SQP, it must not only have only limited quantities of nuclear material, but also no existing or planned nuclear facility. In addition, the new SQPs will require submission by the state of an initial report on nuclear material and notification as soon as a decision has been taken to construct or to authorise construction of a nuclear facility and will permit the Agency to carry out inspections in the state.

IV. *Additional protocols*

As mentioned above, a number of states have concluded additional protocols along the lines of the model additional protocol [INFCIRC/540 (Corr.)]. Those concluded with NNWSs are substantively identical to, and contain all of the measures referred to in, the model. The additional protocols concluded with the NWSs vary in scope and content, ranging from those which include all of the measures, but exclude activities with direct national security significance, to the protocols which contain only those measures which the states have concluded have a relevance to NNWSs. Only two APs have been concluded in connection with INFCIRC/66-type safeguards agreements, one with Cuba, which was signed but not brought into force prior to Cuba's conclusion of an NPT CSA and one signed with India.

D.   Negotiation of safeguards agreements and protocols

While the IAEA is not a nation or a state under international law, it is an entity having an "international personality". That is to say, governments have recognised the IAEA as an entity which has some of the powers and privileges normally associated with a sovereign state. One of the IAEA's recognised powers is to become a party to treaties. In simple terms, a treaty is an agreement between two or more entities, usually governments, having international personality. Thus, the IAEA's safeguards agreements, and the protocols thereto, which are negotiated and concluded between the IAEA and governments of states or other non-governmental entities with international personality (such as EURATOM or ABACC) are treaties.

The process of concluding a safeguards agreement is begun with a request by the state or states concerned that the Secretariat prepare a text in accordance with the particular underlying obligations and commitments of that state or states. The Secretariat then prepares a draft text of the agreement, along with any relevant protocols, and submits it to the state or states for consideration. If necessary, negotiations are held between the Agency and the state authorities with a view to agreeing *ad referendum* to a text that provides for adequate safeguards. In conducting these negotiations, the Secretariat is guided by the policies and practices previously approved by the Board of Governors. Upon conclusion of the negotiations, the safeguards agreement, along with any protocol(s), is presented by the Secretariat to the Board of Governors for its approval.

In approving the text, the Board authorises the Director General to sign and implement the safeguards agreement and protocol(s) where relevant. Depending upon the state and its own national legislation, the agreement/ protocol then enters into force either upon signature or upon receipt by the Agency of notification from the state that its statutory and constitutional requirements for entry into force of the agreement have been met. The choice of mechanism for entry into force is for the state concerned to make.

E. Subsidiary arrangements

INFCIRC/153 agreements expressly require the conclusion of subsidiary arrangements between the state and the IAEA detailing how the procedures in the agreement are to be implemented. These subsidiary arrangements consist of a general part and facility attachments, and generally an attachment or attachments for locations outside facilities, where applicable. Although INFCIRC/66/Rev.2 itself does not refer to "subsidiary arrangements", most recent agreements based on INFCIRC/66/Rev.2 do include a specific reference to them. However, this only formalises the Agency's practice of making detailed arrangements for the implementation of safeguards in all states with such agreements. Subsidiary arrangements are also concluded with NWSs in implementation of their voluntary offer agreements.

The model additional protocol permits, but does not require, the conclusion of subsidiary arrangements with respect to the measures laid down in an additional protocol, unless requested by one of the parties to the safeguards agreement.

The procedures for concluding the subsidiary arrangements are not the same as for the conclusion of the safeguards agreements. The process is generally initiated by the Secretariat before or shortly after the entry into force of the relevant agreement with the drafting of subsidiary arrangements based on standardised texts. Efforts are made to maintain the standardisation of these documents in the interest of non-discrimination, while taking into account the technical differences and circumstances of the individual states. The negotiations are conducted both in writing and in meetings with the state authorities. Agreement on the texts of the subsidiary arrangements is reflected in exchanges of letters, not, as is the case with the safeguards agreements, by formal signature. Nor do they normally require review or approval by the Board of Governors. They may be amended at any time upon agreement between the Agency and the state. The subsidiary arrangements are treated as confidential documents and are not published by the Agency.

F.   Amendment and renegotiation

The parties to an agreement concluded pursuant to INFCIRC/66/Rev.2 are required to consult, at the request of either party, on the amendment of such an agreement. If the Board modifies the safeguards document, the inspectors document or the scope of the safeguards system, the agreement shall be amended if the government(s) party to the agreement so request(s). Amendments to INFCIRC/66/Rev.2 safeguards agreements are usually made for the purpose of extending the duration of the agreement, and occasionally, the scope.

INFCIRC/153 agreements provide that either party (the state or the IAEA) may request consultations on the amendment of the agreement. Any amendment would require the agreement of all parties to the agreement. Entry into force of such an amendment would be subject to the same conditions as entry into force of the agreement. To date there have been no amendments to the substance of INFCIRC/153 agreements, except to add parties to an agreement.

Amendments to APs may be modified in accordance with the same procedures as are provided for in the relevant safeguards agreement, with the exception of amendments to the two annexes to the AP. Annex I [List of Activities referred to in Article 2.a.(iv) of the Model Additional Protocol] and Annex II [List of Specified Equipment and Non-Nuclear Material for the Reporting of Exports and Imports according to Article 2.a.(ix)] may be amended by the Board of Governors upon the advice of an open-ended working group of experts which would be established by the Board. Any such amendment would take effect automatically for all APs four months after its adoption by the Board.

G.   Implementation and analysis

As of 25 June 2010, of the 185 NNWSs party to the NPT, 167 have CSAs in force. Of the 18 remaining NNWS NPT parties, 8 have signed CSAs and 3 more have had a CSA approved by the Board. In addition, each of the NWSs has a voluntary offer agreement in force. The IAEA is applying safeguards under INFCIRC/66-type agreements in three other states.

The programme for strengthening safeguards was originally developed for states with CSAs. However, it was acknowledged early in the evolution of the programme that the implementation of certain of the measures identified thereunder in other states (i.e. the NWSs and the INFCIRC/66 states) could improve the effectiveness and efficiency of the safeguards implemented in such states while enhancing the effectiveness of safeguards implementation in comprehensive safeguards agreement states. This so-called "universality" issue was a central feature in the negotiation of the model additional protocol. Both the Board and the open-ended committee of the Board that negotiated the model additional protocol expressed their expectation that its adoption by CSA states (in its entirety) and by non-CSA states (selected measures) would maintain a certain "parallelism". Several CSA states indicated that evidence of action toward adoption of the model additional protocol in other states would be necessary to obtain approval of an additional protocol in their own countries. As a consequence, during the 15 May 1997 meeting of the Board at which the model additional protocol was approved, each of the five NWSs announced its intention to conclude and AP and indicated which of the measures contained in the model they were prepared to accept.

As of 25 June 2010, the Board of Governors has approved additional protocols with 139 states and Euratom, 132 of which states (and Euratom) have signed them. Of those, additional protocols with 101 states and Euratom have entered into force. All of the VOA APs are in force. The AP signed by India is not yet in force.

Since 1997, the IAEA Secretariat's implementation of APs has required the development of a whole new infrastructure, including:

- the development of guidelines and formats for use by states in the preparation and submission of declarations under APs;

267

- the development of model subsidiary arrangements and model language for required communications to and from states under APs;
- the development of detailed internal guidelines for complementary access; and
- the development of integrated safeguards.

It was recognised early in the field trial phase of Programme 93+2 and acknowledged at several junctures during Committee 24 negotiations that it would be necessary to develop specific guidelines defining the additional, largely qualitative information to be provided by states to the Agency under Article 2 of the model additional protocol. Such guidelines were needed by states to help them formulate internal procedures and regulations to ensure that the necessary information, with the appropriate level of detail and timeliness, would be available to them. For the Secretariat's part, the guidelines were needed to ensure consistency in the declarations from states, both in terms of level of detail and reporting formats. The most recent iteration of the guidelines, "Guidelines and Format for Preparation and Submission of Declarations Pursuant to Articles 2 and 3 of the Model Protocol Additional to Safeguards Agreements" (Services Series 11), was issued in May 2004. This document provides specific guidance on each sub-article including a description of the purpose and use of the information and a definition of reporting format through example. A simplified version of the guidelines for states with SQPs was issued in April 1999.

Guidelines for complementary access were also developed for the internal use of the Secretariat to ensure that complementary access is carried out in an efficient, technically effective and non-discriminatory manner.

Using all of the information available to it, the IAEA carries out annual analysis of the safeguards situation in each state with a safeguards agreement in force. The state evaluation reports reflect the results of those analyses and the conclusions which the IAEA is able to draw from the analyses. These conclusions are collectively summarised and reported to the Board of Governors in the safeguards implementation report in June each year for the previous calendar year.

For those states with only a CSA in force, the Agency draws a conclusion about the non-diversion of declared nuclear material. While the IAEA has the authority to verify the absence of undeclared nuclear material and activities in states with CSAs only and no AP in force, without an AP for a state, the Agency provides assurances only with respect to declared nuclear material in the state. If a state has both a CSA and an AP in force, the IAEA will, after full verification and resolution of any questions or inconsistencies, provide, where appropriate, confirmation not only of the non-diversion of declared nuclear material, but the absence of undeclared nuclear material and activities.

When a state has in place a CSA and an AP, and the IAEA is able to find that there are no indications of the diversion of declared nuclear material and no indications of undeclared nuclear material or activities, it is then in a position to draw what is referred to as the "broader conclusion", i.e. that all nuclear material in the country remains in peaceful activities. In such situations, the IAEA is then able to implement "integrated safeguards" in the state. Integrated safeguards is defined as an optimum combination of all safeguards measures available to the Agency under CSAs combined with APs which achieves the maximum effectiveness and efficiency within available resources in implementing safeguards. The premise of integrated safeguards is that, if the Agency is able to conclude that there are no undeclared nuclear material or activities in the state as a whole, reductions in the IAEA's verification effort with respect to declared nuclear material which would need further processing to make it nuclear weapon usable is possible.

Conclusion

The implementation of strengthened safeguards requires an integrated approach dealing with both efficiency and effectiveness. Evolution of the safeguards implementation criteria has provided for a full integration of the new measures with elements of the traditional system; the elements are now in hand for a greatly strengthened and more efficient safeguards system. The strengthened safeguards system is now more information driven – more qualitative than quantitive – and relies heavily on a vastly improved system of information analysis, based on a state-wide approach, rather than a facility by facility approach.

[7]

The Nuclear Suppliers Group: History and Functioning

DANIEL H. JOYNER*

Since the detonation of atomic bombs over Hiroshima and Nagasaki in 1945, the international community has been concerned about the spread of nuclear weapons and their component parts, and about the inherently destabilising effects on international peace and security caused by such proliferation.[1] Over the succeeding decades there has emerged a web of international agreements and understandings aimed at mediating this threat, some focusing on the limitation and decommissioning of existing nuclear weapons and materials stockpiles held by states, (e.g. SALT I, SALT II, START I, START II, SORT), and others at curbing the proliferation through regular channels of international trade of nuclear materials, weapons-related items and technologies to states not currently possessing them in types and quantities sufficient to construct nuclear weapons. This article is the first of two that will appear in sequential issues of International Trade Law & Regulation describing and analysing the Nuclear Suppliers Group (NSG), an international regime that addresses nuclear proliferation through the co-ordination and normative harmonisation of national nuclear export control laws and policies.[2]

The subject of nuclear export controls has gained a fresh urgency in the mind of policy-makers and general international civil society since the revelations in early 2004 of a long-standing clandestine smuggling ring in nuclear materials and related dual-use goods, headed by the father of Pakistan's nuclear programs Dr Abdul Qadeer Khan. It has since become clear that through this complex system of middlemen and trans-shipment points, both fissile materials and an array of tangible and intangible technologies fit for use in nuclear weapons programs were transferred to countries including Libya, Iran and North Korea.[3] This high profile breach of international norms regulating the transfer of single- and dual-use nuclear-related items prompted Mohammed Elbaradei, Director-General of the International Atomic Energy Agency, to describe the current system of international nuclear export controls as "inadequate", and led US President George Bush to call for a strengthening of Nuclear Suppliers Group norms and an amendment of its procedures to close existing "loopholes".[4]

In the hope of contributing to this important debate, these two articles will provide a background for understanding international nuclear export controls and the Nuclear Suppliers Group in particular, and will offer thoughts on current challenges to, and future prospects for the international nuclear export control regime. The first section of this article outlines the historical and institutional development of the Nuclear Suppliers Group and its relationship and role alongside the Nuclear Non-proliferation Treaty and the Zangger Committee. The next section considers some noteworthy legal issues which have been raised in the context of the character of commitments of members of the NSG, and of the relationship between the NSG and international treaty regimes, notably the Nuclear Non-proliferation Treaty, but including as well the World Trade Organisation. The third section contains a review of the

* Lecturer, University of Warwick School of Law; Senior Research Fellow, University of Georgia Center for International Trade and Security. The author wishes to thank Mike Beck, Cassady Craft, Seema Gahlaut, David Kershaw, and Scott Jones for helpful suggestions and comments on drafts of this article.

1. See S.D. Sagan and K.N. Waltz, The Spread of Nuclear Weapons: A Debate Renewed (W.W. Norton & Co., New York, 2003); D.J. Karl, "Proliferation Pessimism and Emerging Nuclear Powers" (1996/1997) 21(3) International Security 87; J. Seng, "Less is More: Command and Control Advantages of Minor Nuclear States" (1997) 6(4) Security Studies 50; P.D. Feaver, "Neooptimists and the Enduring Problem of Nuclear Proliferation" (1997) 6(4) Security Studies 93; N.E. Busch, No End in Sight: The Continuing Menace of Nuclear Proliferation (University Press of Kentucky, Lexington, KY, 2004). See also J. Goldblat, Arms Control: The New Guide to Negotiations and Agreements (2nd ed., 2002).
2. See generally R. Cupitt and I. Khripunov, "New Strategies for the Nuclear Supplier Group (NSG)" (1997) 16(3)

Comparative Strategy 305–315; F. Schmidt, "NPT Export Controls and the Zangger Committee" (2000) 7(3) Nonproliferation Review, CNS; F. Schmidt, "The Zangger Committee: Its History and Future Role" (1994) 2(3) Nonproliferation Review, CNS; S. Pande, "The Challenge of Nuclear Export Controls" (1999) XXIII(4) Strategic Analysis: A Monthly Journal of the IDSA; C.E. Thorne, ed., A Guide to Nuclear Export Controls (5th ed., 2002); M. Nartker, "Nuclear Suppliers Group Amends Guidelines to Combat Terrorism" Global Security Newswire, December 19, 2002; Inventory of International Nonproliferation Organizations and Regimes, Center for Nonproliferation Studies, 2002, www.nti.org/e_research/official_docs/inventory/pdfs/nsg.pdf; Nuclear Suppliers Group, Nuclear Threat Initiative, Research Library, www.nti.org/db/china/nsgorg.htm; Nuclear Suppliers Group website, www.nuclearsuppliersgroup.org/, www.nsg-online.org/; NSG at Federation of American Scientists, www.fas.org/nuke/control/nsg/; T. Strulak, "The Nuclear Suppliers Group" (1993) 1(1) The Nonproliferation Review 1; Nuclear Suppliers Group at SIPRI, http://cbw.sipri.se/cbw/nsg.htm.
3. See "IAEA Presses N.Korea, Iran on Nuke Threat," www.CNN.com, November 1, 2004; "U.S. Supports Nuclear Pardon," CNN.com, February 5, 2004.
4. See J. Curl, "Stop Spread of Nukes, Bush Urges," The Washington Times, February 13, 2004.

procedural and practical functioning of the NSG, and attempts, in that context, to provide some insight into what has been described as a fairly opaque aspect of the institutional character of all of the multilateral export control regimes, including the NSG.

I. History of the establishment of the arrangement and institutional development

A. The NPT

A history of the Nuclear Suppliers Group must begin with the institution of the Treaty on the Non-proliferation of Nuclear Weapons, also referred to as the Nuclear Non-proliferation treaty (NPT) of 1970, which forms the cornerstone of the modern multilateral nuclear non-proliferation regime.[5] After 25 years of Cold War tension, the NPT was signed for the purposes of providing a normative basis for co-ordination of peaceful uses of nuclear technology; of encouraging international efforts towards disarmament and decommissioning of existing nuclear stockpiles; and of preventing the further proliferation of nuclear weapons.

The NPT's provisions established two classes of state signatories. Art.I obliges five acknowledged nuclear-weapon states (NWS) (the United States, Russian Federation, United Kingdom, France, and China) not to transfer nuclear weapons, other nuclear explosive devices, or their technology to any recipient state not of their number, and prohibits them:

"in any way to assist, encourage, or induce any non-nuclear-weapon State to manufacture or otherwise acquire nuclear weapons or other nuclear explosive devices, or control over such weapons or explosive devices."

Non-nuclear-weapon state (NNWS) signatories to the NPT oblige themselves under Art.II not to acquire from any other states, or produce on their own, nuclear weapons or nuclear explosive devices and not to receive foreign assistance in weapons development programmes.

In order to verify and aid in the implementation of these commitments, Art.III of the NPT provides for two separate mechanisms aimed at preventing the proliferation of nuclear weapons technologies from NWS to NNWS; safeguards in Art.III.1 and export controls in Art.III.2. Under Art.III.1, NNWS are required to accept the imposition of safeguards

administered by the International Atomic Energy Agency (IAEA) to verify compliance with the provisions of the NPT and specifically to detect diversions of nuclear materials from peaceful uses, such as civilian power generation, to the production of nuclear weapons or other nuclear explosive devices. Each NNWS agrees under Art.III.1 to conclude an independent bilateral safeguards agreement with the IAEA. Under the terms of these safeguards agreements, all nuclear materials in peaceful uses at civilian facilities within the jurisdiction of the NNWS must be declared to the IAEA, whose inspectors are to be given regular access to the facilities for purposes of monitoring and inspection. Because of its comprehensive character, this safeguards system is referred to as the "Full Scope Safeguards System" (FSSG).[6] Compliance with IAEA safeguards agreements is verified under this inspection scheme and reports are submitted to the IAEA Board of Governors. If that body determines that there has been a breach either of a safeguards agreement or of the provisions of the NPT itself, it can in accordance with its statutory procedures refer the matter to the United Nations Security Council for that body's deliberation and action, and for its potential authorisation of measures to remedy the breach, including, at the extreme, the use of the Security Council's powers under Chapter VII of the UN Charter.

Article III.2 provides the international legal basis for all nuclear export controls. It specifies that all parties to the treaty will not transfer nuclear (fissionable) materials, as well as "any equipment or material especially designed or prepared for the processing, use or production of special fissionable material" to non-nuclear weapons states, whether treaty signatories or not, for peaceful purposes unless such material is subject to the safeguards specified in Art.III.1. While highly significant as an institutionalisation of nuclear non-proliferation norms in formal international law, this provision, as is customary in broad and binding multilateral conventions, is however quite vague both on the issue of criteria for applying export controls and on the question of exactly what materials should be the subject of export controls.

B. The Zangger Committee

Due to this fact, in March 1971, shortly after the NPT's entry into force, a group of NPT member supplier states and potential supplier states of nuclear materials gathered for the purpose of clarifying the technical implications of NPT export controls, and to establish a continuing forum for interpretation of Art.III.2's broad export control provisions. This meeting was the nucleus of a group

5. Treaty on the Non-Proliferation of Nuclear Weapons, opened for signature July 1, 1968, 21 U.S.T. 483, T.I.A.S. No.6839, 729 U.N.T.S. 161. On the NPT, see J. Goldblat, *Arms Control: The New Guide to Negotiations and Agreements* (2nd ed., 2002) Chs 4–6; *The Nuclear Non-proliferation Regime: Assessment and Prospects* (1997); *Twenty Years of the Non-Proliferation treaty: Implementation and Prospects* (1990); J. Simpson and D. Howlett, eds., *The Future of the Non-proliferation Treaty* (1995).

6. See F. Schmidt, "NPT Export Controls and the Zangger Committee" (2000) 7(3) *Nonproliferation Review*, CNS.

which came to be known as the Zangger Committee, after its first chairman, Professor Claude Zangger. The Zangger Committee continued to meet periodically and eventually established both a set of "Understandings" adopted by all Committee members, and a Trigger List composed of items the export of which should "trigger" the requirement of safeguards. The Committee's declared purpose, from the beginning, has not been to place additional obligations binding upon its members.[7] This fact is evident by the nature of acceptance of the Understandings by each member, which is accomplished through simple exchange of notes and a unilateral declaration that the Understandings will be made effective through national export legislation.[8] Rather, the Committee's role is to provide a forum for harmonisation of export control policies and the setting of minimum standards for the interpretation of the export control provisions of NPT Art.III.2.[9]

The Zangger Committee's Understandings were published in September 1974 as IAEA document INFCIRC/209, and are divided into two separate memoranda addressing export controls on a category of items described in Art.III.2. Memorandum A covers source and special fissionable material. Memorandum B covers equipment and material specifically designed or prepared for the processing, use, or production of special fissionable material. The memoranda provide that nuclear suppliers should, in the context of a transfer of subject items to a non-nuclear weapon state not party to the NPT:

1. obtain assurances from the recipient state that the exported materials will not be used in a nuclear explosion;
2. subject such items and materials on the Trigger List produced through their use to IAEA safeguards; and

3. ensure that items on the Trigger list are not re-exported to a third-party recipient state unless that recipient state meets the criteria laid out in 1 and 2 above.
4. The Trigger List, which clarifies and provides detail regarding the equipment listed in the memoranda is updated regularly in accordance with technological innovations. The Zangger Committee's Trigger List and memoranda together comprised the first major agreement among supplier states regarding nuclear export controls.

C. The London Club/NSG

The explosion of a nuclear device by India in May 1974, together with increased activity among other NNWS towards creating a full nuclear fuel cycle, led to heightened concern among supplier states regarding nuclear proliferation.[10] In 1975 a new group of supplier states met in London with the purpose of supplementing the Zangger Committee's work in the field of nuclear export controls. Over successive meetings, this group became officially known as the Nuclear Suppliers Group (NSG), and unofficially as the "London Club". The chief distinction between the NSG and the Zangger Committee was initially to be found in the character of its membership. The Zangger Committee had from its inception been comprised exclusively of NPT Member States. The NSG by contrast was consciously envisioned to include non-parties to the NPT and, importantly, France, a major supplier state not a party to the NPT and therefore also not a member of the Zangger Committee. The establishment of the NSG thus expanded the number of important voices and interests in deliberations regarding nuclear export control standards.[11]

In 1976, NSG Member States produced a document entitled "Guidelines on Nuclear Transfers", which was accepted by all 15 members in 1977 and published in February 1978 as IAEA document INFCIRC/254. The NSG guidelines incorporated the Zangger Committee Trigger List and largely mirrored the Zangger Committee's Understandings, with the notable addition of going beyond the context of the NPT to cover nuclear transfers to any non-nuclear weapon state. The NSG guidelines further tightened export control standards in a number of areas including the transfer or construction of nuclear facilities and technology supporting them.[12]

The obligational foundation of membership in the NSG is similar to that of the Zangger Committee

---

7. See F. Schmidt, "The Zangger Committee: Its History and Future Role" (1994) 2(3) *Nonproliferation Review*, CNS 38.
8. It has been argued that there is a substantive difference between the joint declaration mode of accession to membership which has been employed in the NSG, and the exchange of note between members which is the modus operandi in the Zangger Committee, the contention being that this exchange of notes creates a more binding foundational understanding among Zangger Committee members. However, an analysis of the notes exchanged as part of this process makes clear that the notes are not intended by their issuers to constitute an understanding of a treaty relationship, which is the only type of agreement enforceable in international law. This understanding of the issuing states governs the issue of creation of a legal relationship in this context as per Arts 11 and 13 of the 1969 Vienna Convention on the Law of Treaties. Thus it is correct to maintain that both the Zangger Committee and the NSG are examples of intergovernmental agreements which are not legally binding as a matter of international law.
9. See F. Schmidt, "NPT Export Controls and the Zangger Committee" (2000) 7(3) *Nonproliferation Review*, CNS 137 ("The Committee does not decide 'ex cathedra' what the export control requirements of the NPT should be. Instead, its members—NPT parties who are major suppliers confronted regularly with the question of how to interpret Art. III.2 obligations—meet to negotiate what minimum requirements should be applied. They seek to harmonize their understandings, aiming at the widest possible membership,

to try to prevent commercial transactions from weakening nonproliferation objectives.")
10. See T. Strulak, "The Nuclear Suppliers Group" (1993). 1(1) *The Nonproliferation Review* 2.
11. *ibid.*
12. *ibid.*, at p.3.

in that no binding legal obligation is undertaken by NSG members in the context of the regime. In this sense the structure of the NSG is very much in keeping with modern trends in security regime design pursuant to which multilateral co-operation on cross-border issues is facilitated through norm-producing arrangements, with the documentary foundations of the regimes themselves being structured with softer, non-binding provisions and procedures in order to allay concerns of national sovereignty impingement.[13] The NSG Trigger List and Guidelines function simply as a harmonised iteration of principles establishing norms to be referenced by Member States in their national export control efforts. All decisions, including those regarding membership and amendments to either the Guidelines or Trigger List, are made by member consensus. Implementation of NSG guidelines is at national discretion, and is carried out through national export control law and policy. However the NSG Guidelines do provide for a mechanism through which members are called upon to consult regarding the implementation of regime norms. Pursuant to this process, members may meet to discuss specific cases of alleged member non-compliance. However, the usefulness of this mechanism for promoting compliance with regime norms has traditionally been hamstrung both by the vagueness of the Guidelines and the ever present necessity of decision-making by consensus.

After the adoption of the guidelines in 1977, the NSG did not meet again officially for 13 years, although during this time the NSG Guidelines were implemented by Member States through national measures, and 12 more states formally accepted the Guidelines. From 1978 to 1990, no changes were made to NSG documents, including updates to the NSG Trigger List, although during the same period the Zangger Committee continued to function and regularly updated its Trigger List.[14] Tadeusz Strulak, chairman of the 1992 meeting of the NSG has noted of this period of relative inactivity:

"In my opinion, the major cause of the group's inactivity was the unwillingness of some NSG suppliers to move beyond the conditions for nuclear exports established in 1977. The motive behind this unwillingness

13. K. Abbot and D. Snidal, "Hard and Soft Law in International Governance" (2000) 54 *International Organization* 421. See A. Stein, "Coordination and Collaboration: Regimes in an Anarchic World" and J. Grieco, "Understanding the Problem of Institutional Cooperation" in D.A. Baldwin ed., *Neorealism and Neoliberalism: The Contemporary Debate* (1993); L.L. Martin, *Coercive Cooperation: Explaining Multilateral Economic Sanctions* (1993); R.T. Cupitt and W.J. Long, "Multilateral Cooperation and Nuclear Nonproliferation", in Zachary S. Davis and Benjamin Frankel, eds, *The Proliferation Puzzle: Why Nuclear Weapons Spread and What Results* (1993); G. Bunn and D. Holloway, *Arms Control Without Treaties?* Stanford University CISAC Working Paper (February, 1998); D.H. Joyner, "Restructuring the Multilateral Export Control Regime System" (2004) 9(2) *Journal of Conflict and Security Law*.
14. See T. Strulak, "The Nuclear Suppliers Group" (1993) 1(1) *The Nonproliferation Review* 3.

was commercial interest. An example to support this view is the case of full-scope safeguards. Discussion on the extent of the safeguards that recipients should be required to agree to as a condition of nuclear supplies dates back to the early NSG period before the acceptance of the guidelines. There was no agreement on this point then, and later attempts in the mid-1980's by some countries to begin a discussion on making full-scope safeguards a condition of export failed as well. Some suppliers unilaterally adopted the requirement of full-scope safeguards".[15]

However, interest in the NSG as a separate institution underwent a revival, and the NSG entered a period of renewed activity in the early 1990s as the Cold War came to an end. With the collapse of the Soviet Union, the chief object of, and uniting purpose for harmonised nuclear export controls among the states at that time composing the NSG disappeared, resulting in something of an identity crisis among a host of international security regimes, including multilateral export control regimes and the NSG. Over subsequent years, the number of states wishing to join the NSG and the other multilateral export control regimes increased, and their characteristics, both in terms of political and social ideology, and in capacity to supply sensitive nuclear related items diversified, resulting in a much more heterogeneous group of states interested in applying harmonised nuclear export controls. Co-operation among this group was seen by many to be better facilitated through the more inclusive frameworks of the Nuclear Suppliers Group.[16]

D. Dual-Use Gap

In addition to these larger geopolitical dynamics, the 1990–91 Gulf War and the lessons learned, particularly by Western supplier states from it, brought home in poignant fashion the necessity of greater attention to harmonisation and tightening of multilateral nuclear export controls.[17] This was particularly so as it became clear that items and technologies directly involved in the processes of weapons manufacture were not the only, or even the most important problem for export control systems to deal with. As the war progressed, and particularly in its aftermath, it became clear that one of the greatest facilitators of the formidable, yet clandestine, Iraqi nuclear weapons programme was the importation, through various methods ranging from open purchase to covert indirect acquisition, of items from Western companies which were not directly nuclear-related but which were dual-use in nature, *i.e.* items which had legitimate

15. *ibid.*
16. T. Perry, *The Origins and Implementation of the 1992 Nuclear Suppliers Group (NSG) Agreement*, Doctoral Dissertation, University of Michigan, Ch. VI (2003).
17. See T. Strulak, "The Nuclear Suppliers Group" (1993) 1(1) *The Nonproliferation Review* 4.

civilian uses but which could also be adapted for use in weapons programmes.[18]

The Trigger Lists and foundational principles of the Zangger Committee and the NSG had up to that point been concentrated on nuclear materials and those items and technologies "especially designed" for their production, as specified in Art.III.2 of the NPT. Now, however, it was realised that a sizeable "dual-use gap" existed between the normative foundations of the multilateral nuclear export control regimes and the realities of the modern security environment.[19] The recognition of this dual-use gap, and a commonly perceived imperative to narrow it, contributed significantly to the revival of the NSG.[20]

At the NSG plenary meeting in The Hague in March 1991, the members agreed to bring the NSG control list up to date by broadening it to include the items which had been added to the Zangger Committee's control list since the last NSG meeting in 1977. The group also decided on the implementation of a revised process of review and consultation (which had been used infrequently up to that point) and also of information exchange.[21] However, the most noteworthy achievement of the Hague meeting was the decision to create a supplementary regime within the NSG framework to control exports of nuclear related dual-use materials and technology. This arrangement was formally adopted by the 27 NSG members at the 1992 plenary meeting in Warsaw, and both the resulting guidelines and trigger list were published by the IAEA in July 1992 as INFCIRC/254/REV 1/Part 2.[22]

The NSG arrangement for dual-use nuclear export controls, now referred to as NSG Part 2, consists of a set of guidelines relating to transfers of nuclear dual-use items and an accompanying list of items including dual-use equipment and technology. The basic principle, as iterated in the guidelines, states that suppliers should not authorise transfers of equipment, materials, software or related technology identified on the list if:

1. they are to be used by a non-nuclear-weapon state in a nuclear explosive activity or an unsafeguarded nuclear fuel cycle;
2. there is in general an unacceptable risk of diversion to such an activity; or

3. the transfers are contrary to the objective of averting the proliferation of nuclear weapons.[23]

Other important provisions in the guidelines specify criteria for assessing the level of risk relevant to application of the Basic Principle, as well as conditions to be imposed upon transfers, (*i.e.* the production of an end-use statement and "an assurance explicitly stating that the proposed transfer or any replica thereof will not be used in any nuclear explosive activity or unsafeguarded nuclear fuel-cycle activity"). A Memorandum of Understanding (MOU) was also adopted at Warsaw, clarifying a number of important matters regarding implementation of the Part 2 guidelines.[24]

In addition to the creation of a new dual-use regime and its related documentation, the Warsaw plenary saw significant steps being taken to strengthen and update the original NSG regime for controlling nuclear transfers (NSG Part 1). Since the signing of the NPT, there had been debate regarding the requirement of full-scope safeguards for transfers of nuclear materials and related items. The text of the NPT requires non-nuclear weapons state parties to undertake a commitment to accept IAEA safeguards on all peaceful nuclear activities. However, this safeguards requirement which NPT parties take upon themselves was not made applicable under the terms of the treaty to non-NPT members receiving exports of nuclear-related items from NPT signatories. Some argued afterwards that the intent of the NPT was to require the same safeguards commitment of non-party recipients, but this interpretation was not widely accepted and state practice in the years following the signing of the NPT indicated that this was not the conclusion of most NPT parties.[25]

However, at the Warsaw meeting in April 1992 NSG members accepted a declaration requiring suppliers not to transfer trigger list items to non-nuclear weapons states (NPT members or not) unless the recipient state had concluded a bilateral agreement with the IAEA implementing full scope safeguards within the recipient state. This declaration, published as IAEA INFCIRC/405, was an important step towards the universalisation of nuclear non-proliferation principles and represented a significant tightening of the nuclear export control regime.

Other important institutional modifications to the NSG which occurred during the 1990s include the extension in 1995 of the "no-undercutting" rule to both NSG Parts 1 and 2. Paragraph 4(b) of the 1992

---

18. J. Holmes & G. Bertsch, "Tighten Export Controls", *Defense News*, May 5, 2003. D. Albright and M. Hibbs, "Iraq and the Bomb, Were They Even Close?" *The Bulletin of Atomic Scientists* (April, 1992) 16; D.A. Kay, "Denial and Deception of WMD Proliferators" (1994) 18(1) *The Washington Quarterly* 90.

19. See T. Strulak, "The Nuclear Suppliers Group" (1993) 1(1) *The Nonproliferation Review* 4.

20. See C.E. Thorne, ed., *A Guide to Nuclear Export Controls* (5th ed., 2002).

21. See T. Strulak, "The Nuclear Suppliers Group" (1993) 1(1) *The Nonproliferation Review* 4.

22. *ibid.*, at 5.

23. *ibid.*

24. *ibid.*

25. F. Schmidt, "NPT Export Controls and the Zangger Committee" (2000) 7(3) *Nonproliferation Review*, CNS 140.

dual-use regime Memorandum of Understanding states that member governments:

> "should not authorise a transfer of equipment, materials, software, or related technology identified in the Annex which is essentially identical to a transfer which was not authorised by another Subscribing Government where this decision was notified pursuant to subparagraph (a), without consulting the Subscribing Government which provided the notice".

The observance of this rule on undercutting transfers is vital to the maintenance of an effective procedure for information sharing in the area of denial notifications. This principle and the other implementing principles of the MOU for "levelling the playing field" among members became available for acceptance by all NSG members in 1997.[26]

II. Legal Discussions

It is worth noting that there has been some discussion within legal circles, and particularly among legal experts in Non-Aligned Movement (NAM) countries regarding the nature of the NSG dual-use regime as being a step removed from the legitimising provisions of Art.III.2 of the NPT in its attempts to regulate trade in dual-use technologies.[27] It will be remembered that Art.III of the NPT addresses export controls upon both nuclear materials and "equipment or material especially designed or prepared for the processing, use or production of special fissionable material". There is no mention within the text of dual-use items, primary uses for which in many cases are only indirectly related to nuclear materials and which are capable of non-nuclear peaceful civilian use.

Trade in such dual-use items is of particular interest to developing states at the early stages of energy production capacities. Many such states have voiced concern that the NSG's regulation in this area is overly restrictive, and on a more fundamental level that the NSG itself is outside of the legal regime for multilateral regulation of nuclear materials, with the NPT as its cornerstone. They have protested against the characterisation of NSG standards and policies as being authoritatively or normatively incumbent upon non-NSG members, whether NPT signatories or not; and against the practice by some NSG members of criticising the policies of non-NSG members on the basis of non-compliance with NSG norms.[28] They have argued that the NSG is essentially a supplier-state cartel

whose policies unduly target states legitimately attempting to develop civilian power-generation facilities.

While their arguments on the motives of NSG members are subject to debate, it must be said that in purely legal terms these commentators are quite correct. Neither the Zangger Committee nor the NSG are legal bodies in the formal sense. Nor are they empowered under the NPT or any other international legal instrument or principle to make decisions authoritatively binding either upon their adherents or upon other states. Any characterisation of NSG norms to the contrary is entirely spurious. However the true import of this legal discussion is not in questioning the legitimacy of the NSG Part 2 framework for Member States of the NSG, which along with Part I falls squarely under the aforementioned paradigm of a non-legally binding political arrangement. States may of course meet to collectively derive interpretations of treaty provisions and to implement harmonised standards in their own national laws, with the understood caveat that since neither the NSG nor the Zangger Committee are part of the formal structure of the international legal regime for nuclear materials proliferation, the weight and effect of these interpretations can extend no farther than the jurisdiction of such national legal systems. As long as characterisations of the norms and policies of these bodies are kept within this framework, particularly by NSG Member State officials, there are no grounds for argument that the arrangements have overstepped their bounds. However, it should be understood that there is no guarantee that interpretations of the NPT adopted by these arrangements would be supported as authoritative should a question involving them be presented to a competent international tribunal. This is the case even as the interpretations touch solely upon matters of member-state national legal systems and *a fortiori* as they are purported to affect the obligations of non-Member States.

Interestingly, the significance of this distinction may be played out in future in the interaction of NSG commitments with obligations under other, more binding instruments specifically addressing issues of general trade in goods. The most notable of these are the agreements comprising the World Trade Organisation, which has yet to specifically address within its framework many issues surrounding export controls for national security and foreign-policy purposes. Currently, Art.XI of the revised General Agreement on Tariffs and Trade provides that:

> "No prohibitions or restrictions other than duties, taxes or other charges, whether made effective through quotas, *import or export licenses* or other measures, shall be instituted or maintained by any contracting party...on the exportation or sale for export of any product destined for the territory of any other contracting party" (emphasis added).

---

26.   T. Perry, *The Origins and Implementation of the 1992 Nuclear Suppliers Group (NSG) Agreement*, Doctoral Dissertation, University of Michigan, Ch.VI (2003).

27.   On the NAM, see *www.nam.gov.za/background/background.htm*.

28.   One basis for such characterisations is provided in the NSG Part 2 Guidelines, para.9, which states "In the interest of international peace and security, the adherence of all states to the Guidelines would be welcome".

Article XI proceeds to provide for a number of fairly broad exceptions to this basic prohibition, with the provisions of Art.XX supplementing these exceptions. These two articles have had the cumulative effect of allowing WTO members to rhetorically justify the application of export restrictions through a variety of means.

However, none of the exceptions in Art.XI or Art.XX specifically addresses export controls for national security and foreign-policy purposes, making these justifications vulnerable to critical appraisal by other WTO members as falling under the general prohibition of Art.XI(1).

Otherwise, countries seeking legal cover under the GATT must look to the security exception provisions of Art.XXI which stipulate that:

> "(n)othing in this agreement shall be construed ... to prevent any contracting party from taking any action which it considers necessary for the protection of its essential security interests ...".

Three seemingly exclusive sub-categories to the exception follow this, two of which have particular relevance to NSG members.

- interests "relating to fissionable materials or the materials from which they are derived ...";
- interests "relating to the traffic in arms, ammunition and implements of war and to such traffic in other goods and materials as is carried on directly or indirectly for the purpose of supplying a military establishment".[29]

The first of these sub-categories would seem to give an effective and fairly uncontroversial exception to implementation of NSG Part I principles in the single-use context. However, as described above, it is the Part II dual-use provisions and their implementation by NSG Member States that has been the source of greatest contention between the developing and developed world, due to the very nature of such goods and technologies as being usable in legitimate power-production processes. The breadth of referenced terms in Art.XXI(b)(ii), as well as its subjectivity, make it a provision ripe for interpretation by a WTO dispute resolution panel.[30]

Ongoing developments in general trading policy among nations and the formation of influential groups, particularly of developing countries, within the framework of the WTO may prompt a strengthening of such voices, and any resulting agreements or normative pronouncements may have to be reconciled with restrictions on trade in dual-use goods laid out in the guidelines and foundational documents of the NSG and of the other multilateral export control regimes.

III. Functioning of the NSG

A. Decision-making, consultation, and information-sharing

In terms of its functional perception, most Member States view the NSG, as well as the other multilateral export control regimes, primarily as a place for consultation and information-sharing among members on matters of nuclear proliferation concern, and not as a place where substantive decisions regarding export controls are made. This is a key distinction between the multilateral export control regimes at their current level of institutional development, and other more formal institutions such as the World Trade Organisation, within which binding rules are made and decisions are taken on discrete cases of alleged non-compliance with institutional norms. Again, in the case of the NSG, the "regime" does not exist in an independent international legal sense but is rather a manifestation of the will of Member States to collectively and normatively do something about the proliferation of nuclear materials. Legal and policy decisions regarding exports are made without exception at the national level, which remains the primary level for the real functioning of the international export control regime system, not only in the nuclear context but in the areas of chemical, biological, missile and conventional weapons and weaponiseable technologies as well.

The decisions of the NSG, like the other multilateral export control regimes, are as a general rule not taken on specific cases, but are rather related to the procedures of the regime itself, to the substantive norms of the regime found in the guidelines, and to the identification of items on the trigger list.[31] These decisions are of course significant, as they are meant to trickle down into national legal systems and policy positions through the processes of national discretionary implementation. However, in terms of its functional utility, the NSG serves most importantly as a forum for consultation and information-sharing among members on matters of nuclear proliferation. From the beginning, these functions have been emphasised and provided for

---

29. See M.J. Hahn, "Vital Interests and the Law of GATT: An Analysis of GATT's Security Exception" (1991) 12 *Mich. J. Int'l L.* 558.

30. See in general the discussion of GATT Art.XXI in Matsushita, Schoenbaum and Mavroidis, *The world trade organization: law, practice and policy* (Oxford University Press, 2003) Ch.10.

31. This is in contrast to the procedure for *ex ante* authorisation of significant exports of sensitive goods which was an institutional feature of the Coordinating Committee for Multilateral Export Controls (COCOM), the Cold War predecessor of the Wassenaar Arrangement. COCOM members wishing to export certain highly sensitive items were required beforehand to submit an application for review and approval by the entire COCOM membership. Unanimous member consent was required for the export to proceed.

in the NSG guidelines, though some modifications have been made over the years.

The original 1978 NSG Part 1 guidelines called for Member States to "maintain contact and consult through regular channels on matters connected with the implementation of these Guidelines". They provided specifically that:

> "Suppliers should consult ... with other governments concerned on specific sensitive cases, to ensure that any transfer does not contribute to risks of conflict or instability".

and held that:

> "In the event that one or more suppliers believe there has been a violation of supplier/recipient understandings resulting from these Guidelines ... suppliers should consult promptly through diplomatic channels in order to determine and assess the reality and extent of the alleged violation".

Through this consultation mechanism, information could be shared within the context of regime processes and simply bilaterally among states, and specific cases of alleged non-compliant proliferation could be addressed using a unified normative framework and set of understandings.

For all its theoretical merits, however, the consultation mechanism in the original NSG guidelines was put to little use by NSG members before the long 13 year period of NSG inactivity ending in 1990. The NSG Part 1 guidelines were crafted so as to rely primarily on the state to which the transfer was directed for guarantees on its legitimate civilian use, even if the government itself was not to be the item's end user. The guidelines stated:

> "Suppliers should authorise transfer of items or related technology identified in the trigger list only upon formal governmental assurances from recipients explicitly excluding uses which would result in any nuclear explosive device".

There was, in essence, a delegation of responsibility from the supplier government to the government of the end user to verify compliance with regime mandates.

When the Part 2 dual-use regime was put into place in 1992 it was clear that, due to the decentralised and generally private nature of commercial trade in many varieties of dual-use goods, this system of state-to-state dealing was insufficient. The Part 2 guidelines went further in requiring supplier states to acquire directly from the end user as a condition of transfer (a) "a statement ... specifying the uses and end-use locations of the proposed transfers," and (b) "an assurance explicitly stating that the proposed transfer or any replica thereof will not be used in any nuclear explosive activity or unsafeguarded nuclear fuel cycle activity". The Part 2 guidelines thus required an extension of supplier states' due diligence efforts to judging the activities and manifestations of private entities within other states.

The switch from state-to-state representations to direct relationships with private entities engaged in international commerce in dual-use goods necessitated a renewed emphasis on information-sharing between members in the Part 2 guideline provisions. The guidelines themselves included a rather curt and vague formal call for information-sharing in para.8. However, in order to provide more procedural specificity to this recognised imperative for information-sharing, along with the Part 2 guidelines in 1992 was adopted the MOU, which became applicable to both NSG Parts 1 & 2 in 1995.

Paragraph 2 of the MOU states that adopting governments:

> "should consult with other Subscribing Governments through regular channels and through the convening of at least one annual meeting. These consultations should address such matters as:
>
> (a) Information exchanges, as appropriate:
>   (i) in pursuit of the Basic Principle and paragraphs 4 and 5 of the Guidelines;
>   (ii) concerning decisions by Subscribing Governments not to authorise transfers of equipment, material or related technology;
>   (iii) on measures taken to implement the Guidelines; and
>   (iv) on proposed and authorised transfers, on a voluntary basis
>
> (b) Additional measures, as referred to in paragraph 7 of the Guidelines, as appropriate.
> (c) Updating the Annex, as necessary".

In addition to simply clarifying the role and purpose of consultations within the NSG framework, the MOU was significant in institutionalising, pursuant to 2(a)(ii) above, the sharing of information on licence denials among NSG members. Until this time, information on licensing decisions had been shared among states only on an ad hoc basis and generally bilaterally. Paragraph 2(a)(ii) of the MOU sought to formally integrate this aspect of information-sharing into the structure of NSG consultations. This information on licensing decisions, and particularly decisions to deny a licence for export of a particular item or technology, was of course particularly vital to the functioning of the previously discussed "no-undercut" provisions also established by the 1992 MOU. Without such information being widely distributed among the membership, there would be no way for a member to recognise:

> "equipment, materials, software, or related technology identified in the Annex which is essentially identical to a transfer which was not authorised by another Subscribing Government ... ".

Interestingly, para.2 of the MOU also called for the sharing of information on "proposed and authorised transfers", meaning those decisions by a Member State to approve transfers of technologies listed in the Appendix. However, unlike the case of denial notifications, this thought was ended by the caveat "on a voluntary basis". Although it is perhaps unnecessary within the context of an essentially voluntary regime, this qualifying language has served to highlight the distinction and relative perceived importance to the functioning of the regime as between state decisions to approve or to deny sensitive materials transfer.

Paragraph 2 finally provides for "at least one annual meeting" for the purposes of such consultation. As a matter of custom, however, the membership of the NSG has met twice per year for this purpose, with one meeting occurring immediately prior to the annual plenary and a second meeting taking place in October of each year at the Japanese Mission in Vienna, during the same week as the annual Zangger Committee meeting.[32]

In order to facilitate this information-sharing, an official Point of Contact (PoC) was established for the NSG, with the Japanese government volunteering its Vienna Mission for this purpose. From 1992 to 1995, NSG members were expected, under the rules of the MOU, to communicate denial decisions for Part 2 dual-use items to the staff of the Japanese Embassy, who would then photocopy the relevant documents and make them available to other NSG members at the IAEA. In 1995, as previously noted, the provisions of the MOU, including the para.2 consultation provisions, were made formally applicable to both the Part 1 and Part 2 guidelines and trigger lists. Thus from 1995 on, the PoC became a clearing house for all NSG denial notification activities.[33]

In 1997, the United States Department of Energy developed a computerised information-sharing network, named the Nuclear Suppliers Group Information Sharing System (NISS). The NISS has now been installed in virtually all NSG Member States and allows the transmission of denial notifications directly to the Japanese mission. The NISS also allows members to access other NSG documents and information, and maintains a record of past denial notifications. Through the sharing of specific information regarding denied technologies and intended parties of receipt, the NISS generally contains sufficient information to put other NSG states on alert regarding the acquisition efforts of states and other parties of proliferation concern.[34]

In addition to the NISS, information-sharing has been facilitated through the efforts of the Information Sharing Working Group at all NSG plenary meetings since 1992. In these meetings, members can discuss specific kinds of sensitive technologies being sought by entities of proliferation concern using both unclassified information and classified information that has been approved for communication in this forum.[35]

B. List Adjustments

Since 1992, changes to the NSG Part 1 single-use trigger list have been made in close parallel with regular changes to the Zangger Committee's trigger list. The NSG and the Zangger Committee are currently composed of an almost identical membership, with the only exception being China, which is only a Zangger Committee member. Membership in the Zangger Committee has customarily been a precursor to membership of the NSG.[36]

Changes to the NSG Part 2 dual-use trigger list have, however, been handled exclusively by the NSG. At the Warsaw plenary in 1992, the NSG membership established the Dual-Use Technical Working Group to lead efforts to update the Part 2 list. The Working Group meets formally and in various subcommittees to review proposed changes to the dual-use list. Its recommendations are forwarded to the Plenary Chair, and decisions on list adjustments are made on a member-consent basis. In 2002, the Dual Use Technical Working Group and the Information Sharing Working group were merged into a new body called the Consultative Group, which is a standing intercessional group tasked with holding consultations on all issues associated with NSG guidelines and technical annexes.[37]

Conclusion

As stated in the introduction, the purpose of the first part of this article on the Nuclear Suppliers Group has been to describe the history, development and functioning of the NSG, a soft-law inter-governmental export control regime that has received comparatively little attention in academic literature, but which has recently once again become the focus of attention among the highest levels of government as an entity with an important role to play in the future of nuclear non-proliferation efforts.

Using this developmental description and analysis as a backdrop, the second part of the article will discuss the reasons for this most recent renaissance of attention to international nuclear export controls, and will offer some observations relative to divergent perceptions regarding the functioning and effectiveness of the NSG. It will discuss a number of difficulties, both internal and external, which the NSG (as well as the other multilateral export control regimes) has faced and which it

32. See C.E. Thorne, ed., *A Guide to Nuclear Export Controls* (5th ed., 2002).
33. T. Perry, *The Origins and Implementation of the 1992 Nuclear Suppliers Group (NSG) Agreement*, Doctoral Dissertation, University of Michigan, Ch. VI (2003).
34. *ibid.*
35. *ibid.*
36. *ibid.*
37. *ibid.*

42 JOYNER: THE NUCLEAR SUPPLIERS GROUP: HISTORY AND FUNCTIONING: [2005] Int.T.L.R.

continues to face in efforts to achieve desired levels of effectiveness in fulfilling its core non-proliferation roles. The article will conclude by offering thoughts on the future of international export controls and the potential for addressing the challenges to regime effectiveness as a part of the international community's overall programme of efforts to prevent the spread and use of weapons of mass destruction.

[8]

NUCLEAR-WEAPON-FREE ZONES: A HISTORY AND ASSESSMENT

by Jozef Goldblat

Jozef Goldblat has been involved in arms control negotiations in Geneva and New York for nearly 40 years, including service for the United Nations. From 1969 to 1989, he directed the arms control and disarmament program at the Stockholm International Peace Research Institute. Since 1989, he has been a Senior Research Fellow at the Geneva Graduate Institute of International Studies and Senior Lecturer at the Geneva Center for Security Policy. He is also Vice-President of the Geneva International Peace Research Institute and consultant to the U.N. Institute for Disarmament Research. His latest publications include **Arms Control: A Guide to Negotiations and Agreements** *(1994) and* **The Nuclear Non-Proliferation Régime: Assessment and Prospects** *(1997).*

The idea of establishing nuclear-weapon-free zones (NWFZs) was conceived with a view to preventing the emergence of new nuclear weapon states. As early as 1958, 10 years before the signing of the Treaty on the Non-Proliferation of Nuclear Weapons (NPT), the Polish government, which feared the nuclearization of West Germany and wanted to prevent the deployment of Soviet nuclear weapons on its territory, put forward a proposal, called the Rapacki Plan (after the Polish foreign minister), for a NWFZ in Central Europe. The zone was to comprise Poland, Czechoslovakia, the German Democratic Republic, and the Federal Republic of Ger-

many, but other European countries would have the opportunity to accede. In the area in question, the stationing, manufacture, and stockpiling of nuclear weapons and of nuclear delivery vehicles would be prohibited. The nuclear powers would have to respect the nuclear-weapon-free status of the zone and undertake not to use nuclear weapons against the territory of the zone.[1] In the political climate of the 1950s, the Rapacki Plan had no chance of becoming a subject of serious international negotiation. Nonetheless, several of its elements were later adopted as guidelines for the establishment of denuclearized zones.

Efforts to ensure the absence of nuclear weapons in other populated

parts of the world have been more successful. By now, three regional denuclearization agreements—the 1967 Treaty of Tlatelolco regarding Latin America, the 1985 Treaty of Rarotonga regarding the South Pacific, and the 1992 Declaration on the Denuclearization of Korea—have entered into force, while two other such agreements—the 1995 Treaty of Bangkok regarding Southeast Asia and the 1996 Pelindaba Treaty regarding Africa—have been opened for signature. Also, certain uninhabited areas of the globe have been formally denuclearized. They include Antarctica under the 1959 Antarctic Treaty; outer space, the moon, and other celestial bodies under the 1967 Outer Space Treaty and the 1979

Jozef Goldblat

Moon Agreement; and the seabed, the ocean floor, and the subsoil thereof under the 1971 Seabed Treaty.[2]

Article VII of the NPT affirmed the right of states to establish NWFZs in their respective territories. The United Nations, in its numerous resolutions, went further by encouraging the creation of such zones, and the 1995 NPT Review and Extension Conference participants expressed the conviction that regional denuclearization measures enhance global and regional peace and security.[3] NWFZs have become part and parcel of the nuclear nonproliferation regime. It is now widely recognized that the universality of this regime, which would require attracting to it the remaining nuclear threshold states (India, Pakistan, and Israel), can be achieved only by establishing denuclearized zones in the regions of South Asia and the Middle East.

In 1975, the U.N. General Assembly recommended that states setting up NWFZ should be guided by the following principles[4]: (a) obligations relating to the establishment of such zones may be assumed not only by groups of states, including entire continents or large geographical regions, but also by smaller groups of states and even individual countries; (b) NWFZ arrangements must ensure that the zone would be, and would remain, effectively free of all nuclear weapons; (c) the initiative for the creation of a NWFZ should come from states within the region, and participation must be voluntary; (d) whenever a zone is intended to embrace a region, the participation of all militarily significant states, and preferably all states, in that region would enhance the effectiveness of

the zone; (e) the zone arrangements must contain an effective system of verification to ensure full compliance with the agreed obligations; (f) the arrangements should promote the economic, scientific, and technological development of the members of the zone through international cooperation on all peaceful uses of nuclear energy; and (g) the treaty establishing the zone should be of unlimited duration.

The United States has laid down its own criteria as conditions for supporting the creation of NWFZ.[5] Among other things, these conditions stipulate that the establishment of the zone should not disturb existing security arrangements to the detriment of regional and international security or otherwise abridge the inherent right of individual or collective self-defense guaranteed in the U.N. Charter. Moreover, a zone should not affect the rights of the parties under international law to grant or deny other states transit privileges, including port calls and overflights; and no restrictions should be imposed on the high seas freedoms of navigation and overflight, the right of innocent passage of territorial and archipelagic seas, and the right of transit passage of international straits.

This article examines the extent to which the above principles and criteria have been observed, given that dissimilar geographical circumstances, as well as different political, cultural, economic, and strategic considerations of the states concerned, prevent any uniform pattern of denuclearized zones. The main differences relate to the scope of the obligations assumed by the parties; the responsibilities of extra-zonal states; the geographical area subject to denuclearization; the verification

arrangements; and the conditions for the entry into force of the zonal agreement, as well as for its denunciation. Although each consecutive NWFZ treaty has brought some substantive improvements, all treaties suffer from shortcomings. These are described below along with suggestions as to how they could be remedied. Current international events highlight the importance of this analysis. The active discussion of new NWFZs, such as in Central Asia, at the 1997 NPT Preparatory Committee meeting in New York, suggests that the breadth of the coverage of these zones may continue to expand.[6] Thus, it is useful to take stock of what zones exist—particularly in inhabited areas of the globe—in order to understand better their significance and relationship to other international nonproliferation efforts.

THE TREATY OF TLATELOLCO

During the 1962 Cuban missile crisis, a draft resolution calling for a NWFZ in Latin America was submitted at the U.N. General Assembly by Brazil but was not put to a vote.[7] In April 1963, at the initiative of the president of Mexico, the presidents of five Latin American countries announced that they were prepared to sign a multilateral agreement that would make Latin America a NWFZ.[8] This announcement received the support of the U.N. General Assembly, and the Latin American nations started negotiations among themselves. On February 14, 1967, at Tlatelolco, a district of Mexico City, the Treaty for the Prohibition of Nuclear Weapons in Latin America was signed by a number of Latin American states. Two Additional protocols annexed to the

Jozef Goldblat

Treaty of Tlatelolco were intended for signature by extra-zonal states.

Scope of the Obligations and Verification

In Article I, the Treaty of Tlatelolco prohibits the testing, use, manufacture, production, or acquisition by any means, as well as the receipt, storage, installation, deployment, and any form of possession of nuclear weapons in Latin America. Encouraging or authorizing or in any way participating in the testing, use, manufacture, production, possession, or control of any nuclear weapon is equally prohibited. Research and development directed towards acquiring a nuclear weapon capability is not expressly forbidden.

Explosions of nuclear devices for peaceful purposes are allowed under the treaty, and procedures for carrying them out are specified in Article 18. However, a proviso is made that such activities must be conducted in conformity with Article 1, which bans nuclear weapons, as well as with Article 5, which defines a nuclear weapon as any device capable of releasing nuclear energy in an uncontrolled manner and having characteristics appropriate for use for warlike purposes. (An instrument that may be used for the transport or propulsion of the device is not included in this definition if it is separable from the device and not an indivisible part thereof.) Most countries interpret these requirements as prohibiting the manufacture of all nuclear explosive devices, unless or until nuclear devices are developed that cannot be used as weapons. For a long time, Argentina and Brazil contested this interpretation. However, in their July 18, 1991 agreement for the exclusive peaceful use of nuclear energy, both countries undertook to prohibit in their respective territories the testing, use, manufacture, production, or acquisition by other means of any nuclear explosive device, as long as no technical distinction can be made between nuclear explosive devices for peaceful purposes and those for military purposes.[9] Thus, the controversy over whether indigenous development of nuclear explosive devices for peaceful purposes is compatible with participation in the Treaty of Tlatelolco has been set aside. It is obvious that allowing any kind of nuclear explosion would defeat the purpose of a NWFZ.

One of the purposes of the treaties establishing zones free of nuclear weapons is to make a nuclear attack against states parties militarily unjustifiable and, consequently, less likely. To achieve this goal, all potential targets of a nuclear strike would have to be removed from the denuclearized areas. These targets include nuclear-weapon-related support facilities, such as communication, surveillance, and intelligence-gathering facilities, as well as navigation installations, serving the nuclear strategic systems of the great powers. The Treaty of Tlatelolco does not, however, specifically ban such facilities.

Each party must conclude an agreement with the International Atomic Energy Agency (IAEA) for the application of safeguards to its nuclear activities (Article 13). The Agency for the Prohibition of Nuclear Weapons in Latin America (OPANAL) is responsible for holding periodic or extraordinary consultations among member-states on matters relating to the purposes, measures and procedures set forth in the treaty and to the supervision of compliance with the obligations arising therefrom. The General Conference, composed of all parties to the treaty, is the supreme organ of OPANAL. It holds regular sessions, as well as special sessions if circumstances so require. The OPANAL Council—able to function continuously—is composed of five members elected by the General Conference. The General Secretary is the chief administrative officer of the Agency (Articles 7 to 11).

Area Subject to Denuclearization

The zone of application of the Treaty of Tlatelolco embraces the territory, territorial sea, airspace, and any other space over which the zonal state exercises sovereignty in accordance with its own legislation (Article 3). Upon fulfillment of several requirements specified in Article 28, it will also include vast areas in the Atlantic and Pacific Oceans, hundreds of kilometers off the coasts of Latin America (Article 4). These requirements are: adherence to the treaty by all states of the region; signature and ratification of Additional Protocols to the treaty by all the states concerned; and conclusion of agreements with the IAEA for the application of safeguards to the nuclear activities of the parties. The extra-continental or continental states that are internationally responsible, *de jure* or *de facto*, for territories lying within the limits of the geographical zone established by the treaty—France, the Netherlands, the United Kingdom, and the United States—have undertaken to apply the statute of military denuclearization to these territories by adhering to Additional Protocol I of the treaty. All nuclear powers have unreserv-

Jozef Goldblat

edly assumed an obligation under Additional Protocol II to respect the denuclearization of Latin America as "defined, delimited and set forth" in the treaty, that is, as covering the designated portions of the high seas as well. However, in statements contradicting this obligation, the signatories of the protocol pointed out that they would not accept any restrictions on their freedom at sea.

Furthermore, since transit of nuclear weapons was not explicitly prohibited by the treaty, the question arose whether such activity is actually permitted. According to the interpretation given in 1967 by the Preparatory Commission for the Denuclearization of Latin America (COPREDAL), it is the prerogative of the territorial state, in the exercise of its sovereignty, to grant or deny permission for transit.[10] In joining Additional Protocols of the treaty, the United States and France made a declaration of understanding to the same effect, while the Soviet Union expressed the opinion that authorizing transit of nuclear weapons in any form would be contrary to the objectives of the treaty. China believes that transport of nuclear weapons through Latin American territory, territorial sea, or airspace is prohibited. Indeed, once nuclear weapons are allowed in transit, even if such transit is limited to port visits or overflights, it will be difficult to maintain that the zone has been totally denuclearized. In any event, since the great powers refuse, as a matter of policy, to disclose the whereabouts of their nuclear weapons, they are unlikely to request permission of transit for specific ships or aircraft carrying nuclear weapons. The right of zonal states to deny permission for transit of nuclear weapons is thus purely hypothetical.

Security Assurances of Extra-Zonal States

Additional Protocol II to the Treaty of Tlatelolco provides for assurances to be given by the nuclear powers not to use or threaten to use nuclear weapons against the parties to the treaty. However, the obligations that the nuclear powers have actually assumed under this protocol are conditional. The United States and the United Kingdom made special interpretative statements at the time of signing and ratifying Protocol II, which reflected their current military doctrines. They reserved the right to reconsider their non-use obligations with regard to any state in the NWFZ in the event of an armed attack by that state carried out with the support or assistance of a nuclear power. The Soviet Union formulated a similar qualification with regard to a party to the treaty committing an act of aggression with the support of, or together with, a nuclear weapon state. For France, its non-use undertaking would present no obstacle to the full exercise of the right of self-defense enshrined in the U.N. Charter.

Entry into Force and Denunciation

The Treaty of Tlatelolco enters into force among states that have ratified it only when certain conditions have been met—the same as are required under Article 28 for the extension of the geographical area of the Treaty's application. These conditions may be waived, and most parties have in fact done so. The treaty became operative in April 1968, when El Salvador joined Mexico in ratifying it and in waiving the requirements for its entry into force.

The treaty is of a permanent nature and is not subject to reservations (Articles 30 and 27). However, any party may denounce it with three-months' notice if, in its opinion, there have arisen or "may arise" circumstances connected with the content of the treaty or of the Additional Protocols that affect its supreme interests or the peace and security of one or more parties (Article 30).

Amendments

In 1992, at the initiative of Argentina, Brazil, and Chile, the General Conference of OPANAL decided to amend the articles relating to verification (Articles 14, 15, 16, 19, and 20) of the Treaty of Tlatelolco. The most important of these amendments concerns the so-called special inspections envisaged in Article 16. According to the original version of this Article, special inspections may be arranged not only by the IAEA—in accordance with the safeguards agreements concluded with the parties—but also by the Council of OPANAL, following a request by a party which suspects that some prohibited activity has been or is about to be carried out in the territory of another party, or following a request by a party which has been suspected of or charged with having violated the treaty. In the latter case, the accused country would have an opportunity to prove its innocence. Inspectors would be granted full and free access to all places and all information necessary for the performance of their duties. The costs of special inspections arranged by the OPANAL Council would normally be borne by the requesting party or parties, except where the Council concludes that in view of the "cir-

Jozef Goldblat

cumstances existing in the case" such costs should be borne by OPA-NAL. According to the amended version of Article 16, the IAEA will have the exclusive power to carry out special inspections. The role of the OPANAL Council will be reduced in this respect to submitting requests to the IAEA to put into operation the mechanisms of inspection. Information regarding the conclusion of the special inspection will be transmitted to the General Secretary of OPA-NAL only after it has been forwarded by the Director General of the IAEA to the IAEA Board of Governors. These modifications may have set an unfortunate precedent for future denuclearization agreements. Certain countries in regions of international tension may be reluctant to entrust the protection of their vital security interests entirely to an international organization, even an organization of such high standing as the IAEA.

Another amendment, adopted in 1990, added to the official title of the Treaty of Tlatelolco the words "and the Caribbean" in order to incorporate the English-speaking states of the Caribbean area into the zone of application of the treaty. By yet another amendment in 1991, all the independent states of the region became eligible to join the regime of denuclearization. (According to the original Article 25, a "political entity," part or all of whose territory was the subject of a dispute or claim between an extra-continental country and one or more Latin American states, could not be admitted.) Owing to this amendment, Belize and Guyana could join the treaty.[11]

Conditions for the entry into force of the amendments are not clearly stated in the treaty. The government

of Mexico, which is the depositary of the treaty, considers the amendments to be in force for those states which have ratified them and waived the requirements specified in Article 28.[12]

THE TREATY OF RAROTONGA

In 1983, in the context of growing concern over the activities of the nuclear powers in the South Pacific, and especially over nuclear test explosions, Australia proposed the establishment of a nuclear-free zone in the region. The proposal was officially submitted at the annual South Pacific Forum, the high-level meeting of independent or self-governing South Pacific countries. It was endorsed the following year. Subsequently, as a result of negotiations among Australia, the Cook Islands, Fiji, Kiribati, Nauru, New Zealand, Niue, Papua New Guinea, the Solomon Islands, Tonga, Tuvalu, Vanuatu, and Western Samoa—all member-states of the South Pacific Forum—a treaty establishing the proposed zone was signed on August 6, 1985, at Rarotonga in the Cook Islands. (Republic of Marshall Islands and Federated States of Micronesia became eligible to sign only upon joining the Forum in 1987.)[13] Three protocols annexed to the treaty were intended for signature by extra-zonal states.

Scope of Obligations and Verification

The South Pacific Nuclear Free Zone Treaty, called the Treaty of Rarotonga, in force since 1986, prohibits, in its Article 3, the manufacture or acquisition by other means, as well as the possession or control, of any nuclear explosive device by

the countries of the zone. It also bans seeking or receiving assistance in the manufacture or acquisition of nuclear explosive devices. Protocol 3, prohibiting tests of any nuclear explosive device anywhere within the zone, was opened for signature by all the nuclear powers, but it was clearly addressed to France, the only state at the time of signing which was engaged in such tests in the region.

By "nuclear explosive device" the treaty means any nuclear weapon or other explosive device capable of releasing nuclear energy, irrespective of the purpose for which it could be used. The term includes such a weapon or device in unassembled and partly assembled forms, but does not include the means of transport or delivery of such a weapon or device if separable from and not an indivisible part of it (Article 1). As in the Treaty of Tlatelolco, research and development directed towards acquiring nuclear-weapon capability are not expressly forbidden.

In addition to banning nuclear explosive devices, the Treaty of Rarotonga contains a ban on dumping radioactive matter at sea anywhere within the South Pacific zone (Article 7); hence the zone is called "nuclear-free," which conveys a notion wider than "nuclear-weapon-free." The relevant provision reflects the concern, often voiced in the United Nations and other international organizations, over the inability of the nuclear industry to dispose safely of its wastes.

As regards weapon-related prohibitions, the Treaty of Rarotonga appears to be stricter than the Treaty of Tlatelolco, because it prohibits the possession or testing of nuclear explosive devices for peaceful purposes. Nevertheless, as in the Treaty

The Nonproliferation Review/Spring-Summer 1997

Jozef Goldblat

of Tlatelolco, the denuclearization measures taken in the South Pacific region have not removed all the potential targets for nuclear attack, because the Treaty of Rarotonga has not prohibited the facilities serving nuclear strategic systems.

Full-scope IAEA safeguards must be applied to nuclear activities of the parties, and no nuclear exports to any non-nuclear weapon state may take place without the application of such safeguards. As distinct from the Treaty of Tlatelolco, safeguards are also required (though not of full-scope type) for nuclear exports to nuclear weapon states (Articles 4 and 8; Annex 2). The Consultative Committee—a forum for consultation and co-operation on any matter arising in relation to the treaty—may be convened to consider complaints by the Director of the South Pacific Bureau for Economic Co-operation, the depositary of the treaty. The Committee, which is constituted of the representatives of the parties, may direct that a special inspection be made by a team of three qualified inspectors, accompanied, if so requested, by representatives of the party complained of. If the Committee decides that there has been a breach of the treaty, the parties shall meet promptly at a meeting of the South Pacific Forum (Articles 9 to 10 and Annex 4).

Area Subject to Denuclearization

Although the Treaty of Rarotonga claims to have set up a nuclear-free zone stretching to the border of the Latin American NWFZ in the east, and to the border of the Antarctic demilitarized zone in the south, it bans the presence of nuclear weapons only within the territories of the South Pacific states, up to the 12-mile territorial sea limit. It does not seek—

as the Treaty of Tlatelolco does through an additional protocol—to have nuclear-weapon prohibitions applied to a larger ocean area. This omission seems to be justified by a specific reference to international law with regard to freedom of the seas, although no law, including the law of the sea, can exclude constraints on any activity, if the constraints are internationally agreed. Establishment of extensive nuclear-weapon-free maritime areas adjacent to nuclear-weapon-free territories would reinforce the sense of security of zonal states.

Article 5 of the treaty allows each party to make an exception for nuclear weapons that may be aboard foreign ships visiting its ports or navigating its territorial sea or archipelagic waters, and for weapons that may be aboard foreign aircraft visiting its airfields or transiting its airspace. The frequency and duration of such permitted visits and transits are not limited. Thus, it is not clear to what extent they differ from the "stationing" (defined in Article 1 as "emplantation, emplacement, transportation on land or inland waters, stockpiling, storage, installation and deployment") of nuclear weapons, which *is* prohibited. Under Protocol 1 to the Treaty of Rarotonga, open for signature by France, the United Kingdom, and the United States, the signatories are to apply the prohibitions contained in the treaty to the territories in the zone for which they are internationally responsible.

Security Assurances of Extra-Zonal States

Protocol 2 to the Treaty of Rarotonga provides for the nuclear powers to give assurances not to use or threaten to use nuclear weapons against the parties. In signing this

protocol, the Soviet Union stated that in case of action taken by a party or parties violating their major commitments concerning the status of the zone, it would consider itself free of its non-use commitments. The same would apply in case of aggression committed by one or several parties to the treaty, supported by a nuclear weapon state, or together with it, involving the use by such a state of the territory, airspace, territorial sea, or archipelagic waters of the parties for visits by nuclear weapon-carrying ships and aircraft or for transit of nuclear weapons. Eventually, the Soviet Union ratified Protocols 2 and 3 without reference to the above statement.

China signed the same protocols with an understanding that it might reconsider its obligations if 'other nuclear weapon states or parties to the treaty took action in gross violation of the treaty and its protocols, thus changing the status of the zone and endangering the security interests of China. This understanding was not referred to at the time of ratification.

The United States stated that its practices and procedures in the South Pacific were not inconsistent with the treaty and its protocols, while the United Kingdom said that it would respect the intentions of the states in the region. In October 1995, both countries and France announced jointly their intention to sign all the protocols in the first half of 1996 (that is, after the planned termination of the last series of French nuclear tests in the Pacific).[14] The signing of the protocols by the three Western nuclear powers took place on March 25, 1996.[15] In its statement of reservation and interpretation, the French government made it clear that it did not consider its inherent right to self-defense to be restricted by the signed documents, and that the assurances provided for in Protocol 2 were the same as those given by France to non-nuclear weapon states parties to the NPT. The U.K. government stated that it would not be bound by its undertaking under Protocol 2 in the case of an invasion or any other attack carried out or sustained by a party to the treaty in association or alliance with a nuclear weapon state, or if a material breach of the nonproliferation obligations under the treaty were committed.[16] The U.S. government signed the protocols without reservation, but its spokesman said that "certain declarations and understandings" would be proposed to the U.S. Senate for incorporation in the resolution of ratification.[17]

Entry into Force and Denunciation

According to Article 15, the Treaty of Rarotonga entered into force upon the deposit of the eighth instrument of ratification. This procedure was much simpler than that provided for in the Treaty of Tlatelolco. Also the denunciation formula of the Treaty of Rarotonga is different. It is more restrictive than that of the Treaty of Tlatelolco, because it concedes the right of withdrawal only in the event of violation of a provision essential to the achievement of the objectives of the treaty, and it requires a 12 months' notice (Article 13). Reservations are not allowed (Article 14).

THE DECLARATION ON KOREA

Whereas the Republic of Korea (South)—which joined the NPT in 1975—has all along been subject to full-scope safeguards, as provided

for in that Treaty, the Democratic People's Republic of Korea (North)—party to the NPT since 1985—refused to sign a safeguards agreement with the IAEA within the time-limit prescribed by the Treaty. It put forward several political conditions for signing that were not directly related to the NPT.

Following the decision by the United States to withdraw most of the tactical nuclear weapons deployed outside its borders and the statement by the South Korean President that there were no such weapons in his country, the government of North Korea finally accepted the NPT safeguards. On January 20, 1992, both Korean states signed a Joint Declaration on the Denuclearization of the Korean Peninsula. The stated aim of the Declaration was to "eliminate the danger of nuclear war" and, in particular, to "create an environment and conditions favorable for peace and peaceful unification of our country."

The parties agreed not to test, manufacture, produce, receive, possess, store, deploy, or use nuclear weapons. They further undertook to use nuclear energy solely for peaceful purposes, and not to possess nuclear reprocessing or uranium enrichment facilities. To verify compliance, each side may conduct inspection of the objects agreed upon by both sides.[18] A South–North Joint Nuclear Control Commission is to be in charge of implementing the Declaration.

The Joint Declaration was to enter into force upon the exchange of appropriate instruments following the completion of the procedures required by each side. This exchange took place in February 1992. However, the March 12, 1993 decision by

North Korea to withdraw from the NPT—although subsequently suspended—placed in jeopardy and, in any event, delayed the realization of the NWFZ agreement.

If brought fully into effect, the Korean Declaration would significantly complement the global nonproliferation regime. Its ban on reprocessing and enrichment activities—which goes beyond the obligations assumed by the parties to other NWFZ treaties—is particularly noteworthy. However, since these activities, which have legitimate civilian applications, are not prohibited by the NPT, they may not be banned in other zonal denuclearization agreements.

THE TREATY OF PELINDABA

On November 24, 1961, in the aftermath of the first French nuclear weapon tests in the Sahara desert, the U.N. General Assembly called on member states to refrain from carrying out such tests in Africa, and from using the African continent for storing or transporting nuclear weapons.[19] Nearly three years later, the African heads of state and government participating in a summit conference of the Organization of African Unity (OAU) solemnly declared that they were ready to undertake, through an international agreement to be concluded under U.N. auspices, not to manufacture or control atomic weapons.[20] The Declaration was endorsed in resolutions of the United Nations, but no concrete action was taken to carry it into effect. Only in 1991, after South Africa—the only country on the African continent possessing the technical capability to produce nuclear weapons—had acceded to the NPT, did real prospects appear for the establishment of an African NWFZ.

In 1995, as a result of several years work, OAU and U.N. experts succeeded in elaborating a draft treaty which, after some amendments, was approved by the OAU Assembly. As in the case of the Treaty of Tlatelolco and the Treaty of Rarotonga, the protocols annexed to the Treaty on the African Nuclear-Weapon-Free Zone are to be signed by extra-zonal states. (The treaty is also called the Treaty of Pelindaba, after the former seat of South Africa's nuclear-weapon-related activities). Other aspects the Treaty of Pelindaba also followed the pattern of the NWFZ arrangements in force in Latin America and the South Pacific. On December 12, 1995, the U.N. General Assembly welcomed the Treaty of Pelindaba,[21] and on April 11, 1996, the treaty was opened for signature.

Scope of Obligations and Verification

The Treaty of Pelindaba prohibits the manufacture, testing, stockpiling, or acquisition by other means, as well as possession and control of any nuclear explosive device (in assembled, unassembled, or partly assembled forms) by the parties. In addition—and this is an important novelty—research on, and development of, such a device are banned. Moreover, the treaty bans seeking, receiving, or encouraging assistance in the above-enumerated activities (Articles 3 and 5). Under Protocol II, open for signature by the five nuclear weapon states, the signatories should undertake not to test or assist in or encourage the testing of any nuclear explosive device within the African zone. Article 1 defines

nuclear explosive device in exactly the same way it is defined in the Treaty of Rarotonga.

In a clear allusion to the past South African nuclear weapon program, Article 6 of the Treaty of Pelindaba requires the dismantlement and destruction of any nuclear device that was manufactured prior to the coming into force of the treaty, as well as the destruction of the relevant facilities or their conversion to peaceful uses. All such operations must take place under the supervision of the IAEA. These provisions aim to dispel any lingering suspicion that some nuclear items have been hidden away in South Africa or that certain prohibited activities are still taking place there. Article 6 sets a precedent for future nuclear weapon-free-zone treaties concluded with the participation of nuclear threshold states.

Like the Treaty of Rarotonga, the Treaty of Pelindaba prohibits the dumping of radioactive matter anywhere within the African zone, but it also contains, in Article 7, an undertaking by the parties to implement or to use as guidelines the measures contained in the Bamako Convention on the Ban of the Import into Africa and Control of Transboundary Movement and Management of Hazardous Wastes within Africa, in so far as it is relevant to radioactive waste. The parties undertake to strengthen the mechanisms for co-operation at bilateral, subregional, and regional levels, with a view to promoting the use of nuclear science and technology for economic and social developments.

While stationing of nuclear explosive devices in the territory of the zonal states is prohibited, visits and

transit by foreign ships and aircraft with nuclear weapons aboard may be allowed by the parties on the rather vague condition that no prejudice should be caused to the purposes and objectives of the treaty (Article 4). Nor is it prohibited in the African zone to establish facilities serving nuclear strategic systems of the nuclear powers.

Verification of the uses of nuclear energy is to be performed by the IAEA, which must apply full-scope safeguards to prevent the diversion of nuclear material to nuclear explosive devices (Annex II).[22] Parties to the treaty may supply nuclear material or equipment to non-nuclear weapon states only if the latter accept full-scope safeguards (Article 9c). Furthermore, the treaty obliges the parties to observe international rules regarding the security and physical protection of nuclear materials, facilities, and equipment in order to prevent their theft or unauthorized use (Article 10). Any action aimed at an armed attack by conventional or other means against nuclear installations in the African zone is forbidden (Article 11).

The African Commission on Nuclear Energy (AFCONE), which will have its headquarters in South Africa, is to be charged with ensuring compliance with all the above undertakings (Article 12). It will be composed of 12 members elected by the parties for a three-year period, bearing in mind not only the principle of equitable geographical distribution, but also the advancement of the members' nuclear programs. The Chairman and Vice-Chairman are to be elected by AFCONE, while the Executive Secretary is to be designated by the Secretary-General of the OAU (Annex III). The Commis-

Jozef Goldblat

sion may request the IAEA to conduct an inspection on the territory of a party suspected of violating its obligations and designate representatives to accompany the Agency's inspection team, but it may also set up its own inspection mechanisms. Established breaches may be referred to the OAU which, in turn, can refer the matter to the U.N. Security Council (Annex IV).

Area Subject to Denuclearization

The Treaty of Pelindaba bans nuclear weapons in the territory of the continent of Africa, island states members of the OAU, and all islands considered in OAU resolutions (presumably also resolutions that may be adopted in the future) to be part of Africa. For the purpose of the treaty, "territory" means land territory, internal waters, territorial seas, and archipelagic waters and the airspace above them, as well as the seabed and subsoil beneath (Article 1). A reference is made to the freedom of the seas (Article 2)—identical to that appearing in the Treaty of Rarotonga; it is clearly intended to preclude restrictions on the presence of nuclear weapons beyond the territorial sea limits of the zonal states. Under Protocol III of the Treaty of Pelindaba, open for signature by France and Spain, the signatories should undertake to apply, in the territories for which each of them is *de jure* or *de facto* internationally responsible and that are situated in the African zone, the denuclearization provisions contained in Articles 3 to 10 of the treaty, and to ensure the application of IAEA safeguards there.

The geographic extent of the application of the Treaty of Pelindaba

and of its protocols is illustrated in a map annexed to the treaty. The main difficulty in drawing up this map was the status of the Chagos Archipelago, including the island of Diego Garcia that harbors a U.S. military base. The Archipelago is covered by the map with a proviso that this is "without prejudice to the question of sovereignty" claimed by both the United Kingdom and Mauritius. It was thus made clear that the resolution of the sovereignty issue would have to take place outside the framework of the treaty. However, the United Kingdom stated that it did not accept the inclusion, without its consent, of the British Indian Ocean Territory, of which Diego Garcia is part, within the African NWFZ, and that it did not accept any legal obligations in respect of that Territory. In a related statement, the United States noted that neither the treaty nor Protocol III applies to the activities of the United Kingdom, the United States, or any other state not party to the treaty on the Island of Diego Garcia or elsewhere in the British Indian Ocean Territories, and that, accordingly, no change was required in U.S. armed forces operations there.[23] Russia, however, pointed out that, as long as a military base of a nuclear power was situated on the Chagos Archipelago islands, and as long as certain nuclear powers considered themselves free from the obligations under the protocols to the Treaty of Pelindaba with regard to these islands, Russia could not regard them as meeting the requirements of nuclear-weapon-free territories.[24]

Security Assurances of Extra-Zonal States

Under Protocol I, open for signature by China, France, Russia, the

United Kingdom, and the United States, the signatories should undertake not to use or threaten to use a nuclear explosive device against any party to the treaty, or any territory within the African zone for which a state that has become party to Protocol III is internationally responsible. However, in signing this protocol, the United States, the United Kingdom, and France declared that they would not be bound by it in case of an invasion or any other attack upon them, carried out or sustained by a party to the treaty in association or alliance with a nuclear weapon state. Russia made a similar statement, but added that it did not consider itself bound by the obligations under Protocol I in respect of the Chagos Archipelago islands.

Parties to the protocols would undertake not to contribute to any act constituting a violation of the treaty or the relevant protocol. This undertaking, however, is unverifiable without the transparency of the nuclear powers' naval and air deployments in the NWFZ as well as in the areas adjacent to the zone.[25]

Entry into Force and Denunciation

The Treaty of Pelindaba is not subject to reservations. It will enter into force on the date of the deposit with the Secretary-General of the OAU of the 28th instrument of ratification. The treaty is of unlimited duration, but any party may withdraw from it at 12-months' notice, if some extraordinary events have jeopardized its supreme interests. The denunciation clause is thus less rigorous than in the Treaty of Rarotonga, which permits withdrawal only in the event of a material breach of the treaty.

THE TREATY OF BANGKOK

In Southeast Asia, the idea of setting up a NWFZ was developed as part of the Declaration on the Zone of Peace, Freedom, and Neutrality (ZOPAN) issued in 1971 by the Association of Southeast Asian Nations (ASEAN). In recent years, states of the region have revitalized the denuclearization proposal,[26] and a working group, established by the Association, engaged in preparatory work to implement the initiative. This work gathered momentum after the United States had closed its military bases in the Philippines and appeared to support the ASEAN project. On December 16, 1995, the Treaty on the Southeast Asia Nuclear-Weapon-Free Zone was signed in Bangkok. It is referred to as the Treaty of Bangkok.

Scope of Obligations and Verification

Parties to the Treaty of Bangkok may use nuclear energy for their economic development and social progress, but are prohibited, both inside and outside the zone, from developing, testing, manufacturing or otherwise acquiring, possessing, or having control over nuclear weapons. (Unlike in the Treaty of Pelindaba, research on nuclear explosive devices is not expressly banned.) The parties will not allow other states to engage in such activities, including the use of nuclear weapons, on their territories. "Nuclear weapon" is defined in somewhat simpler terms than in other denuclearization treaties, namely, as any explosive device that is capable of releasing nuclear energy in an uncontrolled manner. The means of transport or delivery of such a device are not included in this defi-

nition if they are separable from and not an indivisible part thereof. Nuclear explosive devices in unassembled or partly assembled forms are not explicitly covered. Dumping at sea or discharge into the atmosphere within the zone of any radioactive material or wastes is not allowed. Nor is it allowed to dispose radioactive material or wastes on land, unless the disposal is carried out in accordance with IAEA standards and procedures. Seeking or receiving assistance in the commission of acts which would violate the above provisions, as well as assisting in or encouraging the commission of such acts are equally prohibited (Articles 1 and 3).

Parties, which have not yet done so, must conclude an agreement with the IAEA for the application of full-scope safeguards to their peaceful nuclear activities (Article 5). In addition to these safeguards, the control system will comprise reports and exchanges of relevant information; requests for clarification of situations that may be considered ambiguous or may give rise to doubts about compliance; and requests for fact-finding missions to clarify and resolve such situations in accordance with the procedure laid down in the annex to the treaty (Article 10). Prior to embarking on a peaceful nuclear energy program, each party must subject the program to rigorous nuclear safety assessment conforming to the guidelines and standards recommended by the IAEA for the protection of health and minimization of danger to life and property (Article 4b).

A Commission for the Southeast Asia Nuclear-Weapon-Free Zone, composed of all states parties, is to be established to oversee the imple-

mentation of the treaty and ensure compliance with its provisions. The Executive Committee, a subsidiary organ of the Commission—also composed of all parties—is to ensure the proper operation of verification measures, decide on requests for clarification and for a fact-finding mission, set up such a mission (which would consist of three inspectors from the IAEA who are neither nationals of the requesting state nor nationals of the receiving state), decide on its findings, and request the Commission to convene if necessary. The decisions of the Executive Committee and those of the Commission are to be taken by consensus or, failing consensus, by a two-thirds majority of the members present and voting (Articles 8 and 9). In case of an established breach of the treaty, the Commission must decide on measures to cope with the situation, including submission of the matter to the IAEA and—where the situation might endanger international peace and security—to the Security Council and the General Assembly of the United Nations (Article 14.3). Disputes arising from the interpretation of the treaty may be referred to arbitration or the International Court of Justice (Article 21).

Stationing—defined as deploying, emplacing, emplanting, installing, stockpiling, or storing nuclear weapons—in the Southeast Asia Zone is prohibited. However, each party, on "being notified," may decide for itself whether to allow visits by foreign ships and aircraft to its ports and airfields, transit of its airspace by foreign aircraft, and navigation by foreign ships through its territorial sea or archipelagic waters and overflight of foreign aircraft above those waters in a manner not governed by the rights of innocent passage, archipe-lagic sea lanes passage or transit passage (Article 7). As elsewhere, it is doubtful whether the presence of nuclear weapons on foreign ships or aircraft would ever be announced.

Area Subject to Denuclearization

The Southeast Asia Nuclear-Weapon-Free Zone comprises the territories of Brunei Darussalam, Cambodia, Indonesia, Laos, Malay-sia, Myanmar, Philippines, Sin-gapore, Thailand, and Vietnam, as well as their respective continental shelves and exclusive economic zones (EEZ) (Articles 1a and 2.1). The inclusion of continental shelves and of EEZ is a novelty, but, accord-ing to the language of the treaty, the right of states with regard to free-dom of the high seas and innocent passage or transit passage of ships and aircraft, are not to be prejudiced.

Security Assurances of Extra-Zonal States

Under the protocol annexed to the Treaty of Bangkok and open for sig-nature by China, France, Russia, the United Kingdom, and the United States, the signatories would assume the following obligations: to respect the treaty and not to contribute to any act that would constitute its viola-tion, and not to use or threaten to use nuclear weapons against any state party to the treaty and, in general, within the zone. The protocol is of a permanent nature, but each party may withdraw from it, if it decides that extraordinary events related to the subject matter of the protocol have jeopardized its supreme inter-ests.

In the event of a breach of the protocol, the Executive Committee may convene a special meeting of the Commission to decide on appro-priate measures to be taken. No other denuclearization treaty provides for such action.

The United States expressed con-cerns (shared by some other nuclear powers) that because of the geo-graphical extent of the Zone— which it considers inconsistent with the Law of the Sea Convention—regu-lar movement of nuclear-powered and nuclear-armed naval vessels and aircraft through Southeast Asia would be restricted and regional se-curity arrangements disturbed. It is reluctant to provide what it deems to be sweeping security assurances as demanded by the Southeast Asian zonal states. China made known its objection to the geographical scope of the treaty, specifically to the in-clusion of parts of the South China Sea to which it and some ASEAN members have conflicting claims.[27] It is possible that the signatories of the treaty will revise the language of the protocol to make it acceptable to the nuclear weapon states.

Entry into Force and Denunciation

The Treaty of Bangkok will enter into force upon the deposit with the government of Thailand of the sev-enth instrument of ratification (Ar-ticle 16). Reservations are not permitted. The treaty is to remain in force indefinitely, but—like in the Treaty of Rarotonga—each party will have the right to withdraw from it, at 12 months' notice, in the event of a breach by any other party that would be essential to the achieve-ment of the objectives of the treaty (Article 22).

The operation of the treaty is to be reviewed 10 years after its entry into force at a meeting of the Com-mission specially convened for this purpose (Article 20). Amendments can be adopted only by a consensus decision of the Commission (Article 19).

PROPOSALS FOR OTHER DENUCLEARIZED ZONES

In the Middle East—one of the most explosive regions in the world—the concept of a NWFZ was advanced by Iran and Egypt in 1974.[28] Since then, the U.N. Gen-eral Assembly adopted several reso-lutions supporting this concept, and in recent years it has done so by con-sensus.[29] Also the U.N. Security Council cease-fire resolution 687, passed after the 1991 Persian Gulf War, emphasized the need for a de-nuclearized Middle East.

The zone in the Middle East, as envisaged, overlaps, to a large ex-tent, with the NWFZ in Africa, but it is aimed primarily at Israel which re-fuses to join the NPT. Israel ac-knowledges having nuclear weapon capabilities, but has neither con-firmed nor denied the possession of nuclear weapons. It made an am-biguous statement to the effect that "it will not be the first country to in-troduce nuclear weapons into the Middle East."[30] A U.N. study on "effective and verifiable measures which would facilitate the establish-ment of a nuclear-weapon-free zone in the Middle East," published in 1990, suggested that the process of creating the proposed zone should be preceded by confidence-building measures.[31]

In April 1990, President Mubarak of Egypt proposed the establishment in the Middle East of a zone free of all types of weapons of mass destruction.[32] Thus, not only nuclear weapons would be banned in the area in question, but chemical and biological weapons as well, and probably also certain categories of ballistic missiles. In any event, complete and verified denuclearization of the Middle East is not likely to take place before a successful conclusion of the peace process, which would end threats of the use of force in the region.

The proposal for the establishment of a NWFZ in South Asia has been on the agenda of the U.N. General Assembly since the early 1970s, and a number of resolutions have been adopted recommending such a measure. The proposal is aimed at India and Pakistan, the major powers in the region not bound by the NPT.

In 1974, India conducted a test of a nuclear device, which it called a peaceful explosion, but it claims that it has never "weaponized" the results of this test.[33] Nonetheless, according to some reports, India has already manufactured nuclear weapons and perhaps made preparations for another nuclear explosion.[34] Even if these reports are not correct, the very possession of a growing stockpile of nuclear weapon-usable material gives India the ability to "go nuclear" within a short period of time. In retaining the nuclear option India may wish to counterbalance China's nuclear arsenal and its superiority in non-nuclear armaments.

Pakistan has the ability to produce nuclear weapons, and may have already done so,[35] but Pakistani leaders deny it. To demonstrate their good will, they have proposed various denuclearization arrangements with India, such as simultaneous accession to the NPT, mutual acceptance of full-scope IAEA nuclear safeguards, bilateral inspections of all nuclear installations, formal pledges not to manufacture nuclear weapons, and, finally, the establishment of a South Asian zone free of nuclear weapons. India has rejected the above proposals, arguing that without a proper definition of the geographic extent and the security needs of the region (an allusion to the neighboring China), endorsement of the concept of regional denuclearization would be inappropriate. It also considers nuclear disarmament as a matter requiring a global rather than a regional approach.

In Europe, all states have joined the NPT. Moreover, the elimination by the United States and Russia of ground-launched missiles with a range of 500 to 5500 kilometers, in compliance with the INF Treaty, as well as the two powers' unilateral withdrawals of their short-range missiles and most other tactical weapons, have transformed much of the European continent into a zone of considerably thinned-out nuclear armaments. In addition, according to the 1990 Treaty on the Final Settlement with respect to Germany, after the withdrawal of Russian forces from the former German Democratic Republic, no nuclear weapons may be stationed in that part of Germany.[36] Nevertheless, over the years, proposals have been made for a formal denuclearization of different parts of Europe. Recently, the government of Belarus suggested creating a NWFZ that would comprise countries situated between the Baltic Sea and the Black Sea.[37] The suggestion grew out of concern that the planned eastward expansion of the North Atlantic Treaty Organization (NATO) could lead to the deployment of Western tactical nuclear weapons on the territories of the former members of the Warsaw Treaty Organization (WTO). However, there is no consensus among the countries of Central and Eastern Europe about the need for such undertakings. Proposals for a Nordic NWFZ, made repeatedly during the Cold War, were never subject of real negotiation.

The suspected acquisition of nuclear weapons by North Korea gave rise to a discussion about the advisability of setting up a NWFZ in Northeast Asia, which would cover not only the two Korean states but also Japan and Taiwan.

Central Asia, too, has been mentioned by the countries of the region as an area lending itself to denuclearization. Numerous key steps have already taken place, including the tabling of several documents before the United Nations.[38] Most significant among these developments has been the Almaty Declaration of February 28, 1997, in which the presidents of the five states of the region (Kazakstan, Kyrgyzstan, Tajikistan, Turkmenistan, and Uzbekistan) expressed their joint support for the formation of a NWFZ. The five states have created a working group and intend to meet in Tashkent, Uzbekistan, in September 1997 to draw up plans for a formal U.N. resolution announcing their plans and calling on other states for their support in the formation of the zone.[39]

Moreover, an even broader concept of establishing a "nuclear-weapon-free southern hemisphere and adjacent areas" was launched at the 1996 U.N. General Assembly.[40] Finally, proposals for "zones of peace" in the Indian Ocean, the Mediterranean, the South Atlantic, and Central America imply at least some measure of denuclearization in these regions.

Jozef Goldblat

NUCLEAR-WEAPON-FREE COUNTRIES

In 1987, the Parliament of New Zealand decided to establish the New Zealand Nuclear Free Zone.[41] The zone comprises all of the land, territory, and inland waters within the territorial limits of New Zealand; the internal waters and the territorial sea of New Zealand; as well as the airspace above all these areas. In addition to prohibitions on the acquisition, stationing, and testing of nuclear explosive devices in the zone, the Prime Minister may grant approval to the entry of foreign warships into the internal waters of New Zealand only if he is satisfied that the warships will not be carrying any nuclear explosive device upon their entry into these waters. Similarly, approval of landings in New Zealand by foreign military aircraft may be granted by the Prime Minister only if he is satisfied that the aircraft will not be carrying any nuclear explosive device when it lands. Entry into the internal waters of New Zealand by any ship whose propulsion is wholly or partly dependent on nuclear power is prohibited. In this respect, the Parliamentary Act establishing the New Zealand Zone went beyond the restrictions set by other NWFZs; none of them prohibits the presence of nuclear-powered engines.[42]

New Zealand's anti-nuclear posture proved unacceptable to the United States, which canceled its naval exercises with New Zealand, stopped its long-established intelligence relationship with that country, and suspended its security obligations to it. The argument put forward by the United States was that, by barring U.S. warships, New Zealand had placed in jeopardy the collective capacity of the Australia-New Zealand-United States (ANZUS) alliance to resist armed attack.[43]

In his address to the U.N. General Assembly, in September 1992, the President of Mongolia declared the territory of his country a NWFZ. He said that his government would strive to have its status internationally guaranteed.[44]

In response to the above declaration, the United States made a statement in which it noted that, as a non-nuclear party to the NPT, Mongolia benefited from the U.S. commitment to seek Security Council assistance in the event of a nuclear attack, and from the assurances that nuclear weapons would not be used against a non-nuclear weapon state not allied with a nuclear weapon state. The United Kingdom and France made a similar statement. Russia referred to its treaty on friendly relations and co-operation with Mongolia, in which it undertook to respect the policy of the Mongolian government aimed at preventing the deployment of foreign troops as well as of nuclear and other weapons of mass destruction on its territory or their transit through its territory.

In 1988, the Parliament of Denmark passed a resolution requesting the government to notify all visiting warships that they must not carry nuclear arms into Danish ports. In a sense, the resolution merely elaborated on the official Danish policy proclaimed more than three decades earlier, namely, that in time of peace, introduction of nuclear weapons to the country is prohibited. In fact, however, the resolution appeared to reject the practice of "neither confirming nor denying" the presence of nuclear weapons, which is followed by the navies of all the nuclear

weapon powers. Eventually, under pressure exercised within NATO, mainly by the United States and the United Kingdom, Denmark (a member of NATO) agreed as a compromise to proceed on the assumption that its decision to keep its territory free of nuclear weapons in peacetime would be respected by visiting foreign ships or aircraft. Denmark decided not to seek specific assurances.[45]

In neutral Sweden, visiting warships are not permitted to carry nuclear weapons. In 1987, the ruling Social Democratic Party decided that efforts should be made to make the nuclear powers forgo the practice of not giving information regarding presence of nuclear weapons on their warships.

Several other countries as well, including members of the military alliances, have formally prohibited (as have Japan, Iceland, Norway, and Spain) foreign ships or aircraft from entering their territories with nuclear weapons aboard . However, to avoid antagonizing the great powers, the governments of some of these states chose to pretend not to be aware of the presence of nuclear weapons on board the visiting foreign craft.[46]

SUMMARY AND CONCLUSIONS

To the extent that the incentive to acquire nuclear weapons may emerge from regional considerations, the establishment of areas free of nuclear weapons is an important asset for the cause of nuclear nonproliferation. Countries confident that their enemies in the region do not possess nuclear weapons may not be inclined to acquire such weapons themselves. The zones that have been established to date meet other postulates as well. Besides prohibiting the acquisition of nuclear weapons by zonal states, they proscribe (unlike the NPT) the stationing of these weapons in the territories of non-nuclear weapon states. Zonal procedures to verify compliance with the nonproliferation obligations are even stricter than the procedures prescribed by the NPT. Moreover, zonal states benefit from some legally binding security assurances of the great powers.

Nevertheless, as pointed out in the preceding sections, the present NWFZ treaties are deficient in several respects. In particular:

1. None of the treaties specifies that the denuclearization provisions are valid both in time of peace and in time of war.

2. Research on nuclear explosive devices is explicitly prohibited only in the Treaty of Pelindaba.

3. Only the Treaty of Rarotonga and the Treaty of Pelindaba make it clear that the bans cover nuclear explosive devices also in unassembled or partly assembled forms.

4. So-called peaceful nuclear explosions may be allowed by the Treaty of Tlatelolco (though only under certain conditions).

5. Nuclear-weapon-related support facilities serving the strategic systems of the nuclear powers are not banned by any NWFZ treaty.

6. Only the Treaty of Pelindaba prohibits attacks on nuclear facilities.

7. Only the Treaty of Tlatelolco and the Treaty of Bangkok provide for the denuclearization of maritime areas adjacent to the territorial waters of zonal states.

8. All treaties tolerate the transit of nuclear weapons through the territories of zonal states, including visits by foreign ships and aircraft with nuclear weapons aboard.

9. The withdrawal clauses of the Treaty of Tlatelolco and the Treaty of Pelindaba, which refer to the "supreme interests" of the parties, are too permissive. (The Treaty of Rarotonga and the Treaty of Bangkok concede the right of withdrawal only in the event of a material breach of the parties' obligations.)

10. The nuclear powers' undertaking to respect the status of the denuclearized zones is unverifiable.

11. Assurances not to use nuclear weapons against zonal states, as given by the nuclear powers, are not unconditional.

12. Only the Treaty of Bangkok calls for action in the event of violation of the obligations assumed by the nuclear powers.

The above deficiencies could be removed through amendments of the existing NWFZ treaties and should be avoided in the drafting of such new treaties, provided due account is taken of the particularities of each region. Unilateral formal declarations on the denuclearization of individual countries may contain undertakings stricter than treaties. Therefore, they should be encouraged to further strengthen the nonproliferation regime.

¹ A. Albrecht, *The Rapacki Plan—New Aspects* (Poznan, Poland: Zachodnia Agencja Prasowa, 1963).

² A comprehensive discussion of these treaties is beyond the scope of this article, due to space limitations. For an analysis of these areas, see Jozef Goldblat, *Arms Control: A Guide to Negotiations and Agreements* (Oslo and London: PRIO and SAGE, 1994).

³ 1995 NPT Review and Extension Conference document NPT/CONF.1995/32/DEC.2.

⁴ U.N. document A/10027/Add.1.

⁵ U.S. State Department Briefing Document, December 8, 1995.

⁶ See U.N. document NPT/CONF.2000/PC.I/14 (14 April 1997), "Proposed elements for inclusion in the report of the Preparatory Committee on its first session," submitted by Kazakhstan, Kyrgyzstan, Tajikistan, Turkmenistan, and Uzbekistan.

⁷ U.N. General Assembly document A/C.1/L.312/Rev.1-2 and Add.1, 1962.

⁸ U.N. General Assembly document A/5415/Rev.1, 1963.

⁹ PPNN, *Briefing Book*, document G-1, 1993.

¹⁰ A. Garcia Robles, *El Tratado de Tlatelolco*, (Mexico City: El Colegio de Mexico, 1967).

¹¹ For the text of all these amendments, see 1995 NPT Review and Extension Conference document NPT/CONF.1995/10.

¹² By February 26, 1997, only 11 parties to the Treaty of Tlatelolco (out of 32) had ratified all the amendments. These were: Argentina, Barbados, Brazil, Chile, Guyana, Jamaica, Mexico, Paraguay, Peru, Uruguay, and Venezuela. (Information obtained by author from OPANAL.)

¹³ 1995 NPT Review and Extension Conference document NPT/CONF.1995/11.

¹⁴ U.S. Department of State, Office of the Spokesperson, October 20, 1995.

¹⁵ *International Herald Tribune*, March 26, 1996.

¹⁶ Communication from the Legal and Political Officer, South Pacific Forum Secretariat, Suva, Fiji, August 5, 1996.

¹⁷ White House Press Briefing by NSC Senior Director Bell, March 22, 1996.

¹⁸ During negotiations, North Korea rejected South Korea's proposal for a system of challenge inspections to be conducted upon the initiative of the requesting party (L. Niksch and Z. Davis, "North Korean Nuclear Controversy: Defining Treaties, Agreements, and Terms," *CRS Report for Congress* (Congressional Research Service. The Library of Congress, September 16, 1964).

¹⁹ U.N. General Assembly Resolution 1652 (XVI).

²⁰ OAU document AHG/Res.11(1), July 21, 1964.

²¹ U.N. General Assembly Resolution 50/78.

²² So far, four African states—Algeria, Egypt, Libya, and South Africa—have nuclear programs requiring the application of safeguards. Of these, only South Africa is in possession of nuclear power reactors.

²³ PPNN *Newsbrief*, 2nd Quarter 1996.

²⁴ Letter from the Russian Ambassador to the Secretary-General of the Organization of African Unity, Addis Ababa, November 5, 1996.

²⁵ France was the first nuclear power to ratify all the three protocols.

²⁶ U.N. document A/47/80.

²⁷ *International Herald Tribune*, December 9-

Jozef Goldblat

10, 11, 14, and 16-17, 1995.

[28] U.N. General Assembly Resolution A/RES/3263 (XXIX).

[29] For the historical background of this proposal, see M. Karem, *Nuclear-Weapon-Free Zone in the Middle East: Problems and Prospects* (New York: Greenwood Press, 1988).

[30] For a detailed account·of Israel's nuclear weapon capabilities, see Leonard S. Spector, *Nuclear Ambitions* (Boulder, Colo.: Westview Press, 1990), pp.149-174.

[31] U.N. document A/45/435, October 10, 1990.

[32] Conference on Disarmament document CD/989, April 20, 1990.

[33] More tests might be needed to develop a reliable nuclear warhead.

[34] *The New York Times*, December 15 and 16, 1995, and January 9, 1996.

[35] For a detailed account of India's and Pakistan's nuclear weapon capabilities, see Spector, *Nuclear Ambitions*, pp. 63-117.

[36] *NATO Review* (Brussels), No. 5 (October 1990), p. 30.

[37] 1995 Review and Extension Conference document NPT/CONF.1995/SR 3. For an elaboration of this idea, see A. I. Shevtsov, ed., *Analysis of the problem to create a new security system. An initiative to establish a denuclearized zone in Central and Eastern Europe* (Dnepropetrovsk, Ukraine: National Institute of Strategic Studies, 1995); J. Prawitz, "A Nuclear-Free Zone From the Baltic to the Black Sea," *Security Dialogue* 27 (June 1996); and J. Prawitz, PPNN *Issue Review*, No. 10 (February 1997).

[38] See U.N. General Assembly document A/52/112 (March 18, 1997), Annex "Almaty Declaration, adopted by the leaders of Kazakstan, Kyrgyzstan, Tajikistan, Turkmenistan, and Uzbekistan, of 28 February 1997"; also, see U.N. General Assembly document A/C.1/51/L.29 (October 29, 1996) submitted to the First Committee, "Kyrgyzstan and Mongolia: draft resolution. Establishment of a nuclear-weapon-free zone in the Central Asian region."

[39] Information provided by the Center for Nonproliferation Studies at the Monterey Institute of International Studies, based on a trip by senior staff members to the region in May 1997.

[40] U.N. General Assembly Resolution A/RES/51/45.

[41] The New Zealand Nuclear Free Zone, Arms Control and Disarmament Act 1987.

[42] The Act reflected public opinion in New Zealand, where an overwhelming majority of people desired their defense to be arranged in a way that ensured that the country remained nuclear-free (Report of the Defence Committee of Enquiry, *Defence and Security: What New Zealanders Want* and the "Public Opinion Poll on Defence and Security," annexed to the Report, Wellington, July 1986). For a discourse on threat assessment in New Zealand, see Wade Huntley, "The Kiwi that Roared: Nuclear-Free New Zealand in a Nuclear-Armed World," *The Nonproliferation Review* 4 (Fall 1996).

[43] *The Washington Post*, December 18, 1986;

P. Samuel, and F.P. Serong, "The Troubled Waters of ANZUS," *Strategic Review* (Winter 1985).

[44] U.N. document A/47/PV.13.

[45] *Berlingske Tidende* (Copenhagen), April 15, 1988; *Le Monde*, June 9, 1988.

[46] Certain cities have declared themselves nuclear-weapon free, but such declarations are not binding on the governments of the countries concerned.

[9]

Something Old, Something New: The 2006 Semipalatinsk Treaty on a Nuclear Weapon-Free Zone in Central Asia

Marco Roscini*

Abstract

The present article analyses the provisions of the 2006 Semipalatinsk Treaty establishing a nuclear weapon-free zone in Central Asia, explores their different nature and compares them with those contained in the Treaties of Tlatelolco, Rarotonga, Bangkok and Pelindaba. The fundamental question to be answered is whether the Semipalatinsk Treaty will effectively contribute to the non-proliferation of nuclear weapons. The article concludes that the treaty contains lights and shadows: although some positive innovations have been included in the final text, there are loopholes that might weaken the denuclearization regime. The "Great Game" in Central Asia and the tight relations of the regional States with the Russian Federation might also hamper the efforts to obtain the support of the other nuclear powers.

I. Introduction

1. According to the UN General Assembly Resolution 3472(XXX)B of 11 December 1975, a nuclear weapon-free zone is "any zone, recognized as such by the General Assembly of the United Nations, which any group of States in the free exercise of their sovereignty, has established by virtue of a treaty or convention whereby: (a) the statute of total absence of nuclear weapons to which the zone shall be subject, including the procedure for the delimitation of the zone, is defined; (b) an international system of verification and control is established to guarantee compliance with the obligations deriving from that statute".[1] In drafting this

---

* PhD, University of Rome "La Sapienza"; Reader, School of Law, University of Westminster; Visiting Lecturer, Queen Mary University of London and King's College London (email: mroscini@iol.it). This article was completed in April 2008. I am grateful to Dr Yoshifumi Tanaka for reading and commenting a previous version of this article. The usual caveat applies. This article is based on developments as of 30 April 2008 and all websites were also last visited on that date.

1 On this definition, see Sandra Szurek, Zones exemptes d'armes nucléaires et zones de paix dans le tiers-monde, 88 Revue générale de droit international public (1984), 200–203. Art. VII of the 1968 Treaty on the

definition, the General Assembly took inspiration from the Treaty of Tlatelolco, which had been opened for signature in 1967.[2]

2. In 1976, a group of experts appointed by the Conference of the Committee on Disarmament presented a comprehensive study setting out the principles that should be taken into account in order to establish a nuclear weapon-free zone.[3] According to the study, disarmament obligations may be assumed not only by large groups of States, but also by smaller groups and even by individual countries; the agreement must ensure the absence of nuclear weapons in the region; the initiative for the creation of the nuclear weapon-free zone should come from the regional States and participation must be voluntary; all regional States (and in particular those militarily significant) should ideally participate in the initiative; an effective system of verification of compliance must be set up in the agreement; cooperation on all peaceful uses of nuclear energy should be promoted and the treaty should be of unlimited duration.[4]

3. On 30 April 1999, the UN Disarmament Commission adopted by consensus and submitted to the UN General Assembly a report that revises and updates the 1976 study

---

Non-Proliferation of Nuclear Weapons (NPT) recognizes the role of nuclear weapon-free zones by providing that "[n]othing in this Treaty affects the right of any group of States to conclude regional treaties in order to assure the total absence of nuclear weapons in their respective territories".

2   The Treaty of Tlatelolco provides for the establishment of a nuclear weapon-free zone in Latin America and the Caribbean and was opened for signature on 14 February 1967. It entered into force after the conditions contained in Art. 29(1) were met, i.e. with Cuba's ratification (23 October 2002). The regional States could however waive, wholly or in part, those requirements by means of a declaration annexed to their respective instruments of ratification and which could be formulated at the time of deposit of the instrument or subsequently. For those States, the treaty entered into force upon deposit of the declaration, or as soon as those requirements were met which have not been expressly waived (Art. 29(2)). The numeration of articles of the Treaty of Tlatelolco takes into account the amendment adopted by the Agency for the Prohibition of Nuclear Weapons in Latin America and the Caribbean (OPANAL) General Conference on 26 August 1992 (Res 290 (E-VII)).

3   Comprehensive Study of the Question of Nuclear-Weapon-Free Zones in All Its Aspects (Special Report of the Conference of the Committee on Disarmament), UN Doc. A/10027/Add. 1, New York, 1976 (hereinafter "1976 Comprehensive Study"), Annex I.

4   Ibid., para. 90. The United States has drafted its own list of requirements that the nuclear weapon-free zones must possess to obtain Washington's support: (1) the initiative should come from the regional States concerned; (2) all important regional States should participate; (3) the agreement should provide for an effective verification of compliance mechanism; (4) the establishment of the zone should not disturb existing security arrangements and the right of individual or collective self-defense; (5) the treaty should effectively prohibit the development, acquisition and possession of nuclear devices for any purpose; (6) the nuclear weapon-free zone States should be free to decide whether to grant or deny transit privileges within their land, sea and air territory; (7) no restrictions should be imposed on the exercise of rights provided by international law, in particular those related to navigation (Eleanor C. McDowell (ed.), Digest of United States Practice in International Law (Washington, DC: Department of State Publications, 1976), 728–729). These criteria were reaffirmed during the Tashkent Conference of 15–16 September 1997 (www.nti.org/db/nisprofs/shared/canwfz/usstate.htm). China has also indicated its criteria during the Tashkent conference: in particular, the nuclear weapon-free zone treaties should be consistent with the principles and purposes of the UN Charter and should not lead to interferences in the internal affairs of States outside the region; the nuclear weapon-free status should not be conditional on other security mechanisms; the zone should have clear geographical boundaries and an effective verification mechanism including the International Atomic Energy Agency (IAEA)'s safeguards and the nuclear weapon States should provide adequate negative security assurances (LI Jinxian, Principles for the Establishment of New Zones, 20(1) Disarmament: A Periodic Review of the United Nations (1997), 109–110).

in the light of the Treaties of Rarotonga, Bangkok and Pelindaba.[5] These non-binding guidelines, like those of 1976, are meant to guide States in establishing nuclear weapon-free zones but cannot be regarded as exhaustive or be interpreted in such a way as to prejudice the setting up of a nuclear weapon-free zone.[6]

4. It has been argued in an official statement that the nuclear weapon-free zone in Central Asia has been conceived in accordance with the above-mentioned principles and guidelines.[7] The idea of a nuclear weapon-free zone in Central Asia dates back to 1992, when Mongolia declared itself a denuclearized State and manifested its support for other regional disarmament measures, such as a nuclear weapon-free zone.[8] The first formal proposal was however put forward the following year by the President of Uzbekistan at the UN General Assembly.[9] It was then jointly supported by the regional States in the Almaty Declaration of 27 February 1997 and discussed in the Tashkent Conference of September 1997.[10] For the first time, the UN became directly involved in the works to draft a nuclear weapon-free zone treaty.[11] Controversies among the Central Asian States emerged

---

5   Establishment of Nuclear-Weapon-Free Zones on the Basis of Arrangements Freely Arrived at Among the States of the Region Concerned (A/54/42, Annex I) (hereinafter "Report of the Disarmament Commission"), 24 United Nations Disarmament Yearbook (1999), 248-254. The report was eventually adopted by the UN General Assembly (UN Doc. A/RES/55/56A). The treaty establishing a nuclear weapon-free zone in the South Pacific Ocean was signed on 6 August 1985 (40th anniversary of the bombing of Hiroshima) in Rarotonga (Cook Islands), and entered into force on 11 December 1986 with the deposit of the eighth instrument of ratification. The end of the Cold War, the consequent closure of the US military bases in the Philippines and the outrage caused by the French nuclear experiments in the South Pacific led to the conclusion of the treaty establishing a nuclear weapon-free zone in South-East Asia, signed in Bangkok on 15 December 1995 by the Association of Southeast Asian Nations (ASEAN) member States along with Cambodia, Laos and Myanmar. The treaty entered into force on 27 March 1997 with the ratification of the seventh State. The Pelindaba Treaty establishing the African nuclear weapon-free zone, named after the area near Johannesburg where the South African nuclear activities had taken place, was opened for signature on 11 April 1996. Unlike its predecessors, the African treaty, which will enter into force on the date of deposit of the 28th instrument of ratification, is the result of the collaboration between a universal organization (the UN) and a regional one (the then Organisation of African Unity). Such cooperation materialized in the creation of a commission of experts who contributed to the drafting of the treaty and in the UN technical and financial support to the regional States. See Marco Roscini, Le zone denuclearizzate (Torino: Giappichelli, 2003), 8–19.

6   See the words of the South African representative (Disarmament Commission, Press Release DC/2641, 30 April 1999, 20).

7   Statement by the Ministers of Foreign Affairs of the Republic of Kazakhstan, the Kyrgyz Republic, the Republic of Tajikistan, Turkmenistan and the Republic of Uzbekistan, 8 September 2006, cns.miis.edu/pubs/week/pdf_support/060908_ministers_statement.pdf, 2.

8   Scott Parrish, Prospects for a Central Asian Nuclear-Weapon-Free Zone, 8(1) The Nonproliferation Review (Spring 2001), 142.

9   Address by Islam A. Karimov, President of the Republic of Uzbekistan, 6th Plenary Meeting of the United Nations General Assembly, 29 September 1993, UN Doc. A/48/PV.6, 5 October 1993.

10   On the attempts to establish a nuclear weapon-free zone in Central Asia, see Michael Hamel-Green, Regional Initiatives on Nuclear and WMD-Free Zones. Comparative Approaches to Arms Control and Non-Proliferation (Geneva: UNIDIR, 2005), 12–13; Oumirserik Kasenov, On the Creation of a Nuclear-Weapon-Free Zone in Central Asia, 6(1) The Nonproliferation Review (Fall 1998), 144–147; Murat Laumulin, Nonproliferation and Kazakhstani Security Policy, 5(3) The Nonproliferation Review (Spring–Summer 1998), 127; Parrish, above n.8, 141–148.

11   Jozef Goldblat, Denuclearization of Central Asia, 4 Disarmament Forum (2007), 25.

during the negotiations related to the delimitation of the borders between certain States, the legal status of the Caspian Sea and the close relationship with the Russian Federation. At the end of the Samarcanda meeting (25–27 September 2002), the regional States announced that they had reached an agreement,[12] and, on 8 February 2005, the draft text was finally approved in Tashkent. The treaty was opened for signature on 8 September 2006 in Semipalatinsk (Kazakhstan), a former Soviet nuclear weapons test site permanently closed in 1991, and will enter into force 30 days after the deposit of the fifth instrument of ratification.[13] UN General Assembly Resolution 61/88 of 6 December 2006 welcomed the signing of the treaty and considered the establishment of the zone as "an important step towards strengthening the nuclear non-proliferation regime, promoting cooperation in the peaceful uses of nuclear energy and in the environmental rehabilitation of territories affected by radioactive contamination, and enhancing regional and international peace and security" and as "an effective contribution to combating international terrorism and preventing nuclear materials and technologies from falling into the hands of non-State actors, primarily terrorists".

5. The present article discusses the main features of the Semipalatinsk Treaty and investigates whether the treaty will effectively contribute to the non-proliferation of nuclear weapons. First, the article examines the obligations of the Central Asian denuclearized States and explores their different nature. It then goes on to discuss the territorial extension of the nuclear weapon-free zone and the grounds for terminating and suspending the obligations arising from the treaty. The nuclear weapon States' negative security assurances contained in the annexed protocol and the mechanisms to verify and enforce compliance by the States parties are finally analysed. Whenever relevant, the differences between the Semipalatinsk Treaty and the other nuclear weapon-free zone treaties, as well as with the Nuclear Non-Proliferation Treaty (NPT), will be highlighted.

II. The denuclearization obligations of the States parties

6. The object of the basic prohibitions contained in the Semipalatinsk Treaty is "nuclear weapons or other nuclear explosive devices", defined in Article 1(b) as "any weapon or other nuclear explosive device capable of releasing nuclear energy, irrespective of the military or civilian purpose for which the weapon or device could be used". The devices must thus be "explosive", i.e. capable of releasing a considerable amount of nuclear energy in a very short time and in an uncontrolled manner.[14] This excludes from the scope of the prohibitions

---

12   Disarmament Commission, Press Release DC/2842, 30 September 2002.

13   All five Central Asian States have signed the Semipalatinsk Treaty, but only Kyrgyzstan, Turkmenistan and Uzbekistan have ratified it, cns.miis.edu/pubs/inven/pdfs/canwz.pdf. The English version of the Semipalatinsk Treaty can be found at cns.miis.edu/pubs/week/pdf_support/060905_canwfz.pdf.

14   See para. III (e) of the note of the Government of the Federal Republic of Germany issued at the moment of the signature of the NPT: "At the present stage of technology nuclear explosive devices are those designed to release in microseconds in an uncontrolled manner a large amount of nuclear energy accompanied by shock waves, i.e. devices that can be used as nuclear weapons", collections.europarchive.org/tna/20080205132101/www.fco.gov.uk/Files/kfile/024a_NonProliferationNuclearWeapons,0.pdf.

conventional and experimental nuclear reactors, reprocessed nuclear material, depleted uranium ammunitions and radiological weapons, which do not cause a blast or heat wave.

7. There is an important difference between the Treaties of Tlatelolco and Bangkok, on the one hand, and the Treaties of Rarotonga, Pelindaba and Semipalatinsk, on the other. Although the latter expressly include in the definition of "nuclear explosive device" also weapons in unassembled or partly assembled forms (thus prohibiting also the production of the weapon components), the former are silent on this point. Therefore, the prohibitions only apply to completed and ready-to-use devices. All the five treaties, however, specify that the definition of "nuclear explosive device" does not include the means of transport or delivery of the prohibited weapons or devices if they are separable from and not an indivisible part of them. Without the inclusion of this provision, the transit of all vehicles, ships and aircraft big and equipped enough to potentially carry nuclear arms would have been banned from the zone, regardless of whether or not they actually carried the weapons.[15]

8. The basic prohibitions contained in the Semipalatinsk Treaty and common to all nuclear weapon-free zone treaties are the prohibition to manufacture, acquire, possess or otherwise control nuclear explosive devices and the prohibition of stationing those devices within the zone (Article 3(1)). The possession of nuclear explosive devices is prohibited for States parties anywhere, not only on their territories, but also abroad, e.g. in a military base situated in an allied country not included in the nuclear weapon-free zone. Not only formal possession, but also control is prohibited, for instance through a puppet government controlled "by any means" by the denuclearized State. If the relationship between the two States is not of subordination but of cooperation, for instance in the context of a military alliance, one might ask whether this participation involves some kind of control over the alliance's explosive devices and thus violates the nuclear weapon-free zone treaty. During the drafting of the 1976 Comprehensive Study, several experts argued that "such alliances should not be regarded as being in all cases competitive with nuclear-weapon-free zones".[16] The answer would thus depend on the circumstances of each case: if "a treaty or alliance [. . .] does not envisage nuclear retaliation in support of an ally, nor include the stationing of nuclear weapons on the territory of that ally", then it would be "no bar to the creation of a nuclear-weapon-free zone" and in such a case "a non-nuclear weapon State allied to a nuclear-weapon State can [. . .] also be a party to a nuclear-weapon-free zone treaty".[17] In order to avoid assuming conflicting obligations, the denuclearized State

---

15 Alfonso García Robles, El Tratado de Tlatelolco: génesis, alcance y propósitos de la proscripción de las armas nucleares en la América latina (México: El Colegio de México, 1967), XXIV.

16 See the 1976 Comprehensive Study, above n.3, Annex I, para. 92. This conclusion was reasserted by several delegations, including the Italian one (ibid., Annex II, para. 132).

17 1976 Comprehensive Study, above n.3, Annex I, para. 92. According to the Federal Republic of Germany, however, "we do not want to imply a priori that simultaneous membership of a military alliance and of a nuclear-weapon-free zone is impossible in theory. But, in our view, such a simultaneous membership would give rise to considerable and practically insurmountable difficulties" (ibid., Annex II, para. 116).

should however verify that the nuclear weapon-free zone treaty is not in contrast with other agreements to which it is a party.[18]

9. The other fundamental provision common to all nuclear weapon-free zone treaties is the prohibition of stationing nuclear explosive devices within the zone, which is defined in Article 1(c) of the Semipalatinsk Treaty as "implantation, emplacement, stockpiling, storage, installation and deployment".[19] This prohibition constitutes the main difference between the nuclear weapon-free zone treaties and the NPT. Not necessarily does the prohibition of possession assumed by a State involve the denuclearization of its territory. Indeed, the NPT allows China, France, the Russian Federation, the United Kingdom and the United States to deploy nuclear weapons on the territory of non-nuclear weapon States parties, providing that the latter do not have control over them. On the contrary, the Treaties of Tlatelolco, Rarotonga, Bangkok, Pelindaba and Semipalatinsk prohibit the presence of nuclear explosive devices within the zones, whoever owns or controls them. This was one of the problems that blocked for some time the negotiations for the establishment of the Central Asian nuclear weapon-free zone. Kazakhstan, Kyrgyzstan, Tajikistan and Uzbekistan are in fact bound, together with the Russian Federation, by the 1992 Tashkent Collective Security Treaty, Article IV of which provides that the parties will give each other all assistance necessary, including military assistance, in response to aggression.[20] According to Russian officials, this provision allows the deployment of Russian nuclear weapons on the territory of the other parties if, after a joint decision, this was deemed necessary.[21] In the opinion of the United States, the United Kingdom and France, on the other hand, if so interpreted, the provision would undermine the central purpose of establishing a nuclear weapon-free zone.[22] Article

---

18   Report of the Disarmament Commission, above n.5, para. 32. This reference to the compatibility with previous international and regional agreements was deemed necessary by the US, British, French and Polish delegates (Disarmament Commission, Press Release DC/2641, 30 April 1999, 10–12, 22).

19   The definition is identical to that contained in Art. 1(d) of the Bangkok Treaty. Art. 1(d) of the Pelindaba Treaty and Art. 1(d) of the Rarotonga Treaty also include in the definition of stationing the "transport on land or inland waters". While in the Bangkok Treaty transport by States parties is the object of a specific prohibition (even though it is not qualified as a form of stationing), no prohibition of transport is contained in the Semipalatinsk Treaty. The Treaty of Tlatelolco, without using the word "stationing", prohibits "the receipt, storage, installation, deployment and any form of possession of any nuclear weapons, directly or indirectly" (Art. 1).

20   In 2002, the Collective Security Treaty Organization (CSTO) was founded, of which only Turkmenistan is not a member (Uzbekistan rejoined in 2006 after deciding in 1999 not to prolong its participation). Common military exercises were carried out in 2005 and, in October 2007, the creation of a peacekeeping force was agreed. The CSTO States have also increased their cooperation within the framework of the Shanghai Cooperation Organization (SCO), which led to large-scale joint military exercises in 2007 (Martha Brill Olcott, Strategic Concerns in Central Asia, 4 Disarmament Forum (2007), 11). Kazakhstan, Kyrgyzstan, Tajikistan and Uzbekistan are also members of the SCO, along with China and Russia (Iran has applied for membership on 24 March 2008). It has been observed that "the heyday of US military influence in the [Central Asia] region, and likely that of NATO as well, does seem to have passed, at least for the foreseeable future" and that the present trend is towards increased security cooperation with the Russian Federation (ibid.).

21   Parrish, above n.8, 146.

22   Sonia Luthra, Central Asian States Renounce Nuclear Weapons, 36(8) Arms Control Today (October 2006), www.armscontrol.org/act/2006_10/CentralAsian.asp.

12(1) was eventually included in the final text, providing that the Semipalatinsk Treaty "does not affect the rights and obligations of the Parties under other international treaties which they may have concluded prior to the date of the entry into force of this Treaty".[23] At first sight, this appears to be a clause under Article 30(2) of the 1969 Vienna Convention on the Law of Treaties, ensuring that the provisions of the Tashkent Treaty will prevail over those of the Semipalatinsk Treaty, where incompatible. Nonetheless, if the Russian interpretation is correct, i.e. if the Tashkent Treaty does provide for the right to deploy Russian nuclear weapons on the territory of other parties, and if this right is really preserved by Article 12(1) of the Semipalatinsk Treaty, then it would be hard to see how the latter treaty would have any meaning at all. Such an interpretation of Article 12(1) would be absurd and unreasonable and in contrast with the principle of effectiveness, according to which "a treaty must be given an interpretation that enables its provisions to be 'effective and useful', that is, to have the appropriate effect".[24] It is thus this writer's opinion that the first paragraph of Article 12 of the Semipalatinsk Treaty should be interpreted in the light of the second paragraph, which provides that "[t]he Parties shall take all necessary measures for effective implementation of the purposes and objectives of this Treaty in accordance with the main principles contained therein".[25] The combined effect of the two paragraphs of Article 12 is that only those provisions of previous treaties that do not prejudice the effective implementation of the purposes and objectives of the Semipalatinsk Treaty are preserved: therefore, the Central Asian denuclearized States parties to the Tashkent Treaty still have an obligation to provide military assistance to the other parties (including Russia) in case of aggression, but this assistance cannot include the acceptance of nuclear explosive devices on their territory.[26] Of course, assuming that Russia's interpretation of Article IV of the Tashkent Treaty is correct, the States parties to both the Semipalatinsk and the Tashkent Treaties might incur international responsibility under Article 30(5) of the Vienna Convention for the assumption of conflicting obligations.

10. It is worth mentioning that Article 3(1)(a) of the Semipalatinsk Treaty prohibits not only the manufacture, acquisition, possession, control and stationing of nuclear explosive devices but also the conduct of nuclear military research: only the Pelindaba Treaty contains

---

23 A similar provision is contained in Art. 21 of the Treaty of Tlatelolco, according to which "[n]one of the provisions of this Treaty shall be construed as impairing the rights and obligations of the Parties under the Charter of the United Nations or, in the case of States members of the Organization of American States, under existing regional treaties". However, the reference here is to obligations in the framework of the UN and the Organization of American States (OAS), and not to security agreements.

24 Antonio Cassese, International Law (Oxford: Oxford University Press, 2005), 179.

25 This second paragraph was subsequently added by the drafters to accommodate the criticism of France, United Kingdom and United States, which however found this addition insufficient (Goldblat, above n.11, 29).

26 Goldblat suggests another possible solution to affirm the compatibility of the two treaties, i.e. that they do not have the same subject matter: one prohibits the stationing of nuclear weapons within a certain region, the other provides for an obligation to defend an allied country. The presence of nuclear weapons on the territory of the attacked State is not necessary to defend it, as they could be launched from outside the zone (Goldblat, above n.11, 30).

a similar prohibition (Article 3), while the other nuclear weapon-free zone treaties are silent on this point.

11. The denuclearized States are bound not only not to carry out the above-mentioned prohibited activities, but also not to allow the conduct of such activities in their territories by anyone (Article 3(1)(d)) and not to seek or receive assistance or take any action to assist or encourage them (Article 3(1)(b) and (c)). The prohibition of assistance cannot however prejudice the cooperation in the field of the peaceful uses of nuclear energy, even if materials and technology are essentially the same (providing of course that no nuclear explosions are carried out).[27] *A fortiori*, the prohibition of assistance should not be interpreted as prohibiting all scientific or economic cooperation between nuclear weapon and non-nuclear weapon States. The legislative history of the Rarotonga Treaty clearly shows that the words "not to take any action to assist or encourage" do not cover actions having purposes different from those prohibited by the treaty but that could incidentally support them.[28] There appears to be no reason to interpret the Semipalatinsk Treaty differently.[29]

12. Apart from the basic prohibitions contained in Article 3, the Semipalatinsk Treaty imposes other obligations on the States parties. Article 8 requires them to use for exclusively peaceful purposes the nuclear material and facilities which are within their territory, under their jurisdiction or under their control anywhere and to conclude with the IAEA and bring into force a safeguards agreement (INFCIRC/153 (Corr.)) and an Additional Protocol (INFCIRC/540 (Corr.)) no later than 18 months from the treaty's entry into force.[30] Article 8 also requires the parties not to provide any source or special fissionable material or related equipment to any non-nuclear weapon State unless that State has concluded with the IAEA a comprehensive safeguards agreement and related Additional Protocol.[31] The provision of such material or equipment to nuclear weapon States is not prohibited. The Semipalatinsk Treaty is the first nuclear weapon-free zone treaty to refer to the 1997 Additional Protocol providing for more intrusive and comprehensive verification measures. Indeed, under the safeguards system based on INFCIRC/153, the possibility for the IAEA to detect clandestine nuclear activities is limited, as inspections focus on declared nuclear material and on strategic points in declared facilities. Under the Additional Protocol, instead, the IAEA is given the authority to inspect undeclared facilities and to access all parts of a State's nuclear fuel cycle, including uranium mines, as well as any other location where nuclear material is or may be present.

---

27   Art. 7.

28   Nigel Fyfe and Christopher Beeby, The South Pacific Nuclear Free Zone Treaty, 17 Victoria University of Wellington Law Review (1987), 41.

29   Treaties in pari materiæ can be supplementary means of interpretation.

30   Kazakhstan has research reactors at Almaty and Kurchatov and a fabrication unit at Ust-Kamenogorsk, Kyrgyzstan has a processing combine and Uzbekistan has two small research reactors near Tashkent (Hamel-Green, above n.10, 15). On Kazakhstan's civilian nuclear programme, see Laumulin, above n.10, 129–130.

31   Uranium mines are located in Kazakhstan and Uzbekistan (Burkhard Conrad, Regional (Non-)Proliferation: The Case of Central Asia, Conflict Studies Research Centre, April 2000, 2–3, www.da.mod.uk/colleges/arag/document-listings/ca/K29).

13. Unlike the NPT,[32] the Semipalatinsk Treaty also addresses conduct by non-State actors. Under Article 9 of the Semipalatinsk Treaty, each State party undertakes to maintain "effective standards of physical protection of nuclear material, facilities and equipment to prevent its unauthorized use or handling or theft". The measures adopted to this aim must be "at least as effective" as those called for by the 1980 Convention on the Physical Protection of Nuclear Material[33] and by the recommendations and guidelines developed by the IAEA in this field.[34] Article 9 has been included as a measure to fight the increased risk of theft and the possibility to build nuclear arms from raw material.[35] This is particularly important in the Central Asian region, where highly enriched uranium remains present at several sites and where the possibility of theft of nuclear-related materials is high.[36] Central Asia might also become a transit area for terrorist smuggling of nuclear materials.[37] The Semipalatinsk Treaty could as well be seen as a step towards the implementation of Security Council Resolution 1540 of 28 April 2004, which requires all States to adopt effective laws which prohibit any non-State actors to manufacture, acquire, possess, develop, transport, transfer or use nuclear, chemical or biological weapons and their means of delivery and to establish, develop, review and maintain appropriate physical protection measures and effective domestic, border and export controls to prevent trafficking of weapons of mass destruction and related materials.[38]

---

32 Jack I. Garvey, A New Architecture for the Non-Proliferation of Nuclear Weapons, 12 Journal of Conflict and Security Law (2008), 344.

33 The Convention, opened for signature on 3 March 1980 and entered into force on 8 February 1987, requires each contracting party "to take appropriate steps within the framework of its national law and consistent with international law to ensure as far as practicable that, during international nuclear transport, nuclear material within its territory, or on board a ship or aircraft under its jurisdiction insofar as such ship or aircraft is engaged in the transport to or from that State, is protected at the levels described in Annex 1" (Art. 3). The purpose, which is instrumental to Arts I, II and III of the NPT, is to prevent fissile material, usable for the construction of arms from being illegally stolen. Unlike the other Central Asian States, Kyrgyzstan has yet not become a party of the Convention on Physical Protection, ola.iaea.org/factSheets/Country Details.asp?country= KG.

34 The recommendations were prepared for the first time in 1972 by a panel of experts convened by the IAEA Director General and were revised in 1975, 1977, 1989, 1993 and 1997. Even though they are not binding, the implementation of the IAEA recommendations is required by the agreements that the Agency concludes with the States to which it provides assistance and by the bilateral cooperation agreements in the field of nuclear energy.

35 The only other treaty where this provision appears is the Pelindaba Treaty (Art. 10). In Res 1540 (2004), the UN Security Council expressed its concern for "the threat of illicit trafficking in nuclear, chemical, or biological weapons and their means of delivery, and related materials, which adds a new dimension to the issue of proliferation of such weapons and also poses a threat to international peace and security".

36 It has indeed been suggested that "[t]he leading WMD-related risk in Central Asia is the possibility of the theft of materials and their sale by smugglers or through brokers to terrorist or proliferant states" (Togzhan Kassenova, Central Asia: Regional Security and WMD Proliferation Threats, 4 Disarmament Forum (2007), 13). On the proliferation threats in Central Asia, see ibid., 15–17.

37 Scott Parrish and William Potter, Central Asian States Establish Nuclear-Weapon-Free-Zone Despite U.S. Opposition, CNS Research Story, 5 September 2006, cns.miis.edu/pubs/week/060905.htm. For cases of smuggling of radioactive material in the region, see Conrad, above n.31, 3–4.

38 Kazakhstan appears to have the most developed export control system in Central Asia and is also the only State to participate in the Nuclear Suppliers Group control regime (Kassenova, above n.36, 19).

14. Certain obligations contained in other nuclear weapon-free zone treaties have not been included in the Semipalatinsk Treaty: the prohibition of armed attack on nuclear installations (Article 11 of the Pelindaba Treaty), the obligation to declare, dismantle, destroy or convert nuclear explosive devices and the facilities for their manufacture (Article 6 of the Pelindaba Treaty), the obligation to accede to the Convention on Early Notification of a Nuclear Accident (Article 6 of the Bangkok Treaty). Furthermore, the Semipalatinsk Treaty does not expressly prohibit the use of nuclear explosive devices by the States parties. It could however be argued that such prohibition was considered implicit, as, after banning possession, control and any form of acquisition of such weapons, any use by the denuclearized States would be practically impossible. What Article 3(1)(d)(i) of the Semipalatinsk Treaty does expressly say is that the contracting parties must not allow the use of nuclear weapons or other nuclear explosive devices in their territory. This entails an obligation on the Central Asian States to prevent a nuclear weapon State from launching such devices from anywhere within their territory (for instance, from overflying aircraft) regardless of whether the target is located within or outside the nuclear weapon-free zone.

III. The environmental provisions of the Semipalatinsk Treaty

15. By establishing a nuclear weapon-free zone, the regional States aim not only to prevent the dissemination of nuclear weapons and to promote disarmament, but also to protect the natural environment by prohibiting certain activities that might damage it.[39] This ecological element, however, does not always have the same importance: if it plays a significant role in the Treaties of Rarotonga, Bangkok, Pelindaba and Semipalatinsk, it is only of minor significance in the Treaty of Tlatelolco. Indeed, the Cuban missile crisis and the risk of a nuclear war had left other problems in the background.

16. The Semipalatinsk Treaty requires the States parties not to carry out any nuclear weapon test explosion or any other nuclear explosion, to prohibit and prevent any such explosions at any place under their jurisdiction or control and to refrain from causing, encouraging or in any way participating in the carrying out of any nuclear test explosion or any other nuclear explosion by other States (Article 5).[40] The prohibition of nuclear test explosions is usually conceived as a provision aiming to prevent nuclear proliferation by hampering the development of new types of weapons of mass destruction and the modernization of the existing ones. In the nuclear weapon-free zone treaties, however, this prohibition has mostly an environmental purpose. Indeed, these agreements are concluded by States that (with a few exceptions) have never had nuclear ambitions: the inclusion of the prohibition under examination mainly aims to prevent that the ecosystem of certain

---

39   According to the 1999 Report of the Disarmament Commission, "[n]uclear-weapon-free zones may also serve to promote cooperation aimed at ensuring that the regions concerned remain free of environmental pollution from radioactive wastes and other radioactive substances and, as appropriate, enforcing internationally agreed standards regulating international transportation of those substances" (above n.5, para. 17).

40   See also Art. 1 of the Treaty of Tlatelolco, Art. 6 of the Rarotonga Treaty, Art. 3(1) (c) and 3(2)(c) of the Bangkok Treaty and Art. 5 of the Pelindaba Treaty.

regions is damaged by nuclear explosions carried out by the nuclear powers.[41] For instance, the South Pacific nuclear weapon-free zone was established mainly in order to prevent further nuclear tests by France in the region. As far as Central Asia is concerned, it is worth recalling that the Soviet Union conducted more than 450 atmospheric and underground nuclear tests in Semipalatinsk between 1949 and 1989.[42]

17. The Semipalatinsk Treaty requires the States parties not to carry out and to prohibit *any* nuclear explosion, not only those above a certain threshold as provided in the 1974 Threshold Test Ban Treaty and the 1976 Peaceful Nuclear Explosions Treaty, concluded by the United States and the Soviet Union during the Cold War. Furthermore, both underground and atmospheric explosions are prohibited: in that, the Semipalatinsk Treaty takes the 1996 Comprehensive Test Ban Treaty (CTBT) (expressly referred to in Article 5)[43] as a model and differs from the 1963 Partial Test Ban Treaty (PTBT), Article 1 (1) of which prohibits nuclear explosions in the atmosphere, in outer space and under water (including the territorial sea and the high sea) or in any other environment only "if such explosion causes radioactive debris to be present outside the territorial limits of the State under whose jurisdiction or control such explosion is conducted" and thus implicitly allows underground explosions if they do not cause the leakage of radioactivity.[44] The prohibition of all nuclear test explosions solves the problems caused by the absence, in the PTBT, of a definition of "underground" explosions in order to distinguish them from the "atmospheric" ones and by the impossibility to establish in advance whether or not an underground nuclear test explosion will cause the release of radioactive material with transboundary effects.

18. However, the provisions on testing included in the Semipalatinsk Treaty also contain some loopholes. While the other nuclear weapon-free zone treaties simply prohibit the "testing" of nuclear weapons or nuclear explosive devices, according to Article 5 of the Semipalatinsk Treaty the parties undertake not to carry out or cause, encourage or in any way participate in any nuclear *explosion*. Hence, by prohibiting the carrying out of nuclear "explosions" and not simply of "tests", the treaty leaves the door open to simulations. The reasons for this are not clear and it might well be an oversight. Furthermore, to be banned, the test explosion must be "nuclear" and there must be some release of this type of energy: hydrodynamic experiments (where the fissile material of the weapon is replaced by other materials and there is no release of atomic energy) and sub-critical tests (where no self-sustaining nuclear chain reaction can take place even though special nuclear material

41 As acknowledged in the guidelines adopted by the Disarmament Commission in 1999, the nuclear weapon-free zones are "a useful complement to the international regime for the prohibition of any nuclear-weapon-test explosions or any other nuclear explosion" (Report of the Disarmament Commission, above n.5, para. 37).

42 Abel J. González, Radioactive Residues of the Cold War Period: A Radiological Legacy, 40(4) IAEA Bulletin (December 1998), 4.

43 All five Central Asian States have ratified the CTBT.

44 The only other treaty that comprehensively prohibits all nuclear explosions, including underground ones, in its territorial scope of application is the 1959 Washington Treaty on Antarctica (Art. V(1)).

is present) are thus not prohibited.[45] It is also to be noted that, as the definitions of "nuclear weapon" and "nuclear explosive device" contained in the treaties on nuclear weapon-free zones do not include the means of transport or delivery if separable from the weapons and not an indivisible part of them, missile tests are not prohibited. Finally, unlike the Treaties of Rarotonga and Pelindaba and like the Treaties of Tlatelolco and Bangkok, the Semipalatinsk Treaty is not accompanied by a protocol by the ratification of which the nuclear weapon States expressly accept not to carry out nuclear test explosions and to refrain from assisting and encouraging them within the zone.[46]

19. Under Article 3(2) of the Semipalatinsk Treaty, the parties also undertake not to allow the disposal, in their territory, of radioactive waste of other States. "Radioactive waste" is defined in Article 1(e) as "any substance containing radionuclides, that will be or has already been removed and is no longer utilized, at activities and activity concentrations of radionuclides greater than the exemption levels established in international standards issued by the IAEA". This prohibition is however not as broad as its counterpart in other nuclear weapon-free zone treaties, as it does not prohibit the disposal of a State party's radioactive waste in its own territory: indeed, the parties are only required not to allow the disposal of radioactive waste *of other States*.[47] It is not clear whether this was an intentional omission.

20. Unlike the Bangkok Treaty (Article 6), the Semipalatinsk Treaty does not provide for the obligation of early notification of a nuclear accident. On the other hand, the Central Asian treaty contains a "green" provision not appearing in any other nuclear weapon-free zone treaty. According to Article 6, "[e]ach party undertakes to assist any efforts toward the environmental rehabilitation of territories contaminated as a result of past activities related to the development, production or storage of nuclear weapons or other nuclear explosive devices, in particular uranium tailings storage sites and nuclear test sites". The provision refers to the areas contaminated as a result of the nuclear-related activities

---

45   The United States carried out its sixth sub-critical test on 9 February 1999, maintaining its legality under the CTBT because it did not trigger a nuclear chain reaction (Ramesh Thakur, South Asia and the Politics of Non-Proliferation, 54 International Journal (1998–1999), 407). During the sixth NPT Review Conference, however, Switzerland argued that sub-critical and laboratory tests are not consistent with the preamble of the CTBT (Rebecca Johnson, The 2000 NPT Review Conference: A Delicate, Hard-Won Compromise, 46 Disarmament Diplomacy (May 2000), www.acronym.org.uk/46npt.htm).

46   The reason for the inclusion of such a protocol in the Treaties of Rarotonga and Pelindaba is well known: France carried out nuclear experiments in Algeria until 1963, while the South Pacific Ocean was the firing ground for the first atmospheric and then underground nuclear test explosions of the United Kingdom, the United States and France.

47   See Art. 7 of the Rarotonga Treaty, Art. 7 of the Pelindaba Treaty, Art. 3(3) of the Bangkok Treaty. There is no prohibition of dumping in the Treaty of Tlatelolco. The Central Asian States have also ratified the 1997 Joint Convention on the Safety of Spent Fuel Management and on the Safety of Radioactive Waste Management, entered into force in 2001, which aims to ensure that there are effective defenses against hazards related to the management of such materials and to prevent accidents with radiological effects. The Convention applies to both radioactive waste management from civilian applications and to military-spent fuel or radioactive waste if and when such materials are transferred permanently to and managed within exclusively civilian programmes. The Convention also establishes rules for the transboundary movement of spent fuel and radioactive waste.

carried out in Central Asia during the Soviet era, such as weapons storage and testing, uranium mining, plutonium production.[48] The obligation is however a mere obligation of conduct, not an obligation to achieve a precise result (the environmental rehabilitation of contaminated territories) and is presumably triggered by the request for assistance of the State to which the contaminated territories belong. The main problem for the implementation of this provision might be the lack of adequate financial and human resources to fulfil the task.

21. From the above considerations, it should be evident that the Semipalatinsk Treaty, like the other nuclear weapon-free zone treaties, has a composite structure where both localized and non-localized obligations are present:[49] the prohibition of stationing nuclear explosive devices (whoever possesses or controls them) within the zone is a localized obligation, while the prohibitions of possession, control, use, manufacture, military nuclear research, testing, to allow the disposal of radioactive waste, of export of fissile material without safeguards, and the obligations of physical protection of nuclear materials and equipment and to conclude a safeguards agreement with the IAEA are characterized more by a personal than by a territorial nature. This composite structure has consequences on State succession. The localized obligations are transmitted to the successor State(s) under Article 12 of the 1978 Vienna Convention on Succession of States in Respect of Treaties (or the customary norm of identical content).[50] On the contrary, the clean slate rule applies to non-localized obligations.[51] Accordingly, the State that acquires in whole or in part the territory of a denuclearized State will be able to possess, manufacture and use (if such use is consistent with other international law) nuclear explosive devices as long as they are not stationed in the territory formerly belonging to the denuclearized State. The same conclusion applies to States formed from the dismemberment of a denuclearized State and to those incorporating or resulting from the merger of two or more States, of which at least one was party to a nuclear weapon-free zone treaty. Of course, the new State exercising sovereignty over the denuclearized territory might decide to succeed also in the non-localized obligations, but it would be under no international obligation to do so.

---

48 Kassenova, above n.36, 13. The Semipalatinsk nuclear test site in Kazakhstan and the uranium tailings dump in Kyrgyzstan are the most well-known examples of areas in Central Asia contaminated as a result of the Soviet nuclear activities (Alibek Dzhekshenkulov, A Nuclear-Free Zone in Central Asia, 45(4) International Affairs (Moscow) (1999), 54).

49 O'Connell admits the existence of treaties, such as those establishing military bases, where personal and territorial elements are intermingled (Daniel Patrick O'Connell, Recent Problems of State Succession in Relation to New States, 130 Recueil des Cours (1970), 194–195).

50 According to the ICJ, Art. 12 of the Vienna Convention reflects customary international law (Gabčíkovo-Nagymaros Project (Hungary v. Slovakia), ICJ Reports 1997, para. 123).

51 O'Connell maintains that "[t]he transmissible portions of a treaty may be severed from the intransmissible if the two portions (a) deal with separate subject-matters, (b) do not depend upon each other, and (c) are not inseparably connected in the scheme of treaty performance" (Daniel Patrick O'Connell, State Succession in Municipal Law and International Law (Cambridge: Cambridge University Press, 1967), Vol. II, 301). The separability of the different provisions contained in the same treaty is also envisaged in the 1969 Vienna Convention on the Law of Treaties (Art. 44).

IV. The territorial extension of the Central Asian nuclear weapon-free zone and the rights of entry into ports and overflight of foreign nuclear ships, aircraft and missiles

22. According to Article 1(a) of the Semipalatinsk Treaty, the Central Asian nuclear weapon-free zone includes Kazakhstan, the Kyrgyz Republic, Tajikistan, Turkmenistan and Uzbekistan. The treaty is thus not open: only after amending Article 1 could other States adhere to it. A provision envisaging the possible expansion of the zone to neighbouring States was eventually deleted at the insistence of the United Kingdom, the United States and France, which were worried that participation in a nuclear weapon-free zone might be used by Iran in order to shield its nuclear programme.[52]

23. From a geographical point of view, the zone covers "the land territory, all waters (harbors, lakes, rivers and streams) and the air space above them, which *belong*" to the above-mentioned five States (Article 2(a)).[53] It appears that, in the Sapporo meeting of October 1999, the Central Asian States agreed that the zone should not include any portions of the Caspian Sea, the waters of which have not been clearly delimited yet.[54] If interpreted according to the ordinary meaning of the terms employed, however, Article 2(a) does not explicitly (and permanently) exclude the Caspian from the scope of application of the treaty.[55] Indeed, according to the prevalent view,[56] the Caspian is not a "sea" but rather an international lake not governed by the law of the sea, and lakes are included in the list contained in Article 2(a). What presently prevents the Caspian's inclusion in the zone is the fact that no agreement among the littoral States has been reached on the delimitation of its waters and thus no part of them uncontroversially "belongs" to Kazakhstan and Turkmenistan. Nonetheless, once such an agreement will be concluded and relevant portions of the Caspian waters will be determined to belong to the two Central Asian denuclearized States, those waters will constitute part of their territory and will consequently be included in the zone, in accordance with Article 2(a) of the Semipalatinsk Treaty. This interpretation is supported by the inclusion of the precautionary clause contained in the second paragraph of Article 2, according to which "[n]othing in this Treaty shall prejudice or in any way affect the rights of any Central Asian States in any dispute concerning the

---

52   Luthra, above n.22. In February 2008, the Presidents of Tajikistan and Iran issued a joint statement where they support the creation of nuclear weapon-free zones (Tajikistan, Iran Stand for a World without Nuclear Arms, Kazinform, 13 February 2008, www.inform.kz/showarticle.php?lang=eng&id=160537).

53   Emphasis added.

54   Parrish, above n.8, 144. Two littoral States—Kazakhstan and Turkmenistan—are parties to the Semipalatinsk Treaty.

55   The issue is not without importance, as the Russian Federation (a nuclear weapon State) is also a littoral State.

56   William E. Butler, The Soviet Union and the Continental Shelf, 63 AJIL (1969), 106; Robin R. Churchill and Alan V. Lowe, The Law of the Sea (Manchester: Manchester University Press, 1999), 60; Gilbert Gidel, Le droit international public de la mer (Chateauroux: Mellotté, 1932), Vol. 1, at 40; Mariangela Gramola, State Succession and the Delimitation of the Caspian Sea, 14 Italian Yearbook of International Law (2005), 237–238; Paul Tavernier, Le statut juridique de la mer Caspienne: mer ou lac?, Actualité et droit international, 20 October 1999, www.ridi.org/adi/199910a1.htm.

ownership of or sovereignty over lands or waters that may or may not be included within this zone". If read together, the two paragraphs of Article 2 of the Semipalatinsk Treaty seem to say is that the extension of the application of the Semipalatinsk Treaty to any portion of the Caspian depends on the successful conclusion of the negotiations on the delimitation of its waters, matter which is left unaffected by the treaty.

24. It follows from the above considerations and in particular from the qualification of the Caspian as a lake that the law of the sea problems related to the freedom of navigation of foreign ships carrying nuclear weapons through the territorial sea and exclusive economic zones of denuclearized States, emerged in connection with the Treaties of Tlatelolco, Rarotonga, Pelindaba and Bangkok, do not arise with regard to the Semipalatinsk Treaty.[57] The only controversial issue would be the entry of foreign nuclear ships into the denuclearized States' harbours and the overflight of the denuclearized States' territories by aircraft with nuclear weapons on board. Article 4 provides that "[w]ithout prejudice to the purposes and objectives of this treaty, each Party, in the exercise of its sovereign rights, is free to resolve issues related to transit through its territory by air, land or water, including visits by foreign ships to its ports and landing of foreign aircraft at its airfields".[58] This provision introduces an exception to the obligation contained in Article 3(1)(d), i.e. the obligation not to allow on the State party's territory the possession of or control over any nuclear explosive device by anyone. But are the denuclearized States really "free" under international law to allow or deny the visit of nuclear ships and the overflight and landing of aircraft with nuclear weapons on board?

25. It is generally accepted that, under customary international law, there is no obligation on the coastal State to accept foreign ships in its ports: the entry can thus be prohibited.[59] According to the International Court of Justice (ICJ), it is "by virtue of its sovereignty that the coastal State may regulate access to its ports";[60] as these waters have a status identical to that of the land territory as far as the exercise of sovereignty is concerned, there is no obligation to allow access to the ports. Hence, several States' legislations provide that the relevant national authorities can in certain cases deny the authorization to the entry of

---

57 See Roscini, above n.5, 145–256.

58 Compare this provision with Art. 5(2) of the Rarotonga Treaty, Art. 7 of the Bangkok Treaty and Art. 4(2) of the Pelindaba Treaty.

59 See Giuseppe Cataldi, Il passaggio delle navi straniere nel mare territoriale (Milano: Giuffrè, 1990), 86; Louise de La Fayette, Access to Ports in International Law, 11 International Journal of Marine and Coastal Law (1996), 1–2; Rainer Lagoni, Internal Waters, Seagoing Vessels in, in: Rudolf Bernhardt (ed.), Encyclopedia of Public International Law, Vol. II (1999), 1036–1037. It has been noted that "[i]t is at times indeed difficult to make distinction between a simple anchorage of ships and landing of aircraft and their stationing prohibited by the provisions of these Treaties" (Djamchid Momtaz, Nuclear-Weapon-Free Zones in Africa and Asia, in Asian-African Legal Consultative Committee, Essays on International Law (40th Anniversary Commemorative Volume) (1997), 198). Although the language of Art. 4 remains vague and does not specify what distinguishes transit from stationing, it appears that any temporary presence, to qualify as transit, would be restricted to a very short period of time only (Conrad, above n.31, 5).

60 Military and Paramilitary Activities in and against Nicaragua (Nicaragua v. United States), Merits, Judgment of 27 June 1986, ICJ Reports 1986, para. 213.

nuclear-propelled and nuclear-armed ships into the ports.[61] The denuclearized States could of course decide to authorize the entry, but only if this does not prejudice the purposes and objectives of the Semipalatinsk Treaty, as required by Article 4.

26. Customary law, though, admits the entry of ships into the ports and internal waters of a foreign State even without previous authorization in one case, i.e. when the ship is in a situation of force majeure or distress.[62] The former has been defined in Article 23 of the 2001 International Law Commission (ILC) Articles on State Responsibility as "an irresistible force or [...] an unforeseen event, beyond the control of the State, making it materially impossible in the circumstances to perform the obligation", while the latter materializes when "the author of the act in question has no other reasonable way, in a situation of distress, of saving the author's life or the lives of other persons entrusted to the author's care" (Article 24).[63] Modern shipping treaties usually contain a clause providing for the exception of force majeure.[64] In spite of its strictness, even the New Zealand Nuclear Free Zone, Disarmament and Arms Control Act does not limit "the freedom of [...] [a]ny ship or aircraft in distress".[65] According to the Group entrusted with drafting the text of the Rarotonga Treaty, the presence of a ship with nuclear weapons run aground within the nuclear weapon-free zone does not entail the violation of the treaty by the State party to which those waters belong, if it promptly adopts all necessary measures to remove the arms from its territory.[66] However, according to other authors, nuclear ships can be denied entry into the ports and internal waters even in the above mentioned exceptional circumstances because of "an actual risk of criticality, radiation or radioactive contamination of the population of the coastal State, of the installations of the port and of the environment".[67] This view seems to be confirmed by Article 24 of the ILC Articles, that rules out the possibility to invoke distress as a circumstance excluding wrongfulness if "the act in question is likely to create a comparable or greater peril" (the commentary to this provision makes the example of a nuclear submarine with a serious breakdown that might cause the radioactive contamination of the port in which it seeks refuge),[68] and by the declaration issued by the Australian Minister for

---

61 Roscini, above n.5, 197–201.

62 See Lagoni, above n.59, 1040; Daniel Patrick O'Connell, The International Law of the Sea (Oxford: Clarendon Press, 1984), Vol. II, 853–857.

63 The mentioned grounds cannot be invoked to exclude wrongfulness if the State invoking them has provoked, alone or in combination with other factors, the situation of force majeure or distress.

64 O'Connell, above n.62, 857. See also Art. 4 of the 1974 International Convention for the Safety of Life at Sea (SOLAS).

65 Section 12, canterbury.cyberplace.org.nz/peace/nukefree.html.

66 Hisakazu Fujita, The Changing Role of International Law in the Nuclear Age: From Freedom of the High Seas to Nuclear-Free Zones, in: Astrid J.M. Delissen and Gerard Jacob Tanja (eds), Humanitarian Law of Armed Conflict—Challenges Ahead. Essays in Honour of Frits Kalshoven (Dordrecht, Boston, London: Martinus Nijhoff Publishers, 1991), 346.

67 Werner Bischof, Nuclear Ships, in: Bernhardt (ed.), above n.59, Vol. III (1997), 722. See also Alfred-Maurice de Zayas, Ships in Distress, ibid., Vol. IV (2000), 399.

68 Report of the International Law Commission on the work of its 53rd session (23 April–1 June and 2 July–10 August 2001), UN Doc. A/56/10, GAOR, 56th session, Suppl. No. 10, 194.

Foreign Affairs and Trade with regard to the passage of the Japanese ship *Akatsuki Maru* ("[p]ort access is normally granted to ships in distress but safety would be a paramount consideration in deciding whether to grant access to the plutonium ship").[69]

27. As to the overflight of the territory of a State party to the Semipalatinsk Treaty by foreign aircraft carrying nuclear weapons, according to Article 3(c) of the 1944 Chicago Convention (to which all five Central Asian States are parties) State aircraft, including military ones, cannot overfly the territory of another State without its authorization, while Article 35(a) provides that "[n]o munitions of war or implements of war may be carried in or above the territory of a State in aircraft engaged in international navigation, except by permission of such State". States can thus submit to authorization the overflight of their territory and the landing of foreign aircraft, determining the conditions for its granting, among which there could be the absence on board of nuclear arms and materials. State practice confirms this view. The United States granted the authorization of overflight to a French air tanker flying from France to Tahiti only after the French authorities had assured that the cargo "did not include nuclear material or components but rather consisted of naval stores".[70] New Zealand does not allow aircraft with nuclear arms on board to overfly its territory,[71] while in 1979 Australia signed an agreement with the United States authorizing the overflight of B-52 and their call in Darwin: the US government, however, agreed not to provide them with nuclear weapons.[72] Spain has also adopted restrictive legislation in this field.[73]

28. A nuclear warhead can be carried not only by a ship or aircraft, but also by a missile. Two cases must be distinguished, depending on whether the missile passes through the air space only or also through the outer space in order to reach its target.[74] In the former case, the States parties to the Semipalatinsk Treaty are under an obligation to deny permission to the overflight by the nuclear missile, as Article 3(1)(d)(i) requires them not to allow the use of nuclear explosive devices in their territories.[75] The exception with regard to transit contained in Article 4 does not operate as far as missiles with a nuclear warhead are concerned:

---

69 14 Australian YIL (1993), 445.

70 Abram Chayes, Thomas Ehrlich and Andreas F. Lowenfeld, International Legal Process: Materials for An Introductory Course (Boston: Little, Brown & Co., 1968), 1052.

71 New Zealand Nuclear Free Zone, Disarmament, and Arms Control Act, above n.65, Section 10.

72 Australian Foreign Affairs Record, March 1985, 235–236; ibid., September 1985, 863–864.

73 See Art. 70 of Law No. 25 of 29 April 1964 (United Nations Legislative Series—National Legislation and Treaties Relating to the Law of the Sea (ST/LEG.SER.B/16), 1974, 46). In an exchange of notes with the United States, the Spanish government reaffirmed the prohibition to overfly the national territory by aircraft with nuclear material or weapons on board (Javier Díez Hochleitner, Régimen de navegación de los buques de guerra extranjeros por el mar territorial español y de sus escalas en puertos españoles, 38 Revista española de derecho internacional (1986), 567).

74 On the controversial border between air space and outer space, see Daniel Goedhuis, The Problems of the Frontiers of Outer Space and Air Space, 174 Recueil des Cours (1982), 391–402.

75 Ronzitti reaches this conclusion through a different reasoning and in relation to the Treaties of Tlatelolco and Bangkok only (Natalino Ronzitti, Missile Warfare and Nuclear Warheads—An Appraisal in the Light of the 1996 ICJ Advisory Opinion on the Legality of the Threat or Use of Nuclear Weapons, 27 Israel Yearbook on Human Rights (1997), 255).

while the aircraft or ship could simply transport a nuclear explosive device from a location to another, a launched missile necessarily aims to hit a target and must thus be qualified as "use", and not "transit", of nuclear weapons.

29. On the contrary, if the missile, in its trajectory, passes through the outer space above a denuclearized State, this will not be entitled to deny the passage: indeed, the outer space is not subject to national appropriation and is free for exploration and use by all States. It would not be possible to invoke the 1967 Outer Space Treaty, Article IV(1) of which merely prohibits to place in orbit around the Earth or station objects carrying weapons of mass destruction, and does not deal with those flying through outer space in order to reach a target on the Earth: it is necessary for the carrier to be prohibited that it completes at least one orbit around the Earth.[76] The destination exclusively for peaceful purposes provided in para. 2 of Article IV is also not relevant here, as its scope of application is the moon and other celestial bodies and not the outer space in general. What is more, with its inclusion the drafters of the 1967 treaty did not aim to prohibit all military activities, but only those in contrast with the provisions of the UN Charter on the use of armed force.[77]

V. Grounds for terminating the obligations arising from the Semipalatinsk Treaty

30. The right of the contracting parties to terminate their obligations under the Semipalatinsk Treaty can be founded on two legal bases: the general grounds for the termination and suspension of the operation of treaties, codified in the 1969 Vienna Convention on the Law of Treaties, and the withdrawal clause included in the final text of the treaty itself.[78] As to the former, Articles 60 and 62 of the Vienna Convention appear to be of particular importance for disarmament treaties, including those on nuclear weapon-free zones. Article 60(2)(a) states that, unless otherwise provided,[79] a material breach of a multilateral treaty by one

---

76 See Luigi Condorelli and Zidane Mériboute, Some Remarks on the State of International Law Concerning Military Activities in Outer Space, 6 Italian YIL (1985), 9, 20–25.

77 On Art. IV of the Outer Space Treaty, see Sergio Marchisio, Le basi militari nel diritto internazionale (Milano: Giuffrè, 1984), 303–304.

78 A ground for terminating or suspending the Semipalatinsk Treaty neither provided in the treaty itself nor codified in the Vienna Convention on the Law of Treaties is the outbreak of hostilities between parties. The matter is governed by customary international law, but it is unclear what this provides. Aust argues that the inclusion of "political" treaties among those that might be terminated by the outbreak of hostilities (suggested by Lord McNair over 40 years ago) "needs to be re-examined in the light of changes during recent decades, in particular the conclusion of multilateral treaties on disarmament, arms control and demilitarisation" (Anthony Aust, Modern Treaty Law and Practice (Cambridge: Cambridge University Press, 2007), 309). In 2004, the ILC decided to include the topic in its programme of work and appointed Ian Brownlie as Special Rapporteur. On the application of the nuclear weapon-free zone treaties in time of armed conflict, see Roscini, above n.5, 109–116.

79 Art. 60(4). For instance, Art. XII(2) of the Chemical Weapons Convention provides that "[i]n cases where a State Party has been requested by the Executive Council to take measures to redress a situation raising problems with regard to its compliance, and where the State Party fails to fulfil the request within the specified time, the Conference may, inter alia, upon the recommendation of the Executive Council, restrict or suspend the State Party's

of the parties entitles the other parties by unanimous agreement to suspend the operation of the treaty in whole or in part or to terminate it in the relations between themselves and the defaulting State, or as between all the parties.[80] Furthermore, the party specially affected by the breach (e.g. the State whose territory has been reached by the radioactive pollution caused by the material breach) can invoke it as a ground for suspending the operation of the treaty in whole or in part in the relations between itself and the defaulting State (Article 60(2)(b)).

31. If the treaty is "of such a character that a material breach of its provisions by one party radically changes the position of every party with respect to the further performance of its obligations under the treaty", any party other than the defaulting State can invoke the breach as a ground for suspending (but not terminating) the operation of the treaty in whole or in part with respect to itself (Article 60(2)(c)).[81] The main obligations contained in the Semipalatinsk Treaty fall within the scope of this paragraph. Indeed, the prohibitions to station, possess, control, test, manufacture, stockpile, to conduct research on nuclear explosive devices and to seek or receive assistance to these aims can be qualified as "integral" obligations, as they operate "in an all-or-nothing fashion":[82] even though they pursue a collective interest of the group, "each parties' performance is effectively conditioned upon and requires the performance of the other".[83] As Gerald Fitzmaurice puts it, "the obligation of each party to disarm, or not to exceed a certain level of armaments, or not to manufacture or possess certain types of weapons, is necessarily dependent on a corresponding perform-ance of the same thing by all the other parties, since it is the essence of such a treaty that the undertaking of each party is given in return for a similar undertaking by the others".[84]

---

rights and privileges under this Convention until it undertakes the necessary action to conform with its obligations under this Convention". A similar provision is contained also in Art. V(2) of the CTBT.

80 In its Advisory Opinion on the legal consequences for States of the continued presence of South Africa in Namibia notwithstanding Security Council Resolution 276 (1970), the ICJ held that Art. 60 is "in many respects" a codification of existing customary international law (ICJ Reports 1971, para. 94). This view was more recently reasserted in the judgment on the Gabčíkovo-Nagymaros Project case (above n.50, para. 46).

81 Art. 60(2)(c) is echoed in Art. 42(b)(ii) of the 2001 ILC Articles on State Responsibility. As the Special Rapporteur Crawford has noted, the category of integral obligations "has as much relevance for State responsibility as it has for treaty suspension. The other parties to an integral obligation which has been breached may have no interest in its suspension and should be able to insist, vis-à-vis the responsible State, on cessation and restitution" (James Crawford, Fourth Report on State Responsibility, A/CN.4/517, 2 April 2001, 15).

82 Ibid.

83 Report of the International Law Commission on the work of its 53rd session, above n.68, 299. The Commission includes disarmament and nuclear-free zone treaties among the examples of this type of obligations. See also the Report of the International Law Commission on the work of its 18th session (4 May–19 July 1966), UN Doc. A/6309/Rev.1, GAOR, 21st session, Suppl. No. 9, at 255. In legal literature, see Aust, above n.78, 294–295; K. Sachariew, State Responsibility for Multilateral Treaty Violations: Identifying the Injured State and Its Legal Status, 35 Netherlands ILR (1988), 281, who makes the example of the 1963 Nuclear Test Ban Treaty. Paul Reuter has also supported the application of Art. 60(2)(c) to disarmament treaties (Introduction to the Law of Treaties (London and New York: Kegan Paul International, 1995), 38), while Lysén suggests that the application of para. 2(a) of Art. 60 would be preferable (Göran Lysén, The Adequacy of the Law of the Treaties to Arms Control Agreements, in: Julie Dahlitz (ed.), Avoidance and Settlement of Arms Control Disputes (New York and Geneva: UN, 1994), 141).

84 Gerald Fitzmaurice, Second Report on the Law of Treaties, A/CN.4/107, 15 March 1957, 54.

32. Nonetheless, the Semipalatinsk Treaty also contains obligations of a different nature. The prohibitions to allow the disposal of radioactive waste and to provide fissionable material to non-nuclear weapon States without IAEA safeguards and the obligations of physical protection of nuclear material and equipment and of assistance in the environmental rehabilitation of contaminated territories are assumed *erga omnes partes*: like integral obligations, they are expression of a collective interest and are not assumed towards one or more specific parties, but towards the group as a whole.[85] All parties "are recognized as having a common interest, over and above any individual interest that may exist in a given case".[86] However, these obligations differ from integral ones in that, their performance by one member of the group is not dependent on a corresponding performance by the others.[87] These obligations are thus covered not by para. 2(c) of Article 60 of the Vienna Convention, but by paras 2(a) and (b).[88]

33. Whatever the nature of the breached provision, Article 60 only applies to a "material breach": would the acquisition or production of nuclear explosive devices or their stationing within the nuclear weapon-free zone be a "material breach" of the Semipalatinsk Treaty? An affirmative answer appears preferable, if one considers that a "material breach" is a "violation of a provision essential to the accomplishment of the object or purpose of the treaty", and that the object and purpose of the Semipalatinsk Treaty is to ensure the total absence of nuclear explosive devices from Central Asia with the ultimate goal of eliminating those weapons globally.[89]

34. A fundamental change of circumstances could also be invoked by the parties in order to terminate or suspend their participation in the Semipalatinsk Treaty. Article 62 of the Vienna Convention, which is generally thought to reflect customary international law,[90] requires some cumulative conditions for this ground to be invoked: the circumstances must have existed at the time of the conclusion of the treaty and must have constituted an essential basis of the consent of the parties to be bound by the treaty; and the change must be fundamental, "completely" unforeseen and having the effect of radically transforming the extent of obligations still to be performed under the treaty.[91] As acknowledged by the

---

85 Report of the International Law Commission on the work of its 53rd session, above n.68, 320–321.

86 James Crawford, Third Report on State Responsibility, A/CN.4/507, 15 March 2000, 41.

87 Therefore, integral obligations can be considered a sub-category of obligations erga omnes partes (Crawford, above n.86, 47).

88 A nuclear weapon-free zone treaty might also contain obligations of a mainly bilateral character, assumed towards one or more specific parties: an example is the prohibition of armed attack on nuclear installations situated within the zone (Art. 11 of the Pelindaba Treaty).

89 See preamble of the Semipalatinsk Treaty. See also D.N. Hutchinson, Solidarity and Breaches of Multilateral Treaties, 59 BYBIL (1989), 196.

90 Fisheries Jurisdiction (United Kingdom v. Iceland), Jurisdiction, Judgment of 2 February 1973, ICJ Reports 1973, para. 36.

91 Implicit reference to the rebus sic stantibus doctrine appears to have been made by the United States ad abundantiam when denouncing the 1972 Anti-Ballistic Missile (ABM) Treaty (read the US declaration at www. acronym.org.uk/docs/0112/doc01.htm#text). See Rein Müllerson, The ABM Treaty: Changed Circumstances, Extraordinary Events, Supreme Interests and International Law, 50 ICLQ (2001), 539; and the opposite view

ICJ in the *Gabčikovo-Nagymaros* case, though, "[t]he negative and conditional wording of Article 62 [. . .] is a clear indication [. . .] that the stability of the treaty relations requires that the plea of fundamental change of circumstances be applied only in exceptional cases",[92] which might at least partly explain why "the doctrine of fundamental change has extremely rarely been invoked successfully before international judicial bodies".[93] In any case, all five States parties to the Semipalatinsk Treaty have acceded to the 1969 Vienna Convention and are thus required to comply with the procedure spelt out in Articles 65–68 when invoking a ground for termination or suspension provided therein.[94]

35. A further (and easier to invoke) means at the disposal of the parties in order to terminate their obligations under the Semipalatinsk Treaty is expressly provided by the treaty itself. Like all disarmament agreements, the nuclear weapon-free zone treaties contain very broad withdrawal clauses.[95] The inclusion of such clauses in disarmament treaties has been the object of discussion. According to Sims, "[t]he logic of withdrawal clauses implies at least a partial reversibility of the treaties in which they are incorporated. Now, it is by no means generally agreed that a disarmament treaty should be reversible".[96] On the contrary, Cannizzaro doubts that nuclear non-proliferation treaties such as the NPT are irreversible.[97] The (scarce) practice seems to support the latter view. None of the Security Council resolutions concerning the North Korean withdrawal from the NPT qualifies such withdrawal as illegal, but on the contrary they try to persuade the Asian State with different degrees of pressure to retract its announcement and return to the NPT.[98] In the 1993 debates in the Security Council, the North Korean representative affirmed that "[t]he withdrawal of our country from the NPT was based on our full right under the Treaty, a right that belongs to every sovereign Member State"[99] and even the South Korean representative noted that "every party has the right to withdraw from the Treaty".[100] The British representative also did not question "the right of States to withdraw from treaties if such withdrawal is

suggested by Malgosia Fitzmaurice and Olufemi Elias, Contemporary Issues in the Law of Treaties (Utrecht: Eleven Publishing, 2005), 195.

92 Gabčikovo-Nagymaros, above n.50, para. 104.

93 Fitzmaurice and Elias, above n.91, 188–189.

94 On whether or not these procedural requirements reflect customary international law, see Fitzmaurice and Elias, above n.91, 195–198.

95 Art. 54(a) of the Vienna Convention on the Law of Treaties provides that the withdrawal of a party may take place in conformity with the provisions of the treaty itself. It is debatable whether the withdrawal clause allows not only the termination of the treaty but also its suspension (Duncan B. Hollis, Russia Suspends CFE Treaty Participation, ASIL Insight, 23 July 2007, asil.org/insights/2007/07/insights070723.html).

96 Nicholas A. Sims, Approaches to Disarmament: An Introductory Analysis (London: Quaker Peace and Service, 1979), 51–52.

97 Enzo Cannizzaro, Recesso dal Trattato sulla non proliferazione nucleare e minaccia alla pace, 89 Rivista di diritto internazionale (2006), 1081–1082.

98 See SC Resolutions 825 of 11 May 1993, 1695 of 15 July 2006 and 1718 of 15 October 2006.

99 S/PV.3212, 11 May 1993, 7.

100 Ibid., at 30.

614   *Chinese JIL* (2008)

in accordance with the provisions of the treaty concerned".[101] The very fact that the three depositaries of the NPT issued a joint statement questioning the existence of the "extraordinary events" relating to the subject matter of the treaty claimed by North Korea in 1993 seems to suggest that the withdrawal would have been lawful had that requirement been met.[102] Russia did not challenge the legality of the US withdrawal from the ABM Treaty in December 2001,[103] and no State (not even the other parties) seems to have labelled as illegal Russia's statement on the suspension of its obligations under the Treaty on Conventional Armed Forces in Europe (CFE) and related agreements in July 2007.[104]

36. Be that as it may, the fact remains that a withdrawal clause has been included in the final text of the Semipalatinsk Treaty.[105] In the Rarotonga and Bangkok Treaties, the right of withdrawal is triggered by the breach by another party of a provision essential to the achievement of the objectives of the treaty.[106] Taking the Treaties of Tlatelolco and Pelindaba as a

---

101 Ibid., at 54.

102 S/25515, 2 April 1993, reprinted in SCOR, 48th Year, Supplement for April, May and June 1993, at 15.

103 On the contrary, President Putin recognized that "[t]he Treaty does indeed allow each of the parties to withdraw from it under exceptional circumstances", although it qualified the US decision as a mistake, www.acronym.org. uk/docs/0112/doc01.htm#text.

104 Hollis, above n.95. NATO States declared themselves "disappointed" and "deeply concerned" by Russia's decision but did not challenge its legality (NATO Response to Russian Announcement of Intent to Suspend Obligations under the CFE Treaty, NATO Press Release 2007(085), 16 July 2007, www.nato.int/docu/pr/ 2007/p07-085e.html. See also the declaration of the US Department of State's spokesman declaration, Russian Announcement of Intention to Suspend Implementation of Conventional Armed Forces in Europe Treaty, Press Statement 2007/588, 14 July 2007, www.state.gov/r/pa/prs/ps/2007/88417.htm.

105 As to the relationship between an express right of withdrawal included in the treaty and the general grounds for termination, in particular the fundamental change of circumstances, it has been suggested that "the relations between the parties should be governed first and foremost by what they have expressly agreed" (Fitzmaurice and Elias, above n.91, 193). Müllerson, on the other hand, argues that "[e]xpress provisions providing for the possibility of the denunciation of a treaty do not exclude the use of another concept available for treaty termination" (above n.91, 530). Similarly, see Paolo Fois, Il consenso ad obbligarsi nel Trattato sulla non-proliferazione nucleare, 91 Rivista di diritto internazionale (2008), 50. It has also been noted that the concept of "material breach" under Art. 60 of the 1969 Vienna Convention applies to "a more limited number of situations than that covered by the extraordinary circumstances clause", as "the latter might also refer to events which do not involve the responsibility of the other party" (Natalino Ronzitti, Problems of Arms Control Treaty Interpretation, in: Julie Dahlitz and Detlev Dicke (eds), The International Law of Arms Control and Disarmament, Proceedings of the Symposium, Geneva 28 February–2 March 1991 (New York: UN, 1991), 121). The same writer also notes that the extraordinary circumstances clause allows withdrawal from a disarmament treaty in a number of circumstances greater than the rebus sic stantibus doctrine, even though only the operation of the former is conditioned upon giving notice of the intention to withdraw to the other parties (ibid.). The opposite argument is made by Müllerson, who maintains that recourse to a withdrawal clause based on "extraordinary events" and "supreme interests" requires much more concrete threats than the fundamental but broad circumstances required by the rebus sic stantibus doctrine (Müllerson, above n.91, 531).

106 Arts 13 and 22, respectively. The clause contained in the Rarotonga Treaty provides that the right of withdrawal can be exercised also in the case of a violation of the "spirit" of the treaty, which is of difficult interpretation (David A.C. Freestone and J. Scott Davidson, Nuclear Weapon-Free Zones, in: Istvan Pogany (ed.), Nuclear Weapons and International Law (Aldershot, Brookfield, Hong Kong, Singapore, Sydney: Avebury, 1987), 201). It is worth noting that the withdrawal clause contained in the three additional protocols to the Rarotonga Treaty is modelled on that contained in the Treaty of Tlatelolco and allows withdrawal if the party decides that extraordinary events related to the subject matter of the protocols have jeopardized its supreme interests. The withdrawal takes effect three months (not 12, as in the main treaty) after the notification to the Depositary. The same goes for the additional protocol to the Bangkok Treaty, but this provides for a period of 12 months.

model, Article 16 of the Semipalatinsk Treaty provides that "[a]ny Party may, by written notification addressed to the Depositary, withdraw from the Treaty if it decides that extraordinary events, related to the subject-matter of this Treaty, have jeopardized its supreme national interests".[107] The withdrawal takes effect 12 months after the date of receipt of the notification by the Depositary, during which the party must still observe the procedures to review compliance.[108] The lapse of time provision aims to permit consultations and negotiations in order to avoid the withdrawal. Non-compliance with the 12 month term, however, does not necessarily render the withdrawal unlawful: the withdrawal will become effective only after the 12 month period, in spite of the intention of the party to withdraw with immediate effect.[109]

37. The Semipalatinsk Treaty does not set up any mechanism to review the party's decision to withdraw, but requires that the notification of the withdrawal include a statement indicating the "extraordinary events" jeopardizing the party's supreme national interests. Even though the other parties could question the existence of such extraordinary events,[110] the lack of any definition and the vagueness of this concept hardly make it an effective deterrent to the frivolous exercise of the right of withdrawal.[111] However, a role

107 Art. 20 of the Pelindaba Treaty is almost identical to Art. 16 of the Semipalatinsk Treaty, while Art. 31 of the Treaty of Tlatelolco, although very similar, is broader, as it refers to "circumstances" (and not to "extraordinary events"), which may affect not only the supreme interests of the denouncing party but also "the peace and security of one or more Contracting Parties".

108 See, with regard to the NPT, Susan Carmody, Balancing Collective Security and National Sovereignty: Does the United Nations Have the Right to Inspect North Korea's Nuclear Facilities?, 18 Fordham ILJ (1994–1995), 283–284. The Treaty of Tlatelolco provides for an obligation to notify the intention to withdraw to the OPANAL's General Secretary, the Rarotonga Treaty to the Director of the South Pacific Bureau for Economic Co-operation, the Pelindaba Treaty to the Depositary (i.e. the African Union's Secretary-General) and the Bangkok Treaty to the members of the Commission for the South-East Asia Nuclear Weapon-Free Zone. The Latin-American treaty also provides that the withdrawal shall be communicated to the other contracting parties and to the UN Secretary-General, Security Council and General Assembly as well as to the OAS Secretary-General.

109 This situation materialized in January 2003, when North Korea announced its intention to withdraw with immediate effect from the NPT, even though this provides that the withdrawal takes effect three months after the notification to the other parties and to the UN Security Council (Art. X). This was justified by North Korea on the basis of its 1993 announcement to withdraw from the NPT, subsequently suspended. See Cannizzaro, above n.97, 1080.

110 The fact that every State party can "decide" when extraordinary events have jeopardized its supreme national interests does not mean that such decision cannot be scrutinized by the other parties. Otherwise, the circulation of the notification of withdrawal by the Depositary to all the other parties would make little sense (Art. 16(b)).

111 It is not easy to understand what is meant by "extraordinary events". Examples might be new developments in the field of nuclear military technology or the entry into force of a particularly important amendment (Egon Schwelb, The Nuclear Test Ban Treaty and International Law, 58 AJIL (1964), 663). According to Gounelle, as disarmament treaties are based on the balance of forces existing at the moment of negotiations, "[t]out élément qui viendrait troubler cet équilibre accepté est considéré comme un 'événement extraordinaire en relation avec l'objet du traité'" (Max Gounelle, La motivation des actes juridiques en droit international public (Paris: Pedone, 1979), 155). Also the breach of the treaty or the withdrawal exercised by another party have been qualified as "extraordinary events" justifying the withdrawal (Jozef Goldblat and Péricles Gasparini Alves, Responses to Violations of Arms Control Agreements, in: Serge Sur (ed.), Disarmament and Arms Limitation Obligations, Problems of Compliance and Enforcement (Aldershot: Dartmouth; Geneva: UNIDIR, 1994), 284; Fernando Mariño Menéndez, Zonas libres de armas nucleares en el derecho internacional, in Cursos de derecho

616 *Chinese JIL* (2008)

might be played by the ICJ (should its jurisdiction be established over the case), since a controversy among States parties on whether a certain situation amounts to an "extraordinary event" according to Article 16 of the Semipalatinsk Treaty would be a legal dispute concerning the interpretation of a treaty under Article 26(2)(a) of the ICJ Statute. Furthermore, as suggested by Shaker in relation to the NPT, "an act of withdrawal by a Party in order to acquire nuclear weapons could be considered a 'situation which might lead to international friction' justifying an investigation by the Security Council under Article 34 of the UN Charter" and could even be characterized "as a 'threat to the peace' under Article 39, justifying the application of appropriate sanctions under Articles 40, 41 and 42".[112] Of course, not every withdrawal would automatically amount to a threat to the peace. Such a conclusion could only be reached by the Council on a case-by-case basis, taken the existing circumstances into account.

VI. The negative security assurances by the nuclear weapon States

38. Para. II of the above-mentioned Resolution 3472(XXX)B of 11 December 1975, containing the General Assembly's definition of "nuclear weapon-free zone", provides that the nuclear weapon States must "undertake or reaffirm, in a solemn international instrument having full legally binding force, such as a treaty, a convention or a protocol, the following obligations: (a) To respect in all its parts the statute of total absence of nuclear weapons

internacional de Vitoria-Gasteiz 1983 (1985), 162). Lysén argues that "extraordinary events" would be a breach of the treaty, the supervening impossibility of performance, the fundamental change of circumstances and the outbreak of war or armed conflict. To be "extraordinary", the event should also "either be unforeseeable or, though foreseeable, thought by the parties as highly unlikely to occur" (Göran Lysén, The International Regulation of Armaments: The Law of Disarmament (Uppsala: Iustus, 1990), 176–177). Announcing its intention to withdraw from the NPT on 10 January 2003, North Korea qualified the US hostile policy against North Korea as "extraordinary events" jeopardizing North Korean security (Raven Winters, Preventing Repeat Offenders: North Korea's Withdrawal and the Need for Revisions to the Nuclear Non-Proliferation Treaty, 38 Vanderbilt JTL (2005), 1513). In order to justify its withdrawal from the ABM Treaty, the United States seems to have qualified the 11th September events and the possible missile attacks with weapons of mass destruction and without warning against the United States by terrorists or "rogue states" as extraordinary events related to the subject matter of the treaty and jeopardizing US security (13 December 2001), www.acronym.org.uk/docs/0112/doc01.htm#text. Russia also listed the "exceptional circumstances affecting the security of the Russian Federation" and justifying the decision to suspend its participation in the CFE Treaty. The list includes the failure of Eastern European countries to make the necessary changes to the treaty regime in order to take their NATO membership into account; the increased number of NATO States and the "exclusive group" character of the alliance; the US plan to deploy conventional forces in Bulgaria and Romania; the failure to early ratify the Adaptation Agreement and to comply with the Istanbul Agreements by certain CFE parties; and the non-participation of the Baltic States in the CFE Treaty (Information on the decree "On Suspending the Russian Federation's Participation in the Treaty on Conventional Armed Forces in Europe and Related International Agreements", 14 July 2007, www.cdi.org/russia/johnson/2007-161-32.cfm). In the context of the NPT, Germany proposed the conclusion of an agreement clarifying, among other things, what constitutes an "extraordinary event" (Preparatory Committee for the 2005 Review Conference of the Parties to the Treaty on the Non-Proliferation of Nuclear Weapons, Working Paper No. 15, NPT/CONF.2005/PC.III/WP.15, 29 April 2004, www.reachingcriticalwill.org/legal/npt/prepcom04/papers/GermanyWP15.pdf, 2).

112 Mohamed I. Shaker, The Nuclear Non-Proliferation Treaty, Origin and Implementation, 1959–1979 (London, Rome, New York: Oceana Publications, 1980), Vol. II, 896. See also Fois, above n.105, 57–58.

defined in the treaty or convention which serves as the constitutive instrument of the zone; (b) To refrain from contributing in any way to the performance in the territories forming part of the zone of acts which involve a violation of the aforesaid treaty or convention; (c) To refrain from using or threatening to use nuclear weapons against the States included in the zone".[113] When drafting the Treaty of Tlatelolco, the participating States discussed how such commitments should be formalized. Certain States were in favour of a General Assembly resolution approving the establishment of the zone and bounding all States that had endorsed it with their vote. Others preferred a protocol attached to the main treaty, containing the obligations of the nuclear weapon powers towards the denuclearized States.[114] The latter view eventually prevailed and was also adopted by the drafters of the Treaties of Rarotonga, Pelindaba, Bangkok and Semipalatinsk: it can now be maintained that an additional protocol containing (negative) security assurances is an essential component of the model treaty for the establishment of nuclear weapon-free zones in inhabited regions of the world.[115] In its 1996 Advisory Opinion on the *Legality of Nuclear Weapons*, the ICJ unanimously acknowledged that the threat and use of nuclear weapons must be consistent "with the requirements of the international law applicable in armed conflict, particularly those of the principles and rules of international humanitarian law, as well as with specific obligations under treaties and other undertakings which expressly deal with nuclear weapons", where "specific obligations under treaties" can be interpreted as a reference to the protocols additional to the nuclear weapon-free zone treaties and "other undertakings" to the assurances contained in the unilateral declarations issued by the nuclear weapon States in 1995.[116]

113 See also para. 62 of the Final Document of the tenth UN General Assembly Special Session (1978), 17 ILM (1978), 1025. According to the 1976 Comprehensive Study, the security assurances are an important element of a nuclear weapon-free zone (above n.3, Annex I, paras 85 and 115). Some members of the Conference of the Committee on Disarmament argued however that the assurances by nuclear weapon States are not an indispensable requirement for the establishment of a nuclear weapon-free zone and should be given on a case-by-case basis (Bulgaria (ibid., Annex II, para. 101) and Mongolia (ibid., para. 129)). This position was criticized by the Swedish representative (ibid., para. 57). During the negotiations that would lead to the opening for signature of the Treaty of Tlatelolco, Mexico argued that the provision of security assurances by the nuclear powers was extremely useful but not necessary in order to establish the nuclear weapon-free zone, while Brazil took the opposite view and maintained that they were an essential and non-negotiable requirement (Mónica Serrano, Common Security in Latin America—The 1967 Treaty of Tlatelolco (London: Institute of Latin American Studies, 1992), 36–37).

114 Georges Fischer, La non prolifération des armes nucléaires, 13 Annuaire français de droit international (1967), 88; Alfonso García Robles, Mesures de désarmement dans des zones particulières: le traité visant l'interdiction des armes nucléaires en Amérique latine, 133 Recueil des Cours (1971), 66. The nuclear States feared that the inclusion of security assurances in a General Assembly resolution might become a precedent in order to confer binding effect on those instruments (Serrano, above n.113, 41).

115 According to Rosen, however, "[g]iven that a politically if not legally binding NSA [Negative Security Assurance] has been given by the United States and other states in the NPT context, and that the P-5 have all committed to end nuclear weapons testing by signing the CTBT, P-5 participation in most of the current zones awaiting ratification does not add much to the security of regional states" (Mark E. Rosen, Nuclear Weapons Free Zones: Time for a Fresh Look, 8 Duke JCIL (1997–1998), 56–57). In his opinion, the security assurances encourage the use of weapons of mass destruction by "rogue states".

116 Legality of the Threat or Use of Nuclear Weapons, Advisory Opinion, 8 July 1996, ICJ Reports 1996, dispositif, para. 105(2)(D). Although with some language differences, in April 1995 France, Russia, the United Kingdom and the United States declared they would not use nuclear weapons against the non-nuclear weapon States

618   *Chinese JIL* (2008)

39. The security assurances must be distinguished in positive (by which the nuclear powers undertake to assist a non-nuclear weapon State should this be the victim of an attack carried out with nuclear weapons) and negative (by which the nuclear weapon States commit themselves not to use nuclear weapons against non-nuclear weapon States). Only the latter are included in the protocols annexed to the Tlatelolco, Rarotonga, Pelindaba, Bangkok and Semipalatinsk Treaties.[117] However, unlike the negative security assurances issued unilaterally by France, Russia, the United Kingdom and the United States,[118] the protocols attached to the nuclear weapon-free zone treaties contain not only the undertaking not to use nuclear weapons, but also not to threaten their use.[119]

40. Like the protocols additional to the Treaties of Rarotonga, Pelindaba and Bangkok and unlike Protocol II of the Treaty of Tlatelolco, the Semipalatinsk Protocol is addressed only to the five nuclear powers under the NPT, which are expressly named.[120] This is unfortunate, as the consequence is that India and Pakistan will not be expected to give any formal security assurances towards the Central Asian States, even though they possess nuclear weapons and, because of their geographical proximity, would be able to reach the region with their missiles.

41. The beneficiaries of the assurances are the States parties to the nuclear weapon-free zone.[121] The negative security assurances involve a commitment not to threaten or use

parties to the NPT, except in case of an attack carried out by the non-nuclear weapon State allied to or in association with a nuclear weapon State against their territories, armed forces or a State towards which it exists a security commitment. China more comprehensively declared that it would not use nuclear weapons "at any time or under any circumstances" against non-nuclear weapon States (S/1995/261 (Russian Federation), S/1995/262 (United Kingdom), S/1995/263 (United States), S/1995/264 (France) and S/1995/265 (China), reprinted in Tariq Rauf, Nuclear-Weapon-Free Zones (NWFZs), Center for Nonproliferation Studies, Monterey Institute of International Studies (1997), cns.miis.edu/pubs/reports/nwfz.htm, 33–35). The declarations were endorsed by SC Res 984 of 11 April 1995. In a memorandum in connection with Belarus, Kazakhstan and Ukraine's accession to the NPT (5 December 1994), the United States, the United Kingdom and Russia (and France in a separate statement) also affirmed that they would not use nuclear weapons against any non-nuclear weapon State party to NPT "except in the case of an attack on themselves, their territories or dependent territories, their armed forces, or their allies, by such a state in association or alliance with a nuclear weapon state" (ibid., 31). Finally, in October 2000, the five nuclear powers reaffirmed the positive and negative security assurances, as contained in the 1995 unilateral declarations and in SC Res 984 (1995), with regard to Mongolia, that had unilaterally declared itself a denuclearized State in 1992 (Identical letters dated 27 October 2000 from the Permanent Representatives of China, France, the Russian Federation, the United Kingdom and the United States to the UN addressed to the Secretary-General and to the President of the Security Council, A/55/530–S/2000/1052, 31 October 2000, at 2).

117 As observed, "[i]nscrire les garanties positives dans le cadre d'un accord sur une zone exempte d'armes nucléaires revient à cette solution paradoxale que la nucléarisation garantit la dénucléarisation" (Szurek, above n.1, 187). The positive security assurances are recalled in SC Res 255 (19 June 1968) and Res 984 (11 April 1995).

118 See above n.116. Only China committed itself not to threaten the use of nuclear weapons against denuclearized States.

119 Marco Roscini, Threats of Armed Force and Contemporary International Law, 54 Netherlands ILR (2007), 244.

120 Protocol II of the Treaty of Tlatelolco does not list the States that are entitled to sign it, which allows the future adherence by de facto nuclear powers (Héctor Gros Espiell, El derecho de los tratados y el Tratado de Tlatelolco, 4 Anuario hispano-luso-americano de derecho internacional (1973), 324).

121 The protocol annexed to the Bangkok Treaty prohibits the threat and use of nuclear weapons by the nuclear States not only against the parties to the treaty, but also "within the Southeast Asia Nuclear Weapon-Free

nuclear weapons or other nuclear explosive devices not only against their territory, but also against their armed forces wherever they are located, even outside the nuclear weapon-free zone (for instance, a military base situated in a foreign territory or a warship on the high seas).[122] On the other hand, it is unclear whether the Semipalatinsk Protocol prohibits the threat and use of nuclear weapons against those denuclearized States that detain other weapons of mass destruction, such as chemical or bacteriological arms: the fact that the prohibitions do not apply "under any circumstances" (as provided for instance in Article I(1) of the 1993 Chemical Weapons Convention) appears to support the conclusion that, in this case, the threat or use of nuclear weapons would not be inconsistent with the protocol. With regard to the African nuclear weapon-free zone, the Special Assistant to the US President for Arms Control stated that "Protocol I [of the Pelindaba Treaty] will not limit options available to the United States in response to an attack by an African Nuclear Weapons-Free Zone party using weapons of mass destruction".[123] This view also finds support in Judge Schwebel's dissenting opinion on the *Legality of Nuclear Weapons*, where he maintains that "[a]s long as [. . .] 'rogue states' menace the world (whether they are or are not Parties to the NPT), it would be imprudent to set policy on the basis that the threat or use of nuclear weapons is unlawful 'in any circumstance'. Indeed, it may not only be the rogue States but criminals or fanatics whose threats or acts of terrorism conceivably may require a nuclear deterrent or response".[124]

42. Apart from prohibiting the threat or use of nuclear weapons or other nuclear explosive devices against States parties to the Semipalatinsk Treaty, the protocol also requires the five nuclear weapon States not to contribute "to any act that constitutes a violation of the Treaty or this Protocol by Parties to them" (Article 2). The Protocols of Rarotonga and Bangkok employ almost identical wording, while those of Tlatelolco and Pelindaba do not refer to the fact that the act constituting a violation must be committed by another contracting party.

Zone" (Art. 2). This entails the prohibition to launch missiles with a nuclear warhead from ships, submarines or aircraft located within the zone even if the target is situated outside, and also the prohibition to use nuclear weapons against means of transport (even if they belong to a nuclear weapon State) situated in the internal waters, territorial sea and, most importantly, exclusive economic zone of the States parties to the Bangkok Treaty. The nuclear weapon States might also be prevented from using nuclear weapons against a State that has not ratified the Bangkok Treaty but whose land, sea or air territory is included in its territorial scope of application. The United States has thus refused to sign the protocol unless this is amended (Romain Yakemtchouk, Zones dénucléarisées, 50(4–5) Studia Diplomatica (1997), 55). A similar position has been taken by France (Joelle Bourgois, The Role Carried out by the Zones Exempt from Nuclear Arms, in: Péricles Gasparini Alves and Daiana Belinda Cipollone (eds), Nuclear-Weapon-Free Zones in the 21st Century (New York and Geneva: United Nations, 1997), 126). In particular, the nuclear States have requested the deletion of the sentence "not to use or threaten to use nuclear weapons within the Southeast Asia Nuclear Weapon-Free Zone" (Norachit Sinhaseni, Southeast Asia Nuclear-Weapon-Free Zone: Next Steps, 20(1) Disarmament: A Periodic Review of the United Nations (1997), 67–68).

122 This conclusion finds some support in the declarations issued by the nuclear powers in 1995, according to which the security assurances may be withdrawn in case of an attack not only against the nuclear State's territory, but also against its armed forces wherever they are stationed.

123 The White House Special Briefing Topic: ANWFZ—The Africa Nuclear Weapons-Free Zone and the Signing of the Treaty of Pelindaba (11 April 1996), reprinted in Rosen, above n.115, 51–52.

124 Legality of the Threat or Use of Nuclear Weapons, above n.116, p. 329.

43. As to the prospects for the ratification of the Semipalatinsk Protocol by the nuclear weapon States, Russia and China have already declared that they endorse the conclusion of the Semipalatinsk Treaty.[125] On the other hand, the United Kingdom, the United States and France have withdrawn their support to the initiative because previous security arrangements like the 1992 Tashkent Collective Security Treaty might prejudice the application of the Semipalatinsk Treaty in case of armed conflict.[126] Negotiations are thus still going on in order to secure the participation of all nuclear weapon States in the denuclearization of Central Asia, which is the reason why the protocol has not yet been opened for signature.

VII. The verification and enforcement mechanisms

44. General Assembly Resolution 3472(XXX)B of 11 December 1975 recalls that one of the essential elements of a nuclear weapon-free zone treaty is an international system of verification that ensures compliance with the denuclearization obligations. According to the 1976 Comprehensive Study, "[t]he viability of the nuclear-weapon-free zone will largely depend on an effective system of verification and control that ensures the nuclear-weapon-free status of the zone". The scope and nature of the system would necessarily differ from region to region and would depend upon the obligations assumed, but it should in any case extend to all nuclear activities of the States parties.[127] The 1999 Guidelines also emphasize that "[a] nuclear-weapon-free zone should provide for the effective verification of compliance with the commitments made by the parties to the treaty, *inter alia*, through the application of full-scope IAEA safeguards to all nuclear activities in the zone", as provided in the IAEA documents INFCIRC/153 and INFCIRC/540.[128]

45. Verification has been defined as "a process covering the entire set of measures aimed at enabling the Parties to an agreement to establish that the conduct of the other Parties is not incompatible with the obligations they have assumed under that agreement".[129] According to Krass, "[t]he verification process consists of two major components: monitoring, which is the primarily technical process of gathering and analyzing evidence on compliance behavior;

---

125 Ministry of Foreign Affairs of the Russian Federation, Press Release, 8 September 2006, cns.miis.edu/pubs/week/pdf_support/060908_russian_press_statement.pdf; Foreign Ministry Spokesman QIN Gang's Comments on a Treaty on the Central Asia Nuclear Weapon Free Area to Be Signed by the Five Central Asian Countries, 7 September 2006, www.fmprc.gov.cn/eng/xwfw/s2510/t270714.htm.

126 See above Section II, para. 9. The United Kingdom, the United States and France were the only States to vote against the adoption of GA Res 61/88 of 6 December 2006 welcoming and supporting the opening for signature of the Semipalatinsk Treaty.

127 1976 Comprehensive Study, above n.3, Annex I, paras 123, 128. The importance of an effective verification mechanism was emphasized by Czechoslovakia (ibid., Annex II, para. 47), Soviet Union (para. 72), Mongolia (para. 122) and the United Kingdom (para. 144).

128 Report of the Disarmament Commission, above n.5, para. 34.

129 Serge Sur, Introduction, in: Serge Sur (ed.), Disarmament and Arms Limitation Obligations. Problems of Compliance and Enforcement (Aldershot: Dartmouth; Geneva: UNIDIR, 1994), 2. In 1995, the UN Secretary-General published a study on verification (Verification in All Its Aspects, including the Role of the United Nations in the Field of Verification. Report of the Secretary-General, A/50/377 and Corr. 1, A/52/269, A/54/166, A/54/555).

and evaluation, which is the process of weighing and interpreting the evidence to determine whether or not a violation has occurred".[130] In the nuclear weapon-free zone treaties, these tasks are usually performed by two parallel mechanisms, one entrusted to the IAEA and the other to regional organs established by the treaty or—as in the Rarotonga Treaty—already existing. This two-pronged system is due to the fact that the IAEA safeguards agreements, conceived in relation to Article III of the NPT, were not meant to monitor compliance with the broader obligations contained in a nuclear weapon-free zone treaty.[131] The two mechanisms, thus, do not overlap, but have different competences: the IAEA detects the diversion of fissile materials from peaceful to military uses, while the regional organs monitor compliance with the other denuclearization obligations, in particular with the prohibition of stationing nuclear weapons within the zone.[132]

46. In the Semipalatinsk Treaty, the role of the IAEA is outlined in Article 8, according to which—as already noted[133]—States parties are under an obligation to conclude with the Agency and bring into force a comprehensive safeguard agreement (INFCIRC/153 (Corr.)) and an Additional Protocol (INFCIRC/540 (Corr.)) no later than 18 months from the treaty's entry into force. The IAEA safeguards constitute a confidence-building measure and an early warning mechanism that might trigger responses by the international community in case of breach of non-proliferation obligations. They include on-site inspections of declared and, under the Additional Protocol, undeclared sites, on-going monitoring and evaluation. With regard to the Central Asian States, if Kazakhstan, Kyrgyzstan, Turkmenistan and Uzbekistan have already concluded both the comprehensive safeguards agreement and the Additional Protocol with the IAEA, Kyrgyzstan has so far only signed the Protocol.[134]

47. As to the regional verification mechanism referred to in Article 10 and described in the annex of the Semipalatinsk Treaty, it neither envisages the establishment of an international organization nor relies on existing ones, but simply provides for annual consultative meetings to review compliance, with decisions taken by consensus.[135] Extraordinary consultative meetings can also be convened at the request of any party (when the motion is seconded by two other parties) to discuss matters related to the implementation of the treaty and its violations. The need to convene the extraordinary meeting must be explained. The five nuclear weapon States under the NPT and the representatives of relevant international

---

130 Allan S. Krass, Arms Control Treaty Verification, in: Richard Dean Burns (ed.), Encyclopedia of Arms Control and Disarmament (New York: Charles Scribner's Sons, 1993), Vol. I, 297.

131 XIA Liping, Nuclear-Weapon-Free Zones: Lessons for Nonproliferation in Northeast Asia, 6(4) The Nonproliferation Review (Fall 1999), 84.

132 Marie-Françoise Furet, Le désarmement nucléaire (Paris: Pedone, 1973), 181. The Rarotonga Treaty explicitly states that the regional mechanism, and in particular special inspections, "shall not duplicate safeguards procedures to be undertaken by the IAEA" (Annex 4, para. 5).

133 Above Section II, para. 12.

134 www.iaea.org/OurWork/SV/Safeguards/sg_protocol.html.

135 It appears that earlier drafts of the treaty provided for the establishment of an organization entrusted with verification, but these provisions were eventually deleted and do not appear in the final text (Parrish, above n.8, 145).

622   *Chinese JIL* (2008)

organizations can participate as observers with the consent of the States parties, and the meetings' decisions are reflected in outcome documents in Russian and, if needed, in English. A record of the consultative meetings may be transmitted, with the consent of all parties, to all interested international organizations as well as to the observers. One cannot however fail to note that, although the regular meetings of the parties might play a positive role and "attenuate rivalries among the countries in the region and foster the good neighbourly relations necessary for the planned regional cooperative undertakings in the field of environmental security",[136] the regional machinery could have been more elaborate and intrusive, in particular by establishing verification organs with the authority to conduct inspections as in the other nuclear weapon-free zone treaties.[137]

48. If a violation of the nuclear weapon-free zone treaty is detected through the mechanisms described above, the breached obligation must be enforced so that compliance is ensured. Even though there is no specific enforcement mechanism envisaged in the Semipalatinsk Treaty, enforcement could still be achieved in two ways: multilaterally or unilaterally. With regard to the former, the States parties might react to a violation in the framework of a competent international organization, such as by resorting to the UN Security Council or General Assembly.[138] Indeed, several Security Council resolutions have qualified the proliferation of weapons of mass destruction and of their means of delivery as a threat to international peace and security.[139] In the Semipalatinsk Treaty, no role of the UN main organs in the enforcement process is expressly envisaged, which marks a difference with other nuclear weapon-free zone treaties. However, this would not prevent the Security Council from dealing with a violation of the denuclearization regime should this be qualified as a threat to the peace: even in the absence of a specific provision contained in a treaty, any UN member State (and even a non-member which is a party to the dispute and accepts to settle it peacefully) can bring any dispute, or situation which might lead to international friction or give rise to a dispute, to the attention of the Security Council or of the General Assembly (Article 35 of the UN Charter). The IAEA Board of Governors might also report to the Security Council and to the General Assembly cases of non-compliance with obligations towards the IAEA (Article XII (C) of the IAEA Statute).

---

136 Goldblat, above n.11, 32.

137 On the inspection mechanisms in the other nuclear weapon-free zone treaties, see Roscini, above n.5, 355–358.

138 James Crawford, The International Law Commission's Articles on State Responsibility (Cambridge: Cambridge University Press, 2002), 302. The above-mentioned Comprehensive Study refers to the need to coordinate the nuclear weapon-free zone treaties with the UN collective security system (1976 Comprehensive Study, above n.3, Annex I, paras 123, 135, 144.).

139 See SC Res 825 of 11 May 1993 (linking "progress in non-proliferation" to the maintenance of international peace and security) and the more explicit Resolutions 1540 of 28 April 2004, 1695 of 15 July 2006 and 1718 of 14 October 2006. In Res 1540, the Council also affirmed "its resolve to take appropriate actions against any threat to international peace and security caused by the proliferation of nuclear, chemical and biological weapons and their means of delivery". For a critical discussion of Res 1540, see Daniel H. Joyner, Non-proliferation Law and the United Nations System: Resolution 1540 and the Limits of the Power of the Security Council, 20 Leiden JIL (2007), 508–515.

49. States parties might also react unilaterally to a breach of the denuclearization regime and adopt countermeasures under the conditions provided in customary international law.[140] In particular, the State party taking the countermeasure might react in kind and breach the same provision initially violated by the wrongdoer providing that this obligation is not *erga omnes partes*.[141] Furthermore, the State party might breach other treaties in force with the wrongdoer, such as those providing for economic cooperation. In any case, the limits highlighted in Articles 50 and 51 of the 2001 ILC Articles on State Responsibility, which reflect customary international law, must be respected. In particular, Article 50 provides that a State taking countermeasures is not relieved from fulfilling its obligations "under any dispute settlement procedure applicable between it and the responsible State". In this context, Article 11 of the Semipalatinsk Treaty should be recalled, as it contains the obligation to settle disputes involving the interpretation or application of the treaty "through negotiations or by any other means as may be deemed necessary by the Parties".

VIII. Conclusions

50. The opening for signature of the Semipalatinsk Treaty marks the successful conclusion of the negotiations for the establishment of a nuclear weapon-free zone in Central Asia, the first situated entirely in the northern hemisphere and sharing borders with two nuclear weapon States. Although it is true that—as Goldblat suggests—"this treaty may help build up geopolitical stability and security in Central Asia" and is thus "a valuable asset for the cause of non-proliferation",[142] it contains however lights and shadows. It is the first of its kind to require the States parties to comply with the CTBT and the Additional Protocol on IAEA strengthened safeguards. It prohibits not only ready-to-use nuclear explosive devices, but also their components. It is the only nuclear weapon-free zone treaty providing for an obligation of assistance in the efforts towards the rehabilitation of radioactively contaminated territories. The obligation of physical protection of nuclear material, facilities and equipment included in Article 9 could also make the Semipalatinsk Treaty an effective tool against the risk of nuclear terrorism. Finally, unlike in the Treaties of Tlatelolco, Rarotonga and Bangkok, military nuclear research is expressly prohibited.

51. On the downside, the verification mechanism provided in the annex is disappointing, as it only provides for consultative meetings to review compliance, with decisions taken by consensus. Furthermore, there is no protocol attached to the Semipalatinsk Treaty by the

---

140 See Roscini, above n.5, 370–381.

141 On the erga omnes partes character of certain obligations contained in the Semipalatinsk Treaty, see above Section V, para. 32.

142 Goldblat, above n.11, 32. According to Enkhsaikhan, the establishment of the Central Asian nuclear weapon-free zone might have "a positive impact on maintaining and strengthening the overall balance and stability in the subregion and its strategically important adjacent areas" (Jargalsaikhany Enkhsaikhan, Central Asia—Future Perspectives, in: Gasparini Alves and Cipollone (eds), above n.121, 97). The First Deputy Foreign Minister of Kyrgyzstan also observed that "if implemented, this initiative would make for deep positive movements on the global, regional and subregional levels, as well as in the sphere of bilateral relations of countries in our region" (Dzhekshenkulov, above n.48, 54).

ratification of which the nuclear weapon States commit themselves not to carry out nuclear test explosions within the zone, and the disposal of a State party's radioactive waste in its own territory is not prohibited. The list of provisions contained in other nuclear weapon-free zone treaties but not in the Semipalatinsk Treaty also includes the prohibition of armed attack against nuclear installations situated within the zone, the obligation to declare, dismantle and destroy or convert nuclear explosive devices and facilities for their manufacture and the obligation to accede to the Convention on Early Notification of a Nuclear Accident.

52. However, even though the Semipalatinsk Treaty is far from being perfect, one should see the glass half full, not half empty. Each nuclear weapon-free zone treaty necessarily reflects the specific characteristics of the region to which it applies and, if it aims to be successful, has to strike a compromise between the interests of the regional States and those of the nuclear powers. After years of gestation, the Semipalatinsk Treaty has finally been opened for signature. The perfect is sometimes the enemy of the good.

[10]

ARMS CONTROL LAW IN CRISIS? A STUDY OF THE NORTH KOREAN NUCLEAR ISSUE

Masahiko Asada*

ABSTRACT

The North Korean nuclear issues have exposed the international community to a great proliferation risk for more than ten years. They have grown particularly serious since North Korea (Democratic People's Republic of Korea, DPRK) reportedly admitted in October 2002 that it had clandestinely pursued development of nuclear weapons based on uranium enrichment. Legally speaking, the North Korean proliferation risk reached its worst point in January 2003, when Pyongyang announced its withdrawal from the Nuclear Non-Proliferation Treaty (NPT). However, that was not the first instance in which North Korea had declared withdrawal. They had done so in March 1993, but at that time the declared withdrawal was suspended one day before its effectuation (withdrawal takes effect three months after its notification). Given the complicated nature of the situation, there can be several ways of interpreting the North Korean status under the NPT. This article tries to examine four such interpretations, including those given by North Korea itself and by the International Atomic Energy Agency (IAEA). It will also give some thought to the North Korean obligation to accept IAEA safeguards under the Safeguards Agreement with the Agency and under other legal and political arrangements.

1 INTRODUCTION

The 11 September 2001 terrorist attacks on the World Trade Center have led to the United States adopting a new national security concept.[1] In an attempt to apply the new concept, the US government started a war against Iraq in March 2003 to contain the perceived proliferation risks of weapons of mass destruction (WMD).

Contemporaneously, a no less grave WMD-related issue revealed itself in East Asia. It was reported in October 2002 that when US Assistant Secretary of State James Kelly visited North Korea (Democratic People's Republic of Korea, DPRK), one of his counterparts, Deputy Foreign Minister Kang Sok Joo, admitted that the DPRK has clandestinely pursued development of nuclear weapons based on uranium enrichment.[2] This was the prelude to a renewed nuclear crisis on the Korean Peninsula. The crisis reached a climax when Pyongyang announced its withdrawal from the Nuclear Non-Proliferation Treaty (NPT) on 10 January 2003.

This was, however, not the first instance in which the DPRK declared its intention to withdraw from the NPT. It had already done so in March 1993. At that time,

---

* Professor of International Law, Kyoto University, Japan.

[1] See, e.g., White House, *The National Security Strategy of the United States of America*, September 2002, 5–7, 13–16; *National Strategy to Combat Weapons of Mass Destruction*, December 2002, 3.

[2] *Washington Post*, 17 October 2002; *New York Times*, 17 October 2002.

332   *Masahiko Asada*

Pyongyang decided later to 'suspend' the effectuation of its withdrawal from the NPT after conducting bilateral talks with the United States. This time, no such decision was made. Notwithstanding, there is a debate as to whether North Korea has already withdrawn from the NPT or still remains a party to the Treaty. There is even an attempt to deliberately obfuscate the legal situation with regard to North Korean status under the NPT.

This article will analyse the legal arguments that have been put forward on the question of the DPRK's legal status under the NPT as well as other related issues. In doing so, it will try to show how difficult it would be to resolve the problems involved and, at the same time, how flawed some of the legal arguments that have been propounded are. Such an exercise would also shed light on the political intentions behind the international community's decision to leave the legal question aside for the resolution of the immediate crisis. Before going into the detailed analysis of the legal arguments, it would be pertinent to trace the historical development of the North Korean nuclear issue.

2 HISTORY OF NORTH KOREAN NUCLEAR DEVELOPMENT

2.1 North Korea's Incorporation in the Nuclear Non-Proliferation Regime

It was in 1965 that North Korea started to operate its first nuclear research reactor at Yongbyon, a place that later became a nuclear development centre of the country that caused much concern in the 1990s. Although the first reactor was provided by the Soviet Union, North Korea started to construct a graphite-moderated reactor for itself late in the 1970s, since the country produces both natural uranium and graphite that are needed for operating that type of reactor.

At the same time, Pyongyang embarked on a project of light-water reactors after deciding to regard them as the main means of electricity production in the country.[3] The Soviet supply of light-water reactor to North Korea was conditioned on the latter's accession to the NPT[4] because North Korea, a member of the International Atomic Energy Agency (IAEA) since September 1974,[5] had been outside the NPT regime. Pyongyang accepted this deal and acceded to the NPT on 12 December 1985. However, the light-water reactor project itself encountered

---

[3]   UN doc. S/2003/91, 27 January 2003, 5.

[4]   *Ibid.*

[5]   According to Professor Michael Mazarr, Pyongyang's accession to the IAEA was calculated to create an image of compliance among members of the international community and magnify world pressure on South Korea to abandon its nuclear programme, which was motivated by the Nixon or Guam Doctrine of 1968 and the ensuing US troop reduction in South Korea. Michael J. Mazarr, *North Korea and the Bomb: A Case Study in Nonproliferation* (1995), 25–30.

financial problems and was frustrated with the demise of the Soviet Union, while the fact that Pyongyang had acceded to the Treaty remained.

According to article 3 of the NPT, non-nuclear-weapon state parties are obliged to accept full-scope safeguards by concluding an agreement with the IAEA. They must conclude the agreement no later than 18 months after the entry into force of the Treaty for them. In the North Korean case, they had not done so more than six years after acceding to the Treaty. They attributed the cause for the failure partly to the presence of US tactical nuclear forces in the South.

On 27 September 1991, President Bush of the United States announced a drastic set of decisions and proposals for US and Soviet nuclear forces. They encompassed the elimination of the US 'entire worldwide inventory of ground-launched, short-range nuclear weapons'. It resulted in the complete withdrawal of US nuclear weapons from South Korea and the latter's complete denuclearisation.[6] The US decisions and proposals were mainly motivated by the danger in which Soviet tactical nuclear weapons were placed after the failed coup in August 1991 in that country,[7] but might also have been aimed at responding to the North Korean concern as an additional factor.

With the realisation of denuclearised South Korea, and presumably of the denuclearised Korean Peninsula, the North and South proceeded on 20 January 1992 to sign a denuclearisation agreement entitled, 'Joint Declaration on the Denuclearization of the Korean Peninsula'.[8] This Declaration, though only politically binding,[9] went further than the usual nuclear-weapon-free zone treaties. Unlike the latter treaties, the Joint Declaration was not only to prohibit the testing, manufacture, production, receipt, possession, storage, deployment and the use of nuclear weapons, but it was also to proscribe the possession of nuclear reprocessing and uranium enrichment facilities even for peaceful purposes. This Declaration entered into force on 19 February 1992.

At around the same time, Pyongyang moved finally to conclude a safeguards agreement with the IAEA, which was signed on 30 January 1992 and entered into

---

[6] Although the US government did not formally declare that South Korea is now nuclear free because of its 'Neither Confirm Nor Deny (NCND)' policy, South Korean President Roh Tae Woo announced on 18 December 1991 that 'there do not exist any nuclear weapons whatsoever, anywhere in the Republic of Korea'. Mazarr, *op.cit.*, 67–68.

[7] Jack Mendelsohn, 'Bush Announces Unilateral Cuts in Tactical Weapons' Alerts' (1991) 21(8) *Arms Control Today* 21.

[8] For the text of the Joint Declaration, see CD/1147, 25 March 1992, 8–9. While this CD document says that the Joint Declaration was signed on 20 January 1992, there are other materials that say that the Joint Declaration was signed on 31 December 1991. See, e.g., Leon V. Sigal, *Disarming Strangers: Nuclear Diplomacy with North Korea* (1998), 32.

[9] That the Joint Declaration is a political and non-legal document was confirmed by Ambassador Chun Yung-woo, Deputy Permanent Representative of the Republic of Korea to the United Nations, in an interview by the author on the occasion of the UN Conference on Disarmament Issues in Osaka, 21 August 2003. Incidentally, there could be no state-to-state relations between the two Koreas, according to the preamble to the 'Agreement on Reconciliation, Non-aggression and Exchanges and Cooperation between the South and the North', signed on 13 December 1991. CD/1147, 25 March 1992, 2.

334   *Masahiko Asada*

force on 10 April of the same year – nearly five years later than required. As an element leading to these developments, it was important that the United States and the Republic of Korea had repeatedly signaled that they would cancel for that year the US-South Korean military exercises, 'Team Spirit', if the North signed the IAEA agreement or the inter-Korean talks on nuclear issues progressed.[10] 'Team Spirit' exercises had been conducted annually since 1976 and were labelled by the North as a nuclear war rehearsal against it.

2.2 First North Korean Nuclear Crisis (Phase-1): Announcement of Withdrawal from the NPT and Its Suspension in the US-DPRK Joint Statement in 1993

Pursuant to article 62 of the Safeguards Agreement between North Korea and the IAEA, Pyongyang submitted on 4 May 1992 the Initial Report on nuclear material subject to safeguards under the Agreement; and pursuant to article 71, the IAEA began *ad hoc* inspections in May to verify the correctness and completeness of the information contained in the Initial Report. As a result of the inspections, some inconsistencies were revealed in July between the information contained in the Initial Report and the findings of the Agency's inspection activities.

According to the Agency Director General, Hans Blix, the inconsistencies included the following points:

- Nuclear waste which was stored within the compound of the Radio-chemical Laboratory (reprocessing facility) proved to have an isotopic composition indicating that some plutonium should exist which has not been declared;

- Sample analysis of the plutonium which has been declared indicates that there should be some nuclear waste which has not yet been made available for sampling and analysis.[11]

After several exchanges of letters and visits between the IAEA and North Korea, ambiguities still remained. With the North Korean refusal to provide access to the specified additional sites on the ground that they are non-nuclear and military sites, Director General Blix on 9 February 1993 requested North Korea to accept a special inspection in accordance with article 73 of the Safeguards Agreement.[12] On 25 February 1993, after being faced with the North Korean refusal of the request,

---

[10]   In fact, the Korean Central News Agency (KCNA) specifically referred to the South Korea-US decision on the 'Team Spirit' as an important element that led to the North Korean signing of the Safeguards Agreement with the IAEA. UN doc. S/2003/91, 6.

[11]   See 'Statement of Hans Blix, Director General, IAEA, at Informal Briefing of United Nations Security Council regarding the Democratic People's Republic of Korea (DPRK)', New York, 6 April 1993.

[12]   Western intelligence agencies' provision of information to the IAEA about suspected nuclear waste storage sites which North Korea had failed to declare to the Agency also contributed to the Agency Director General to request a special inspection. Dunbar Lockwood and Jon Brook Wolfsthal, 'Nuclear Developments and Proliferation' (1993) *SIPRI Yearbook*, 244.

the Agency's Board of Governors adopted a resolution (GOV/2636), calling upon Pyongyang to respond positively and without delay to the Director General's request.[13] Special inspections are those that may be conducted 'if the Agency considers that information made available by the Democratic People's Republic of Korea ... is not adequate for the Agency to fulfil its responsibilities under [the Safeguards] Agreement'.[14] And they would involve access to information and locations other than those for *ad hoc* and routine inspections.

The DPRK responded to these demands by declaring on 12 March 1993 its decision to withdraw from the NPT. In doing so, it referred to 'a grave situation' created and 'abnormal situation' prevailing in North Korea, specifically citing the resumption of the 'Team Spirit' joint military exercises in 1993 and the IAEA's passing of a resolution aimed at forcing a 'special inspection' of North Korean military installations as well as some of the IAEA officials' lack of 'impartiality and strict neutrality'. Regarding the IAEA officials, Pyongyang claimed that they are biased because they stubbornly insist on a special inspection of North Korean military bases while ignoring the North's demand for an inspection of the US nuclear bases in the South.[15]

According to the NPT, a withdrawal would not take effect immediately but three months after its notification to all other parties to the Treaty as well as to the UN Security Council (art. 10). During this three-month period, the international community would endeavour to have the withdrawing party change its decision.

On 1 April 1993, the IAEA's Board of Governors adopted a resolution (GOV/2645) by a vote of 28 to 2 (China and Libya), with 4 abstentions (India, Pakistan, Syria and Vietnam). In the resolution, the Board found that the DPRK was in non-compliance with its obligations under the Safeguards Agreement and that the IAEA was not able to verify that there had been no diversion of nuclear material to nuclear weapons, and decided to report these findings to the Security Council of the United Nations as required by article 12 C of the IAEA Statute.[16] The Security Council, in turn, adopted a resolution (S/RES/825) on 11 May 1993 with 13 in favour and 2 abstentions (China and Pakistan). It simply called upon the DPRK to 'reconsider' the announced decision to withdraw from the NPT and to honour its non-proliferation obligations under the Treaty and comply with its safeguards agreement with the IAEA.[17]

It was the United States that made the final attempt with moderate success to persuade Pyongyang to change its mind. On 11 June 1993, the eve of the withdrawal taking effect, the United States and North Korea issued a Joint Statement, providing that North Korea 'has decided unilaterally to suspend as long as it considers necessary the effectuation of its withdrawal from the [NPT]'.[18]

---

[13] GOV/2636, 25 February 1993, reproduced in UN docs. A/48/133-S/25556, 12 April 1993, 52–53. This resolution was adopted without a vote.

[14] Article 73 (b) of the Safeguards Agreement.

[15] UN doc. S/25407, 12 March 1993, Annex.

[16] GOV/2645, 1 April 1993, reproduced in INFCIRC/419, 8 April 1993, Annex 1.

[17] SC Res. 825, 11 May 1993.

[18] 'Joint Statement of the Democratic People's Republic of Korea and the United States of America', New York, 11 June 1993.

336   *Masahiko Asada*

However, this represented only partial success, because North Korea did not revoke its withdrawal from the NPT, but simply 'suspend[ed]' its effectuation in the Joint Statement. This is one of the bases on which Pyongyang later began to claim a 'unique status' under the NPT, meaning, according to the North, that it is no longer obliged to allow the inspectors to carry out their work under the Safeguards Agreement and that it would accept inspections only to those facilities it chooses.[19] Moreover, the Joint Statement did not address, let alone resolve, the questions of verification inconsistencies and of special inspections that had led to the first nuclear crisis on the Korean Peninsula. In that sense, there remained causes which might again precipitate the North Korean nuclear issue into a major crisis.

2.3 First North Korean Nuclear Crisis (Phase-2): De-fuelling of the Reactor and the Agreed Framework in 1994

As feared, notwithstanding the calls of the IAEA and the international community for the North Korean acceptance of comprehensive safeguards as required under its Safeguards Agreement,[20] Pyongyang restricted IAEA inspectors in their verification activities. It declared that the acceptance of inspection was not based on its Safeguards Agreement but rather on its 'unique status' under the NPT. In order to break the stalemate, the IAEA adopted a resolution (GOV/2711) on 21 March 1994 to re-submit the North Korean nuclear issue to the UN Security Council, by a vote of 25 to 1 (Libya), with 5 abstentions (Brazil, China, India, Indonesia, and Lebanon).[21] It is worth noting that China abstained this time, unlike the previous resolution submitting the issue to the Security Council in April 1993, when it had voted against it.

Despite such an international pressure, Pyongyang in May 1994, announced and actually moved to begin de-fuelling the 5 megawatts (MW) graphite-moderated research reactor, the only graphite reactor in operation at Yongbyon, without having IAEA inspectors present.[22] The United States and the IAEA had insisted that inspectors should be present for such an action, because spent fuel could potentially be reprocessed for use in nuclear weapons. Some time in June, North Korea appears to have completed the removal of 8000 rods of spent fuel

---

[19]   IAEA, 'Fact Sheet on DPRK Nuclear Safeguards', Media Advisory 2002/52, 16 December 2002.

[20]   For instance, the General Assembly adopted by an overwhelming majority a resolution urging the DPRK to cooperate with the IAEA in the full implementation of the safeguards agreement. GA Res. 48/14, 1 November 1993. It was adopted by a vote of 140 to 1 (DPRK), with 9 abstentions.

[21]   GOV/2711, 21 March 1994. This time, the Security Council responded to the IAEA submission not by adopting a resolution but by making a Presidential Statement. S/PRST/1994/13, 31 March 1994.

[22]   According to Professor Leon Sigal, this move of Pyongyang was a provocative way to draw world attention to its nuclear potential and away from its nuclear past. Sigal, *op.cit.*, 113.

(containing plutonium enough for producing 5 to 6 atomic bombs) from the research reactor without the IAEA presence and, even worse, placed them in cooling ponds in such a way that the IAEA could not verify the history of the past North Korean reprocessing activities. In a letter of 2 June to the Security Council, Director General Blix asserted that as a result of the de-fuelling of the reactor in the way North Korea did it, the IAEA's opportunity to segregate and secure fuel rods for later measurements had been lost and accordingly 'the Agency's ability to ascertain, with sufficient confidence, whether nuclear material from the reactor had been diverted in the past has also been lost'.[23]

Against this background, it was natural that the international community moved toward sanctions against North Korea, which had been alluded to for some time and against which Pyongyang had warned by saying that '[s]anctions mean war, and there is no mercy in war'.[24]

It was the IAEA that applied the first institutional sanctions against Pyongyang. On 10 June 1994, it decided to suspend non-medical technical assistance to the DPRK.[25] North Korea responded to this decision three days later by announcing its withdrawal from the Agency.[26] This did not mean that North Korea was released from obligations under the Safeguards Agreement, because the application of IAEA safeguards in a state or region is not conditioned by its membership in the IAEA.[27] It simply means that it does not participate in IAEA activities as a member state.

Many observers expected that the next step would be UN sanctions sponsored by the Security Council. Since China abstained from voting on the IAEA sanction against North Korea rather than voting against it, it was expected that it might do the same in the Security Council, too.

What helped overcome this crisis and prevented a drift toward an eventual 'war' was a visit by former US President Jimmy Carter to Pyongyang from 15–16 June 1994. He met with North Korean leader Kim Il Sung and struck a deal, which was later to be codified as the Agreed Framework. With the confirmation of the content of the deal by Ambassador-at-Large Robert Gallucci, the drive for sanctions was suspended.

After some delay due to the sudden death of Kim Il Sung on 8 July, 'the Agreed Framework between the United States of America and the Democratic People's Republic of Korea' was signed on 21 October 1994 in Geneva as a non-legal, political document.[28] The heart of the Agreed Framework lies in a deal under

23 UN doc. S/1994/656, 2 June 1994, Annex, 3.
24 Mazzar, *op.cit.*, 160.
25 (1994) 36(3) *IAEA Bulletin*, 58. The sanctions were decided upon by a vote of 28 to 1 (Libya) with 4 abstentions (including China).
26 INFCIRC/447, 21 June 1994.
27 For instance, Taiwan has accepted IAEA safeguards though it is not a member of the IAEA.
28 According to the State Department, it deliberately chose the word 'decided', instead of 'agreed', as the language introducing the operative clauses in order to show that the document is non-legally binding. Unites States General Accounting Office, *Nuclear Nonproliferation: Implications of the U.S./North Korean Agreement on Nuclear Issues* (Letter Report, 10/01/96, GAO/RCED/NSIAD-97–8), Letter 3 and Appendix III.

which North Korea will freeze its nuclear programme by first freezing and eventually dismantling its three graphite-moderated reactors – with a generating capacity of 5 MW, 50 MW and 200 MW, the former two located in Yonbyon and the latter in Taechon, and the latter two being under construction at that time – and two related facilities (the reprocessing facility and the fuel fabrication plant);[29] in return, the United States will make arrangements for the provision to the DPRK of a light-water reactor (LWR) project with a total generating capacity of approximately 2,000 megawatts. The target date of 2003 was set for the completion of the LWR project. The United States also committed itself to provide 500,000 tons of heavy oil annually to cover the energy shortage to be caused by the freeze of the graphite reactors.[30] To finance and construct the above project an international consortium of states, called the Korean Peninsula Energy Development Organization (KEDO), was established in March 1995 by an Agreement on the Establishment of the KEDO (hereinafter cited as the 'KEDO Agreement') among the United States, South Korea and Japan.

Regarding the North Korean status under the NPT, the Agreed Framework stated that the 'DPRK will remain a party to the Treaty ... and will allow implementation of its safeguards agreement under the Treaty'. But it only required North Korea to 'come into full compliance with its safeguards agreement', including taking all steps that may be deemed necessary by the IAEA, '[w]hen a significant portion of the LWR project is completed, but before delivery of key nuclear components'.

2.4 Second North Korean Nuclear Crisis: Announcement of Withdrawal from the NPT in 2003

Although the KEDO and the DPRK successfully concluded an Agreement on Supply of a Light-Water Reactor Project to the DPRK (hereinafter cited as the 'Supply Agreement') on 15 December 1995, the project suffered delays for a number of reasons. But since the start of the construction phase in February 2000, the project had been on schedule.[31] With the delivery of 'key nuclear components'[32] in prospect, the IAEA started to urge North Korea to extend its full cooperation with the Agency. On 18 September 2000, for instance, on the occasion of the

---

[29] What 'related facilities' specifically mean is not provided for in the Agreed Framework itself but is said to be spelt out in the Confidential Minutes signed by both sides at the same time as the Agreed Framework was signed.

[30] It is said that 500,000 tons of heavy oil roughly corresponds to the three reactors to be frozen in terms of electricity generated.

[31] IAEA, 'Fact Sheet on DPRK Nuclear Safeguards', Media Advisory 2002/52.

[32] What constitutes the 'key nuclear components' is not provided for in the Agreed Framework itself but is said to be spelt out in the Confidential Minutes signed by both sides of the Agreed Framework, and is later incorporated in the Supply Agreement (Annex 3, para. 4). According to it, 'key nuclear components' are the components controlled under the Export Trigger List of the Nuclear Suppliers Group.

forty-fourth Session of the IAEA General Conference, Director General Mohamed ElBaradei stated that since the entire verification process in North Korea may take between three and four years, '[w]e therefore need to start our work now'.[33]

While North Korea had not positively responded to such a call, a policy change had come to be expected soon on the part of the other party to the Agreed Framework with the victory of George W. Bush in the US Presidential election in November 2000. As expected, President Bush reviewed the US policy toward North Korea, and announced the result of the review on 6 June 2001 by saying that the United States would pursue an 'improved implementation of the Agreed Framework relating to North Korea's nuclear activities',[34] an implicit call for North Korea's early acceptance of special inspections.

At the same time, the Bush administration started to advocate a new national security strategy. On 1 June 2002 at West Point and on 19 July at Fort Drum, New York, President Bush suggested that preemptive action would be necessary to combat those with weapons of mass destruction.[35] Earlier in his State of the Union speech on 29 January of the same year, the President had mentioned North Korea as 'a regime arming with missiles and weapons of mass destruction' and as part of the 'axis of evil'.[36]

Against this backdrop, the North agreed to resume the suspended talks with the United States when Foreign Minister Paek Nam Sun met with Secretary of State Colin Powell on the sidelines of the foreign ministerial meeting of the ASEAN Regional Forum (ARF) in Brunei on 31 July 2002. After a discussion with South Korea regarding the specifics of the proposed trips to North Korea, Assistant Secretary of State for East Asian and Pacific Affairs James Kelly was sent to Pyongyang from 3 to 5 October.

On 16 October 2002, Assistant Secretary Kelly disclosed the North Korean confession that it was pursuing a programme to build nuclear weapons using enriched uranium. More precisely speaking, according to State Department's Spokesman Richard Boucher, when Assistant Secretary Kelly and his delegation advised the North Koreans that 'we had recently acquired information that indicates that North Korea has a program to enrich uranium for nuclear weapons', North Korean officials 'acknowledged that they have such a program'.[37]

---

33   IAEA, 'Statement to the Forty-fourth Regular Session of the IAEA General Conference 2000 by IAEA Director General Dr. Mohamed ElBaradei', 18 September 2000. For its part, North Korea maintained that 'three to four months would be enough for inspections'. *Asahi Shinbun*, 21 August 2002.

34   Office of the Press Secretary, White House, 'Statement by the President', 6 June 2001.

35   The idea was later elaborated in the *National Strategy to Combat Weapons of Mass Destruction* in December 2002. It says that: 'Because deterrence may not succeed, and because of the potentially devastating consequences of WMD use against our forces and civilian population, US military forces and appropriate civilian agencies must have the capability to defend against WMD-armed adversaries, including in appropriate cases through *preemptive measures*' (emphasis added). *Ibid.*, 3.

36   White House, 'President Delivers State of the Union Address', 29 January 2002.

37   US State Department, 'Press Statement by Richard Boucher, Spokesman: North Korean Nuclear Program', 16 October 2002.

In response to this revelation, not only the United States but also South Korea and Japan denounced it as a 'violation' of relevant agreements to which North Korea is a party.[38] In the light of the violations, the KEDO Executive Board decided on 14 November 2002 to suspend heavy oil deliveries to North Korea as of the December shipment.[39] Moreover, the IAEA's Board of Governors adopted a resolution (GOV/2002/60) on 29 November without a vote, which recognised that the programme to enrich uranium for nuclear weapons or any other covert nuclear activities would constitute a violation of the DPRK's international commitments, including its Safeguards Agreement with the IAEA, and urged Pyongyang to 'give up any nuclear weapons programme'.[40]

At least officially, however, the DPRK has not confirmed its reported acknowl-edgement. Instead, it issued a press release saying that: '[p]roviding no concrete evidence, the US special envoy asserted that we were violating the DPRK-US Agreed Framework by engaging in a programme to enrich uranium with a view to manufacturing nuclear weapons', and that '[w]e clearly told the US presidential special envoy that we are entitled to have nuclear weapons and more powerful weapons'.[41] The DPRK also responded to the above moves by sending two letters to the IAEA's Director General in December:[42] one expressing disappointment about the Agency's unilateral and unfair approach; and the other conveying its decision to lift the freeze of its nuclear facilities as of 13 December in the light of the US suspension of the heavy oil supply pursuant to the Agreed Framework. As a first step to proceed as announced, Pyongyang started to cut the seals and disable surveillance cameras on 22 December, and then ordered the IAEA inspectors on 27 December to leave the country (they in fact left North Korea on 31 December 2002).

In the light of these developments, the IAEA's Board of Governors adopted a further resolution (GOV/2003/3) on 6 January 2003 by consensus, deploring 'in the strongest terms' the DPRK's unilateral acts to remove and impede the functioning of containment and surveillance equipment at its nuclear facilities, and calling for its urgent and full cooperation with the Agency.[43] But it stopped short of submit-ting the issue to the UN Security Council.

---

[38]   See, e.g., 'Joint US-Japan-ROK Trilateral Statement', Los Cabos, Mexico, 26 October 2002.

[39]   KEDO, 'KEDO Executive Board Meeting Concludes', 14 November 2002.

[40]   GOV/2002/60, 29 November 2002.

[41]   'North Korean Spokesman Issues Press Statement on Nuclear Issue', *BBC Worldwide Monitoring*, 25 October 2002. See also Kenneth Boutin, 'North Korean Crisis: Fallout for Verification' (Jan–Feb 2003) 106 *Trust & Verify* 1.

[42]   One letter was received on 4 December from the DPRK's Foreign Minister, Paek Nam Sun, and the other on 12 December from the Director General of the General Department of Atomic Energy of the DPRK, Ri Je Son. IAEA, 'Fact Sheet on DPRK Nuclear Safeguards'. Media Advisory 2002/52.

[43]   GOV/2003/3, 6 January 2003.

North Korea responded on 10 January, declaring the resolution 'unjust'. At the same time, it announced that it was withdrawing from the NPT. In a letter of 10 January 2003, to the President of the Security Council, the DPRK informed the latter that it decided to revoke the 'suspension' on the effectuation of its withdrawal from the NPT and accordingly 'the DPRK's withdrawal from the NPT will be effectuated fully from 11 January 2003'. The 'Statement of the Government of the Democratic People's Republic of Korea' (hereinafter cited as the 'Statement of the DPRK Government'),[44] which was issued on the same day and a copy of which was enclosed with the DPRK's letter to the President of the Security Council, explained the background and reasons behind the decision. It was also made clear in the Statement that 'the DPRK withdrawing from the NPT is totally free from the binding force of the safeguards accord with the IAEA under its article 3 [providing for cooperation between the DPRK and the IAEA]'.[45] Pyongyang further announced later in January that it would reactivate the reactors to secure electricity supply that had been lacking due to the stop of heavy oil delivery from the KEDO.[46]

Faced with these announcements, the IAEA Board of Governors finally decided in its resolution of 12 February 2003 to report to the UN Security Council the DPRK's non-compliance and the Agency's inability to verify non-diversion of nuclear material.[47] The resolution was adopted by an overwhelming majority with no objection with only Russia and Cuba abstaining.[48] The Security Council has not acted on this IAEA submission yet in the form of a resolution or a Presidential Statement at the time of writing.

In the meantime, according to the Korean Central News Agency (KCNA), a Spokesman of the North Korean Foreign Ministry told the KCNA on 5 February 2003 that the DPRK restarted and normalized the operation of its nuclear facility to generate electricity. On 26 February 2003, the US government ascertained the restart of the 5 MW graphite reactor in Yongbyon that had been frozen under the Agreed Framework.[49]

---

[44] 'Statement of the Government of the Democratic People's Republic of Korea dated 10 January 2003', in UN doc. S/2003/91, 3–4.

[45] This part of the 'Statement of the DPRK Government' is slightly different between its Korean Central News Agency version ('Statement of DPRK Government on its withdrawal from NPT', *Korean News*, 11 January 2003) and that of the Security Council document (UN doc. S/2003/91, 3–4). The former is adopted in the text because it is more logical.

[46] *Asahi Shinbun*, 12 January 2003.

[47] IAEA, 'IAEA Board of Governors Adopts Resolution on Safeguards in North Korea', Media Advisory 2003/48, 12 February 2003.

[48] *Yomiuri Shinbun*, 13 February 2003.

[49] *Asahi Shinbun*, 5 February 2003; *Yomiuri Shinbun* (evening edition), 27 February 2003.

342 *Masahiko Asada*

3 NORTH KOREAN STATUS UNDER THE NPT

3.1 The Withdrawal Clause of the NPT and Four Possible Interpretations of North Korea's Status under the NPT

With the above facts established, we now consider the status of North Korea under the NPT. Perhaps, the following three facts are most relevant here:

(1)   North Korea announced its decision to withdraw from the NPT on 12 March 1993 (first announcement);

(2)   It suspended the announced withdrawal from the NPT in the US–DPRK Joint Statement on 11 June 1993, one day prior to its effectuation; and

(3)   It informed the Security Council on 10 January 2003 that it revoked the suspension of the effectuation of the withdrawal (second announcement).

The withdrawal clause of the NPT, article 10, paragraph 1, stipulates as follows:

Each Party shall in exercising its national sovereignty have the right to withdraw from the Treaty if it decides that extraordinary events, related to the subject matter of this Treaty, have jeopardized the supreme interests of its country. It shall give notice of such withdrawal to all other Parties to the Treaty and to the United Nations Security Council three months in advance. Such notice shall include a statement of the extraordinary events it regards as having jeopardized its supreme interests.

Thus, we can identify three procedural requirements that a state party must satisfy before withdrawing from the NPT: (1) a statement of extraordinary events that have jeopardised its supreme interests must be included in its notice of withdrawal; (2) the notice must be given to all other Parties to the Treaty and the UN Security Council; and (3) a period of three months must elapse before the noticed withdrawal takes effect.

Based on the relevant facts and in the light of the above provisions of the NPT, one can think of at least the following four interpretations on the North Korean status under the NPT:

(a)   North Korea withdrew from the NPT as of 12 June 1993 (three months after the first announcement);

(b)   It withdrew from the NPT as of 11 January 2003 (one day after the second announcement);

(c)   It withdrew from the NPT as of 10 April 2003 (three months after the second announcement); and

(d)   North Korea still remains party to the NPT.

3.2 North Korean Argument and the IAEA's Response

North Korea itself interprets the situation as follows: since it decided to 'unilaterally suspend' its 12 March 1993 notice of withdrawal 'as long as it considers necessary' in the US-DPRK Joint Statement on 11 June 1993, one day before its effectuation, and since its 10 January 2003 announcement revoked that 'suspension', the withdrawal fully took effect on the following day of the 2003 announcement, i.e., on 11 January 2003 (interpretation (b)).[50]

The reason for lifting the moratorium in 2003 was explained in the 'Statement of the DPRK Government'. It said that 'now that the United States has unilaterally abandoned its commitments to stop nuclear threats and renounce hostility towards the DPRK in line with the [11 June 1993] statement', it declared an 'automatic and immediate effectuation of its withdrawal from the NPT'.[51] Here Pyongyang was referring to the fact that in the US-DPRK Joint Statement of June 1993 both sides agreed, among other things, to the principle of 'assurances against the threat and use of force, including nuclear weapons'.[52] Thus, an attempt was made to establish a connection between the June 1993 Joint Statement (on the suspension of the withdrawal) and the January 2003 announcement (on the lifting of the suspension). Such an explanation was also made by the North Korean Permanent Representative to the United Nations, Pak Gil Yon, at the press conference on 10 January 2003.[53]

The IAEA challenged such explanations by the DPRK and argued that 'the NPT contains no provision for the "suspension" of a notice of withdrawal from the NPT'. It then made reference to the fact that 'Article 68 of the Vienna Convention on the Law of Treaties provides only for the revocation of an instrument or notification of withdrawal from a treaty', and maintained that '[t]hus, it may be concluded that the 11 June 1993 "moratorium on the effectuation of its withdrawal from the NPT" by the DPRK should be treated as a revocation of its notice of withdrawal'.[54] The IAEA argument stopped short of indicating whether North Korea

---

[50] See 'Letter dated 10 January 2003 from the Minister for Foreign Affairs of the Democratic People's Republic of Korea addressed to the President of the Security Council', in UN doc. S/2003/91, 2.

[51] 'Statement of the Government of the Democratic People's Republic of Korea dated 10 January 2003' in *ibid.*, 4.

[52] 'Joint Statement of the Democratic People's Republic of Korea and the United States of America', New York, 11 June 1993.

[53] United Nations, 'Press Briefing: Press Conference by Democratic People's Republic of Korea', 10 January 2003.

[54] GOV/2003/4, 22 January 2003, para. 7. Due note should be taken of the fact that the IAEA's interpretation on the North Korean status under the NPT is contained in the 'Report by the Director General [of the IAEA]'. It was not formally approved by any organs of the IAEA and, as such, does not necessarily represent the views of its member States or Board of Governors. The Board simply said in its resolution of 12 February 2003, that it has 'considered the report of the Director General (GOV/2003/4)'. Nonetheless, it could be assumed from the same resolution that the Board members overwhelmingly agreed to the conclusion that the North Korean argument of immediate withdrawal was not acceptable, because it confirms that the Agency's Safeguards Agreement with the DPRK pursuant to the NPT 'remains binding and in force'.

344   *Masahiko Asada*

would leave the NPT three months after the second announcement. This argument of the IAEA[55] would raise a couple of questions relating, respectively, to the acquiescence of the other parties and to the intent of the announcing party.

First, it is true that there is no system of suspension of withdrawal provided for in the NPT. However, it may be permissible, generally speaking, to agree among the parties to a treaty, explicitly or tacitly, on a special treatment of a special case of political importance even in the absence of specific provisions in the treaty to that effect, unless that would run counter to the object and purpose of the treaty or its relevant provisions.

Perhaps, what comes to one's mind as an example of such deviation from treaty provisions would be the case of the Syrian readmission to the United Nations that was effected in a way variant from UN Charter provisions. When Syria, after having established the United Arab Republic (UAR) with Egypt in 1958, decided to become an independent state again in 1961, the UAR (Egypt) kept its seat at the United Nations, leaving the question of the readmission of Syria. In that case, the readmission, which should have occurred in accordance with the Charter procedure for admission, took place through a simplified procedure, with no intervention of the Security Council and no formal decision of the General Assembly. What happened was that the President of the General Assembly simply asked whether there were any objections to restoring the seat of the country, and after taking note of the unanimous approval, he invited Syria to take its seat again. What enabled this to happen was the 'ability of acquiescence of States to remedy even the most obvious illegal acts of the organs' as Professor Conforti points out.[56]

Likewise, it could be said that what happened in 1993 regarding the North Korean suspension of withdrawal from the NPT was the acquiescence of the other parties to the North Korean argument of unilateral suspension of withdrawal in that particular case. Of course, there are objections to the North Korean argument at present, but there were apparently no such objections at the time of the announcement of suspension, for the obvious reason that an objection virtually meant the support for the withdrawal. Indeed the President of the Security Council even issued a consensus statement, which 'welcome[d] the joint statement of the DPRK and the United States of 11 June 1993, which included the DPRK's decision to *suspend* the effectuation of its withdrawal from the [NPT]'.[57]

Such recourse to the doctrine of acquiescence should not be sustained if the result would run counter to the object and purpose of the NPT or its relevant provisions. But that does not seem to have been the case. On the contrary, it would have been in nobody's interest to refuse the DPRK's statement on the suspension of withdrawal, because the refusal would have meant that a Party to the NPT suspected of developing nuclear weapons was leaving the Treaty. As such, the

[55]   Sweden put forward a similar argument by saying that the States Parties to the NPT do not recognise that it should be possible to 'save' a portion of the 90-day withdrawal period from one occasion to another, and accordingly North Korea is still a party to the NPT. CD/PV.918, 30 January 2003, 30. See also note 96 below.

[56]   Benedetto Conforti, *The Law and Practice of the United Nations* (2000), 38, 45.

[57]   S/PRST/1994/13, 31 March 1994. Emphasis added.

acquiescence in 1993 (the North Korean case) arguably takes on more legitimacy than the one in 1961 (the Syrian case). It has been said that the withdrawal clause of the NPT was formulated so that parties to the Treaty could not withdraw from it easily and quickly.[58] Thus, suspending the effectuation of withdrawal would not contradict the object and purpose of that clause, either.

Perhaps, it may even be argued that the other Parties to the NPT, or more precisely those who were Parties at that time, would now be estopped by their acquiescence[59] in 1993 from objecting to the North Korean argument of 'immediate effectuation' of its withdrawal in 2003.

The second point that could be raised regarding the IAEA refutation of the North Korean logic is related to the IAEA argument that the DPRK's 'suspension' of withdrawal should be treated as its 'revocation'. As a unilateral declaration, the meaning of the North Korean announcement should be interpreted according to its terms and the intent of its author as well as the circumstances of its making,[60] none of which seems to support the IAEA argument.[61]

Moreover, the IAEA might previously have accepted the North Korean argument for the suspension of withdrawal, albeit reluctantly. According to Professor Sigal, '[t]he IAEA preferred to have North Korea abandon the Nonproliferation Treaty altogether than remain partially in and partially out'.[62] This was his analysis of a statement made by Mr. Pellaud, the IAEA's Deputy Director General, who had reportedly said in July 1994 that the DPRK's departure from the Treaty would at least clarify its non-compliance status. Thus, the IAEA seems to have seen the DPRK's status under the NPT as somewhat half in and half out as a result of its suspension of withdrawal from the Treaty.

In contrast with this, North Korea seems to have had every reason to believe that it had been given a 'unique status' under the NPT.[63] Although the decision of suspension itself was made 'unilaterally' by North Korea, that decision was included in a 'Joint Statement' with the United States, implying the latter's tacit endorsement of the decision in general terms. The Presidential Statement from the Security Council mentioned above also seems to have endorsed the suspension by welcoming the Joint Statement. The Agreed Framework subsequently signed between North Korea and the United States provided a further basis leading Pyongyang to believe that it was in a unique position *vis-à-vis* the NPT, because it

---

[58] See 3.3 below.

[59] For the relationship between estoppel and acquiescence, see D.W. Bowett, 'Estoppel before International Tribunals and its Relation to Acquiescence' (1957) 33 *BYBIL* 197; I.C. MacGibbon, 'The Scope of Acquiescence in International Law' (1954) 31 *BYBIL* 147.

[60] Regarding the interpretation of a unilateral declaration in general, see Gerald Fitzmaurice, *The Law and Procedure of the International Court of Justice* (vol. I, 1986), 363–6.

[61] A similar argument for revocation might have been more tenable if it had been based on paragraph IV.1 of the Agreed Framework, because it states that 'The DPRK will remain a party to the [NPT]'. But here too, Pyongyang's intention was clearly not to that effect.

[62] Sigal, *op.cit.*, 97.

[63] See CD/PV.918, 31 (DPRK).

346 *Masahiko Asada*

granted the DPRK a moratorium on the full implementation of its Safeguards Agreement with the IAEA as noted earlier.

3.3 Other Possible Interpretations

Despite all that has been said, a hard fact remains that the North Korean arguments have not been supported by other states, at least openly. With this fact taken as given, one can think of two other possible interpretations of the North Korean declaration of 'suspension' of its withdrawal from the NPT.

One would be that since there is no system of suspension of withdrawal provided for in the NPT, an announcement to that effect would have no legal effect at all. One logical consequence of this interpretation should be that Pyongyang withdrew from the NPT on 12 June 1993 (interpretation (a) above). For if the announced suspension had no legal effect, then the withdrawal notice of 12 March 1993 must have taken effect three months later in accordance with the NPT.

However, this does not conform with subsequent events: Pyongyang's membership in the NPT was confirmed by various international documents and state practices after that date. For instance, the 1994 Agreed Framework expressly provided that '[t]he DPRK will remain a party to the [NPT]'. The North Korean membership in the NPT was further confirmed on the occasion of the NPT Review and Extension Conference in 1995. Pyongyang sent its delegation to that Conference and there was no objection raised regarding its participation. To the contrary, the DPRK was listed in the Final Report of the Credentials Committee to the Conference as one of the participating 'States parties'.[64] Thus, interpretation (a) is not supported by any state, including North Korea itself, although it is logically possible.

The other possible interpretation of the North Korean 'suspension' of withdrawal is the one put forward by the IAEA: namely, that the North Korean decision of 'suspension' of its withdrawal from the NPT should be treated as that of 'revocation' of the withdrawal – an interpretation not really persuasive as discussed above. But if one takes the IAEA interpretation as given, there are still two further possible interpretations as to the North Korean status under the NPT, depending on how one interprets and treats the January 2003 declaration of North Korea lifting the moratorium on the effectuation of its withdrawal from the NPT.

One possible interpretation would be to treat the 2003 declaration as a *new* notice of the North Korean withdrawal from the NPT. In this case, it would follow that Pyongyang withdrew from the NPT as of 10 April 2003, three months after the new announcement of withdrawal (interpretation (c) above). The other possible interpretation would be that despite the renewed announcement, North Korea still remains a party to the NPT even after 10 April 2003, because the new announcement did not meet all the requirements for a valid notice of withdrawal under the

---

[64] NPT/CONF.1995/CC/1, 10 May 1995, in NPT/CONF.1995/32 (Part II), New York, 1995, 413–15.

NPT (interpretation (d) above). There could be several arguments in support of this last interpretation and some of them have in fact been put forward by some states, including Japan and the United Kingdom.[65]

Recalling the withdrawal clause of the NPT, it provides for two major requirements to be satisfied by the withdrawing party in addition to the timeline of three months. They are: a statement of the extraordinary events the withdrawing party regards as having jeopardized its supreme interests and the notification of the intended withdrawal to all other parties to the Treaty and the UN Security Council. Both of these requirements could possibly be considered as not being fulfilled by the North Korean announcement of January 2003.

First, the 2003 announcement was, according to North Korea, purported to lift the moratorium it had placed in June 1993 regarding its withdrawal from the NPT. As the North Korean did not intend to make a *fresh* declaration of withdrawal in 2003, it may not necessarily contain 'a statement of the extraordinary events' that was *currently* existing at the time of the 2003 declaration of withdrawal. Thus, Japan has reportedly cast doubt about North Korean satisfaction of this aspect of the withdrawal procedure by maintaining that there is no statement of extraordinary events that North Korea regards as having jeopardised its supreme interests in its 2003 notice to Japan.[66]

Second, in terms of the procedure of giving notice to 'all other Parties to the Treaty' and to the UN Security Council, several states have reportedly raised that point.[67] According to them, the North Korean announcement of withdrawal in 2003 did not reach 'all other Parties to the Treaty'. In fact, Romania has sometimes been mentioned as one of those Parties to the NPT that have not received the North Korean notice in 2003.

If one attaches great importance to one or both of these aspects of the withdrawal procedure, it would logically follow that the North Korean notice of 2003 did not meet the requirements under the withdrawal clause and could never result in the DPRK's departure from the NPT.

However, there could be a counter-argument to such a strict application of the withdrawal clause. Under article 10 of the NPT, each Party has the 'right to withdraw' from the Treaty in exercising its 'national sovereignty'. In that sense, the fact that some of the other parties to the Treaty did not receive the notice of withdrawal or that 'the extraordinary events' were not fully spelled out in the notice, should not be treated as something that would completely invalidate a party's notice of withdrawal. China reportedly stands along this line, stating that 'withdrawal [from the Treaty] is a matter of national sovereignty'.[68] As Professor Frederic Kirgis argues in the context of the three-month notice requirement, '[n]oncompliance with the notice requirement does not necessarily mean that the

---

[65] For Japan, see below; for the United Kingdom, letter from Simon N. Brown, Political Section, British Embassy in Tokyo, 7 May 2003.

[66] *Yomiuri Shinbun*, 11 April 2003.

[67] *Yomiuri Shinbun* (evening edition), 26 April 2003.

[68] *Ibid.*

withdrawal from the NPT is invalid'.[69] In other words, the notice requirements should not be treated as conditions to be met for a withdrawal notice to be valid, but rather as procedural obligations a violation of which would only give rise to some form of reparation, though in theory.[70]

This is not to say that procedural requirements are all immaterial and can be dismissed; in fact some of them are really critical. Whether a particular procedural requirement is critical or not is perhaps dependent on its purposes. It seems that one of the purposes of requiring the withdrawing party to notify the withdrawal 'to all other Parties to the Treaty' is to inform the latter of that important decision and to give them the opportunities to persuade the withdrawing party to reconsider the decision.[71] If so, the fact that a handful of parties to the Treaty have not received the notice should not be regarded as fatal. It could also be considered as remedied by the North Korean notice to the Security Council and the latter's circulation of it to other UN member states.[72] As the International Court of Justice held in the Case concerning Application of the Genocide Convention, a procedural defect that could easily be remedied 'matters little'.[73]

There is arguably a parallel procedural requirement provided for in article 51 of the UN Charter regarding the right of self-defence. And the requirement to report to the Security Council the measures taken in the exercise of the right of self-defence is usually not respected by states exercising that right.[74] Would an act of self-defence cease to be as such if the measures taken were not reported to the Security Council as required by article 51 of the Charter? Or is it just a matter of procedural non-compliance of the obligation that would not deprive the act of the nature of self-defence? Similar arguments based on the principle of *de minimis non curat praetor* or *de minimis non curat lex* seem to apply here, too.

In addition, the argument that failure to notice all other parties to the Treaty would invalidate the notice itself might be seen as somewhat opportunistic and arbitrary in the particular context of North Korea. In fact, the same argument of procedural nature could have been put forward when Pyongyang declared its intention to withdraw from the NPT for the first time in 1993. For it was reported that not all members of the NPT had been notified at that time.[75] But no states appear

---

[69] Frederic L. Kirgis, 'North Korea's Withdrawal from the Nuclear Nonproliferation Treaty', *ASIL Insights*, January 2003.

[70] *Ibid*.

[71] For the drafting history of article 10 of the NPT with comments, see Mohamed I. Shaker, *The Nuclear Non-Proliferation Treaty: Origin and Implementation 1959–1979* (vol. II, 1980), 883–99.

[72] See UN doc. S/2003/91.

[73] *Case concerning Application of the Convention on the Prevention and Punishment of the Crime of Genocide (Preliminary Objections)*, ICJ Rep. 1996, 612, para.24. See also *Appeal relating to the Jurisdiction of the ICAO Council*, ICJ Rep. 1972, 69–70, para.45.

[74] As Professor Jean Combacau points out, the obligation to report the measures taken to the Security Council is rarely complied with. Jean Combacau, 'The Exception of Self-Defence in UN Practice', in A. Cassese (ed.), *The Current Legal Regulation of the Use of Force* (1986), 14–16.

[75] Lockwood and Wolfsthal, *op.cit.*, 245.

to have raised the point as far as the author is aware. And this assumption seems most plausible in the light of the US-DPRK Joint Statement of June 1993, in which North Korea decided to suspend the effectuation of its withdrawal from the NPT. If some parties to the Treaty had raised a point of procedural anomaly that could invalidate the North Korean withdrawal notice, and if that was taken as a legitimate argument, then that itself must have been seen as enough to retain the DPRK in the NPT regime and have made it unnecessary to prescribe on the 'suspension' of the withdrawal in the Joint Statement. Thus, the fact that the North Korean suspension of withdrawal was included in the Joint Statement implies that its earlier notice of withdrawal was considered as valid despite the fact that not all had been duly notified.

With regard to the requirement to include 'a statement of the extraordinary events' in the withdrawal notice, the purpose and significance of such a statement was explained during the drafting of the NPT that since withdrawal would be a step of vital importance, other parties would have a strong and legitimate interest in knowing why such action was being taken.[76]

There are two points to be mentioned in this regard. One is that although the North Korean letter to the President of the Security Council dated 10 January 2003 itself did not necessarily spell out the events that led to the decision to announce its withdrawal from the NPT, the 'Statement of the DPRK Government,' a copy of which was enclosed with the letter, explained in detail not only the logic of 'automatic and immediate effectuation' of the withdrawal but also the situation that led to the decision. It began by saying that: '[a] dangerous situation where our nation's sovereignty and our State's security are being seriously violated is prevailing on the Korean peninsula due to the vicious, hostile policy of the United States of America towards the Democratic People's Republic of Korea'. It specifically referred to the alleged fact that the IAEA termed North Korea 'a criminal' in its resolutions as well as the fact that the United States listed the DPRK as part of an 'axis of evil' and, according to Pyongyang, singled it out as a target of pre-emptive nuclear attack.[77]

The second and more important point is that the ultimate authority to determine whether there exists 'extraordinary events' that would justify the withdrawal of a party from the NPT lies with the withdrawing party itself, though customary international law arguably imposes a good faith requirement on that party. This interpretation of the NPT withdrawal clause seems to have received unanimous agreement among writers.[78]

Of course, it is legally tenable and politically possible that the Security Council would respond to the withdrawal notice by adopting a resolution deciding to nullify it under chapter VII of the UN Charter. But one could at least point out that it would not be usual for the Security Council to exercise its power to negate the legal

[76] Shaker, *op.cit.*, 897.
[77] UN doc. S/2003/91, 3–4.
[78] See, e.g., Nicolas Sims, 'Withdrawal Clauses in Disarmament Treaties: A Questionable Logic?' (Dec. 1999) 42 *Disarmament Diplomacy* 16; Kirgis, *op.cit.*; Shaker, *op.cit.*, 898.

effect of a withdrawal announcement on the ground that the stated reasons are not sufficient to justify the withdrawal.

In this connection, it is worth mentioning that the three depositary governments of the NPT – the US, UK and Russia – issued a statement on 1 April 1993 regarding the North Korean announcement of withdrawal in that year. It said that: 'We question whether the DPRK's stated reasons for withdrawing from the Treaty constitute extraordinary events relating to the subject-matter of the Treaty'.[79] It must be pointed out, however, that contrary to the possible impression that this statement may convey, the depositary governments are not legally entitled to question the withdrawing party's reasons for withdrawal, simply because that is not provided for in the NPT.[80] Thus, it could ultimately and daringly be said that if the withdrawing party considers something to be an 'extraordinary event,' so it actually is in legal terms, barring an exceptional case of Security Council intervention.

In summing up, if one thinks that the questions raised regarding the procedural requirements under article 10 would not prevent North Korea from withdrawing from the NPT, the DPRK would have actually withdrawn from the Treaty on 10 April 2003. But if not, it would follow that Pyongyang still remains a party to the NPT. Clearly, the former interpretation is more persuasive than the latter as shown above.

4 NORTH KOREA'S OBLIGATION UNDER THE IAEA SAFEGUARDS AGREEMENT

North Korean membership in the NPT is closely linked to its obligations under the Safeguards Agreement. The Safeguards Agreement between North Korea and the IAEA clearly stipulates that it 'shall remain in force as long as the Democratic People's Republic of Korea is party to the [NPT]' (art. 26).[81] This means that as long as North Korea remains party to the NPT, the Safeguards Agreement must apply to the DPRK in its entirety as the IAEA has been arguing consistently. However, things are not so simple as they argue, due particularly to the existence of the Agreed Framework between the United States and North Korea and other relevant agreements.

The Agreed Framework provides on the IAEA safeguards in three different

---

[79] UN doc. S/25515, 2 April 1993, 2.

[80] In this connection, the observations made by the United Kingdom and the United States regarding 'General Comment 24' adopted by the Human Rights Committee merit particular reference. In responding to the Committee's General Comment to the effect that the Committee should determine whether a specific reservation is compatible with the object and purpose of the Covenant, they argued that the Committee would not have such power as is not provided for in the Covenant. See UN doc. A/50/40, 3 October 1995, 129 (General Comment), 131–132 (US), 138, para.12 (UK).

[81] INFCIRC/403, May 1992, reproduced in UN doc. A/48/133-S/25556, 12 April 1993, Annex 2, 25.

ways.[82] One is the general statement that the DPRK 'will remain a party to the [NPT]' and 'will allow implementation of its safeguards agreement under the Treaty'. Secondly, with regard to the graphite reactors and related facilities frozen under the Agreed Framework, the IAEA will be allowed to 'monitor this freeze', with the DPRK's full cooperation to the Agency for this purpose, as from the date of the Agreed Framework. And thirdly, with respect to the 'facilities not subject to the freeze,' *ad hoc* and routine inspections will resume under the Safeguards Agreement 'upon conclusion of the supply contract',[83] and pending conclusion of the supply contract, inspection required for the continuity of safeguards will continue at those facilities.

Thus, the DPRK was not required by the Agreed Framework to accept the *whole* system of safeguards under its agreement with the IAEA. On the contrary, as the Agreed Framework itself clearly provides, the DPRK was required to 'come into full compliance' with the IAEA Safeguards Agreement only '[w]hen a significant portion of the LWR project is completed'.[84]

Apparently, the arrangement introduced by the Agreed Framework was not in conformity with the DPRK's obligations under its Safeguards Agreement with the IAEA. That is partly why the IAEA's Board of Governors and General Conference resolutions have repeatedly expressed their deep concern over the DPRK's 'continuing non-compliance' with the Safeguards Agreement and reiterated their calls to the DPRK to 'comply fully and promptly' with it.[85]

At the same time, the IAEA had conducted monitoring of the freeze of the graphite reactors and related facilities as provided for in the Agreed Framework. This might be seen as if the IAEA had tacitly endorsed the arrangement made by the Agreed Framework so that it had no longer been in a position to call to the DPRK to comply fully with the Safeguards Agreement.

However, this does not seem to be the case. As the IAEA explains, its monitoring of the freeze was not based on the provisions of the Agreed Framework directly; instead, it was based on the request of the UN Security Council, as some of the IAEA resolutions explicitly refer to.[86] More specifically, the IAEA's monitoring activities at specified facilities in the DPRK had been based on the Presidential Statement of the UN Security Council made on 4 November 1994. In that Statement, the Security Council 'request[ed] the IAEA to take all steps it may

---

82   Agreed Framework, paras IV.1, I.3, and IV.2, respectively.

83   The 'supply contract' was concluded in December 1995 in the form of the Supply Agreement between the DPRK and the KEDO. See UN doc. S/2003/91, 8.

84   Agreed Framework, para. IV.3.

85   For some of the recent examples, see, e.g., GC(44)/RES/26, September 2000, para. 4; GC(45)/RES/16, September 2001, paras 4, 5; GC(46)/RES/14, September 2002, paras 4, 5; GOV/2002/60, 29 November 2002, para. 1; GOV/2003/3, 6 January 2003, para. 1.

86   For instance, GC(46)/RES/14 of September 2002 commends the Secretariat for its continuous efforts to monitor the freeze of specified facilities in the DPRK 'as requested by the United Nations Security Council' (para. 2).

deem necessary as a consequence of the Agreed Framework to monitor the freeze', after receiving an oral report from the IAEA's Director General apparently to the effect that the said monitoring activities are within the scope of the IAEA-DPRK Safeguards Agreement.[87] Thus, for the IAEA the monitoring activities were steps having their direct basis in the Council request and having been taken within the framework of the Safeguards Agreement with the DPRK. As such, the IAEA monitoring activities in North Korea *per se* did not entail any particular elements of its endorsement of the special arrangement introduced by the Agreed Framework.

A second question that may be posed with regard to the IAEA safeguards activities in the DPRK is: whether such a political document as the Agreed Framework could change the obligations under such a legal instrument as the Safeguards Agreement, or whether North Korea has been in non-compliance with the IAEA Safeguards Agreement for a decade, as the IAEA claims, even if it *fully* complies with the provisions of the Agreed Framework.

Legally, there is no doubt that the latter is the case. But then, what did the Agreed Framework mean at all? Did the United States make an arrangement with the DPRK contrary to the latter's legal obligations under the Safeguards Agreement, thus having induced the latter to breach international law? If the Agreed Framework is a mere political instrument and cannot change or terminate any legal obligations that the DPRK has assumed elsewhere, then did it have no legal implications whatsoever? Perhaps the only possible legal implication it may have would be that as far as the United States is concerned, it could not invoke, as a member of the IAEA, the legal responsibility of the DPRK resulting from its non-compliance with the Safeguards Agreement as a consequence of its *full and faithful* compliance with the Agreed Framework.

However, the above explanation based essentially on the legal-political dichotomy could become unconvincing when one recalls the fact that some of the provisions of the Agreed Framework have been incorporated in legal documents, such as the KEDO Agreement and the Supply Agreement. Indeed, the latter Agreement has incorporated almost all provisions of the Agreed Framework that are related to the DPRK's safeguards undertaking as a mutual condition for the provision of the LWR project; and it clearly states that it 'shall constitute an international agreement between the KEDO and the DPRK, and shall be binding on both sides under international law'.[88] Thus, it could be said that there are two *legal* regimes concerning the DPRK's safeguards obligations.

Important in this regard is the fact that the KEDO is not a closed organisation but an organization open to states or international organizations that support its purpose and offer assistance.[89] It started functioning in March 1995 with the three states of the United States, South Korea and Japan as original members, but now

---

[87]   S/PRST/1994/64, 4 November 1994.
[88]   Supply Agreement, art. 3, para. 1, Annex III and art. 18, para. 1.
[89]   KEDO Agreement, art. 5 (b).

its membership has grown to be as many as 12 states and one international organisation, i.e., the European Union having a membership of 15 states. Thus the legal authority of the special safeguards regime for the DPRK rooted in the Agreed Framework has gained a relative weight as the membership of the KEDO rises. And to change the scheme provided for in the Supply Agreement, a consensus or, if it is not achievable, a majority vote of the Executive Board members (US, Japan, South Korea, and the EU) is needed for the KEDO side alone.[90]

Notwithstanding such a development, it could still be argued that there is nothing wrong for the IAEA to express concern over the continuing non-compliance of the DPRK with the IAEA Safeguards Agreement, since the Agency is a party to the Safeguards Agreement, but a third party in relation to the Agreed Framework and the KEDO-related agreements after all. Beyond such IAEA perspectives, however, the general picture remains blurred, as would often be the case with the application of successive treaties relating to the same subject-matter.[91]

Suppose that North Korea is definitely out of the NPT, it no longer assumes the full scope safeguards obligations under the NPT. And the picture would become clear to that extent. But there may arise equally or more difficult questions, including the validity of the KEDO Agreement and other KEDO-related agreements that may be questioned based on the doctrine of material breach or *rebus sic stantibus*.

5 CONCLUSIONS

The present article examined legal aspects of the nuclear issues that have been raised with regard to North Korea for more than ten years. As a result, it has become clear that they are full of uncertainties and ambiguities. Such uncertainties and ambiguities have created particularly serious problems with regard to the North Korean status under the NPT.

Recently, there was a rare opportunity in which nearly all the complicated legal questions involved could have been resolved, i.e., the Preparatory Committee for the 2005 NPT Review Conference held from 28 April to 9 May 2003 in Geneva. However, parties to the NPT decided on 25 April, just before the opening of the Committee, not to draw any legal conclusion at the Committee on the question of the North Korean withdrawal from the Treaty.[92] They further decided that the nameplate for the DPRK would not be put on the delegations desk in the conference room but placed under the administrative 'custody' of the Chairman of

---

[90] KEDO Agreement, art. 6 (a) and (e). At the same time, it is also true that the LWR project would not complete without the US and the DPRK concluding an agreement concerning peaceful uses of nuclear energy.

[91] Ian Sinclair describes this question as '[a] particularly obscure aspect of the law of treaties'. Ian Sinclair, *The Vienna Convention on the Law of Treaties* (2nd edn, 1984), 93.

[92] *Yomiuri Shinbun* (evening edition), 26 April 2003.

354 *Masahiko Asada*

the Preparatory Committee.[93] At the Committee meeting, the Chairman's state-ment to this effect[94] was taken note of.[95]

From an international legal perspective, there seems to be little question about removing the whole uncertainties and ambiguities by all means for the sake of legal clarity. In fact, as mentioned earlier, the IAEA once hinted that it would even prefer to see the DPRK completely out of the NPT rather than remaining partially in and partially out.

On the other hand, there have been strong counter-argument that it would not necessarily be wise to clarify the legal situation regarding the North Korean status under the NPT. For instance, US State Department Spokesman Richard Boucher on 9 April 2003 said in a press briefing as follows: '[t]he [US] administration has not taken a position on whether North Korea's withdrawal notification meets the requirements of Article 10 [of the NPT]. For the present, we see no need to try and reach agreement on North Korea's legal status under the [NPT]. Debate on this legal question could sidetrack ongoing multilateral consultations . . . It is import-ant to remain focused on the real strategic issue, . . . denuclearization of the penin-sula. . . . That's not really a matter of a legal interpretation of the treaty'.[96]

The present author would not hesitate to agree to the thrust of what Spokesman Boucher said, if he intended to confine his statement to a short-term objective. In the short-term, it would perhaps be more important to keep North Korea on this side of the point of no return by whatever means, however strange it would be in legal terms, than to definitely conclude that North Korea is now out of the NPT regime. The latter course of action might well lead North Korea to reach the point of no return. And even if Pyongyang decides to return later, it might try to make conditions for its re-accession to the Treaty. If so, legal considerations should perhaps give way for the moment to political considerations for an overall benefit of international peace and security in the region.

However, in the longer term, it is doubtful whether such an approach would

---

93   *Ibid.* See also Rebecca Johnson, 'Rogues and Rhetoric: The 2003 NPT PrepCom Slides Backwards' (June/July 2003), 71 *Disarmament Diplomacy* 6.

94   The Chairman of the second session of the Preparatory Committee, after reporting that the consultations that he had carried out revealed 'diverging views on the status of the Democratic People's Republic of Korea in the NPT', stated as follows: 'It is my conviction that a debate on the issue would only serve to the detriment of the purpose of the Preparatory Committee, namely . . . . In light of the above, the Chair has the intention, under his own responsibility, not open a debate on this issue and to retain the nameplate of the said country temporarily, in his custody. The Chair has therefore asked the Secretariat to hold the nameplate in the conference room for the duration of the second session of the Preparatory Committee. This is in no way meant to prejudice the outcome of on-going consultations on the issue'. NPT/CONF.2005/PC.II/CRP.1, 7 May 2003, para. 6.

95   *Ibid.*

96   US Department of State, 'Transcript: State Department Noon Briefing, 9 April 2003 (Iraq, Russia, North Korea, China), State Department Spokesman Richard Boucher briefed', 9 April 2003. According to Spokesman Boucher, the US position regarding the North Korean status under the NPT is that it 'took a position that the immediate withdrawal announcement was not effective' but it has 'not taken a position on whether the three-month withdrawal is legally operational or not'. *Ibid.*

really serve the objective of arms control and disarmament, and ultimately the objective of the maintenance of international peace and security. If a state were to be allowed to be nebulous about whether it has assumed such important legal obligations as not to manufacture or otherwise acquire nuclear weapons under the NPT, that would not only undermine the NPT itself but might also affect other legal regimes prohibiting and regulating weapons and weapons systems.

What the international community is now doing is deliberately refraining from clarifying North Korean status under the NPT. Although the case was submitted to the Security Council, it has taken no concrete measures so far. This has been said to be all for the sake of a peaceful and diplomatic solution of the problem. Such an exercise might prove successful this time. But it would surely leave impressions that the NPT might not work in a real contingency situation, and that it might be possible to leave the Treaty any time without strict sanctions imposed. More generally, the North Korean case might adversely affect arms control and the disarmament law system as a whole by setting a bad precedent.

6 POSTSCRIPT

Since mid-2003, the world has witnessed the worsening nuclear situation on the Korean Peninsula. Pyongyang claimed that it resumed and completed reprocessing of the spent fuel rods previously frozen at Yongbyon, and later publicly said that the resulting fissile material would be used to bolster its 'nuclear deterrent force,' although there is no independent confirmation of North Korea's claim. Without any positive development in actual terms, the KEDO Executive Board decided on 21 November 2003 to suspend the LWR project in the DPRK for a period of one year, beginning 1 December 2003. The future of the project is to be decided by the Board before the expiration of the suspension period.

In the meantime, there has been an endeavour going on to resolve the North Korean nuclear issue diplomatically through multilateral talks among the states most concerned. In April 2003, the first such talks were held in Beijing with the participation of North Korea, the United States and China. In August 2003, South Korea, Japan and Russia joined the process, making it six-party talks. During the six-party talks in August, North Korea agreed to the eventual elimination of its nuclear programmes if the United States were first willing to sign a bilateral 'non-aggression treaty' and meet various other conditions, including the provision of substantial amounts of aid and normalisation of relations. The North Korean proposal was unacceptable to the United States, which insisted on a multilateral resolution to the issue and refused to provide benefits for North Korea to abide by its previous international obligations. A hinted shift in the US policy was revealed in October 2003 when President Bush said that he would be willing to consider a multilateral written security guarantee in the context of North Korea's complete, verifiable and irreversible elimination of its nuclear programme. Despite such a development and despite the convening of the second round of six-party talks in February 2004, there is no clear prospect for a final resolution to the issue.

[11]

Why Less is More:
Law and Policy Considerations on the Iranian Nuclear Issue

Daniel H. Joyner[1]

In late 2002, the world learned from Iranian opposition groups in exile that Iran had concealed from the International Atomic Energy Agency (IAEA) for eighteen years the existence of facilities at Natanz and Arak engaged in experiments involving uranium enrichment and plutonium separation. Upon a report by IAEA inspectors detailing their findings on the undeclared activities, the IAEA Board of Governors reached the conclusion in a Resolution passed November 26, 2003 that, due to this concealment and to other reporting omissions, Iran had "in a number of instances" failed to meet its obligations under its safeguards agreement with the agency.[2] In its resolution the Board further recognized that Iran had a particular onus of cooperation and transparency in order to "provide and maintain the assurances required by Member States" and "restore confidence." Iran subsequently agreed to a temporary suspension of its uranium enrichment activities and in December 2003 signed the IAEA Additional Protocol.

Despite these concessions, Iran has continuously maintained that all of its work with fissile materials and related technologies, including work at these undeclared sites, has been aimed at furthering its capacity to produce civilian nuclear energy. Iran's leaders have thus argued, notwithstanding Iran's failure to comply with reporting requirements under its safeguards agreement, that Iran has always been in compliance with its substantive obligations under the 1968 Nuclear Non-proliferation Treaty (NPT). In this argument, they have relied specifically upon the inalienable right of all states to engage in peaceful uses of nuclear technologies recognized in Article IV, paragraph 1, of the NPT.[3]

However, suspicions have become widespread, particularly among Western states and Israel, that the uranium enrichment work which Iran has carried out is intended not solely for use in peaceful energy production, but for the creation of nuclear weapons.

---

[1] Associate Professor, University of Alabama School of Law. The author would like to thank Adam Lebovitz and the staff of the Harvard Law and Policy Review Online for helpful comments on an earlier draft of this article.

[2] IAEA Document GOV/2003/81.

[3] For an analysis of the legal arguments surrounding Iran's nuclear program, see Daniel H. Joyner, INTERNATIONAL LAW AND THE PROLIFERATION OF WEAPONS OF MASS DESTRUCTION, 50–55 (2009).

2   *HARVARD LAW AND POLICY REVIEW ONLINE*

Notwithstanding these suspicions, IAEA inspectors have to date found no conclusive evidence to support allegations of a clandestine nuclear weapons program in Iran.[4]

Despite this lack of evidence of a weapons program, on February 4, 2006, the IAEA Board of Governors decided to refer Iran's case to the U.N. Security Council. This referral, without a supporting report by IAEA inspectors providing evidence that Iran was in breach of its substantive NPT obligations or that it was in continuing breach of its safeguards agreement, led some to criticize the Board's decision as premature. However, on July 31, 2006 the Security Council passed Resolution 1696 in which, acting under Article 40 of Chapter VII of the U.N. Charter, it demanded that Iran suspend all uranium enrichment-related and reprocessing activities and requested a report from the IAEA Director-General by August 31 to confirm this suspension.

Iran's failure to abide by the terms of this resolution and its insistence that its activities are firmly within its rights under NPT Article IV have led the Security Council to issue additional resolutions under Chapter VII, which impose trade restrictions and other economic sanctions on Iran and on specified Iranian individuals and business entities. Tensions between Iran and Western powers have recently been aggravated by Iran's disclosure in September 2009 that it has for some years been constructing a facility near Qom intended as an additional uranium enrichment facility to supplement its primary enrichment facility at Natanz.

In this article I will first briefly review the international legal issues surrounding Iran's development of uranium enrichment capacity. I will conclude that Iran is currently in breach of its international legal obligations to cease uranium enrichment, due to the passage of Security Council Resolution 1696. I will then go on to consider the policy positions that Western governments and Israel in particular have taken in light of this illegality and will argue that none of the policy positions that have so far been adopted or proposed are likely to be effective in stopping Iran from acquiring nuclear weapons capability if indeed that is Iran's intent. I will conclude by arguing for a more minimalist approach by Western governments and Israel toward Iran and a greater reliance on the influence of international civil society on internal Iranian politics and social movements. I argue that, in the end, internal political change represents the only realistic potential source of meaningful change to Iran's nuclear posture.

I.   Law

First, in consideration of the legal merits of Iran's claim that its nuclear activities are justified by Article IV of the NPT, it is important to note that uranium enrichment, when declared to the IAEA, is not an NPT violation *per se*. Certainly when uranium is enriched to a U-235 presence of less than 20%, and can thus still be classified as Low-Enriched Uranium (LEU), that enrichment activity is one that is fully includable within the Article IV inalienable right to engage in peaceful uses of nuclear technologies. This understanding was clear at the time of the drafting of the NPT. As the Director of the

---

[4] *See also* OFFICE OF THE DIR. OF NAT'L INTELLIGENCE, DECEMBER 2007 NATIONAL INTELLIGENCE ESTIMATE, IRAN: NUCLEAR INTENTIONS AND CAPABILITIES, *available at* http://www.dni.gov/press_releases/20071203_release.pdf.

U.S. Arms Control and Disarmament Agency told the Senate Foreign Relations Committee in 1968:

> It may be useful to point out, for illustrative purposes, several activities which the United States would not consider per se to be violations of the prohibitions in Article II. Neither uranium enrichment nor the stockpiling of fissionable material in connection with a peaceful program would violate Article II so long as these activities were safeguarded under Article III. Also clearly permitted would be the development, under safeguards, of plutonium fueled power reactors, including research on the properties of metallic plutonium, nor would Article II interfere with the development or use of fast breeder reactors under safeguards.[5]

Japan and a number of other Non-nuclear Weapon State (NNWS) parties to the NPT have carried out enrichment of uranium for the purpose of nuclear power generation for many years without complaint from the IAEA Board of Governors. Japan has in fact separated and stockpiled at least 43.1 tons of plutonium and has a robust and productive gas centrifuge program for uranium enrichment at its facility in Rokkasho, Aomori prefecture. This example serves to further illustrate that even the overproduction and stockpiling of fissile materials is deemed permissible by the IAEA.[6] It is only when this enrichment activity by an NNWS is undeclared to the IAEA that a violation of an IAEA safeguards agreement results. Even this, however, is not a violation of the NPT *per se*. Only if enrichment proceeds to the production of Highly-Enriched Uranium (HEU), at approximately 20% presence of U-235, does it produce a weapons-usable material. Undeclared enrichment of weapons-usable HEU would create a *prima facie* case of breach of Article II of the NPT, and such activity would not be justifiable by reference to Article IV.

As a matter of law Iran was therefore quite correct in its interpretation of the coverage of its uranium enrichment activities by Article IV of the NPT until July 31, 2006. The basis of Iran's case was not altered by previous IAEA urgings that Iran cease uranium enrichment, as the IAEA's only legal competence is in the administration of safeguards agreements, and the continuation of uranium enrichment in declared sites, under IAEA safeguards, poses no challenge to the provisions of Iran's safeguards agreement. The legal landscape did change, however, on July 31, 2006 with the passage

---

[5]*Treaty on the Nonproliferation of Nuclear Weapons: Hearings Before the S. Comm. on Foreign Relations*, 90th Cong. 39 (extension of remarks by Mr. Foster in response to question regarding nuclear explosive devices).

[6] *See Japan's "Separated" Plutonium Stockpile Increases to 43 Tons*, KYODO NEWS AGENCY, available at http://www.redorbit.com/news/science/231519/japans_separated_plutonium_stockpile_in creases_to_43_tons/index.html. Uranium enrichment through centrifuge cascade is also carried out, for example, at the Almelo facility in the Netherlands, and at the Gronau facility in Germany.

of Security Council Resolution 1696, in which the Council exercised its authority under Chapter VII of the U.N. Charter to order Iran to cease uranium enrichment.

Regardless of prudence or other merit of this demand by the Council, in passing this resolution the Council changed the legal underpinnings of Iran's case for justifying its enrichment activities by reference to NPT Article IV. This issue can be approached legally under a number of different theories. However, perhaps the most persuasive theory for the superiority of Chapter VII resolutions over the rights of NPT Article IV is simply to be found in the reasoning that the rights defined in Article IV are not creations alone of the treaty terms of the NPT, but are rather rights recognized by the terms of the treaty, yet existing independently within the bundle of rights inherent in the attributes of a state. Under this reasoning, while the Article IV rights are important features of the sovereign character of all NPT parties, they are nonetheless categorizable along with all other general state rights. By a state's consent to the terms of Article 25 of the U.N. Charter, such general state rights are made surmountable by and subject to the authority of the Security Council acting under Chapter VII.[7] Any other understanding of the relationship between the generally inherent rights of states and Article 25 of the Charter would render the Security Council unable to authorize any remedial force under Articles 41 and 42 as a consequence of its determinations under Article 39 of threats to international peace and security.

In summary, then, Iran is currently in violation of international law in its refusal to abide by Security Council Resolution 1696 and subsequent resolutions in which the Security Council has required Iran to suspend all uranium enrichment-related and reprocessing activities.

II.   Policy

In spite of the various efforts that have been undertaken to pressure Iran into compliance with Resolution 1696, including additional resolutions imposing trade restrictions and other economic sanctions, the leadership of Iran has shown no sign of changing course in its nuclear-related activities. Indeed, the pace of uranium enrichment has increased significantly over the past few years, and there are plans to begin operation of an additional enrichment facility near Qom by 2011. In the face of Iran's resistance to international pressure and in light of their suspicion that Iran's nuclear program has military aspects, the leaders of Western countries including the United States, the United Kingdom, France, and Germany, as well as Israel, have taken up the almost mantric refrain that a nuclear armed Iran is "unacceptable" to them. This statement is frequently and forcefully made to draw a policy line in the sand, and is clearly meant to communicate that these states are committed to taking all necessary measures to prevent this unacceptable eventuality from coming to pass.

From a policy perspective, this position seems problematic. It appears to expose a gap between rhetoric and reality on the question of what Western governments can realistically hope to do to prevent Iran from acquiring nuclear weapons, if indeed that is

---

[7] Article 25 states that "[t]he Members of the United Nations agree to accept and carry out the decisions of the Security Council in accordance with the present Charter."

Iran's intention. In fact, there are likely no realistic options for externally preventing Iranian acquisition of nuclear weapons if Iran's intent is sufficiently fixed on this goal.

First to a consideration of that intent. A variety of evidence has been adduced of Iran's involvement in research and possible development of nuclear weapons related technologies.[8] The most recent such allegation was made on December 14, 2009 in an article published by *The Times* of London. In this article, reporter Catherine Philp claims to have obtained a 2007 "technical document" from an office in Iran's Defense Ministry that "describes the use of a neutron source, uranium deuteride, which independent experts confirm has no possible civilian or military use other than in a nuclear weapon."[9] As with other allegations of evidence supporting the claim of a military aspect to Iran's nuclear program, this document's authenticity is difficult to confirm. Moreover, even if this document or other pieces of evidence are determined to be authentic, it is even more difficult to show that any Iranian nuclear weapons work has moved beyond the research stage and into development or manufacture. Thus far no weapons-grade HEU or other single use fissile material, or manufactured nuclear explosive devices or components thereof, have been found in Iran. Then there is the December 2007 U.S. National Intelligence Estimate, in which the U.S. intelligence community judged "with high confidence" that Iran halted its nuclear weapons program in the fall of 2003.[10] This assessment—vigorously disagreed with by Israel in particular—casts doubt on much of the evidence of an ongoing Iranian nuclear weapons program. Iran itself has repeatedly stated that it does not desire to acquire nuclear weapons and that all of its nuclear work is peaceful in purpose.

However, let us assume for the sake of argument the worst-case scenario: that Iranian officials are lying, and that Iran does indeed intend to acquire nuclear weapons. Or, more realistically, let us assume that what Iran intends to obtain is the latent capability to construct nuclear weapons within a relatively short time. As Ariel Levite has described it, this is a policy of nuclear hedging.[11] Nuclear hedging means having the knowledge and capacity to produce a sufficient amount of weapons-grade fissile material and manufacture the warhead hardware of a nuclear weapon in a matter of weeks once the political decision to construct a weapon has been made. This status of nuclear hedging is almost certainly a more realistic goal for Iran than is the manufacture and maintenance of one or more completed nuclear weapons. The nuclear hedging policy, pursuant to which the knowledge and capacity to manufacture a nuclear weapon are obtained but no concrete steps are taken in construction of a weapon, would keep Iran's

---

[8] See Dafna Linzer, *Strong Leads and Dead Ends in Nuclear Case Against Iran*, WASHINGTON POST, Feb. 8, 2006.

[9] Catherine Philp, *Secret Document Exposes Iran's Nuclear Trigger*, TIMES (London), Dec. 14, 2009, *available at* http://www.timesonline.co.uk/tol/news/world/middle_east/article6955351.ece.

[10] OFFICE OF THE DIR. OF NAT'L INTELLIGENCE, *supra* note 4, at 6.

[11] Ariel Levite, *Never Say Never Again: Nuclear Reversal Revisited*, INTERNATIONAL SECURITY, Winter 2002-03, at 59-88.

nuclear programs technically legal under NPT law. This would in turn serve to defuse negative international opinion and would avoid giving the West a justification for war or other serious pressuring efforts. However, it creates in the hedging state a real capability that, if known or suspected by others, confers many of the same strategic benefits of nuclear weapons possession, including deterrent value against aggressors.

We come then to the gap between rhetoric and reality presented by statements of Western states and Israel that a nuclear armed Iran is unacceptable and by the concomitant pledge to take all necessary measures to prevent Iran from acquiring nuclear weapons capability. There would appear in fact to be no realistic means available to these unaccepting states whereby they might externally prevent Iran from obtaining nuclear hedging status if that is indeed Iran's intent. None of the options that have been discussed for doing so—strengthened economic sanctions, targeted airstrikes on Iranian nuclear facilities, and diplomatic accords—are likely to achieve significant results or alternatively achieve benefits which outweigh their costs.

A.   Sanctions

As noted above, the United Nations Security Council has imposed several rounds of economic sanctions on Iran and on Iranian individuals and business entities in response to Iran's failure to abide by the terms of the Council's Resolution 1696. These sanctions have largely been focused on Iran's nuclear program itself and have included an international prohibition on supply of nuclear-related materials to Iran as well as a freeze on the overseas assets of named Iranian individuals and businesses. There have been a number of voices arguing for a stepping up of the sanctions regime against Iran, with some calling for the Security Council to institute a wide-ranging international embargo of trade with Iran, similar to that imposed upon Iraq by the Security Council in the aftermath of the 1990-91 Gulf War.[12]

However, in the specific case of Iran and its policy regarding its nuclear program, economic sanctions are not likely to be effective in changing Iran's policy of nuclear hedging if that is indeed its intent. In the leading academic study of the use of economic sanctions as a tool of foreign policy, the authors found that economic sanctions have historically achieved success in changing target state behavior in only thirty-four percent of cases.[13] However, when one considers the particular facts of the Iranian case, the expected likelihood of a stepped up sanctions program significantly influencing Iran's nuclear policy would be considerably less than that.

Iran is a large and regionally powerful country. It is led by an essentially autocratic government, founded upon religious principles. The specific issue in question —the state's nuclear policy—is an issue of the highest political and security sensitivity, particularly if one assumes that there is a military aspect to that policy. It is also one that is a focus of nationalist pride among much of the population of the country. On these

---

[12] Orde Kittrie, *Using Stronger Sanctions to Increase Negotiating Leverage with Iran*, ARMS CONTROL TODAY, December 2009, at 18.

[13] GARY CLYDE HUFBAUER ET AL., ECONOMIC SANCTIONS RECONSIDERED 158 (3rd ed. 2007).

facts, even stepped up sanctions are highly unlikely to be an effective tool in influencing the policies and behavior of Iran's leaders.[14] As the authors of the abovementioned study conclude:

> Policymakers often have inflated expectations of what sanctions can accomplish. This is especially true of the United States today and was true of the United Kingdom in an earlier era. At most there is a weak correlation between economic depravation and political willingness to change. . . . Sanctions are seldom effective in impairing the military potential of an important power or in bringing about major changes in the policies of the target country. . . In high policy cases, the costs of compliance for the target are high, both sender and target are intensely interested in prevailing, and the sender must be able to either threaten or impose unusually high costs on a defiant target in order to prevail.[15]

Specifically with regard to cases in which the target state is led by an autocracy, the authors note:

> It is hard to bully a bully with economic measures. The evidence from the cases suggests that democratic regimes are more susceptible to economic pressure than autocratic ones and that economic weakness and political instability in the target country can make it still more vulnerable, but the evidence on this last point is weaker than expected.[16]

The case of Iran's nuclear program is therefore disanalogous to many of the economic sanction success stories held up by proponents of this foreign policy tool; for example, the role of Security Council authorized economic sanctions in bringing down the Apartheid government of South Africa. Even within the international security issue area, the economic sanctions success stories, including Iraq, do not provide particularly encouraging precedents. In these cases the economic sanctions regimes imposed upon the target states tend to be comprehensive and draconian. This is particularly true in the case of Iraq in the 1990s. And even with such crushing economic sanctions, the success of that program could only be determined after many years of its maintenance. Thus, economic sanctions should be considered likely to be effective in changing state behavior in high politics and military related cases only in the long term, and only through high-cost and comprehensive sanctioning programs that cause massive societal disruption and privation for the civilian populace of the target state. In the case of Iran's nuclear program, causing the Iranian people to suffer a decade of poverty just to see if this will

---

[14] See generally Martin Matishak, *House Approves Gasoline Cutoff Bill on Iran Despite Warnings*, GLOBAL SECURITY NEWSWIRE, Dec. 16, 2009, *available at* http://gsn.nti.org/gsn/nw_20091216_7976.php.

[15] HUFBAUER ET AL., *supra* note 13, at 162.

[16] *Id.* at 166.

have any effect upon the autocratic ideologues who run their country's government hardly seems proportionate to the feared potential that Iran will achieve a status of nuclear hedging.

In this cost/benefit analysis, one must also consider how Iran is likely to react to a strengthened sanctions regime. If a comprehensive trade embargo were imposed, Iran might consider this action tantamount to an armed attack against it. Iran has declared that in such a case, it would move to block access to the Straits of Hormuz, potentially severely restricting the flow of oil out of the Persian Gulf and causing chaos in world energy markets. To an international economy struggling to pull itself out of a deep worldwide recession, such an energy crisis could be devastating.

In sum, the unlikely benefits to be gained by significantly ratcheting up the international sanctions regime against Iran, when compared with the massive potential costs of maintaining such a coordinated and sustained sanctions program and the collateral damage it would inevitably inflict on the Iranian civilian populace, makes this an unrealistic option for externally changing Iran's policy of acquiring a nuclear hedging capability, if indeed that is Iran's intent.

B.   Airstrikes

Another possibility for changing the direction of Iran's nuclear policies is of course the military option, and specifically the option of targeted airstrikes on Iranian nuclear facilities. This possibility is periodically mentioned by government officials in the West, usually in a dismissive sense, but is still among the options that are "on the table." Israeli officials are at times more candid about their willingness to use force if they perceive that Iran has crossed some threshold of nuclear weapons capability.

The idea of addressing the Iranian nuclear question through the use of targeted airstrikes is also unlikely to achieve benefits that outweigh its costs. The only benefit that targeted airstrikes might achieve is the destruction of known nuclear facilities. However, these known facilities likely comprise only a part of the overall Iranian nuclear complex. There are almost certainly hidden or underground facilities about which Western intelligence sources know little or nothing. Destroying Iran's known facilities is not likely to lead to a permanent change in Iran's nuclear policies. At best such a military strike would amount to a temporary setback to some of Iran's nuclear capabilities, a setback that could likely be overcome by a few years of rebuilding.

In terms of costs, this will depend largely on how Iran reacts to such a strike. It would almost certainly strike back at its attackers, likely Israel, precipitating a military conflict of unpredictable scope and duration. The cost in human life and national infrastructure could be significant for both Iran and Israel.

The diplomatic consequences of a military strike against Iran would be of long duration. It would essentially foreclose any future diplomatic engagement on the nuclear issue. Such an attack, which would itself almost certainly be a breach of international law, would undermine the perceived legitimacy of the West's umbrage at Iran's own violations of international law and negatively affect international support for further pressuring efforts against Iran.[17]

The unrealistic nature of the targeted airstrikes option for changing the course of Iran's nuclear policies is not lost upon most leaders in the West, and it is highly unlikely that any Western governments will participate directly in such a military action against Iran. However, Israel's willingness to take such drastic measures, if in its opinion Iran passes some threshold of nuclear weapons capability, is much less predictable.

C.   Diplomatic Accord

Efforts by Western states to influence Iranian nuclear policy have thus far focused on diplomatic negotiation, looking toward some international accord pursuant to which Iran will agree either to cease uranium enrichment entirely or to at least take other meaningful steps toward restoring the confidence of Western leaders that its nuclear intentions are purely peaceful. The most recent of such efforts have been directed at a compromise plan, under which Iran would ship approximately seventy percent of its existing LEU out of the country to be further enriched and then processed into fuel rods for use in its medical isotope producing reactor in Tehran. To the West, acceptance of this plan by Iran would show a willingness on Iran's part to make confidence-building concessions, and it would also remove a significant quantity of Iran's known LEU reserves out of the country, preventing them from being used in the manufacture of a nuclear weapon. Iran has so far rejected this proposal.

However, even if Iran were to accept this proposal or some similar international accord focused on neutralizing its LEU stockpile, this would not necessarily represent a change in Iran's assumed policy of nuclear hedging. The problem that all such international accords pose is that they are only as good as their verifiability by IAEA inspectors. Again, it is likely, in light of Iran's decades-long maintenance of clandestine facilities at Arak and Natanz and the recent revelation of the centrifuge facility at Qom, that the full extent of Iran's nuclear complex is not known to Western intelligence agencies. Thus, an agreement to neutralize known LEU stockpiles, or even to cease uranium enrichment work at known facilities, will not provide evidence of a true change in Iran's assumed policy of nuclear hedging. The IAEA is simply not equipped to act as an investigative agency, uncovering facilities and activities which a safeguarded state wishes to keep clandestine. Any such international accord focusing on known fissile materials or facilities would be suspected as being only for diplomatic appearances, with nuclear activities continuing at undeclared locations. This problem cannot be overcome through the deployment of any number of international inspectors inside Iran.

While diplomacy should of course continue in an effort to resolve the nuclear standoff between Iran and the West through low-cost peaceful means, diplomatic accords and confidence-building measures themselves can only potentially be seen as limited evidence of a change in Iran's nuclear policy.

---

[17] Such an attack would be in many ways analytically similar to the 2007 Israeli attack on a suspected nuclear facility in Syria. On this case, see Daniel Joyner, *North Korean Links to Building of a Nuclear Reactor in Syria: Implications for International Law*, ASIL INSIGHTS, Apr. 28, 2008, *available at* http://www.asil.org/insights080428.cfm.

D.   Internal Change

In considering the several policy options that have been put forward for externally influencing Iran's assumed intention to achieve nuclear hedging status, none appear to be realistically likely to achieve significant results, or alternatively to achieve benefits that outweigh their costs. Rather, the only possibilities for realistic change to Iran's assumed intent to obtain a latent nuclear weapons capability lie internally in Iran.

One possibility for internal policy change is a decision by the current government in Tehran to reverse course in its nuclear weapons desires and forego the acquisition of a latent nuclear weapons capability. This possibility is not without precedent. Though imperfectly analogous in important ways, there are historical examples of nuclear reversal decisions of this kind. Brazil, South Africa, Argentina, Libya, and Egypt all reversed course on their nuclear weapons programs after varying degrees of progress down the nuclear path. Understanding why these states chose nuclear reversal is difficult due to the variety of factors present in each individual case.[18] However, if lessons can be learned from these past cases, they probably caution against optimism that Iran will follow this course.

If Iran does desire nuclear weapons and is working toward that end, it is primarily because of significant regional and international security interests. Iran wants to strategically strengthen its hand against Israel and Western states it perceives as hostile towards its interests. By acquiring a nuclear deterrent, Iran would level the playing field with Israel, which up to now has enjoyed the upper hand in regional security dynamics as the only state in the region with nuclear weapons. Iran is thus not comparable to North Korea, a financially ruined country that seems to have pursued nuclear weapons largely as a tool of leverage to force economic concessions from other states and which at times seems to be willing to forego its nuclear weapons program if the foreign financial inducement for doing so is sufficient. Iran's interests in nuclear weapons are far more rational and strategic and are unlikely to be changed by any carrot that can be offered by the West. The only meaningful carrot that could be offered to assuage Iran's regional security concerns would be an offer by Israel to completely disarm Israel's own nuclear arsenal. However, this is certain not to occur. And Iran is also, as discussed above, unlikely to be significantly influenced by any of the practical sticks (e.g. stepped up sanctions or targeted military strikes) the West can bring to bear for this purpose.

The other possibility for internal policy change on the nuclear issue, and perhaps the more realistic possibility, is a more fundamental change to the current Iranian political regime that results in a change in Iran's overall approach to the region and to the West, including a decision to reverse course on the desire for a latent nuclear weapons capability. The social and political schisms within Iran that were revealed in the protests and government crackdown following the June 2009 presidential election appear to be the

---

[18] *See* Levite, *supra* note 11, at 59-88.

deepest since the 1979 revolution. Time will tell whether these schisms run deep enough to threaten the ruling political regime in fundamental ways, as some have argued.[19]

The current policy of the West toward Iran should be informed by an understanding that the only realistic possibilities for change to Iran's assumed intent to acquire latent nuclear weapons capability lie in social and political change inside Iran. This understanding argues for a halt to the escalation of economic sanctions against Iran, as well as for a change in Western political rhetoric towards Iran. Specifically, the rhetoric of deadlines, take-it-or-leave-it offers, and implicit threats of sanctions and military force should be abandoned. Export controls on nuclear-related items and technologies can remain in place to avoid actively contributing to any potential nuclear weapons program, and diplomatic dialogue should continue with an eye toward communication, transparency, and understanding. However, the best hope for change to Iran's nuclear weapons ambitions is real internal political change in Iran.

Supporting that change will require a paradigm shift for Western policy officials, particularly in the United States. No Western government can be seen to explicitly or directly support social and political change movements inside Iran, as this would give the government in Tehran a pretext to crack down on these change elements. In this situation, only international civil society efforts by groups that are not connected to or identifiable with Western governments— i.e. NGOs—are likely to be effective in supporting movements for political change in Iran from the outside. Thus, in the final analysis, the best action that Western governments can take to realistically effect change to Iran's assumed intent to acquire latent nuclear weapons capability is as little action as possible.

This will admittedly be a bitter pill to swallow for leaders of Western governments, who want to be seen politically to be doing something about the perceived threat of Iran's nuclear ambitions. However, these officials must remember that acting aggressively and confrontationally to address a problem of conflicting state interests in international relations is seldom the most effective policy choice. Often, aggressive confrontation will only make things worse by triggering primal psychological reactions of defiance and self-preservation in the leaders of the confronted state. The most effective opposition strategy is usually a policy of resolution of fundamental conflicts of interest through cooperation when possible or a policy of calculated efforts of passive opposition when interests cannot be compromised and cooperation is not possible. In the case of Iran's nuclear ambitions, a policy of passive opposition through reliance on international civil society groups and the Iranian people themselves to work a fundamental change to the Iranian political regime, is more likely to bring about meaningful change than are any efforts of external pressuring by Western states and Israel.

---

[19] E.U. Institute for Security Studies, *Analysis Paper: The Iranian Elections and the Aftermath* (June 2009) (*prepared by* Rouzbeh Parsi), *available at* http://www.iss.europa.eu/uploads/media/Iranian_elections_and_the_aftermath.pdf.

12   *HARVARD LAW AND POLICY REVIEW ONLINE*

Preferred Citation: Daniel H. Joyner, *Why Less Is More: Law and Policy Considerations on the Iran Nuclear Issue*, 4 HARV. L. & POL'Y REV. (Online) (Mar. 24, 2010), http://hlpronline.com/2010/03/joyner_iran/.

Part III
Chemical and Biological Weapons

[12]

Chemical and Biological Weapons

Julian Perry Robinson

This chapter presents a synoptic view of chemical and biological weapons (CBW), their threats to our security, and international efforts to contain them. In preference to "weapons of mass destruction" (WMD), a concept of "governance regime" is used to frame the issues. For while some CBW can properly be treated as WMD, all CBW are WMD only when eccentric meanings are given to these two technical terms. The original 1947–48 United Nations definition of WMD, for example, some of which is followed in present-day U.S. legislation on the subject, embraces only "lethal" chemical and biological weapons, whereas the CBW disarmament treaties of 1972 and 1993 have no such limitation, covering lethal and "nonlethal" CBW alike. This chapter therefore warns that express pursuit of WMD nonproliferation may damage the existing CBW governance regime, which is aimed at suppressing CBW and has proved largely successful in so doing. "Nonproliferation" is itself another technical term that is problematic in its application to CBW, for international law is now either approaching or, depending on one's view, has long since reached the point at which any possession of CBW is illegal. To posit nonproliferation of CBW as a policy objective is therefore to imply that this legal regime is failing. There is no evidence whatsoever for this. Nor, in contrast to nuclear weapons, does any state have license to possess CBW, not even the permanent members of the UN Security Council (UNSC).

So the present chapter does not fit easily into a book about WMD nonproliferation. It starts with an account of what sets CBW apart from other weapons. It then explains its concept of "CBW governance regime" and goes on to consider the challenges facing the regime. It closes with discussion of how the regime might best be strengthened.

The Peculiarities of CBW

CBW are weapons whose intended means for causing harm is either the toxicity of chemicals or the infectivity of disease-causing micro-organisms (including viruses, prions, and other such biological agents that are not, in the strict meaning of the expression, living organisms). There are other categories of biological and chemical that, although highly aggressive in their properties, are not useful in either toxic or infective weapons and which are therefore disregarded in the present chapter: napalm, white phosphorus, smoke agents, malodorants, high explosives, propellants, bacteria that can damage inanimate materials, and many more besides. They all lie beyond the scope, too, of the CBW disarmament treaties just mentioned.[1] Article II of the 1993 Chemical Weapons Convention (CWC) limits the chemicals covered by the treaty to "toxic chemicals and their precursors," qualified by a general purpose criterion (GPC) that reads "except when intended for purposes not prohibited under this Convention, as long as the types and quantities are consistent with such purposes." Article II goes on to define a toxic chemical as "any chemical which through its chemical action on life processes can cause death, temporary incapacitation or permanent harm to humans or animals." The corresponding provision in Article I of the 1972 Biological and Toxin Weapons Convention (BWC) is worded less tightly but also uses a GPC: it extends to all "microbial or other biological agents, or toxins whatever their origin or method of production, of types and in quantities that have no justification for prophylactic, protective or other peaceful purposes."

Readers needing detailed descriptive information about CBW that is reliable and sufficiently extensive to go to the heart of the problems that the weapons present for security—international, national, and human security—are well advised to turn first to three authoritative international texts on CBW—that of the UN secretary-general in 1969, which heralded the BWC negotiation, and those of the World Health Organization (WHO), initially produced as input into the secretary-general's report and later rewritten for the post–Cold War, post–9/11 world.[2] The 2004 WHO volume allows one to understand what makes CBW so peculiar today and why the security and health impacts of CBW armament could be so heavy. Three features in particular stand out from that text.

First and foremost, CBW may resemble other categories of weapon in that they can attack life, killing their victims no less dead than bullets or bayonets, but they may also be targeted to disrupt individual processes that contribute to life, which other weapons cannot do save by accident, not design. The nerve gases, for example, target nerve-signal transmission; the blood gases, cellular respiration. Advances in the life sciences and in those allied technologies that allow the analysis and construction of complex biologically active molecules could eventually make it possible to design a CBW agent that will interfere with *any* life process that can be understood in molecular terms, whether it be the process of development, inheritance, reproduction, locomotion, sensation, cognition, or indeed any other process that keeps us functioning properly, according to expectations. The potential is there, inasmuch as it has not materialized already, for inducing many different forms of malfunction, maybe even ones that discriminate between ethnic groups of human beings. It is this potential for manipulating at will our very humanity, in pursuit of who-knows-what strategy of adversary subjugation, repression, or coercion, that makes CBW especially menacing.[3] Science has a way to go yet before the full horrors can be upon us, but the writing is clearly on the wall. For example, the most obvious motivation that can be imputed to Iraq's program in the 1980s to weaponize aflatoxin is a desire to harm through latent liver cancer a subsequent generation of anticipated adversaries. As one UN Special Committee on Iraq (UNSCOM) commissioner put it, the objective must have been a weapon of delayed genocide.[4] Artillery shells charged with aflatoxin are said to have been used during the suppression of the Shi'ite uprising in March 1991. This has not been confirmed.

The second outstanding characteristic is that, as destroyers of life on a large scale, some CBW are WMD. When first used, on April 22 and 23, 1915, the device that brought chemical warfare out from its prehistory, namely massed cylinders of liquefied chlorine gas that could simultaneously be opened into the wind, reportedly asphyxiated five thousand French and Canadian troops at Ypres in Belgium and harmed a further fifteen thousand. Comparable numbers of people are said to have fallen victim to Iraqi mustard and nerve gas in the Kurdish town of Halabja after chemical air raids during March 16–18, 1988. For biological weapons there has been no similar experience, but during 1964–68 the United States conducted unprecedentedly large field trials over open sea of aircraft germ weapons, each of which was found capable of laying down a cross-wind line source of pathogenic microbial aerosol tens of kilometers long that was able to infect experimental animals at sea level over a distance of several tens of kilometers downwind.[5] That could translate into an infective threat to every person living within an area on the order of thousands, even tens of thousands, of square kilometers. In other words, it appeared from experimental data that some biological weapons would be capable of producing effects comparable in their magnitude to the life-destroying potential of nuclear weapons. Within the North Atlantic Treaty Organization (NATO) at that time, defense scientists were also anticipating a new generation of *chemical* weapons having comparable area effectiveness.[6] Yet the actual historical record of CBW employment is not at all dominated by episodes of mass destruction. Published military doctrine shows that most of the military and other utilities for which user-services have valued possession of CBW have depended on aggressive properties other than mass killing. One may view the available target effects of CBW as lying along spectra that have highly localized, say, or low-casualty effects at one end and large-area or mass-casualty effects at the other. Where along a spectrum a given chemical or biological weapon would manifest its effects is determined by the characteristics of the toxic/infective agent being used (such as the contagiousness of any disease it can cause) and the manner of its use, and by the vulnerability of the threatened population, this reflecting such factors as the health status of the population and degree of preparedness for protecting itself against the disseminated agent. It remains the case today that, in the design of CBW, increasingly severe technological constraints set in as the mass-destruction end of the spectrum is approached: the greater and more assured the area-effectiveness sought for the weapon, the greater the practical difficulties of achieving it. This is why the notion of mass-destruction terrorism using CBW is less plausible than its portrayals have often suggested.

The third outstanding characteristic of CBW is the existence of a uniquely wide array of societal constraints on CBW armament. This array has been building up over time in the law and custom of nations, so that damaging opprobrium is likely to fasten on any future users of CBW. Only nuclear weapons share this feature, but they have not yet attracted anything approaching the proscription of CBW. Some states speak with pride about their nuclear weapons.

From this third characteristic of CBW there stem elements of widely accepted law tending to suppress biological and chemical warfare. This is the "CBW governance regime" referred to earlier: an accretion of norms, rules, and procedures, both national and international, the whole constituting an entity ("regime") that individual states, through their various internal political processes, may judge themselves to be better off inside than outside. Its emergence can be explained in different ways. One of them is in terms of an ancient cross-cultural taboo, evident in different literatures over the millennia, against weapons that exploit disease, whether infectious or noninfectious.[7] One may well imagine this taboo having become transformed into a norm of international behavior, providing a basis for the further development of international law that is uncommonly strong in this peculiar field of armament. Weapons of any type are designed to harm, and there is no obvious reason for regarding one type of weaponized harm as more (or less) reprehensible than another. Is it worse to be the victim of unnatural disease than, say, to be shattered by shell fragments? One may ask this and then be surprised that so strong an obloquy should nevertheless have attached to disease weapons and not to other weapons. There is an irrationality here whose very strength and depth is characteristic of taboo.

The Existing CBW Governance Regime

The more recent milestones in that development of CBW-related law are here identified in turn, the focus being on the major multilateral elements of the regime. The regime has also been extended by developments that have not, in contrast, rested on wide international consensus, following instead from "pluri-lateral initiatives" and from a sequence of unilateral renunciations.

The 1925 Geneva Protocol, which is an international treaty whose states par-ties have agreed among themselves not to use CBW against one another, is the bedrock of the existing CBW governance regime. More properly known as the Protocol for the Prohibition of the Use in War of Asphyxiating, Poisonous or Other Gases, and of Bacteriological Methods of Warfare, it was negotiated dur-ing a League of Nations conference in Geneva on the arms trade and was signed on June 17, 1925. According to a communication in October 2002 from the Ministry of Foreign Affairs of France, which is the depositary of the treaty, it has 130 states parties (not counting Taiwan) including the five permanent members of the UNSC and one additional signatory state.[8] The Geneva Protocol builds on earlier international agreements, such as ones from the 1899 and 1907 peace conferences in The Hague, and is now widely considered to have entered cus-tomary international law, thereby becoming binding on all states whether they have or have not formally joined the treaty. The fact that the definition of war crimes in the Rome Statute of the International Criminal Court extends to use of chemical but not biological weapons is a reflection less of the state of customary law in 2000 than of a North-South political deal cut during the negotiation on account of nuclear weapons.

The 1972 Biological Weapons Convention is an international treaty ratified by 155 of the 171 states that, by September 2006, had signed it, thereby renouncing germ weapons in order to "exclude completely" the possibility of such weap-ons being used against human beings, other animals, or plants. It reflects the renunciation of biological weapons by the defeated Axis powers after the Sec-ond World War, as in the 1954 revised Brussels Treaty as well as the unilateral renunciations by the United States in 1969 and France (which did not join the treaty until 1984) in 1972. The BWC extended the regime of CBW no first use established by the Geneva Protocol by explicitly outlawing development, pro-duction, and stockpiling of biological and toxin weapons, but it has rather few of the ancillary provisions that are nowadays often thought essential: means of monitoring, even enforcing, compliance with its prohibitions and prescriptions of procedure for implementing its other rules, or of international organization for assisting states parties to discharge their obligations. Opportunities for extending the regime during the review conferences for which the BWC provides were, however, soon taken up, as with the institution of a consultative procedure in the event of problems arising, and also a variety of "confidence-building mea-sures" characterized as "politically binding." But subsequently confirmed reports of gross violation of the BWC by the USSR, as well as intelligence on Iraqi biological weapons (BW), promoted the belief that such measures could never in themselves be sufficient. This led, in 1995, to the opening of negotiations for an agreement among the states parties on a legally (as opposed to "politically") binding instrument that would strengthen the treaty by establishing verification or other compliance-promoting procedures. These Compliance Protocol negotiations collapsed in 2001.[9]

The 1977 EnMod Treaty, as the Convention on the Prohibition of Military or Any Other Hostile Use of Environmental Modification Techniques is commonly known, among other things prohibits warfare with chemicals toxic to plants, "having widespread, long-lasting or severe effects." This treaty entered into force in 1978 but is at present subscribed to by less than a majority of the world's states, though among the permanent members of the UNSC only France is a nonparty.

The 1993 Chemical Weapons Convention, like the BWC, originated in intergovernmental talks on CBW that commenced in 1968.[10] It prohibits development, production, and stockpiling of weapons toxic to human beings or other animals, or assistance in acquiring such weapons, and obliges parties to the treaty not only to institute domestic compliance-assuring measures, including penal legislation, but also to participate in a verification system operated by an international agency that the treaty established in The Hague, the Organization for the Prohibition of Chemical Weapons (OPCW). The OPCW includes a trained international inspectorate of 150–200 people. The treaty further extends the 1925 Geneva Protocol by including among its provisions an express prohibition of any use of toxic chemical weapons, including the use in reprisal or in retaliation, that the protocol could not outlaw. Together with the BWC, the CWC is the core of today's CBW governance regime. Initially inspired by the Vietnam War and heavily marked by the Cold War, both treaties are, in terms of membership, nearing universality, but with important holdouts, most conspicuously North Korea, Egypt, Israel, and Syria.[11] Both treaties seek to preclude international transfers of prohibited items, these being defined by their purpose because of the general purpose criteria that the two treaties use to set their scope in order not to interfere with dual-use goods meant for unprohibited purposes. Such an approach to governance of dual-use technology had become more fully developed by the time of the CWC, so much so that the CWC expressly outlaws factories for chemical weapons. The BWC had made no similar provision, its negotiators having been nervous about inhibiting vaccine production and commerce in products of biotechnology. Nor, in contrast to the CWC, does the BWC require disclosure of past biological weapons programs, though one of the confidence-building measures adopted in 1991 provides for it.[12]

80   *Julian Perry Robinson*

Empowerment of the UN Secretary-General to Investigate Use Allegations.   In November 1987 the UN General Assembly reaffirmed the powers of the UN secretary-general to investigate allegations of CBW use.[13] Such investigations took place on several occasions in Asia and Africa during 1981–93.[14] Since April 1997, the OPCW has been able, at the request of member states, to investigate allegations of chemical warfare. It has not yet formally done so. What happens if a UN investigation verifies an allegation is left for decision by the processes of international politics. Express provision for sanctions is largely absent from the overall regime.

UNSC Resolution 1540 (2004) and its implementing machinery are elements of the international response to perceptions of impending WMD terrorism. As regards CBW, the resolution seeks to universalize parts of national BWC- and CWC-implementing legislation (including transfer provisions) in regard to non-state entities. Even states not parties to the treaties, being bound as all UN member states are by UNSC resolutions, are now under obligation to enact and enforce such legislation.

Those are the six main components of today's CBW governance regime, all multilateral. Additional components have stemmed from unilateral renunciations outside the treaties and also from three plurilateral initiatives—the Global Partnership against the Spread of Weapons and Materials of Mass Destruction, the Proliferation Security Initiative, and, exclusively concerned with CBW, the Australia Group (AG). The AG began its work in May 1985 at the Australian embassy in Brussels after a year of preparatory activity both there and in other Western capitals. It seeks to harmonize supply-side controls on dual-use technology applicable to CBW by promoting common standards for the formation and implementation of national export-control policies.[15] It was inspired by the discovery that the chemical weapons used by Iraq in its war with Iran were not USSR-supplied but homemade, put together from dual-use commodities and know-how imported from the global marketplace. Its membership and range of activities have expanded over the years, most notably in the early 1990s, when it took on biological as well as chemical export controls and also agreed to controls on specific dual-use equipment applicable to the production and dissemination of CBW agents.[16] As the BWC and the CWC advance closer toward universality of membership, the AG will presumably come to serve mainly as a safety net against noncompliance with the technology-transfer provisions of the two treaties.

The international norm underlying the overall governance regime is CBW nonarmament and, in the case of former CBW possessor states, CBW disarmament. A principle of the regime is that it be nondiscriminatory, making no distinction between the "haves" and "have-nots" among its member states On the chemical side all of this has been developed into a respected international organization overseeing implementation and compliance procedures, hampered though it is by some remaining gaps in its legal foundation and by the ever-present possibility of governments (or their voters) losing awareness or appreciation of the OPCW's raison d'être.[17] On the biological side, in contrast, there is no such implementing organization to put into effect the terms of the BWC, which on its face is not much more than a statement of the norm plus obligations serving to enhance it that states parties have not always observed. To say this is not at all to disparage the BWC or to suggest that the biological side of the regime is feeble; on the contrary, the norm has clearly drawn much strength from state practice and the support of internationally organized civil society.[18] As Ambassador Donald Mahley, former chief U.S. CBW negotiator, said in Geneva during his valedictory statement on April 28, 2006, civilization, norm, and law are now such that there would be a massive reaction against the use of biological weapons by anyone, whether state or terrorist, in the future.[19] But the BWC regime certainly suffers, as its critics rightly observe, from an "institutional deficit"—the absence of an "OPBW" or anything like it charged with those routine activities of information exchange, assistance networking, and shared international procedure that would embed responsibility for the norm and the obligations within the bureaucracies and legislatures of BWC states parties.

Supranational threats to security, such as these weapons pose, require global solutions involving active international cooperation, as the UK government observed in 2002 in its green paper on strengthening the BWC.[20] Nothing less can suffice. Surprisingly successful though the regime has been, it still needs enlightened policymaking for its further development, not least in view of the newly emergent challenges that are described in the following section.

Challenges to the CBW Governance Regime

A development or change that causes a state to question its continuing allegiance to the CBW governance regime is, by definition, a challenge to that regime. The challenge may be to the regime as a whole or to particular parts of it. If major or many states start such questioning, the challenge is serious, requiring a collective response if the regime is to remain in good order, properly adapted to its ever-changing environment of international relations. For each state party the constant question is whether the benefits flowing from the regime continue to outweigh the attendant costs and also any penalties there may be to the national interest—are we still better off inside the regime than outside it? With that as a framing concept, particular challenges can be identified. Three big ones stand out at present: the emergence of new utilities for CBW, proliferation in a variety of forms, and the creeping legitimation of non-WMD CBW.

New Utilities for CBW

Disarmament, especially WMD disarmament, is an objective widely seen as beneficial, but armament can bring benefit by preserving security. Under some circumstances that could include CBW armament. Military options forgone through renunciation of CBW capabilities might then be significant on the cost side of remaining within the CBW governance regime. The taboo associated with disease weapons means that most states are content with CBW disarmament—except that circumstances now seem to be creating utilities for CBW not previously considered.

At least three types of new utility may now be discerned, and examples of all three seem evident in recent conflicts or in preparedness for war. The first is a consequence of wider changes in the nature of warfare, rather as the shift from "massive retaliation" to "limited war" doctrine in the late 1950s elevated the status of CBW in Western military thinking. A new type of organized violence is taking the place of, for example, those confrontations between highly disciplined and technologically advanced armed forces that characterized the later Cold War. Conflicts these past two decades in the Balkans, the Caucasus, the Horn of Africa, Rwanda, Liberia, Sierra Leone, Angola, Afghanistan, and Iraq have eroded formerly clear distinctions between war, organized crime, and large-scale violation of human rights. These new wars are fought by seeking political control through the displacement or worse of civilian populations and through the sowing of fear and hatred.[21] Because CBW can lend themselves particularly effectively to such objectives, they may have a greater affinity to the new wars than they did to the old, so, notwithstanding the CBW governance regime, they may have an expanding future.[22] This is an additional reason why the latest CBW use allegations, emanating from Sudanese, Israeli, Palestinian, Baluchi, and Lebanese sources, should not remain uninvestigated.

The CWC, though not the BWC, has a compliance-verification system run by the OPCW and its international inspectorate that ought in principle to countervail the new-utility challenge. But the routines of that system were designed against Cold War–period conceptions of utility, meaning that the lists of chemicals and types of industrial facility that the OPCW now has under its immediate surveillance are dictated by the types of chemical weapon that fitted old-war, not new-war, requirements. Basically that meant focusing on toxic chemicals that were so intensely aggressive in their effects that weapons disseminating them would be competitive, in casualty-producing terms, with conventional weapons. Not a great many such toxicants exist, so their coverage in the CWC schedules that govern routine OPCW verification allowed people to suppose that the main threats had thereby been brought under control. In the new wars, however, it is not so much relative aggressivity that determines the utility of CW but rather such other factors as accessibility or availability and terrorizing potential. A whole host of toxic industrial chemicals and other chemicals not hitherto regarded as CW agents might thus find application in new-war contexts. The fact that most of these chemicals are not listed in the CWC control schedules does not mean that their use for CW purposes is not prohibited, nor that the CWC is unavailing against them. It means only that the routine international verification procedures run by the OPCW may not see them. The GPC that the CWC uses to define its scope obliges the national authorities of states parties to ensure that no toxic chemical is abused. The challenge to the regime therefore lies in the degree to which such national controls may fail to exert a constraining effect.

A second major source of novel utility for CBW is the propensity of newly gained knowledge in the life sciences for suggesting novel modes of attack that could be the basis for militarily or politically attractive new forms of weapon. For example, if a hitherto unknown molecular pathway serving a process of life comes to be identified, chemical or biological agents capable of interfering with that pathway might also become identifiable and thus form the basis for a novel weapon. Of course, many considerations other than novelty of effect determine the usefulness of a new weapon, so the new science is not itself the challenge to the regime that is here suggested. But it would be a step toward it, and many such steps can be envisaged.[23] This prospect is not necessarily remote. We should not, for example, disregard the statement reliably attributed to a "former high-level Defense Department official" commenting on the feasibility of U.S. attack on Iranian underground facilities: "We can do things on the ground, too, but it's difficult and very dangerous—put bad stuff in ventilator shafts and put them to sleep."[24] Again, it is the GPC as used in the BWC and in the CWC that is the safeguard provided by the CBW governance regime against such challenges.

A third type of novel utility now becoming manifest is the emerging role of CBW, not so much in the hands of terrorists or other new-war aggressors, but for purposes of counterterrorism. This utility has demonstrably become a stimulus to rich-country questioning of the regime. It is rooted in past counterinsurgency applications of toxic chemicals, which reach back through the Vietnam War to British, French, Italian, and Spanish use of toxic chemicals in colonial situations—a utility that the CWC was intended to suppress. Its reemergence in counterterrorist guise is perhaps to be seen in the proliferation of weapons based on Agent CR, evident each year in that part of the OPCW Annual Report addressing declarations of "riot control agents," for the potency and other properties of CR have caused it to be widely rejected as suited to civil police use. The utility is also evident in the vigorous advocacy to be heard in some quarters for the arming of counterterrorist forces with more advanced types of "nonlethal" CBW. The readiness with which the U.S. Marine Corps has taken to toxin weapons of this type—devices disseminating Agent OC—is further indication.[25] So is the absence of any serious criticism of the Russian government for having authorized use of toxic chemicals other than riot-control agents by the *spetznaz* forces that, on October 26, 2002, liberated 634 of the theatergoers taken hostage by Chechen separatists in Moscow. The other 129 hostages were killed by the toxicant used, which is said to have been an agent "based on derivatives of fentanyl" that had been developed by USSR special services.[26]

Proliferation of CBW

Nowadays when people speak of CBW proliferation it is not always clear what they are talking about. The concerns expressed most commonly are probably about clandestine acquisition of CBW by nonstate entities, such concerns having supplanted or perhaps augmented earlier concerns about "rogue states." The characteristics that have caused states to be described as rogues include their supposed interest in acquiring CBW, so the concern could have been at root a questioning of the efficacy of the CBW governance regime, in turn becoming stimulus to the various plurilateral initiatives that have since contributed to the regime. Latterly these initiatives have been directed also against nonstate entities. Such entities include business corporations heedlessly serving a lucrative marketplace, criminal organizations feeding a black market, and terrorist groups seeking new weapons.

Proliferation of CBW to terrorists is, for reasons addressed earlier, probably myth. While it is known that certain terrorist groups have indeed looked at CBW options, such intent as they have to acquire CBW has not been translated into capability. Thus far, other means for terrorist violence have proved more attractive or more accessible to them and, since the aberration of Aum Shinrikyo in the 1990s, only the most footling attempts to acquire CBW have been observed.[27] This is not to say that it could not happen: the lesson to draw from the still unresolved "anthrax letters" affair in the United States during late 2001 is that biological weapons can put potential for great harm into the hands of technically competent and skilled individuals.[28] The CWC and BWC in fact place useful tools at the disposal of counterterrorism by obliging states parties to introduce and enforce effective controls on access and use of toxic and infective materials by persons within their jurisdictions. Yet it is at the state level that CBW proliferation is still, on the available evidence, a more serious challenge to the CBW governance regime.

Here it is necessary to differentiate between "vertical" and "horizontal" proliferation. Vertical proliferation describes the process whereby states possessing CBW weapons expand or upgrade existing CBW capabilities. It thus refers solely to states that have opted to remain outside the regime and, for those that have done so in order to preserve CBW capability (as opposed to lack of interest or even awareness), the challenge to the regime is serious on several counts. Above all, it strengthens pro-CBW constituencies in both national and bureaucratic politics, thereby increasing the political costs to the country's leadership if it were to advocate joining the regime. Most probably this process is operating in Egypt, Israel, and Syria, where it has been greatly complicated by nuclear weapons. Syria has been uniquely forthcoming about its avowed CW capability, starting in November 1996 when its ambassador to Egypt told a lecture audience in Alexandria that Syria would retaliate with chemical weapons against Israeli nuclear attack or threat.[29] President Bashar Assad has spoken recently about Syrian rights to possession of CBW as a safeguard against "Israeli aggression."[30] Nor have Israeli officials been reticent about their view of Syrian CW and, by implication, the counter-chemical weapons value of Israeli nuclear weapons.

Horizontal CBW proliferation presents an altogether different kind of challenge to the CBW governance regime, one that is rooted in the otherwise mostly beneficial tendency of industrial and other technologies to diffuse rapidly around the world under the various influences of globalization. The capability of individual states to acquire CBW weapons, if they so choose, is thereby enhanced, and if they still need specialized assistance, clandestine procurement networks have now gained increasingly dense cover within which to operate. That networks of this type can indeed spring up to meet demand was clearly shown by the UNSCOM/UNMOVIC (UN Monitoring, Verification, and Inspection Commission) investigation of Iraqi CBW acquisition and by the Libyan CW program.[31] At the level of know-how and other intangible technology, comparable assistance is increasingly available from another quarter as well. A great proliferation of competence in technological matters relating to CBW is currently underway in the United States as thousands of millions of dollars are dedicated annually to countermeasures against bioterrorism, a competence that may by now surpass whatever is left from the Soviet BW program.[32] Even states that have no immediate wish to acquire CBW may nevertheless move to take advantage of these various possibilities as a hedge against circumstances changing—by, for example, building what could serve as "breakout capacity" into their industrial infrastructure rather as the

USSR created "mobilization capability" for manufacturing BW within its bio-tech industry during 1973–92. Iran, victim on a terrible scale to Iraqi chemical weapons during 1983–88, very probably falls into this category while at the same time being among the most vocal supporters of the CBW governance regime and, especially on the medical side, a proactive participant in its international procedures.[33] Nor is there any clear impropriety in such a position, for all the in-dustrial powers, including ones that menace Iran, have manufacturing industries to which they could turn at short notice for CBW agents (whose full weaponiza-tion would, however, be more demanding). The fact nevertheless remains that horizontal proliferation of this type is a threat to confidence in the regime and therefore a serious challenge to it for as long as the problem of dual use persists.

Creeping Legitimation of Non-WMD CBW

In the ability of CBW agents to target themselves on particular life processes, there is growing scope for users of weapons based on them to "tailor" the nature or severity of their effects to a strategic objective. In that such tailoring could, as has been seen, open the way to weapons suited to hugely malign purpose, CBW present a long-term danger that demands an alert and strong CBW gov-ernance regime. That same tailoring can, however, provide weapons of an al-together more acceptable character, including ones having effects gentler than most other means of violence. Examples include the "tear gas" of police forces; the psychochemical weapons that, according to past U.S. Army teaching, would cause the enemy to "linger in overpowering reverie";[34] and the entirely mythical knockout agents of "war without death" that have figured in science fiction since the nineteenth century. Add to these chemicals the various infective agents that can induce highly debilitating diseases of low mortality, and a category of CBW is created whose features seem far distant from those of WMD, whose possession may appear desirable, and whose constraint by the regime may therefore come to seem a substantial liability, notwithstanding the abyss into which the tailoring could also take us.

A rather wide variety of commercial, political, and military interests stand to benefit from exclusion of some or all of these non-WMD CBW from the gover-nance regime. Sub rosa campaigning to that end has long been under way, most notably during the last months of the CWC negotiation in mid-1992, when the new protagonists of nonlethal warfare (NLW) came up against governmental of-ficials charged with securing consensus on those parts of the CWC text that dealt with "riot control agents" (RCAs). The issue turned then on whether RCA should or should not fall within the definition of "toxic chemicals," subject, thereby, to the GPC that would serve to regulate the duality of their application either in warfare (prohibited) or in law enforcement (permitted). The United States favored exclusion but, finding itself isolated in this position within the Western group, secured a compromise in which the CWC expressly prohibited use of RCA "as a method of warfare" but remained silent on the toxic character of RCAs, thus perpetuating a semblance of ambiguity on whether the toxicity criterion fundamental to the CWC did or did not capture RCAs. The way became open for determined NLW protagonists to argue that, if tear gas was not proscribed by the CWC, then neither should the more modern varieties, for which they coined the category label "advanced RCA technology" (ARCAT). Subsequent ARCAT development projects funded by the U.S. government included work on the fentanyls and other such intensely supertoxic chemicals. The process that can be seen here is a surreptitious equation of toxicity with lethal toxicity, and in this attempt to loosen the CWC constraint on the weaponization of other forms of toxicity we have started to see a creeping legitimation of non-WMD CBW, which is a most serious challenge to the regime. A situation in which some types of toxic weapon are allowed but not others is certain to be unstable.

Strengthening the CBW Governance Regime

Two features stand as bulwarks against the challenges to the CBW governance regime. The first is an OPCW that, despite severe budgetary constraints and opaque operating methods but having constructive U.S. support, is now an effective multilateral institution that is actively suppressing chemical warfare armament in most of the world. Second, in regard to disease warfare more generally, modern customary and conventional international law has transformed an ancient taboo into an enforceable norm of international behavior. Together these are the principal reasons why chemical and biological warfare are rare occurrences even in today's conflict-ridden world. Because of what CBW could become, they are treasure that must not be frittered away.

Loose talk of CBW "nonproliferation" is, as has been seen, a step in that direction, for it carries the implication—no doubt unintended by most of those who use the term—that some states have a right to possess disease weapons; and there are indeed certain states in which some leadership figures actually seem to believe this to be so, at least in the case of disabling chemical weapons having counterterrorist application. Yet as a step in the wrong direction this one is surely far outpaced by that other tendency mentioned earlier, treating CBW as though they can properly be regarded as a subset of WMD. The hazard here is not only the suggestion that non-WMD CBW are acceptable—that as long as CBW do not kill us in large numbers they are legitimate instruments of security. Nor is it only the danger that the fuzzy concept of WMD is now supplanting that long-standing precept of the laws of war whereby weapons employment that does not discriminate between combatant and noncombatant is impermissible, on whatever scale it may occur. No less pernicious is a third implication: that, being in the same category, nuclear weapons are a legitimate, even a necessary, counter to CBW, whether as deterrent instrument of retaliation or as means for destroying CBW capability. We can see this implication displayed in the current pressure in the United States for acquisition of "bunker busting" nuclear weapons and in the entry into the declared national policy of some of the NWS (China is in fact the only clear exception) of stated willingness to use nuclear weapons in response to CBW attack. There is further reason beyond the legitimation it seems to offer for nuclear armament why this last is so dangerous a policy. Any decision on such nuclear release would have to rest on what recent events have shown to be very uncertain ground indeed: intelligence about supposed adversary CBW behavior. Ambiguities, uncertainties, and other peculiarities attach to CBW to such a degree that the methods of intelligence assessment that seem to work adequately outside the CBW field do less well within it. The oddities of CBW, which are rooted mainly in the dual-use nature of much of their contributing technology, are too obtrusive to be swept under a collective WMD carpet. Professional CBW intelligence analysts of course recognize this; it is at the interface between them and their political masters that the attendant misapprehensions are liable to become dangerously misleading or, if not that, the uncertainties then become subordinated to the political imperatives of the moment. The failure to find CBW in Iraq after the last coalition invasion; the cruise-missile bombardment of Al-Shifa Pharmaceutical Industries in the Sudan before that; and, from still earlier times, the Yellow Rain fiasco in which President Reagan's administration mistook bee excrement for BW—all of these and more are cautionary tales.

The sixth BWC review conference (November 20–December 8, 2006) stimulated much work on how best to strengthen the biological side of the present CBW governance regime, and the second CWC review conference (April 7–18, 2008) has begun to do the same for the chemical side. The U.S. government, which has faced criticism for its seemingly hostile attitude toward the BWC since 2001, has put forward suggestions, albeit chiefly of a plurilateral rather than multilateral kind. The often contrasting recommendations of the WMD Commission chaired by Hans Blix of Sweden also merit the most careful attention.[35]

Ordering principles for these and the many other proposed ways forward are needed and, for this, an attractive logic is to prioritize around the two bulwarks of the regime: to put most effort into (a) enhancing the OPCW and (b) strengthening the norm. In comparison, the various other sorts of proposals, such as codes of conduct for scientists, seem mere tinkering at the edges, useful though they are as topics for international discourse at times when real progress is politically difficult.

Enhancing the OPCW means soliciting maximal support for the organization in national politics and as much freedom for it to get on with its CWC-assigned tasks as the international system can countenance. Enhancing the OPCW also means ensuring that, in its necessary pursuit of adaptation to changing international relations, it is protected from having to compromise on principles or procedures that lie at its heart. Undoubtedly the best judge of how to do this is the OPCW technical secretariat. But its institutional memory is now severely challenged by the secretariat having to implement an employment policy that admits only a seven-year job tenure. For this reason, and especially for matters that impinge on political sensitivities and on which the secretariat may therefore be unable to develop its own recommendations, "scapegoat" study by outside specialists may become essential. A clear case in point is the question of how the OPCW should best respond to NLW technology. A second (and not unrelated) example is study of why so many OPCW member states have difficulty implementing the GPC or even recognizing it as the source of the comprehensive nature of the CWC's prohibitions, which is the vital safeguard against adverse technological change and against abuse of dual technology.[36] Both are topics that civil-society friends of the OPCW will expect the second CWC review to examine most carefully. Meanwhile the OPCW's own projects for strengthening the norm should receive the widest possible outside assistance, including that of civil society: the action plans for promoting universality of the CWC and for improving implementation of CWC Article VII on national measures.

Strengthening the norm means, first, not weakening the norm and, second, promoting mechanisms that will ensure the norm is not disregarded at the national level and is more enforceable than it is at present at the international level. How is it possible to weaken a norm that seems to rest on so strong a taboo? Perhaps by fragmentation: by treating BW and CW as though they were entirely different from one another instead of variations on a single theme, that of disease weapons; or by differentiating lethal and "nonlethal" CBW, or WMD and non-WMD. Sometimes, certainly, different types of CBW will require different practical arrangements; but, in the interests of norm integrity, the default position, so to speak, must surely be common treatment wherever possible. Nor is that an unnatural default. As scientific disciplines, chemistry and biology are converging. And the BWC and the CWC anyway overlap strongly in their scope: toxins, for example, are covered by both treaties; and it is not unreasonable to contemplate the routine international procedures of the OPCW being extended into the domain of toxins and other inanimate biological agents.

Beyond that, two different forms of strengthening may now be judged worth-while. The first is the mechanism noted earlier: machinery for entrenching responsibility for the norm and rules of the BWC into the bureaucracies and legislatures of BWC states parties. For such machinery the CWC has a demonstrably workable model in the obligation it has placed on its states parties to designate or establish national authorities for liaising with other states parties, and with the OPCW, empowered by penal legislation to implement the provisions of the treaty within their jurisdictions. A number of OPCW member states have gone further and created formal lines of communication between their national authorities, their legislatures, their industries, and their civil society, as in the UK's National Authority Advisory Committee. Some of the CWC national authorities already include BWC cells. The necessary precursor of the mechanism being proposed here is an international campaign to ensure that BWC states parties take Article IV more seriously than many seem to do at present. That article contains the obligation upon each state party to "take any necessary measures to prohibit and prevent" all BWC-violative activity within its jurisdiction. The European Union (EU) has already agreed to a joint action to this end and further pressure is emanating from UNSC Resolution 1673 (2006) that has extended 1540 (2004).[37] All that would then be lacking to complete the norm-strengthening mechanism would be some form of standing international secretariat for the BWC. Though there has in the past been resistance to creating any such body, times have now changed, and the BWC institutional deficit has become a disgrace to the states that created it. Their affirmations of support for the BWC are no longer credible.

The second, and complementary, means for strengthening the norm is machinery for better enforcement. Sovereign states do not readily commit themselves in advance to punitive or other reactive sanctions against one another, so a possible way forward is a mechanism for holding *individuals* personally accountable for any such violations. The individual-responsibility approach is already a discernible trend in international affairs. Individuals, or at least substate entities, in their identity as persons involved in WMD proliferation, are the main target of UNSC Resolution 1540 (2004). The former president of Iraq, Saddam Hussein, was found guilty of charges arising out of the CW attacks on Halabja and executed. From among the several categories of stakeholder in the development of biotechnology, individual scientists are being made responsible for impeding access to dual-use materials judged helpful to bioterrorists. All of this is surely good for the norm. Yet the defining feature of a universal norm is not that it should dictate how particular individuals or groups behave but rather how *everyone* should behave, high or low, head of state or simple citizen. All of us are responsible for the continued well-being of the norm against the weaponization of disease, and the onus is therefore on us all, individually, to uphold it. It is all very well saying (as many people continued to do at the time of the 2005 BWC intersessional meetings) that scientists need to think more about conceivable end-applications of their work and be taught about the international treaty that is meant to suppress BW. That treaty, the BWC, codifies the norm, but like the Geneva Protocol and the CWC, it places its primary constraints on the behavior of states, not of individuals. If the norm is to be strengthened, the overall regime must be developed so that its relevance to the individual as well as to the state becomes clear to all. And unless this is done in step with the current moves toward codes of conduct and principles of practice for scientists, those moves will merely become empty acts of discrimination, unpopular and ignored. A more compelling way of inserting the sanction of individual accountability into the regime is needed.

Now that international criminal law is emerging from the constraints of the Cold War, just such a mechanism has become possible. It is a very simple one indeed: a new international convention that would confer on national courts jurisdiction over individuals present in their national territory, regardless of their nationality or official position, who order, direct, or knowingly lend substantial assistance to the acquisition, production, or use of CBW anywhere. Such a convention might take various forms. One possible text, prepared with advice from an international group of eminent jurists, is the Harvard Sussex Draft Convention.[38] This has already attracted favorable notice from a number of governments and now constitutes the basis for a possible further initiative in the WMD area by the EU.

If support could indeed be mustered for the several norm-strengthening and organization-enhancing measures just described, the CBW governance regime would surely be better able to resist the challenges that now face it, even the ultimate challenge of emergent CBW that can change human identity.

Notes

1. The texts of the two treaties are available in many places, including the Web site of the Harvard Sussex Program on CBW, http://www.sussex.ac.uk/Units/spru/hsp, which is cited here because some of the literature referenced later in this chapter, including the CBW Conventions Bulletin, is posted on it.

2. United Nations, Chemical and Bacteriological (Biological) Weapons and the Effects of Their Possible Use, report of the secretary-general (New York: United Nations, 1969); World Health Organization, Health Aspects of Chemical and Biological Weapons: Report of a WHO Group of Consultants (Geneva: World Health Organization, 1970); World Health Organization, Public Health Response to Biological and Chemical Weapons: WHO Guidance (Geneva: World Health Organization, 2004).

3 See also Matthew Meselson, "Averting the Hostile Exploitation of Biotechnology," *CBW Conventions Bulletin* 48 (June 2000): 16–19.

4 See "News Chronology: May through August 1997," May 6, 1997, entry, *CBW Conventions Bulletin* 37 (September 1997): 16.

5 Ed Regis, *The Biology of Doom* (New York: Henry Holt, 1999).

6 North Atlantic Treaty Organization, standing group, von Kármán Committee, *Future Developments in Chemical Warfare*, report of Working Group 10 on Chemical, Biological and Radiological Defence, March 1961, as distributed to the UK Ministry of Defence Advisory Council on Scientific Research and Technical Development, paper no. SAC 1928, February 11, 1969, in the National Archive, Kew, file WO195/16864

7 M A Marin, "The Evolution and Present Status of the Laws of War," *Académie de Droit International: Receuil des Cours* 92, no. 2 (1957): 633–749.

8 See World Health Organization, *Public Health Response*, 109–10, 335–40.

9 For the definitive account of the protocol negotiations, see Jez Littlewood, *The Biological Weapons Convention: A Failed Revolution* (Aldershot, UK: Ashgate, 2005).

10 For an unrivaled description of the CWC, see Walter Krutzsch and Ralf Trapp, *A Commentary on the Chemical Weapons Convention* (Dordrecht: Martinus Nijhoff, 1994).

11 North Korea is party to the BWC but not the CWC. Both Egypt and Syria have signed but not yet ratified the BWC; neither has signed or ratified the CWC Israel has signed but not yet ratified the CWC; it has not signed or ratified the BWC. All four countries are understood to have developed CW and/or BW capability.

12 On which see in particular Nicolas Isla, *Transparency in Past Offensive Biological Weapon Programmes: An Analysis of Confidence Building Measure Form F 1992–2003*, Hamburg Centre for Biological Arms Control Occasional Paper 1, June 2006, http://www.biological-arms-control.org/download/FormF_1992-2003.pdf.

13 UN General Assembly resolution 42/37C.

14 For references see World Health Organization, *Public Health Response to Biological and Chemical Weapons*, 129

15 Recently the Australia Group (AG), hitherto a secretive organization, has established its own Web site at http://www.australiagroup.net.

16 Robert J Mathews, "The Development of the Australia Group Export Control Lists of Biological Pathogens, Toxins and Dual-Use Equipment," *CBW Conventions Bulletin* 66 (December 2004): 1–4.

17 For a detailed account of the formation of the OPCW and of how the first eight years of its existence proceeded, see the quarterly reviews published as "Progress in The Hague," *Chemical Weapons Convention Bulletin* 19 (March 1993) through the *CBW Conventions Bulletin* 67 (March 2005): 6–11

18 See, for example, Julian Perry Robinson, "The Impact of Pugwash on the Debates over Chemical and Biological Weapons," in *Scientific Cooperation, State Conflict: The Roles of Scientists in Mitigating International Discord*, ed. Allison L. C. de Cerreño and Alexander Keynan (New York: New York Academy of Sciences, 1998), 224–52.

19 Graham Pearson, "Report from Geneva: The Preparatory Committee for the Sixth BWC Review Conference," *CBW Conventions Bulletin* 71 (May 2006): 6–15 (14)

20. United Kingdom, Secretary of State for Foreign and Commonwealth Affairs, *Strengthening the Biological and Toxin Weapons Convention: Countering the Threat from Biological Weapons*, Cm 5484, April 29, 2002, http://www.brad ac.uk/acad/sbtwc/other/fcobw.pdf.

21. Mary Kaldor, *New and Old Wars: Organized Violence in a Global Era* (Cambridge, UK· Polity, 1999).

22 See also Julian Perry Robinson, "The General Purpose Criterion and the New Utility of Toxicants as Weapons," paper presented at the 15th workshop of the Pugwash Study Group on Implementation of the CBW Conventions, Oegstgeest, the Netherlands, June 23–24, 2001.

23. For a particularly rich recent source of information on advances in technology that may be applicable to CBW, see the Institute of Medicine and National Research Council, and the Committee on Advances in Technology and the Prevention of Their Application to Next Generation Biowarfare Threats (Stanley M. Lemon, and David A. Relman, cochairs), *Globalization, Biosecurity, and the Future of the Life Sciences* (Washington, DC: National Academies Press, 2006).

24. Seymour M. Hersh, "The Iran Plans: Would President Bush Go to War to Stop Tehran from Getting the Bomb?" *New Yorker*, April 17, 2006, 30–31, http://www.newyorker.com/archive/2006/04/17/060417fa_fact

25 See "News Chronology. February–May 1996," March 22, 1996, entry, *CBW Conventions Bulletin* 32 (June 1996). 27

26. Julian Perry Robinson, "Disabling Chemical Weapons A Documented Chronology of Events," paper for private distribution, Harvard-Sussex Program, November 1, 2003, 139–42.

27. For an informed review of the evidence of interest in CBW by actual terrorist groups today, see Milton Leitenberg, *Assessing the Biological Weapons and Bioterrorism Threat*, Strategic Studies Institute of the U.S Army War College, December 2005, 21–42.

28. See, further, Martin Rees, *Our Final Century: Will the Human Race Survive the Twenty-first Century?* (London: Heinemann, 2003); and Milton Leitenberg, *The Problem of Biological Weapons* (Stockholm: Swedish National Defence College, 2004, 137–55.

29. See "News Chronology: November 1996 through February 1997," November 25, 1996, entry, *CBW Conventions Bulletin* 35 (March 1997)· 24.

30 See "News Chronology. November 2003 through January 2004," January 6, 2004, entry, *CBW Conventions Bulletin* 63 (2004): 37.

31 On UNSCOM investigations, see especially Tim Trevan, *Saddam's Secrets: The Hunt for Iraq's Hidden Weapons* (London· HarperCollins, 1999); Graham Pearson, *The UNSCOM Saga: Chemical and Biological Weapons Non-Proliferation* (London· Macmillan, 1999); Graham Pearson, *The Search for Iraq's Weapons of Mass Destruction: Inspection, Verification and Non-Proliferation* (Basingstoke, UK: Palgrave Macmillan, 2005); Scott Ritter, *Iraq Confidential* (New York: Nation Books, 2005).

32. Stephanie Chang and Alan Pearson, *Federal Funding for Biological Weapons Prevention and Defense, Fiscal Years 2001 to 2007*, Center for Arms Control and Non-Proliferation, June 21, 2006, http://www.armscontrolcenter.org/assets/pdfs/fy2007_bwbudget.pdf.

33. International Institute for Strategic Studies, *Iran's Strategic Weapons Programmes: A Net Assessment* (London: Routledge. 2005).

34. U S. Army Chemical Center and School, Fort McClellan, "New Chemical Agents and Incapacitating Agents," lesson plan LP6075, undated (ca. 1965).

35 Weapons of Mass Destruction Commission, *Weapons of Terror: Freeing the World of Nuclear, Biological and Chemical Arms*, final report (Stockholm, Sweden Weapons of Mass Destruction Commission, June 1, 2006).

36. On these functions of the GPC, see United Kingdom Department of Trade and Industry, *Operation of the Chemical Weapons Act 1996: Annual Report 2004*, 26–28, July 2005, http://www.berr.gov.uk/files/file26554.pdf

37. Council of the European Union, *Council Joint Action 2006/184/CFSP*, February 27, 2006, http://eur-lex.europa.eu/LexUriServ/ LexUriServ.do?uri=OJ:L:2006:065:0051:0055 :EN:PDF

38. Matthew Meselson and Julian Robinson, "A Draft Convention to Prohibit Biological and Chemical Weapons under International Law," in *Treaty Enforcement and International Cooperation in Criminal Matters*, ed. Rodrigo Yepes-Enriquez and Lisa Tabassi, 457–69 (The Hague: TMC Asser, 2002).

[13]

THE ORGANIZATION FOR THE PROHIBITION OF CHEMICAL WEAPONS: MOVING CLOSER TOWARDS AN INTERNATIONAL ARMS CONTROL ORGANIZATION? A QUANTUM LEAP IN THE INSTITUTIONAL LAW OF ARMS CONTROL

Eric P.J. Myjer[*]

I. Introduction

Someone had stuck a piece of paper on the wall of the *Congresgebouw* in The Hague where the PrepCom working groups of the Organization for the Prohibition of Chemical Weapons (OPCW) were meeting on a daily basis in order to fill in the basic structure of the Chemical Weapons Convention (CWC)[1] to be presented to the First Conference of States Parties for approval. The paper indicated how far one still had to come in order to attain the necessary 65 ratifications before the entry into force of the Convention. After that point was finally reached on 31 October 1996 by the deposit of the Hungarian instrument of ratification[2] the paper was replaced by a calender "which ticked away" the days up to the required 180 days after the deposit of this 65th instrument of ratification when "EIF" (entry into force) of the Convention would be attained on 29th of April 1997. In the meantime at the Catsheuvel, an open spot almost opposite the *Congresgebouw*, builders were - finally- busily laying their concrete foundations for the OPCW building.

Since that time the building has been completed, and, after more than four years of PrepCom work, the First Conference of States Parties has been held,[3] the initial declarations have been submitted and the inspection teams have started their work.

After the many years of negotiations it somehow seems a miracle that this point finally has finally been reached, for the international community has been rather reticent about achieving quick results in this area. It took 20 years after the Biological Weapons Convention was concluded as well as the end of the Cold War before the negotiations in the Conference on Disarmament led to the

---

[*] This is an updated version from the seminar.

This contribution is tributed to Bert Vierdag, Professor Emeritus of Public International Law and International Relations at the University of Amsterdam, for his stimulating role in the advance of research into and teaching of arms control law.

[1] Convention on the Prohibition of the Development, Production, Stockpiling and the Use of Chemical Weapons and on Their Destruction, 32, *ILM*, pp. 800-873.

[2] *Ibid*, Art. XXI.

[3] From 6 May - 23 May 1997.

Chemical Weapons Convention (CWC) as signed in January 1993.[4] "The significance of this achievement lies in the fact that it is the first multilaterally negotiated treaty which provides for the ban of an entire category of weapons of mass destruction under strict and universally applied international control".[5] The total ban on chemical weapons, in other words on a complete category of weapons of mass destruction, is to be realized by prohibiting the development, production or retention of chemical weapons. The scope of the CWC is much wider than that of the BWC for biological weapons for it also includes a commitment *never under any circumstances to use* chemical weapons. A complete disarmament of this category of weapons is foreseen as States which possess such weapons will have to destroy all the existing chemical weapons as well as the production facilities. The use and production of certain chemicals will be restricted because they might be used as precursors in the development of chemical weapons. Control of these restrictions will of necessity involve civilian chemical industries. This first comprehensive ban on both the possession as well as the use of a complete category of weapons therefore not only involves the military establishment, but also large sections of States Parties' civilian chemical industries. This raises the problem of the protection of confidential business information.[6]

No such expansive agreement, however, would have been possible without agreement on an effective mechanism to control compliance with these undertakings. For that purpose this Convention at the same time establishes the Organization for the Prohibition of Chemical Weapons (OPCW), a specialised international organization, within the UN family, with as its sole[7] purpose the supervision of compliance with the core ("general") obligations of States

---

[4] For a comprehensive compilation of documents and decisions on the Convention see L. Woollomes Tabassi (ed.), *OPCW, The Legal Texts* (1999). For general commentaries see for instance: D. Bardonnet (ed.), Hague Academy of International Law, *The Convention on the Prohibition and Elimination of Chemical Weapons: A Breakthrough in Multilateral Disarmament* (1995); W. Krutzsch and R. Trapp, *A Commentary on the Chemical Weapons Convention* (1994); B. Kellman and E.A. Tanzman, *Manual for National Implementation of the Chemical Weapons Convention* (1998) (2nd); M. Bothe, N. Ronzitti and A. Rosas (eds), *The New Chemical Weapons Convention- Implementation and Prospects* (1998).

[5] A.J.J. Ooms, History of the Negotiations of the Chemical Weapons Convention, unpublished paper, at 1.

[6] To which element also the US Senate attaches great importance. See Condition 16 (Protection of Confidential Information), Ratification Resolution, *Senate Congressional Record*, April 24, 1997, at S 3655.

[7] Notwithstanding the role of the OPCW under Article X regarding the provision of assistance and protection against chemical weapons. The formulation in Article VIII A (1) suggests an autonomous task for the OPCW beyond supervision of compliance of the core commitments under Article I, by the provision of a forum "for consultation and cooperation among States Parties". This, however, should be viewed as functional in the context of supervision of compliance.

E. MYJER 63

Parties under Article I.[8] Thereto this international organization -the OPCW- has wide powers for verifying compliance locally, on a Member State's territory, not only routinely on-site (routine inspections) at predetermined places, but also at the request of States Parties via challenge inspections to be undertaken by the standing international inspectorate of the OPCW.

It is remarkable that States Parties were willing for the common good (the ban on chemical weapons) or because of their interdependence[9] to allow for these inroads into their territorial sovereignty. Features like these give the CWC compliance-control mechanism its unique character.

Another outstanding feature, and for political purposes highly necessary, is the universal character of this treaty which is reflected in the high number of required ratifications (65) before the treaty enters into force and in the high number of States Parties (139[10] at the time of writing) and Signatory States (35), which may lead to an almost universal membership. This aspect of universality is also reflected in the fact that the organization will be part of the UN system as reflected in the special agreement between the United Nations (UN) and the OPCW.[11] It is, however, an independent, autonomous international organization.

---

[8] It appears to be an international organization of which, in the words of I. Seidl-Hohenveldern, the *raison d'être* is the control of member states' compliance with a certain purpose. For him this is even the *raison d'être* of any international organization for "These entities were established to grant their member states a better control of each other's activities towards the fulfilment of a given purpose". Another example would be the Commission for the Navigation of the Rhine. In: N. Blokker & S. Muller, *Towards More Effective Supervision by International Organizations* (essays in honour of H.G. Schermers) (1994) at 255. I agree with Blokker/Muller (at 275) that this function, supervision of rule compliance by the member states, is a "classical function of International organizations". But I differ, however, with Seidl-Hohenveldern that this is always the *raison d'être*, for an important function of a general international organization also lies in its ability for decision-making and acting as a forum.

[9] Writing about supervision by International Organizations in general :"Interdependence has forced states to accept encroachments of sovereignty; not only by the formulation of international obligations, but also by some degree of surveillance over their observance of these obligations and even, to a limited extent, the possibility of sanctions being imposed in case of non-compliance. Thus, interdependence is the bridge between supervision and sovereignty. It is the magic word which reconciles these two seemingly irreconcilable concepts."Blokker/Muller, *supra* n. 8, at 310.

[10] As of September 2000.

[11] "The United Nations recognises that the OPCW, by virtue of the Convention, shall function as an idependent, autonomous international organization in the working relationship with the United Nations established by this Agreement." (Article I, para. 2), *Agreement Concerning the Relationship between the United Nations and the Organization for the Prohibition of Chemical Weapons*, signed 17 October 2000. In view of an earlier decision by the Conference (C-IV/DEC.4, 2 July 1999), the Executive Council recommended the Conference to approve the draft of this agreement and authorized the Director to sign it for provisional application pending approval by the UN General Asssembly and by the

64   E. MYJER

Aspects like these led to the OPCW being appraised from many sides as a unique international organization both from a political point of view as well as from a legal point of view.[12] This in itself is sufficient reason to take a closer look at this organization. Another reason being that this CWC mode of supervision has already been applied in the case of the Comprehensive Test Ban Treaty (CTBT) with its Comprehensive Nuclear Test-Ban Treaty Organization[13] and that attempts are made to foresee a comparable supervisory mechanism for the Biological Weapons Convention (BWC) that does not yet have any supervisory mechanism,[14] since at the time of concluding the BWC the military usefulness of these weapons was anyhow considered to be low. Furthermore, the International Atomic Energy Agency (IAEA) in considering strategies to strengthen the effectiveness of NPT safeguards had an independent expert group (SAGSI) appointed that came up with the recommendation "that the CWC offers approaches for verification and investigation that may be adaptable to the NPT".[15] Developments like these make necessary an analysis of the OPCW as a model for future international organizations with a supervisory role in the sphere of arms control. Such an analysis is the main purpose of this contribution. I will thereby (also) look into the question whether the OPCW as an international organization in the area of arms control with its specific supervisory purpose is as unique as it appears.

For analytical purposes I will make use of the concept of supervision as used with regard to international economic organizations with its three separate functions. These functions are the *review function* (evaluating State behaviour for its conformity with an agreed rule of international law); the *correction*

Conference (EC-MXI/DEC.1.,1 September 2000).

[12] Compare Krutzsch et al., n. 4 at 125; Also Bernauer, *The Chemistry of Regime Formation: Explaining International Cooperation for a Comprehensive Ban on Chemical Weapons* (1993): The International Institute for Strategic Studies (London) called CWC "the most ambitious disarmament agreement ever negotiated", International Institute for Strategic Studies (IISS), *Strategic Survey 1992-1993*, at 214.

[13] Compare Article II (the Organization) of the Comprehensive Test Ban Treaty and its extensive Protocol with annexes that are integral to the treaty, opened up for signature September 24, 1996, 35 *ILM* 1439-1478. See G. den Dekker, *Internationale controle en handhaving van het verbod op kernproeven*, Utrecht University (1997) (ISBN 90-5213-095-7).

[14] Compare the "mechanism" contained in Article V of the BWC on consultation and cooperation between States Parties "in solving any problems which may arise in relation to the objectives of, or in the application of the provisions" and in Article VI that foresees the lodging of a complaint with the Security Council by a State Party "which finds that another State Party is acting in breach of obligations deriving from the Provisions of the Convention".

[15] See for an extensive comparative analysis: D.S. Gualtieri, B. Kellman, K.E. Apt and E.A. Tanzman, Advancing the law of weapons control - comparative approaches to strengthen nuclear non-proliferation, 16 *Michigan Journal of International Law*, (1995) at 1029-1111.

E. MYJER 65

function (the correction of State behaviour, when it is established that a state has violated an international obligation); and the *creative function* (interpretation or clarification of the rules). For the sake of clarity, however, I will, add a fourth function, namely the *collection function*, which leads me to the following distinction: (1) collection function; (2) review function; (3) creative function; (4) correction function.

Chapter II will provide a historical description of the stages involved in the control of chemical weapons; *Chapter III* describes the general structure of the Convention and *Chapter IV* that of the OPCW in particular. *Chapter V* contains an analysis of the OPCW as an organization established to supervise compliance with the core obligations under the CWC. Thereby the focus will be on the four separate functions of the concept of supervision, respectively: the *collection function* (para. 2); the *review function* (para. 3); the *correction function* (para. 4) and the *creative function* (sources) (para. 5). Chapter VII will draw some general conclusions with regard to the CWC model of supervision. In so doing a comparison will be made with the "management model" of Chayes and Chayes. And what, in particular, can be concluded with regard to the international law of arms control? Chapter VIII ends with some concluding remarks.

II.The control of chemical weapons: historical development

1. The 1925 Geneva Protocol

The 1925 Geneva Protocol,[16] which is generally regarded as a landmark agreement in the prevention of the use of poisonous gases and bacteriological weapons, came into being as a reaction to the extensive use of poison gas in World War I, resulting in over a million casualties and over 100,000 deaths.[17] This protocol is a typical example of an arrangement which is generally regarded as belonging to the law of armed conflict,[18] for it is an agreement that

---

[16] The Protocol for the Prohibition of the Use in War of Asphyxiating, Poisonous or Other Gases, and of Bacteriological Methods of Warfare was signed on June 1925 and entered into force on 8 February 1928. It was originally a Protocol to the 1925 Convention for the Supervision of the International Trade in Arms and Ammunition and in Implements of War, Jozef Goldblat, *Arms Control, A Guide to Negotiations and Agreements* (1994) at 91. The United States only ratified in 1976 and deposited its instrument of ratification two weeks after it deposited its ratification of the Biological Weapons Convention respectively March 26 and April 10, 1975.

[17] T. Bernauer, *The Projected Chemical Weapons Convention: A Guide to the Negotiations in the Conference on Disarmament*, UNIDER (1990) at 11; Arms Control and Disarmament Agreements, texts and histories of the negotiations, United States Arms Control and Disarmament Agency (1996), further ACDA, at 95.

[18] L.C.Green, *The Contemporary Law of Armed Conflict* (1993), at 37. *Humanitarian Law in Armed Conflicts*- manual- Federal Ministry of Defence of the German Federal Republic (1992), at 17, 43.

66 E. MYJER

restricts the use of a certain type of weapon as a means of combat.[19] However, it is also considered under arms control,[20] for at the same time it controls a (whole) category of weapons of a State Party. It is, in other words, the archetypal example of a treaty belonging to the international law of military security.

Whereas under The Brussels Declaration of 1874 and The Hague Conventions of 1899 and 1907[21] the use in war of toxic substances was already prohibited,[22] and under the 1899 Hague Declaration 2 the use of projectiles the sole object of which is the diffusion of asphyxiating or deleterious gases,[23] the use of both chemical and biological weapons are banned under the 1925 Geneva Protocol.[24] Emphasizing the demands made by humanity in justly condemning the use in war of these already prohibited substances[25] and "[..]that this prohibition shall be universally accepted as a part of International Law",[26] the Protocol also extends this prohibition to the use of bacteriological methods of warfare.[27] Given that the Protocol's terms leave considerable room for diverse interpretations,[28] there have been attempts to clarify the scope of the prohibition obligations under it.[29] The Protocol, however, is limited to a

---

[19] On the restriction of the right of parties to an armed conflict to choose means (and methods) of warfare, compare: Article 22 Hague Regulations, annex to Hague Convention IV of 18 October 1907 respecting the Laws and Customs of War on Land, in A. Roberts and R. Guelff, *Documents on the Laws of War* (1989), at 52; Article 35 para. 1 1977 Geneva Protocol I Additional to the Geneva Conventions (1949), in Roberts (et al.), at 409.

[20] Compare arms control handbook / manuals like J. Goldblat, Arms Control Agreements (1983) at 124; Goldblat, Arms Control, *supra* n. 17, for instance at 91-92, ACDA *supra* at 5.

[21] See Article 23(a) forbidding the employment of poison or poisoned weapons and Article (e) the employment of arms, projectiles and materials calculated to cause unnecessary suffering, in: Roberts (et al.) *supra* n. 19 at 39. Both the 1899 Hague Convention II and the 1907 Hague Convention contained general principles of customary international law prohibiting the use of poison and materials causing unnecessary suffering. *Ibid*, at 35.

[22] Bernauer, *supra* n. 17 at 11.

[23] A. Roberts et al., *supra* n. 19, at 35.

[24] See also B.V.A. Röling and O. Sukovic, *The Law of War and Dubious Weapons*, SIPRI (1976), in particular 11 et seq.

[25] "Whereas the use in war of asphyxiating, poisonous or other gases, and of all analogous liquids, materials or devices, has been justly condemned by the general opinion of the civilized world; [...] [W]hereas the prohibition of such use has been declared in Treaties to which the majority of Powers of the World are Parties;..", 1925 Geneva Protocol, preambular.

[26] "[..]To the end that this prohibition shall be universally accepted as a part of International Law, *binding alike the conscience and the practice of nations*". [emphasis added], 1925 Geneva Preambular Protocol; Röling, *supra* n. 24 at 11.

[27] "Declare:[..] agree to extend this prohibition to the use of bacteriological methods of warfare and agree to be bound as between themselves according to the terms of this declaration", 1925 Geneva Protocol.

[28] Roberts, et al, *supra* n. 19, at 137.

[29] Compare the 1969 Resolution 2603 A (XXIV) adopted by majority in the General Assembly. See also Roberts, et al., *ibid*, at 138 and Goldblat, *supra* n. 16 at 91.

situation of war and between the parties to it. The non-universal character of the Protocol therefore weakens its force. Furthermore, numerous States have made the reservation that it is binding only in relation to other States bound by it and ceases to be binding if the enemy or its allies fail to respect the prohibitions of the Protocol.[30] In other words they reserved the right to a "second strike" (a retaliatory strike). The dominant view, however, is that the ban under the Geneva Protocol evolved into a customary rule.[31] Furthermore, there are no mechanisms to verify compliance. Since the 1980s, however, this gap has been filled by the UN resolutions empowering the UN Secretary-General to investigate reports on possible violations of the Geneva Protocol.[32] In a joint statement on the Non-proliferation of Chemical Weapons the United States and the Soviet Union confirmed their intention to provide active support to the UN Secretary-General in conducting investigations into reported violations of the Protocol. They affirmed their intention to consider the imposition of sanctions against the violators of the Protocol, including, interestingly, those under Chapter VII of the UN Charter.[33]

---

[30] Compare reservations of the kind made by Parties to the Protocol like the UK ("The protocol is only binding on the United Kingdom as regards the powers which have signed and ratified or who have acceded to it and it ceases to bind the United Kingdom towards any Power whose armed forces or the armed forces of whose allies fail to respect the prohibitions", *Manual of Military Law* (1958) at 216). In other words, use in second strike would remain possible. Similar ones were made by countries like Canada, Belgium, France, the Netherlands or the USSR. The Protocol was "regarded by such states as containing not an absolute prohibition on the use of such weapons, but only as an agreement not to use such weapons first", Roberts et al., *supra* n. 19, at 138.

[31] Compare Roberts et al., *ibid.* at 138. No controversy regarding the ban on any use, also in second strike, is possible in the case of the CWC with its ban on use under any circumstances and exclusion of reservations. In the case of the BWC the question regarding the reservations was not solved as it does not contain a ban on its use, but concerns non-possession and production. However, notwithstanding the fact that there are 131 States Parties to the 1925 Convention (as of 1 July 1988 according to the US Department of State (and 114 according to the depositary) (Roberts et al., *supra* n. 19 at 21 and 144), whereas there are 91 States Parties to the BWC (ACDA *supra* n. 16 at 104) there does not appear to be much controversy nowadays about a ban on its use, either conventionally, or customary. According to F. Kalshoven (Arms, Armaments and International Law, *Recueil des Cours*, 1985-II, at 267) "(T)hese restrictions on application of the prohibition, and in particular the condition of reciprocity, have largely lost their significance with the entry of the prohibition into the body of customary international law". Compare also L. C. Green, *The Contemporary Law of Armed Conflict* (1993) at 131, or Röling, *supra* n. 24 at 7. See also the Final Declaration of the Conference of States Parties to the 1925 Geneva Protocol and Other Interested States and on the Prohibition of Chemical Weapons of 11 January 1989, 28 *ILM* (1989) pp. 1020-1022 as well as UN Doc. SIRES (1991) p. 1687, preambular.

[32] Goldblat, *supra* n. 16, at 92. This points to another coincidence of the law of collective security and the law of armed conflict.

[33] Soviet Union-United States joint statement on non-proliferation, issued June 4, 1990, 29 *ILM* 932-933.

The Protocol was reconfirmed once more in 1989, when in an attempt to speed up the process of negotiating a chemical weapons convention France, the depositary of the 1925 Geneva Protocol, convened a conference of States Parties to the Protocol and other interested States on the prohibition of chemical weapons. Besides giving an impetus to a prospective CWC the States Parties reaffirmed in their Final Declaration[34] the prohibition as established in the Protocol. Furthermore, they "reaffirm their full support for the Secretary-General for carrying out his responsibilities for investigations in the event of alleged violations of the Geneva Protocol".[35]

This development strengthens the majority view that the prohibitions contained in the Protocol have become part of customary law.[36] According to Roberts, however, some are of the opinion that the controversy over its interpretation and its reservations "have reduced the Protocol's usefulness as a guide under customary international law".[37] However, it retains the ban on first use.

2. The Biological Weapons Convention

Under the 1925 Protocol, prohibiting the *use* of both chemical and bacteriological weapons, States were still allowed to *possess* chemical and bacteriological weapons and to develop and stockpile them. After the adoption of the Protocol, the prevalent opinion has been that also the *possession* of chemical and bacteriological (biological) weapons should be prohibited simultaneously.[38] For there was the fear "that if one of them were to become the object of a prohibition it might look like a legitimisation of the other.[39] Since many States had reserved the right to use chemical and/or bacteriological agents in reply, and because, unlike biological weapons, chemical weapons had actually been used in war, many States maintained chemical weapons in their arsenal to deter the use of this type of weapons against them, and to provide a retaliatory capacity if deterrence failed. The aim of a simultaneous prohibition of both chemical and biological weapons therefore blocked progress, because many States were reluctant to give up their capability of chemical weapons "without reliable assurance that other nations were not developing, producing, and stockpiling chemical weapons".[40] In the 1960s, however, the conviction

---

[34] Final Declaration of the Conference of States Parties to the 1925 Geneva Protocol and other interested States on the prohibition of chemical weapons, Paris 7-11 January 1989, *ILM.* 1020-1022 (1989).

[35] *Ibid*, at 1022.

[36] See for instance Goldblat, *supra* n. 16, at 92. Bernauer, *supra* n. 17, at 12.

[37] Roberts et al., *supra* n. 19, at 139.

[38] J. Goldblat, The 1993 Chemical Weapons Convention: A Significant Step in the Process of Multilateral Disarmament, in Bardonet, *supra* n. 4, at 16.

[39] Ooms, *supra* n. 5, at 5.

[40] ACDA, *supra* n. 5, at 95.

grew that this deadlock should be broken and to opt for separate instruments for the control of biological weapons and chemical weapons respectively, for it was assumed that since a ban on biological weapons did not require intrusive verification it could therefore be concluded quickly.[41]

In 1969 the UK submitted to the Eighteen-Nation Disarmament Committee (ENDC) a draft convention concentrating solely on biological weapons. There was, however, no general acceptance of this approach, especially amongst the East Europeans. In the same year, however, the US renounced all biological weapons[42] and this was followed subsequently by countries like the UK.[43] Finally, in 1971 the Soviet Union and its allies agreed to concentrate first on a convention on biological weapons. This considerably speeded up the process, for shortly thereafter - after having worked out an agreed draft - the US and the USSR submitted separate but identical texts for a possible convention[44] to the Conference of the Committee on Disarmament (CCD[45]). This led to the Biological Weapons Convention,[46] which was the first international agreement since World War II to provide for the elimination of an entire class of weapons.[47] The Convention was opened for signature in 1972 and entered into force on 26 March 1975. In the BWC parties undertake not to develop, produce, stockpile, or acquire biological agents or toxins of types and in quantities that have no justification for prophylactic, protective, and other peaceful purposes, as well as weapons and means of delivery.[48] All such *matériel* is to be destroyed within nine months of the Convention's entry into force.[49] Interestingly, the Convention does not forbid the use of these weapons. It reconfirms, however, the prohibition of the 1925 Protocol on the use in war of chemical and bacteriolocial (biological) weapons, whereby *first use* was already forbidden; a prohibition that can now be regarded as one of customary

---

[41] Goldblat, *supra* n 16, at 93. According to Ooms, (*supra* n. 5, at 3) a role played whereby although these weapons had not been used on the battlefield during the Second World War there appeared "a renewed attention to this manner of warfare due to the use of riot control agents and herbicides by the United States in Vietnam and of the use of presumably mustard gas by Egypt in the Yemen".

[42] In November 1969 the President declared that the United States unilaterally renounced the first use of lethal or incapacitating chemical agents and weapons and unconditionally renounced all methods of biological warfare. "Henceforth the U.S. biological program would be confined to research on strictly defined measures of defense, such as immunization". ACDA, *supra* n. 17, at 95.

[43] ACDA, *ibid*, at 95.

[44] ACDA, *ibid*, at 96.

[45] The Eighteen-Nation Disarmament Commission was renamed after its enlargement to 26 members in August 1969. (ACDA, *ibid*. at 96). See also n. 60.

[46] Convention on the prohibition of the development, production and stockpiling of bacteriological (biological) and toxin weapons and on their destruction, of 10 April 1972.

[47] Goldblat, *supra* n. 16, at 96.

[48] Article I, BWC.

[49] Article II, BWC.

70   E. MYJER

law.[50] But after States Parties would have destroyed their weapons in accordance with Article II, and not being allowed to acquire biological agents or toxins as agreed under Article I, both first and second strike use would in practice be excluded. Effective verification of the ban on the possession of biological (bateriological) weapons under the BWC, however, is lacking, for the BWC does not have any supervisory mechanism. Although within nine months after entry into force the States Parties will under Article II either have to destroy substances or "to divert to peaceful purposes", there is no duty to declare possession, nor is there any mechanism to control compliance. For that States Parties are dependent on their National Technical Means (NTMs). Especially this lack of a supervisory mechanism has been the subject of discussion, both at Review Conferences and by *ad hoc* groups.[51] The Second Review Conference of September 1986 led to a meeting of scientific and technical experts[52] with the task to develop procedures for implementing annual data exchanges.[53] The Third Review Conference of 1991 in its turn led to an *ad hoc* group of governmental experts "to identify, examine and evaluate from a scientific and technical standpoint potential verification measures with respect to the prohibitions of the convention": the VEREX group. The *ad hoc* group met four times in 1992 and 1993 and submitted a consensus report.[54] In September 1994 a special conference was convened to discuss this report and the Conference agreed to establish an *ad hoc* group to consider appropriate measures and draft proposals to strengthen the Convention and to be included in a legally binding instrument.[55] This led to two substantive meetings in 1995 with additional meetings in 1996. Interestingly it is the supervisory system of the CWC that acts as the model.

---

[50] See above at pp. 66-67 and in particular nn. 30 and 31.

[51] See for instance Winfried Lang, Verhinderung von Erfüllungsdefiziten im Völkerrecht, in Festschrift für Herbert Schambeck, *Verhinderung von Erfüllungsdefiziten im Völkerrecht Beispiele aus Abrüstungs und Umweltschutz* (1994), at 825-827.

[52] 31 March-15 April 1987.

[53] This led to the exchange of data as a Confidence Building Measure, in other words a voluntary system. The participation of states is low. See T. Stock et al. in *SIPRI Yearbook 1995*: Armaments, Disarmament and International security at 743-744.

[54] *Ad Hoc* Group of Governmental experts to Identity and Examine Potential Verification Measures from a Scientific and Technical Standpoint, Report, BWC/CONF.III/VEREX/9, Geneva 1993.

[55] This Ad Hoc Group should, inter alia, consider a system of measures to promote compliance with the Convention. "[M]easures should apply to all relevant facilities and activities. They should be reliable, cost effective, non-discriminatory and as non-intrusive as possible, consistent with the effective implementation of the system and should not lead to abuse; [..]", Special Conference of States Parties to the Convention on the Prohibition of the Development, Production and Stockpiling of Bacteriological (Biological) and Toxin Weapons and on Their Destruction, Geneva 19-30 1994, Final Report, BWC/SPCONF/1 at 9-10. In: *SIPRI Yearbook 1994*, at 746.

E. MYJER 71

Interesting from the perspective of chemical weapons control, is the fact that the Biological Weapons Convention repeats the previously mentioned purpose of controlling both chemical weapons and biological weapons jointly,[56] as well as States Parties' explicit undertaking to conclude an early agreement on a chemical weapons convention.[57] In spite of this commitment certain great powers remained rather reluctant to divest themselves of chemical weapons[58] which were regarded as militarily useful, in contrast to biological weapons. It would take another 20 years and the end of the Cold War before the negotiations in the Conference on Disarmament finally led to the CWC as signed in January 1993.

3. Towards a ban on chemical weapons

Ever since 1969[59] at the Conference on Disarmament (CD), the Geneva-based multilateral forum for arms control negotiations, and its successors,[60] negotiations had taken place to reach an early agreement on the control of chemical weapons. Discussions only took place in plenary meetings of the CD and during informal consultations. However, when in 1980 a special subsidiary body of the CD (*ad hoc Working Group on Chemical Weapons*) was established the negotiations began to speed up, especially when in 1984 agreement was reached on the structure of a joint preliminary draft text.[61] In

---

[56] Compare the preambular Paragraph of the BWC that expresses States Parties' conviction "[..] that the prohibition of the development, production and stockpiling of *chemical and bacteriological (biological)* weapons and their elimination, through effective measures, will facilitate the achievement of general and complete disarmament under strict and effective international control, [...] (Emphasis added.)" Striking is also the para. that refers to "an agreement on the prohibition of *bacteriological (biological)* and toxin weapons "as" (emphasis added) a first possible step towards the achievement of agreement on effective measures also for the prohibition of the development, production and stockpiling of chemical weapons", which also expresses the determination to continue negotiations to that end.

[57] "Each State Party to this Convention affirms the recognized objective of effective prohibition of chemical weapons and, to this end, undertakes to continue negotiations in good faith with a view to reaching early agreement on effective measures for the prohibition of their development, production and stockpiling and for their destruction, and on appropriate measures concerning equipment and means of delivery specifically designed for the production or use of chemical agents for weapons purposes", Article IX, BWC.

[58] Goldblat, *supra* n. 38, at 16.

[59] Bernauer, *supra* n. 12, at 25 and "After the conclusion of the NPT in 1968, the Eighteen-Nation Disarmament Committee placed the question of chemical and biological weapons on its agenda under the heading "non-nuclear measures", at 24.

[60] Goldblat, *supra* n. 16, at 8. The Conference on Disarmament is the successor to the Ten-Nation Committee on Disarmament (1959-1960), the Eighteen-Nation Committee (1962-1969), the Conference of the Committee on Disarmament (1969-1978), and the Committee on Disarmament (1979-1983).

[61] Bernauer, *supra* n. 17, at 1.

72   E. MYJER

1984 the name of the Working Group was changed to *Ad Hoc Committee on Chemical Weapons*. Its new mandate was "to start the full and complete process of negotiations, to develop and work out the Convention, except for its final drafting".[62]

In the meantime the US and the USSR, the possessors of the most expansive stocks, held several bilateral talks to see on what issues they were in agreement. In the end two issues stood out. First, there was substantial disagreement on the degree of intrusiveness of the verification of compliance, for instance via mandatory on-site inspection. Second, these countries wanted to maintain a residual stock of chemical weapons, until all chemical weapon-capable states had joined the projected multilateral convention.[63] Especially this latter aspect was not acceptable to the negotiating states, for the projected chemical weapons treaty had to be of a non-discriminatory nature unlike the Non-Proliferation Treaty. At the 1989 Paris Conference of the Parties to the 1925 Protocol specially convened by France to speed up the negotiating process the parameters for a universally acceptable convention were outlined. The participating states stressed:

> "[..] the necessity of concluding, at an early date, a Convention on the prohibition of the development, production, stockpiling and use of all chemical weapons, and on their destruction. This Convention shall be global and comprehensive and effectively verifiable. It should be of unlimited duration. [..]"[64]

In 1990 the US and the USSR signed a bilateral agreement.[65] The obvious aim of this agreement was to set -as done before with regard to many multilateral arms control agreements- the preconditions (minimum requirements) pertaining to a multilateral treaty. This treaty thereby contained measures to facilitate the early conclusion of a multilateral chemical weapons convention.[66] The principal obligations assumed by the US and the USSR in their bilateral agreement were to halt the production of chemical weapons; to reduce chemical weapon stockpiles to equal, low levels; and to accept measures necessary to

---

[62] Bernauer, *ibid*. at 6.

[63] See Goldblat, *supra* n. 16, at 99-101.

[64] Final declaration of the Conference of States Parties to the 1925 Geneva Protocol and other Interested States on the Prohibition of Chemical Weapons, January 11, 1989 sub. 3, 28 *ILM* (1989), at 1022. See also Goldblat, *ibid*, at 102.

[65] Agreement between the United States of America and the Union of Soviet Socialist Republics on Destruction and Non-production of Chemical Weapons and on Measures to Facilitate the Multilateral Convention on Banning Chemical Weapons, 1 June 1990, 29 *ILM* 934 (1990).

[66] Goldblat, *supra* n. 16, at 97.

verify compliance.[67] In spite of the fact that there was substantial agreement on reduction, each side wanted to keep 5,000 metric tons of chemicals. Furthermore, the technical capacity to manufacture chemical weapons was not restricted. Both parties were at the time not willing to give up the option under the 1925 Geneva Protocol to use weapons in retaliation. With regard to the prospective multilateral convention they appeared unwilling to unconditionally destroy all of their chemical weapons and production facilities. Both States went as far as to agree to reduce their stockpiles to 500 tons within eight years after the entry into force of the multilateral convention, but wanted to maintain a veto on a decision on the elimination of the remaining stock.[68] After the US abandoned this position in 1991 the multilateral negotiations speeded up and in September 1992 there was agreement on a draft Convention.

The scope of this Convention is much wider than the BWC and also includes the commitment never under any circumstances to use chemical weapons, thereby restricting the more limited non-use commitment of the 1925 Protocol (with its reservations). It foresees furthermore a ban on the production of a complete category of weapons, i.e. chemical weapons, the complete disarmament of States possessing such weapons via the destruction of the actual weapons and their production facilities within a period of 10 years, as well as the control of certain chemical substances (mainly) in the civilian industry that might be used as precursors in the development of chemical weapons. This is the first comprehensive ban not only to "disarm" a complete category of weapons, but also forbidding their use. It will, furthermore, not only involve the military establishment, but also large sections of State Parties' civilian chemical industry, which raises the touchy problem of the protection of confidential business information.

---

[67] " ..(a) to cooperate regarding methods and technologies for the safe and efficient destruction of chemical weapons; (b) not to produce chemical weapons; (c) to reduce their chemical weapons stockpiles to equal, low levels; (d) to cooperate in developing, testing, and carrying out appropriate inspection procedures; and (e) to adopt practical measures to encourage all chemical weapons-capable states to become parties to the multilateral convention" (Article I, Agreement between the United States of America and the Union of Soviet Socialist Republics on Destruction and Non-production of Chemical Weapons and on Measures to Facilitate the Multilateral Convention on Banning Chemical Weapons, 1 June 1990, 29 *ILM* 934 (1990). Goldblat, *supra* n. 16, at 97.

[68] Goldblat, *ibid.*, at 99. In an agreed statement attached to the 1 June 1990 agreement this was carefully worded.

74   E. MYJER

III. The CWC: its substantive law

1.General

The system of the Convention is relatively straightforward. First of all, it contains the primary obligations, which deal with the central disarmament and non-proliferation obligations, including the "carrot and stick" obligations of Articles X (assistance and protection against chemical weapons) and XI (economic and technical development). The second category of obligations, the supporting or procedural obligations, support the operation of these central obligations and provide for the necessary elements to allow for the supervision of compliance with the core provision. It is, however, this very intricate system of supervision that lends the Convention its special character. On the one hand, there is a constant stream of -declared- information. On the other hand, this information is constantly being assessed, thereby providing actual information as to the state of compliance with the Convention. This substantially raises confidence[69] in the actual implementation of the treaty which is a prerequisite for obtaining universal membership. This is essential if chemical weapons are to be banned completely. A further element contributing to this end by raising confidence in the system of supervision is that it is recognized that the confidentiality of certain information obtained needs to be guaranteed. This not only concerns information that is provided by States Parties themselves, but also information collected by inspectors during the course of their inspection duties, be it in the civil chemical industry or not. The importance attached thereto follows not only from the fact that one of the Annexes to the Convention relates to confidentiality but also that one of the first subsidiary organs to be appointed is the Confidentiality Commission. To allow for an effective system of supervision the Convention foresees the creation of two types of institutions, namely at the national level in a National Authority and at the international level in the OPCW. Pivotal, in this respect, is the position of the OPCW. Furthermore, States Parties have to adopt national implementation measures.

The Convention itself is concise, counting only 24 Articles. There are, however, three annexes, the Annex on Chemicals, the Annex on Implementation and Verification (Verification Annex) and the Annex on the Protection of Confidential Information (Confidentiality Annex). The reason to opt for such a combination can be explained by the different amendment

---

[69] According to Chayes transparency 'may operate to promote treaty compliance'. In particular it provides reassurance that Parties will not be taken advantage of when complying and it deters actors from contemplating non-compliance. Abraham Chayes & Antonia Handler Chayes, *The New Sovereignty, Compliance with International Regulatory Agreements* (1995) at 135. See *infra*.

procedures to be applied to the Convention and to the Annexes respectively. For in the annexes we find the regulations with regard to the more technical and administrative details, which need to be able to be changed relatively easily. The Convention and annexes, however, only provide for the essential framework (structure) while the Preparatory Commission for the OPCW (PrepCom), which was established by the Paris resolution[70] at the signing ceremony of the CWC, was tasked with a mandate for the further elaboration of rules and policies for approval by the First Conference of States Parties,[71] such as the further development of inspection procedures,[72] or a confidentiality policy. The PrepCom, during the more than four years of its work, held 16 plenary meetings. It met for the first time from 8-12 February 1993 and held its final meeting from 9-15 April 1997. The actual work of the PrepCom was, however, carried out in between the sessions in its different "thematic" working groups. It did not succeed, however, in completely fulfilling its mandate and a number of unresolved issues were left for the consideration of the First Conference.[73] For a complete understanding of the system of the Convention it may therefore be necessary to consult both the reports of the 16 PrepCom plenary sessions as well as the decisions taken by both the First and the consecutive Conferences, both on the resolved and the unresolved issues, since some of the issues were not resolved at the First Conference and were either decided upon at one of the consecutive conferences or are still unresolved.

From a systematic point of view, within the Convention four main areas can be distinguished, namely *States Parties' obligations*; *States Parties' rights* (including protection and benifits); *supervision* or compliance control (including the establishment of the OPCW); and *treaty-related technicalities*.

---

[70] Resolution establishing the Preparatory Commission for the Organization for the Prohibition of Chemical Weapons, adopted in Paris during the signing ceremony of the Convention on the Prohibition of the Development, Production, Stockpiling and use of Chemical Weapons and on their Destruction 13-15 January 1993, *Legal Series PC-OPCW 1, 1994.*

[71] "..for the purpose of carrying out the necessary preparations for the effective implementation of the Convention[..] and for preparing for the first session of the Conference of the States Parties to that Convention", Paragraph 1, Paris Resolution, *ibid.*

[72] "The Commission shall develop, *inter alia*, the following draft agreements, provisions and guidelines for consideration and approval by the Conference of the States Parties....(a) Guidelines on detailed procedures for verification and for the conduct of inspections, in accordance with, *inter alia*, Part II, Paragraph 42, of the Verification Annex;[..] Recommendations for procedures to be followed in case of breaches or alleged breaches of confidentiality, in accordance with paragraph 18 of the Confidentiality Annex.", Paragraph 12 Paris Resolution, *ibid.*

[73] See Final Report of the Preparatory Commission for the Organization for the Prohibition of Chemical Weapons to the First Session of the States Parties of the Organization for the Prohibition of Chemical Weapons and to the First Meeting of the Executive Council of the Organization for the Prohibition of Chemical Weapons, *PC-XVI/37*, 15 April 1997. at 47-54.

76   E. MYJER

Summarily one could therefore group the articles of the Convention in the following way:

> *Obligations*: Articles I, III, IV, V and VI and also the Annex on Chemicals and the Verification Annex, provide and elaborate the central obligations.
>
> *Rights*: These cannot only be found in Article X (the assistance and protection against chemical weapons) and Article XI (economic and technological development) (protection and benefits), but also in Article VI (activities not prohibited under this convention).
>
> *Supervision*: Articles VIII (the organization), IX and XII (measures to redress a situation and to ensure compliance) and the two annexes, the one on verification, and the one on confidentiality, concern the machinery by which to ensure compliance with the Convention.
>
> *Final clauses and treaty-related technicalities*; This category concerns, as such, the technical aspects of the treaty.[74] Article II provides definitions and criteria, Articles XIII (relation of the CWC to other agreements), XIV (settlement of disputes), XV (amendments), XVI (duration and withdrawal), XVII (status of the annexes), XVIII (signature), XIX (ratification), XX (accession), XXI (entry into force), XXII (reservations), XXIII (depositary) and XXIV (authentic texts).

This sub-division is introduced in order to clarify the general outline of the Convention and to systematize its different aspects. It cannot, however, be applied too rigorously since, for instance, States Parties' obligations not only concern their obligations relating to chemical weapons and related substances, but also those in relation to verification and compliance. The focus will therefore be on States Parties' obigations (paragraph 2), States Parties' rights (paragraph 3) concerning the central role of supervision (paragraph 4) and on the final clauses (paragraph 5), albeit summarily. Supervision in the above broad sense will be the issue of Chapter IV on the central role of the OPCW and on its institutional aspects and Chapter V in which the different functions of the OPCW in relation to compliance control (supervisory functions) will be analyzed.

2.Obligations of the States Parties

Article I contains the central obligation not to have, develop or in any other way obtain, chemical weapons and never to use them. Furthermore, it obliges States Parties never to assist in the transfer of such weapons. A noteworthy

---

[74] Articles XIII through XXIV are known as "housekeeping articles", D. Mahley, The Chemical Weapons Convention: an Overview, at 4: in: A.E. Smithson, The Chemical Weapons Convention Handbook, The Henry L. Stimson Center (1993).

exception to the general ban is the States Parties' undertaking not to use "riot control agents" as a method of warfare, meaning that they can be used for internal purposes, a purpose not prohibited under the Convention.[75] Each State Party furthermore undertakes to destroy the chemical weapons it owns or that it has abandoned on other states' territories, as well as any chemical weapons production facility. With regard to old and abandoned chemical weapons a special regime exists, as detailed in Annex Part IV (B). This general obligation falls into two parts. The first of these is the destruction of the existing chemical weapons and of the production facilities. The second obligation concerns the ban on future production of chemical weapons and their precursors. The former obligation is finite and will cease to exist under the Convention after a period of 10 years;[76] the latter obligation is infinite, and will involve the civilian chemical industry on a continuous basis, since that is the place where "listed" chemicals may be produced and consequently it is there that the continuing verification of compliance with regard to the non-production of chemical weapons and their precursors will take place.

One further obligation needs to be specifically mentioned, namely that of Article VII concerning the national implementation measures. To start with, each State Party will have to implement its core obligations and prohibit natural and legal persons anywhere on its territory or in any place under its jurisdiction from undertaking any activity prohibited for that State Party under the CWC,[77] and not to permit such activity in any place under its control.[78] Violators will have to be penalized, even if it concerns nationals that are outside its territorial jurisdiction.[79]

Furthermore, States Parties will have to establish a National Authority "to serve as the national focal point for effective liaison with the Organization".[80]
As the main (principal) obligations of the States Parties to the CWC the following can be distinguished:

primary obligations:

* non-development, non-production, non-stockpiling (I para. 1(a);

---

[75] "Purposes not prohibited under this convention" means: ..(d) Law enforcement including domestic riot control purposes". Article II, para. 9 (d).

[76] A State Party may submit a request for the extension of the deadline up to a maximum of 15 years. See Verification Annex, Part IV (A), paragraphs 24-28.

[77] Article VII, (1)(a).

[78] Article VII, (1)(b).

[79] Article VII, (1)(c).

[80] Article VII, (4). See also *Handelingen Tweede Kamer der Staten Generaal*, vergaderjaar 1994-1995, 23 910 (R 1515), nrs.1-2. In the Netherlands the Ministry of Economic Affairs is the appointed National Authority.

78   E. MYJER

* non-use, both first use and retaliatory use (I para. 1(b); no transfer, directly or indirectly, to anyone (I para. 1(a); not to engage in any military preparation to use them (I para. 1 (c);

* not to assist, encourage or induce anyone to do anything prohibited for States Parties (I para. 1(d);

* destruction of existing stocks which it owns or possesses, or that are located in any place under its jurisdiction or control (I para. 2);

* destruction of abandoned stocks on the territory of another party (I para. 3);

* destruction of production facilities it owns or possesses, or that are located in any place under its jurisdiction or control (I para. 4);

* no restrictions impeding trade, development and promotion of scientific and technological knowledge in the field of chemistry for industrial, agricultural, research, medical, pharmaceutical or other peaceful purposes (XI, para 2(c));[81]

* facilitate the exchange of chemicals, equipment and scientific and technical information for non-prohibited purposes (XI);

* facilitate the exchange of equipment, material and scientific and technological information concerning means of protection against chemical weapons (X);

* provide information on programmes for protective purposes (X);

* provide assistance through the OPCW (X);

supporting or procedural (secondary) obligations such as:

* declaring possession of inventories of chemical weapons and production facilities (III paras. 1 (a),(b),(c);

* declaring any transfer of chemical weapons out of or into its territory (III para. 1 (a)(iv));

* drawing up of plans for the destruction and the execution thereof of weapons and destruction facilities (III paras. 1 (a)(v) and (c)(v));

* with regard to activities not prohibited, declaring relevant chemicals and facilities (development, production etc.) (VI);[82]

* allow for on-site inspections and/or monitoring with on-site instruments (IV paras. 4,5; V paras. 6, 7(b), 15; VI paras. 3,4,6; IX para. 10);

---

[81] "Developing states note that access to commercially valuable chemical technology is an important part of a larger effort to facilitate industrial development.[..] Nevertheless, it does not rule out the continuation of collective efforts to control the export of high-risk chemicals and technologies. (Author: Australia Group)."(Mahley, *supra* n. 74, at 4).

[82] See Mahley, *ibid*, at 1.

* institute national implementation measures, insuring compliance by natural and legal persons within its territory and under its jurisdiction (VII);
* establishing confidentiality standards for information received (VII);
* reviewing existing national regulations in the field of trade in chemicals for consistency with the object and purpose of CWC (XI);
* controlling the production of chemicals in the civilian industry (VI, para. 2);

3. Rights of the States Parties

Although it can be held that the obligations in the Convention are central, there would never have been a Convention if it did not also contain certain rights which are reciprocal to the obligations mentioned. They concern rights like the right to receive information or to have a situation clarified,[83] or indeed the right to a challenge inspection.[84] These are crucial rights with regard to the compliance control of other States Parties' obligations and are therefore instrumental in obtaining States Parties' compliance with the Convention. Furthermore, there are rights that are either exceptions to the duty not to produce chemical substances suitable for chemical weapons production, like the right to a controlled use or production of Schedule 1, 2 or 3 chemicals, or rights that were included in the Convention in order to stimulate technically less advanced states to join. This is what has been referred to as the "carrot and stick" provisions.

In the former case States Parties are allowed to make use of toxic chemicals and their precursors for purposes not prohibited by the Convention.[85] These include industrial, agricultural, research, medical, and pharmaceutical purposes, protective purposes, military purposes,[86] or law enforcement purposes.[87]

The latter case concerns Articles X and XI, as the debates, both in the context of the PrepCom as well as in the US Senate,[88] concerning the "rights

---

[83] Article IX, paras. 2-6.

[84] Article IX, para. 8.

[85] "To develop, produce, otherwise acquire, retain, transfer and use"(VI para. 1).

[86] Not connected with the use of chemical weapons and not dependent on the use of the toxic properties of chemicals as a method of warfare (Article II, para. 9 (c)).

[87] Including domestic riot control purposes, Article II, 9 (d).

[88] See for instance Senator Ashcroft: "There are the requirements, particularly in Articles X and XI of the treaty, which require us to share technology, to share information, and to share, in particular, the defensive technology of chemical weaponry. There is an anomaly in chemical weaponry which is challenging. It is that when you provide the defensive technology for chemical weapons, you are providing one of the essential components of delivering chemical weapons.[..] If a rogue state wants to deliver chemical weapons, one of the things they need to do is to acquire the defensive technology to defend against them and to protect their soldiers in delivery. That seems to me one of the substantial problems contained

issue" and the possible negative consequences thereof have shown. Article XI (Economic and Technological Development) is about the right to access to commercially valuable chemical technology and chemicals, whereas Article X concerns assistance and protection against chemical weapons. In particular, it concerns the right to participate in "the fullest possible exchange of equipment, material and scientific and technological information concerning means of protection against chemical weapons"[89] in case of being threatened with a chemical weapons attack or having suffered an attack.[90] A commentator notes that this provision "enables the treaty to nullify any potential political or military advantage of either a non-party developing chemical weapons or a party clandestinely developing chemical weapons". And that it is "one of the reasons why states should not waste their time, money, or effort trying to solve real or perceived national security problems by developing chemical weapons".[91] Especially these measures are intended as an incentive for the industrially less developed states. It is therefore curious to note that during the PrepCom a number of these countries blocked progress because they were of the opinion that Article XI was being interpreted too narrowly, thereby not offering enough (too little). In contrast, those opposed to the Convention in the American Senate, which almost led to non-ratification, based their opposition almost exclusively on Articles X and XI as offering too much. Furthermore, it is striking that in the preparatory phase most of the problems did not concern the actual issue of disarmament obligations, but rather the incentive issue: the rights.

Article X deals with protection against chemical weapons if ever they would be used against a State Party. For this purpose States Parties are allowed to conduct research. Central are Article X, paragraph 5 obliging the Technical Secretariat (TS) to provide a State Party with expert advice and assistance; and Article X, paragraph 6 concerning the right of States Parties to request and provide assistance bilaterally. Article X, paragraph 7, obligates States Parties "to provide assistance" through the OPCW. The measure of assistance, however, is voluntary ("and to this end elect one or more of the following measures"). This may amount to a financial contribution ("contribute to the voluntary fund for assistance)", or to declare within 180 days after the entry into force the kind of assistance it might provide.[92] It is therefore completely up to States Parties to decide for themselves, as the Convention does not oblige

---

in Articles X and XI. The risks far exceed the benefits." *Congressional Record, Senate,* April 24, 1974, at S3651. The resolution of ratification of April 24, 1997, therefore also contains expansive conditions relating to these Articles X and XI like under 7 (Continuing vitality of the Australia Group and national export controls) and 15 (assistance under Article X).

[89] Article X (3).
[90] See Smithson, *supra* n. 74, at 20.
[91] Mahley, *supra* n. 74, at 4.
[92] Article X, para. 7(c).

them to provide specifically described chemical assistance. The U.S. Senate did so by stipulating that the U.S. would not contribute to the voluntary fund for assistance under Article X, paragraph 7(a) and that for States Parties ineligible for certain assistance under the Foreign Assistance Act only limited assistance would be available.[93]

With regard to Article XI there exists the controversy surrounding the ending of the export controls of the Australia Group, since these would be contrary to the supposed lifting of trade restrictions under Article XI of the CWC.[94] (This "rights"issue therefore clearly constitutes an "obligation" issue for certain States Parties). To explain this issue a few words are necessary about the Australia Group. The Australia Group came into existence when it appeared in the eighties that in the Iraq-Iran War commercial trade in dual-use chemicals by Western countries was fuelling programs to develop and produce chemical weapons.[95] The original Australia Group of 15 members, that met informally for the first time in 1985, in 1986 adopted a 35-chemical warning list and in 1987 a core-list of 8 chemicals. All participants would formally control the core list of chemicals, whereas the warning list would be issued to the chemical industry for voluntary action.[96] Decisions by the Australia Group are not legally binding, they are taken by majority and there is no formal charter or constitution.[97] New members, however, need to have unanimous approval. By 1996 15 more members were admitted and the two previously mentioned lists were merged and by 1992 there were 54 chemicals listed. Furthermore, a list was drawn up for the control of dual-use chemical equipment.[98] The scope of its controls was furthermore extended by drawing up a list to also control the proliferation of biological weapons.

With the Australia Group regime still in force many developing countries regard the CWC as discriminatory. Why is it necessary, they claim, that States

---

[93] [..] for any State Party the government of which is not eligible for assistance under chapter 2 of part II (relating to military assistance) or chapter 4 of part II (relating to economic support assistance) of the Foreign Assistance Act of 1961- (i) no assistance under paragraph 7 (b) of Article X will be provided[..]; and (ii) no assistance under paragraph 7(c) of Article X other than medical antidotes and treatment will be provided[..]. Ratification Resolution, of April 24 1997, under 15, *Congressional Record Senate*, at S3655.

[94] "[T]he use of export controls, the Australia Group and the CWC have become mirred in controversy" , A.E. Smithson, *Separating Fact from Fiction: The Australia Group and the Chemical Weapons Convention* (The Henry L. Stimson Center (1997) at 6).

[95] Smithson, *ibid*, at 7 and "[..] companies and individuals from West Germany, Great Britain, Japan, Austria, Belgium, the Netherlands, Italy, Switzerland, France, and the United States, among other countries, had sold Iraq and Libya products that facilitated their proliferation aim" at 7-8, referring to Australia Group Document AG/Dec92/Press/Chair/9 (Paris: 22 December 1992).

[96] Smithson, *ibid*, at 8-9.

[97] Smithson, *ibid*, at 10, referring to different sources.

[98] See for the Australia Group Control List of Dual-use Chemical Manufacturing Facilities and Equipment and Related Technology, Smithson, *ibid*, annex 2, pp. 36-43.

that have agreed to chemical weapons disarmament would still be subject to an export control system aimed at exactly the same end? Illustrative in this respect is the clear position Brazil took in the following statement:

> "The second category of commitments - that is those related to free trade and cooperation among States Parties - is clearly defined in Article XI. These commitments have a logical ground, because many States, especially those that do not possess chemical weapons, would not be willing to give all the assurances of compliance with their disarmament and non-proliferation commitments under the Convention - by means of declarations and inspections - if, at the same time, they would be subject to trade restrictions as if they were not abiding by the Convention. Article XI is even more explicit thereon than Article X of the Biological Weapons Convention."[99]

After having made clear that non-restriction of free trade is crucial to the Convention, Brazil then concludes in a rather sharply-worded warning that all commitments have a similar binding character, are equal, and that some cannot be treated as a bit more equal than others:

> "The provisions of international treaties are not to be divided into "more important" and "less important", "hard" and "soft" ones. Once the Convention is in force, States Parties that do not comply with a given provision, including those contained in Article XI, will be violating the Convention."[100]

Against this position it is held that there is no positive duty under the CWC to disband the Australia Group, and neither is there any positive obligation to trade in any chemical that some State Party might demand or to share any technological know how. The CWC, so goes the argument, does not foresee a centrally controlled think-tank or stock, which would anyhow be contrary to the very idea of a free market.

Another counter argument used by Australia Group members stresses that the non-proliferation of chemical weapons, and under the BWC the same with regard to biological weapons, is one of the most important provisions under

---

[99] "In case there is a suspicion of non-compliance by an importing State Party, the exporting country that is also a Party to the Convention should bring the issue to the attention of the Executive Council of the Organization. This is not a question which demands unilateral action and should not be treated as a trade issue. On the contrary, suspicion of non-compliance is a question that affects the security concerns of all States Parties to the Convention". And "In other words, a parallel export control regime with schedules and scope exceeding those of the Convention is only admissible if applied and oriented to States not Parties to the Convention. Of course, these States, which voluntarily insist on remaining outside the Convention regime, cannot have recourse to the free trade assurances contained therein". Statement by the delegation of Brazil, at the XIIIth Plenary Session (March 1996) of the Preparatory Commission for the Organization for the Prohibition of Chemical Weapons.

[100] Statement by the delegation of Brazil, *ibid*.

E. MYJER 83

these treaties.[101] Smithson refers to Article XI that "[..]clearly stipulates that efforts to enhance free trade among treaty parties must not be "incompatible with the obligations undertaken under this Convention". She then points to the non-proliferation commitment in Article I of the Convention and concludes that "this wording allows the Australia Group and other unilateral exports controls intended to stem the proliferation of chemical weapons to continue since they are "wholly compatible" with the CWC's principle objectives".[102] The least that can be said against this argument is that the export controls of the Australia Group that are directed at the same non-proliferation goal are not incompatible, but that maintaining them amongst States Parties is not logical for it questions the (effectiveness of the) very non-proliferation system of the CWC with its verification system, by arranging for an additional non-proliferation system alongside the CWC's system. The argument that export controls are integral to the operation of the CWC appears fallacious as the export controls included in the Convention all concern non-State Parties.

What seems reasonable, however, is that until full compliance with the Convention has been assessed and established it would be unrealistic to force States Parties to work on the – unverified - assumption that universal compliance is already in its place from the very first day of the entry into force. Only when it appears that there is full compliance will a review of the respective national regulations in the field of trade in chemicals "to render them consistent with the object and purpose of this Convention"[103] seem imperative, or in the words of what was stated on behalf of the Australia Group, namely, the intent to review its export control policy toward those states that comply fully with the CWC.[104] That such may be a difficult process is apparent from the position taken by the US Senate in its elaborate condition "7" regarding the Australian Group and national export controls as contained in the ratification resolution, whereby it even declared "that the collapse of the informal forum of states known as the "Australia Group", would amount to a fundamental change in circumstances affecting the object and purpose of the Convention",[105] which

---

[101] Smithson, *supra* n. 94, at 23-24.

[102] Smithson, *ibid*, at 27.

[103] Article XI 2(e).

[104] CD/PV.629 (Geneva: 6 August 1992)(16-7) in Smithson *supra* n. 94, at 20. In this vain the Dutch government stated as regards Article XI that it is being interpreted by members of the Australia Group so that in future, when it appears that States Parties appear to completely comply with their treaty obligations, then export controls that were not based on the treaty, may be either eased or terminated. *Memorie van Toelichting*, Tweede Kamer 1994-1995, 23 910 (R.15 15), nr 3 at 41.

[105] "[..](7). *Continuing Vitality of the Australia Group and National Export Controls. - (A) Declaration. -* The Senate declares that the collapse of the informal forum of states known as the "Australia Group", either through changes in membership or lack of compliance with common export controls, or the substantial weakening of common Australia Group export controls and non-proliferation measures in force on the date of United States ratification would constitute a fundamental change in circumstances affecting the object and purpose of

84   E. MYJER

clearly refers to the doctrine of *rebus sic stantibus*[106] as a ground to be invoked for terminating or withdrawing from the CWC.

4. Supervision

Crucial to the operation of the Convention is an intricate system devised to ensure compliance. In this supervisory system the specially established international organization, the Organization for the Prohibition of Chemical Weapons (OPCW),[107] occupies a central role. Furthermore, States Parties will have to cooporate closely by providing, for instance, declarations, information and clarification. The basic rules for the operation of compliance control can be found in Article VIII on the OPCW, in Article IX on consulation, cooperation and fact-finding, in Article XII on measures to ensure compliance and in the Annex on Verification and the Confidentiality Annex. Supervision not only concerns the destruction of weapons and weapons facillities, but also the production of chemicals.

In order to allow for compliance control of the core obligations to destroy existing chemical weapons, including old and abandoned chemical weapons, and production facilities, first of all an inventory of these weapons, and production and destruction facilities is in order. States Parties will therefore have to start by declaring to the OPCW the "state of affairs" with regard to chemical weapons, and chemical weapons related matters. Such an inventory is also essential to allow for compliance control of future non-production, also when existing stocks and production facilities have not yet been destroyed after the projected 10-year period. For these inventory purposes States Parties will have to declare within 30 days after the entry into force of the Convention whether they own or possess chemical weapons and to indicate the "location, aggregate quantity and detailed inventory"[108] and declare the same with regard to chemical weapons production facilities.[109] These declarations will have to

the Convention". Furthermore is interesting - (B) *Certification requirement*. - Prior to the deposit of the United States instrument of ratification, the President shall certify to Congress that-[..](iii) the Convention preserves the right of State Parties, unilaterally or collectively , to maintain or impose export controls on chemicals and related chemical production technology for foreign policy or national security reasons, notwithstanding Article XI(2); and (iv) each Australia Group member, at the highest diplomatic levels, has communicated to the United States Government its understanding and agreement that export control and non-proliferation measures which the Australia Group has undertaken are fully compatible with the provisions of the Convention, including Article XI(2), and its commitment to maintain in the future such export controls and non-proliferation measures against non-Australia Group members" [...], Ratification Resolution, April 24, 1997, *Congressional Record Senate*, at S3653.

[106] As expressed in Article 62 of the Vienna Convention on the Law of Treaties.
[107] Article VIII.
[108] Article III 1(a); Verification Annex, Part IV (A).
[109] Article III 1(c); Verification Annex, Part V.

contain a general plan "for the destruction" of the chemical weapons".[110] For old and abandoned weapons there is a special regime.[111] With regard to the weapons' production facilities the declaration will have to "provide its general plan for the destruction " of any chemical production facility, "specify actions to be taken for the closure of any chemical weapons production facility" and "provide its general plan for any temporary conversion" into a chemical weapons destruction facility.[112] With regard to the destruction of chemical weapons *per se* Article IV provides detailed procedures and Article V does so with regard to the chemical weapons production facilities. A detailed *Declaration Handbook* has been developed providing detailed explanations as well as instructions for the completion of initial, annual and other declarations.[113]

The implementation of the core-obligations - destruction or conversion of weapons production facilities - will be carried out under the close scrutiny of the OPCW, which at this stage introduces the Verification Annex. To begin with, "physical" supervision already starts immediately after the declaration phase, for States Parties will immediately have to "provide access to chemical weapons specified" for the purpose of "systematic verification of the declaration through on-site inspection" by inspectors of the OPCW. This is also the case in the period before destruction because for purposes of systematic on-site verification access will have to be provided. The destruction will have to start within two years after entry into force and will have to have been completed not later than 10 years after entry into force.[114] Detailed plans for the destruction will have to be submitted not later than 60 days before each annual destruction period begins. States Parties will have to make declarations regarding the implementation of these plans and after the destruction process has been completed.[115]

With regard to chemical weapons that are owned or possessed by another State Party a State Party "shall make the fullest efforts to ensure that these chemical weapons are removed from its territory not later than one year" after

---

[110] Article III 1 para. (v).

[111] Old chemical weapons produced before 1925: Article III 1 (b)(i); Verification Annex, Part IV (B). Old chemical weapons produced between 1925-1946 that have deteriorated to such an extent that they can no longer be used as chemical weapons (Article II 5 (b)): Article III 1 (b)(i); Verification Annex, Part IV (B). Abandoned chemical weapons: Article III 1(b)(ii)(iii); Verification Annex, Part IV (B).

[112] Article III 1(c) (v), (vi) and (vii) respectively.

[113] Declaration Handbook for the Convention on the Prohibition of the Development, Production, Stockpiling and Use of Chemical Weapons and on their Destruction, PTS-OPCW, revised 1996-11-14 with appendices to sections A, B, and C and Section F. (Declaration/information concerning old chemical weapons produced between 1925-1946) (draft 17 March 1997).

[114] Article IV, para. 6.

[115] Article IV, para. 7.

86   E. MYJER

the entry into force of the CWC (Article IV, para. 11). The arrangements in Article V with regard to chemical weapons production facilities are structured along the same lines of Article IV concerning chemical weapons. Central of course is the States Parties' duty "to cease immediately all activity" at these plants[116] and start destruction within one year and to finish it not later than 10 years after entry into force. These facilities may, however, temporarily be converted into destruction facilities. "In exceptional cases of compelling need" the Conference of States Parties may allow chemical weapons production facilities to be used for purposes not prohibited under the Convention. All converted facilities shall be subject to systematic verification (V para. 15).

Chapter IV of this contribution deals with the institutional aspects of the OPCW, whereas its functions will be analyzed in chapter V. Both the Convention and its Verification Annex foresee detailed arrangements regarding verification in this respect. As Perry Robinson, however, rightly points out the verification measures set out in the Convention cover only a fraction of the prohibitions enunciated in Article I (1).[117] This leads him to remark that "responsibility for overseeing compliance with the remaining fraction must therefore fall to the individual States parties".[118]

5. Final clauses

Of the remaining clauses Article XIII concerns the relationship between the CWC, the 1925 Geneva Protocol and the Biological Weapons Convention, respectively. It stipulates that nothing in the CWC shall be interpreted as in any way limiting or detracting from the obligations assumed by States under the other mentioned instruments.

Article XIV deals with the settlement of disputes concerning "the application or the interpretation" of the CWC. This clause will be dealt with more extensively in para. 6 of Chapter IV.

Article XV concerns the ammendment procedures.

For the Convention and for its Annexes different amendment procedures are applicable, namely *amendments* and *changes* respectively.[119] In the Annexes we find the regulations with regard to the technical and administrative details, which need to be able to be changed relatively easily. In order "to ensure the viability and the effectiveness"[120] of the Convention it therefore foresees a "light" procedure for such proposed changes. Proposed changes of an

---

[116] Article V, para. 4.

[117] J.P. Perry Robinson, The Verification System For The Chemical Weapons Convention, in: Bardonnet (ed.), *supra* n. 4, at 492.

[118] Perry Robinson, *ibid*, at 492.

[119] See Article XV, para. 1.

[120] Article XV, para. 4.

"administrative or technical nature"[121] will be examined thoroughly both by the Director-General for its "possible consequences for the provisions of the CWC and by the Executive Council".[122] If the Executive Council recommends to all States Parties that the proposal be adopted "it shall be considered approved if no State Party objects to it within 90 days after receipt of the recommendation".[123] Changes in the Annexes that are not of an administrative or technical nature need to be made via *amendments*[124] as well as all changes to the Convention. The CWC amendment procedure is special in that it has tried to find a balance between the normal rule that amendments do not bind States Parties that did not participate in amending the treaty and the application to all States Parties of amendments accepted by majorities.[125] Amendments to the Convention shall therefore enter into force when they have been adopted at the Amendment Conference by a positive vote of a majority of all States Parties, with no State Party casting a negative vote and when accepted or ratified by the States Parties casting a positive vote.[126]

This amendment procedure of Article XV CWC therefore "will bind all States Parties, none of them against its declared will, with a requirement for ratification modified to the extent that it applies only to States Parties demonstrating an active interest in the procedure."[127]

Of the remaining articles Article XVII concerns the status of the Annexes, which form an integral part of the Convention, and Article XXII stipulates that the Articles of the Convention are not subject to reservations and that the Annexes shall "not be subject to reservations incompatible with its object and purpose". This leaves Article XVI (Duration and withdrawal), Article XVIII (Signature), Article XIX (Ratification), Article XX (Accession), Article XXI (Entry into force) and the three annexes that have been dealt with so far: the Annex on Chemicals; the Annex on Implementation and Verification (Verification Annex) and the Annex on the Protection of Confidential Information (Confidentiality Annex). The Annex on Chemicals contains the guidelines for

---

[121] Sections A and C of the Confidentiality Annex , Part X of the Verification Annex, and those definitions in Part I of the Verification Annex which relate exclusively to challenge inspections, are excluded from this "light" procedure. See Article XV (4).

[122] Article XV, para. 5 (a)-(d).

[123] "If the Executive Council recommends that the proposal be rejected, it shall be considered rejected if no State Party objects to the rejection within 90 days after receipt of the recommendation", Article XV, para. 5(d).

[124] Krutzsch et al., *supra* n. 4, at 242 comments that "all modifications of the Articles and such modifications of the of the Annexes which are of a more than administrative or technical nature shall be made by amendments". He thereby incorrectly suggests that also changes with regard to the Convention would be possible via the "light" procedure.

[125] See Krutzsch et al., *ibid*, at 241.

[126] See Article XV, especially paras. 1-3.

[127] Krutzsch et al., *supra* n. 4, at 241.

88   E. MYJER

schedules of chemicals as well as the actual schedules of chemicals themselves. The Verification Annex has already been referred to extensively and details the rules relating to the inspections, declarations and so on. It is a sizable document more than twice the size of the Convention. The special case of the Confidentiality Annex with its Confidentiality Commission will be dealt with in Chapter IV paragraph 6 (ii) concerning dispute settlement.

IV. The OPCW: the institutional aspects

1. General functions

Under Article VIII of the CWC States Parties are to establish an international organization - the Organization for the Prohibition of Chemical Weapons (OPCW) - in order to:

> "achieve the object and purpose of this Convention, to ensure the implementation of its provisions, including those for international verification of compliance with it, and to provide a forum for consultation and cooperation among States Parties".[128]

Of these functions the verification of compliance with the core obligations of the Convention is the central one. Running "[..] the most comprehensive verification regime ever devised for a global treaty" will be one of the principal tasks of the OPCW.[129] It is for that reason that the OPCW could be typified as a specialized "single-purpose"[130] organization, the purpose being the implementation of the Convention,[131] with the very specifically related purpose of supervision. That function will be analyzed in Chapter V. This Chapter aims to focus on the institutional framework of this international organization. In order to be able to appraise the special character of the OPCW as an international organization *per se,* this Chapter will focus on some aspects of the institutional structure that all international organizations have in common, namely *the constitution* (para. 2); *membership* (para. 3); *the organs* (para. 4); *legal personality* (para. 5); *decision making* (para. 6); *privileges and immunities* (para. 7) and *dispute settlement* (para. 8). In these paragraphs also some other aspects (inter alia Headquarters Agreement and liability) will also be touched upon.

---

[128] Article VIII, para. 1.

[129] Terrence Taylor, The Chemical Weapons Convention and Prospects for Implementation, 42 *International and Comparative Law Quarterly*, October 1993, at 912.

[130] T. Bernauer, The Organization for the Prohibition of Chemical Weapons (OPCW): Structured, Functions, and Potential Deficiencies, in: Bardonnet (ed.), *supra* n. 4, at 334. Compare also footnote 7.

[131] Compare Krutzsch et al., *supra* n. 4, at 128.

E. MYJER 89

2.*The Constitution and the comptences of the organs*

The Constitution of the OPCW is contained in Article VIII of the CWC. This means that the CWC general amendment procedure also applies to Article VIII. Also the general rules of treaty interpretation will apply to the Constitution, although the ICJ made it clear in its advisory opinion on the WHO that the constituent treaty of an international organization "can raise specific problems of interpretation "owing, *inter alia*, to their character which is conventional and at the same time institutional".[132] This may lead to special attention when interpreting these constituent treaties.[133] However, given the clear wording of the Convention, its context and object and purpose, it is not expected that problems shall arise with regard to the determination of compteneces. Furthermore, as far as the supplementary means of interpretation are concerned, documentation abounds as regards the preparatory work of the Convention. The experience so far regarding the competences of the organs does not suggest that they have been formulated too narrowly or that there are any grey areas. It therefore seems unlikely that in the near future the doctrine of implied power needs to be applied in order to define more clearly the powers of principal organs. Perphaps also the fact that the OPCW is not a general purpose organization like the United Nations has contributed to this clear delimitation of these competences, for the object and purpose of the CWC are quite clear: banning chemical weapons.

As regards the Convention, one could, however, witness during the PrepCom phase a curious process that may have led to a creeping shift in reading and interpreting its terms and thereby also the Constitution and consequently the competences of the organs. It concerns a process that cannot be explained away as the mere practice of the organization (to be). For some of the participating States Parties were not at the time reading and interpreting the terms of the CWC in accordance with the clear "ordinary meaning to be given to the terms of the treaty in their context and in the light of its object and purpose",[134] but rather used the principle of consensus[135] as a bargaining tool in deciding almost routinely on any issue, like the ones mentioned in the Paris Resolution that had to be decided upon within the framework of the text of the

---

[132] Legality of the use by a state of nuclear weapons in armed conflict (WHO/Nuclear Weapons case), International Court of Justice, Advisory Opnion, 8 July 1996, para. 19.

[133]"...the very nature of the organization created, the objectives which have been assigned to it by its founders, the imperatives associated with the effective performance of its functions, as well as its own practice, are all elements which may deserve special attention when the time comes to interpret these constituent treaties". *Ibid.*

[134] Art. 31 The Vienna Convention on the Law of Treaties.

[135] "All decisions of the Commission should be taken by consensus", Art. 6 The Paris Resolution, *supra* n. 70.

90   E. MYJER

Convention.[136] The Paris Resolution, establishing the PrepCom for the OPCW, describes in detail its tasks which are as diverse as the drafting of "staff rules for recruitment and service conditions" for the personnel of the Technical Secretariat, and the development of draft agreements, provisions and guidelines, such as detailed procedures for verification and for conducting inspections.

By constantly doing this during a preparation process lasting four years, whereby States had to seek agreement on the basis of consensus, unavoidably some compromises crept in, thereby watering down, or changing some of the clear intentions of the States that had agreed to the Convention in 1992. Some of the issues that would appear uncontestable but that according to the Final Report of the PrepCom remained unresolved[137] are illustrative of this process. Take, for instance, the fact that there was no agreement on "the timing of the notification of challenge inspections".[138] According to Article IX, paragraph 15 the Director-General "shall transmit the inspection request to the inspected State Party not less than 12 hours before the planned arrival of the inspection team". The stalemate was caused by the position taken, on the one hand, by States like Iran, India, China and Pakistan, that were of the opinion that there should be earlier notification, for reasons like national holidays or time-zones, with, on the other hand, the postition taken by States like France, Germany, the US, the UK and the Netherlands that notification had to take place in a non-discriminatory manner.

The effect of this process is that the so-called "ordinary meaning" of the Convention is encroachingly being reread in the light of these compromises, thereby effectively reinterpreting the Convention, and thereby also the Constitution of the OPCW. From the point of view of the competences of the organs of the OPCW this development is important to note, as the work in the PrepCom extensively dealt with rules of procedure involving the Technical

---

[136] Illustrative in this respect was an attempt by a few States - Cuba, India, Pakistan and Iran - to hold the adoption of a Draft Final Report of the PrepCom hostage in order to have included in this document not only agreed texts on the issues referred to in the Paris resolution, but also the respective arguments for not agreeing on certain issues. As a result of this attitude the Committee on Preparations for the First Session of the Conference of the States Parties could not agree by consensus on the adoption of such a report, to be approved by the plenary PrepCom in order to present it to the First Conference of States Parties. There was also no agreement on the inclusion in the document of what had already been agreed upon by consensus at the previous fifteen plenary meetings of the PrepCom. Finally, at the final PrepCom a compromise was agreed upon to have included in the Final Document a mere reference to the outstanding issues, as had already been previously suggested during the Committee phase. Compare also Smithson, *supra* n.134, at 6, describing a previous attempt by Pakistan to hold the CWC, as then negotiated, hostage for national policy reasons.

[137] Final Report of the Preparatory Commission for the Organization for the Prohibition of Chemical Weapons to the First Session of the Conference of States Parties and to the First Meeting of the Executive Council, Section Four, unresolved issues pp. 47-53, PC-XVI/37.

[138] *Ibid*, 123, p. 53.

Secretariat or the Executive Council. Sometimes it appeared that pre-Geneva debates were again being opened up. From the point of view of the building phase (gestation period) of an international organization this could be looked upon as merely interesting practice. This process of changing by interpretation the terms of the CWC and thereby also the Constitution of the OPCW took place in a PrepCom that could not be regarded as a "provisional organ", but with "legal capacity" and being something more than a negotiating body. Remarkable, however, is that it concerns a body that was composed of all the signatories, including those that might have no intention whatsoever of ratifying (they already knew that they could not or would not do so), or at least for an indeterminate period like Israel. These latter signatories, in other words, could leave their mark, although it is difficult to pinpoint exactly where. The counter-argument that whatever the case may be, in the end it would be the First Conference of States Parties that would take the formal decisions, is fallacious, for the First Conference could not in two weeks go to the same length as the PrepCom had done in the four years of its operation.[139]

Even if via the "light" amendment procedure changes are brought about in one of the Annexes, it is not to be expected that this would lead to an extension of the powers of the OPCW organs, for all modifications to the Annexes which are more than of an administrative or technical nature have to be made by amendment.[140] The only area in which the OPCW seems to have some room for manoeuvre is in the question of Article X (assistance and protection against chemical weapons).

3. Membership

The principal aim of the negotiators in the Conference on Disarmament was to produce a treaty banning chemical weapons that would be universally acceptable. The OPCW is consequently an open organization. Given the large number of States Parties and of Signatory States[141] to this Convention they have undoubtedly succeeded in this aim of universality. It led, however, in the words of Taylor, to "an element of flexibility, or some would say constructive ambiguity, built into the text without which the Convention would not have been concluded".[142]

---

[139] The same tendency could be seen regarding the issues that could not be resolved during the PrepCom phase (unresolved issues) like equipment-related issues. The Conference adopted the list of approved equipment "in the understanding that the issues contained in paras. 118 and 119 of the Final Report of the PrepCom remain unresolved for the time being", C-I/DEC.71, 23 May 1997.

[140] See Article XV, para. 4 and Krutzsch et al., *supra* n. 4, at 242. Also see Chapter III, para. 5.

[141] As of September 2000 there are 139 States Parties and 35 Signatory States.

[142] Taylor *supra* n. 129, at 913.

92   E. MYJER

All States Parties to the Convention are automatically members of the OPCW. There is therefore no special procedure for a State's admission to membership.[143] The CWC explicitly makes clear that no State Party shall be deprived of its membership.[144] With Krutzsch I am also of the opinion that this also excludes any suspension of membership, for a suspension might have the very negative effect that States Parties wanted to prevent in the first place by excluding deprivation of membership,[145] namely non-universal application of the Convention.[146] Given the object and purpose of this Convention – the total disappearance of chemical weapons - it is clear that this can only be achieved via universal membership. Therefore under no circumstances could it be possible for States Parties to be deprived of their membership as a sanction, for instance for non-payment by a member of its financial contribution, or non-compliance with any other obligation.[147] A different thing altogether is that a State Party may maintain its right to withdraw from the Convention "if it decides that extraordinary events, related to the subject-matter of the Convention, have jeopardized the supreme interests of its country."[148] In the absence of such a clause it could have been held that a State Party would have no right to withdraw from the organization.[149]

4. The Organs of the OPCW

The OPCW has the following organs: the Conference of the States Parties, the Executive Council and the Technical Secretariat.

(i) The Conference of the States Parties

The Conference is the plenary organ of the OPCW and is composed of all members of the Organization. It is the representative organ of the Organization in which all of its members are represented on an equal footing. It meets

---

[143] Krutzsch et al., *supra* n. 4, at 128.

[144] Article VIII(A)(2).

[145] Krutzsch et al., *supra* n. 4, at 128.

[146] Compare also "Determined [...] to exclude completely the possibility of the use of chemical weapons, through the implementation of the provisions of this Convention [...]" (preamble).

[147] "The rationale for this provision is: a State Party, insensitive for the Organization's urgent appeals to bring itself into compliance with provisions of the Convention, might if stripped of membership, falsely conclude that it was free from obligations undertaken under the convention. In addition, an organization which by virtue of its existence has to strive towards universal adherence, would by a policy of expulsion defeat its main purpose", Krutzsch et al., *ibid*, at 128.

[148] Article XVI, para. 2.

[149] See: H.G. Schermers & N.M. Blokker, *International Institutional Law* (1995), pp. 91-94; N.D. White, *The Law of International Organizations* (1996), at 63.

E. MYJER 93

annually in regular sessions and may furthermore meet in special sessions, for instance at the request of the Executive Council.[150]

It is the principal organ of the Organization.[151] It oversees the implementation of the Convention, and acts in order to promote its object and purpose.[152] In particular, it shall,

> "[t]ake the necessary measures to ensure compliance with this Convention and to redress and remedy any situation which contravenes the provisions of this Convention, in accordance with Article XII"[153]

It is therefore important to note that the Conference is allowed to establish such subsidiary organs as it finds necessary for the exercise of its functions in accordance with the CWC.[154] It oversees, furthermore, the activities of the Executive Council and the Technical Secretariat and may issue guidelines in accordance with the CWC to either of them.[155] "[..]It may make recommendations and take decisions on any questions, matters or issues related to the Convention raised by a State Party or brought to its attention by the Executive Council".[156] The CWC sums up a number of other decisions which the Conference has to take, such as: consideration and adoption of the report, programme and budget of the OPCW,[157] appointment of the Director-General of the Technical Secretariat,[158] election of the members of the Executive Council.[159] Decisions to be taken that stand out are those that it had to consider and approve at its first session, like any draft agreements, provisions and guidelines developed by the PrepCom.

The Conference is furthermore called upon to hold, at regular intervals, review conferences to review the operation of the CWC, taking into account any relevant scientific and technological developments.[160] It is clear from the Convention that the Conference is the authoritative forum to decide upon extraordinary questions or to overcome specific crisis situations connected with compliance disputes.[161]

---

[150] Article VIII, para. 12.

[151] Article VIII, para. 19.

[152] Article VIII, para. 20.

[153] Article VIII, para. 21(k).

[154] Article VIII, para. 21(f).

[155] Article VIII, para. 20.

[156] Article VIII, para. 19.

[157] Article VIII, para. 21(a).

[158] Article VIII, para. 21(d).

[159] Article VIII, para. 21(c).

[160] Article VIII, para. 22.

[161] Krutzsch et al., *supra* n. 4, at 136 (in particular footnote 3). See under Chapter V. In particular see Articles V, para. 13; VIII, paras. 21 (k), 36; IX, paras. 7, 23, 24, 25; XII; XIV paras. 4, 5; Verification Annex: Part IV (A), 22, 26, 34, 58; Part V, 39, 68, 75, 82.

94   E. MYJER

(ii)The Executive Council

The Executive Council is the executive organ of the OPCW with limited membership, which is responsible to the Conference. Its composition was a main point of discussion during the negotiations.[162] A balance had to be struck between the need for a small body that could act effectively and the wish of States Parties to sit frequently on the Council. Furthermore, the interests of States with extensive chemical industries had to be taken into account. Therefore it was decided to have the relatively high number of members, namely 41, to be divided under the five regional groups, taking into account States Parties with the most significant chemical industries. These general principles can be found in paragraph 23 of Article VIII: "In order to ensure the effective functioning of this Convention, due regard being specially paid to equitable geographical distribution, to the importance of chemical industry, as well as to political and security interests [..]". This leads to a mix of regional representation - nine from Africa, nine from Asia, five from Eastern Europe, seven from Latin America and the Caribbean and ten from among Western Europe and other States Parties located in this region. Of these, 41 seats, respectively three, four, one, three, and five shall be the ones "with the most significant national chemical industry in the region".[163] Each State Party has the right, in accordance with the principle of rotation, to serve on the Council. They shall be selected for a period of two years. The Composition and decision-making of the Executive Council "has perhaps been the most controversial and sensitive issue of the negotiations".[164] The final result is built upon the "main elements identified in previous discussions" like the "right of all members to serve on the Board, rotation, election, equitable geographical distribution, importance of chemical industry as well as political and security interests".[165] Krutzsch points to the importance of the PrepCom phase for the smooth functioning of the provisions.[166]

Interestingly, the CWC contains a provision that allows the Conference to review the composition of the Executive Council "taking into account developments related to the principles specified in paragraph 23".[167] Given the

---

[162] Tweede Kamer, *supra* n. 104, no. 3, p. 34.

[163] Article VIII, para. 23.

[164] Krutzsch et al., *supra* n. 4, at 148. "Although it was the subject of discussions for many years, the efforts to arrive at a balanced and generally acceptable compromise had to be continued until the last minute."

[165] *Ibid*, at 149.

[166] "Since these elements and their interrelationship are not clearly defined, the interpretation of their meaning by common understanding, gentleman's agreement and established practice, starting during the preparation period, will be crucial for the smooth functioning of this provision", *ibid*, at 149.

[167] Article VIII, para. 25. It could be questioned, however, whether this provision allows for

central role of the Executive Council with its substantional powers, one may assume this to be a matter of substance, which therefore in principle has to be decided upon by consensus.

The Executive Council shall carry out the powers and functions entrusted to it under the CWC, as well as those functions delegated to it by the Conference. It shall do so "in conformity with the recommendations, decisions and guidelines of the Conference and assure their proper and continuous implementation."[168] The Council shall promote the effective implementation of the CWC and compliance with it and shall furthermore supervise the activities of the Technical Secretariat, cooperate with the National Authority of each State Party and facilitate consultations and cooperation among the States Parties at their request.[169] Not surprisingly the CWC puts great emphasis on the central role of the Executive Council with regard to questions of compliance and non-compliance.[170] The Executive Council shall consult with the States Parties involved and as appropriate "request the State Party to take measures to redress the situation within a specified time". In case it considers further action to be necessary it shall decide on which measure to take, like informing all States Parties of the issue or matter; bringing the issue or matter to the attention of the Conference or making recommendations to the Conference regarding measures to redress the situation and to ensure compliance.[171] As will be discussed[172] the Executive Council may also bring the issue to the attention of the UN General Assembly and the UN Security Council in cases of "particular gravity and urgency".[173] Another important task of the Executive Council is its role in relation to the conclusion of arrangements and agreements. For it is the Executive Council which shall, on behalf of the OPCW, and subject to the prior approval of the Conference, conclude agreements and arrangements with States and International Organizations.[174] It shall conclude agreements with States Parties concerning the procurement of assistance as foreseen under Article X. It will also have to approve the agreements or arrangements relating to the implementation of verification activities as negotiated by the Technical Secretariat

---

a change in the composition via the normal rules of decision-making. According to Krutzsch and Trapp an amendment procedure is still necessary: "Amendments of its text must be subject to the procedure generally provided for in Article XV. Paragraph 25 does not dispense with this article", *supra* n. 4 at 152. The contrary argument, however, is why provide in detail for this specific possibility and criteria if it is not meant as an exception to the amendment rule, but as a normal case of amendment. In the latter case this reference is superfluous.

[168] Article VIII, para. 30.
[169] Article VIII, para. 31.
[170] Article VIII, para. 35.
[171] Article VIII, para. 36 (a)(b) and (c).
[172] See under Chapter V, the correction function.
[173] Article VIII, para. 36, final section.
[174] Article VIII, para. 34 (a).

96   E. MYJER

with the States Parties.[175] Like any serious executive body it will also take care
of technical matters like submitting to the Conference the draft programme and
budget of the OPCW[176] or the draft report of the OPCW on the implementation
of the CWC.[177]

(iii)The Technical Secretariat

The Technical Secretariat is the substantial and permanent body which is
subordinated to the Conference and the Executive Council[178] and which
foresees the necessary technical and administrative know how.[179] Since the
Inspectorate is a unit of the Technical Secretariat,[180] it manages the inspection
teams. It is the centre for receiving declarations[181] and takes care of the initial
and routine inspections. It assesses reports and generally keeps an ear to the
ground. The Technical Secretariat, in short, embodies the OPCW as an
organization.

> "The Technical Secretariat shall assist the Conference and the Executive
> Council in the performance of their functions. The Technical Secretariat shall
> carry out the verification measures provided for in this Convention [..] as well as
> those functions delegated to it by the Conference and the Executive Council."[182]

The Technical Secretariat shall inform the Executive Council of, inter alia,
doubts, ambiguities or uncertainties concerning compliance with this
Convention that have come to its notice in the performance of its verification
activities and that it has been unable to resolve or clarify through its consultations with the State Party concerned.[183] Furthermore, it shall negotiate
agreements or arrangements relating to the implementation of verification
activities with States Parties. It will also play a central and coordinating role
with regard to the provision of assistance under Article X of the Convention.[184]
Since, according to Bernauer, the functions of the Technical Secretariat were
rather vaguely specified in the treaty text, much was left to the PrepCom and
the Provisional Technical Secretariat (PTS).[185] In his opinion the problem with
regard to the Secretariat pertains not so much to technical issues, but concerns

---

[175] Article VIII, para. 34 (c).
[176] Article VIII, para. 32.
[177] As well as the report on the performance of its own activities and all such special reports
as it deems necessary, or which the Conference requests.(Article VIII, paragraph 32 (b)).
[178] Article VIII, D, para. 37.
[179] See in general Article VIII paras 38 and 39.
[180] Article VIII, para. 42.
[181] Article VII, para. 38 (c).
[182] Article VIII, para. 37.
[183] Article VIII, para. 40.
[184] Article VIII, para. 39.
[185] Bernauer, *supra* n. 130, at 340.

"the degree to which the Secretariat will be able to act independently and in an activist manner".[186]

The Technical Secretariat shall be headed by a Director-General,[187] who is responsible to the Conference and the Executive Council for the appointment of the staff and the organization of the Technical Secretariat. The Inspectorate shall act under the supervision of the Director-General. The Director-General fulfils an important role with regard to the handling and protection of confidential information.[188]

5. Decisions and decision- making

The two essential types of decisions are the ones taken by the Conference, as the prime representative organ, and those by the Executive Council. Of these two categories of decisions the ones by the Conference are the most important ones, for the Conference not only has the general task of overseeing the implementation of the Convention, it also oversees the activities of the Executive Council and the Technical Secretariat and may issue guidelines in accordance with the CWC to either of them in the exercise of their functions.[189] Furthermore, it elects the members of the Executive Council and appoints the Director-General.[190] The Conference decides on procedural questions by a simple majority of the members present and voting.[191] Matters of substance "should be taken, as far as possible, by consensus". If consensus is not attainable, the Chairman shall defer any vote for 24 hours. During this period he shall do his utmost to facilitate the attaining of consensus. Within this period he shall report to the Conference. If no consensus can be reached at the end of the 24-hour period a majority decision will be taken if the Convention does not specify otherwise. This decision shall be taken by "a two-thirds majority of

---

[186] "... that is, to what extent the Secretariat can or will lobby Governments to join the Convention; what role it will play in the process of initiating inspections and evaluating their results; how it will deal with cases where Parties provide incomplete or no information on their relevant behaviour; and how it will handle cases of various forms on non-compliance". Bernauer, *ibid*, at 340.

[187] Article VIII, para. 41.

[188] The Director-General shall have prime responsibility for ensuring the protection of confidential information and shall establish a stringent regime governing the handling of confidential information by the Technical Secretariat (Confidentiality Annex (A)(2)): See more in particular the Confidentiality Annex and *infra* paragraph 6 (ii) (p 99 et seq.) the case of the Confidentiality Commission.

[189] Article VII, para. 20.

[190] Article VIII, para. 21 (c), (d).

[191] Article VIII, para. 18. Also under the CTBT the Conference of the States Parties of the Comprehensive Nuclear Test-Ban Treaty Organization (CTBTO) (Article II, para. 22). Different is that the adjective "simple" before the word "majority" has been omitted, perhaps a sign that it has become the standard procedure!

members present and voting".[192] The Executive Council shall take decisions on matters of substance by a two-thirds majority of all its members.[193] Decisions on questions of procedure shall be taken by a simple majority of all its members.[194] Decisions taken in accordance with the Convention are binding on the Member States. Remarkable is the fact that two of the organs (including its most important one) of an international organization in the sphere of national (military) security are allowed to take majority decisions! Even more remarkable is that under Article IX, paragraph 17 of the Convention, decisions of the Council *against* carrying out a challenge inspection shall be made by a three-quarters majority of all its members.[195] The required greater majority to block a challenge inspection underlines the central importance that is being attached to this element of challenge inspection. This is understandable because the possibility of a challenge inspection was crucial in order to have the Convention agreed upon in the first place. Furthermore, it underlines the non-discriminatory nature of this Convention by allowing a single vote at both levels for each State Party represented.[196] All of these innovative institutional elements were obviously included in the CWC in order to stimulate universal accession to the Convention, which is essential from the point of view of effective arms control.[197]

6. Dispute settlement

(i)General

Although the Convention's central dispute settlement clause as contained in Article XIV was mentioned above[198] and dispute settlement will also be touched upon in Chapter V concerning the creative function, given the central

---

[192] Article VIII, para. 18. Also under the CTBT the Conference of the States Parties of the CTBTO (Article II, para. 22).

[193] Article VIII, para. 29. Accordingly rule 36 of the Rules of Procedure of the Executive Council, C-I/DEC.72, 23 May 1997. Also under the CTBT the Executive Council of the CTBTO (Article II, para. 36).

[194] Article VIII, para. 29. Also under the CTBT the Executive Council of the CTBTO (Article II, para. 36). Different is that the adjective "simple" in front of "majority" has been omitted like is the case with the Conference, see *supra* n.191.

[195] Rule 38 of the Rules of Procedure of the Executive Council, C-I/DEC.72, 23 May 1997.

[196] A member of the Council that is in arrears in the payment of its contribution to the OPCW, however, shall have no vote in the Council "if the amount of its arrears equals or exceeds the amount of the contribution due from it for the preceding two full years unless the Conference permits such a member to vote in accordance with Article VIII, para. 8 of the Convention", rule 35 Rules of Procedure Executive Council, C-I/DEC.72, 23 May 1997.

[197] Compare "general and complete disarmament under strict and effective international control".

[198] See p. 86.

role of the Executive Council and the Conference a few more words are in order in the context of the institutional framework of the OPCW. Article XIV deals with the settlement of disputes concerning "the application or the interpretation"[199] of the CWC. When there is a dispute between States Parties, or between one or more States Parties and the Organization, they shall consult together with a view to the expeditious settlement of the dispute via negotiation or by other peaceful means" of their choice. This apparently refers to the methods of Article 33 of the UN Charter, or more generally to Chapter VI, given the general reference in paragraph 1 of Article XIV to the duty to settle disputes in conformity with the provisions of the Charter. They can furthermore involve the organs of the OPCW and, by mutual consent, submit the dispute to the adjudication of the ICJ.[200] This clause appears to refer to dispute settlement related to treaty technicalities and not to compliance issues.

The point of departure is therefore that the above mentioned disputes shall be settled in conformity with the provisions of the UN Charter, in other words via the peaceful settlement techniques contained in Article 33. As will be seen when discussing the supervisory functions of the OPCW, use is made of these techniques from the very first moment in the collection phase. In other words, there is a constant process of dispute settlement.[201]

A dispute may arise at different levels. It may already arise during the review phase of a possible case of non-compliance or it may occur when the Conference has decided on a case. A dispute may also arise regarding a breach of confidentiality. Or it may concern a dispute between the host country and the Organization. A central role is attributed to the two central organs of the OPCW, the Executive Council and the Conference. States Parties may seek the settlement of a dispute via recourse to the appropriate organs of the OPCW.[202] The Executive Council may contribute to the solution of a dispute by whatever method it deems fit, including by offering its good offices.[203] The Conference shall consider questions brought to its attention, and can under Article VIII, paragraph 19 take decisions on any matters or issues related to the Convention brought to its attention by States Parties or by the Executive Council. The Conference may furthermore establish subsidiary organs with tasks related to the settlement of disputes. With the consent of the UN General Assembly the Executive Council or the Conference are empowered to request

---

[199] This formula is taken to include reference to "any legal question arising within the scope of the activities of the Organization" as referred to in Article XIV para. 5 concerning the possiblity of requesting an advisory opinion from the ICJ.

[200] Article XIV, para. 2.

[201] See also E.P.J. Myjer, Supervisory mechanisms and dispute settlement, in: J. Dahlitz, *Avoidance and Settlement of Arms Control Disputes* (1994), at 166. In general 158 et seq.

[202] Article XIV, para. 2. It refers, however, to the appropriate organs "of this Convention", where "of the Organization" would have been more appropriate.

[203] Article XIV, para. 3.

100   E. MYJER

an advisory opinion from the ICJ.[204] In general, however, it can be determined that the CWC is weak as regards judicial dispute settlement.

(ii)The case of the Confidentiality Commission

Given that the CWC is weak as regards judicial dispute settlement, an interesting element of the CWC is the special place of its Confidentiality Commission. The Confidentiality Commission is an autonomous subsidiary organ of the Conference,[205] which is specifically mentioned in the Convention.[206] The fact that the Convention has an Annex specially devoted to the protection of confidential information (the Confidentiality Annex) already underlines the special character of this convention. This not only concerns confidential information in the area of military security, but also confidential business information. Verification of the chemical industries is essential in order to realize the purpose and principles of the CWC. Since, therefore, the civilian chemical industry would be heavily involved in the supervision process (viz. declarations or the inspections of chemical plants) there was strong pressure from the chemical industries to preserve the confidentiality of the information. States Parties and their private industries had to be certain that there would be a sufficient deterrent that the verifying inspectors, the Technical Secretariat and even the States Parties, who had received information, would protect its confidential character.[207] This led to the Confidentiality Annex and the establishment of the Confidentiality Commission. Reference to obligations in this respect can also be found in the Convention in Article VIII, paragraph 5 for the OPCW and in Article VII, paragraph 6 for each State Party.[208] The Annex contains General Principles for the handling of confidential information. This has been detailed in an extensive document: *OPCW Policy on Confidentiality*.[209] It foresees individual secrecy agreements for staff members. The Director General has a central position in case of breach or alleged

---

[204] Article XIV, para. 5.

[205] Confidentiality Annex, D, para. 23. See E.P.J. Myjer, The Settlement of Disputes under the Chemical Weapons Convention and the Case of the Confidentiality Commission, in Bardonnet, *supra* n. 4, at pp.537-553.

[206] Para. 23 of the Annex on the Protection of Confidential Information (Confidentiality Annex) to the CWC.

[207] That this issue is regarded as politically sensitive can be assessed from the fact that also in this area some issues remained unresolved. See PrepCom's Final Report, PC-XVI/37, section four (unresolved issues), paragraph IV (Confidentiality), 115-117, p. 52. See also the debate in the US Senate, *supra* n. 133, p. S 3655-S3656; Also B. Kellman, D.S. Gualteri, E.A. Tanzman, Disarmament and Disclosure: How Arms Control Verification can proceed Without Threatening Confidential Business Information, 36 *Harvard J.Int'l.L.*, pp.71-126.

[208] These requirements are elaborated in the provisions detailing verification procedures like Article VI, para. 10, paras. 56 and 62, Part II of the Verification Annex, and para. 48, Part X, Verification Annex.

[209] C-I/Dec.13/6 May 1997.

breaches of confidentiality. He shall impose punitive and disciplinary measures on staff members who have violated their obligations to protect confidential information. Remarkable is the disclaimer, as discussed, contained in the Annex with regard to the liability of the OPCW in case of a breach of confidentiality committed by members of the Technical Secretariat.[210] The US Senate formulated extensive conditions regarding the protection of confidential information in the ratification resolution.[211] The Confidentiality Commission deals with breaches of confidentiality involving a State Party and the OPCW. Its single task is the settlement of these disputes.

In cases of complaints regarding a breach of confidentiality by the OPCW or by some State Party the Confidentiality Commission may receive a complaint. This Commission, however, is not a kind of joint consultative committee, which we can find in different arms control treaties.[212] It is a real dispute settlement body. The twenty members of the Commission come from different fields of expertise and are appointed by the Conference in their personal capacity for a period of two years. Whenever there is a complaint it is up to the Commission to decide to convene a meeting. According to their extensive operating procedures,[213] drawn up by the Commission and approved by the Conference, there is a refined system for dispute settlement in place, ranging from mediation up to conciliation or even arbitration. Although the Commission can only take binding decisions if the parties so desire, it is essentially a dispute settlement body. And that is what it is supposed to look like. For the Conference was even willing to go along with the proposal by the Commission to appoint the International Bureau of the Permanent Court of Arbitration as an independent Registry to receive the complaints, which otherwise might have to be received by the TS, the very organ against which the complaint might be made.[214] To the author's knowledge this is the first time, and certainly in the area of arms control, that the one international organization (the OPCW) has signed an agreement[215] with another international organization (the Permanent Court of Arbitration) in order to assure the independence of a dispute settlement procedure within a particular regime. And

---

[210] Confidentiality Annex, D, 23. See above.

[211] For instance, in case of a breach of confidentiality the President will have to certify to Congress that the Confidentiality Commission has been established to consider the breach. Ratification Resolution, *Congressional Record Senate*, April 24, 1997, at S 3655.

[212] Compare the Standing Consultative Commission (Article XVII, SALT II), the Verification Commission (Article XIII, INF Treaty), and the Joint Consultative Group (Article XVI, CFE Treaty).

[213] Operating Procedures of the Confidentiality Commission, C-III/DEC.10, published in *The Legal Texts*, *supra* n. 4 at pp.498-512.

[214] In its decision of 5 December 1997 (C-II/DEC.14) the Conference appointed the International Bureau of the Permanent Court of Arbitration in The Hague to serve as the Registry of the Confidentiality Commission. See *The Legal Texts*, *ibid*. at 512.

[215] Registry Agreement between the OPCW and the Permanent Court of Arbitration, dated 9 December 1998. See EC-XII/DEC.6 of 9 October 1998.

102   E. MYJER

this brings in the management aspect, as will be discussed later,[216] because the very appearance of a fair dispute settlement procedure with regard to a possible breach of confidential information may serve as a "confidence-building measure" which may induce not only the States Parties, but also the national chemical industries to cooperate fully with the CWC regime. So within the essentially non-adversarial supervisory system, a potentially adversarial dispute settlement body has been created with detailed operating procedures, although as a matter of course it is primarily equipped with non-judicial techniques. But having said that, it is still adversarial in character.

7. Some general issues

"The organization shall enjoy on the territory and in any other place under the jurisdiction or control of a State Party such *legal capacity* [emphasis added] and such privileges as is necessary for the exercise of its functions",[217] a formulation quite similar to that of Articles 104 and 105 of the UN Charter. Seen in conjunction with paragraph 50, which refers to agreements between the Organization and the States Parties in which the legal capacity, privileges and immunities shall be defined, this reference in the Convention apparently refers to legal capacity at the non-international level.[218] Reference to this capacity does not seem surprising for, as Amerasinghe argues, "[w]ithout personality an organization would not be able to appear in its own right in legal proceedings, whether at the international or non-international level".[219] As regards the international level, as with most international organizations legal personality is not explicitly referred to in the constituent treaty but can nevertheless be presumed. This follows from the functions and powers of the Organization, like the ability to conclude agreements or arrangements[220] and the privileges and immunities for the Director-General and the staff of the Organization.[221] To presume international legal personality is in accordance

---

[216] See p. 127 et seq..

[217] Article VIII, para. 48.

[218] "The legal capacity, privileges and immunities referred to in this Article shall be defined in agreements between the Organization and the States Parties as well as in an agreement between the Organization and the State in which the headquarters of the Organization is seated.[..]", Article VIII, para. 50. See Krutzsch et al., *supra* n. 4, at 169.

[219] "There would also not be a single international person as such having the capacity in its own right to have rights, obligations and powers, whether implied or expressed, both at the international level and at the non-international level. Such rights, obligations and powers would be vested collectively in all the creating States, which may not have been the intention behind the creation of the organization, and also could create unnecessary practical problems, particularly in the area of responsibility, both active and passive." C.F. Amerasinghe, *Principles of the Institutional Law of International Organizations* (1996), at 69.

[220] See Article VIII, paras. 34 and 39 (a).

[221] "Delegates of States Parties, together with their alternates and advisers, representatives

with "the prevalent view", according to which it is implicitly given if there is no specific constitutional attribution.[222] This position finds support in the well-known advisory opinion of the ICJ.[223] It is relatively rare for an intergovernmental organization to state that it has personality "indeed there appears no need for an express provision in the constituent treaty of an organization for it to be deemed to possess personality".[224]

Given that the Constitution of the OPCW makes clear that the OPCW has a certain legal capacity, both at the national and the international level, but at the same time excludes its liability, the question can be raised what is then left of the concept of legal personality if it is at the same time restricted? For, interestingly, as regards a possible breach of confidentiality committed by a member of the Technical Secretariat the Confidentiality Annex makes it quite clear that the OPCW shall not be held liable for such breaches.[225] Since such possible breaches of confidentiality may only occur with regard to the information of Member States, or of facilities under their jurisdiction, there seems to be nothing against States Parties agreeing to have the liability of the OPCW restricted towards themselves. It would, however, have been different if States Parties had restricted the organization's general liability. Still, in this way the created international legal personality appears to be rather unbalanced with, on the one hand, rights but, on the other, fairly restricted duties.

The Organization shall enjoy the usual privileges and immunities on the territory of a State Party and in any place under its jurisdiction or control.[226] The privileges and immunities shall be defined in agreements between the OPCW and the States Parties as well as in the Headquarters Agreement.[227]

---

appointed to the Executive Council together with their alternates and advisers, *the Director-General and the staff of the Organization shall enjoy such privileges and immunities as are necessary in the independent exercise of their functions in connection with the Organization*", Article VIII, para 49 [emphasis added]. Also Krutzsch et al., *supra* n. 4, at 127: "The Organization is equipped with all the attributes of an international legal personality, as contained in Article 104 and 105 of the UN Charter. The Organization is the addressee of rights and obligations provided for by the Convention."

[222] Schermers & Blokker, *supra* n. 149, at 979.

[223] *Reparation for Injuries Suffered in the Service of the United Nations*, ICJ Rep. 1949 at 174. See Schermers & Blokker, *ibid.* at 979-980.

[224] White, *supra* n. 149, at 27. Also Amarasinghe, *supra* n. 219 at 78: "International personality is very rarely dealt with explicitly or impliedly in the constitutions of international organizations". See, however, Article 4 of the Rome Statute of the International Criminal Court, wherby the Court is established as an international organization and explicitly granted international legal personality (see Article 4 Rome Satute, A/Conf.183/9).

[225] Confidentiality Annex, D (22).

[226] Article VIII, para. 48

[227] Article VIII, para. 50. OPCW Headquarters Agreement (C-I/DEC.59, 14 May 1997): inter alia, Article 4 (Immunity from legal process); Article 5 (Immunity of property from other actions, inviolability of the archives, samples, equipment, and other material); Article 7 (law and authority in the headquarters); Article 10 (facilities and immunities in respect of

104   E. MYJER

Notwithstanding these regulations, in the Verification Annex[228] detailed arrangements are contained regarding the privileges and immunities of the inspectors and inspection assistants in the carrying out of their inspection duties. During the carrying out of verification activities the immunities of the Director-General and the staff of the TS are accordingly extended.[229]

In its external relations with States and other international organizations under Article VIII para. 34 the OPCW has the capacity to conclude agreements or arrangements. An important example of these is the Relationship Agreement between the United Nations and the OPCW.[230]

V. The supervisory functions of the OPCW

1.General: supervision as a model

In the previous chapters we have looked at the Convention and described its core obligations and we looked at the OPCW as the international organization that is established under this treaty primarily[231] to ensure compliance with these obligations. It aims, in other words, to control compliance with these obligations. Lang refers to compliance control as a relatively new concept, which he does not define, however, but which is rooted in the English term "compliance" and which is linked to the French term "*contrôle*".[232] This is exactly what the concept of supervision is about. More in particular it is about supervision by an international organization in contradistinction to States exercising supervision over each other. The international organization which the OPCW is fulfils a number of sub-functions, all aimed at the overarching goal of supervision of the behaviour of the Member States. This function of supervision is realized via these sub-functions. The techniques applied in these

---

communications and publications); Article 11 (exemption of the OPCW and its property from taxes and duties); Article 12 (freedom of financial assets from restrictions); Article 13 (exemption from import and export restrictions); Article 14 (transit and residence); Article 15 (permanent missions to the OPCW); Article 16 (privileges and immunities of heads of delegations, permanent representatives to the OPCW and staff members of permanent missions); Article 17 (privileges and immunities of delegates and alternates for and advisers attached to heads of delegation); Article 18 (privileges and immunities of the Director-General and other officials of the OPCW); Article 19 (privileges and immunities of experts).

[228] Verification Annex II, part B.

[229] Article VIII, para. 51.

[230] The Relationship Agreement between the UN and the OPCW, *supra* n. 11.

[231] Also in the sphere of cooperation under Article X the OPCW has a function.

[232] "Compliance-control is a relatively new concept; it is rooted in the English term "compliance" and links it to the term "contrôle", which is the focal point of many French-language writings on this subject", W. Lang, Compliance with Disarmament Obligations, *Zeitschrift für Öffenliches Recht und Völkerrecht*, no. 55/1, 1995, at 69.

sub-functions are all directed to this particular end. "Their main purpose is to evoke compliance behaviour from the subjects of the legal order".[233] The institutional structure of the OPCW regulates the carrying out of these different sub-functions. The OPCW can therefore be held to be first and foremost an international organization that embodies the institutional structure of this supervisory mechanism. This section aims to analyze the sub-functions of this compliance control organization.[234]

Lately much has been written about compliance control, especially by social scientists.[235] Interestingly, it often concerns fields of international law like arms control, trade or environmental protection.[236] No attempt will be made to add more theoretical expositions on compliance control,[237] since the only aim of this section is to analyze the functions of the OPCW in this respect. In order to do so for analytical purposes I will use the concept of supervision, as applied with regard to international economic organizations,[238] with its three separate functions. These functions being the *review function* (judging State behaviour for its conformity with an agreed rule of international law)[239] the *correction function* (the correction of State behaviour, when it is established that a State has violated an international obligation)[240] and the *creative function* (interpretation or clarification of the rules).[241] I have, however, come to the conclusion that for the sake of clarity a fourth function should be added, namely the *collection function*. This function refers to the collection of information, be it the collection of information regarding the behaviour of States Parties, their

---

[233] T.M.R. Chowdhury, *Legal Framework of International Supervision* (Thesis, University of Stockholm (1986)), at xvi.

[234] Also referred to as "monitoring agency", A. Smithson, *supra* n. 94, at 6.

[235] "In the past few years many social scientists interested in cooperation have turned their attention to the problem of compliance in international regulatory regimes. Much of the empirical research in this area has been conducted by a group composed mainly of qualitative political scientists and scholars interested in international law", Downs et al., *infra* n. 237, at 379. An exception in the legal field are the Chayes. See Chayes et al., *supra* n. 69 and *infra* n. 237.

[236] See Lang, *supra* n. 232, at 69. Downs, *infra* n. 237, at 3, 84.

Downs argues that, contrary to what "the managerialists" might argue, "at least with respect to the relationship between enforcement and depth of cooperation, the areas are not as different as one might imagine or as some might hope", *ibid* at 390.

[237] Compare George W. Downs, David M. Rocke, and Peter N. Barsoom, Is the Good News about Compliance Control Good News About Cooperation?, 50 *International Organization*, 3, summer 1996, pp. 379-406; Abram Chayes and Antonia Handler Chayes, On Compliance, 47 *International Organization*, 2, spring, 1993, pp. 175-205.

[238] See P. van Dijk (ed.), *Supervisory Mechanisms in International Economic Organizations* (1984).

[239] But also the accuracy of the information provided.

[240] Compare M. Koskenniemi, Breach of Treaty or Non-Compliance?, Reflections on the Enforcement of the Montreal Protocol, *Yearbook of International Environmental Law*, Vol.3, (1992) at 123-126.

[241] Van Dijk et al., *supra* n. 238 at pp. 11-39.

agents or those legal and natural persons under their jurisdiction. The concept of supervision thus applied appears to provide maximum clarity.[242]

Nollkaemper, writing about environmental law, also makes the distinction between collection of information and its review, where for analytical purposes he divides provisions into three categories corresponding to the three main stages of compliance control by international fora: the *compilation of information* (provisions which aim to ensure that international fora obtain adequate information on the degree to which states comply with their obligations); *review of compliance* (provisions which govern the review of compliance) and *enforcement* (provisions which make it possible that in case of non-compliance obligations are enforced).[243] He does not, however, deal with the creative function separately. Elements thereof can be found in the respective functions like where the review procedure contributes to the clarification of the State's obligations[244] and thereby elucidates the contents of the obligation.

The distinction used by myself is therefore the following: (1) *collection function*; (2) *review function*; (3) *creative function*; and (4) *correction function*. Such a distinction in four (sub-) functions can be applied in various fields of international law,[245] but especially in the field of disarmament and arms control it is indispensable because it allows us better to understand the, for that area, highly developed and pivotal concept of "verification" and to distinguish it from sanctions to be applied in case of a breach of treaty obligations. With regard to verification of arms control agreements Sur, who regards verification as a process,[246] distinguishes three aspects of this process namely: (1) establishments of the facts; (2) their legal assessment; and (3) consequences to be drawn in the event of an established violation. He then presents three possible concepts: the "minimalist concept", which is limited to the hard-core that constitutes establishment of the facts";[247] the "intermediate concept", which incorporates legal assessment;[248] and the "extensive concept", which adds the reactions emanating from the determination of a violation.[249] He is of the opinion that the intermediate concept is the dominant one.

---

[242] See for instance E.P.J. Myjer, The Law of Arms-Control and International Supervision in 3 *LJIL* (1990) at 99-123 / M. Brus et al., The United Nations Decade of International Law (1991), at 99-123; *supra* n. 201, at 149-169 and E.P.J. Myjer, *New Procedures of International Dispute Resolution*, in: ASIL/NVIR Proceedings (1997), at 355-363.

[243] A. Nollkaemper, *The Legal Regime for Transboundary Water Pollution: Between Discretion and Constraint* (1993) p. 256 et seq.

[244] Nollkaemper, *ibid*, at 268.

[245] Like human rights or protection of the environment. On the application of different concepts in the various fields of international law see Lang, *supra* n. 232, at 69.

[246] See *supra* n. 293, at 150.

[247] S. Sur, *A Legal Approach to Verification in Disarmament or Arms Limitation*, Research Paper no. 1 UNIDER (1988), at 8.

[248] Sur, *ibid*, at 8.

[249] Sur, *ibid*, at 8.

E. MYJER 107

Lang, writing about compliance with regard to *disarmament obligations*, in clarifying different notions in this area[250] makes a distinction whereby "verification represents an external approach aimed at checking facts" but not envisaging the consequences of failure to comply.[251] He refers to Sur's three concepts of verification - the minimalist, the intermediate and the extensive - and is of the opinion that *verification* should be restricted to the first two of these variations since problems arising in the third field "... considerably differ from issues of fact finding and legal assessment".[252] Adoption of the extensive concept would then lead back to his (broader) concept of compliance control.[253] This concept of compliance control comes close to that of verification, but also encompasses the consequences in case of non-compliance.

The four functions of supervision as applied by myself come closest to the compliance control concept of Lang and to Sur's extensive concept. However, it disects the different functions and restricts verification to the collection of facts. Furthermore, in distinguishing the correction function it allows one to separate the more political character of the consequences to be drawn, as rightly demonstrated by Sur. With regard to the CWC we find two of these "steps", viz. the collection function and the review function, clearly set out in the four sub-systems that Perry Robinson.[254] distinguishes in the verification system of the Chemical Weapons Convention: 1) *the system of data collection*, whereby "individual States Parties monitor relevant activities within their own jurisdictions"; 2) the system of declarations, whereby prescribed categories of information are reported by individual States Parties to the Technical Secretariat ;[255] 3) *the system of validation*, "which is operated by the Technical secretariat to check the accuracy of State declarations by means of routine on-site inspection"; and 4) *the system of requested inspection*. As will be clear Perry Robinson's system of validation and the system of requested inspection partly coincide with my review function.

---

[250] Notions like compliance control, implementation, application, verification, supervision, monitoring and inspection, Lang, *supra* n. 232, at 69-70.

[251] Lang, *ibid*, at 70.

[252] Lang, *ibid*, at 81.

[253] "Adopting the "extensive concept" would lead back to the broader idea of compliance control already discussed [..]", Lang. *ibid*, at 81.

[254] J.P. Perry Robinson, *supra* n. 117, at 491.

[255] He then continues "which then processes the information and disseminates it to all States Parties", at 491. In my opinion the information will, if necessary, be automatically updated after inspections, as will also be the case after the "validation" and after the challenge inspection.

108   E. MYJER

2. The collection function

This function refers to the actual collecting of all relevant information. A wealth of information is collected within the context of the CWC. This is done both by individual States Parties and by the OPCW respectively. States Parties will have to collect the information they need to declare within their own (national) jurisdictions. They will have to provide this information subsequently to the OPCW via the system of declarations.[256] In principle this information will be validated by the OPCW via routine on-site inspections.[257] Here, indeed, one enters the review function, with the validated information coming back via the collection function as factual information. Furthermore, information will be collected via inspections upon request, which will not take place upon the initiative of the OPCW but rather upon that of the States Parties. States Parties will receive on request, for instance in case they ask for clarification from the OPCW - the Executive Council -[258] the information assembled by the OPCW. With regard to the collection function, Perry Robinson's, sub-systems mentioned in the previous paragraph are illustrative, but not comprehensive since collection of information is also possible outside these systems, e.g. via clarification, on-site monitoring or collation of information. Of the different methods the following are the most prominent:

* national data collection
In order to be able to fulfil its obligation to provide for the requested relevant information States Parties will have to arrange for that nationally. This, in Perry Robinson's words, is *the system of data collection*. With regard to declarations under Article III, State Parties that fall in the "yes" category[259] will normally already have the information required at hand. With regard to Article VI (activities not prohibited under this Convention) in all probability it will mainly concern civilian chemical industries. This information will have to be obtained via national legislation.[260]

---

[256] In order to provide the National Authorities of States Parties to the CWC with detailed explanations on declaration requirements with regard to initial, annual and other declarations a Declaration Handbook has been developed (PTS-OPCW, rev. 1996-11-14).

[257] Notwithstanding initial inspections.

[258] Compare Article IX para. 3.

[259] According to Krutsch the first part of the declaration is a "yes-no" declaration. "Each of the elements *individually* triggers an affirmative or negative declaration, *supra* n. 4 at 48.

[260] Article VII (1) contains the general implementation obligation. Article VI, para. 2 and the Verifacation Annex in Parts VI(D), VII(A), Paragraph VIII(A), IX (A) are specific regarding the declarations.

E. MYJER   109

*via declarations by States Parties[261]

In different articles the CWC details the information (reports) which States Parties will have to submit to the OPCW, and the period within which this will have to be done after the entry into force of the CWC. It concerns information about chemical weapons, on old and abandoned chemical weapons, on chemical weapons production facilities and on other facilities,[262] which under Article III will have to be declared within 30 days after entry into force. For instance, with regard to chemical weapons, inter alia, the precise location and aggregate quantity will have to be declared.[263] With regard to chemical weapons production facilities the requested information concerns any facility under its jurisdiction since 1 January 1946.[264] Furthermore, each State shall submit detailed plans for the destruction of chemical weapons[265] and chemical weapons destruction facilities.[266] With respect to riot control agents "the chemical name, structural formula and Chemical Abstracts Service registry number"[267] will have to be specified. To ensure that toxic chemicals and their precursors are not used for the production of chemical weapons these chemicals, as listed in Schedules 1, 2 and 3, and the related facilities will have to be declared.[268] This means that declarations will not only have to be submitted with regard to weapons and facilities, but also with regard to certain chemicals of which controlled use is allowed for purposes not prohibited under the Convention.[269] Such use, however, is controlled and subject to specific provisions. In order to allow for different degrees of intensity of verification and for the "reporting threshold' (declaration duty) chemicals are ranked in order of risk into three categories, namely Schedule 1, Schedule 2 and Schedule 3 chemicals. Furthermore, there is also the category "discrete organic chemicals". *Schedule 1* lists twelve chemicals that are key to nerve and blister agents[270] and that are unlikely to be of any industrial interest.[271] *Schedule 2*

---

[261] See for instance note by the Executive Secretary on the information required from States Parties Immediately or soon after Entry Into Force, PC-XVI/10, 1 April 1997.

[262] Article III and Parts IV(A), IV(B) and V of the Verification Annex.

[263] Article III, para. (a)(ii).

[264] Article III, para. (c).

[265] Article IV, para. 7 (a). Furthermore, a State Party shall submit declarations annually regarding the implementation of its plan for the destruction (sub. (b)) and certify not later than 30 days after the destruction process has been completed (sub. (c)).

[266] Article V, para. 9 (a) "Not later than 180 days before the destruction of each facility begins").

[267] Article III, para. 1 (e).

[268] Article VI, para. 7. See for instance regarding the projected activities and anticipated production for the coming year of Schedule 1 activities, Verification Annex, Part VI.16 and 20.

[269] States Parties maintain as a principle their right "to develop, produce, otherwise acquire, retain, transfer and use toxic chemicals and their precursors..", Article VI, para. 1.

[270] "This category includes all known nerve gasses, mustard agents, lewisites and some key precursors, R.G. Sutherland, The Chemical Weapons Convention: The Problems of

110   E. MYJER

contains fourteen chemicals of significant risk that are not widely used in industry, whereas *Schedule 3* lists seventeen precursors and chemicals that are frequently used in industry, but still pose a risk.[272] Since these categories determine the level of involvement of the civilian chemical industry and becasuse of its complex nature, the following in particular can be said with regard to these categories:

Schedule 1: Because these chemicals present the greatest risk to the CWC's object and purpose,[273] activities with regard to Schedule 1 chemicals are banned, with the exception of permitted activities for a limited number of purposes,[274] which will be closely monitored. Each party is not allowed to have more than 1 tonne of Schedule 1 chemicals. Production exceeding 10 kg can only take place in a single small-scale production facility for research, medical, pharmaceutical and protective purposes.[275] Production facilities for Schedule 1 chemicals fall under the regime of systematic on-site inspections and monitoring with on-site instruments.[276] Also the transfer of Schedule 1 chemicals is subject to severe transfer restrictions.[277] The transfer of these chemicals to non-States Parties is forbidden.[278] The initial declaration will have to take place within 30 days after the entry into force of the CWC; initial declarations on new facilities shall be provided 180 days before operations are to begin.[279] Furthermore, States Parties, will have to make declarations annually concerning the activities of the facility for the previous year.[280]

Schedule 2: There are no production limits for Schedule 2 and 3 chemicals that are being produced commercially, but there are thresholds above which production must be declared.[281] For Schedule 2, the "reporting thresholds"

Implementation, 7 *Pacific Research*, no. 1, 1994, at 8.

[271] Sutherland, *ibid* at 8.

[272] Smithson, *supra* n. 74 at 7.

[273] Kellman et al., *supra* n. 4 at 34.

[274] *Ibid*, at 34.

[275] See Part VI Verification Annex (Activities not prohibited under this convention in accordance with Article VI. Regime for schedule 1 chemicals and facilities related to such chemicals) under A.1. Para. 11 states that "at facilities approved by the State Party production of chemicals in quantities of more than 100 g per year may be carried out for research, medical or pharmaceutical purposes outside a single small-scale facility in aggregate quantities not exceeding 10 kg per year per facility".

[276] See Article VI, para. 3.

[277] Kellman et al., *supra* n. 4 at 39.

[278] Verification Annex, VI,(B)(3).

[279] Verification Annex, Part VI, (d)(13).

[280] Verification Annex, Part VI (D)(15).

[281] See in particular Verification Annex: Part VII under A.3 (Activities not prohibited under this convention in accordance with Article VI, Regime for schedule 2 chemicals and facilities related to such chemicals) and Part VIII under A.3 (Activities not prohibited under this convention in accordance with Article VI, Regime for schedule 3 chemicals and facilities related to such chemicals). Sutherland, *supra* n. 270 at 8.

range from one kilogram to one tonne. The "inspection threshold", however, is "about tenfold larger".[282] Also Schedule 2 chemicals are subject to export controls. This obligation shall take effect three years after the entry into force of the CWC.[283] During that period "end-user certificates" are required. Declarations will have to be made initially within 30 days after entry into force, and furthermore annually within 90 days after the end of the previous calender year as well as declarations on anticipated activities not later than 60 days before the beginning of the following calendar year. Initial declarations will have to include all plants which have produced at any time since 1946.

Schedule 3: The declaration threshold is thirty tonnes, with an "inspection threshold" of about 200 tonnes.[284] The export controls with regard to Schedule 3 chemicals are less strict. Each State Party shall, however, adopt the necessary measures to ensure that the transferred chemicals shall only be used for purposes not prohibited under the CWC.[285]

Discrete organic chemicals: other chemical plant sites where compounds of these chemicals are made and which contain phosphorus, sulpher or fluorine (PSF) in amounts greater than thirty tonnes will have to be declared, as will plants which produce more than 200 tonnes of unscheduled discrete organic chemicals. Such plants will be liable to CWC inspection after the Convention has been in force for three years.[286] Declarations will have to be made initially within 30 days after the CWC enters into force and annually not later than 90 days after the previous calendar year,[287] as well as declarations on anticipated activities not later than 60 days before the beginning of the following calendar year. Initial declarations will have to include all plants which have produced at any time since 1946.[288]

The duty to declare does not only imply initial declarations, but also annual declarations on past activities as well as on anticipated activities.[289] If the facilities are privately owned, States Parties will have to arrange for the collection of that information via national legislation. To provide the respective National Authority with such information may be made a legal requirement.[290]

---

[282] Sutherland, *ibid* at 8.

[283] Verification Annex, VII, (B)(31).

[284] Verification Annex, Part VIII, B, 12. Sutherland, *supra* n. 270 at 8.

[285] Verification Annex, Part VIII, (C)(26).

[286] Verification Annex, Part IX, C, 22. Sutherland *supra* n. 270 at 9.

[287] Declarations on aggregate national data, on plant sites as well as on past production. See Verification Annex, Part VIII (A).

[288] See Verification Annex, Part IX (Regime for other chemical production facilities).

[289] See verification annex Part VIII, A (4).

[290] See above under "national data collection"; Kellman et al., *supra* n. 4, especially at 41. Compare for the Netherlands the *Uitvoeringswet Verdrag Chemische Wapens*, Tweede Kamer, vergaderjaar 1994-1995, 23 911, nrs. 1-2, especially Articles 4, 5, and 7. Any violation is punishable under the *Economic Offences Act*.

112   E. MYJER

Since the requested information is detailed[291] formats have been developed in order to standardise the information.[292]

*via inspections

As described above the first reports thus obtained will in the first instance be verified via initial inspections[293] by an OPCW inspection team. The purpose of this inspection is not only to verify information, but also to "obtain any additional information needed for planning future verification activities at the facilities, including on-site inspections and continuous monitoring, and for preparing the facility agreements.[294] Of course the very aspect of "verifying information" falls under the review function. The latter aspect - collection of information *per se* - falls under the collection function. The same will be the case for information collected on site during routine or challenge inspections. In accordance with the facility agreements inspectors will receive information, such as, if necessary, "[..]samples taken at their request from any devices, bulk containers and other containers at the destruction facility or the storage facility thereat".[295]

Under the CWC four different kinds of verification inspections can be distinguished:
   -   systematic verification of chemical weapons and their production facilities through on-site inspection and monitoring with on-site instruments;[296]

---

[291] Compare regarding chemical weapons: "The declaration of chemical weapons by a State Party pursuant to Article III, para. 1 (a) (ii), shall include the following: (a) The aggregate quantity of each chemical declared; (b) The precise location of each chemical weapons storage facility, expressed by: (i) Name; (ii) Geographical coordinates; and (iii) A detailed site diagram, including a boundary map and the location of bunkers/storage areas within the facility; (c) The detailed inventory for each chemical weapons storage facility including: (i) Chemicals defined as chemical weapons in accordance with Article II; (ii) Unfilled munitions, sub-munitions, devices and equipment defined as chemical weapons; (iii) Equipment specially designed for use directly in connection with the employment of munitions, sub-munitions, devices or equipment specified in sub-para. (ii); (iv) Chemicals specifically designed for use directly in connection with the employment of munitions, sub-munitions, devices or equipment specified in sub-para. (ii)." Verification Annex, Part IV (A)(1).

[292] In order to provide the National Authorities of States Parties to the CWC with detailed explanations on declaration requirements with regard to initial, annual and other declarations a Declaration Handbook has been developed (PTS-OPCW, rev. 1996-11-14: *Declaration Handbook related to Industrial Declarations.*)

[293] "Each declared facility subject to on-site inspection pursuant to Articles IV (chemical weapons, author), V (chemical weapons production facilities, author), and VI (Activities not prohibited under this convention, author), shall receive an inspection promptly after the facility is declared", Verification annex, Part III, A (1); Verification Annex Part IV (A) D (38).

[294] Verification Annex, Part III, A (1).

[295] Verification Annex (A), IV D 70(c).

[296] See: Article IV, para. 3 (chemical weapons); Article V, para. 3 (chemical weapons

- routine inspections of certain chemical facilities;[297]
- challenge inspections;[298]
- investigations in case of alleged use of chemical weapons.[299]

Of these types of inspection the first two primarily concern data control. That will not necessarily be the case with the challenge inspection and investigations in case of alleged use.

There are two categories of inspections, namely the *initial* and the *routine inspections* at the initiative of the Organization, as well as the *challenge inspections* at the request of States Parties. The purpose of the initial inspection is "to verify information provided and to obtain any additional information needed for planning future verification activities at the facility, including on-site inspections and continuous monitoring with on-site instruments" and to prepare the facility agreements.[300] Facility agreements are agreements between the Organization and States Parties relating to specifically declared facilities subject to on-site verification pursuant to Articles IV, V and VI.[301]

(1) initial and routine inspections

All declared locations at which chemical weapons are stored or destroyed, as well as all chemical weapons production facilities shall receive an initial inspection promptly after the facility has been declared.[302] For each declared facility that is subject to on-site inspections[303] a facility agreement will be concluded with the Organization. These facilities are subject to systematic verification through "on-site inspection and monitoring with on-site instruments".[304] The destruction of these weapons, which will have to take place within a period of two to ten years after the entry into force of the Convention, and one to ten years for the production facilities respectively, will be closely monitored. The routine inspections will take place at short notice and not less than 24 hours in advance of the planned arrival of the inspection team at the point of entry.[305] Old and abandoned weapons are subject to a different regime.

Initial inspections will also take place with regard to the "second line" - not chemical weapons as such - of chemical substances, namely chemicals that are used to make pharmaceuticals, pesticides, fertilizers and other everyday

---

production facilities); Article VI, para. 3 (Schedule 1 chemicals and facilities).

[297] Article VI, paras. 2, 4, 5 and 6.

[298] Article IX, para. 8 ("of any facility or location").

[299] Article X, paras. 8-11.

[300] Verification Annex, Part III under A.1.

[301] Verification Annex, Definitions, 7.

[302] Part III, A 1, Verification Annex.

[303] Pursuant to Articles IV, V and VI, para. 3.

[304] Article IV, para. 3 and Article V, para. 3.

[305] Part III, C 17, Verification Annex.

commercial products, but which can also be used to make chemical weapons.[306]

(2)Challenge inspections

Challenge inspections, remarks Kellman, "are the Convention's safety net".[307] "For the sole purpose of clarifying and resolving any questions concerning possible non-compliance" with the provisions of the CWC each State Party has the right to request an on-site challenge inspection of any facility or location in the territory or in any other place under the jurisdiction or control of any other State Party.[308] These inspections will have to be conducted anywhere without delay by an inspection team designated by the Director-General. The State Party to be inspected will not be notified less than 12 hours before the planned arrival of the inspection team at the point of entry.[309] Within 12 hours after having received the inspection request the Executive Council may "decide by a three-quarter majority of all its members against carrying out the challenge inspection if it considers the inspection request to be frivolous, abusive or clearly beyond the scope" of the CWC.[310] States Parties are under the obligation to keep the inspection request within the scope of the CWC and "shall refrain from unfounded inspection requests, care being taken to avoid abuse".[311] The request shall contain all appropriate information on the basis of which concern has arisen regarding possible non-compliance with the CWC. Therefore it is expected that "[t]hese inspections are not regular, nor, presumably frequent".[312]

For its part the inspected State Party shall have "the right and obligation to make every reasonable effort to demonstrate its compliance with this Convention and, to this end, to enable the inspection team to fulfil its mandate".[313] The inspection team and the inspected State Party need to come to an agreement on the requested perimeter of the inspection site.[314] Access, however, is "managed"[315] ostensibly which "allows inspectors enough access to determine whether the site is indeed involved in prohibited activity while also allowing the facility under inspection to protect sensitive information unrelated to the Convention".[316] Accordingly, in the Verification Annex it is stated

---

[306] Smithson, *supra* n.74, at 7.

[307] Kellman et al., *supra* n. 4, at 131.

[308] Article IX, para. 8.

[309] Article IX para. 15.

[310] Article IX, para. 17

[311] Article IX, para. 9.

[312] Kellman et al., *supra* n. 4, at 131.

[313] Article IX, para. 11 (a).

[314] Verification Annex, Part X, (B)(14)-(21).

[315] Declared facilities under Articles IV, V, and VI use different managed access procedures. See Verification Annex, X (c)(52); Kellman et al., *supra* n. 4, at 140.

[316] Smithson, *supra* n. 74, at 32.

that "[..] The inspected State Party has the right under managed access to take such measures as are necessary to protect national security".[317] But also that these provisions "may not be invoked by the inspected State Party to conceal evasion of its obligations not to engage in activities prohibited under this Convention"! This means that the extent of access to any particular place or places within the site, the exact nature of inspection activities, and the information that the host officials are to provide to the inspection team are subject to negotiations between host officials and the inspection team.[318]

*via monitoring with on-site instruments

Monitoring with on-site instruments is possible with regard to chemical weapons[319] that are stored at some facility, chemical weapons production facilities[320] and with regard to Schedule 1 chemicals.[321] Accordingly, arrangements have to be made in the facility agreement.

*via compilation

The Technical Secretariat with its specialized knowledge, complete overview of the declarations, its highly advanced information system and other information (for instance, results of scientific research), will generate "new" information of its own accord.

In conclusion it can be said that under the CWC a wealth of information is collected. That, in itself, is not sufficient. There is, for example, no automatic assurance that the information collected nationally will be correct.

> "The success or failure of routine verification will therefore largely be determined by how conscientiously States Parties conduct their national monitoring in the first place, and otherwise prepare themselves for submitting full and accurate declarations. If garbage is what they feed into the verification system, then garbage is what will come out of it, no matter how skilful and dedicated the OPCW Technical Secretariat may be."[322]

---

[317] Verification Annex, Part X (41).

[318] Smithson, *supra* n. 74, at 32.

[319] Verification Annex IV (A) D 42 ("The systematic verification shall be initiated as soon as possible after the declaration of chemical weapons is submitted and shall continue until all chemical weapons have been removed from the storage facility. It shall in accordance with the facility agreement, combine on-site inspections and monitoring with on-site instruments"); 51; 59.

[320] Verification Annex Part V, C (46);(56);(60)(83) (concerns the conversion of chemical weapons production facilities to purposes not prohibited under the CWC).

[321] Verification Annex Part VI E (22) ("The facility shall be subject to systematic verification through on-site inspection and monitoring with on- site instruments") and the same with regard to other facilities referred to in paras. 10 and 11(29).

[322] Perry Robinson, *supra* n. 117, at 491.

116   E. MYJER

What therefore has to be done is to assess a) whether the information provided is correct and b) whether that information confirms a State Party's compliance with the Convention. In other words, whether that information reflects State behaviour, or behaviour for which a State is responsible, and whether that information conforms to the norm. That assessment will take place within the review function.

3. The Review Function

In general the "review function" refers to judging State behaviour as regards its conformity with an agreed rule of international law. This also includes an assessment of the accuracy of the information provided. In our case it concerns the question whether States Parties fulfil their obligations under the CWC. In general the review will take place via three stages involving the three organs of the OPCW, namely, and in this order, via the TS, the Executive Council and the Conference. The methods to be applied appear to be of a non-judicial dispute settlement character. The normal situation, however, is that there is no problem with the information provided and that information confirms a State Party's compliance with the Convention. In that case there is no need for the TS to involve either the Executive Council or the Conference and this is where the review ends. With regard to the information to be assessed, a distinction can be made as regards the way in which this information is obtained because certain information has to be handed in as a hard and fast rule ("routinely") while other information is obtained in special cases.

The following situations can be distinguished:

routine

-   information provided in declarations has to be compared with the results of initial and routine inspections. Assessed has to be the "actual state of affairs". This has to be weighed against the norms of the Convention. This should lead to either a "yes compliance" or "no non-compliance" situation. If it would result in an "uncertain/don't know situation", additional information may then be necessary or something is inherently wrong with the collection mechanism;[323]

---

[323] From this should be distinguished the situation whereby it appears that incorrect information had been provided, but that on the basis of correct information the State Party has acted in conformity with the norm, in other words: only the declaration was mistaken.

special

- information obtained via challenge inspections confirms, via the same assessment procedure as in the routine situation, a breach of treaty norms;
- a case of actual use is established;

The organs of the OPCW are involved in reviewing in the following way:

* The role of the TS

The Convention does not contain a separate article exclusively devoted to the review function. Even Article VIII paragraph 40 regarding the role of the Technical Secretariat in informing

> "[..] the Executive Council of any problem that has arisen with regard to the discharge of its functions, *including doubts, ambiguities or uncertainties about compliance* with this Convention that have come to its notice in the performance of its verification activities and that it has been unable to resolve or clarify through its consultations with the State Party concerned" [emphasis added]

is not exclusively devoted to compliance problems. "Information on *specific cases concerning compliance* will be only a portion of the Activities stipulated in this Article".[324] According to Krutzsch "any problem", in this paragraph, has a rather broad meaning and "also relates to shortcomings in organization and structure of the TS, budgetary problems as well as inexpedient verification procedures or instruments".[325] He is of the opinion that with regard to "doubts, ambiguities or uncertainties about compliance", in Article VIII, Paragraph 40 as quoted above, "uncertainties" is the most important and objective term, the meaning of which covers the other two terms.[326] Interestingly, paragraph 40 contains an important qualification, for the Executive Council will only have to be informed when the TS has been unable to resolve or clarify those uncertainties through its consultations with the State Party. It can therefore be held that the first stage in the review process already takes place during the collection phase, when the TS tries to resolve or clarify uncertainties. In order to be able to do so, almost "by definition" a measuring against specific norms needs to take place. It will thereby use dispute settlement techniques like asking for clarification and making use of the technical fact-finding by the inspectors and (designated) laboratories. The TS, however, will have to decide on whether or not it is satisfied within the confines of the TS, rendering it a non-public, and

---

[324] Krutzsch et al., *supra* n. 4, at 165.
[325] Krutzsch et al., *ibid*, at 165.
[326] Krutzsch et al., *ibid*, at 165.

118   E. MYJER

therefore non-transparent, procedure. The actual decisionmakers, however, are international civil servants. And only when the TS is not satisfied will the Executive Council be informed. This leads one to wonder whether this review stage will be documented and whether it will be accessible to States Parties, for instance when they ask for clarification under Article IX under Paragraph 3. A similar reference to "uncertainties" is contained in the Verification Annex, Part II, paragraphs 64 and 65 concerning the inspection reports.[327]Also here elements of a (provisional) review are evident when the inspectors have to decide which "facts are relevant to compliance".[328] It is of course during the reporting phase by the inspector that actual doubts about compliance may (begin to) grow. The final report[329] together with observations (in other words not only factual information) that an inspector may attach to the report will immediately be submitted to the inspected State Party. "Any written comments which the inspected State Party may immediately make on its findings shall be annexed to it."[330] This report is then presented to the Director-General of the TS within 30 days after the inspection. The Director-General, on his part, shall approach the inspected State Party for clarification "should the report contain uncertainties".[331] If these cannot be removed "or the facts established are of a nature to suggest that obligations under this Convention have not been met"[332] the Director-General shall inform the Executive Council.

* The role of the Executive Council

Other instances[333] whereby information relevant for consideration under Article VIII paragraphs 35-36 will be brought to the attention of the Executive Council are: the case of a challenge inspection, when the Director-General has to transmit the final report of the inspection team promptly to the Executive Council[334] and the above mentioned case of the Verification Annex[335] part II, paragraph 65,[336] which according to Krutzsch should be regarded as being included under

---

[327] Krutzsch and Trapp obviously find it an "empty" requirement for they refer to it as "[t]he requirement of fruitless efforts aimed at the solution of uncertainties..", *ibid*, at 165.

[328] Verification Annex, part II, para. 62.

[329] "Including information as to the manner in which the State Party inspected cooperated with the inspection team", Verification Annex, part II, paragraph 62.

[330] Verification Annex, Part II, para. 63.

[331] " [..] or should cooperation between the National Authority and the inspectors not measure up to the standards required [..]", Verification Annex, part II, para. 64. It is not clear why this reference was included. In order to have the national authorithy punished?

[332] Verification Annex, Part II, para. 65.

[333] Krutzsch et al., *supra* n. 4, at 157-158.

[334] Article IX, para. 21. In paras. 22-25 in particular the review is detailed.

[335] Verification Annex, Part II, para. 65.

[336] Krutzsch et al., *supra* n. 4, at 165: "For consistency, the interpretation of paragraph 35

Article VIII paragraph 35. In these cases the Executive Council is involved in the review of inspection reports. Other cases that involve the Executive Council are when States Parties request the Executive Council to assist in the clarification of situations which may be considered ambiguous or give rise to a concern about the possible non-compliance of another State Party;[337] when it is requested to obtain clarification from another State Party;[338] or in case a State Party requests assistance in the clarification of a situation that has given rise to its possible non-compliance.[339] The Executive Council shall consider any issue or matter within its competence affecting the Convention and its implementation "including concerns regarding compliance, and cases of non-compliance".[340] Whereas under Article VIII paragraph 31 - under *powers and functions* - the general task of the Executive Council of promoting adherence with the Convention is set out ("[..] *shall promote* the effective implementation of, and compliance with, this Convention"[..]), paragraph 35 is about actual or potential breaches ("[..] *shall consider* any issue [..] affecting this Convention, including concerns regarding compliance [..]").[341] This is elaborated upon in paragraph 36. What then are the "review" methods to be applied by the Executive Council? In contradistinction to the TS-phase, and not withstanding the essential protection of confidential information, it will be done via a semi-public procedure, for the Executive Council with its 41 members is a representative organ of the OPCW.[342] Like in the case of the Director-General who can seek clarification (see above) the Executive Council "shall consult" with the States Parties involved and, as appropriate, request the State Party to take measures to redress the situation within a specified period.[343] With the exception of consultation - a non-judicial dispute settlement technique - no specific method for review is suggested by the Convention. It may be assumed therefore that the objective facts established by the TS and the (technical) assessment made by it, which has led to doubts about compliance, together with the ensuing comments by States Parties that are not considered to be satisfatcory form the basis ("the file of the case") for a review by the Council. Furthermore, it may be assumed that the norm to be applied is uncontested and if not, that also the opinion of the legal council of the Organization would be

---

should also cover the content of the provision of Verification Annex, Part II, paragraph 65."

[337] Article IX, para. 3.

[338] Article IX, para. 4.

[339] Article IX, para. 5.

[340] Article VIII, para. 35.

[341] Emphasis added.

[342] Compare the case of the United Nations Commission on Human Rights with its 43 members: "..although the procedure under Resolution 1503 is confidential, it is certainly not secret. Every communication is seen in summary by the forty-three government representatives on the Commission.", A.H. Robertson & J.G. Merrills, *Human Rights in the World*(1992), at 76

[343] Article VIII, para. 36.

120   E. MYJER

included. But who, one might wonder, then weighs this opinion on the level of the Executive Council? The Convention is silent on this point.[344] This clearly involves the creative function.

This information will then have to lead the Executive Council to a decision, a matter of substance, therefore to be taken by a two-thirds majority.[345] Here we find a mix of review and correction as the Executive Council may opt for an extended review by the Conference or by the UN GA or SC. Even in the case whereby it recommends a particular course it may be assumed that an extended review first takes place within the context of the Conference. The measures[346] to be applied are:

(a) inform all States Parties of the issue or matter;
(b) bring the issue to the attention of the Conference;
(c) make recommendations to the Conference regarding measures to redress the situation and to ensure compliance.

Informing all States Parties of the matter (*sub. a*) is designed to attract the attention of the membership of the OPCW to the case. It can also be regarded as a "moral sanction".[347] The difference between *sub. b* and *sub. c* may be that in the case of *sub.b* "... the Conference's action may be required, be it that the Council was unable to come to a conclusion on how to assess a contested behaviour ... .[348] In the case of *sub. c* the Council has been able to decide on a course of action. Krutzsch is of the opinion that "[s]uch action would be required if the authority of the Conference and concerted actions of the members of the Organization are needed to overcome the resistance of the State Party involved to bring its behaviour into harmony with its obligations under the Convention".[349] A more simple explanation may be that it concerns a situation in which the Council has already asked the State Party to take measures to redress a situation and it is the Conference and not the Executive Council that is empowered under Article XII to decide on the necessary

---

[344] Also the Rules of Procedure of the Executive Council do not elaborate on this. It has to be assumed that questions concerning compliance will be dealt with just as any other question which the Executive Council has to consider. Rule 12 refers to meeting at short notice under these circumstances. Furthermore, rule 18 makes clear that each matter "brought to the attention of the Council by the Director-General or proposed for inclusion in the agenda by any member of the Organization, the United Nations or a State or an international organization with which the Organization has a relationship agreement *shall be accompanied by an explanatory memorandum and, if possible, by basic documents or by a draft decision or recommendation*", C-I/DEC.72, 23 May 1997. The least that one may assume is that the explanatory memorandum, the draft decision or recommendation will have passed the desk of the legal advisor (TS) of the OPCW.

[345] Article VIII, para. 29.

[346] Article VIII, para. 36.

[347] Krutzsch et al., *supra* n. 4 at 160.

[348] "[..]or that the decision of the principal organ is needed on a problem of general importance", *ibid*. at 160.

[349] *Ibid*, at 160.

measures. In cases of "particular gravity" the Executive Council may bring the matter, including relevant information and conclusions, directly to the GA and the SC.

The rather open way of reviewing is illustrated in the case of a challenge inspection where the Convention rather vaguely stipulates that the Executive Council "shall review" the inspection report and the comments made thereto "*in accordance with its powers and functions*".[350] It should be remembered, however, that it is the Conference that decides on the powers and functions both of the Executive Council and the TS.[351]

* The role of the Conference

Under "powers and functions" of the Conference in Article VIII the central position of the Conference regarding compliance is established: "The Conference shall review compliance with this Convention." This is not surprising for the Conference is the principal organ of the OPCW at which each member is represented. Furthermore, the Conference, being the principal organ of the OPCW, may take decisions on "any questions, matters or issues related to this Convention raised by a State Party or brought to its attention by the Executive Council".[352] For that it shall take the necessary measures to ensure compliance and redress and remedy any situation in contravention of the CWC.[353] It appears that the Conference is completely free to organize this review stage. It could even decide to establish a subsidiary organ for this purpose.[354]

On the basis of what information will the Conference take its decisions? If we take the case of the "challenge inspection" to guide us, it will have a varied "file" at its disposal. This will not only contain the factual findings of the inspector as well as an assessment by the inspection team "of the degree and nature of access and cooperation granted for the satisfactory implementation of the challenge inspection"[355] but also the comments made by the requesting State Party, the inspected State Party and those by other States Parties.[356] Furthermore, in considering the necessary measures under Article XII the Conference "shall take into account all information and recommendations[357]

---

[350] Article IX, para. 22.

[351] Article VIII, para. 19.

[352] Article VIII, para. 19.

[353] Article VIII, para. 21 (k).

[354] Article VIII, para. 21 (f).

[355] Article IX, para. 21.

[356] Article IX, para. 21.

[357] It is not clear from the wording of Article XII whether or not a recommendation is essential before the Conference can decide on this matter. The most logical seems to be that the Conference also can decide without any recommendation and that the Conference "[..]

122 E. MYJER

submitted on the issues by the Executive Council".[358] When reviewing the case before it decides on any such measure the Conference will therefore also have the opinion of the Executive Council to hand, as otherwise it could not recommend measures in cases of non-compliance. No effective review therefore seems to be possible without a proper hearing and having received a complete file, in other words essential elements for due process.

4.The correction function

The next question is what can actually be done to correct a State Party's behaviour if the conclusion is that it has breached the Convention? In that respect the supervisory system under the CWC does not seem so much different from general international law for it appears rather weak on actual enforcement. It is, however, important to note that the CWC actually addresses the question of reactions in the event of a breach, be it decisions of a binding or of a recommendatory character, and that it concerns reactions by the compliance control organization: the OPCW. Article XII deals with "measures to redress a situation and to ensure compliance including sanctions". Referring to the negotiations of the Convention Krutzsch mentions that although several attempts were made to draw up a list of possible sanctions these failed, but that it became clear that an organization "for the implementation of a disarmament treaty" did not have economic services or benefits available, like an organization for economic assistance and co-operation and development to restrict or suspend.[359] To start with, a State Party may not be deprived of its membership in the Organization as a sanction,[360] which is not surprising given that it is essential to preserve the universal character of the Convention.[361] Accordingly a member should be allowed to be able to fulfil its major rights under this Convention under Article IX. However, in cases where a State Party has been requested by the Executive Council to take measures to redress a situation "raising problems with regard to compliance" and fails to accommodate such a request, the Conference could restrict or suspend the State Party's right and privileges under the Convention until it is in compliance with the CWC.[362] Within the system of the Convention this appears as the crucial sanction.

---

the Executive Council", (Krutzsch et al., *supra* n.4, at 222).

[358] Article XII, para. 1.

[359] Krutzsch et al., *supra* n. 4 at 224.

[360] Article VIII, para. 2. This also includes suspension of membership. See Krutzsch, *ibid*, at 128.

[361] Also Krutzsch et al., *supra* n. 4 at 128 "[..]an organization which by virtue of its existence has to strive towards universal adherence, would by a policy of expulsion defeat its main purpose". Furthermore, they give as the rationale that a State Party stripped of its membership might falsely conclude that it was free from its obligations under the Convention.

[362] Article XII, para. 2. See Krutzsch et al., *ibid*, at 223.

E. MYJER 123

Which rights and privileges under the Convention are of sufficient weight to give it such prominence?

- The case which first springs to mind revolves around Article XI on economic and technological developments, especially the suspension of "the right to participate in the fullest possible exchange of chemicals, equipment and scientific and technical information relating to the development and application of chemistry for purposes not prohibited under this Convention" (para. 2(b)), as well as a recommendation to Member States for restrictions in trade concerning chemicals, equipment and know how under Article XI paragraph 2 (c).[363] The heated debates during the PrepCom about the obligations under Article XI at least suggest the contentious character of any such measures.
- Another sanction would be the suspension of the rights to assistance and protection against chemical weapons under Article X.
- Also as a sanction one might treat a State Party as a non-treaty Party as far as the transfer of chemicals is concerned, viz. non-trade in Schedule 2 chemicals, because three years after entry into force only the transfer of chemicals to States Parties is permitted.[364] Also Schedule 1 chemicals may only be transferred to another State Party for the objectives indicated in the Verification Annex.[365] And with regard to Schedule 3 chemicals, States Parties shall adopt measures that ensure that the transferred chemicals shall only be used for non-prohibited purposes,[366] whereby after five years after entry into force States Parties shall consider the need to establish "other measures" regarding the transfer of Schedule 3 chemicals to States not Party to the Convention!
- In breaching its duty to maintain the confidential character of information received a suspension of the right to receive confidential information, for instance under Article IX paragraph 3, seems logical.
- In cases where "serious damage to the object and purpose" of the CWC may result from activities prohibited under the CWC, in particular the ones mentioned by Article I, the Conference may "recommend collective measures to States Parties in conformity with international law."[367] This clearly points to

---

[363] See, Krutzsch et al., *ibid*, at 224. "The right to participate in the fullest possible exchange of chemicals etc. pursuant to Article XI, para. 2 (b), can be restricted with regard to Schedule 2 chemicals when a State Party fails to comply with the provisions of the Verification Annex, Part VII, paragraphs 31 and 32, concerning the transfers of such chemicals to States not Party to this Convention", Article IX, para. 23 allows for financial compensation for the costs of challenge inspections in case of abuse. Krutzsch et al. (at 224) also mention the financial costs resulting from non-cooperation with the inspection team under the Verification Annex, Part II 35 and 36. They do not, however, provide any basis therefor.
[364] Verification Annex, Part VII, C, para. 31.
[365] Verification Annex, Part VI, B, 3.
[366] Verification Annex, Part VIII, C, 26.
[367] Article XII, para. 3.

the recommendation to States Parties of countermeasures not contrary to international law like retorsion. These measures, however, are of a non-binding recommendatory character,[368] for instance a recommendation "monitored by the verification mechanism of the Organization"[369] to withhold from the non-complying State Party the export of certain chemicals or equipment, or technical knowledge. The Conference and the Executive Council here seem to have a maximum of flexibility, as long as these recommendations fit the purpose and principles of the Convention and are not contrary to international law.[370] This even seems not to exclude the recommendation of classic sanctions under international law in not directly related areas.[371]

- And "in cases of particular gravity" the Conference shall (the only time "shall" is mentioned in Article XII, author) bring the issue together with the file on the matter to the attention of the General Assembly and the Security Council. A similar provisional correction could already be undertaken by the Executive Council "in case of particular gravity and *urgency*".[372] In the Relationship Agreement between the OPCW and the UN both cases are specifically mentioned. In these cases the OPCW shall notify the Secretary-General of the UN, who shall bring the question to the attention of the General Assembly and the Security Council which will act as appropriate, in accordance with their own mandates. Of course this reference to the UN General Assembly or Security Council cannot create any competence for these organs that they do not already have under the Charter. These measures should be regarded as complementary to the aforementioned ones under the Convention on which the Conference decides in close cooperation with the Executive Council. The Relationship Agreement between the UN and the OPCW, however, assures that the UN will give the matter proper consideration and that the OPCW will provide the UN with any additional information which may be necessary.[373] Consideration by the Security Council may lead to

---

[368] M. Kamto, Discussion in: Bardonnet (ed.), *supra* n. 4, at 403: "As for recommendations under Article XII, para. 3, they fall within the category of classic non-binding recommendations". Mahiou, however, mentions "even if it is not known whether the word "recommendation" is used in Article XII in its usual sense or whether it means that there is an obligation", *ibid*, at 402.

[369] Krutzsch et al., *supra* n.4, at 226.

[370] According to Krutzsch et al. "in conformity with international law" "carries the message that the prerogatives of the UN Security Council should be respected", *ibid* n. 4, at 225. I am of the opinion, however, that the simple meaning is that such measures should not be contrary to international law.

[371] For instance via reprisals. On countermeasures under Article XII see A. Rosas, Reactions in the Event of Breach, in Bardonnet (ed.), *supra* n. 4, at 577-589.

[372] Article VIII, para. 36. Emphasis is added.

[373] "1. The United Nations and the OPCW, recognising the need to work jointly to achieve mutual objectives, and with a view to facilitating the effective exercise of their responsibilities, agree to cooperate closely within their respective mandates and to consult on

decisions of the Security Council under Chapter VII of the UN Charter, like sanctions or if necessary enforcement actions to redress a situation.

5. The creative function

This function of the OPCW could be regarded as the tool to assist any of the other functions discussed, because in any of these functions a rule may need to be clarified. Often a rule of law needs to be clarified before the collection, review and correction function can become operative. It may appear that what is meant is a technique to interpret a rule of law comparable to the rules contained in Articles 31-33 of the Vienna Convention on the Law of Treaties which deal with the interpretation of treaties. But the quintessential difference is that there is an ongoing process within the context of an international organization in the execution of its principal task of compliance control, or supervision of States Parties' commitments under the CWC. Therefore one of the supervisory functions of the OPCW is the shaping of the law. Bernauer seems to refer to this same function when he remarks: "[o]ne of the most important functions of international organizations is to serve as fora where the parties can engage in the interpretation and modification of agreements and decide on actions to be taken in the implementation process".[374] As we have seen when discussing the other supervisory functions, there is a constant referral back and forth between States Parties and the OPCW. Thereby a constant use is being made of diplomatic dispute settlement techniques like consultation, or clarification (compare Article IX), both of which are forms of negotiation. More in general it can be held that this wide use of dispute

---

matters of mutual interest and concern. To that end, the United Nations and the OPCW shall cooperate with each other in accordance with the provisions of their respective constituent instruments.

2. Cooperation between the United Nations and the OPCW, in particular, shall require that:

(a) cases of particular gravity and urgency which, in accordance with paragraph 36 of Article VIII of the Convention, shall, including relevant information and conclusions, be brought directly to the attention of the General Assembly and the Security Council by the Executive Council, through the Secretary-General in accordance with the existing United Nations procedures;

(b) cases of particular gravity which, in accordance with paragraph 4 of Article XII of the Convention, shall, including relevant information and conclusions, be brought to the attention of the General Assembly and the Security Council by the Conference of the States Parties through the Secretary-General in accordance with the existing United Nations procedures;

[...]

3. The OPCW, within its competence and in accordance with the provision of the Convention, shall cooperate with the General Assembly and the Security Council by furnishing them, at the request of either, such information and assistance as may be required in the exercise of their respective responsibilities under the United Nations Charter.

[...]", Article II, Relationship Agreement between the UN and the PCW, *supra* n.11.

[374] Bernauer, *supra* n. 130, at 335.

126 E. MYJER

settlement techniques is characteristic of the system of supervision under the CWC. Not surprisingly (in this vain) also disputes concerning "the application or the interpretation" of the CWC will have to be settled in conformity with the provisions of the UN Charter, viz. Article 33 or more generally Chapter VI. Also disputes between two or more States Parties or between the OPCW and one or more States Parties concerning the interpretation or application of the CWC will according to Article XIV have to be settled via negotiation or other means of their choice, including recourse to appropriate organs. This appears also to refer to the subsidiary organs that the Conference by virtue of Article XIV, paragraph 4 may establish[375] (or entrust) with the task of settlement of disputes brought to its attention by the Executive Council or raised by States Parties. Elsewhere[376] I have argued that given the structure of Article XIV and of its close link with Article 33 (1) of the Charter it is obvious that these tasks seem to refer to fact finding, conciliation and arbitration, modes of settlement contained in Article 33 (1) of the Charter but not explicitly mentioned in Article XIV. Given the strong provisions of the CWC with regard to *collection* there does not appear to be any direct necessity for the establishment of a subsidiary organ for fact finding; with regard to the creative function it is not even necessary. All the more so for the effective execution of the creative function of the OPCW some institutional basis for conciliation or arbitration, either *ad hoc* or semi-permanent via a subsidiary organ is in order, as this will provide the necessary institutional basis for these two modes of dispute settlement.

States Parties may, by mutual consent, also refer a dispute to the ICJ. Given that only States may be parties before the Court[377] this excludes disputes involving the OPCW. Under Article XIV, paragraph 5 both the Conference and the Executive Council may request the ICJ for an advisory opinion on "any legal question within the scope of the activities of the Organization". For this, however, on each occasion authorization is needed by the General Assembly of the UN.[378]

---

[375] On the basis of Article VIII, para. 21 (f).

[376] Myjer, *supra* n. 205, at p. 541.

[377] Article 34, Statute of the International Court of Justice.

[378] This is an interesting feature, for the OPCW is apparently not to be regarded as a specialized agency with a general authorization under Article 96 (compare L.M. Goodrich and E. Hambro, *Charter of the United Nations, Commentary and Documents* (1946), at 267) but as an "independent autonomous international organization", that will be dependent on authorization from the GA in each separate case. Compare the Relationship Agreement UN-OPCW (*supra* n. 11): "The UN recognizes that the OPCW, by virtue of the Convention, shall function as an independent, autonomous international organization in the working relationship with the UN established by this Agreement", (Article I, para. 2), and also the position taken by the Legal Advisor of the OPCW, when discussing the Headquarters Agreement. At that time Pakistan insisted that an explicit reference would be made in it concerning the

Furthermore, the Executive Council may contribute by whatever means it considers appropriate, including offering its good offices.[379]

VI. CWC supervision as a management model and the quantum leap in the institutional law of arms control

1. General

Are there, apart from the few specific characteristics mentioned, other reasons to regard the OPCW as an international organization so special that it was not only used to model the CTBTO upon, but that also the IAEA was looking at the system of the CWC for answers to improve its function as well as the States Parties to the BWC? The answer seems to lie in the fact that the OPCW is more than a simple verification organization. For even though we are dealing with what could be called a single purpose organization,[380] the single purpose is, however, of a rather broad nature. It is not only fulfilling a single aspect of the process of supervision, viz. the verification by the inspectors and the TS of compliance by States Parties with the Convention. The OPCW represents an organization, whereby the technical verification via inspections is only one aspect. The sum of the different stages of supervision offers more in terms of effective supervision than suggested by the respective sub-functions apart, for all four - collection, review, correction and creation - are woven together. From the very first moment that States Parties hand in their declarations and the initial inspections take place, there is a constant referral back and forth providing additional information and explanation. There is contact between the suspicious and the suspected State Party asking for clarification, which may ultimately culminate in a challenge inspection, not as a favour but as a right. It

---

adjudication of the ICJ. In its reply the Legal Advisor did not agree for he was of the view that "due to the Article 96 of the UN Charter (only organs of the UN and specialized agencies are entitled to request advisory opinions) the OPCW will not receive general authorisation and will be obliged to ask the General Assembly in each *separate case* (emphasis added) to consider its application and to give authorisation to request the advisory opinion". (PC-XVI/A/2). Since he thought this to be a too cumbersome and time-consuming mechanism, he did not want to recommend this as a dispute settlement mechanism in the Headquarters Agreement. It would, however, be interesting to hear whether also the GA would agree to that and under which paragraph the possibility for these separate requests would then fall. For Article 96, para. 1 refers to the GA or SC requesting such an advisory opinion and Article 96 para. 2 concerns other organs of the UN and specialized agencies. The UN/OPCW Relationship Agreement is not clear in that respect: "The UN and the OPCW agree that each such request for an advisory opinion shall first be submitted to the GA, which will decide upon the request in accordance with Article 96 of the Charter," (Article VII, para. 2), *supra* n. 11.

[379] Article XIV, para. 3.

[380] A special organization to perform specific functions. See Schermers & Blokker, *supra* n. 149 at 43.

128   E. MYJER

involves active participation in all stages, be it for fact finding, review or correction purposes, by the different organs of the OPCW. And in all of these stages use is made of dispute settlement techniques in order to ensure compliance within the system of the Convention. Via the different functions of the OPCW it appears possible to maximize States Parties' compliance. All of this happens within the framework of this specialized international organization, that indeed has a single purpose, this being control over compliance, in all its aspects, with the central norms of the Chemical Weapons Convention. The interesting aspect is that compliance is primarily being controlled within the system by making use of methods of dispute settlement, and less by making use of the more traditional coercive methods to enforce compliance. This process is constantly in operation, whereby via the element of information and clarification compliance is constantly being assessed.[381] This whole process is somehow reminiscent of *musyawarah*,[382] an Indonesian indigenous way of decision-making via deliberation and discourse.

The CWC system of supervision adheres to Chowdhury's observation that

> "[..] the effectiveness of a legal order is not exclusively dependent on the effectiveness of sanctions; effectiveness and availability of the techniques and procedures for detection of breach are equally important".[383]

This is the case since it represents a comprehensive system of continuous control whereby from the very first moment dispute settlement techniques are used. Of these the fact finding via on-site inspection is of course of primordial importance.

The CWC with the OPCW thereby resemble a self-contained regime.[384] This leaves us, however, with some of the pertinent questions raised by Koskenniemi in his challenging article on the comparable enforcement of commitments under environmental law,[385] how special non-compliance

---

[381] Den Dekker (*supra* n. 13) in his current research is developing a model of supervision, which partly explains the constancy, by pointing out that the element of control is constantly in operation. Regardless of the clarification of possible disputes, the "run of the mill" verification continues.

[382] Literally: 1. meeting, conference; 2. discussion, deliberation. It is closely linked with local law (*adat*), which is based on decisions taken in the village council after a process of deliberation (*musyawarah*) and consensus seeking (*mufakat*)", J. Van Reenen, *Central Pillars of the House* (thesis Leyden, 1996), at 35.

[383] Chowdhury, *supra* n. 233, at xvi.

[384] Compare the discussion on self-contained regimes in L.A.N.M. Barnhoorn and K.C. Wellens (ed.), *Diversity in Secondary Rules and the Unity of International Law* (1995).

[385] "Recent treaties have set up bodies for monitoring and information gathering, reporting and inspection of party performance. Such bodies rarely possess formal power for

procedures relate to using traditional remedies for breach of treaties. For, after all, he argues, a breach of an international obligation is an internationally wrongful act, and wrongfulness gives rise to responsibility:

"As far as traditional law is concerned, this is the long and the short of "non-compliance": Breach entails wrongfulness; wrongfulness calls for responsibility which in turn may be realized either through recourse to third-party settlement or, in certain circumstances, by taking counter-measures against a non-performing party. Where, then, is the need for specific provisions on non-compliance?"[386]

2. The management model

With this conclusion on the type of compliance control model the CWC system of supervision represents we have entered the quite specific debate on compliance control by regime theorists[387] for this characterisation of the OPCW appears to correspond to the "management model" - in contradistinction to the "coercive model"[388]- of the managerial school[389]- as developed by social scientists and of which, amongst lawyers, the Chayes'[390] are proponents - that considers "arrangements featuring enforcement as a means of eliciting compliance"[391] as not of much use in international society. "Those compliance problems that do exist are best addressed as management rather than enforcement problems."[392] Instances of apparent non-compliance are problems to be solved, rather than violations that have to be punished.[393] Downs and co. who establish a connection between the depth of cooperation represented by a given treaty and the amount of enforcement that is needed[394] are of the opinion that "this suggests that evaluating the importance of enforcement by examining the level of compliance is misleading".[395] Instead we need to worry about the possibility that:

---

enforcement, but instead rely on their "capacity to bring to bear a form of community pressure and international accountability". Koskenniemi, *supra* n. 240, p.123.

[386] Koskenniemi, *ibid*, at 125.

[387] On regime theory and international law see for instance A. Hurrell, International Society and the Study of Regimes: A Reflective Approach, in: R.J. Beck et al., *International Rules, Approaches from International Law and International Relations* (1996).

[388] See review of Chayes, by Harold Hongju Koh, in 91 *AJIL* (1997), at 389-391.

[389] Downs, *supra* n. 237, at 379 refers to this group of social scientists as the managerial school.

[390] Chayes, *supra* n. 69. See inter alia also Chayes & Chayes, On compliance, *supra* n. 237, pp 175-205.

[391] O. Young quoted in Downs, *supra* n. 237, at 381.

[392] *Ibid*, at 379.

[393] *Ibid*, at 381.

[394] *Ibid*, 382 et seq.

[395] *Ibid*, at 387.

> "[..] both the high rate of compliance and relative absence of enforcement threats are due not so much to the irrelevance of enforcement as to the fact that states are avoiding deep cooperation [..] because they are unwilling or unable to pay the costs of enforcement."[396]

The most prominent aspects of the CWC regime, as described above, fall into place and can be explained by looking at it through the prism of the management model, like the discursive nature of the compliance control model, as well as its intrinsically transparent character. Taking a closer look at some of the central elements of Chayes' management strategy, in particular at the elements of *transparency, dispute settlement, capacity building* and the uses of *persuasion*, is illustrative. There is the element of ensuring transparency via, for instance, the development of data on "the performance of the parties as to the principal treaty norms and on the general situations of concern to the regime",[397] mostly done via self-reporting, and verification. Under the CWC the first element is found in the *collection function* of the OPCW, the second element in the *review function*. Dispute settlement under the management strategy may concern situations "where ambiguity or vagueness in treaty language creates compliance problems [..]".[398] Albeit via binding procedures or not, what counts is that treaty regimes foresee an "authoritative interpretation of controverted provisions".[399] This is exactly what happens under the *creative function*. Capacity building refers to technical, bureaucratic or financial assistance where it concerns difficulties of domestic enforcement of measures adopted in compliance with international environmental obligations.[400] In the case of the CWC reference could, for instance, be made to the establishment and maintenance of permanent stockpiles of emergency goods and humanitarian assistance by States Parties (against chemical weapons) in accordance with Article X paragraph 7 (b) and (c), or to training courses for National Authorities that have been voluntarily organized. Furthermore, it can be held that the whole process of supervision in itself leads to greater transparency.[401] "These disparate elements - transparency, dispute settlement, capacity building - [..] can be considered to be parts of a management strategy. They merge into a broader process of "jawboning" - the effort to *persuade* the miscreant to change its ways - that is the characteristic method by which international regimes seek to induce compliance".[402] It is this element of persuasion that can be traced back in the different functions of the OPCW, like when information is

---

[396] *Ibid*, at 387.

[397] Chayes, *supra* n. 69, at 23.

[398] *Ibid*, at 24.

[399] *Ibid*, at 24.

[400] *Ibid*, at 25.

[401] In Article X(4) where it concerns the provision of information reference is even made to "transparency" ("for the purposes of increasing *transparency*"). (Emphasis added).

[402] Chayes, *supra* n. 69, at 25.

exchanged and clarification is being asked for, culminating as a last resort in the *correction function*. Compliance further seems to benefit from the two levels of management, namely at the international level by the OPCW and by the States Parties and at the national level by the respective National Authorities, which leads to the greater "interwoveness" of rules and procedures between these two levels. The focus on management to ensure compliance, instead of on coercive strategies, compensates under the CWC regime for the lack of a real enforcement mechanism, although I have to agree with Hongju Koh that management and the elements of coercion are not alternatives, but complement one another,[403] which is the way correction via the UN should be looked upon.

The Chayes' refer to a *New Sovereignty*. According to Hongju Koh they "suggest that sovereignty now means not freedom *from* external interference, but freedom *to* engage in international relations as members of international regimes. A state's sovereignty thus becomes contingent upon its *ongoing web* [emphasis added] of international ties and obligations".[404] And here we enter the institutional law of arms control, that appears to be beginning to be shaped via the compliance control models of an OPCW kind like the CTBTO,[405] which hang together within the broader context of the outer boundaries of the international law of military security - only arms to allow for quintessential exceptions (both conventional and customary) to the use of force, namely the use of force for collective security and for self-defence.[406] Compliance control models of the OPCW type seem to offer the best possible opportunity to realize compliance with the central treaty norms regarding chemical disarmament. The least that can be said is that given the delicate nature of national security and States' disinclination to allow for inroads on their sovereignty, this seems at present the maximum system of supervision which is attainable. This leads me to conclude that the OPCW with its specifically organized supervisory functions can be regarded as a model for future compliance

---

[403] Hongju Koh, *supra* n. 388 at 391. Compare A. Mahiou, Discussion in: Bardonnet (ed.), *supra* n. 4, at 402 in particular. This power of the sanction is extremely important even if it is not known whether the term "recommendation" is used in Article XII in its usual sense or whether it means that there is an obligation. Kamto, *supra* n. 369, however, is of a different opinion: "As for recommendations under Article XII, para. 3, they fall within the category of classic non-binding recommendations."

[404] Hongju Koh, *ibid* at 390. "The process [of persuasion, author] works because modern states are bound in a tightly woven fabric of international agreements, organizations, and institutions that shape their relations with one another and penetrate deeply into their internal economics and politics. The integrity and reliability of this system are of overriding importance for most states, most of the time", Chayes, *supra* n. 69 at 26.

[405] Or the one discussed with regard to the BWC, namely an organization for the Prohibition of Biological Weapons (OPBW), the effect on IAEA and so on. See p. 64.

[406] See also Introduction p.3.

control in the area of arms control. Given the multiplication of international organizations with this special compliance control function, thereby creating for States in the sphere of international security a web of "international ties and obligations",[407] one feels tempted to typify it as the prototype for an (essential) international arms control organization. In comparing it with the *International Disarmament Organization* as proposed by the Netherlands at the United Nations Special Session on Disarmament,[408] several similarities are apparent.

3. An International Disarmament Organization

For this UN Special Session on Disarmament the Netherlands tabled a working paper on the establishment of an international disarmament organization. In it "...an international disarmament organization is envisaged as the operational framework for the implementation of international arms control and disarmament treaties, with functions mainly in the field of verification. In addition it is thought that such an organization could be instrumental to the preparation and organization of review conferences already provided for in several disarmament treaties and could serve as a clearinghouse for information on disarmament."[409] The suggested approach was to initially set up an international disarmament organization for the implementation of a particular disarmament treaty, and then gradually to give it more functions "dependent on emerging needs and taking into account experience gained".[410] With regard to the possible functions for such an organization a possible future chemical weapons convention was mentioned, which would "probably provide for rather extensive notification and verification procedures" and with regard to a treaty banning nuclear tests,"[a]n international seismic system will in all probability be established to exchange and process seismic data", which would make necessary a consulatative organ with respect to technical and organizational problems of the seismic system.[411] As a first step it is then proposed that in the final document of the Special Session the Secretary-General of the UN "is requested to seek the views of member States with respect to the functions and organization of a possible

---

[407] Hongju Koh, *supra* n. 388, at 391.

[408] Tenth Special Session of the General Assembly, New York, 23 May-1 July 1978 (First Special Session devoted to disarmament). See Final Document of the Tenth Special Session of the General Assembly of 30 June 1978 (A/RES/S – 10/2) 125 (GG). Also A/S – 10/AC.1/37, para. 186.

[409] Study on the establishment of an international disarmament organization, Netherlands working paper, 5 April 1978, reproduced in: Ministerie van Buitenlandse Zaken (Netherlands Ministry of Foreign Affairs) no. 122 (1979), *Verslag over de Tiende Bijzondere Zitting van de Algemene Vergadering der Verenigde Naties*, at p. 97.

[410] *Ibid.*

[411] *Ibid.*

international disarmament organization...".[412] This proposal with regard to the implementation of disarmament agreements failed to be included in the Final Document,[413] however, because of Soviet Resistance to the Dutch proposal, which was procedural in nature.[414]

When comparing the OPCW with this proposed international disarmament organization the most noticeable similarity is that it also foresaw a permanent organization to streamline the consultations[415] and the implementation measures, with functions mainly in the field of verification and that it was also supposed to serve as a clearing-house for information on disarmament.[416] The proposal was then to start with a single disarmament treaty and to gradually expand it by also giving it certain tasks concerning other treaties. Looking at the OPCW this may occur in the future, but the need to build one single Disarmament Organization seems less pressing today not only because of the highly developed information systems (technology), but also because of the fact that experience has taught us that it is better to have a few active and streamlined organizations, than one single organization which, like the UN, may be considered to be top-heavy. Perhaps the above mentioned web of ties and obligations in the field of arms control or - more generallly - in the field of security, by States with different organizations of the OPCW type and between such organizations themselves offers the best guarantee for compliance. Given the present state of the art in international law where international security is concerned, or more explicitly the international law of military security, and especially with regard to the law of arms control, the CWC with its OPCW

---

[412] *Ibid.*

[413] See *supra* n. 408.

[414] Ministry of Foreign Affairs, *supra* n. 409 at 4. Also earlier, in 1973, both the Netherlands (CCD/PV 617 and CCD/410 of 13 July 1973) and Sweden (Document CCD/PV 601 of 13 April 1973) and CCD/PV 610 of 5 July 1973) had already expressed detailed views on this subject in the Conference of the Committee on Disarmament. Interestingly *"[T]he standing disarmament organ, as proposed by the Netherlands, would firstly be entrusted with the verification of a treaty banning chemical weapons.* However, it was envisaged from the beginning that such an organ could take upon itself other tasks, such as the verification of other arms control and disarmament treaties as well as the organization of review conferences provided for such treaties.In the absence of prospects, at that time, for substantial multilateral disarmament agreements as well as for other reasons, the ideas put forward by Sweden and the Netherlands were not pursued to any further degree", *ibid*, at p. 97. (Emphasis added).

[415] *Ibid*, at 98.

[416] Regarding this clearing-house function it is further elaborated: "(f). Relevant information with respect to the implementation of arms control and disarmament agreements could be combined in one organization. Data on various disarmament measures, such as for instance stockpile-destruction, seismic data, results of inspections and fact-finding missions could be stored with one organization which would act as a clearing-house for information on all implementation efforts in the field of disarmament", *ibid*, at 98.

134   E. MYJER

adds a new dimension by presenting some very specific outlines for the institutional law of arms control. As such, the OPCW can be regarded as
constituting a quantum leap in the institutional law of arms control.

VII. Concluding remarks

1. The relevance of initial organizational practice

Before drawing some general conclusions it should be stressed that these will
primarily be based on an analysis of a theoretical model, as presented in the
previous chapters when charting the CWC, the OPCW and analyzing the
supervisory functions of the OPCW. As is often the case with any analysis of
theoretical models the total picture may seem rather overly neat and tidy,
whereas State and organizational practice may be less perfect and may lead to
undesired consequences. For a proper assessment of a given regime, therefore,
such practice should also be taken into consideration. The CWC regime,
however, is still too much in its infancy to have already accumulated enough
practice to be able to weigh properly how it will function in real terms.[417]
There are, however, already some indications that the non-fulfilment by States
Parties of some basic procedural obligations may affect the very delicate
compliance process in all its aspects and make the management process less
transparent and thereby it will undoubtedly suffer. This can be demonstrated
by the example of the initial practice concerning handing in the necessary
declarations, which is illustrative of possible undesired consequences. It
thereby concerns the crucial and supposedly simple task of actually handing in
declarations ("not later than 30 days after the Convention enters into force")
for which States Parties had all the time to prepare (given that the CWC was
signed in January 1993 and entered into force in May 1997). These
declarations, however, remain sluggishly forthcoming. According to the report
for the Fourth Conference on the implementation of the convention, by the end
of 1998 one third of the States Parties had still failed to hand in the
declarations that were due.[418] The report notes that this issue had become "a
point of serious political concern for the OPCW by the end of 1998." Earlier,
in his opening statement to the Third Conference, Director-General Bustani
voiced his frustration in unequivocal terms by explicitly mentioning the

---

[417] As a sequel to their Commentary on the CWC (Krutszch et al. supra n. 4) recently a first
commentary on verification in practice by Krutsch and Trapp was published: W. Krutzsch
and R. Trapp, Verification Pratice under the Chemical Weapons Convention. (1999)

[418] "By the end of 1998 a total of 86 States Parties had submitted their initial declarations to
the Organization. While all of the declared chemical weapons possessor States and, with one
notable exception, all States with a sizable chemical industry, had submitted their declarations
to the OPCW in the period under review, approximately one third of States Parties had still
failed to report their declarable activities to the Organization." C-IV/5, 2 July 1999, p. 2.

United States[419] and by urging it to submit declarations with regard to its chemical industry as it had blocked any inspection of the American chemical (civilian) industry. This led States Parties that had already fulfilled their obligations to grumble about the frequency of the inspections of their facilities[420] and voices were even heard to place budgetary constraints on the number of inspections of Schedule 2 facilities. The possible negative impact of a non-declaration by a leading country on the delicate structure of supervision, for instance non-compliance by other States Parties that would welcome this as an excuse, may explain the rather strongly worded call by the Director-General when he expressed "a feeling of uneasiness in relation to what appears to be the temptation, on the part of some States Parties, to use this current situation to place artificial limits on the number of industry inspections".[421] He urged States Parties to continue to demonstrate understanding and political generosity of spirit and not to hold "the verification regime of the Convention [..] hostage to this issue".[422] The Director-General's message therefore seems to have had a wider purpose aimed at all States Parties by stressing that it is "becoming critically important to close the remaining gaps in the verification regime, caused by the absence of declarations and by incomplete declarations. If the present situation is allowed to persist, confidence in the regime will begin to erode [..]".[423]

---

[419] "The stated source of this dissatisfaction with industry inspections is the fact that the United States of America, the State Party with the largest chemical industry in the world, has - due to legislative difficulties - not submitted declarations with respect to its chemical industry under Article VI of the Convention, and has not exposed its chemical industry to inspections. Fortunately, the primary cause of this problem, the absence of national implementing legislation for the Convention in the United States of America, has now been removed. In order to establish the "level playing field" foreseen in the Convention, it is, however, essential for the Government of the United States of America to take the necessary action to ensure that it can meet its obligations with respect to its chemical industry declarations at the earliest opportunity. I urge the Government of the United States of America, therefore, to take whatever action is necessary to achieve this goal soon." Statement by the Director-General to the Conference of the States Parties at its Third Session, C-III/DG.12, 16 November 1998. By the time of the Fifth Conference the US was pleased to state that it had "(…) at last submitted long-overdue Article VI declarations". (C-V/NAT.2, 18 May 2000).

[420] "It is an open secret that, for some national chemical industries and their respective governments, the first experience of industry verification was less than satisfactory, not because of the quality of the inspections which they received, but due to the uneven application of the verification regime across States Parties. In the interests of the Convention, it is imperative that this situation be redressed as soon as possible, and I believe that there are now good chances that this will happen", *ibid.*

[421] *Ibid.*

[422] "..I also urge other States Parties with a concern in relation to this issue, in particular those which have so far borne the bulk of the industry inspections, to continue to demonstrate understanding and political generosity of spirit. In particular, I would ask them not to hold the verification regime of the Convention, and the OPCW Programme of Work and Budget, hostage to this issue". *Ibid.*

[423] *Ibid.* In a statement to the First Committee of the UN (19 October 1990), the Director-

136   E. MYJER

Also other instances similar to these, where States Parties not completely fulfil their commitment, may harm the supervisory mechanism.[424] Some States Parties may, for instance, still have difficulties in fully complying, for instance regarding challenge inspections, as a result of national constitutional impediments, or slowly forthcoming or inadequate national implementation legislation.[425] Observations like these, however, do not lead to the conclusion that the actual process of supervision does not function or is ineffective. At this stage - the CWC only entered into force in April 1997 - and on the basis of the (open) information available, one cannot yet answer this question. One is, however, reminded that even a refined theoretical model may encounter difficulties in practice.

The outlook, however, is positive, for there is already an international organization in place and operational and if one only goes by the sheer size of the number of inspections the system seems to work well.[426] But given the almost universal membership it also points at some of the limitations of this inherently transparent compliance control model.

2. General Conclusions

— Looking at its structure as an international organization the OPCW does not seem so remarkable: it was created by States Parties via a treaty, containing its constitution, describing clearly both its functions as well as the tasks and competences of the respective organs. Of these organs the Conference as the plenary is the classic representative one, the Executive Council the executive one and the Technical Secretariat the classic permanent body foreseeing both the technical and administrative support structure. Given the necessary universal application of the Convention, the OPCW is an open organization of which all States Parties are automatically members. The organization enjoys privileges and immunities, with special arrangements for the inspectors in carrying out their duties. Given the subject matter of the Convention and

---

General of OPCW stated when referring to what might happen if the current situation were to continue for "yet another year": "I have no doubt that the very soul of the Convention's verification regime would be at stake".

[424] "It is also my sincere hope[..] that, in the very near future the United States of America will take action to rectify those aspects of its implementing legislation - in relation to the issues of challenge inspections, out of country analysis and low concentration thresholds - which, in our eyes and in the eyes of many, are not in accordance with the spirit of the Convention." *Ibid.*

[425] States Parties, however, are bound to comply fully with the CWC, which may not be subject to reservations (Article XXII). On the issue of national implementation see M. Bothe, National Implementation of the CWC: Some Legal Considerations, in Bothe et al., supra n. 4, in particular pp. 545-546 (on the relationship between treaties and the constitution) and pp. 551-552 (on the need for appropriate implementation legislation).

[426] For only 1998 the 200 inspectors of the OPCW made a total of 261 inspections of 198 sites in 26 States Parties, amounting to 16,927 inspector days! C-IV/5, 2 July 1999.

specifically the element of challenge inspection the extensive arrangements in this respect are functional and essential for the fulfilment of its purposes and functions.[427] Furthermore, the OPCW can be regarded to have both an internal and an external legal personality, with ensuing rights, like a treaty-making capacity,[428] and duties. A special feature in this respect is the fact that the liability of the OPCW for any breach of confidentiality committed by a member of the TS is excluded.[429] Special, and essential from the point of view of arms control, is the fact that no State Party can be deprived of its membership, for instance as a reaction to non-compliance. With regard to decision making we have noted the possibility of decision making by a two-thirds majority, which is especially remarkable in the area of security. Furthermore, that which has stood out is the three-quarters majority which is required to block a challenge inspection and the non-discriminatory character of allowing each State Party an equal vote, all aimed at achieving the aspect of universality.

— From the dogmatic point of view of the law of international organizations the OPCW does not therefore have many characteristics that make it stand out as an international organization. After all, within that area of the law one already finds all forms of transfer of state power to an international organization, whereby the ultimate form of transfer is the creation of a supranational international organization in a certain area. However, given the fact that arms control commitments deal with the security interests of States, and thereby impact on a State's security concept, allowing for compliance control in this very security area is by its very nature a delicate issue. It

[427] See Amarasinge, *supra* n. 219, at 370.

[428] Compare "The Executive Council shall: (a) Conclude agreements or arrangements with States and international organizations..."(Article VIII, para. 34). See for instance the OPCW Headquarters Agreement (C-I/DEC.59, of 14 May 1997) or the draft Relationship Agreement between the United Nations and the OPCW. See *supra* n. 11. On the possession of personality by international organizations and treaty-making capacity see White, *supra* n. 149 at 28: "[..] although the possession of personality by international organizations may produce certain common core features in the sense of rights, principally treaty-making capacity, privileges and immunities, limited *locus standi* before international tribunals and capacity to bring claims, and duties in the sense of the "responsibility of the organization for its own illegal acts, the extent of the personality of a particular organization depends on its constituent document [..]", at 28. Also I. Brownlie, *Principles of Public International Law* (1990), at 683-684: "The existence of legal personality does not of itself support a power to make treaties, and everything depends on the terms of the constituent instrument of the organization."

[429] This, however, does not exclude the responsibility of the OPCW. (Compare *supra* n. 149 Schermers & Blokker at 991). It deals with a complicated question that touches upon Member States' liability which was the issue in the case of the insolvent Tin Council. See Schermers & Blokker, *ibid*, at 990 et seq, in particular 993-994 and 1009-1010. On responsibility and liability also see extensively Amerasinghe, *supra* n. 219. With regard to the Tin Council especially at 259 et seq.

138   E. MYJER

therefore appears remarkable that the CWC allows for such a substantial encroachment into States Parties' national sovereignty by allowing for on-site monitoring, on-site routine inspections and even on-site challenge inspections, which at after all take place within States Parties' domestic jurisdiction. It may then seem even more remarkable that although the primary organs - the Executive Council and the Conference - primarily aim to achieve decisions by consensus, they *can* take decisions by a two-thirds majority. One observes therefore, in other words, that in the supervision of States Parties' compliance with the material obligations of the CWC, responsibility is primarily allocated to the international organization and its organs rather than to States Parties separately. These apparently paradoxical commitments, however, emanate from the very fact that it concerns commitments in the area of security. States Parties were only willing to allow for such a fundamental encroachment upon their sovereignty, as well as the substantial financial costs this supervisory mechanism entails, because of the very fact that in the area of arms control they need maximum certainty that all States Parties will comply. This could be classified as a principle of arms control law.

— Under the CWC a supervisory mechanism has been developed whereby a central role is allocated to the OPCW. In all respects its role is that of a supervisory organization *pur sang* and is not restricted to that of a verification organization. As a model it has several similarities with the 1978 Dutch proposal for an *International Disarmament Organization*. It could even be argued that the OPCW goes further and is more comprehensive in the supervisory functions it exercises.

— The supervisory system in the case of the CWC, with its central role for the OPCW, demonstrates essentially a non-adversarial process whereby there is a mix between, on the one hand, States Parties which are bound to declare a certain state of affairs with, on the other, organs of this international organization which have a reviewing capacity. But not only does the organization actively review, the States Parties also do so when asking for clarification or initiating a challenge inspection. Characteristic of this supervisory system is that in this process with regard to all of the supervisory functions (collection, review, correction, creative) there is constant referral back and forth to the States Parties in question, be it the inspected or the requesting State, and also between the different phases of this process of supervision. Within this process all elements like the declarations, the clarifications or the inspections are essential.

— This process acts as a constant "guardian" of the collective security interests of the States Parties and will undoubtedly have a beneficial effect on the prevention of formal disputes. This is important, for the CWC is weak as regards judicial dispute settlement.

— The supervision model under the CWC actually presents an example of compliance management in the sense of Chayes & Chayes, which is cooperative rather than adversarial in character. Applying this model makes the most prominent aspects of the CWC regime, like its non-adverserial and transparant character fall into place. It also explains the very strength of the CWC model, whereby the different stages of supervision offer more in terms of effective supervision than suggested by the respective sub-functions on their own, as all four functions are interwoven.

— The OPCW's Confidentiality Commission, with its special Registry Agreement, is at the same time illustrative of how essential it is, if only from the point of view of confidence building, also to have a proper - potentially adverserial and coercive - dispute settlement system in place.

[14]

THE SHORTCOMINGS OF INDETERMINACY IN ARMS CONTROL REGIMES: THE CASE OF THE BIOLOGICAL WEAPONS CONVENTION

*By Jack M. Beard**

I. Biological Weapons, Indeterminacy, and Design Elements for Arms Control Regimes

In 1972 a historic attempt to create the world's first international legal regime banning the development and possession of an entire class of weapons of mass destruction (WMDs) culminated in the conclusion of the Biological Weapons Convention (BWC).[1] Crippled by key compromises made by the great powers in pursuit of various self-interested security objectives in the context of the Cold War, the Convention is fundamentally flawed. Although the BWC purports to outlaw the development and possession of all biological weapons, deadlier and more sophisticated biological weapons than were imaginable in 1972 can now be and have been produced, as evidenced in October 2001 by two letters sent to the Capitol Hill offices of Senators Tom Daschle and Patrick Leahy.[2] These letters reportedly contained threatening notes and a dangerous and sophisticated form of "weapons-grade" anthrax spores.[3] Even though both the sender of these letters and the source of the anthrax remain unknown, the technical sophistication of the spores led some experts to suggest that the attacker was supported by a U.S. "biodefense" laboratory or an advanced foreign-state-run biological weapons (BW) facility because the spores could not have been produced by an amateur working in his basement.[4]

* Professorial Lecturer, University of California at Los Angeles; former Associate Deputy General Counsel (International Affairs), U.S. Department of Defense. The views expressed herein are those of the author alone and do not reflect the views of the Department of Defense or the U.S. government. The author appreciatively acknowledges useful comments by David Koplow, Maximo Langer, and Kal Raustiala on earlier drafts. I am also grateful to Scott Dewey and Emmy Levens for research assistance.

[1] Convention on the Prohibition of the Development, Production and Stockpiling of Bacteriological (Biological) and Toxin Weapons and on Their Destruction, Apr. 10, 1972, 26 UST 583, 1015 UNTS 163 [hereinafter BWC].

[2] A study by the Central Intelligence Agency reports that advances in science and technology since 1972 have resulted in genetically engineered pathogens with the ability to cause effects "worse than any disease known to man." John Mintz & Jody Warrick, *U.S. Unprepared Despite Progress, Experts Say*, WASH. POST, Nov. 8, 2004, at A1.

[3] A diverse group of sixteen biodefense scientists published a paper describing the Senate anthrax powder as an exceptionally deadly "weapons-grade" version of the bacterium with "high spore concentration, uniform particle size, low electrostatic charge, treated to reduce clumping." Thomas V. Inglesby et al., *Anthrax as a Biological Weapon, 2002: Updated Recommendations for Management*, 287 J. AM. MED. ASS'N 2236, 2237 (2002); *see also* Dan Eggen & Guy Gugliotta, *FBI Secretly Trying to Re-create Anthrax from Mail Attacks*, WASH. POST, Nov. 2, 2002, at A9 (describing the particles as "astonishingly pure"); Gary Matsumoto, *Anthrax Powder: State of the Art?* 302 SCIENCE 1492, 1492–94 (2003); Reynolds M. Salerno et al., *A BW Risk Assessment: Historical and Technical Perspectives*, NONPROLIFERATION REV., Fall/Winter 2004, at 25, 53 n.50.

[4] Although the FBI originally suggested that the anthrax powder could have been produced by a lone amateur working in a basement laboratory, this theory soon came to be regarded as unlikely and was abandoned. Guy

In addition to the empirical evidence of new "super" biological weapons, the failings of the BWC are further manifested by the growing significance that countries like the United States attach to the BW threat,[5] allegations by senior U.S. government officials that terrorists and rogue states possess biological weapons,[6] and contentious review conferences of BWC states parties that have been unable to resolve cheating and compliance concerns. Furthermore, a significant number of states have not yet joined the BWC and few have joined in recent years, prompting statements of concern about its lack of universality.[7]

The BWC is commonly said to have failed because it lacks mandatory transparency measures and a dedicated monitoring organization.[8] This explanation, which is well grounded in arms control practice, international relations theory, and theoretic game models, posits that a state actor is unlikely to forgo a particular class of weapons permanently unless it receives assurances that adversary states are reciprocally so committed and an effective monitoring regime is in place to ensure against a "surprise defection," that is, cheating.[9] Perceived security threats and asymmetrical information may generate or enlarge incentives for states to renege, making the Pareto-optimal outcome of mutual disarmament decidedly unstable and transparency a critical factor in ensuring that one state does not take advantage of the other.[10] In spite of this recognized need for transparency, the states parties to the BWC have been unable to agree on any mandatory transparency measures and the United States in particular has blocked serious efforts at reform.[11] While the lack of transparency is thus widely cited as a reason for the BWC's

Gugliotta & Gary Matsumoto, *FBI's Theory on Anthrax Is Doubted; Attacks Not Likely Work of 1 Person, Experts Say*, WASH. POST, Oct. 28, 2002, at A1. The spores were also reportedly identified as belonging to a highly virulent strain of anthrax used in U.S. biodefense research programs. Eileen Choffnes, *Bioweapons: New Labs, More Terror?* BULL. ATOM. SCI., Sept./Oct. 2002, at 28. After more than five years without an arrest, however, some FBI officials have reportedly questioned the sophistication of the anthrax powder used in the attacks. Allan Lengel & Joby Warrick, *FBI Is Casting a Wider Net in Anthrax Attacks*, WASH. POST, Sept. 25, 2006, at A1.

[5] Four of the top five "Nightmares for Disaster Planning" developed by the Department of Homeland Security involve BW attacks. Eric Lipton, *U.S. Lists Possible Terror Attacks and Likely Toll*, N.Y. TIMES, Mar. 16, 2005, at A1. The perceived BW threat also figured prominently—and erroneously—in the arguments of senior U.S. officials justifying an invasion of Iraq. *E.g.*, Steven R. Weisman, *Powell, in U.N. Speech, Presents Case to Show Iraq Has Not Disarmed*, N.Y. TIMES, Feb. 6, 2003, at A1.

[6] President Bush has flatly stated that "[r]ogue states and terrorists possess these weapons and are willing to use them." George W. Bush, Statement on Strengthening the International Regime Against Biological Weapons, 37 WEEKLY COMP. PRES. DOC. 1580, 1580 (Nov. 5, 2001).

[7] The Secretary-General: Message to the Fifth Review Conference of the States Parties to the Biological Weapons Convention (Nov. 19, 2001), *available at* <http://www.opbw.org> [hereinafter BWC Web site].

[8] The lack of verification mechanisms has been criticized and debated by BWC states parties since at least 1986, resulting in intensive, but unsuccessful, efforts by the "Ad Hoc Group" from 1994 to 2001 to develop a protocol to the BWC that would have established various legally binding declaration, visit, and continuous monitoring procedures. *See infra* notes 77–84 and corresponding text.

[9] Looking at the role that information can play in strategic interactions between states acting with mixed motives, legal scholars have used the well-known Prisoners' Dilemma and other models drawn from noncooperative game theory to gain valuable insights into the meaning and function of arms control agreements generally. *See, e.g.*, Kenneth W. Abbott, *"Trust But Verify": The Production of Information in Arms Control Treaties and Other International Agreements*, 26 CORNELL INT'L L.J. 1 (1993).

[10] ARTHUR A. STEIN, WHY NATIONS COOPERATE: CIRCUMSTANCE AND CHOICE IN INTERNATIONAL RELATIONS 142 (1990). Transparency is also linked to rationalist explanations of state compliance with international law that rely on reputational concerns. *See* Kal Raustiala, *Compliance and Effectiveness in International Regulatory Cooperation*, 32 CASE W. RES. J. INT'L L. 387, 402 (2000).

[11] The U.S. government abruptly ended a seven-year-long reform in July 2001 by effectively ending consideration of the BWC draft protocol. *See infra* notes 80–84 and corresponding text.

lack of success, this article argues that another, equally important factor contributes to the ineffectiveness of the BWC and other disarmament or arms control regimes that operate in environments where member states perceive their security to be threatened: the use of indeterminate[12] language in key provisions, a phenomenon that is sometimes characterized as a dimension of "soft law."

There is substantial disagreement among legal scholars about the definition, status, and role of soft law;[13] however, many argue that it considerably influences the behavior of states and displays significant advantages over "hard law" in different areas of international practice.[14] The term "soft law" is often used to denote principles, standards, or arrangements of a nonlegally binding nature.[15] But the absence of formal legal obligation is arguably only one characteristic of a continuum of softness: the term "soft law" is also used by scholars to refer to hortatory language[16] and to imprecise, ambiguous, vague, or otherwise indeterminate formulations,[17] even when found in legally binding agreements like the BWC.[18] Key structural deficiencies in international agreements, such as the failure of the BWC to provide for any mandatory mechanisms to enhance transparency and enforcement, are also sometimes associated with soft law when the elements of an international agreement

---

[12] I use the term "determinacy" to encompass concepts of both precision and clarity and I refer to determinate provisions as those that clearly convey their message, communicate their intent, and help "shape that intent into a specific situational command." Thomas M. Franck, *Legitimacy in the International System*, 82 AJIL 705, 725 (1988).

[13] Commentators have long suggested that "soft law" can manifest itself in an "infinite variety" of forms. *See* R. R. Baxter, *International Law in Her "Infinite Variety,"* 29 INT'L & COMP. L.Q. 549 (1980). Sufficient variations of soft law now exist for scholars to suggest that there is "no acepted definition." Dinah L. Shelton, *Normative Hierarchy in International Law*, 100 AJIL 291, 319 (2006).

[14] *See* Andrew T. Guzman, *A Compliance-Based Theory of International Law*, 90 CAL. L. REV. 1823, 1880 (2002) ("[M]any instruments that are not considered 'law' under the classical definition have a substantial impact on the behavior of states."); Geoffrey Palmer, *New Ways to Make International Environmental Law*, 86 AJIL 259, 269 (1992) (describing soft law solutions as "useful steps on a longer journey" and the point where "international law and international politics combine to build new norms"); Anne-Marie Slaughter et al., *International Law and International Relations Theory: A New Generation of Interdisciplinary Scholarship*, 92 AJIL 367 (1998) (emphasizing the advantages of nonbinding soft law in the context of international governance and the generation of norms by supranational institutions and their dissemination by nongovernmental organizations); David Weissbrodt & Muria Kruger, *Norms on the Responsibilities of Transnational Corporations and Other Business Enterprises with Regard to Human Rights*, 97 AJIL 901, 914 (2003) (noting the impact of soft law on the interpretation of treaties and on the establishment of customary international law in areas such as human rights).

[15] Shelton, *supra* note 13, at 319.

[16] Edith Brown Weiss, *Introduction* to INTERNATIONAL COMPLIANCE WITH NON-BINDING ACCORDS 1, 3 (Edith Brown Weiss ed., 1997) [hereinafter INTERNATIONAL COMPLIANCE].

[17] *See* Kenneth W. Abbott & Duncan Snidal, *Hard and Soft Law in International Governance*, 54 INT'L ORG. 421, 422 (2000) (arguing that "'soft law' begins once legal arrangements are weakened along one or more of the dimensions of obligation, precision, and delegation"); Prosper Weil, *Towards Relative Normativity in International Law?* 77 AJIL 413, 414–15 n.7 (1983) (stating that "[i]t would seem better to reserve the term 'soft law' for rules that are imprecise and not really compelling"); Shelton, *supra* note 13, at 319 (noting that "[t]he term 'soft law' is also sometimes employed to refer to the weak, vague, or poorly drafted content of a binding instrument"). Unlike hortatory or purely aspirational language, however, such indeterminate provisions retain a legally binding character and are not soft law in the sense that an adjudicative body with jurisdiction would decline to apply them on the grounds that they do not entail a legal obligation whose content can be ascertained by resort to established interpretive techniques.

[18] FRIEDRICH KRATOCHWIL, RULES, NORMS, AND DECISIONS 200–01 (1989); Christine Chinkin, *Normative Developments in the International Legal System*, in COMMITMENT AND COMPLIANCE: THE ROLE OF NON-BINDING NORMS IN THE INTERNATIONAL LEGAL SYSTEM 21, 25–26 (Dinah L. Shelton ed., 2000) [hereinafter COMMITMENT AND COMPLIANCE].

are viewed as a whole.[19] While these different variants of soft law are often merged to such an extent that some scholars appear to find little reason to distinguish between them,[20] others argue that such a merger impedes the study of law's relative influence on state behavior because it conflates the legally binding nature of agreements with other issues such as their substance or structure.[21] However it is characterized, the fusion of a "hard," legally binding agreement with "soft," indeterminate language is a common, yet problematic, trade-off[22] that merits separate analysis, particularly in the context of arms control regimes that attempt to regulate potentially destabilizing technology with both peaceful civilian uses and devastating military applications.[23] This article thus focuses on indeterminate language in legally binding agreements, which represents one choice that states may make from a range of options for designing arms control and disarmament regimes.

One approach to resolving indeterminate legal terms involves delegating authority to judicial bodies to interpret ambiguous language. Since some degree of rule indeterminacy is common in the domestic context, judges in domestic courts are often called upon to apply and interpret broad standards or to engage in the case-by-case administration of justice.[24] Similarly, some international adjudicative bodies may also apply broad standards that require considerable interpretation and filling in of gaps.[25] The resolution by third-party adjudication, however, of issues arising from indeterminate language in the arms control context generally represents an unacceptable threat to the sovereignty and national security of states, particularly the most powerful ones. State actors operating in an anarchic and unforgiving security environment pursue policies with respect to international cooperation on the basis of their own self-interested motives or preferences,[26] and so approach disarmament regimes and other restrictions in the "high politics" arena of war and peace with great suspicion. While states may conclude that their interests are advanced by joining security regimes, the terms of governing international agreements are invariably subject to scrutiny and compromise. In this regard, states—especially the most powerful states, which are accustomed to setting the rules of most

---

[19] *See* Kal Raustiala, *Form and Substance in International Agreements*, 99 AJIL 581, 582 (2005) (suggesting that legality, substance, and structure can be viewed as "distinct design elements" that should be treated holistically in evaluating the effectiveness of international agreements).

[20] Atsuko Kanehara, *Some Considerations Regarding Methods of International Regulation in Global Issues: Sovereignty and 'Common Interests,' in* INTERNATIONAL COMPLIANCE, *supra* note 16, at 81, 83.

[21] Raustiala, *supra* note 19, at 582, 589–90.

[22] Whatever term is used to describe the result, if a broad conceptual framework is applied to the architecture of international agreements, placing indeterminate provisions in a legally binding agreement may be characterized as one of several possible "systematic trade-offs" between form and substance that states make in designing their international commitments. *Id.* at 581.

[23] The security dilemmas that states routinely face in arms control regimes are likely to be significantly more pronounced or acute when such complex dual-use technology is regulated. *See infra* note 91 and corresponding text.

[24] Louis Kaplow, *Rules Versus Standards: An Economic Analysis*, 42 DUKE L.J. 557 (1992); Cass R. Sunstein, *Problems with Rules*, 83 CAL. L. REV. 953 (1995); Robert Weisberg, *The Calabresian Judicial Artist: Statutes and the New Legal Process*, 35 STAN. L. REV. 213 (1983).

[25] The WTO Appellate Body, for example, applies and interprets some indeterminate language in the context of economic regulation. Joel P. Trachtman, *The Domain of WTO Dispute Resolution*, 40 HARV. INT'L L.J. 333, 337–38 (1999). Similarly, "friendship, commerce and navigation" treaties contain standards that are sometimes interpreted by the International Court of Justice. *See* Kenneth J. Vandevelde, *A Brief History of International Investment Agreements*, 12 U.C. DAVIS J. INT'L L. & POL'Y 157, 164–65 (2005).

[26] Underlying state motivations may be described as "preferences" as to goals or outcomes as opposed to strategies or ways to reach goals. Robert Powell, *Anarchy in International Relations Theory: The Neorealist-Neoliberal Debate*, 48 INT'L ORG. 330 (1994).

international regimes according to their interests[27]—are generally unwilling and unlikely to entrust their most important security interests to other states or to adjudication by international institutions.[28]

In view of the high stakes associated with international security cooperation, it is useful to assess the design of arms control regimes in the context of preferences that may underlie self-interested state behavior. This article undertakes such an assessment and uses the BWC to explore the choices states make along a continuum of options that include various dimensions of soft and hard law. In doing so, it illuminates the hazards of choosing indeterminate language to perform critical regime functions amid unstable security conditions.

Many scholars proclaim the virtues of soft law, including that dimension characterized by indeterminacy of language. In the area of arms control, some suggest that different types of soft law may at least be no less effective than hard law, especially when widely supported norms are involved,[29] or that they may in fact offer distinct advantages over hard law.[30] While indeterminate language may serve as a useful tool for states in certain negotiations and agreements, this article shows that it is fatal to the success of arms control in general, and multilateral disarmament agreements in particular. Even with all the transparency measures imaginable (including intrusive monitoring and verification mechanisms), indeterminacy of the language delineating permissible behavior will doom arms control to failure. Such indeterminacy not only robs commitments of credibility—making it impossible to solve the security dilemma— but also is likely to exacerbate the security dilemma, breeding more of the mistrust that feeds it. By cloaking defection in plausible legality, many acts of noncompliance may be legitimized. Moreover, indeterminacy permits discriminatory application of key rules, favoring powerful states and deterring weaker states from joining the regime. This set of problems is illustrated below by consideration of the indeterminate language that has helped undermine the BWC and may have worsened the BW arms race.

Part II of this article briefly reviews the development of international legal prohibitions related to biological weapons and examines the origins and nature of the indeterminate BWC legal framework. Using the BWC to illustrate the process whereby states make various substantive and structural trade-offs in designing international regimes, it analyzes the compromises that led to the adoption of this framework. Part II concludes by summarizing the regime's

---

[27] *See* Stephen D. Krasner, *Structural Causes and Regime Consequences: Regimes as Intervening Variables, in* INTERNATIONAL REGIMES 1 (Stephen D. Krasner ed., 1983); *see also* Stephen D. Krasner, *Global Communications and National Power: Life on the Pareto Frontier*, 43 WORLD POL. 336 (1991).

[28] Bilateral arms control treaties help illustrate how states generally prefer recourse to unilateral measures or bilateral dispute resolution procedures rather than entrusting third parties with the power to interpret terms that relate to national security in such agreements. *See, e.g.*, Note, *Legal Models of Arms Control: Past, Present, and Future*, 100 HARV. L. REV. 1326 (1987) (noting that the ABM, SALT I, and SALT II treaties all established a Standing Consultative Commission (SCC) to interpret ambiguous phrases but that the USSR and the United States never invited other parties to participate in SCC proceedings); Angela M. Bradley, *Opposing Interpretations of an International Treaty: The Anti-ballistic Missile Treaty Controversy*, 2 CHI. J. INT'L L. 295, 296 (2001).

[29] *See, e.g.*, Richard L. Williamson Jr., *Is International Law Relevant to Arms Control? Hard Law, Soft Law, and Non-law in Multilateral Arms Control: Some Compliance Hypotheses*, 4 CHI. J. INT'L L. 59, 63 n.14 (2003) (further arguing that "[l]ittle in arms control seems to depend on whether one thinks of this category as a subset of soft law or just very mushy hard law").

[30] *See* Barry Kellman, *Protection of Nuclear Materials, in* COMMITMENT AND COMPLIANCE, *supra* note 18, at 486, 494–95 (arguing that soft law makes a better framework than hard law for the regulation of nuclear materials protection); Abram Chayes & Dinah Shelton, *Multilateral Arms Control: Commentary, in id.* at 521, 526 ("Soft law can make an important contribution because it can more quickly respond to changing weapons technologies that create uncertainty about the risks of the future strategic situation and the mechanisms to minimize them.").

problematic and indeterminate provisions and provides an overview of the unsuccessful performance of the BWC to date.

Parts III, IV, and V analyze the combined effects on arms control regimes of indeterminacy and lack of transparency in the context of three groups of states, as defined by their preferences: defensive defectors, offensive defectors, and compliant or conformist states. This examination demonstrates how psychological and rational mechanisms associated with indeterminate language can enlarge existing security dilemmas, undermine cooperation, and impede the universality of arms control regimes. The analysis of the negative effects of indeterminacy on arms control regimes in the context of these three preference groups is then applied to the particular case of the BWC regime. Taking into account the possibilities for improved performance suggested by the assessment of indeterminate arms control regimes in highly insecure environments, parts III, IV, and V evaluate, within the three respective preference groups, the role that determinate provisions could play together with transparency in addressing the observed deficiencies of the BWC regime. The United States recently abandoned its support for BWC reform efforts that were consistent with such an approach and instead placed itself as the main obstacle to these widely accepted reform measures, expressing unilateralist sentiments and broad national security concerns that also reflected the opposition of the U.S. pharmaceutical industry to such measures.

Part VI concludes by briefly contrasting the experience of the BWC with that of other multilateral disarmament regimes to illustrate how states are increasingly using determinacy to regulate complex dual-use technology problems (that is, technology that can be used either for building prohibited weapons or for legitimate, peaceful purposes) related to WMDs, and it further considers the complementary role that determinacy must play in successful BW nonproliferation efforts generally.

II. THE ORIGINS OF THE INDETERMINATE AND INEFFECTIVE BWC REGIME

The First Prohibition Against the Use of Biological Weapons

Although its use in warfare has been relatively rare, disease is said to have been employed as a weapon as early as the Middle Ages.[31] Practical considerations, however, greatly limited the use of biological agents as weapons, particularly as they were difficult to produce, store, and deploy, and were as likely to harm friendly forces as the enemy. Nascent efforts by states to regulate the increasingly destructive new weapons near the end of the nineteenth century included agreements banning the use of certain poisons and asphyxiating gases but not biological weapons.[32] In spite of early efforts to ban asphyxiating gases, chemical weapons (CW) were used extensively in World War I and caused hundreds of thousands of casualties. After

---

[31] There are various primitive examples of biological warfare. *See* ROBIN CLARKE, THE SILENT WEAPONS 14 (1968); GEORGE DEAUX, THE BLACK DEATH: 1347, at 1444 (1969); Jeffery K. Smart, *History of Chemical and Biological Warfare: An American Perspective, in* 16 TEXTBOOK OF MILITARY MEDICINE: MEDICAL ASPECTS OF CHEMICAL AND BIOLOGICAL WARFARE 9, 12 (Frederick R. Sidell et al. eds., 1997).

[32] Convention with Respect to the Laws and Customs of War on Land, July 29, 1899, 32 Stat. 1803, 1 Bevans 247 (prohibited, inter alia, the use of poison or poisoned arms); Declaration Concerning Asphyxiating Gases, July 29, 1899, TEXTS OF THE PEACE CONFERENCES AT THE HAGUE, 1899 AND 1907, at 81 (James Brown Scott ed., 1908), 1907 Gr. Brit. TS No. 32 (Cd. 3751) (banned "the use of projectiles the sole object of which is the diffusion of asphyxiating gases"); Convention Respecting the Laws and Customs of War on Land, Oct. 18, 1907, 36 Stat. 2277, 1 Bevans 631 (included a declaration outlawing the use of asphyxiating gases).

the war, widely publicized accounts of the suffering and death associated with CW led to various attempts by states formally and effectively to outlaw the use of all chemical weapons.

At a multilateral arms control conference in 1925 addressing the nonuse of poisonous gases, a prohibition on "the use of bacteriological methods of warfare" was proposed for the first time.[33] The work of this conference resulted in the conclusion of the Geneva Protocol for the Prohibition of Poisonous Gases and Bacteriological Methods of Warfare on June 17, 1925 (Geneva Protocol), which banned the use of both chemical and biological weapons.[34] However, banning biological weapons, in contrast to chemical weapons, was a new legal concept in 1925. Since any practical threat presented by these weapons in 1925 was merely imagined, the authors of the Geneva Protocol in effect sought to ban a weapon of the *future*.[35] In doing so, states demonstrated the power of biological weapons to cause considerable fear and insecurity on a largely abstract level.

As an international agreement, the Geneva Protocol was significantly limited in the scope of its application. The text banned the use, in war,[36] of biological weapons only against other states parties (not states generally),[37] and did not ban the possession or development of these weapons. Many states also made reservations declaring that the obligations under the Protocol would cease to be binding on them if enemy states failed to respect its prohibitions, effectively making it a prohibition on the "first use" of chemical and biological weapons.[38] Thus, the Protocol's de facto recognition of a potential defensive or deterrent basis for these weapons—coupled with the absence of any prohibition on their development, acquisition, possession, manufacture, or transfer—resulted in a legal framework that allowed states to conduct BW research, develop new biological weapons, and ultimately engage in BW arms races.

---

[33] 1st and 2nd meetings of the General Committee of the Conference for the Supervision of the International Trade in Arms and Ammunition and in Implements of War, League of Nations Doc. A.13.1925.IX. Although the term "bacteriological" has a narrower scientific definition than "biological," in legal contexts the two terms have been used interchangeably in disarmament negotiations since before World War II. *See* A. BOSERUP, CBW AND THE LAW OF WAR 43 (Stockholm International Peace Research Institute [SIPRI], The Problem of Chemical and Biological Warfare Vol. 3, 1973). The broad, modern international legal definition of biological weapons encompasses several known categories of pathogens and toxins and also includes those that may come from as yet undiscovered sources, "regardless of any technical developments." *See* GA Res. 2603A (XXIV) (Dec. 16, 1969); *see also infra* note 39. The broad scope of this general prohibition has been repeatedly reaffirmed by states at BWC review conferences.

[34] Protocol for the Prohibition of the Use in War of Asphyxiating, Poisonous or Other Gases, and of Bacteriological Methods of Warfare, June 17, 1925, 26 UST 571, 94 LNTS 65.

[35] As a forward-looking ban, the prohibition on the use of biological weapons envisioned by the Geneva Protocol was comprehensive in spirit. *See* BOSERUP, *supra* note 33, at 40–41. The all-inclusive scope of the prohibition was reinforced by the term *methods* of warfare, potentially extending its coverage to a wide variety of means, processes, designs, delivery systems, and types of targets. *Id.* at 71.

[36] By agreeing to prohibit the use of biological weapons only "in war," the parties to the Geneva Protocol left open the possibility of using biological weapons in noninternational armed conflicts, or in other contexts not amounting to "war." *See id.* at 28–33.

[37] Although the prohibition against the use of asphyxiating, poisonous, or other gases was viewed by some as a reaffirmation of an existing norm, the prohibition against biological weapons was an innovation that had not yet attained that status, leaving the parties bound in this area only "as between themselves according to the terms of this declaration." *Id.* at 21–23.

[38] See, for example, the reservations of France, the Soviet Union, and the United Kingdom, Geneva Protocol Reservations, SIPRI, High Contracting Parties to the Geneva Protocol (2005), *available at* <http://www.sipri.org/contents/cbwarfare/cbw_research_doc/cbw_historical/cbw_historical.html>. Although forty-two states originally made reservations to the Protocol, many would later withdraw them upon becoming a party to the BWC.

278   THE AMERICAN JOURNAL OF INTERNATIONAL LAW   [Vol. 101:271

The BW Arms Race

The fears generated by biological weapons and the security dilemmas that states have faced in arming against BW threats have historically been compounded by fundamental identification problems associated with the development of these weapons. Since disease occurs naturally, a troubling question of intention has often arisen when the scientific or military establishments in adversary states have been reported to be in possession of components or technology with BW applications.[39] It was in fact the fear of *nonexistent* weapons, the *potential* impact of technological advances, and the *misperception* of threats that first inspired several states to begin to develop their own BW programs shortly after the legal ban on their use was formalized in 1925.[40] In a remarkable testament to the power of these concerns, "misperceptions of enemy interest" appear to have compelled several states to begin building biological weapons soon after the Geneva Protocol was signed.[41]

Events in World War II further demonstrated the power of BW misperceptions to magnify security dilemmas and motivate states to pursue BW programs. Although after the war the lack of any large-scale German BW program was established, both Britain and the United States had misperceived a serious German BW threat during the war and responded by developing their own BW programs.[42] Both countries also concluded that the best defensive arsenal should include offensive biological weapons and in 1942 Britain conducted tests that for the first time proved the effectiveness of bombs with BW agents.[43]

American efforts at the close of World War II to limit access to captured scientists responsible for Japan's infamous BW experiments on humans increased Soviet suspicions of U.S. intentions regarding new BW capabilities and set the stage for the Cold War BW arms race.[44] While the United States had not shown great interest in BW research programs in the 1930s, efforts to build a BW program expanded rapidly at the end of World War II and funding was dramatically increased.[45] After adopting a policy in 1956 to be "prepared to use chemical and

---

[39] The regulation of biological weapons has always been complicated by the requirement of intention, while no such requirement is stated for chemical weapons. *See* INGRID DETTER, THE LAW OF WAR 258 (2d ed. 2000). Thus, the UN General Assembly has defined prohibited biological agents of warfare as "living organisms, whatever their nature, or infective material derived from them—which are *intended* to cause disease or death in man, animals or plants." GA Res. 2603A (XXIV), *supra* note 33 (emphasis added).

[40] J. PERRY ROBINSON & M. LEITENBERG, THE RISE OF CB WEAPONS 332 (SIPRI, The Problem of Chemical and Biological Warfare Vol. 1, 1971) (arguing that during the interwar years groups of individuals in the most powerful states decided that potential enemy countries were interested in biological warfare when in fact it appears that in most countries other than Japan biological weapons were "at most the part-time concern of very small groups of people").

[41] *Id.* at 332–33.

[42] SHELDON H. HARRIS, FACTORIES OF DEATH: JAPANESE BIOLOGICAL WARFARE 1932–45 AND THE AMERICAN COVER-UP 161 (1995); *see also* Barton J. Bernstein, *Churchill's Secret Biological Weapons*, BULL. ATOM. SCI., Jan./Feb. 1987, at 46, 47–49.

[43] Early U.S. BW planners concluded that "the best defense is offense and the threat of offense." U.S. National Academies, War Bureau of Consultants, Final Report (1942), *quoted in* ED REGIS, THE BIOLOGY OF DOOM: THE HISTORY OF AMERICA'S SECRET GERM WARFARE PROJECT 177 (1999). Britain conducted tests in which 25-pound anthrax bombs were dropped among tethered sheep on Gruinard Island off the coast of Scotland. TOM MANGOLD & JEFF GOLDBERG, PLAGUE WARS 30 (2001); Bernstein, *supra* note 42.

[44] DANIEL BARENBLATT, A PLAGUE UPON HUMANITY: THE SECRET HISTORY OF AXIS JAPAN'S GERM WARFARE OPERATION 207–09 (2004); MANGOLD & GOLDBERG, *supra* note 43, at 27–28, 44; REGIS, *supra* note 43, at 107–11.

[45] Bernstein, *supra* note 42, at 49; Henry L. Stimson Center, History of the U.S. Offensive Biological Warfare Program (1941–1973), *available at* <http://www.stimson.org/cbw/?sn=CB2001121275>.

bacteriological weapons in general war,"[46] the United States embarked on extensive programs to test the lethality, survivability, and dispersal characteristics of biological agents.

Choosing Indeterminacy and No Transparency: The Creation of the BWC

At the height of the massive BW arms race in the midst of the Cold War, President Richard M. Nixon took the dramatic and unexpected step on November 25, 1969, of unilaterally renouncing the possession and use by the United States of "lethal biological agents and weapons, and all other methods of biological warfare," and declaring that all biological research in the future would be confined to "defensive measures such as immunization and safety measures."[47] Although the stated goal was to advance world peace, the questionable military utility of biological weapons significantly influenced the opinions of U.S. decision makers. In spite of newly developed practical applications, President Nixon and U.S. military leaders had serious reservations about the effectiveness of biological weapons and believed that nuclear forces provided both sufficient and superior strategic deterrence for the United States.[48]

As the United States proceeded to destroy its BW arsenal, the United Kingdom continued its attempt to achieve a worldwide treaty banning biological weapons.[49] In 1969 the British and Americans were able to agree on the final wording of such a treaty, but the Soviet Union adamantly opposed the effort even after the British removed language requiring enforceable verification measures.[50] In August 1970, the Soviets suddenly dropped their objections to the proposal, and within a year the Americans, the British, and the Soviets were able to report the draft BWC to the United Nations for its approval.[51] The BWC was opened for signature on April 10, 1972, and the United States became a party on January 22, 1975.[52]

Cold War scenarios, often modeled in game theory as iterated, two-person Prisoners' Dilemmas, might suggest that the United States and its allies became a party to the BWC to achieve what they hoped would be a Pareto-optimal disarmament arrangement with the Soviet

---

[46] National Security Council, Reg. NSC 5062/1 (Mar. 15, 1956), *quoted in* REGIS, *supra* note 43, at 177. This new policy appeared to be broad enough to envision the first use of biological weapons.

[47] Richard M. Nixon, Statement on Chemical and Biological Defense Policies and Programs, 1969 PUB. PAPERS 461, 461 (Nov. 25, 1969). The renunciation was later extended to cover the use and production of all biological toxins as well. MANGOLD & GOLDBERG, *supra* note 43, at 56 n.22 (citing White House Press Release (Feb. 14, 1970)).

[48] MANGOLD & GOLDBERG, *supra* note 43, at 55, 61. U.S. military officials believed that biological weapons were not likely to be useful for either tactical applications or strategic deterrence. President Nixon is quoted as telling his staff, "We'll never use the damn germs, so what good is biological warfare as a deterrent? If somebody uses germs on us, we'll nuke 'em." William Safire, *Essays; Iraq's Ton of Germs*, N.Y. TIMES, Apr. 13, 1995, at A25.

[49] In August 1968, the United Kingdom proposed a convention banning biological weapons by submitting a working paper to the Eighteen-Nation Disarmament Committee. Susan Wright, *Evolution of Biological Warfare Policy, 1945–1990, in* PREVENTING A BIOLOGICAL ARMS RACE 26, 38 (Susan Wright ed., 1990).

[50] MANGOLD & GOLDBERG, *supra* note 43, at 57.

[51] On December 16, 1971, the General Assembly approved the treaty by a vote of 110-0. GA Res. 2826 (XXVI) (Dec. 16, 1971).

[52] Following the Senate's advice and consent, President Gerald Ford ratified the treaty for the United States and also took the long-overdue action of ratifying the Geneva Protocol, doing so with no reservations regarding the use of biological weapons.

280   THE AMERICAN JOURNAL OF INTERNATIONAL LAW   [Vol. 101:271]

Union.[53] Such paradigms do not, however, fully explain this Cold War transaction, particularly since its impact on third parties significantly informed U.S. preferences.[54] As a balance-of-power issue, the spread of biological weapons was seen by American strategists as an undesirable way for relatively weak countries to obtain great destructive capability, while at the same time reducing the U.S. advantages in the acquisition and deployment of expensive conventional and nuclear forces.[55] Believing that most states were not yet in a position to develop advanced biological weapons, the United States and Britain sought to negotiate the BWC with the Soviet Union quickly, in part to lock in existing strategic advantages over less developed states.[56]

While the Soviets obtained their key objective by eliminating any mandatory transparency measures in the BWC regime, the United States and Britain obtained what they thought was a critical Soviet concession by signing a "hard" legally binding instrument. In hindsight, this was a dubious achievement for the Western powers since a legally binding agreement gave the Soviets a deceptive legal cover for a massive offensive BW program when an informal arrangement might not have falsely raised such expectations of their compliance. From the outset, Soviet acquiescence in a legally binding BWC appears to have been a cynical maneuver that enabled the clandestine building of the largest BW research and armament program in history.[57] The Soviet Union was not, however, the only state to seek compromises that would ultimately weaken the BWC.

In negotiating the design of agreements, states may face a wide range of trade-offs in substance, structure, and obligation that include hard and soft levels of legalization, and thus yield different types of commitments and different degrees of difficulty in achieving these agreements.[58] Various forms of soft law are touted by scholars as an easier way for states facing these choices to achieve desired objectives, to accommodate different interests through short-term compromises, and to provide the flexibility to address uncertainties and other issues.[59] In the case of the final compromise BWC text, the design elements chosen by the drafting parties—hard legally binding obligations, soft structure (lacking any

---

[53] Although there are at least seventy-eight different two-person, two-strategy games, game theorists and political scientists have often focused on the Prisoners' Dilemma and its associated problems, even though it does not apply to most conflicts. WILLIAM POUNDSTONE, PRISONER'S DILEMMA 129 (1992). The Prisoners' Dilemma in fact became so commonly associated with nuclear arms rivalry that it was "oversold" as a paradigm for Cold War relations, sometimes overshadowing the realities of arms races. *Id.*

[54] Many arms races are not true Prisoners' Dilemmas since relativistic assessments of mutual armament and disarmament may appear to provide higher returns to one of the parties, resulting in a zero-sum game in which the equilibrium outcome is no longer Pareto-deficient. STEIN, *supra* note 10, at 126–27. While a *disarmament* agreement is more likely to meet the requirements for a true Prisoners' Dilemma, the parties negotiating such agreements may not be genuinely focused on reducing competition between themselves but may instead be more interested in achieving relative advantages over third parties. *Id.* at 133.

[55] *See* Letter from Matthew S. Meselson to Henry A. Kissinger, national security adviser (Sept. 1969), *quoted in* JUDITH MILLER ET AL., GERMS: BIOLOGICAL WEAPONS AND AMERICA'S SECRET WAR 62 (2001); Susan Wright, *Introduction: In Search of a New Paradigm of Biological Disarmament, in* BIOLOGICAL WARFARE AND DISARMAMENT: NEW PROBLEMS/NEW PERSPECTIVES 3, 7 (Susan Wright ed., 2002).

[56] *See* Susan Wright, *Geopolitical Origins, in* BIOLOGICAL WARFARE AND DISARMAMENT, *supra* note 55, at 313, 323 (drawing largely on declassified UK government biological arms control studies).

[57] *See* Anthony Rimmington, *The Soviet Union's Offensive Program: The Implications for Contemporary Arms Control, in* BIOLOGICAL WARFARE AND DISARMAMENT, *supra* note 55, at 103, 121.

[58] *See* Abbott & Snidal, *supra* note 17, at 436.

[59] *Id.* at 423, 436 (noting how soft law can serve as a "compromise at a point in time" that can accommodate "different interests and values, different time horizons and discount rates, and different degrees of power"); Raustiala, *supra* note 19, at 586, 613; Weiss, *supra* note 16, at 6.

access to transparency measures), and soft indeterminate language—reflected a complex set of preferences. Both the United States and Britain, like the Soviet Union, were clearly not eager to accept the sovereignty costs and security limitations associated with either precise requirements or intrusive inspections.[60]

Ambiguity in the BWC advanced important security objectives for the United States and Britain. The Western militaries in particular were unwilling to accept any clarifying distinctions between "peaceful" and prohibited BW activities, which resulted in the intentional placement by the Western powers of a fatal ambiguity at the heart of the BWC.[61] While indeterminate provisions and a lack of transparency created a real possibility of future undetected defections, the ultimate national security interests of the Western powers were thought to be safeguarded in 1972 by powerful strategic nuclear deterrents. In the context of bipolar Cold War security and competition, the BWC drafting parties thus perceived a rational basis for eschewing both precision in their commitments and serious monitoring mechanisms, but this decision would have far-reaching consequences for the BWC regime when it was forced to confront BW proliferation challenges beyond the Cold War paradigm.

Overview of the Indeterminate Provisions in the BWC

The central obligation of the BWC is found in Article I, which requires each state party "never in any circumstances to develop, produce, stockpile or otherwise acquire or retain . . . [m]icrobial or other biological agents, or toxins whatever their origin or method of production."[62] This comprehensive ban, however, is limited in the same sentence to apply only to agents or toxins if they are "of types and in quantities that have no justification for prophylactic, protective or other peaceful purposes."[63] The BWC offers no definitions of or clarifying rules on the types of biological agents that have "no justification for prophylactic, protective or other peaceful purposes."[64] Similarly, both the obligation imposed upon states parties in Article II to destroy or convert to peaceful purposes all prohibited agents, toxins, weapons, or equipment in their possession and the prohibition in Article III preventing states parties from transferring prohibited agents, toxins, weapons, or equipment are explicitly made dependent on what might be included within the scope of the indeterminate phrase "peaceful purposes" found in Article I.

To provide for domestic enforcement of its treaty obligations, each BWC state party is required to take the necessary measures within its territory to prohibit and prevent the

---

[60] For a review of formerly classified internal documents detailing the British government's deliberations on joining the BWC and its assessment of the legal, political, and military implications of biological and chemical disarmament, see Wright, *supra* note 56, at 313–42. For a variety of reasons, including a desire to protect both commercial and military secrets, the Western powers were also reluctant to accept highly intrusive verification measures. *Id.* at 335.

[61] *Id.* at 336; Jonathan B. Tucker, *A Farewell to Germs: The U.S. Renunciation of Biological and Toxin Warfare, 1969–70*, 27 INT'L SECURITY 107, 124 (2002) (discussing the desire of U.S. military planners to maintain a sufficient BW program to "avoid technological surprise by an enemy").

[62] BWC, *supra* note 1, Art. I(1).

[63] *Id.*

[64] Weapons, equipment, or means of delivery of agents and toxins are also prohibited, provided that they are "designed to use such agents or toxins for hostile purposes or in armed conflict." *Id.*, Art. I(2).

development, production, stockpiling, acquisition, or retention of unlawful agents, toxins, weapons, and equipment.[65] Once again, however, determining the extent of this prohibition depends on the vagaries of the term "peaceful purposes" as set forth in Article I. With respect to international enforcement, the BWC provides that a state party may submit a complaint of noncompliance to the UN Security Council, but the Convention does not specify any clear legal requirements or rules to invoke in lodging such a complaint, which must establish a "breach of obligations deriving from the provisions of the Convention."[66]

The lack of any determinate rules or criteria in the BWC also raises troubling issues with respect to the obligation of states parties to facilitate "the fullest possible exchange of equipment, materials and scientific and technological information for the use of bacteriological (biological) agents and toxins for peaceful purposes."[67] With no definition of what constitutes "peaceful purposes," how can any state determine precisely what should be exchanged to the fullest possible extent, on the one hand, and what should be restricted, on the other, to prevent the proliferation of biological weapons? The lack of such a definition similarly complicates the obligation to implement the BWC so as to avoid hampering international cooperation and exchanges in "peaceful" biological activities.[68]

Cheating Under the BWC, Insecurity, and the Failure of Reform Efforts

Less than a year after it signed the BWC, the Soviet Union embarked on a massive clandestine cheating effort in which it concealed a vast network of BW research, development, testing, and production facilities within its existing civilian and military structures under the direction of an organization known as Biopreparat.[69] Only after a major accident at a military microbiology factory in Sverdlovsk in 1979 and the subsequent defection of key scientists did the size and scope of the secret Soviet effort begin to become apparent.[70]

By the time the second BWC review conference of the states parties met in September 1986,[71] allegations of Soviet treaty violations, growing suspicions about the easily concealed

---

[65] The BWC envisions that states parties will do much of the policing, requiring each one to take "any necessary measures to prohibit and prevent the development, production, stockpiling, acquisition, or retention of the agents, toxins, weapons, equipment and means of delivery specified in article I of the Convention, within the territory of such State, under its jurisdiction or under its control anywhere." *Id.*, Art IV.

[66] *Id.*, Art. VI(1). Without UN action, resolution of disputes between states parties is subject only to voluntary consultation and cooperation under Article V.

[67] *Id.*, Art. X(1). In addition, the states parties are encouraged to cooperate in contributing to the "further development and application of scientific discoveries in the field of bacteriology (biology) for prevention of disease, or for other peaceful purposes." *Id.*

[68] *Id.*, Art. X(2).

[69] Rimmington, *supra* note 57, at 108–13; *see also* AMY E. SMITHSON, TOXIC ARCHIPELAGO: PREVENTING PROLIFERATION FROM THE FORMER SOVIET CHEMICAL AND BIOLOGICAL WEAPONS COMPLEXES 10 (Henry L. Stimson Center Report No. 32, Dec. 1999), *available at* <http://www.stimson.org/cbw/pdf/toxicarch.pdf>; Jonathan B. Tucker et al., *Biological Weapons Proliferation from Russia: How Great a Threat? in* REPAIRING THE REGIME: PREVENTING THE SPREAD OF WEAPONS OF MASS DESTRUCTION 217, 217–19 (Joseph Cirincione ed., 2000).

[70] Michael Moodie, *The Soviet Union, Russia, and the Biological and Toxin Weapons Convention*, NONPROLIFERATION REV., Spring 2001, at 59, 60–61.

[71] States parties held a review conference five years after the BWC's entry into force to assure its provisions were being "realized." BWC, *supra* note 1, Art. XII. The first review conference was held in Geneva on March 3–21, 1980, and subsequent review conferences have since been held every five years.

nature of recent advances in biotechnology, and the absence of effective BWC verification mechanisms led to the adoption of several voluntary confidence-building measures (CBMs) that called for the exchange of information about research centers and laboratories with high-containment facilities and data on unusual outbreaks of disease.[72] Amid continuing allegations of noncompliance, the third review conference in 1991 established a second set of CBMs, calling on states to provide information voluntarily on past offensive BW programs, vaccine production facilities, and relevant BW legislation, regulations, and other measures.[73] The "Ad Hoc Group of Governmental Experts" (referred to as "VEREX") was also established to identify and examine potential verification measures from a scientific and technical standpoint.[74] The need for such measures, as well as the shortcomings of the voluntary CBM process, was dramatically exposed a few months later, in early 1992, when Russian president Boris Yeltsin made a series of startling admissions about Soviet violations of the BWC.[75]

By 1994 it was generally acknowledged that voluntary CBMs were a failure,[76] prompting a Special Conference of States Parties to establish the "Ad Hoc Group of States Parties" (Ad Hoc Group) to negotiate a more effective and legally binding verification regime for the BWC.[77] The weakness of the existing BWC regime was made more apparent in the summer of 1995 when Iraq acknowledged that it had maintained an offensive BW program from 1975 until January 1991, even though it had previously claimed that it did not possess any biological weapons.[78] Amid rising concerns about the BWC's ineffectiveness and Iraqi defiance of new UN inspections, the fourth review conference met in late 1996 and discussed the work of the Ad Hoc Group. After four and a half more years of negotiations, a "composite text" of a BWC draft protocol containing compromise language for outstanding bracketed issues was submitted by the chairman of the Ad Hoc Group and considered in April 2001.[79]

---

[72] Second Review Conference of the Parties to the BWC, Final Document: Part II, Final Declaration, Doc. BWC/CONF.II/13/II (1986), *available at* BWC Web site, *supra* note 7. These voluntary exchanges were conducted as a "consultation" activity under Article V.

[73] Third Review Conference of the Parties to the BWC, Final Document: Part II, Final Declaration, Annex, Doc. BWC/CONF.III/23 (Part II Annex) (1991), *available at* BWC Web site, *supra* note 7.

[74] *Id.*, Final Declaration, Doc. BWC/CONF.III/23 (Part II), Art. V. In September 1993, VEREX issued a report concluding that a combination of twenty-one verification and assurance measures (including information monitoring, data exchange, remote sensing, inspections, and continuous monitoring) could help strengthen the BWC through increased transparency. *See* Ad Hoc Group of Governmental Experts to Identify and Examine Potential Verification Measures from a Scientific and Technical Standpoint: Summary Report, Doc. BWC/CONF.III/VEREX/8, at 7–8 (1993), *available at* BWC Web site, *supra* note 7.

[75] Graham S. Pearson, *The Essentials of Biological Threat Assessment, in* BIOLOGICAL WARFARE 55, 75–78 (Raymond A. Zilinskas ed., 2000).

[76] *See* Jonathan B. Tucker, *The BWC New Process: A Preliminary Assessment*, NONPROLIFERATION REV., Spring 2004, at 26, 28, *available at* <http://cns.miis.edu/pubs/npr/vol11/111/111tucker.pdf> (noting that since the first CBMs were developed in 1986, "only a small minority of member states have submitted the CBM declarations on a consistent basis").

[77] For a review of the Ad Hoc Group's unsuccessful attempt to develop a BWC verification protocol and an examination of its different components, see JEZ LITTLEWOOD, THE BIOLOGICAL WEAPONS CONVENTION: A FAILED REVOLUTION (2005).

[78] Richard Butler, *Inspecting Iraq, in* REPAIRING THE REGIME, *supra* note 69, at 175, 175–78. Iraq signed the BWC on May 11, 1972, and finally ratified it on June 19, 1991, after being directed to do so by the UN Security Council. SC Res. 687, paras. 8–10 (Apr. 3, 1991).

[79] Protocol to the BWC, Doc. BWC/AD HOC GROUP/CRP.8 (draft, Apr. 3, 2001), *available at* BWC Web site, *supra* note 7. The proposed legally binding text included provisions requiring states to make declarations regarding their biodefense programs and relevant facilities, to submit to routine site visits and challenge-type investigations of suspect facilities, and to permit investigations of suspicious outbreaks of infectious disease.

284   THE AMERICAN JOURNAL OF INTERNATIONAL LAW   [Vol. 101:271

On July 25, 2001, the U.S. ambassador to the twenty-fourth session of the Ad Hoc Group stunned delegates by unexpectedly rejecting the composite text of the draft protocol, arguing that it "would put national security and confidential business information at risk" and that it would "do little to deter those countries seeking to develop biological weapons."[80] Other than noting general national security risks and the proprietary concerns of the U.S. pharmaceutical industry, the United States offered no specific reasons for its actions, leading domestic and international observers to complain that the decision had been heavily influenced by the drug companies.[81] The U.S. criticism of the draft protocol's ineffectiveness was all the more unexpected in view of the many changes that had previously been made in the text based on American objections.[82] When the fifth review conference convened on November 19, 2001, the United States sought to terminate the Ad Hoc Group's discussion of legally binding multilateral measures altogether. Rejecting the draft protocol as a "flawed text" that would neither detect nor deter proliferators, the U.S. representative also named specific states that he said were not complying with the BWC obligations.[83] With the draft protocol effectively dead, the fifth review conference was hastily adjourned and any further discussion of similar multilateral initiatives was suspended.[84]

Unsuccessful BWC reform efforts thus have been accompanied by allegations of extensive noncompliance, underscoring the regime's failings while exacerbating perceived threats that can contribute to further defections. In the absence of both effective transparency measures and determinate rules to define illicit activity, governments and nonproliferation experts remain in substantial disagreement over which states to accuse of misconduct or to include on lists of states possessing or pursuing BW programs.[85] Although the U.S. government has obviously not included itself on any list of states of BW concern, many nonproliferation experts

---

[80] Ambassador Donald Mahley, Statement to the Ad Hoc Group of Biological Weapons Convention States Parties (July 25, 2001), *at* <http://www.state.gov/t/ac/rls/rm/2001/5497.htm>.

[81] *See, e.g.*, Editorial, *Germ-Warfare Abdication*, BOSTON GLOBE, Nov. 16, 2002, at A18 (arguing that both the Clinton and Bush administrations "bought the dubious argument of representatives of the pharmaceutical industry that an aggressive system of international inspections might result in the disclosure of trade secrets"); Rachel Giese, *Fear and Secrecy Along 49th Parallel*, TORONTO STAR, Dec. 6, 2001, at A35.

[82] Michael Crowley, Letter to the Editor, *Iraq's Weapons*, INDEPENDENT (London), Dec. 5, 2001, at 2 (senior analyst, British American Security Information Council, noting that "the US consistently watered down suggestions for intrusive investigations due to concerns over national security and the protection of its pharmaceutical industry. It then rejected and effectively destroyed the whole protocol process on grounds that it would 'not improve our ability to verify compliance'.").

[83] John R. Bolton, Remarks to the 5th Biological Weapons Convention RevCon Meeting (Nov. 19, 2001), *available at* <http://www.state.gov/t/us/rm/janjuly/6231.htm>. The states that the United States accused of pursuing prohibited BW programs were Iran, Iraq, Libya, North Korea, Sudan, and Syria. The United States has continued to make such allegations against several of these countries, most recently at the sixth review conference in 2006.

[84] *See* Fifth Review Conference of the States Parties to the BWC, Final Document, Doc. BWC/CONF.V/17 (2002), *available at* BWC Web site, *supra* note 7. States parties have since been engaged in brief meetings designed to "discuss, and promote common understanding and effective action" on voluntary measures. *Id.*, para. 18(a). Delegates to the sixth review conference in 2006 continued to avoid discussing any initiatives similar to the draft protocol and agreed on little beyond the need for continuing to talk. *See* Peter Crail, The Sixth Review Conference of the Biological Weapons Convention: Success or Failure? [interview of Jonathan B. Tucker] (Jan. 4, 2007), *at* <http://cns.miis.edu/pubs/week/070104.htm> (observing that the fact that the conference was hailed as a success "suggests how dysfunctional the biological arms control process has become").

[85] With a lack of determinate rules and no monitoring mechanisms to confirm suspicions, there is predictable disagreement among experts about which states are states of BW concern. Various research institutes and nonproliferation experts list approximately a dozen states that, to varying degrees, could be considered of BW concern, with a higher level of consensus on the following nine countries: China, Egypt, India, Iran, Israel, North Korea, Russia, Syria, and, with growing reservations, Cuba. *See* JOSEPH CIRINCIONE ET AL.,

disagree and contend that the United States is itself contributing to an insecure BW environment by conducting research in expansive "biodefense" programs that appears to violate the BWC.[86]

III. INDETERMINATE ARMS CONTROL REGIMES AND DEFENSIVE DEFECTORS

Indeterminacy in Multilateral Disarmament Regimes and Acute Security Dilemmas

Security cooperation and state preferences. Given the dangers posed by surprise defections, states might be expected to pursue arms control activities with their rivals by establishing highly institutionalized hard law regimes that contain explicit definitions of cheating and specify elaborate verification and monitoring procedures.[87] Contrary to these expectations, however, some scholars argue that states use a wide variety of forms of soft law in the area of arms control[88] and that soft law may serve just as well as hard law for various types of arms control regimes or even offer distinct advantages.[89] States may in fact be tempted to choose different dimensions of soft law as design elements for multilateral disarmament regimes for many of the same reasons they choose them in other areas of cooperation, perceiving these soft options as an easier way to promote maximum participation in such regimes while better addressing potential advances in technology or other uncertainties.

Although multilateral disarmament and bilateral arms control regimes share many common characteristics, the latter are usually associated with agreements between the United States and the Soviet Union that were based on nuclear parity, benefited from a variety of bilateral dynamics across many different fields of cooperation, and could rely on carefully scripted reciprocal behavior between the two parties that is hard to replicate in complicated multilateral relationships. Multilateral disarmament agreements present many similar security problems but must address more complex compliance issues and involve more complicated game theory models.[90]

DEADLY ARSENALS: TRACKING WEAPONS OF MASS DESTRUCTION 68 (2d ed. 2005); Arms Control Association, Chemical and Biological Weapons Proliferation at a Glance (2002), *at* <http://www.armscontrol. org/factsheets/>; Federation of American Scientists, States Possessing, Pursuing or Capable of Acquiring Weapons of Mass Destruction (2000), *at* <http://www.fas.org/irp/threat/wmd_state.htm>; Center for Nonproliferation Studies, Chemical and Biological Weapons: Possession and Programs Past and Present (2002), *at* <http://cns.miis.edu/research/cbw/>; Henry L. Stimson Center, Biological Weapons Proliferation Concerns (2007), *at* <http://www.stimson.org/cbw/?sn=CB2001121274>.

[86] *See, e.g.,* Seth Brugger, Briefing Paper on the Status of Biological Weapons Nonproliferation (Arms Control Association, Sept. 2002, updated by Kerry Boyd, May 2003), *available at* <http://www.armscontrol.org/pdf/bwissuebrief.pdf>; *see also* Milton Leitenberg et al., *Biodefense Crossing the Line*, 22 POL. & LIFE SCI. 1, 1–2 (2004).

[87] *See* STEIN, *supra* note 10, at 97, 40; Guido den Dekker, *The Effectiveness of International Supervision in Arms Control*, 9 J. CONFLICT & SECURITY 315 (2004).

[88] *See* Chayes & Shelton, *supra* note 30, at 523–24 (arguing that "some of the most elaborate 'soft' international law" is in the area of arms control).

[89] *See supra* notes 29 and 30.

[90] Williamson, *supra* note 29, at 64 (suggesting that "[t]he role of law in fostering compliance may be quite different in bilateral arms control than in multilateral arms control"). Game theory suggests that in contrast to two-player scenarios, multistate Prisoners' Dilemma may be more difficult for participants to overcome. Further complications are created by increased monitoring costs and the likelihood of increased "undetected or unredressed free-riding." JACK L. GOLDSMITH & ERIC A. POSNER, THE LIMITS OF INTERNATIONAL LAW 36 (2006).

In spite of the many proponents and purported advantages of soft law in other contexts, its indeterminate dimension appears to be a dangerous choice for a design element in multilateral disarmament regimes, particularly when member states face acute security dilemmas and effective transparency measures are not available. The classic security dilemma, in which efforts by states to improve their own security lead other states to feel threatened, is heightened when dual-use technology problems further obscure states' intentions and make it more difficult to distinguish between defensive and offensive postures, the more so if offensive capabilities may involve a devastating new military advantage.[91] While transparency measures designed to detect and discourage cheating may assist a regime operating in such an environment, an even more unstable environment for cooperation may be created by combining this lack of transparency with reliance on indeterminate language. The impact of indeterminacy on egoist state actors in these circumstances varies in accordance with the preferences underlying the strategies of states participating in the regime.

A state's preferences for compliance with obligations under a security regime or for noncompliance—referred to as "defection" from cooperation in game theory parlance—are often difficult to discern and defy rigorous scientific analysis. On the one hand, states are likely to have some identifiable self-interested security objectives that inform their preferences and underlie related weapons strategies. On the other hand, rationality does not necessarily provide a clear and unambiguous guide to their behavior, since states may make different rational assessments of their interests and of other states' actions.[92] It is this "conflict of rationalities" that has made the Prisoners' Dilemma such a popular game theory for modeling international relations problems when states are uncertain about the actions of other state actors and must choose between cooperation and defection, particularly in the context of security regimes.[93]

Since the preferences of individual egoist state actors are based on their own imperfect assessments of their interests and of other states' behavior, three broad groups of state actors that reflect the sometimes overlapping preferences underlying weapons strategies constitute a useful lens for evaluating the impact of indeterminacy and lack of transparency on multilateral disarmament regimes. These three groups, defensive defectors, offensive defectors, and compliant or conformist states, are further divided into several subgroups for purposes of analysis.

The problem of defensive defection. Arms control agreements are often modeled as Prisoners' Dilemmas in which fear of exploitation contributes to a dominant strategy of cheating by state actors.[94] While the Prisoners' Dilemma is applied to many different types of international situations, certain characteristics of the security context make cooperation in the area of disarmament uniquely problematic and more likely to inspire defensive defections. The inherently relative nature of military power creates intensely competitive conditions in a high-stakes security environment with little room for error.[95] Furthermore, state actors face difficulties in evaluating their own security and in accurately determining what other states are doing, especially

---

[91] *See* Robert Jervis, *Cooperation Under the Security Dilemma*, 30 WORLD POL. 167, 186–206 (1978).

[92] STEIN, *supra* note 10, at 97. Thus, rational arguments may be made by states both for cooperation and for defection in any particular situation. *Id.*

[93] *Id.* While mutual cooperation is a Pareto-superior outcome to mutual defection, a state may also rationally choose to pursue a dominant strategy of defection regardless of other states' actions or it may choose to defect on a defensive basis to ensure that it at least achieves its maximum possible outcome in the context of feared noncooperation. *Id.*

[94] *Id.* at 40.

[95] *See* Robert Jervis, *Security Regimes*, *in* INTERNATIONAL REGIMES, *supra* note 27, at 173, 174.

when offensive and defensive motives are hard to distinguish and often result in similar policies perceived as threatening to other states.[96] This potential for misperceiving the motives of other states and taking actions that inadvertently threaten others can lead to a "spiral model" of international politics: the influence of both perceptual and structural factors on the interaction of security-seeking states makes that security difficult for any of the actors to attain.[97] Facing such a security dilemma, a member of a multilateral disarmament regime may have to contend with strong incentives to stage a successful surprise defection yet must remain on guard against having its own national security interests seriously damaged by another state's possible defection.[98]

Commentators have suggested a variety of techniques and structures to assure the mutuality of states' commitment to regimes and thus help to overcome the Prisoners' Dilemma in different areas of international concern.[99] In the field of arms control, scholars have suggested that fears giving rise to defensive defections may be decreased by a system of "assurance" measures in which states inform potential adversaries about capabilities and facilitate or engage in actions that demonstrate their continuing compliance with the regime's obligations.[100] Any transparency measures designed to provide assurances, however, may be undermined by the substance of those obligations. By using language designed to preserve flexibility and produce a widely accepted multilateral disarmament convention, states may sacrifice determinacy and incur costs that relate to the problem of defensive defections. On a foundational level, indeterminate normative standards in international regimes may be said to entail significant legitimacy costs[101] while obfuscating what is expected of states for them to satisfy the regime's requirements.[102] These qualities enhance neither overall confidence in a regime nor the ability of its members to provide mutual assurances of compliance in highly unstable security conditions, even if supported by strong transparency measures.

In addition to the uncertainty of states about the expectations regarding their compliance with indeterminate provisions, a fundamental related problem is the type of commitment a state signals by proposing an agreement containing such language. Other states that are asked to rely on this type of commitment, particularly in a multilateral security context, are likely to prefer an agreement that does a better job of providing assurances of compliance and demonstrating costs that the proposing state would bear if the agreement were violated. "Credible

---

[96] *Id.*

[97] *See* Robert Jervis, *Realism, Neoliberalism, and Cooperation: Understanding the Debate*, 24 INT'L SECURITY 42, 49 (1999).

[98] Chayes & Shelton, *supra* note 30, at 521.

[99] *See, e.g.*, Jeffrey L. Dunoff & Joel P. Trachtman, *The Law and Economics of Humanitarian Law Violations in Internal Conflict*, 93 AJIL 404 (1999) (suggesting that an agreement providing enhanced individual responsibility for human rights violations in internal conflicts could overcome Prisoners' Dilemmas and help suppress incentives for states to defect when it is accompanied by commitment techniques that provide some assurance that the agreement will be performed, such as universal jurisdiction or some kind of mandatory "extraterritorial" jurisdiction); Laurence R. Helfer, *Exiting Treaties*, 91 VA. L. REV. 1579, 1631–32 (2005) (suggesting that the Prisoners' Dilemma may be overcome in some multilateral agreements by better ensuring iteration or an increased "shadow of the future" by restricting exit opportunities).

[100] Abbott, *supra* note 9, at 4–5.

[101] As Thomas Franck notes, indeterminacy also has costs and these costs are usually "paid in the coin of legitimacy." THOMAS M. FRANCK, THE POWER OF LEGITIMACY AMONG NATIONS 53–54 (1990). Franck further suggests that "[t]he degree of determinacy of a rule directly affects the degree of its perceived legitimacy," and that "the more determinate the standard, the more difficult it is to resist the pull of the rule to compliance and to justify noncompliance." Franck, *supra* note 12, at 716, 714.

[102] FRANCK, *supra* note 101, at 54–55.

commitments" are said to respond to this need and are often modeled in the Prisoners' Dilemma and other theoretic game models involving strategic interaction, and have other applications in contracting theory, business, and government.[103] In interest-based theoretic models, international relations scholars use the term "credible commitment" to explain situations in which a state, after binding itself or otherwise constraining its ability to act, communicates this undertaking to another state to give that state an incentive to change its behavior.[104]

To convey a credible commitment, the commitment a state makes in an international agreement to help induce another state to behave as it otherwise might not have done must be perceived by that other state as both genuine and costly to retract. Some scholars consider a legally binding agreement with the highest degree of formality to be the most convincing way for a state to express a credible commitment, and they view treaties and their related ratification process as the best way for states to signal such intentions.[105] But the psychological effects of indeterminate language impair its ability to communicate such commitments even if packaged in formal legal documents. As modeled in game theory and analyzed in bargaining dynamics, imprecision ultimately undermines the credibility of both threats and promises however they are expressed.[106]

Credible commitments and the overall prospects for successful cooperation by members of disarmament regimes are weakened when key indeterminate provisions make the requirements for compliance difficult to identify, further complicating existing security dilemmas. As shown in iterated versions of theoretic game models, successful cooperation cannot emerge if players are unable to *recognize* defection when it occurs.[107] Recognition problems in theoretic game models often translate into rule changes related to improved transparency or revised payoff structures, but in this situation the same lack of clear definitions that obscures defection also makes such rule changes ineffective.

In addition to the limited ability of various forms of soft law to convey credible commitments, some of its purported advantages may also be illusory in the context of arms control and disarmament agreements. One of the professed benefits of soft law is its ability to adapt to change so that states can first commit themselves to various forms of discourse and procedure

---

[103] *See* THOMAS C. SCHELLING, THE STRATEGY OF CONFLICT 21–52 (1960); OLIVER WILLIAMSON, THE MECHANISMS OF GOVERNANCE 48–49 (1985).

[104] *See, e.g.,* James D. Fearon, *Signaling Foreign Policy Interests: Tying Hands Versus Sinking Costs,* 41 J. CONFLICT RESOL. 68 (1997); Slaughter et al., *supra* note 14, at 386 (noting how Institutionalists focus on credible commitments in international relations theory as one of several mechanisms that can reduce the opportunity for cheating).

[105] *See* Charles Lipson, *Why Are Some International Agreements Informal?* 45 INT'L ORG. 495, 508, 511 (1991) (noting that states use treaties to "signal their intentions with special intensity and gravity," to "underscore the durability and significance of the underlying promises," and as "a conventional way of raising the credibility of promises by staking national reputation on adherence"); *see also* Jack L. Goldsmith & Eric A. Posner, *International Agreements: A Rational Choice Approach,* 44 VA. J. INT'L L. 113, 127 (2003).

[106] JON HOVI, GAMES, THREATS & TREATIES 16 (1998); SCHELLING, *supra* note 103, at 21–52. In terms of psychological mechanisms, experiments have demonstrated that a clear message that seems to make sense will be accepted regardless of its source, while a message with less clear content is more likely to be accepted only if it comes from a respected source. ROBERT JERVIS, PERCEPTION AND MISPERCEPTION IN INTERNATIONAL POLITICS 123 (1976).

[107] *See* ROBERT AXELROD, THE EVOLUTION OF COOPERATION 140 (1984) (suggesting that recognizing defection is an important requirement in promoting cooperation and that the "scope of sustainable cooperation can be expanded by any improvements in the players' ability to recognize each other from the past, and to be confident about the prior actions that have actually been taken").

that may eventually lead to the acceptance of deeper, legally binding rules;[108] but the time continuum required for this successful transition is not at all certain, nor are the consequences of delay in different areas of cooperation. In some cases, it is possible that the losses associated with the increased propensity of states to violate soft law may not overshadow the gains from clearer and more effectively monitored commitments.[109] Over time and in different contexts, however, soft law may prove to be less beneficial. In the case of multilateral disarmament agreements that must regulate dual-use technology, soft design elements selected as short-term compromises will ultimately fail if they cannot address the fears and insecurity that generate strong incentives for defensive defections.

Although various forms of soft law are promoted as superior design elements for regimes as enabling states in the short term to bridge the gaps between technological uncertainties and solutions, in the long term indeterminate soft law may in fact make it harder for states to manage risks associated with advances in technology in complex, legally binding arms control and disarmament regimes. When the scope of technological challenges becomes more certain, the parties to such agreements may be more likely to benefit from determinate provisions that establish a mechanism for managing and sharing risks and can also more readily take advantage of new technological improvements in related monitoring and verification capabilities.[110] Bilateral arms control regimes in particular have demonstrated the importance of determinacy in helping to adapt to new security and technology developments and thus preventing disputes that could lead to defections.[111] Although dynamic changes under multilateral disarmament regimes generally present a more complicated situation,[112] determinacy is a critical requirement for these regimes in successfully adapting to dynamic technological, political, and strategic changes and preventing these changes from inevitably enlarging perceptions of threat.

Defensive quasi-defectors. A variant of defensive defection may arise in multilateral disarmament regimes when key rules are so vague or leave so much to discretion that states, especially the most advanced industrial ones, may engage in activities that could appear to be unlawful but arguably are consistent with their own self-serving interpretations of those rules. With their advanced technology, these defensive "quasi-defectors" can exploit the soft limits of indeterminate restrictions through sophisticated auto-interpretation of a regime's scientific and technical requirements, pursuing advanced research projects with offensive applications under the guise of strictly defensive measures.

---

[108] *See* Abbott & Snidal, *supra* note 17, at 446; Chayes & Shelton, *supra* note 30, at 526.

[109] *See* Raustiala, *supra* note 19, at 611.

[110] *See, e.g.*, AXELROD, *supra* note 107, at 140 (noting that the technical difficulties in monitoring nuclear explosions and distinguishing them from earthquakes under applicable test ban treaties were eventually overcome by advances in technology); Mohamed ElBaradei [IAEA director general], Nuclear Technology in a Changing World: Have We Reached a Turning Point? (Nov. 3, 2005), *at* <http://www.iaea.org/Archive/DgStatements/2005.html> (noting the key role of advanced technology in IAEA efforts to prevent nuclear weapons proliferation, such as the use of advanced nuclear forensic techniques to help to "reconstruct the chronology and nature of past nuclear activity, and to verify the origin of the associated nuclear material").

[111] If the terms of a bilateral arms control agreement are sufficiently determinate, states have shown themselves able to establish procedures to control related technology even if it is currently unknown. *See, e.g.*, Treaty on the Limitation of Anti-ballistic Missile Systems, Agreed Interpretations, Common Understandings and Unilateral Statements, Statement D, May 26, 1972, U.S.-USSR, 23 UST 3435, 3456, 944 UNTS 13 (committing the parties to conduct additional negotiations with a view to establishing appropriate limitations for future antiballistic missile systems if based on technologies utilizing physical principles not present at the time the treaty enters into force).

[112] *See* Edwin M. Smith, *Understanding Dynamic Obligations: Arms Control Agreements*, 64 S. CAL. L. REV. 1549, 1604 (1991).

While a preference for defensive quasi defection by great powers may be motivated in part by the same perceptions and fears that drive other states to pursue BW programs, it may also be inspired by the forces that have inexorably driven powerful industrial states to conclude that, as a matter of security policy, they must develop or acquire the most advanced science and technology with potential military applications.[113] Fearing technological inferiority itself and confronted with an "asymmetric diffusion of military technology" that can give an innovator a significant (if only temporary) advantage, great powers have historically sought the latest that science can offer and the best military technology that their opponents might possess.[114]

In an earlier era when security under bilateral arms control agreements was firmly based on mutual assured nuclear destruction, states sometimes intentionally cultivated uncertainty about their new technological capabilities so as to suggest additional deterrent capabilities. In the modern, post–Cold War environment where states confront security dilemmas under a multilateral disarmament regime with only indeterminate obligations, actions that create uncertainties about technological advances are more likely to inspire defections than deterrence.

Some legal scholars argue that precision itself is advantageous in international agreements, primarily as it relates to review structures and as it is applied by institutions charged with subsequently developing corresponding standards.[115] However, in hard legally binding multilateral disarmament regimes operating in highly unstable security environments, the effect and significance of soft indeterminate provisions appears to extend beyond dependence on review structures to affect the preferences and security policies of states by generally making obligations harder to understand, credible commitments harder to convey, and noncompliance harder to recognize and easier to justify. Furthermore, while imprecision may not alter the formal legal status of a legally binding agreement, it may make it possible for a state to use the legality of the agreement itself to help create false expectations in other parties, thus assisting a noncompliant state in more successfully cheating on its obligations.

Indeterminate language may also considerably affect the behavior of states under legally binding arms control and disarmament agreements by creating loopholes through incomplete regulation. Imprecise or otherwise indeterminate language may effectively leave some weapons systems or related technology unregulated, just as some arms control and disarmament regimes explicitly remove certain weapons systems or technology from their coverage. Since agreements do not eliminate underlying state preferences and rivalries, language that fails to regulate related and strategically attractive weapons systems has historically had the effect of channeling arms races into those unregulated areas rather than ending the arms races themselves.[116]

---

[113] As long as the possibility exists that conflict will be conducted by force, "competition in the arts and the instruments of force" will take place. KENNETH N. WALTZ, THEORY OF INTERNATIONAL POLITICS, ANARCHIC ORDERS AND BALANCES OF POWER 180 (1979) (further suggesting that this competition will produce a tendency toward sameness of competitors and that contending states will imitate the military innovations of the country of greatest capability and ingenuity); *see also* JOHN J. MEARSHEIMER, THE TRAGEDY OF GREAT POWER POLITICS 231–32 (2001).

[114] MEARSHEIMER, *supra* note 113, at 231.

[115] *See, e.g.,* Raustiala, *supra* note 19, at 583 n.10.

[116] *See* STEIN, *supra* note 10, at 133. A frequently cited example is the experience of the Washington Naval Armaments Treaty of 1922 in which the major naval powers of the world agreed to limit the construction of a variety of different types of ships then in existence, resulting immediately in a major arms race in the classes of ships not covered by the agreement. Charles H. Fairbanks et al., *Arms Control to Arms Reductions: The Historical Experience,*

Defensive Defectors and the BWC

Because the highly insecure environment in which offensive and defensive BW activities are difficult to distinguish and misperceptions about dual-use biotechnology can aggravate security dilemmas, states have historically had considerable incentives to develop their own BW programs for defensive or deterrent purposes. The BWC regime, lacking any mandatory transparency measures, also lacks structural mechanisms to provide assurances of compliance to address those incentives, which may lead to a downward spiral of defections. This shortcoming is magnified by key indeterminate terms that make it harder for states to give each other credible commitments of compliance.

Inasmuch as the combination of soft structure and substance has made it difficult to detect and define noncompliance, the existing BWC framework has proved to be a highly ineffective design approach to reducing incentives for defensive defection in spite of its "hard" or legally binding status. These difficulties, in turn, have created an unstable and corrosive atmosphere of allegations and denials that has further diminished confidence in the regime and made it even more difficult for regime members facing acute security dilemmas to provide each other with assurances or credible commitments of compliance. Controversial, vague, and uncorroborated allegations by the United States have been particularly destructive.[117] In the context of a regime already diminished by admitted acts of cheating and the failure of its members to agree on any appropriate reforms, continuing allegations of noncompliance aggravate the fears and misperceptions that have historically generated BW arms races and risk a chain reaction of more defensive defections that would create even more acute security dilemmas.[118] Confidence has been further eroded by the continuing perception that the indeterminate BWC framework is unequal to addressing dynamic technological changes.[119]

The full scope of the problem of defensive defection under the BWC is impossible to establish through rigorous scientific methods. Clearly, however, numerous factors contribute to such defections, including various regional and historical rivalries. More states in the Middle East are widely considered to be of BW concern than in any other region of the world, making conflicts there the most important regional rivalries to involve states with potential BW capabilities.[120] Most of the Middle Eastern states are BWC states parties. Those that are not parties display a tentative or defensive legal posture toward biological weapons, having signed but not

WASH. Q., Summer 1987, at 59 (noting that the Washington Naval Treaty ironically encouraged the extraordinarily rapid emergence of the aircraft carrier).

[117] Unsubstantiated allegations by the U.S. representative at the fifth review conference in 2001 that six specific states were pursuing illegal BW programs were accompanied by vague assertions of other noncompliant states that were not publicly identified. *See* Bolton, *supra* note 83. These U.S. allegations were widely criticized as selective and politically motivated. Richard Wolffe, *US Names Iran as Chief State Sponsor of Terror*, FIN. TIMES (London), May 22, 2002, at 1. U.S. nonproliferation experts would also later claim that BW and other WMD intelligence had been exaggerated to make a case for unilateral American action against countries such as Cuba and Iraq. Steven R. Weisman, *In Stricter Study, U.S. Scales back Claim on Cuba Arms*, N.Y. TIMES, Sept. 18, 2004, at A5; Sonni Efron, *Harsh Critic of U.N. Named Ambassador*, L.A. TIMES, Mar. 8, 2005, at A1.

[118] *See* Richard Falk, *Inhibiting the Reliance on Biological Weaponry: The Role and Relevance of International Law*, *in* PREVENTING A BIOLOGICAL ARMS RACE, *supra* note 49, at 241, 244.

[119] As early as 1986, the BWC Conference of States Parties officially noted "apprehensions" about developments in microbiology, genetic engineering, and biotechnology, but could not agree on any serious reforms to address them. *See* Final Declaration, *supra* note 72, Art. I.

[120] Egypt, Israel, and Syria are widely viewed by nonproliferation experts and many governments as having offensive BW research programs or some level of BW capability. *See supra* note 85.

ratified the BWC, while being obligated to refrain from the first use of biological weapons under the Geneva Protocol.[121]

Although a detailed examination of Middle Eastern security policies is beyond the purview of this article, considerable evidence suggests that a variety of defensive and deterrent motivations may inform the preferences of states there with respect to biological weapons. These factors include the legacy of several conflicts that have involved the use of chemical weapons, another weapon of mass destruction.[122] Even states that commentators frequently associate with purely aggressive, expansionist, or offensive motives and policies, such as Iran[123] and Saddam Hussein's Iraq,[124] may have decided to develop or maintain BW programs at least in part to advance various defensive or deterrent objectives. Rather than being perceived by states as an integral part of strategic or tactical offensive forces or as an effective means to threaten other states, BW capabilities, on closer examination, may be of interest to many states in the region largely on the basis of their perception of a dangerous environment.[125] To whatever extent defensive or deterrent motives underlie preferences that lead states in the Middle East or any other region to violate their BWC obligations, the regime remains inadequate to deal with this problem, as key indeterminate language and a lack of transparency measures impede the provision of assurances to reduce incentives for defensive defection.

Defensive Quasi Defectors and the BWC

As described above, fear of technological developments that could give an innovator a significant advantage appears to have been a major factor contributing to the participation of advanced industrial states in even the earliest BW arms races. The United States further justifies its current development of advanced technology with BW applications by incorporating an

[121] All states in the region are parties to the BWC except Egypt, Israel, Syria, and the United Arab Emirates (UAE); however, Egypt, Israel, and Syria are parties to the Geneva Protocol. *See* SIPRI, *supra* note 36. Egypt and Syria have signed but not yet ratified the BWC. *See* BWC Web site, *supra* note 7. Although Israel is a nonsignatory, it attends BWC review sessions as an observer.

[122] One of these legacies in the Middle East appears to be that WMDs are most likely to be used against states and populations that do not possess them, creating the strategic perception that the best deterrent against such weapons is the ability to launch an in-kind response. Peter Sabin, *Restraints on Chemical, Biological, and Nuclear Use: Some Lessons from History, in* NON-CONVENTIONAL-WEAPONS PROLIFERATION IN THE MIDDLE EAST: TACKLING THE SPREAD OF NUCLEAR, CHEMICAL, AND BIOLOGICAL CAPABILITIES 13, 15 (Efraim Karsh et al. eds., 1993) [hereinafter NON-CONVENTIONAL-WEAPONS PROLIFERATION].

[123] The alleged involvement of Iran in BW and CW programs apparently began as defensive measures in response to the extensive and devastating use of chemical weapons against it during the Iran-Iraq war (1980–1988) and is widely suspected of continuing. *See* Central Intelligence Agency, Unclassified Report to Congress on the Acquisition of Technology Relating to Weapons of Mass Destruction and Advanced Conventional Munitions, 1 January Through 30 June 2001 (2001), *available at* <https://www.cia.gov/cia/reports/archive/reports_2001.html>. Iran's interests in biological weapons thus did not originate in a strategy to use them to threaten other states in the region.

[124] The considerable deterrent value that Iraq perceived with respect to its apparent chemical weapons capabilities was extensively (and ironically) documented by U.S. investigators interviewing former Iraqi officials and reviewing Iraqi government records after the U.S. invasion of Iraq. *See* Transmittal Message, *in* 1 COMPREHENSIVE REPORT OF THE SPECIAL ADVISOR TO THE DCI ON IRAQ'S WMD 1 (2004) [hereinafter CIA COMPREHENSIVE REPORT], *available at* <https://www.cia.gov/cia/reports /iraq_wmd_2004/>. Saddam's view that WMDs had helped to save his regime on multiple occasions helps explain why he "purposely gave an ambiguous impression about possession as a deterrent to Iran," although this approach would have unexpected consequences for his regime in its relations with both the United Nations and the United States. *Id.* at 9.

[125] *See* Susan Wright & Richard Falk, *Rethinking Biological Disarmament, in* BIOLOGICAL WARFARE AND DISARMAMENT, *supra* note 55, at 413, 421.

expansive version of self-defense in aggressive counterproliferation policies. Without determinate criteria, the restrictive phrase "peaceful purposes" does nothing to moderate the incentives powerful states may have to pursue questionable and expansive biodefense programs in pursuit of technological superiority.

Revelations of formerly secret U.S. biodefense projects form an empirical framework for examining the potentially limitless expanse of quasi cheating under the BWC and the related negative effects of indeterminacy in the highly insecure BW environment. After a series of articles appeared in the *New York Times* in September 2001,[126] the U.S. government admitted that it had recently conducted two clandestine projects, and was planning a third, which were designed to simulate offensive BW activities as part of U.S. biodefense efforts.[127] Project Bachus was managed by the Department of Defense and resulted in the construction of a fully functional BW production facility at a Nevada test site.[128] Project Clear Vision was managed by the Central Intelligence Agency and focused on building and testing a biological bomb based on a Soviet design.[129] Project Jefferson was managed by the Defense Intelligence Agency and resulted in plans to develop a modified, vaccine-resistant strain of anthrax modeled after a Russian version.[130]

The biodefense projects revealed in 2001, which were not declared by the United States under applicable confidence-building measures, were widely criticized as either a clear violation of BWC obligations or a dangerous precedent that blurred the distinction between permissible defensive and prohibited offensive activities.[131] In the aftermath of the attacks of September 11, 2001, several projects managed by the Department of Homeland Security and undertaken at the newly established National Biodefense Analysis and Countermeasures Center apparently involved the production of "small amounts" of weaponized microbes (and perhaps genetically engineered pathogens as well) and were also criticized as skirting the edges of BWC obligations.[132] U.S. government officials have defended all U.S. biodefense projects as being "in compliance" with existing treaties.[133] Such claims, however, highlight both the lack of clear rules under the BWC regime and the likelihood that powerful states will continue to use their advanced

---

[126] Judith Miller et al., *U.S. Germ Warfare Research Pushes Treaty Limits*, N.Y. TIMES, Sept. 4, 2001, at A1; Judith Miller, *When Is a Bomb Not a Bomb? Germ Experts Confront U.S.*, N.Y. TIMES, Sept. 5, 2001, at A5 [hereinafter Miller, *Not a Bomb*].

[127] Victoria Clarke, assistant secretary of defense for public affairs, U.S. Department of Defense, Regular Briefing (Sept. 4, 2001), *available in* LEXIS, Federal News Service File.

[128] Judith Miller, *Next to Old Rec Hall, a 'Germ-Making Plant,'* N.Y. TIMES, Sept. 4, 2001, at A6. Project Bachus was designed to assess the difficulties in constructing a BW facility using only commercially available components and to find out whether it emitted "signatures" for identification purposes. *See* MILLER ET AL., *supra* note 55, at 297–99; Miller et al., *supra* note 126.

[129] MILLER ET AL., *supra* note 55, at 290–96; Miller et al., *supra* note 126.

[130] MILLER ET AL., *supra* note 55, at 308–12; Vernon Loeb, *U.S. Seeks Duplicate of Russian Anthrax; Microbe to Be Used to Check Vaccine*, WASH. POST, Sept. 5, 2001, at A16.

[131] *See* Miller, *Not a Bomb*, *supra* note 126 (quoting a former U.S. arms control official as saying that other countries would call it "a dangerous violation of the treaty," and that "it surely appears to be a violation of the treaty in terms of common interpretation"); *see also* Seth Brugger, *International Reaction to Secret U.S. Bio-weapons Research Muted*, 31 ARMS CONTROL TODAY, Oct. 2001, at 22, 22 (quoting a European official as saying that the projects made "gray areas grayer still" when attempting to distinguish offensive from defensive activities under the BWC); Oliver Meier, *On the Wrong Side of the Line?* BULL. ATOM. SCI., Nov./Dec. 2001, at 19, 21.

[132] Joby Warrick, *The Secretive Fight Against Bioterror*, WASH. POST, July 30, 2006, at A1 (quoting one arms control expert as saying that "[i]f we saw others doing this kind of research, we would view it as an infringement of the bioweapons treaty").

[133] Loeb, *supra* note 130.

industrial capabilities to engage in quasi cheating to address perceived security threats or preemptively seek technological superiority. Even if a multilateral monitoring regime were present, the failure of the BWC clearly to define what is prohibited and what is "peaceful" leaves uncertain the status of many sophisticated biodefense research programs, underscoring the importance of combining determinate provisions and transparency measures to correct the regime's deficiencies.

The quest for technological BW superiority by powerful states that in turn leads to a quest for technological dominance can, if unchecked, also manifest itself in a search for new pathogens that "express traits that would render existing defenses useless."[134] Apparent U.S. efforts to develop "defenses" under the BWC not only against *known* pathogens but also against imagined or futuristic ones, as evidenced by work performed on a genetically modified form of vaccine-resistant anthrax, are a case in point.[135] The lack of evidence that any terrorist organization has the resources to develop genetically engineered bioweapons[136] has led some commentators to suggest that U.S. efforts to develop such weapons in "biodefense programs" stem from other than purely defensive preferences. In addition to creating or aggravating perceived security threats, novel pathogens that owe their existence to the failure of indeterminate language in the BWC may also undermine overall BW nonproliferation efforts by advancing societal acceptance of the idea that the generation of new biological weapons is a normal and appropriate activity.[137]

The problem of incomplete regulation manifests itself in the BWC through the indeterminate phrase "peaceful purposes." Like other limited disarmament agreements that have inspired arms races in key areas that were not regulated, the BWC contains loopholes spawned by indeterminate language that can encourage the most powerful states to use their advanced technology to develop new biological weapons purportedly within those unregulated areas. By dangerously blurring distinctions between offensive and defensive designs and creating new and greater perceived BW threats for other states, these quasi defections further exacerbate the security dilemmas under the BWC.

Hard Solutions for the BWC: Applying Determinacy to Defensive Defectors

As seen above, although some scholars suggest that a hard legally binding agreement with the highest degree of formality is the most convincing way for states to signal a credible commitment,[138] the formality of the treaty process actually allowed the Soviets to misrepresent the importance and durability of their commitment, illustrating the dangers of relying on hard legally binding agreements with soft substance and structure.[139] While arms control theory posits that hard structures may also offer solutions to the problem of defensive defections, history suggests that even if mandatory transparency measures had been present, they would have

[134] Susan Wright, *Taking Biodefense Too Far*, BULL. ATOM. SCI., Nov./Dec. 2004, at 58, 63.

[135] *Id.* at 63–64.

[136] Leitenberg et al., *supra* note 86, at 3.

[137] Wright, *supra* note 134, at 65.

[138] *See* Goldsmith & Posner, *supra* note 105, at 124–25; *see also* Chayes & Shelton, *supra* note 30, at 526–27 (arguing that some evidence in arms control cases suggests that legally binding norms create their own compliance pull and that "a norm in a treaty may induce more conforming state behavior than one that is purely non-binding").

[139] Lipson, *supra* note 105, at 511 (noting that while treaty commitments can be used to deceive unwary states and create false presumptions of compliance, "[i]nformal agreements are less susceptible to these dangers. They raise expectations less than treaties and so are less likely to dupe the naive.").

been undermined by the indeterminate standards in the BWC that make noncompliance difficult to recognize.[140]

If legally binding agreements and hard structures are insufficient, states may use hard, determinate legal commitments themselves as instruments for providing assurances, particularly in arms control regimes where the potential for damaging defections is high. To the extent that the legally binding nature of commitments may be used as an "*ex ante* sorting device" that helps a state to identify itself as a party that is less likely to defect, determinate provisions in such a commitment will probably make that device more credible and effective.[141] Closely related to the role they can play as signaling and sorting devices, determinate provisions may provide further assurances through their expected impact on states that are tempted to defect in highly insecure environments. In this sense, determinate rules that clearly convey normative content can improve confidence in a regime and reduce overall incentives for defection by encouraging "gratification deferral."[142] If states in highly unstable security situations fear that their adversaries will be tempted to take advantage of opportunities to defect from cooperation under a disarmament regime, parties are likely to choose to comply with the rules and forgo the gratification of defection only if they have a longer-term interest in seeing a potentially beneficial rule reinforced.[143] States can be expected to defer the attainable short-term gains of defection only if the regime's rules are sufficiently determinate to allow those states to foresee future situations in which the rules will operate to their advantage and benefits will be derived from strengthening and complying with the rules in the present.[144]

Another potential advantage of determinacy in combating defensive defections in an unstable security environment is its greater ability in some cases to deal with dynamic changes. In 1972 the flexibility of imprecise language was perceived by the drafting states (particularly the United States and the United Kingdom) as a mechanism for dealing with a variety of risks and technological uncertainties. The potential character and scope of advances in biotechnology and genetic engineering are now much better known, as is the nature of the once-imagined BW threat. In addition, these advances not only create potential incentives for states to pursue BW programs, but also offer the possibility of new restraints on their development through improved monitoring technology and verification methods.[145]

---

[140] This problem was demonstrated by the contentious efforts of the British, Americans, and Russians to inspect each others' BW facilities in the early 1990s without the benefit of agreed BWC benchmarks. *See infra* notes 181–83 and corresponding text.

[141] Lipson, *supra* note 105, at 508 (noting that states desiring to signal a binding commitment use formal agreements to raise the political costs of noncompliance and that these costs "are highest when the agreement contains specific written promises"); *see also* Raustiala, *supra* note 19, at 582 (noting how trade-offs between *ex ante* credibility and *ex post* flexibility are central to functionalist analysis).

[142] *See* Franck, *supra* note 12, at 721 (noting that rules that lend themselves to broad interpretations, even for humane or rational reasons, are "unlikely to inhibit any state from pursuing every opportunity for short-term interest gratification"); Claire R. Kelly, *The Value Vacuum: Self-Enforcing Regimes and the Dilution of the Normative Feedback Loop*, 22 MICH. J. INT'L L. 673, 706 (2001).

[143] Franck, *supra* note 12, at 716.

[144] *Id.*

[145] Malcolm R. Dando, *New Developments in Biotechnology and Their Impact on Biological Warfare, in* ENHANCING THE BIOLOGICAL WEAPONS CONVENTION 21 (Oliver Thränert ed., 1996) [hereinafter ENHANCING THE BWC].

296   THE AMERICAN JOURNAL OF INTERNATIONAL LAW   [Vol. 101:271

The experience of bilateral arms control agreements demonstrates that the parties must be able to address themselves to a number of "dynamic obligations" and must be prepared to monitor and adapt to changes in both the strategic and the technological contexts.[146] Many of these agreements involve highly determinate attempts to regulate weapons systems, together with elaborate and intrusive inspection procedures that are structured to provide an adequate basis for responding to such changes and minimizing the associated risks. A bilateral arms control or multilateral disarmament regime that does not regulate clearly defined weapons, facilities, and related materials can neither effectively transmit information to its members about mutual compliance with obligations nor effectively communicate important political, technological, or strategic changes related to those weapons in member states. Such changes may be particularly relevant in the BW context.

The ability of hard law to provide a basis for positively responding to dynamic changes may be especially important in the Middle East where, as previously noted, there appear to be incentives for defensive defection from the BWC. Determinacy, together with legally binding transparency measures, might assist both in providing better assurances of compliance to states and reducing incentives for defection, and in promoting deeper cooperation by taking advantage of new political, technological, or strategic developments that relate to diminished or reevaluated interest in biological weapons in the region.

Several recent developments, including the confirmed elimination of all weapons of mass destruction in Iraq[147] and the apparent abandonment of all WMD programs in Libya, may now provide an impetus for states in the Middle East to reappraise the utility of BW programs and the desirability of joining legal regimes to prohibit them. Many of the same factors that have historically limited the effectiveness of biological weapons elsewhere have an even larger presence in the Middle East, making BW unlikely weapons of choice there, thus potentially the subject of greater and more willing regulation by states.[148] Some commentators have observed that BW programs may be less attractive to many states in the region than has been assumed.[149] Moreover, as Egypt and Israel appear to be taking renewed, if only tentative, steps in the direction of increased cooperation regarding the BWC,[150] determinacy and transparency

---

[146] Smith, *supra* note 112, at 1582. As regards regulation of future technologies, see *supra* note 111.

[147] With its demonstrated ballistic missile technology, proclivity for CW use, and previously declared BW arsenal, Saddam Hussein's Iraq constituted a particularly difficult strategic predicament for states in the region, especially for Israel. Avner Cohen, *Israel: Reconstructing the Black Box, in* BIOLOGICAL WARFARE AND DISARMAMENT, *supra* note 55, at 181, 192–95.

[148] *Id.* at 190 (noting that Israeli military strategists reportedly concluded that biological weapons could not be relied on for strategic deterrence or as an effective strategic or tactical military weapon, especially since most wars in the Middle East have been decisively terminated in a matter of days and leave no military use for "such uncertain weapons with a long incubation time"). The proximity of interdependent populations in a relatively small space has led others to argue that the use of WMDs such as biological weapons in the Middle East would be "highly irrational." Yezid Sayigh, *Middle Eastern Stability and the Proliferation of Weapons of Mass Destruction, in* NON-CONVENTIONAL-WEAPONS PROLIFERATION, *supra* note 122, at 179, 180.

[149] *See* Jonathan B. Tucker, *Motivations for and Against Proliferation: The Case of the Middle East, in* BIOLOGICAL WARFARE, *supra* note 75, at 27, 33–35 (noting the uncertain military utility of biological weapons, the significant difficulties in delivering and preserving them in adverse meteorological conditions, and their very limited deterrent value compared to other WMDs and even conventional weapons). Experts note that Israel in particular, because of its nuclear weapons capability, now has little strategic reason to maintain BW capabilities or a posture of "CBW ambiguity." Cohen, *supra* note 147, at 202.

[150] Despite Egypt's status as only a BWC signatory state and Israel's status as a nonsignatory observer, both countries participated in the fifth and sixth review conferences and Egypt actively participated in the work of the Ad Hoc

appear to be critical and timely tools for making the BWC framework better able to provide assurances, reduce incentives for defection, and positively reflect dynamic changes in the security environment. In the absence of such reforms, voluntary, self-reporting CBMs such as those now attached to the BWC do little to enhance cooperation and may instead be used or perceived as a source of disinformation that can worsen suspicions and give rise to more defensive defections.[151]

Hard Solutions for the BWC: Applying Determinacy to Defensive Quasi Defectors

While quasi defections are less likely to occur if transparency and determinacy are incorporated into the BWC regime, a powerful state may be deterred from adopting a hard law approach for any multilateral disarmament regime by various trade-offs that include forgoing perceived national security benefits derived from the continued exploitation of indeterminate language and structural deficiencies in transparency. At the same time, determinate rules and mandatory transparency provisions will probably not be adopted and succeed in the BWC without the support of the great powers, which is likely to be based on a calculated judgment that multilateral regulation is superior to individualistic behavior.[152] Such a judgment may involve various factors but will doubtless depend on a self-interested evaluation by each state of its national security interests. To forgo individualistic security measures, states such as the United States must perceive such measures as more costly than the burdens imposed by determinate hard law, increased multilateral regulation, and the resulting sovereignty costs. Hard law often incurs sovereignty costs by fundamentally encroaching on a state's exclusive control over matters such as national security.[153] Furthermore, even a limited delegation of authority, such as of certain responsibilities to an outside monitoring organization, may entail additional or unanticipated sovereignty costs.[154] These costs will probably be important factors in evaluating the trade-offs inherent in choices along a continuum of options that include various dimensions of what can be described as hard and soft law.[155]

While a political Realist might suggest that the U.S. rejection of the BWC draft protocol resulted inevitably from the prevalence of national interests over those of a multilateral regime, powerful states may nonetheless join such a regime and embrace determinate, hard law commitments if they decide to seek long-term security benefits over maximizing short-term or myopic interests.[156] The United States is one of many states that support the principles and objectives of the BWC; it begins its evaluation of the long-term benefits with strong incentives

Group. Three signatories in the region, Egypt, Syria, and the UAE, were also invited to participate in the preparatory work for the sixth review conference.

[151] *See* Laura Drake, *The Middle East: Integrated Regional Approaches to Arms Control and Disarmament, in* BIOLOGICAL WARFARE AND DISARMAMENT, *supra* note 55, at 151, 166–67.

[152] Jervis, *supra* note 95, at 176.

[153] *See* Abbott & Snidal, *supra* note 17, at 438 ("Even the most powerful states recognize that legalization will circumscribe their autonomy.").

[154] *Id.*

[155] General, but unexplained, concerns about such costs were expressed by the United States in rejecting the final composite text of the BWC draft protocol in 2001. *See* John R. Bolton, The U.S. Position on the Biological Weapons Convention: Combating the BW Threat (Aug. 26, 2002), *at* <http://www.state.gov/t/us/rm/13090.htm> (saying that the draft protocol "would have compromised national security").

[156] Noting that Realists such as Hans J. Morgenthau have observed that "the national interest wins out over the international objective" in many areas, Robert Keohane suggests that such views ignore the possibility that states may nonetheless choose international cooperation by defining their interests more broadly and by eschewing immediate or "myopic" interests. ROBERT O. KEOHANE, AFTER HEGEMONY 99 (1994).

298   THE AMERICAN JOURNAL OF INTERNATIONAL LAW   [Vol. 101:271]

to make the BWC regime more effective and to discourage BW proliferation, even at the expense of some immediate interests.[157] Further, the United States originally led efforts to strengthen the BWC and has accepted hard law commitments and subjected itself to intrusive inspection and monitoring measures under other arms control and disarmament agreements like the Chemical Weapons Convention (CWC).[158] Notwithstanding the advancement of many worthy goals, this apparent self-abnegation is likely to have been based on a rational and studied pursuit by the United States of its own security interests. Such efforts also involved a view of long-term interests that does not appear to have been dominated by any one American business interest, unlike the influence apparently exercised by the U.S. pharmaceutical industry with respect to BWC reform initiatives.

In contrast to the national security benefits that may flow from determinacy and transparency, powerful states may incur national security costs in choosing to continue the individualistic pursuit of expansive biodefense programs under the indeterminate provisions of the BWC. For example, biodefense programs may themselves present troubling limitations and risks relevant to calculating the costs of national security trade-offs. While these programs are strongly supported by the U.S. government, many BW experts argue that it is virtually impossible to protect an entire civilian population from a surprise biological attack and note that this problem contributed to the original decision by the United States to renounce its BW programs in 1969.[159] Vaccination programs are problematic since they are unlikely to be able to develop and administer effective vaccines to protect a civilian population against a variety of specific *unknown* biological agents.[160] On the other hand, vaccines are essential for personnel working on *offensive* BW programs and may be viewed as particularly suspect by other countries when they are developed by military organizations.[161] Countermeasures against those vaccines can also lead to qualitative BW proliferation, as states attempt to circumvent the protection provided by other states' immunization programs.[162] Even if states believe they are taking legitimate defensive actions, without agreed-upon determinate rules and transparency measures, extensive biodefense programs such as those pursued in new U.S. secret research centers may

---

[157] *Id.* at 107.

[158] Convention on the Prohibition of the Development, Production, Stockpiling, and Use of Chemical Weapons and on Their Destruction, Jan. 13, 1993, S. TREATY DOC. NO. 103-21 (1993), 32 ILM 800 (1993) [hereinafter CWC].

[159] *See* Laura Reed & Seth Shulman, *A Perilous Path to Security? Weighing U.S. "Biodefense" Against Qualitative Proliferation, in* BIOLOGICAL WARFARE AND DISARMAMENT, *supra* note 55, at 57, 59. The unpredictable nature of the threat and the related inability of civil biodefense to prevent outbreaks from spreading out of control were important factors in the U.S. decision to renounce BW programs in 1969 and have continued to inform U.S. BW policy since that time. *Id.* at 59–60.

[160] *Id.* at 72 ("[I]t has been frequently pointed out that vaccines are useful only in the face of positive intelligence with respect to the nature of the hostile agent; similarly, treatment with drugs such as antibiotics is useful only for bacteria and only after the isolation and testing of the organism.").

[161] *See* Victor W. Sidel, *Defense Against Biological Weapons: Can Immunization and Secondary Prevention Succeed? in* BIOLOGICAL WARFARE AND DISARMAMENT, *supra* note 55, at 77, 81 (noting that other nations may negatively view the intense interest shown by U.S. military researchers in vaccines intended to counter specific and rare organisms that are unlikely to cause public health problems unless intentionally spread); Richard Novick & Seth Shulman, *New Forms of Biological Warfare? in* PREVENTING A BIOLOGICAL ARMS RACE, *supra* note 49, at 103, 112 (noting that since vaccines are more useful against agents contemplated for use as offensive weapons, their possession inevitably serves to "unbalance the international biological warfare situation"); *see also* Jonathan King & Harlee Strauss, *The Hazards of Defensive Biological Warfare Programs, in id.* at 121.

[162] Reed & Shulman, *supra* note 159, at 68; *see also* Sidel, *supra* note 161, at 81 (noting that such circumvention appears to have motivated the Russians' search for a new strain of anthrax).

easily raise suspicions in other countries that will exacerbate already dangerous security dilemmas.[163] These concerns, together with fears about the safety and security of biodefense programs, have led some scientists to conclude that a more effective defense against these weapons may be improving the overall effectiveness of public health programs in the United States.[164]

A final national security trade-off that may be implicated by a powerful state's rejection of hard law to exploit the indeterminacy of the BWC is the inadvertent role of expansive biodefense programs in helping terrorist groups to acquire biological weapons. This threat appears to merit significant consideration in current U.S. national security calculations in light of the likely involvement of advanced, state-run biodefense labs in the 2001 anthrax letter attacks. Effective biological weapons capable of causing catastrophic casualties remain difficult to produce and deploy, and terrorist groups probably cannot launch such attacks *on their own.*[165] Accidents at U.S. biodefense facilities may pose another threat to public health and national security, as evidenced by recent incidents involving the reappearance of relatively rare infectious diseases in America linked to state-run BW research facilities and state-funded BW research projects.[166]

IV. INDETERMINATE ARMS CONTROL REGIMES AND OFFENSIVE DEFECTORS

Indeterminate Rules, Cheaters, and Rogues

One much-analyzed preference, modeled in game theory, that is displayed by some states is to defect offensively from regime cooperation, that is, to cheat secretly and thus secure an advantage over other states that remain bound by the obligations of that regime. Indeterminate provisions that leave the rules of cooperation uncertain and make it easier to evade obligations are tempting devices for states to use in pursuing strategies based on

---

[163] *See* Warrick, *supra* note 132 (noting that critics of the NBACC fear that "its work fuels suspicions that could lead other countries to pursue secret biological research"). Such suspicions are increased by the close ties of the National Biodefense Analysis and Countermeasures Center to the U.S. intelligence community and the assignment of special CIA advisers to the lab. *Id.* While national security officials may be quick to draw inferences about aggressive behavior from the military posture of adversary states, they are often not inclined to apply this reasoning to their own behavior, incorrectly assuming that other states are aware of their peaceful intentions and see no threat or menace in their actions. JERVIS, *supra* note 106, at 68.

[164] Choffnes, *supra* note 4, at 29 (arguing that expanding U.S. biodefense activities risks training and equipping would-be bioterrorists).

[165] *Id.* (noting that "[t]errorists who want to mount a major attack with bioweapons would need substantial help from state sponsors to do so"); Malcolm Dando, *The Bioterrorist Cookbook*, BULL. ATOM. SCI., Nov./Dec. 2005, at 34, 36 (describing "barriers to entry" as potentially quite high for terrorists seeking to develop "weapons on a destructive scale comparable to those developed by states for military use"); DANA A. SHEA & FRANK GOTTRON, SMALL-SCALE TERRORIST ATTACKS USING CHEMICAL AND BIOLOGICAL AGENTS: AN ASSESSMENT FRAMEWORK AND PRELIMINARY COMPARISONS, at CRS–11 (Congressional Research Service, 2004), *available at* <http://fpc.state.gov/documents/organization/33629.pdf> (noting that some experts suggest that "development of weaponized biological agents presents remarkably high hurdles, particularly in mass dissemination, which would require teams of scientists with state backing to overcome").

[166] For example, the disease glanders had not been reported in English-language medical literature since 1949 until a young microbiologist was hospitalized in Maryland in March 2004. This incident reportedly occurred in the context of "research on agents of biological warfare." Arjun Srinivasan et al., *Glanders in a Military Research Microbiologist*, 345 NEW ENG. J. MED. 256, 256 (2001) (further noting that labs face difficulties in recognizing potential agents of biological warfare and that this case may serve as a harbinger of the resurgence of nearly forgotten diseases). In another incident in 2004, three laboratory workers at Boston University were exposed to the bacterium that causes tularemia. The workers were reportedly working on a vaccine to protect against bioterrorist attacks. Scott Shane, *Exposure at Germ Lab Reignites a Public Health Debate*, N.Y. TIMES, Jan. 24, 2005, at A13.

300   THE AMERICAN JOURNAL OF INTERNATIONAL LAW   [Vol. 101:271

this preference.[167] Structural mechanisms including assurance devices that might otherwise be relevant to this problem will probably not be of assistance once a state adopts defection as its dominant strategy since in effect such a state is no longer an interdependent actor that can be influenced by the correction of misperceptions through confidence-building measures or other mechanisms for dispensing useful information about compliance.[168] The need to reduce the likelihood of successful offensive defections in these circumstances primarily implicates intrusive inspection, monitoring, and other "verification" measures rather than assurance devices, particularly when states fear that other states have achieved, or may achieve, significant technological advances related to the development of advanced weapons systems.[169] When a preference for cheating is adopted, however, indeterminacy in key provisions can undermine these structural safeguards by making it more difficult to detect and identify violations.

A subgroup of offensive defectors could be characterized as states that maintain a preference not only for violating their obligations under a specific arms control or disarmament regime, but also for disregarding their legal obligations generally. States that engage in aggressive, defiant, and lawless behavior have been given numerous labels but are often described by U.S. government officials and many other commentators as "rogue states."[170] While the term "rogue state" has no international legal standing and has been defined and used in many different ways,[171] it is used here to characterize a state as "a perennial violator" of international rules.[172] Such states may have various reasons for violating international norms and rules, including overall dissatisfaction with the status quo,[173] yet their motives are often described as "irrational."[174] If rogue states are irrational actors, they are presumably even less likely than other defecting states to respond to assurances, threats, or any other information from or about their

---

[167] Franck, *supra* note 12, at 714, 718.

[168] *See* STEIN, *supra* note 10, at 65.

[169] Abbott, *supra* note 9, at 16 (noting that concern for offensive defections will be especially pronounced when states fear technological advances by other states that are "capable of producing one-time gains large enough to offset the likely future costs or, in the extreme case, to end the game").

[170] The Department of State abandoned the term "rogue state" in 2000 in favor of other terms such as "state of concern." *See* Robert S. Litwak, *What's in a Name? The Changing Foreign Policy Lexicon*, 54 J. INT'L AFF. 375, 377, 379 (2001). The term has since been resurrected by the Bush administration and used prominently in official policy statements. *See* NATIONAL SECURITY STRATEGY OF THE UNITED STATES 13 (Sept. 2002), *available at* <http:// www.whitehouse.gov/nsc/nssall.html> [hereinafter 2002 NATIONAL SECURITY STRATEGY] ("new deadly challenges have emerged from rogue states and terrorists").

[171] The term "rogue state" has been so overused that some scholars have argued that it is often little more than "an ideological tag with no content." Anthony Clark Arend, *International Law and Rogue States: The Failure of the Charter Framework*, 36 NEW ENG. L. REV. 735, 735 (2002).

[172] *Id.*; *see also* 2002 NATIONAL SECURITY STRATEGY, *supra* note 170, at 14.

[173] Although the terms "rogue state" and "revisionist state" are sometimes used interchangeably, a revisionist state is best defined as a rational one that nonetheless takes risks and violates international norms in an effort to change the status quo, as exemplified by imperial Japan and Nazi Germany and their use of force to achieve greater power and influence in the 1930s. *See* Richard Falk, *Re-framing the Legal Agenda of World Order in the Course of a Turbulent Century*, 9 TRANSNAT'L L. & CONTEMP. PROBS. 451, 458 (1999). While rogue states are also likely to be dissatisfied with the status quo, they tend to be marginal actors that threaten regional stability without the capabilities of a Hitler or a Stalin to challenge the entire international system. *See* Litwak, *supra* note 170, at 387.

[174] For example, North Korea is a rogue state that is often characterized by U.S. government officials and other commentators as irrational. *See* Denny Roy, *North Korea and the 'Madman Theory,'* 25 SECURITY DIALOGUE 307, 316 n.15 (1994) (noting that "the great majority of analysts implicitly or explicitly accept the premise of North Korean irrationality"); *see also* Victor D. Cha, *Hawk Engagement and Preventive Defense on the Korean Peninsula,*

adversaries, including attempts at deterrence.[175] This conduct is consistent with theoretic game models suggesting that threats of penalties for noncompliance are not likely to be effective against irrational actors.[176] Similarly, U.S. national security policies emphasizing preemptive military action reflect the perceived irrationality of rogue states and their inability to be deterred.[177] By definition rogue states are not inclined to cooperate with other states or to comply with the obligations of a legal regime, arguably making even the most strictly enforced, verifiable, and hard legal obligations irrelevant to their conduct.

The presumed inability of any diplomatic or legal initiatives to influence the behavior of rogue states remains dependent on the characterization of these states as irrational actors. If instead they are motivated by any rational preferences, such as a desire to obtain economic concessions or technical assistance in exchange for compliance, indeterminate provisions cannot yield the clear rules needed to establish workable arrangements with other regime members to facilitate such exchanges. Distinguishing between activities that must be abandoned and those that may be assisted will probably be impeded by indeterminate provisions, especially if alleged violators can claim an inalienable or guaranteed right to pursue various peaceful activities involving dual-use materials, such as chemical components, biological agents, and nuclear technology, under applicable multilateral disarmament regimes.

Offensive Defectors and the BWC

Confronting the unrelenting efforts of states to maximize their relative power to secure their survival, the designers of international security regimes have long struggled with the problem of offensive defectors. While assurance measures are most closely linked with efforts to address defensive defections through the exchange of useful information related to compliance, more intrusive methods such as on-site inspections are often described as "verification" measures and are commonly associated with efforts to improve compliance by detecting cheating by states engaged in offensive defection.[178] In both practice and theory, however, these two systems are closely related and are often combined in arms control and disarmament agreements so as to promote transparency more effectively.[179] In attempting to remedy the much-criticized structural deficiencies of the BWC in this respect and to address the problem of potential offensive

---

27 INT'L SECURITY 40, 46 (2002) (noting that the irrationality of the North Korean regime is commonly argued to be a threat to peace on the Korean Peninsula).

[175] *See* Winston P. Nagan & Craig Hammer, *The New Bush National Security Doctrine and the Rule of Law*, 22 BERKELEY J. INT'L L. 375 (2004); Elaine Sciolino & Steven Lee Myers, *U.S. Study Reopens Division over Nuclear Missile Threat*, N.Y. TIMES, July 5, 2000, at A1 (quoting senior U.S. officials as rejecting deterrence against countries like North Korea because their leaders were "capable of irrational self-destructive behavior").

[176] *See* SCHELLING, *supra* note 103, at 130.

[177] In contrast to strategies for dealing with a status quo adversary in the Cold War, U.S. policy was revised in 2002 to reflect the view that "deterrence based only upon the threat of retaliation is less likely to work against leaders of rogue states more willing to take risks, gambling with the lives of their people, and the wealth of their nations." 2002 NATIONAL SECURITY STRATEGY, *supra* note 170, at 15.

[178] Abbott, *supra* note 9, at 4.

[179] *Id.* at 5. States will often have reasons to use both systems. Many bilateral arms control regimes are designed to mesh with various other external monitoring procedures and capabilities (such as satellites or other "national technical means"), the most extensive verification measures being dependent on the active cooperation of the parties under observation. *Id.*

defections, the rejected BWC draft protocol envisioned a hybrid system of both assurance and verification measures.[180]

The current BWC framework appears to offer an inviting target for offensive defectors, as demonstrated by the ability of the Soviet Union and Iraq to develop illicit BW programs. While undetected cheating in such cases may often highlight the lack of transparency measures, the historical experience of the BWC also suggests that a lack of determinate rules and requirements will impede attempts to establish a meaningful verification process. Thus, in 1992 the United States, Britain, and Russia undertook to ascertain BWC compliance through a series of voluntary visits to nonmilitary sites of concern under the nonbinding "Trilateral Framework Agreement."[181] This process quickly ended in failure after several visits demonstrated Russia's unwillingness to give a full account of Soviet BW activities and accusations by both sides only intensified mutual suspicions.[182] The absence of determinate rules or criteria contributed substantially to this failure, as participants could not agree on the implications of what they had observed during their visits.[183]

Even with transparency measures and determinate rules, the BWC regime would presumably not be able to affect offensive defectors characterized as "rogue" or outlaw states whose pursuit of BW programs is based on irrational motives. North Korea, for example, is often described as a particularly dangerous rogue and is also regarded by many governments and experts as a state of BW concern.[184]

In rejecting the BWC protocol, the U.S. government argued that a reformed BWC with access to some level of monitoring and clearer requirements would not deter determined cheaters and specifically accused North Korea of being such a cheater.[185] While the United States also purportedly based this rejection on perceived flaws in the text and additionally cited the overarching concerns of the pharmaceutical industry, to the extent that it relied on the argument that such reforms cannot counter rogue states it remains dependent on the core assumption that these would-be cheaters are irrational and cannot be influenced by diplomatic efforts, or that arms control measures are useless in this area against any state, or both. The U.S. government continues to emphasize that *no* arms control or disarmament regime would deter any state that is determined to engage in illicit

---

[180] The BWC draft protocol incorporated many of the twenty-one identified verification and assurance measures recommended by VEREX. *See supra* note 74.

[181] David C. Kelley, *The Trilateral Agreement: Lessons for Biological Weapons Verification*, 2002 VERIFICATION Y.B. (Verification Research, Training and Information Centre) 93, 96–97.

[182] *Id.*; *see also* Moodie, *supra* note 70, at 66. U.S. officials found what they considered to be clear evidence of continuing offensive BW programs during their visits to several Russian facilities. Contentious Russian visits to Pfizer Corporation facilities in Indiana and Connecticut later resulted in accusations by Russian state media that Pfizer was producing biological weapons. *See* MILTON LEITENBERG, BIOLOGICAL WEAPONS ARMS CONTROL 11 n.17 (PRAC Paper No. 16, 1996), *available at* <http://www.cissm.umd.edu/papers/files/prac.pdf>. Although the trilateral process began in 1992, no further visits occurred after 1994 owing to disagreements over visits to military facilities.

[183] Moodie, *supra* note 70, at 66.

[184] *See* Bolton, *supra* note 83. For the findings of nonproliferation and research institutes regarding possible or alleged North Korean BW programs, see *supra* note 85. North Korea was also designated by the United States as a dangerous member of an "axis of evil." George W. Bush, State of the Union Address (Jan. 29, 2002), 38 WEEKLY COMP. PRES. DOC. 133, 135 (Feb. 4, 2002), *available at* <http://www.gpoacces.gov/sou/index.html>.

[185] *See supra* note 85.

biological weapons development,[186] a view that conforms with a visceral dislike of international regimes that has sometimes been famously reflected in other comments by key U.S. officials. This attitude presents the question whether a stronger BWC regime would offer *any* benefits in addressing the threat of determined offensive defectors and what costs or trade-offs, if any, would be incurred by adopting more determinate provisions and mandatory transparency measures.

Hard Solutions for the BWC: Applying Determinacy to Offensive Defectors

The possibility of mixed motives and their importance. Selecting design elements for an effective international regime is difficult when some members appear to have a preference for offensively defecting from cooperation to secure advantages over others. Even in such cases, however, the possible nuances in each state's preferences must be carefully evaluated if more effective legal regimes and sustained cooperation are to be achieved.[187] Rather than reflecting a single motivation, the behavior of most states is more likely to be based on a constellation or combination of preferences.[188]

Russia is a country that may harbor a combination of preferences related to its BW programs. To the extent that it apparently continues to pursue offensive BW programs that it inherited from the Soviet Union, a preference for offensive defection remains a highly plausible motivation for some Russian actions.[189] But Russia may also have some of the "great power" motives of a defensive quasi defector like those displayed by the United States, exploiting the indeterminate language of the BWC to be the first to acquire new, arguably permitted military technology and so avoid the unknown risks of any technological inferiority.[190] In addition, Russia may be influenced somewhat by defensive or deterrent motives, and some writers even suggest that the Soviets were influenced by such factors.[191] Finally, to some degree Russia may share some of the interests of many compliant states in ensuring the nonproliferation of biological weapons.[192]

---

[186] Robert G. Joseph, under secretary of state for arms control and international security, Remarks to Carnegie International Nonproliferation Conference (Nov. 7, 2005), *available at* <http://www.state.gov/t/us/rm/56584.htm> ("The traditional arms control verification approach . . . . would not have deterred those who would seek to violate the [Biological Weapons] Convention.").

[187] *See* Jervis, *supra* note 97, at 42, 53.

[188] STEIN, *supra* note 10, at 48. Even ancient Athens, whose aggressive conquests as recounted by Thucydides continue to be related by modern political Realists, was influenced by a combination of different motives. *See Speech of the Athenians, in* 1 SIMON HORNBLOWER, A COMMENTARY ON THUCYDIDES i.75.3, at 120 (1991) ("fear was our first motive, afterwards honour, and finally advantage").

[189] The Russian Ministry of Defense steadfastly continues to refuse to allow any access to four of its facilities (in Kirov, Sergiev Posad, Ekaterinburg, and St. Petersburg) that appeared to be at the center of the Soviet offensive BW program. *See* Rimmington, *supra* note 57, at 117.

[190] According to a prominent defector involved in the post-BWC Soviet BW program, many Soviet generals were not originally convinced of the military utility of biological weapons but felt that it was "dangerous, if not outrageous, to be behind the West in anything." *See* KEN ALIBEK WITH STEPHEN HANDELMAN, BIOHAZARD 41 (1999).

[191] There is some evidence even suggesting that the U.S. government may have deliberately attempted to create a false impression of continuing work on BW programs to encourage the Soviets to dedicate resources on BW work rather than on other military programs. *See* Raymond L. Garthoff, *Polyakov's Run*, BULL. ATOM. SCI., Sept./Oct. 2000, at 40; Rimmington, *supra* note 57, at 109.

[192] *See* Leonid A. Skotnikov, permanent representative of the Russian Federation to the Conference on Disarmament, Statement to the Fifth Review Conference of the States Parties to the BWC (Nov. 19, 2001), *available*

304   THE AMERICAN JOURNAL OF INTERNATIONAL LAW   [Vol. 101:271

The Russian BWC case illustrates the difficulties in discerning the specific preferences of states, especially when they may have incentives for secrecy and misrepresentation. To the extent, however, that states like Russia may be more than pure offensive defectors and may be motivated by a combination of preferences, determinacy and transparency in the BWC are likely to promote their cooperation with other similarly motivated parties. Strategies based on a more complicated set of preferences may account for Russia's continuing support of a legally binding multilateral monitoring agreement to strengthen the BWC and its insistence that such a document incorporate more precise or objective terms.[193]

The rogue or outlaw state. Although North Korea is often characterized as an irrational rogue or outlaw state and thus not influenced by factors that affect the behavior of other self-interested states, a considerable amount of unpredictable, risky, or apparently irrational behavior by rogue states has been seen to be the product of miscalculations or misassessments.[194] Using the term "rogue" to attribute irrationality to a potentially diverse group of aggressive or lawless states and then relying on that designation to establish policies may obscure an understanding of the individual motives or preferences that underlie the actions of each of these states.[195]

While the intensely secret and closed nature of the North Korean government defies efforts to explain its behavior or analyze its preferences fully, a sizable body of evidence suggests that rational decisions may nonetheless underlie many, if not all, of its strategies,[196] all the more since its aggressive and threatening behavior has often served it well in its negotiations with more powerful countries.[197] A rational state may find it quite useful to appear irrational, stubborn, or angry in a variety of circumstances.[198] A combination of rational motives may therefore underlie many North Korean preferences, including those related to BW activities, which

at BWC Web site, *supra* note 7 (expressing concern about BW proliferation, calling for approval of legally binding multilateral verification measures for the BWC, and noting the enactment of criminal sanctions and export control laws to implement the BWC in Russia).

[193] *Id.* ("[W]e would like to emphasize once more the importance that we have been and still are giving to the inclusion of terminology and objective criteria into the Protocol.").

[194] Predicting other states' capabilities and intentions involves inherent uncertainties and a "probabilistic assessment of an uncertain and unknown future," potentially leading to "bad predictions, miscalculations, and misassessments" by any state actor, including a rogue state. *See* STEIN, *supra* note 10, at 60–61.

[195] *See* Litwak, *supra* note 170, at 376, 379 (arguing that in the absence of a Cold War adversary, U.S. policymakers have used the term "rogue state" to demonize a disparate group of states in an effort to mobilize international and domestic political support for the adoption of "hard-line policies" against these states, potentially obscuring a better understanding of these states and distorting policy); *see generally* Zbigniew Brzezinski et al., *Differentiated Containment*, FOREIGN AFF., May/June 1997, at 20.

[196] Some critics question the assumption that the North Korean regime is irrational when it clearly seems interested in its own self-preservation and the United States has successfully contained it on the Korean Peninsula for many years. *See* Jihwan Hwang, *Offensive Realism, Weaker States, and Windows of Opportunity: The Soviet Union and North Korea in Comparative Perspective*, WORLD AFF., June 22, 2005, at 39; David C. Kang, *Rethinking North Korea*, 35 ASIAN SURVEY 253 (1995); Steven Mufson, *Threat of 'Rogue' States: Is It Reality or Rhetoric?* WASH. POST, May 29, 2000, at A1.

[197] Although North Korea is criticized for taking irrational risks, some commentators argue that it is a classic example of the effective use of threats, bluffs, blackmail, and brinksmanship to create crises in order to extract maximum concessions from more powerful countries. SCOTT SNYDER, NEGOTIATING ON THE EDGE (1999); Roy, *supra* note 174.

[198] Jack L. Goldsmith & Eric A. Posner, *A Theory of Customary International Law*, 66 U. CHI. L. REV. 1113, 1135 (1999) ("Weak states with idiosyncratic domestic arrangements—like Iraq, Serbia, or North Korea—may benefit from being unpredictable or irrational."); Benedict Kingsbury, *The Concept of Compliance as a Function of Competing Conceptions of International Law*, *in* INTERNATIONAL COMPLIANCE, *supra* note 16, at 49, 55.

presents possibilities for self-interested North Korean participation in a reformed BWC regime. Recent initiatives by the United States to engage Iran and North Korea by offering various incentives for better behavior, while hardly enthusiastic, suggest fundamental reconsideration by U.S. officials of the presumption of the irrationality of rogue states.[199]

One potentially important self-interested motive behind some alleged WMD activities of North Korea may be the desire to obtain maximum advantages or compensation from the international community in exchange for its participation in disarmament regimes,[200] an approach facilitated by regimes that guarantee states the right to pursue "peaceful" research, development, exchange, and other activities closely related to prohibited undertakings. The BWC offers such guarantees,[201] as do other agreements like the Treaty on the Non-proliferation of Nuclear Weapons (NPT).[202] Under this type of regime, a state might demand concessions for an agreement to forgo otherwise permitted "peaceful" activities, arguing that full enjoyment of such activities would represent a trade-off or a form of "compensation" for the state's original willingness to subject itself to the terms of a disarmament agreement.[203]

Given the unproven military utility of biological weapons and the inherent limitations of a BW arsenal serving as an effective strategic deterrent, particularly when compared with nuclear weapons,[204] North Korea could rationally conclude that BW programs are not essential for national security purposes yet at the same time decide that demonstrating full compliance with BWC obligations could be profitable. The incentives for a rogue state to behave in this way are potentially greater than for it to engage in any type of genuine security cooperation,

---

[199] *See* Peter Baker & Anthony Faiola, *U.S., S. Korea Find Unity Against North's Nuclear Arms Program*, WASH. POST, Nov. 17, 2005, at A20 (noting how two years of six-party negotiations resulted in an offer of "economic incentives" in exchange for abandonment by North Korea of its nuclear weapons program). On February 13, 2007, North Korea is reported to have agreed to take certain incremental steps with respect to its nuclear programs, including shutting down the Yongbyang reactor and readmitting international nuclear inspectors, in exchange for energy aid and other inducements. Glenn Kessler & Edward Cody, *U.S. Flexibility Credited in Nuclear Deal with N. Korea*, WASH. POST, Feb. 14, 2007, at A11. In the aftermath of an apparent North Korean nuclear weapons test, the UN Security Council appears to continue to display a belief in the ability of North Korea to make rational assessments by imposing a variety of sanctions designed to change its behavior. *See* SC Res. 1718 (Oct. 14, 2006). With respect to the Council's attempts to influence the behavior of the Islamic Republic of Iran and that country's continuing pursuit of economic and other concessions in exchange for actions related to its nuclear activities, see *infra* notes 273–76 and corresponding text.

[200] Efforts by North Korea to obtain various economic and other concessions have been a major part of its often aggressive negotiating positions with the international community with respect to its nuclear activities. *See* Nancy E. Soderberg, Op-Ed, *Escaping North Korea's Nuclear Trap*, N.Y. TIMES, Feb. 12, 2003, at A37 ("The history of negotiation with North Korea is one in which the international community has repeatedly offered incentives to North Korea to rein in its nuclear programs."). North Korea's vice foreign minister stated the issue bluntly: "Our demand is also for the U.S. to make due compensation for the freeze and dismantlement of nuclear facilities that we have built with huge investment, tightening our belts." Colum Lynch, *North Korea Resists Talks on Nuclear Arms; Meeting by U.S. Election Is Unlikely*, WASH. POST, Sept. 28, 2004, at A21.

[201] *See supra* notes 67–68 and corresponding text.

[202] Treaty on the Non-proliferation of Nuclear Weapons, Arts. IV(2), X(2), July 1, 1968, 21 UST 483, 729 UNTS 161 [hereinafter NPT]; *see infra* notes 262–63 and corresponding text.

[203] David A. Koplow & Philip G. Schrag, *Carrying a Big Carrot: Linking Multilateral Disarmament and Development Assistance*, 91 COLUM. L. REV. 993, 1034–35 (1991). For example, non-nuclear states such as Iran may argue that part of their "compensation" under the NPT for agreeing not to exercise their right to develop nuclear weapons is an inalienable right to acquire all forms of "peaceful" nuclear technology. *See* Henry Sokolski, *Taking Proliferation Seriously*, POL'Y REV., Oct. 1, 2003, at 18.

[204] *See* Tucker, *supra* note 149, at 33–34 (noting that it is highly unlikely that biological weapons could ever provide the same level of deterrence as nuclear weapons since nuclear retaliation is immediate, devastating, and effective against military equipment as well as troops, while biological weapons are "slow, uncertain in their effects, and incapable of destroying military hardware and buildings").

306   THE AMERICAN JOURNAL OF INTERNATIONAL LAW   [Vol. 101:271

which comports with the view of scholars who argue that states like North Korea are probably more motivated to join a regime by profit than by security interests.[205] While a self-interested North Korean regime might possibly be encouraged to participate in a reformed BWC regime, history has demonstrated that such a regime would require legally binding, precise hard law terms with access to verification measures as insurance that the international community will "receive" from North Korea what it "pays" for.[206]

The advantages of determinacy in enhanced enforcement. Even a strong international regime supported by a spectrum of self-interested member state preferences may at some point benefit from the availability of sanctions for noncompliance, especially if incentives for offensive defection grow as cooperation deepens.[207] In this regard, determinacy may contribute to improving the BWC's limited enforcement mechanisms. Although reputational sanctions are clearly more effective when a regime imposes determinate, hard law obligations and has access to monitoring mechanisms so that violations are known to other state actors,[208] reputational costs are less likely to affect states that are already viewed as cheaters or rogues.[209] If, however, rational states are making a choice either to honor or to violate their international commitments, the availability of other, more effective sanctions could improve compliance by making the possible costs of a breach outweigh the costs of compliance, thus altering a state's payoffs.[210]

Few sanctions or enforcement options are available under the existing BWC framework. Beyond notoriously ineffective voluntary consultation procedures and domestic criminal penalties,[211] the Convention contemplates the possibility of sanctions by enabling states parties to lodge a complaint with the Security Council in case of a breach of obligations under the Convention by another state party.[212] Without determinate provisions to identify violations when

---

[205] Randall L. Schweller, *Unanswered Threats, A Neoclassical Realist Theory of Underbalancing International Security*, 29 INT'L SECURITY 159, 165 (2004); *see also* Randall L. Schweller, *Bandwagoning for Profit: Bringing the Revisionist State Back In*, 19 INT'L SECURITY 72, 87– 89 (1994).

[206] The nonbinding "Agreed Framework," under which North Korea promised in 1994 that it would verifiably freeze certain nuclear-processing activities in exchange for Western assistance, collapsed in 2002 after North Korea refused to deny claims that it was secretly enriching weapons-grade uranium. Key ambiguous terms, especially those related to the timing and sequence of activities and assistance, had been disputed by both sides for many years and undermined effective cooperation. *See Korean Reactions*, FIN. TIMES, Aug. 9, 2002, at 14 ("[T]he Agreed Framework clearly contains many flaws and ambiguities that have stalled its implementation."). Beyond initial energy aid, receipt by North Korea of additional assistance under the agreement reached on February 13, 2007, appears to depend on meeting more determinate requirements than those found in the 1994 Agreed Framework. *See Faces Saved All Around—The North Korean Nuclear Deal*, ECONOMIST, Feb. 17, 2007, at 28, 30 (quoting the chief American negotiator as having repeatedly told the North Koreans "that America needed to know 'precisely' what was happening with uranium enrichment").

[207] George Downs et al., *Is the Good News About Compliance Good News About Cooperation?* 50 INT'L ORG. 379, 397 (1996) (noting that "[c]ooperation in arms, trade, and environmental regulation may begin with agreements that require little enforcement, but continued progress seems likely to depend on coping with an environment where defection presents significant benefits").

[208] *See* Guzman, *supra* note 14, at 1860.

[209] Reputational models have been criticized as overused or incomplete and the reputational costs associated with violation of international law in particular have been described as exaggerated or too heavily relied upon by scholars. *See* GOLDSMITH & POSNER, *supra* note 90, at 102.

[210] Guzman, *supra* note 14, at 1860.

[211] The BWC relies on each state party to enact implementing legislation with appropriate criminal penalties under Article IV and to participate on a voluntary basis in additional consultation and confidence-building measures; most states have declined to participate in these voluntary measures. *See supra* note 76.

[212] BWC, *supra* note 1, Art. VI(1). No state has ever availed itself of this right.

they occur and without the benefit of any agreed multilateral monitoring mechanisms to confirm noncompliance, a state is unlikely to be able to submit a complaint that includes "all possible evidence confirming its validity."[213] Although the BWC requires no action on such complaints other than carrying out an investigation and informing states of the results,[214] the Security Council has identified the proliferation of biological weapons and other WMDs as a "threat to international peace and security"[215] and would thus be able to impose a variety of enforcement measures on that basis if violations could be determined—and if no permanent member vetoed those measures.

To the extent that legally binding agreements with more precise obligations are credited by some scholars with an increased capacity for enforcement by bodies that are delegated that responsibility,[216] determinacy in the BWC could make the possibility of Security Council action a more effective sanction, particularly if combined with transparency measures. The quasi-judicial or legalistically formal language in the BWC requiring the demonstration of a "breach of obligations" reinforces the need for determinate provisions that allow both allegations and potential defenses to be tested by agreed legal rules or requirements.[217] As currently constituted, however, the indeterminate BWC framework makes the threat of sanctions almost nonexistent, projecting little deterrence to offensive defectors; this threat is further diminished by the BWC's lack of mandatory transparency measures.

Determinacy and drawing lines. Some legal scholars have suggested that international law itself is intrinsically indeterminate, essentially constituting a rhetorical fabric used by powerful actors to engage in international politics as they see fit.[218] Although some degree of indeterminacy appears to be inevitable in any set of rules and too much precision may even undermine a rule's effectiveness, some outer boundary of a rule's elasticity must be established for it successfully to convey a message regarding required or prohibited conduct,[219] especially as regards arms control. A certain degree of indeterminacy is inherent in any arms control or disarmament regime, but a high degree of indeterminacy is likely to undermine the regime's objectives, particularly if it is impossible to draw *any* bright lines between prohibited and permitted conduct. The limited experience of the Treaty on Outer Space, a multilateral agreement that attempts to control arms and military activities by relying on the term "peaceful purposes" while providing no clarifying rules or criteria, suggests that such an indeterminate approach in this area is highly problematic.[220]

---

[213] *Id.* Each state party to the BWC undertakes in Article VI, paragraph 2, "to cooperate in carrying out any investigation which the Security Council may initiate, in accordance with the provisions of the Charter of the United Nations, on the basis of the complaint received by the Council."

[214] *Id.*

[215] SC Res. 1540 (Apr. 28, 2004).

[216] *See* Abbott & Snidal, *supra* note 17, at 427.

[217] *Id.* (noting that legal review in the context of agreed rules and procedures is also more likely to increase the reputational costs associated with violations).

[218] *See, e.g.,* David Kennedy, *A New Stream of International Law Scholarship,* 7 WIS. INT'L L.J. 1 (1988). Kennedy further argues that international law has become obsessively process oriented and inappropriately state centered when in fact the state might be better viewed as a "linguistic relationship between law and politics." *Id.* at 2, 49; *see also* DAVID KENNEDY, THE DARK SIDES OF VIRTUE: REASSESSING INTERNATIONAL HUMANITARIANISM (2004).

[219] *See* FRANCK, *supra* note 101, at 53, 56–57.

[220] *See* BIN CHENG, STUDIES IN INTERNATIONAL SPACE LAW 513–22 (1997). Cheng describes definitional problems related to the phrase "for peaceful purposes only" in Article IV of the Outer Space Treaty as giving rise to "grave anxiety." *Id.* at 513. The United States has chosen to interpret "peaceful purposes" in this Treaty as meaning "non-aggressive" (rather than "non-military"), an expansive view that leaves the door open to controversies over

308   THE AMERICAN JOURNAL OF INTERNATIONAL LAW   [Vol. 101:271

Although achieving a higher degree of rule determinacy in the BW context is not a simple task because of the difficulty of distinguishing between some offensive and defensive or "peaceful" BW activities, broad differences between related BW programs can be identified and key elements that are common to offensive programs can be subjected to restrictions or special scrutiny through appropriate transparency measures.[221] Four areas for which such criteria and rules could be established are large-scale dissemination trials of BW agents, large-scale BW production activities, work on BW delivery systems, and efforts to enhance the potency of pathogens.[222] Inside these four areas, "bright lines" could be drawn setting forth specific restrictions and transparency measures for certain activities or items, including the size or volume of certain types of equipment necessary to produce pathogens (such as fermenters and centrifugal separators), the quantity of certain types of manufacturing materials (such as the media needed to grow pathogens), and the research equipment and facilities necessary for developing BW delivery systems (such as aerosol inhalation chambers, spraying and fogging systems, and aerosol-generating units).[223]

While not without challenges, lines could be drawn between key prohibited BW activities and permitted peaceful biotechnological activities, allowing mechanisms to be established to monitor compliance by using determinate rules and requirements that incorporate these distinctions. Critics of such an approach argue that even measures that incorporate clearer rules and requirements will not be effective in verifying compliance or in deterring violations by the most determined cheaters. Foremost among these critics are U.S. government officials who opposed the monitoring provisions in the BWC draft protocol on those grounds.[224] Incongruously, some of these same officials had previously expressed support for such measures to

---

the defensive nature of weapons and military activities, and one that Cheng describes as "needless, wrong, and potentially noxious." *Id.* at 520. Article IV does, however, provide the following clarifying language: "The establishment of military bases, installations and fortifications, the testing of any type of weapons and the conduct of military manoeuvres on celestial bodies shall be forbidden." Treaty on Principles Governing the Activities of States in the Exploration and Use of Outer Space, Art. IV, Jan. 27, 1967, 18 UST 2410, 610 UNTS 205. The limiting term "peaceful purposes" in the Antarctic Treaty similarly has the potential to raise definitional concerns, although Article I of that Treaty prohibits "any measures of a military nature" and further provides that specific prohibitions set forth in that agreement are, as Cheng explains, "exemplificative and not exhaustive." Antarctic Treaty, Art. I, Dec. 1, 1959, 12 UST 794, 402 UNTS 71; CHENG, *supra*, at 517.

In spite of attempts to establish parameters for the term "peaceful purposes," both the Antarctic and Outer Space Treaties also contain potentially problematic exemptions for these clarifying elaborations in subsequent provisions. *See* Antarctic Treaty, *supra*, Art. I(2) (providing: "The present Treaty shall not prevent the use of military personnel or equipment for scientific research or for any other peaceful purpose."); Outer Space Treaty, *supra*, Art. IV (providing: "The use of military personnel for scientific research or for any other peaceful purposes shall not be prohibited.").

[221] *See* Graham S. Pearson, *Biological Weapons: Their Nature and Arms Control, in* NON-CONVENTIONAL-WEAPONS PROLIFERATION, *supra* note 122, at 99, 117 (noting that "the depth of understanding and the scale of work has to be much greater to support an offensive programme"). Subjecting key elements of offensive BW programs to restrictions or special scrutiny does not require, and should not be used to promote, the establishment of lists or definitions of types or quantities of *permitted* biological agents or toxins, since such an action could be used to undermine the scope of the BWC's general prohibitions.

[222] *See* D. L. Huxsoll et al., *Medicine in Defense Against Biological Warfare*, 262 J. AM. MED. ASS'N 677 (1989), *cited in* Pearson, *supra* note 221, at 294. An initial attempt to establish rules based in part on these key elements was made, unsuccessfully, in the BWC draft protocol.

[223] These and other useful potential restrictions are suggested by the Australia Group's existing control lists and could serve to clarify not only what is prohibited under the BWC but also what is appropriate for exchange and transfer. *See infra* notes 251–56 and corresponding text.

[224] *See* Bolton, *supra* note 83; Mahley, *supra* note 80 (stressing that the "draft Protocol will not improve our ability to verify BWC compliance").

Congress, stating that effective verification was never the goal of the BWC draft protocol, but rather "greater transparency" in "dual-capable activities and facilities," and that there was "real value" in increased transparency measures that could "complicate the efforts of countries to cheat on their BWC obligations."[225]

Prior to the U.S. invasion of Iraq, some commentators and U.S. government officials pointed to the failure of UN inspections in Iraq as evidence of the futility of monitoring efforts in deterring the development of BW and other WMD programs by a rogue state. There is now some irony in these arguments in light of the U.S. government's own findings (subsequent to the invasion) indicating that these and other UN activities did in fact contribute to impeding or complicating the development of Iraqi BW programs.[226] Furthermore, while some nascent BW research activities may be difficult to detect even with determinate rules and transparency measures, that is not true of the later stages of BW research and production and the integration of these weapons into military strategy and training.[227] On balance, while no design elements can ensure that resolute cheaters will not violate the BWC regime, determinacy and transparency together can significantly contribute to promoting the regime's objectives, improving its effectiveness, and making cheating more difficult and more detectable.

V. INDETERMINATE ARMS CONTROL REGIMES AND COMPLIANT AND CONFORMIST STATES

Perceived Discriminatory Effect on Developing Countries

To advance the complete elimination of a class or type of weapon, multinational disarmament regimes strive to achieve universal membership and attract nonstates parties that are acting in conformity with the regime's obligations. Persuading these "conformist states" to join a regime formally and become compliant states parties may be impeded by the effect of indeterminacy on the attractiveness of membership. On one level, the real, alleged, and feared defections that characterize the failure of a legally binding multinational disarmament regime dependent on soft indeterminate terms and soft structure, that is, one lacking transparency mechanisms, may make that regime less attractive generally. On another level, many developing states that have no interest in the weapons banned by a particular regime may also have little

---

[225] Donald A. Mahley, Testimony, Biological Weapons Convention, *in Hearing Before the Subcomm. on National Security, Veterans Affairs and International Relations of the House Comm. on Government Reform*, 106th Cong. (2000), *available in* LEXIS, Transcripts Library, Fed. Doc. Clearing House File, *available at* <http://www.fas.org/spp/starwars/congress/2000_h/testimony_of_ambassador_donald_a.htm>. *But see* Barbara Hatch Rosenberg & Gordon Burck, *Verification of Compliance with the Biological Weapons Convention, in* PREVENTING A BIOLOGICAL ARMS RACE, *supra* note 49, at 300, 305 (noting that while no BWC verification regime will detect all violations, "[a]dequate verification will deter violation of the Convention, make illegal actions difficult and limit their scale, and provide workable means for international investigation of concerns that may be raised through national intelligence").

[226] *See, e.g.,* 3 CIA COMPREHENSIVE REPORT, *supra* note 124, at 39 (noting that as early as 1992, UN sanctions, inspections, mandatory declarations, and monitoring of the importation and use of media needed for the growth of bacterial BW agents created "impediments for any Iraqi biological production effort").

[227] Rosenberg & Burck, *supra* note 225, at 304 (arguing in addition that the difficulties in monitoring BW activities at the research level have been overstated).

interest in becoming bound by its obligations.[228] These states may also believe that such a regime could have a negative effect on their access to dual-use technologies and other materials. Just as powerful egoist states are unlikely to join a regime that does not advance their security interests, so other states are unlikely to join unless the regime provides incentives for conscientious potential members to participate and fully comply with its obligations.[229]

While some suggest that not much is learned from empirical evidence of compliant behavior by states like Benin and Burkina Faso under a regime like the Outer Space Treaty, the unwillingness of many developing states to become parties to certain multilateral disarmament regimes may tell us something about the impact of indeterminate and *interdependent* provisions on the attractiveness of those regimes to such states. Powerful states may encourage less developed states to join disarmament regimes by promising them the widest possible access to dual-use technology and materials for peaceful purposes, in exchange for their abiding by related restrictions on weapons-related uses. Yet powerful nations may also treat the indeterminate terms of a disarmament regime as flexible and expansive so that they can pursue questionable bioweapons research while treating those terms as hard, narrow, and restrictive when it comes to attempts by developing states to gain access to restricted dual-use technologies.

By thus having it "both ways," powerful states may make a regime vulnerable to complaints by developing states that it discriminates against them by imposing obligations that are not coterminous with their disarmament responsibilities. Such perceived discriminatory conduct, in turn, may undermine the developing world's support for a regime and impede efforts to achieve universal membership by discouraging conformist nonsignatory states and compliant signatory states from taking the actions necessary to join or become full states parties.

Compliant and Conformist States and the BWC

Currently, 155 of the 192 member states of the United Nations are parties to the BWC.[230] Relatively few of them have ever been alleged to be states of BWC concern and thus almost all of them can generally be described as compliant parties.[231] An additional 16 states have signed the BWC but have not yet ratified it or otherwise taken the necessary steps to become parties.[232] Most of these states are also widely regarded as complying with their BWC obligations: only Egypt and

---

[228] Compliant signatory states in the developing world that have not yet completed the formal processes necessary to become parties to disarmament regimes, like conformist nonsignatory states, may find full membership in such regimes unattractive.

[229] KEOHANE, *supra* note 156, at 103 ("Insofar as regimes create incentives for compliance, they also make it more attractive for conscientious potential members to join them.").

[230] *See* Status of Multilateral Arms Regulation and Disarmament Agreements, *at* <http://disarmament2.un.org/TreatyStatus.nsf>. A state that is not a member of the United Nations, the Holy See, is a party to the BWC. *Id.*

[231] Even U.S. officials quick to allege violations by other states have conceded that "the vast majority of the BWC's parties have conscientiously met their commitments." John R. Bolton, Beyond the Axis of Evil: Additional Threats from Weapons of Mass Destruction, Remarks to the Heritage Foundation (May 6, 2002), *available at* <http://www.state.gov/t/us/rm/9962.htm>.

[232] The 16 states that have signed the BWC but not yet become parties are Burundi, the Central African Republic, Côte d'Ivoire, Egypt, Gabon, Guyana, Haiti, Liberia, Madagascar, Malawi, Myanmar, Nepal, Somalia, Syria, Tanzania, and the UAE. *See* Status of Multilateral Arms Regulation and Disarmament Agreements, *supra* note 230. As signatories, these states are obliged to refrain from acts that would defeat the object and purpose of the BWC pending their ratification, acceptance, or approval of the Convention or until it "shall have made its intention clear not to become a party to the treaty." *See* Vienna Convention on the Law of Treaties, Art. 18(a), May 23, 1969, 1115 UNTS 331. There are currently 108 states parties, including Egypt, Syria, and 5 other BWC signatory states.

Syria have been alleged to be of BW concern.[233] Of the 21 nonsignatory states, only Israel has been alleged to be of BW concern.[234] The remaining 20 states are generally regarded as conformist nonsignatories, states that do not have BW programs and do not appear to be pursuing them.[235]

Almost all of the 20 apparently compliant nonsignatory states are poor, fragile, or economically distressed, and most are classified among the least-developed or poorest countries of the world.[236] Most of the 14 apparently compliant BWC signatory states also fall into that category.[237] Both of these groups of states may have more incentives to adopt preferences related to economic and technical development than to the acquisition of a new, uncertain, and expensive unconventional weapons capability.[238] While unlikely to be interested in BW programs, these states are also no longer moved by any of the incentives to join the BWC based on affiliation with one of the two camps of Cold War adversaries. Uninterested in biological weapons but unmotivated to become a party to the BWC, these poor or fragile states nonetheless prevent the BWC regime from achieving universality.

In recent years, few states have ratified or acceded to the BWC.[239] Beyond the considerations listed above, two other factors that are linked to the failure of indeterminate regimes in acute security dilemmas are likely to contribute to this apparent lack of motivation. First, the BWC regime can be described as unattractive to possible new members because of its widely perceived failure to address noncompliance issues and the continuing failure of the states parties to make necessary reforms. Second, developing states may find the BWC regime unattractive because they perceive the regime's indeterminate and *interdependent* provisions as having a discriminatory impact on their access to health care and biotechnology resources. Most of the developing states that remain outside the BWC not only have limited financial resources but also would probably prefer to obtain access to vaccines, diagnostic equipment, advanced biotechnology, and various pharmaceutical products than to join a treaty regime that does not improve—and may be viewed as impeding—their access to health sciences and biotechnology.

---

[233] *See supra* note 85.

[234] The 21 members of the United Nations that have not signed the BWC are Andorra, Angola, Cameroon, Chad, the Comoros, Djibouti, Eritrea, Guinea, Israel, Kazakhstan, Kiribati, the Marshall Islands, Mauritania, Micronesia, Mozambique, Namibia, Nauru, Samoa, Trinidad and Tobago, Tuvalu, and Zambia. *See* Weapons of Mass Destruction, *at* <http://disarmament.un.org/wmd/>.

[235] *See supra* note 85. One nonsignatory, Kazakhstan, is not generally regarded as a state of BW concern but is one of several states that inherited a significant amount of BW infrastructure from the former Soviet Union. *See generally* SMITHSON, *supra* note 69.

[236] Twelve of the 21 BWC nonsignatory states are listed by the United Nations as "least developed countries." *See* UN Office of the High Representative for the Least Developed Countries, List of Least Developed Countries, *at* <http://www.un.org/special-rep/ohrlls/ldc/list.htm> [hereinafter LDC List]. An additional 5 are listed in the World Bank's lowest two of five categories of economic development. *See* World Bank, Data and Statistics (2007), *at* <http://www.worldbank.org/countries> [hereinafter World Bank Data].

[237] Ten of the 16 BWC signatory states are listed by the United Nations as least-developed countries. *See* LDC List, *supra* note 236. An additional 4 are listed in the World Bank's lowest two of five categories of economic development. *See* World Bank Data, *supra* note 236.

[238] Contrary to a view popularized in Western countries, the advanced science and technology required for BW programs make biological weapons an unlikely component in the arsenals of developing countries. *See* Wright, *supra* note 55, at 6 (finding "some irony" in describing biological weapons as the "poor man's nuke" in view of their development by industrialized countries).

[239] Only 12 UN member states have become parties to the BWC since 2000. *See* Status of Multilateral Arms Regulation and Disarmament Agreements, *supra* note 230. All of the 16 signatory states that have failed to com-

As seen above, despite arguments that soft law facilitates wider participation in regimes and more easily permits reluctant states to join and comply with regime requirements,[240] soft indeterminate provisions in legally binding agreements like the BWC may have the opposite effect for developing states. The ambiguities in Article I permit powerful industrial states to advance their own security interests by undertaking questionable BW research activities for "prophylactic, protective or other peaceful purposes," while broadly prohibiting the exchange of various dual-use materials through export controls coordinated by the Australia Group (AG).[241] Although developing countries enjoy the right under Article X to "the fullest possible exchange of equipment, materials and scientific and technological information for the use of bacteriological (biological) agents and toxins,"[242] in practice the developed industrial states have used the indeterminate conditional phrase "for peaceful purposes" in that article to justify the imposition of whatever AG-coordinated restrictions they deem appropriate on the transfer and export of dual-use materials, technology, and information. AG member states argue that these export controls merely implement Article III of the BWC by preventing the transfer of any of the agents, toxins, weapons, equipment, or means of delivery specified in Article I.[243] However, no rules or criteria established collectively by BWC states parties inform this implementation process.

Although Article X further requires that the BWC be "implemented in a manner designed to avoid hampering the economic or technological development of States Parties to the Convention," this requirement again applies only to indeterminate "peaceful bacteriological (biological) activities."[244] For purposes of export control, the AG has turned interdependent and vague terms in the BWC into precise national rules by imposing standardized end-user undertakings through common lists of export-controlled biological agents and dual-use biotechnology. Developing states argue that many of the prohibited items on these lists are necessary for disease control and public health improvements and that AG export control measures are applied in a discriminatory manner, contravening their rights under the BWC to the free exchange of materials, technology, and expertise.[245]

Advanced industrial states thus exploit the interdependent term "peaceful purposes" so that it remains indeterminate and flexible when applied against them under Article I but specific

plete the necessary procedures to become a member of the BWC originally signed the Convention in 1972 or 1973 immediately after it was opened for signature. *Id.*

[240] Shelton, *supra* note 13, at 319; pt. V, "Perceived Discriminatory Effect on Developing Countries," *supra.*

[241] BWC, *supra* note 1, Art. I(1). The AG is an informal consultative arrangement of states that was founded in 1984 after events in the Iran-Iraq war revealed that some countries were producing chemical weapons with materials obtained through international trade and a lack of uniform licensing measures. The AG first sought to impede the proliferation of chemical weapons through coordinated national export control laws and later expanded its mandate to include biological weapons. All thirty-eight states that participate in the AG are parties to the BWC and the CWC and include most of the states of the world with advanced biological and biotechnology industries. *See* AG, Origins of the Australia Group, *at* <http://www.australiagroup.net>.

[242] BWC, *supra* note 1, Art. X(1).

[243] *See* AG, Objectives of the Group, *at* <http://www.australiagroup.net>.

[244] BWC, *supra* note 1, Art. X(2).

[245] *See, e.g.,* Sha Zukang, head of the Chinese Delegation, Statement to the Fifth Review Conference of the States Parties to the BWC (Nov. 19, 2001), *available at* BWC Web site, *supra* note 7, at 3 (criticizing advanced countries for "stubbornly sticking to existing discriminatory practices" that were "detrimental . . . to the legitimate rights of states parties"); John Zarocostas, *Gaps Remain in Weapons Ban Talks,* UPI, Feb. 23, 2001, *available in* LEXIS, Wire Service Stories Library.

and hard when broadly applied through export controls against developing states under Articles III and X. Besides being widely perceived as discriminatory, this practice cannot advance the achievement of universality.[246] It arguably also creates incoherence, which undermines the legitimacy of the BWC regime itself.[247] Current BWC states parties in the developing world that participated in the Ad Hoc Group emphasized these concerns by showing less interest in the draft protocol's verification measures than in its attempts to establish lines distinguishing the types of equipment and materials that are—and are not—properly subject to transfer restrictions under the Convention.[248] Without more determinate language to draw such lines, developing states parties attempting to import biotechnological and pharmaceutical materials for peaceful purposes will continue to face restrictions that are not coterminous with the problem of biological weapons, creating a confrontational situation that over time will be hard to contain under a multilateral disarmament agreement.[249] For developing nonparty states, the rational mechanisms associated with the BWC's indeterminate and interdependent terms are likely to perpetuate their perception of the BWC's discriminatory application, fueling their disincentives to participate in the regime.

Hard Solutions for the BWC: Applying Determinacy to Compliant and Conformist States

The problems for compliant and conformist nonparty states that are caused by the discriminatory application of indeterminate terms in the BWC cannot be solved by the Western approach of using different definitions for the same language in key articles, since developing and many other states clearly view these articles as inseparably linked.[250] Instead, determinacy in the BWC framework, in conjunction with greater transparency, has the potential to resolve this problem by allowing developing states greater access to technology and materials that are not subject to BWC regulation, while at the same time clarifying restrictions on prohibited activities. Some determinate, line-drawing solutions to perceived BWC discrimination problems are suggested by the Australia Group's own codification efforts. From the perspective of

---

[246] *See, e.g.*, Rakesh Sood, head of Delegation of India, Statement to the Fifth Review Conference of the States Parties to the BWC (Nov. 20, 2001), *available at* BWC Web site, *supra* note 7, at 5 ("The promotional aspects of Article X are, we believe, a crucial element in strengthening the Convention and even perhaps in achieving universal adherence.").

[247] *See* FRANCK, *supra* note 101, at 153.

[248] *See* Oliver Thränert, *Enhancing the Biological Weapons Convention*, *in* ENHANCING THE BWC, *supra* note 145, at 17 (further noting that many African countries perceive greater threats from diseases like HIV and Ebola than from BW programs); Zarocostas, *supra* note 245 (quoting Ambassador Tibor Tóth, chairman of the Ad Hoc Group, as saying that export controls "were debated in a heated manner," with emphasis by developing countries on the need for access to technology related to diseases).

[249] *See* Chayes & Shelton, *supra* note 30, at 525 ("Long-term stability and efficiency require that arms control regimes be built upon mutual interests and relationships, not confrontation.").

[250] *See* Celina M. Assumpção de Valle Pereira, ambassador, Statement to the Fifth Review Conference of the States Parties to the BWC (Nov. 19, 2001), *available at* BWC Web site, *supra* note 7 (describing nonproliferation and technological cooperation as viewed as the "two main pillars" of the BWC); Sood, *supra* note 246, para. 7 (describing Articles III and X as "two mutually inseparable aspects of any disarmament agreement that deals with a dual-use technology"); Sha Zukang, *supra* note 245, at 3 (arguing that nonproliferation activities and the promotion of peaceful uses of biotechnology "should be complementary and mutually reinforcing," while noting with regret that "a minority of countries have gone out of their way to separate the two issues"); Abdul Basit, acting permanent representative of Pakistan, Statement to the Fifth Review Conference of the States Parties to the BWC (Nov. 19, 2001), *available at* BWC Web site, *supra* note 7, para. 10 (emphasizing that Pakistan "cannot agree to an interpretation of Article III that is in any manner at variance with the provisions of Article X").

many developing and other states that seek fully to implement the free exchange of technology envisioned in the BWC, certain types of protective and containment equipment listed as AG-controlled items have important applications for public health.[251] From the perspective of powerful states that already benefit from advanced biotechnology and are more interested in security, the export of such items to developing states would be less problematic if it were covered by mandatory transparency measures such as some form of monitoring requirements.

Unlike protective equipment, however, other types of AG-controlled items appear to be more useful for BW programs than for disease control or peaceful medical activities, particularly when quantitative requirements and rules are applied. These items include fermenters with specified high capacities,[252] centrifugal separators with specified capabilities including high flow rates,[253] aerosol inhalation chambers with specified high capacities,[254] and other items necessary for the development of BW delivery systems such as spraying and fogging systems and aerosol-generating units.[255] Thus, many items on the AG-controlled list were logically included on mandatory declaration lists in the final composite text of the BWC draft protocol.[256]

While bringing determinacy and consistency to the BWC through more precise technological specifications presents challenges, the common items of equipment that appear on both the AG-controlled list and the mandatory declaration list of the draft protocol suggest that the BWC states parties could collectively agree on at least some types of equipment that should be subject to prohibitions or increased scrutiny under Article I and to denial of transfer or export under Articles III and X. The establishment of monitoring mechanisms could give AG member states corresponding incentives to abandon their conflicted approach to several items they find acceptable for themselves yet not for transfer or export to other states. From the self-interested perspective of these developed states, the continued use of only their own guidelines to prohibit transfers (rather than a complementary and collective agreement by BWC states parties on critical ambiguous terms) continues to risk undermining the disarmament regime they seek to reinforce.[257] While powerful states can be expected to pursue their own interests, AG member

---

[251] Protective and containment equipment includes complete containment facilities (at the "containment" or "maximum containment," known as the P3 and P4, levels, as specified by the WHO) and various types of protective suits and biological safety cabinets or isolators. AG, Control List of Dual Use Biological Equipment and Related Technology, §§I.1, I.6 (Apr. 2005), *at* <http://www.australiagroup.net>.

[252] *Id.* §I.2.

[253] *Id.* §I.3.

[254] *Id.* §I.7.

[255] *Id.* §I.8. Other items of concern that seem unlikely to be used primarily for peaceful civilian activities have been included on AG-controlled lists so as to raise the awareness of the industry, including equipment for the microencapsulation of live microorganisms and toxins in the range of one to ten microns particle size; fermenters that have small capacities but are part of aggregate orders or are designed for use in combined systems would similarly justify special treatment. *Id.*, Items for Inclusion in Awareness Raising Guidelines, paras. 1–2.

[256] For example, each state party with specified facilities would have been required under the protocol to declare production of designated agents using bioreactors/fermenters with total internal volume of 50 liters or more, *see* Protocol to the BWC, *supra* note 79, at 19–20, and would also have been required to supply information concerning various other types of equipment present at or used in a declared facility, including specified types of continuous or semicontinuous centrifuges with throughput capacity greater than 100 liters per hour, *see id.* at 118.

[257] BWC developing states strongly criticize this extraregime regulatory approach, arguing that "the transfer of dual-use materials for medical, diagnostic and treatment purposes should be regulated on the basis of guidelines to be negotiated and accepted by all States Parties." *See* Sood, *supra* note 246, para. 7. For its part, the

states may be taking a myopic view of those interests by not seeking to clarify these key ambiguities, by maintaining BW export control lists outside the BWC regime, and, in the case of the United States, by opposing a legally binding BWC monitoring regime that also attempts to establish some determinate rules and requirements.[258]

In view of the probable scant interest of most compliant and conformist nonparty states in joining the BWC, the scarcity of their resources for engaging in major disarmament initiatives, and their likely competing preferences, the question arises of the willingness of such states to embrace a reformed BWC regime even with the inclusion of determinate provisions. The experience of other regimes may shed some insight on this question. Twenty-four of the thirty-one poorest developing countries that are not parties to the BWC have nonetheless expended scarce governmental resources and shown sufficient interest in limiting the spread of WMDs to become parties to the CWC, and all thirty-one have become parties to the NPT.[259] Like the BWC, both are multilateral disarmament agreements that address access to complex dual-use technology and materials capable of generating acute security dilemmas.

That all but seven of the thirty-one developing states that have not become parties to the BWC over the last forty years have chosen to join the CWC regime since it was opened for signature in 1997 may reflect various calculations and assessments, but calls particular attention to the more determinate rules of the CWC and its developed oversight and monitoring mechanisms.[260] While the regulation of materials and technology related to biological weapons presents a number of challenges, the success of the more recently established CWC regime at least suggests that the BWC's relative lack of determinacy—the absence of rules, schedules, or criteria for distinguishing peaceful biotechnology from prohibited BW programs—is not the inevitable result of these challenges.[261]

United States has argued that the guidelines in the draft protocol "could undermine U.S. regulations against the export of sensitive technology used in bioweapons." Glenda Cooper, *U.S. Rejects Biological Arms Ban Protocol*, WASH. POST, July 26, 2001, at A1. Some arms control experts, however, have questioned why the draft protocol's clearer requirements for export controls would undermine AG efforts rather than support them. *See* Brugger, *supra* note 86.

[258] "Myopic" self-interest refers to a state's perception of the relative costs and benefits of alternative available courses of action with respect to a particular issue when the assessment of that issue is made in isolation from others. KEOHANE, *supra* note 156, at 99. The apparent anomaly of egoistic states acting in ways that appear to be inconsistent with their interests may often be explained by the fact that they are complying with rules that conflict with their immediate or "myopic" self-interests. *Id.*

[259] *See* Status of Multilateral Arms Regulation and Disarmament Agreements, *supra* note 232. Only one state, Angola, has signed neither the CWC nor the BWC; two other BWC nonparties, the Comoros and Israel, have signed but not yet ratified the CWC. *Id.* As noted above, thirty-one of the thirty-seven UN member states that are not parties to the BWC are designated as least-developed countries by the United Nations or are in the World Bank's bottom two categories of economic development. *See* LDC List, *supra* note 236; World Bank Data, *supra* note 236. Yet only seven of these poorest developing states (Angola, the Central African Republic, the Comoros, Egypt, Myanmar, Somalia, and Syria) are not parties to the CWC. *See* Status of Multilateral Arms Regulation and Disarmament Agreements, *supra* note 232.

[260] *See infra* text at notes 280–85.

[261] Mikhail Berdennikov, special advisor to the director-general, *The Experience of the Organization for the Prohibition of Chemical Weapons, in* THE IMPLEMENTATION OF LEGALLY BINDING MEASURES TO STRENGTHEN THE BIOLOGICAL AND TOXIN WEAPONS CONVENTION 103, 107 (Marie Isabelle Chevrier et al. eds., 2004) [hereinafter IMPLEMENTATION OF LEGALLY BINDING MEASURES]; Graham S. Pearson, *The Key Elements of a Legally Binding Instrument to Strengthen the Biological and Toxin Weapons Convention, in id.* at 55, 77 ("A comparison of the BWTC legally binding instrument regime and the CWC regime has shown that the two regimes are indeed comparable and effective.").

VI. CONCLUSION

A brief review of other multilateral disarmament regimes that must address the instability generated by easily confused military and civilian applications of regulated technology indicates that such regimes rely increasingly as they mature on harder language—namely, more determinacy—and harder structures—namely, legally binding verification and transparency measures—to ensure the clarity of fundamental obligations under the regime. The regulation of nuclear weapons under the NPT offers a case in point. The NPT is a legally binding agreement that, among other things, obligates non-nuclear weapons parties not to acquire such weapons and requires international inspections of all their nuclear activities to verify compliance and ensure the peaceful use of any nuclear materials.[262] Just as the BWC guarantees various rights with respect to peaceful uses of regulated dual-use materials, so the NPT affirms an "inalienable right of all the Parties to the Treaty to develop research, production and use of nuclear energy for peaceful purposes" and guarantees the "fullest possible exchange of equipment, materials and scientific and technological information for the peaceful uses of nuclear energy."[263] As under the BWC, some NPT-regulated materials may have both military and peaceful applications, increasing the risk of defensive defections based on misperceived threats. The high security stakes at issue in the NPT and the "prestige" and power associated with nuclear weapons also present temptations for offensive defectors, and this temptation is not reduced by the status that several powerful countries continue to enjoy as nuclear weapons states under the NPT.[264] Structures and measures to identify and detect cheating are thus design elements for an effective NPT regime.

Specific procedures and detailed requirements designed to ensure verification of the fulfillment of a state's obligations under the NPT are incorporated into the legally binding comprehensive safeguards agreement that each non-nuclear weapons party is required to negotiate with the International Atomic Energy Agency (IAEA).[265] As the NPT has matured, the IAEA has "hardened" the regime's transparency requirements by continually extracting deeper and more precise commitments from member states through legally binding additional protocols that are designed to reinforce the safeguards agreements.[266] The IAEA developed the Model Additional Protocol in 1997 in response to Iraq's successful concealment of its pre-1991 nuclear program.[267]

[262] NPT, *supra* note 202, Arts. II, III.

[263] *Id.*, Art. IV(1), (2).

[264] Unlike biological weapons, nuclear weapons are widely viewed as an effective strategic deterrent and have become an integral part of the security policies of NPT nuclear weapons states parties. Moreover, biological weapons are less likely to inspire the "ferocious nationalistic pride" that nuclear weapons and energy generate in some states. *See* Christopher Dickey et al., *Iran's Rogue Rage, Nukes: Iranians Want Nuclear Know-How—and Seem to Be Daring the West to Stop Them*, NEWSWEEK, Jan. 23, 2006, at 26, 26.

[265] The IAEA is a UN-related organization whose safeguards system is intended to verify NPT compliance. As of March 22, 2007, thirty-one NPT non-nuclear weapon states had not yet brought into force a comprehensive safeguards agreement with the IAEA. NPT Comprehensive Safeguards Agreement: Overview of Status (Mar. 22, 2007), *at* <http://www.iaea.org/Publications/Factsheets/English/nptstatus_overview.html>.

[266] One hundred and eleven UN member states have signed additional protocols and seventy-seven are currently in force; a protocol with Iran is being implemented pending its formal entry into force, although Iran recently curtailed most access to its facilities. *See id.*

[267] *See* IAEA Staff Reports, More States Sign Safeguards Agreements and Additional Protocols (Nov. 28, 2005), *available at* <http://www.iaea.org/NewsCenter/News/2005/safeguardsrights.html>.

In the case of Iran's controversial uranium enrichment and reprocessing activities and related deceptive practices, the IAEA has sought more detailed and precise information and an even more comprehensive level of access than is required by the safeguards agreement and additional protocol.[268] Such additional detailed transparency and verification measures form a critical part of the maturing and hardening of the NPT regime as it has continued to attract new members: only 4 of the 192 members of the United Nations are nonparties to the NPT and remain outside its legally binding obligations.[269]

Even as the NPT has progressively become harder, the regime has suffered setbacks in some important cases where the IAEA has relied on both nonlegally binding instruments and indeterminate language. For example, after years of failing to meet its obligations under its safeguards agreement,[270] the Iranian government was nonetheless initially able to escape referral by the IAEA to the UN Security Council for its apparent NPT violations in September 2003 by agreeing merely to a vague nonbinding statement that it would voluntarily suspend its suspect uranium enrichment and processing activities.[271] On January 10, 2006, Iran reneged on this nonbinding commitment and announced that it had broken the internationally monitored seals at its nuclear sites and would resume "research activities" with equipment that included centrifuges capable of enriching uranium for use in a nuclear bomb.[272] On June 6, 2006, the five permanent members of the Security Council and Germany offered Iran a package of incentives accompanied by an array of possible penalties aimed at persuading it to freeze some of its most important questionable nuclear activities.[273] After Iran rejected a proposed incentives package and refused to halt its enrichment and reprocessing activities, the UN Security Council, on July 31, 2006, adopted a resolution calling on Iran to

[268] The IAEA Board of Governors urged Iran to adopt these additional transparency measures on September 24, 2005, noting that "Iran's full transparency is indispensable and overdue." IAEA Res. GOV/2005/77, pmbl., para. 4 (Sept. 24, 2005), at <http://www.iaea.org/Publications/Documents/Board/2005/gov2005-77.pdf>. Subsequent board resolutions have continued to stress the need for Iran to implement all required transparency measures and support ongoing board investigations. See, e.g., IAEA Res. GOV/2006/14 (Feb. 4, 2006), at <http://www. iaea.org/Publications/Documents/Board/2006/gov2006-14.pdf>. The UN Security Council has repeatedly affirmed that Iran must comply with IAEA Res. GOV/2006/14 in order "to build confidence in the exclusively peaceful purpose of its nuclear programme and to resolve outstanding questions." SC Res. 1696, para. 1 (July 31, 2006); SC Res. 1737, para. 1 (Dec. 27, 2006); SC Res. 1747, para. 1 (Mar. 24, 2007).

[269] India, Israel, and Pakistan have not signed the NPT; North Korea joined the NPT in 1985, but in January 2003 announced its intention to withdraw. See Status of Multilateral Arms Regulation and Disarmament Agreements, supra note 230.

[270] IAEA Director General, Implementation of the NPT Safeguards Agreement in the Islamic Republic of Iran, IAEA Doc. GOV/2005/67 (Sept. 2, 2005), at <http://www.iaea.org/Publications/Documents/Board/2005/gov2005-67.pdf> (detailing how over many years Iran had failed to meet its obligations under its safeguards agreement by not reporting nuclear material, its processing, and its use; not declaring related processing and storage facilities; not providing design information; and engaging in "extensive concealment activities").

[271] Statement by the Iranian Government and Visiting EU Foreign Ministers, para. 2(b)(i) (Oct. 21, 2003), available at <http://www.iaea.org/NewsCenter/Focus/IaeaIran/statement_iran21102003.shtml>. Iran's chief nuclear negotiator noted that Iran had "won a crucial change to reflect the fact that the freeze of its enrichment program was 'not legally binding.'" Elaine Sciolino, Iran Backs away from a Demand on A-Bomb Fuel, N.Y. TIMES, Nov. 29, 2004, at A1.

[272] Steven R. Weisman & Nazila Fathi, Iranians Reopen Nuclear Centers, N.Y. TIMES, Jan. 11, 2006, at A1.

[273] Nazila Fathi & Elaine Sciolino, Iran Open to Incentives on Nuclear Talks, with a Hedge, N.Y. TIMES, June 7, 2006, at A14. Subsequent attempts by the European Union to work out an "incentives package" with Iran led to Iranian requests for specific details on "verification" and "sequencing." See Judy Dempsey, Iranian and Europe Envoy Open Talks on Uranium Enrichment, N.Y. TIMES, Sept. 28, 2006, at A14.

suspend these activities.[274] Confronted with Iranian defiance, the Security Council approved additional resolutions in December 2006 and March 2007, which imposed mild sanctions and threatened tougher ones if Iran continued to fail to comply with the Council's demands.[275]

As the Iranian nuclear crisis continues to unfold at the writing of this article, concerned NPT members face considerable risks and challenges in designing a supplemental framework to ensure that Iran will comply fully with regime requirements as it continues to engage in "peaceful" nuclear activities. Since Iran enjoys an "inalienable right" to the peaceful use of nuclear energy—which its leaders argue includes uranium enrichment processes that can produce both fuel for nuclear reactors and fissionable material for nuclear weapons—continuing efforts to persuade Iran to forgo that right are likely to involve proposed incentives, rewards, or compensation, in addition to the threat of possible sanctions.

The design of an incentives or compensation package to encourage Iran to comply with its NPT obligations and permit related inspections will probably require determinacy to establish the requisite behavior, the contours of the incentives, and the penalties involved. *Both* sides in such a transaction appear to have a fundamental interest in ensuring determinacy, as demonstrated by the initial response of Iran's chief nuclear negotiator to the package of incentives and penalties proposed on June 6, 2006, when he expressed concern about the removal of some "ambiguities."[276]

Another example of applied determinacy and transparency in a multilateral disarmament regime charged with the regulation of dual-use materials is the CWC. The CWC enjoys the benefit of a dedicated full-time oversight authority, the Organization for the Prohibition of Chemical Weapons (OPCW),[277] as well as an elaborate verification regime containing mechanisms and procedures for conducting eleven different types of inspections that can take advantage of several reinforcing layers of determinate rules. In addition to obligations in the text, annexes to the CWC spell out, with as much clarity and precision as possible, critical definitions, guidelines, criteria, and schedules of chemicals to be used in regulating the elimination of chemical weapons.[278] The CWC also contains an Annex on the Protection of Confidential Information and an Annex on Implementation and Verification, which establish various criteria and definitions pertaining to regulated equipment, buildings, and personnel.[279]

As with other regulated weapons, various incentives for defection by states from CW disarmament cooperation can easily be identified. For example, the military and civilian applications of many chemicals and their precursors may elicit misperceived threats and

---

[274] SC Res. 1696 (July 31, 2006). Iran failed to comply with the Council's sixty-day deadline for suspension of these activities. *See* Dafna Linzer & Colum Lynch, *Iran Continues Nuclear Work Despite Deadline, Sanction Threat*, WASH. POST, Feb. 22, 2007, at A14.

[275] *See* SC Res. 1737 (Dec. 27, 2006) (prohibiting trade with Iran in nuclear materials and ballistic missiles and freezing financial assets of ten key Iranian entities and twelve individuals associated with these programs); SC Res. 1747 (Mar. 24, 2007) (banning all Iranian arms exports and freezing financial assets of fifteen Iranian individuals and thirteen entities linked to Iranian military and nuclear agencies).

[276] Fathi & Sciolino, *supra* note 273.

[277] The OPCW includes the Conference of States Parties, Executive Council, Technical Secretariat, Confidentiality Commission, and advisory boards on science and administrative and financial matters.

[278] An integral part of the CWC is a detailed Annex on Chemicals that includes Guidelines for Schedules of Chemicals. The guidelines in part I of the annex contain specific criteria for determining whether toxic chemicals or precursors should be included in one of three different schedules or levels of regulation in part II of the annex. These schedules identify chemicals for the application of extensive verification measures according to the provisions of the detailed Verification Annex. *See* CWC, *supra* note 158, Annex on Chemicals.

[279] *See* CWC, Annex on the Protection of Confidential Information; *id.*, Annex on Implementation and Verification.

defensive defections. In addition, unlike biological weapons, chemical weapons have a history of demonstrated military utility, particularly in some recent conflicts in the Middle East, and thus present a real risk that a state will cheat to gain a decisive military advantage. Unlike the BWC regime, the CWC regime has been forced to deal with weapons that in many cases were deployed in sizable numbers and often presented complex questions about their safe removal and disposal.[280] In spite of the CWC's recent entry into force, the incentives for noncompliance, and the complexity and expense of safe and environmentally sound CW disposal, the regime has achieved striking success. The CWC has already attracted 179 UN members as states parties, and in the ten years since its entry into force in 1997 all CW production facilities declared by states have been inactivated, all declared CW stockpiles have been inventoried and verified, and 59 of the 65 declared CW production facilities have been either destroyed or converted for peaceful purposes.[281] In addition, nearly twenty-eight hundred inspections have taken place at nearly two hundred CW-related facilities and at over 850 industrial sites on the territory of 77 states parties.[282] As the CWC regime matures and cooperation deepens, determinacy plays an increasingly important role in the success of inspections, the regulation of chemical agents, the elimination of CW stockpiles, and related assistance activities.

Although states have succeeded in making other multilateral disarmament regimes progressively harder, the collapse and failure of collective state action to reform the BWC has coincided with calls by some legal scholars to focus less attention on governmental actions and more on the role that individual scientists, businesses, trade organizations, academic groups, and other nongovernmental actors in civil society can play in preventing BW proliferation and in protecting human health and the environment.[283] Consistently with the view that rejects states as primary and unitary actors in international affairs in favor of a disaggregated model that emphasizes the role of nonstate actors and the importance of transnational societal interaction,[284] some commentators have suggested that the appearance of new and reemerging infectious diseases has demonstrated the limitations of Westphalian governance,[285] while highlighting the growing significance of nonstate actors in a new framework of "global health

---

[280] David A. Koplow, *How Do We Get Rid of These Things?: Dismantling Excess Weapons While Protecting the Environment*, 89 NW. U. L. REV. 445, 451 (1995).

[281] *See* Status of Multilateral Arms Regulation and Disarmament Agreements, *supra* note 230; Organisation for the Prohibition of Chemical Weapons, Declarations and Inspections, and Chemical Weapons Destruction Under Way (Mar. 16, 2007), *at* <http://www.opcw.org/factsandfigures/index.html> (further noting that "[o]ver 30% of the 8.6 million chemical munitions and containers covered by the Convention have been verifiably destroyed").

[282] Organisation for the Prohibition of Chemical Weapons, Declarations and Inspections, *supra* note 281.

[283] *See* Wright & Falk, *supra* note 125, at 433 (arguing for "a heightened mobilization of global civil society" as with conclusion of the antipersonnel land mines treaty as only way to avoid a biological arms race); *see also* Kenneth Anderson, *The Ottawa Convention Banning Landmines, the Role of International Non-governmental Organizations, and the Idea of International Civil Society*, 11 EUR J. INT'L L. 91 (2000); Richard Price, *Reversing the Gun Sights: Transnational Civil Society Targets Land Mines*, 52 INT'L ORG. 613 (1998).

[284] *See* Anne-Marie Slaughter Burley, *International Law and International Relations Theory: A Dual Agenda*, 87 AJIL 205, 225 (1993); Andrew Moravcsik, *Taking Preferences Seriously: A Liberal Theory of International Politics*, 51 INT'L ORG. 513, 522 (1997); Anne-Marie Slaughter, *A Liberal Theory of International Law*, 94 ASIL PROC. 240 (2000).

[285] *See generally* David P. Fidler, *SARS: Political Pathology of the First Post-Westphalian Pathogen*, 31 J. L. MED. & ETHICS 485 (2003).

governance."[286] In fact, transnational societal efforts to prevent BW proliferation continue to be pursued, including through codes of conduct for scientists, guidelines for corporations in the biopharmaceutical sector, and various other initiatives designed to provide more safety and security in biotechnology.

Notwithstanding their increasing importance in some areas, transnational societal efforts have made uneven progress across different fields of international cooperation[287] and may be especially limited in the area of national security, where states play the dominant role and continue to develop dangerous weaponized pathogens on the basis of their own security-driven, self-interested preferences. Furthermore, many transnational societal efforts related to BW nonproliferation are affected by the large amounts of funding that governments now provide to universities, companies, and other nonstate actors for their participation in BW-related programs, including expansive and sometimes questionable biodefense programs.[288] Their many financial and other interests may prevent these transnational societal efforts from being consistently or universally directed toward the same goals.[289] One important group of nonstate actors that supports many transnational biosecurity and biosafety issues, the U.S. pharmaceutical industry, has also been a major force in opposing efforts to strengthen the BWC regime. In comments reflecting the concerns of this group, the U.S. government stated that it opposed the BWC draft protocol in part because it would negatively affect the pharmaceutical and biotech industries by putting "confidential business information at risk."[290]

In the long term, however, determinacy may offer solutions for some of the nonstate actors that now oppose a harder BWC regime. For instance, while some concerns expressed by the U.S. pharmaceutical and biotech industries regarding the draft protocol may be legitimate, the experience of the U.S. chemical industry in implementing the CWC suggests that corporations can protect their business secrets and function reasonably well under a broadly similar disarmament regime if clearly stated, determinate requirements underlie applicable monitoring measures. While biological and chemical weapons present some different challenges, the

---

[286] *See* David P. Fidler, *Constitutional Outlines of Public Health's New World Order*, 77 TEMP. L. REV. 247, 267 (2004) (noting how nonstate actors performed key monitoring functions and provided accurate data on the SARS outbreak in China in 2003, eventually forcing China to deal more openly with the outbreak and causing similar embarrassment for the governments of Thailand and Indonesia).

[287] While transnational societal factors may contribute to the larger phenomenon of globalization or the cross-national convergence of national economic and regulatory systems, state interests continue to play a critical role, and this globalization is not proceeding evenly either across the globe or across economic sectors or other regulatory topics. *See* Richard H. Steinberg, *Trade-Environment Negotiations in the EU, NAFTA, and WTO: Regional Trajectories of Rule Development*, 91 AJIL 231, 232 (1997).

[288] The U.S. government's financial involvement with academic institutions in this area began in 1942 with contracts for secret work at over two dozen major U.S. universities. *See* Barton J. Bernstein, *Origins of the Biological Warfare Program*, in PREVENTING A BIOLOGICAL ARMS RACE, *supra* note 49, at 9, 12. By 1968, U.S. government involvement in both chemical and biological weapons programs had made such weapons "big business" for industry and higher learning. CLARKE, *supra* note 31, at 8. Massive increases in U.S. biodefense spending in recent years involve numerous government agencies and nonstate institutions. In the civilian biodefense sector alone, the government has dramatically increased spending since 2001. Joby Warrick, *Custom-Built Pathogens Raise Bioterror Fears*, WASH. POST, July 31, 2006, at A1 ("Five years after the Sept. 11 attacks, the federal government budgets nearly $8 billion annually—an 18-fold increase since 2001—for the defense of civilians against biological attack.").

[289] Steve Charnovitz, *Nongovernmental Organizations and International Law*, 100 AJIL 348, 348 (2006) (noting that "[t]oday, overwhelming NGO support for the international rule of law can no longer be assumed. NGOs follow their own stars.").

[290] Mahley, *supra* note 80 ("In our assessment, the draft Protocol would put national security and confidential business information at risk.").

pharmaceutical industry might find determinacy in the BWC regime to be as desirable as the chemical industry and member governments have found it to be in the CWC regime.[291] Nongovernmental organizations and nonstate or transnational actors that strongly support BW nonproliferation efforts may also support hard rules since they can provide these actors with a range of new strategies and facilitate enforcement actions against both governmental and nongovernmental entities.[292]

While transnational actors will continue to contribute to BW nonproliferation efforts and are likely to benefit from determinate rules in the BWC, state actors with security-driven preferences hold the key to establishing an effective ban on biological weapons. In 1972, in an attempt to achieve various short-term security objectives in the context of bipolar Cold War strategies, the most powerful state actors chose the short-term benefits and expediency of soft indeterminate provisions and soft structural approaches in designing a "hard" legally binding BWC regime. In the context of modern BW proliferation problems, however, these states now have a self-interested security basis for eschewing this type of soft law approach. The United States in particular has reason to reevaluate, in light of its long-term national security interests, the rejection of BWC reform policies that it embraced prior to adopting a position based on myopic interests and unilateralist sentiments. Although a soft law approach based on indeterminacy may be beneficial in other contexts, the long-term impact of its psychological and rational mechanisms in modern arms control and multilateral security instruments presents fundamental problems that pose a different research agenda.

---

[291] *See* Tibor Tóth, *The Requirement to Strengthen the Biological and Toxin Weapons Convention, in* IMPLEMENTATION OF LEGALLY BINDING MEASURES, *supra* note 261, at 9, 13 (arguing that the industry players involved in BWC-related activities "will need clear-cut rules of the game" and that "these companies and industrial actors would prefer clarity in the rules of the game that are applicable globally").

[292] *See* Abbott & Snidal, *supra* note 17, at 451 (private demandeurs will normally press for hard law, other things being equal, to raise the costs of violation for other parties and to facilitate enforcement against resister groups and governments, including their own).

[15]

CBW Export Controls: Towards Regime Integration?

Alexander Kelle
Lecturer, Queen's University, Belfast

Introduction

Even after a cursory look at the debate on export controls in general and those aimed at chemical and biological dual-use materials, technologies and services in particular, one cannot avoid the impression that much of that debate is dominated by either rhetoric or ignorance (Roberts 1995). The rhetoric is provided by fundamental and dogmatic critics of these controls, many of which are to be found in the Non-Aligned Movement (NAM) and who equal export controls with a strategy of export denial. Their criticism, however, has not been substantiated with figures as to how big a trade volume has been denied to them. Even the enumeration of a set of instances, in which exports were denied and end-uses were very obviously and unambiguously peaceful, has not been forthcoming from the camp of dogmatic export control critics. This – as well as the fact that most of the states who are accused of withholding essential technologies and material from developing states are trading states who have an interest in free, and not restricted trade – very much nurtures the suspicion that export controls are either misunderstood or misrepresented when they are portrayed primarily as a means to implement a strategy of export denial. This rhetoric has led many export control proponents to ignore these criticisms as outlandish and politically motivated, rather than based in fact. This perception, in turn, has prompted the mantra-like reiteration of the well-known western position that export controls are a mere manifestation of the non-transfer norms (see below) contained in the nuclear weapons control regime and the chemical and biological weapons prohibition regimes. As a result, a constructive debate on chemical and biological weapons-related export controls has been taking place only to a limited extent.

Such a constructive debate might usefully start with an explication of the functions that export controls on dual-use goods, technologies and services serve. Their primary goal is to ensure the civil application of exported commodities and services and to deter recipients from using them in military programmes. In order to fulfil this function domestically, that is in the supplying state, export control measures have to be capable of identifying illegal exports and of threatening the potential exporter with a level of punishment that exceeds any gain from such an illegal export. Although export controls on dual-use goods and equipment pursued in isolation from other non-proliferation measures cannot prevent the acquisition of WMD by a determined proliferant, they can slow down the procurement process and increase the proliferant's costs. When coordinated among supplier states, export controls provide a level playing field for potential suppliers in different states, thereby greatly increasing the hurdles for a proliferant. Harmonized export controls – such as in the Australia Group – make it more difficult to play one supplier against the other, since the individual exporters do not have to face comparative disadvantages because of unequal export control guidelines (Müller et al. 1993; Roberts 1998).

Export controls are but one part of the more comprehensive control (in the case of nuclear weapons) or prohibition regimes (in the case of chemical and biological weapons). As there are a number of different understandings and usages of the term 'regime' in the academic literature (Hasenclever, Mayer and Rittberger 1997), let alone in the political arena, it is necessary to briefly outline its usage in this chapter: international regimes are an issue area specific subset of international institutions 'around which actor expectations converge in a given issue area' (Krasner 1982, 185). International regimes display a four-part structure, consisting of principles, norms, rules and procedures. As Krasner has summarized:

> Principles are beliefs of fact, causation, and rectitude. Norms are standards of behaviour defined in terms of rights and obligations. Rules are specific prescriptions or proscriptions for actions. Decision-making procedures are prevailing practices for making and implementing collective choice (Krasner 1982, 186).

Understood in this way, international regimes shape expectations, prescribe roles, guide behaviour and thus create an order in a particular issue area among actors on the international level (Müller 1993).

In the issue areas of chemical and biological weapon prohibition, the core underlying principle is that the use of chemical and biological weapons (CBW) constitutes an abhorrent act of warfare and, as such, has to be prohibited. Since the late nineteenth century this principle has found its way into a number of international treaties which culminated in the Biological and Toxins Weapons Convention (BTWC) 1972 and the Chemical Weapons Convention (CWC) 1993. Both BTWC and CWC form the central pillars of the two prohibition regimes, which will be discussed in detail in the third part of this chapter. The preceding section will analyse the activities of the Australia Group in the area of chemical and biological export controls. The final part of the chapter will summarize the state of play and assess prospects for a higher degree of regime integration as regards the non-transfer norms contained in the two regimes and the Australia Group's functions.

Chemical and Biological Weapons Export Controls and the Australia Group

The Australia Group (AG) was founded in 1985, following an Australian initiative. The AG's original purpose was to harmonize national controls on the trade in dual-use chemical warfare agents. It was created in response to the rapid proliferation of chemical weapons, their repeated use in the Iran–Iraq war, and the limited progress in negotiations on the CWC (Robinson 1992; Smithson 1997). The AG consisted originally of 15 states[1] plus the European Union (EU) in an observer role. However, even among these states, the harmonization and deepening cooperation on expanded export controls was not uncontroversial, as some EU member states questioned whether the cooperation among AG participants was in conformity with other obligations they had already undertaken, most notably EU membership, where one of the founding treaties, the Rome Treaty, in its Article 223 gives exclusive authority to member states in matters of defence (Robinson 1992, 159). Despite these initial worries, the AG continuously expanded both its membership and the range of goods and technologies covered by its harmonized controls.

Membership of the Group has more than doubled from the 15 founding members. While initial growth in membership was restricted geographically to Europe, with the addition of Argentina in 1993 and South Korea in 1996, the AG expanded into the Americas and Asia. The latest member Ukraine, which took part in AG proceedings for the first time in April 2005, brings current AG membership to 39 states plus the European Union (Australia Group 2005). Initially, the AG met bi-annually, but later moved to an annual meeting schedule. It is noteworthy that the AG is not an international organization in the formal sense. It does not have a budget, standing bureaucracy or permanent office buildings. Rather, the Australian embassy in Paris acts as contact point, providing secretarial services for the annual meetings.

> The Australia Group is an informal arrangement. Participants do not undertake any legally binding obligations: the effectiveness of the cooperation between participants depends solely on their commitment to CBW nonproliferation goals and on the effectiveness of measures implemented nationally which aim at preventing the spread of chemical and biological weapons (Australia Group, 2000).

In 1990 AG participants agreed to expand their controls to cover biological weapon agents and toxins, as well as dual-use equipment necessary for their production. In 1992 control lists were agreed upon which covered 18 bacteria, four rickettsiae, 25 viruses and 14 toxins. In addition, dual-use equipment like fermenters, centrifuges, aerosol chambers and filter and freeze-drying equipment with certain technical specifications were subjected to controls (Robinson 1992). The following year, the AG agreed on a so-called no-undercut policy which relies on 'procedures for ensuring that denials of an export of a listed item for CBW non-proliferation reasons by one member would be respected by all other members' (Australia Group 1993). The meeting in October 1995 reflected the increased risk of terrorists acquiring chemical and biological weapons, as evidenced by the Aum Shinrikyo sarin gas attack in the Tokyo subway system earlier that year – a topic the AG would return to a few years later in the aftermath of the anthrax mailings in the United States in the autumn of 2001. In addition to the growing terrorist threat continuous reviews and updates of the AG's procedures, guidelines and control lists were necessitated by advances in science and technology and changes in the international regulatory environment

(Australia Group 2001). Thus the AG had to bring its controls on the transfer of chemical mixtures in line with the parameters agreed upon by the Organization for the Prohibition of Chemical Weapons (OPCW) member states during the 5th session of the Conference of State Parties in 2000.

Australia Group controls made a quantum leap in 2002 when its participants agreed on a new set of measures which went considerably beyond those previously agreed upon. First of all, the AG adopted 'formal guidelines governing the licensing of sensitive chemical and biological items' which included a so-called 'catch-all' provision, supplementing the exclusively list-based approach pursued before (Australia Group 2002). These guidelines were subsequently made publicly available (Australia Group 2004). In addition, the AG agreed to control 'for the first time, the intangible transfer of information and knowledge which could be used for chemical and biological weapons purposes'. The group furthermore agreed to tighten controls on certain equipment, such as fermenters, for which the volume threshold at which controls would be started to apply was lowered from 100 to 20 litres, and to add more toxins to its control list (Australia Group 2002).

Overall, two decades of efforts to control sensitive biological and chemical items in order to prevent their use in chemical and biological weapons programmes of either states or sub-state groups, such as terrorist organizations, has resulted in the formulation of export control guidelines, to which all AG participants adhere, and a set of six control lists covering dual-use chemical manufacturing facilities and equipment and related technology, chemical weapons precursors, dual-use biological equipment and related technology, biological agents, animal pathogens and plant pathogens (all lists available at <www.australiagroup.net>). From the point of view of critics of the AG's activities in the chemical realm, it is not only the controls on manufacturing equipment that they regard as contravening the letter and spirit of the CWC but also the fact that 24 of the 63 precursors on the AG list are not listed on any of the CWC's three schedules on chemicals. This gives the appearance that the AG chemical weapons precursor control list covers a wider area than the CWC schedules and, one could argue, in conjunction with its application to CWC state parties, runs counter to Article XI of the CWC (see below).

The Chemical and Biological Weapons Prohibition Regimes

The Chemical Weapons Prohibition Regime

Regime Structure[2]   As already mentioned above, the principles of an international regime are the shared beliefs of regime participants about the issue area which they want to regulate through the regime. In the case of the chemical weapons prohibition regime, the belief that the use of chemical weapons constitutes an abhorrent act of warfare – sometimes referred to as chemical weapon taboo (Price 1997) – is the central regime principle. It leads to the central regime goal: in the words of the preamble of the CWC, 'for the sake of all mankind, to exclude completely the possibility of the use of chemical weapons'. The second regime principle reflects the recognition that the peaceful uses of chemistry are a legitimate undertaking. However, as peaceful uses of chemistry cannot be taken for granted, two additional principles have been agreed upon: first, defences against the threat or use of chemical weapons are a legitimate undertaking, and secondly the acknowledgement that regime compliance by state parties needs to be verified. Finally, due to the nature and speed of scientific and technological advances in chemistry and the life sciences more generally, state parties share an understanding of the dynamic character of the issue area that the chemical weapon prohibition regime is set up to regulate.

The regime norms are derived from these five principles. They are to guide state behaviour in the issue area and thereby lead to the achievement of the regime goals. From the recognition that the use of chemical weapons constitutes an abhorrent act of warfare, a couple of core regime norms follow: first of all, states which possess chemical weapons have to destroy their stockpiles completely (the disarmament norm). State parties who do not possess chemical weapons commit themselves not to acquire them (the non-acquisition norm). All state parties agree never to use chemical weapons (the non-use norm) and – central to the argument of this chapter – not to transfer materials or technology that will aid a third party in chemical weapon production (the non-transfer norm).

The verification principle in turn has lead state parties to submit information related to chemical weapons and chemical industry (the declaration norm) to the OPCW. Likewise, state parties allow the OPCW's secretariat to perform on-site inspections (the inspection norm) of the accuracy of the declarations, the progress of CW destruction, and other obligations they have undertaken.

The principle that civilian applications of chemistry are legitimate informs the CWC's cooperation norm, which prescribes that the implementation of the Convention must not impede the civilian applications and free trade in chemicals for purposes not prohibited under the CWC. In cases of the threat or use of chemical weapons against a state party to the CWC, the provision of assistance to be provided by those in a position to do so has been included in the text of the CWC (the assistance norm). The consultation norm takes on two different forms in the chemical weapons prohibition regime: firstly, CWC state parties commit themselves to consultation in case of problems in implementing the treaty. Secondly, in the context of the Australia Group, of which only some CWC members are participating, states have agreed to consult one another in case of a transfer request which threatens to contribute to the proliferation of chemical and biological weapons. Furthermore, the internalization norm requires state parties to the CWC to translate the stipulations contained in the Convention into their national legal systems. Lastly, but not least, state parties are under an obligation to keep the regime current with respect to developments in science and technology (S&T) of relevance to the regime (the adaptation norm).

The rules and procedures of the chemical weapons control regime are so numerous that discussion of these rules and procedures is well beyond the scope of this chapter. However, some of the rules and procedures that relate to the non-transfer norm will be addressed in subsequent sections.

CWC Transfer System and Australia Group Controls   In the final stages of negotiating the CWC, the then ambassador of Australia to the Conference on Disarmament, Ambassador O'Sullivan made a statement in August 1992 on behalf of the Australia Group, according to which its members would review its activities in the field of export controls 'with the aim of removing such measures for the benefit of State Parties to the Convention acting in full compliance with their obligations under the Convention' (Conference on Disarmament 1992). As Feakes (2001, 47) has pointed out, this statement was not greeted with universal optimism by NAM members. However, in the end it proved useful in securing the approval of the CWC's text.

Non-transfer-related regulations are contained in a number of Articles of the Convention. According to Article I (1), 'each State Party to this Convention undertakes never under any circumstances: (a) To ... transfer, directly or indirectly, chemical weapons to anyone'. Following Article VI (2), '[e]ach State Party shall adopt the necessary measures to ensure that toxic chemicals and their precursors are only ... transferred ... for purposes not prohibited' under the CWC. In addition, Article XI (2) tasks state parties in section (e) to 'undertake to review their existing national regulations in the field of trade in chemicals in order to render them consistent with the objective and purpose of this Convention'.

More detailed transfer guidelines are found in the Verification Annex, Parts VI, VII and VIII. Part VI contains the 'Regime for Schedule 1 Chemicals and Related Facilities', according to which 'a State Party may transfer Schedule 1 chemicals outside its territory only to another State Party and only for research, medical, pharmaceutical or protective purposes. Chemicals transferred shall not be retransferred to a third State'.

In Part VII of the Verification Annex, the regime for Schedule 2 chemicals and related facilities is spelled out. Section C on 'Transfers to States Not Party to this Convention' stipulates that Schedule 2 chemicals shall only be transferred to or received from state parties. This obligation has taken effect three years after entry into force of the CWC, that is, in the spring of 2000. During the interim three-year period, each state party had to require an end-user certificate for transfers of Schedule 2 chemicals to states not party to the CWC. Such end-user certificates had to state: that the transferred chemicals will only be used for purposes not prohibited under the CWC; that they will not be retransferred; their types and quantities; their end-use(s); and the name(s) and address(es) of the end-user(s).

Similarly, Part VIII of the Verification Annex contains the regime for Schedule 3 chemicals and related facilities. It states that when transferring Schedule 3 chemicals to states not party to the CWC, each state party shall adopt the necessary measures to ensure that the transferred chemicals shall only be used for purposes not prohibited under the CWC. A requirement – comparable to the one for Schedule 2 chemicals – exists for demanding an end-user certificate from the recipient state. Five years after the CWC's entry into force – that is, in April 2002 – the Conference of State Parties (CSP) had to consider the question of whether to establish other measures regarding transfers of Schedule 3 chemicals to states not party to the CWC. Although Feakes notes a correlation between the number of new accessions to the CWC in 2000 and the enactment of trade restrictions for Schedule 2 chemicals (Feakes 2001, 51), this did not seem to provide a big enough incentive for CWC state parties to restrict trade in Schedule 3 chemicals. Rather, reflecting many state parties interest in the chemical trade, April 2002 came and went without any additional trade-restricting measures being agreed upon.

A similar pattern of behaviour could be observed in relation to the transfers to non-state parties of mixtures containing Schedule 2 chemicals. A decision had to be reached on this matter because of the above-mentioned trade restrictions taking effect three years after the CWC's entry into force. According to the decision reached at the 5th session of the CSP in May 2000, transfers to non-state parties are permitted firstly, if the products contain 1 per cent or less of a Schedule 2A or 2A chemical; secondly, if the products contain 10 per cent or less of a Schedule 2B chemical or; thirdly, if products are identified as consumer goods packaged for retail sale for personal use or packaged for individual use (OPCW 2000).

The continued dissatisfaction of some NAM states with the export controls of the Australia Group applied to CWC member states was brought to the fore during the 3rd Session of the Conference of State Parties of the OPCW in November 1998. During this meeting of CWC state parties, Iran, Cuba and Pakistan submitted a draft resolution in which the Conference was asked to emphasize that the CWC 'has not envisaged any export control restriction in chemical trade between State Parties for peaceful purposes', that 'the OPCW should be seen as the sole responsible body to verify the compliance of the State Parties with their obligations undertaken under the Convention' and that CWC state parties 'should abide by the provisions of the Convention and abolish existing export control regimes against state parties in order to render their national regulations ... consistent with the obligations undertaken in accordance with the Article XI of the Convention' (Iran, Cuba and Pakistan 1998). The draft resolution went on to request that state parties complete their review of national regulations so as to render them consistent with the above quoted stipulation of Article XI of the CWC. Predictably, this resolution was not adopted by the CSP. Instead, the OPCW's Executive Council was tasked to deal with the matter. Thus, form this point onwards export controls were explicitly on the Council's agenda, but no discernible action has been taken by that body. However, it has to be assumed that this trilateral initiative has been the motivator behind the Australian, Canadian, Swedish and US national papers that were presented to the 4th CSP session in outlining their respective national implementation mechanisms of Article XI including the review of their national export control regulations (Australia 1999; Canada 1999; Sweden 1999; United States of America 1999). Somewhat surprisingly NAM critics received some backing for their position from the Director-General of the OPCW's Technical Secretariat in his opening statement to the 5th Session of the CSP:

> As more states join the CWC, and as their chemical producers support it, the arguments originally advanced for the maintenance of restrictions outside a credible reliable international legal framework become increasingly redundant. Given this fact, the continuing existence of export controls by some State Parties against others is hard to understand and very difficult to justify.[3]

The First CWC Review Conference in April and May 2003 then witnessed another replay of the by now decades-old debate about whether the Australia Group violates the stipulations of the CWC and should be abolished without delay – or whether the AG represents an important instrument for CWC state parties to fulfil their non-proliferation obligations stemming from the Convention. The distribution of roles in this almost ritualistic exchange of arguments was entirely predictable: Brazil, India, Iran, Malaysia (on behalf of the NAM and China) and Pakistan criticized the AG; the United Kingdom and the US, among others, defended the need for its continued existence. Given the hardened fronts in this debate, the Review Document is confined to a reiteration of text contained in the CWC, urging the EU to 'continue its facilitation efforts to reach early agreement on the issue of the full implementation of Article XI' (OPCW 2003).

The Biological Weapons Prohibition Regime

Regime Structure[4]   Four regime principles of the biological weapons prohibition regime, which are very similar to the ones identified earlier for the chemical weapons prohibition regime, can be identified. The first is related to the conviction of regime participants that the use of biological weapon agents constitutes an abhorrent act of warfare and is therefore prohibited. It was first expressed in the 1925 Geneva Protocol and later reiterated in the Biological and Toxins Weapons Convention (BTWC) preamble, in which BTWC state parties confirm their determination, 'for the sake of all mankind, to exclude completely the possibility of bacteriological (biological) agents and toxins being used as weapons, [c]onvinced that such use would be repugnant to the conscience of mankind'.

According to the second principle, on which the biological weapons control regime is based, peaceful uses of the biosciences are a legitimate undertaking. The wording of the prohibitions contained in Article I of the BTWC reflect this peaceful uses principle. Accordingly:

> Each State Party to this Convention undertakes never in any circumstances to develop, produce, stockpile or otherwise acquire or retain: (1) Microbial or other biological agents, or toxins whatever their origin or method of production, of types and in quantities that have no justification for prophylactic, protective or other peaceful purposes.

This so-called general purpose criterion makes it clear not only that peaceful uses of the biosciences are legitimate undertakings for state parties to the BTWC, but makes them such even if they involve pathogenic organisms or toxins in quantities and for purposes other than use as weapons.

The third regime principle expresses the assumption of states subscribing to the regime that defences against the threat or use of biological and toxin weapons are permitted, which is also expressed in the above quote from Article I of the Convention. This principle is rooted in the belief that the peaceful uses of biosciences cannot be taken for granted – be it for the lacking universality in membership or for a state party cheating on the obligations it has assumed. However, while this underlying belief has led, in both the nuclear non-proliferation regime and the chemical weapons control regime, to the manifestation of yet another principle, the verification principle, this has not materialized in the biological weapons context. Neither the 1925 Geneva Protocol nor the BTWC makes explicit reference to such a principle. The final principle underlying the BTWC control regime is the complementarity principle which is clearly stated in preambular paragraphs 2 to 4 of the BTWC: the 1925 Geneva Protocol and the BTWC complement one another.

Central to the biological weapons control regime is the non-use norm, which is explicitly spelled out in the 1925 Geneva Protocol and implicitly contained in Article I of the BTWC. Although this article of the Convention makes explicit reference only to the non-acquisition norm, it can be inferred from it that non-use is prohibited as well. The disarmament norm is contained in Article II of the BTWC. It requires that all state parties either destroy or divert to peaceful purposes all agents, toxins, equipment and means of delivery related to their biological weapons holdings within nine months after entry into force of the BTWC.

The non-transfer norm is contained in Article III of the BTWC, according to which state parties forswear to 'transfer to any recipient whatsoever, directly or indirectly, and not in any way to assist, encourage, or induce' any actor to acquire any of the items specified in Article I of the BTWC. The non-transfer norm is additionally strengthened through Article IV of the BTWC which calls for national implementation measures (internalization norm) to put the basic obligations under the Convention into effect. It is these two normative guideposts that members of the Australia Group regard as the legal basis for their activities.

In addition, the cooperation norm is spelled out in Article X of the BTWC, representing, from the point of view of many BTWC state parties (mostly from the developing world), the flip side of the non-acquisition and non-transfer norms. The assistance norm is contained in Article VII. It stipulates that state parties will come to each other's assistance in case of the use or threat of biological or toxic weapons against one of them. The consultation norm is spelled out in Article V of the BTWC, in which state parties agree to 'consult one another and to cooperate in solving any problems which may arise in relation to the objective of, or in the application of the provisions of, the Convention'.

Efforts to Strengthen the Regime   What is clearly absent from the above enumeration of regime principles and norms is the existence of the verification principle and its corresponding declaration and inspection norms. This shortcoming in the regime structure was recognized by BTWC state parties and led the Third BTWC Review Conference in 1991 to establish a Group of Governmental Experts to identify and assess potential verification measures from a scientific and technical viewpoint (VEREX). Only when the report of that group was discussed during a Special Conference of the State Parties to the BTWC in September 1994, did the question of trade restrictions and export controls take centre stage (Special Conference 1994). It became apparent that several BTWC state parties were not too supportive of the idea of establishing a verification system for the BTWC. A group of developing countries

Arms Control Law

– which seemed to be more concerned about the financial burden of a verification system and questions of national sovereignty than of a neighbouring state secretly developing biological weapons – successfully managed to include in the mandate of a new Ad Hoc Group the task to negotiate measures to strengthen the implementation of Article X of the BTWC, that is, the cooperation norm of the regime. Thus, in light of the special interests of BTWC member states, the Ad Hoc Group, was tasked to consider, *inter alia*, 'specific measures designed to ensure effective and full implementation of Article X, which also avoid any restrictions incompatible with the obligations undertaken under the Convention' (Special Conference 1994).

Negotiations of the Ad Hoc Group started in January 1995 and progressed until July 2001, when the overall approach taken in the negotiations up to that point was rejected by the US administration and the draft Protocol text decreed for parties to reduce rather than increase security against biological weapons. The negotiations proceeded in four phases (Toth 1999): during the first phase which lasted until mid-1997, potential elements of a compliance protocol were identified. From mid-1997, negotiations were based on a rolling text, which was developed further during the negotiating sessions of the Ad Hoc Group. During the third phase in 1999, the formal structure of the protocol was negotiated and in the fourth phase, compromise language on the less controversial issues under negotiation was integrated in the rolling text. In order to create additional momentum for the Ad Hoc Group to enter into an end-game during which also the more controversial issues could be tackled, the chairman of the Ad Hoc Group developed a compromise text which he presented to delegations in spring of 2001 (Pearson, Dando and Sims 2001).

The July 2001 session of the Ad Hoc Group was scheduled to have a debate of the compromise text submitted by the Ad Hoc Group chairperson. While some delegations were criticizing specific elements of the document presented by Ambassador Toth, the US delegate, Ambassador Donald Mahley, concluded in his remarks:

> that the Chairman's text was not an adequate basis for completing the Protocol, that it could not be made an adequate base for further negotiation and, furthermore, that the whole conceptual framework on which the negotiations had been conducted, would have to be changed (quoted in Dando 2002, 175).

This conclusion was based on the assessment that the protocol 'would threaten national security and commercial proprietary information; and it would threaten the dual-use export control regime of the Australia Group' (Rosenberg 2001). This effectively ended the Ad Hoc deliberations. The so-called 'new process' which was initiated after the collapse of Ad Hoc negotiations does not address the non-transfer norm or its relation to the cooperation norm.

Non-Transfer and Cooperation Provisions in the Compliance Protocol and Australia Group Controls[5]   With respect to strengthening the implementation of the norms expressed in both Article III (non-transfer) and X (cooperation) of the BTWC, a relatively small number of working papers were submitted by state parties participating in the Ad Hoc Group, which then found their way into the rolling text for the BTWC Compliance Protocol. As Littlewood points out, one has 'to understand that the debate in the Ad Hoc Group was a proxy discussion about the existence of the Australia Group and the perception of broken promises from the final stages of the negotiations on the CWC' (Littlewood 2005, 139).

Thus, it does not come as a surprise that when measures to enhance the implementation of Article III were discussed in some detail during the March 1997 session of the Ad Hoc Group, India introduced a working paper (India 1997a), proposing a number of far-reaching measures to strengthen the non-transfer norm, which amounted to nothing less than abrogating the present export control practice. They included a substantial transfer of national sovereignty to a future BTWC organization, which would have been empowered to decide on all biological weapons-related transfers. Under the scheme proposed by India, the BTWC organization and not the individual member state would have been the central decision-making organ. Following from that, if national export controls would become obsolete, so would harmonized national controls, that is, those of the Australia Group.

A more moderate approach to strengthening Article III of the BTWC was presented by Austria and New Zealand. In their working paper (Austria and New Zealand 1997), the two Australia Group members advocated to include in the future protocol an obligation for each state party to declare annually 'the national legal measures it has adopted in order to implement Article III of the BTWC' and to 'report to the Organization on an annual basis on its administrative and other related national implementation measures with regard to Article III of the BTWC to ensure that transfers of agents, toxins, and equipment are only authorized in compliance with the provisions of the Convention'. If such measures were implemented, not only would the decision-making power continue to reside with the state parties, but the declarations would also be limited to national measures. Harmonized measures, such as the ones of the Australia Group, would not be touched upon and, consequently, state parties would not be obliged to become more transparent to states outside this group.

As these positions were well known and did not change over the course of the Ad Hoc Group negotiations, it does not come as a surprise that only about a dozen of more than 450 working papers submitted to the group were dealing with the strengthening of the BTWC's Article III.[6] Littlewood reports that the politicized nature of Australia Group export controls even spilled over into other areas of the Ad Hoc Group's work and that 'negotiation on this issue was avoided because every debate on it soured the relationship between delegations on all other subjects' (Littlewood 2005, 147). This led to a situation where the portion of the rolling text dealing with the strengthening of the BTWC's Article III was still heavily bracketed even in May 2001, indicating still prevailing major disagreements among negotiating parties (Ad Hoc Group 2001a, 73–8).

The compromise proposal on the BTWC's Article III contained in the composite text presented by the chairperson of the negotiations (Ad Hoc Group 2001b, 396–400) foresaw, first, the revision and – if necessary – amendment of national legislation to regulate transfers of dual-use biological weapons agents, equipment and technology by state parties in order to bring national measures in line with the protocol. Secondly, it contained transfer guidelines, including specific measures which may be taken by state parties. In other words, adoption of the measures was not mandatory, but left to the discretion of individual states. The same applies to the notification of transfers and consultations among state parties on the implementation of these provisions. In sum, the proposed text contained hardly any legally binding obligations. Rather, one has to think of these stipulations as suggestions for best practice, which, as Littlewood has noted (2005, 154) conferred some legitimacy to the Australia Group's activities.

Thinking the Unthinkable? Prospects for Regime Integration

This chapter started with the assertion that much of the controversy over chemical and biological weapons export controls is fuelled by either rhetoric or disinterest, an assessment originally provided by Roberts a decade ago. As the debates in the context of both the CWC and the BTWC protocol negotiations since then have shown, this verdict holds true largely today. Some NAM states are still demanding the immediate cessation of 'parallel' export control regimes, that is the Australia Group, and instead advocate reliance on the transfer mechanisms, such as those provided by the CWC or which would have been provided for under the BTWC protocol had negotiations been concluded successfully. Likewise, apart from a somewhat higher degree of transparency – achieved in part by the establishment of a website and the publication of some key documents, such as the transfer guidelines – AG members continue to regard a fundamental rethink of their approach to export controls which could result in a move away from harmonized national export controls as something akin to heresy. This does not bode well for the integration of AG export controls into any of the two chemical and biological weapons prohibition regimes.

For any attempt at integration to stand a chance of succeeding, it will have to separate the harmonization function from the information or intelligence sharing function, because the assessment of Roberts of the biological weapons prohibition regime remains valid, that is, '[s]o long as proliferation is a concern of such scope and immediacy, and so long as the BTWC remains a weakly implemented regime, the functions of the AG cannot readily be transferred to the BTWC with any sense of optimism that the basic purposes and objectives of the treaty would be well served' (Roberts 1998, 247).

The same applies to the chemical weapons prohibition regime. Neither of the two regimes provides a regulatory framework which is conducive to sharing sensitive intelligence data, although a potential proliferator could be a regime member. Although the CWC contains a challenge investigation procedure to address concerns of non-compliance, up to date this procedure has not been invoked, neither on the basis of procurement activities, nor on the basis of other available information. This clearly shows that some state parties who claim to have information on potential violations of other regime members are reluctant to use this information to trigger a challenge inspection. This unwillingness to share such information with as large a group of countries as there are regime members in either of the chemical or biological weapons prohibition regimes can be expected to remain a defining feature of export control policies.

Still there are differences as to the prospects for and the degree to which regime integration with a view to the export control harmonization function of the AG might take place and would actually make sense. These are largely due, first of all, to the different states of development of the chemical and biological weapons prohibition regimes. As the biological weapons prohibition regime currently does not have any of the organizational structures or mechanisms available that are contained in its chemical weapons counterpart, there is very little to consolidate AG biological weapon-related controls with. The CWC, in contrast, has an implementing organization at its disposal, which the BTWC does not. Furthermore, there are precise rules and procedures to guide state action available in the chemical weapons context, which again are missing in the biological weapons realm. As has been noted above, in the initial stages of CWC implementation, 70 to 80 per cent of import and export data reported by state parties did not match, pointing to considerable implementation problems on the national level. So long as this ratio will not have been at least reversed, and more than three quarter of all data sets on exports and imports match one another, it is inconceivable that AG participants would consider merging their control efforts with the transfer mechanism established under the CWC. One obvious issue that would have to be tackled relates to the fact that AG control lists and CWC schedules overlap, but are not identical. Given the scientific and technical expertise assembled in the OPCW's Scientific Advisory Board (SAB), this would be the obvious subsidiary body to consider the matter – together with experts and representatives from AG participants and other interested state parties. Article XV, paragraphs 4 and 5 provide a simplified amendment procedure which would be applicable for changes in the CWC's three schedules.

Somewhat more problematic is the integration of the AG list on dual-use chemical manufacturing facilities and equipment and related technology. Although licensing the export of such items and technology is well within the purview of the CWC's general purpose criterion, no comparable list of items to be controlled exists within the CWC context. The addition of a new schedule to the CWC, however, is very unlikely to fall under the simplified amendment procedure of Article XV and would instead have to go through an amendment conference. Alternatively, the Conference of State Parties could take a decision that state parities are expected to licence such dual-use equipment in order to be in compliance with the obligation undertaken in Article I, paragraph 1(d) of the CWC, that is, the stipulation, not to 'assist ... in any way, anyone to engage in any activity prohibited to a State Party under this Convention'. Such a decision, of course, would not carry the legal weight of a formal amendment, which would have to be ratified by CWC state parties.

These different stages of regime development are, at least partially, a reflection of the differences in the substance matter which is to be prevented from being misused for proliferation purposes. In the chemical weapons context, there are a number of past chemical weapons programmes on which the control efforts could be based, whereas in the biological weapons area, the composition of Australia Group control lists is largely informed by the 'intrinsic risk posed by a particular pathogen or toxin, rather than knowledge that it had been sought for proliferation purposes' (Mathews 2004, 3). In contrast to chemical warfare agents, pathogens and toxins occur in the natural environment which also makes it more difficult for export controls to restrain the proliferation of chemical and biological weapons. In addition, as reflected by the continuous additions to the AG biological weapons-related control lists, the revolution in the life sciences and advances in biomedical research make the biological weapons area a highly dynamic one. In contrast, chemical warfare agents and their precursors are well known and technological surprises which would necessitate additions to control lists for licensing purposes are therefore less likely.

One of the key issues surrounding AG export controls as they relate to the chemical and biological weapons prohibition regimes is the question of transparency or the lack thereof, even if only so perceived. As noted above, four AG participants submitted national papers to the OPCW concerning the review of their national implementation of CWC Article XI, some of which contained information on the actual denials of transfers. It should not be too difficult for all states participating in the AG to provide this kind of information on a regular basis. Such a step is not required by any of the declarations foreseen in the CWC, but it might serve to underscore the point made by the AG that export controls do not restrict legitimate trade, but rather enable it. A higher degree of transparency which shows that these licensing requirements are applied in a fair manner can in turn be expected to contribute to the robustness of the chemical weapon prohibition regime. Thus, it would be a small investment for AG participants to make, upon which they could, at a later stage and if the political will to do so materializes, build further integrating AG controls into the chemical weapons prohibition regime. With respect to the biological weapons prohibition regime, suitable structures for a perhaps future merger with AG licensing requirements would have to be created in the first place. After the abandonment of the Ad Hoc Group negotiations and the current minimalist approach to 'strengthening' the BTWC, it is very likely that AG biological weapons-related export controls will remain the only available 'multilateral' export control mechanism for the foreseeable future.

References

Ad Hoc Group (2001a), 'Procedural Report of the Ad Hoc Group of State Parties to the Convention on the Prohibition of the Development, Production and Stockpiling of Bacteriological (Biological) and Toxin Weapons and on Their Destruction', BTWC/AD HOC GROUP/56-1, 18 May 2001, <www.opbw.org>.
——(2001b), 'Appendices [to Ad Hoc Group 2001a]', BTWC/AD HOC GROUP/56-2, 18 May 2001, <www.opbw.org>.

Australia (1999), 'Chemical Weapons Convention (CWC) Implementation Adjustment of Australian Export and Import Licensing Measures', C-IV/NAT.5, 17 June 1999, <www.opcw.org/html/global/c_series/csp4/civ_nat5.html>.

Australia Group (1993), 'Press Release: Australia Group Meeting', AG/Jun93/Press/Chair/10, <www.australiagroup.net/en/releases/ninety_three.htm>.

—— (2000), 'Background Paper. Export Licensing Measures on Materials Used in the Manufacture of Chemical and Biological Weapons', AG/May00/Press/Chair/18, <www.australiagroup.net/en/releases/background.htm>.

—— (2001), 'Press Release: Australia Group Meeting', AG/Oct01/Press/Chair/24, <www.australiagroup.net/en/releases/2001.htm>.

—— (2002), 'Press Release: Australia Group Meeting', <www.australiagroup.net/en/releases/press_2002_06.htm>.

—— (2004), 'Guidelines for Transfer of Sensitive Chemical or Biological Items', <www.australiagroup.net/en/guidelines.html>.

—— (2005), 'Media Release: 2005 Australia Group Plenary', <www.australiagroup.net/en/releases/press_2005.htm>.

Austria and New Zealand (1997), 'Working Paper by Austria and New Zealand', BTWC/AD HOC GROUP/WP.142, 14 March 1997, <www.opbw.org>.

Brazil (1996), 'Working Paper Submitted by Brazil: Article X Implementation in A BTWC Compliance Regime: Aspects of a Cooperative Approach', BTWC/AD HOC GROUP/WP.104 17, September 1996, <www.opbw.org>.

Canada (1999), 'Canadian Review Under Article Xl Paragraph 2(e): Canada's Export and Import Controls on CWC Chemicals and Precursors', C-IV/NAT.4, 15 June 1999, <www.opcw.org/html/global/c_series/csp4/civ_nat4.html>.

Conference on Disarmament (1992), 'Chemical Weapons: Final Records (PV) 1992 Session', CD/PV659, 10 August 1992.

Cuba (1995a), 'Working Paper Submitted by Cuba: Some Elements Associated to the Promotion of Science and Technology with Peaceful Aims within the Framework of the BTWC', BTWC/AD HOC GROUP/WP.4, 28 November 1995, <http://www.opbw.org>.

—— (1995b), 'Working Paper Submitted by Cuba: Rights and Obligations of the State Parties to the BTWC within the Framework of the Economic and Technological Development and in the Field of International Cooperation and Assistance, BTWC/AD HOC GROUP/WP.5, 28 November 1995, <www.opbw.org>.

Dando, M.R. (2002), *Preventing Biological Warfare: The Failure of American Leadership*, Palgrave, Basingstoke.

Fahmy, N. (1996), 'Export Control Regimes: A Critique', in J. Brown (ed), *Arms Control in a Multi-Polar World*, VU University Press, Amsterdam.

Feakes, D. (2001), 'Export Controls, Chemical Trade, and the CWC', in J. Tucker (ed.), *The Chemical Weapons Convention: Implementation Challenges and Solutions*, Monterrey Institute of International Studies, Monterrey, CA.

Hasenclever, A., Mayer, P. and Rittberger, V. (1997), *Theories of International Regimes*, Cambridge University Press, Cambridge.

India (1997a), 'Working Paper by India: Guidelines to Ensure Compliance with Obligations under Article III of the Convention on the Prohibition of the Development, Production and Stockpiling of Bacteriological (Biological) and Toxin Weapons and on Their Destruction (BTWC)', BTWC/AD HOC GROUP/ WP.126, 5 March 1997, <www.opbw.org>.

—— (1997b), 'Working Paper by India: Measures to Strengthen Implementation of Article X of the BTWC', BTWC/AD HOC GROUP/WP.131, 10 March 1997, <www.opbw.org>.

Ireland (1996), 'Working Paper Submitted by Ireland on Behalf of the European Union. European Community Collaboration with Developing Countries in the Field of Biotechnology', BTWC/AD HOC GROUP/WP.75, 18 July 1996, <www. opbw.org>.

Islamic Republic of Iran (1997), 'Working Paper submitted by the Islamic Republic of Iran: Article X. Economic and Technological Development', BTWC/AD HOC GROUP/WP.149, 20 March 1997, <www.opbw.org>.

Islamic Republic of Iran, Cuba and Pakistan (1998), 'Draft Resolution Submitted by Islamic Republic of Iran, Cuba and Pakistan: Fostering of International Cooperation for Peaceful Purposes in the Field of Chemical Activities', C-III/ NAT.4, 19 November 1998.

Japan (1995), 'Working Paper Submitted by Japan: Japanese Cooperation in the Field of Biotechnology', BTWC/AD HOC GROUP/24, 13 July 1995, <www. opbw.org>.

Kelle, A. (1998), 'Strengthening the Biological Weapons Convention: A Role for Export Controls?', *The Monitor: Nonproliferation, Demilitarization and Arms Control*, Vol. 4, Nos. 2–3.

Kelle, A. (2003), 'Strengthening the Effectiveness of the BTW Control Regime – Feasibility and Options', *Contemporary Security Policy*, Vol. 24, No. 2.

—— (2004), 'Assessing the Effectiveness of Security Regimes: The Chemical Weapons Control Regime's First 6 Years of Operation', *International Politics*, Summer 2004.

Krasner, S. (1982), 'Structural Causes and Regime Consequences: Regimes as Intervening Variables', *International Organization*, Vol. 36, No. 2.

Littlewood, Jez (2005), *The Biological Weapons Convention: A Failed Revolution*, Ashgate, Aldershot.

Mathews, R.J. (1993), 'A Comparison of the Australia Group List of Chemical Weapon Precursors and the CWC Schedules of Chemicals', *Chemical Weapons Convention Bulletin*, No. 21.

—— (2004), 'The Development of the Australia Group Export Control List of Biological Pathogens, Toxins and Dual-Use Equipment', *Chemical and Biological Weapons Conventions Bulletin*, No. 66, pp. 1–4.

Morel, B. (1992), 'How Effective is the Australia Group?', in K. Bailey and R. Rudney (eds), *Proliferation and Export Controls*, University Press of America, Lanham, MD.

Müller, H. (1993), *Die Chance der Kooperation. Regime in den Internationalen Beziehungen*, Wiss. Buchgesellschaft, Darmstadt.

Müller, H. et al. (1993), 'From Black Sheep to White Angel? The New German Export Control Policy', *PRIF Reports*, No. 32, Peace Research Institute Frankfurt, Frankfurt/Main.

Netherlands (1995), 'Working Paper Submitted by the Netherlands: Implementation of Article X of the BTWC', BTWC/AD HOC GROUP/WP.45, 7 December 1995, <www.opbw.org>.

OPCW (2000), 'Decision, Implementation of Restrictions on Transfers of Schedule 2 and Schedule 3 Chemicals to and from States not Party to the Convention', C-V/Dec.16, 17 May 2000, <www.opcw.org/html/global/c_series/csp5/cv_dec16.html>.

—— (2003), 'Report of the First Special Session of the Conference of the State Parties to Review the Operation of the Chemical Weapons Convention 28 April – 9 May 2003', RC-I/5, 9 May 2003, <www.opcw.org/docs/rc105.pdf >.

Pearson, G.S., Dando, M.R. and Sims N.A. (2001), 'The Composite Protocol Text: An Effective Strengthening of the Biological and Toxin Weapons Convention', Evaluation Paper No. 21, University of Bradford, Bradford, July 2001, <http://www.brad.ac.uk/acad/sbtwc>.

Price, R.T. (1997), *The Chemical Weapons Taboo*, Cornell University Press, Ithaca, NY.

Roberts, B. (1995), 'Rethinking Export Controls on Dual-Use Materials and Technologies: From Trade Restraints to Trade Enablers', *The Arena*, No.2, CBACI, Alexandria, VA.

—— (1996), 'Technology Diffusion and International Security', in J. Brown (ed.), *Arms Control in a Multi-Polar World*, VU University Press, Amsterdam.

—— (1998), 'Export Controls and Biological Weapons: New Roles, New Challenges', *Critical Reviews in Microbiology*, Vol. 24, No. 3.

Robinson, J.P.P. (1992), 'The Australia Group: A Description and Assessment', in H.G. Brauch, H.J. v. d. Graaf, J. Grin, and W. Smit (eds), *Controlling the Spread and Development of Military Technology*, VU University Press, Amsterdam.

Rosenberg, B. (1996), 'Incorporation of Dual-Use Export Controls in a Compliance Regime for the Biological Weapons Convention', *Chemical Weapons Convention Bulletin*, No. 33.

—— (2001), 'Allergic Reaction: Washington's Response to the BTWC Protocol', *Arms Control Today*, <www.armscontrol.org/act/2001_07-08/rosenbergjul_aug01.asp>.

Smithson, A. (1997), 'Separating Fact from Fiction: The Australia Group and the Chemical Weapons Convention', Occasional Paper No. 34, The Henry L. Stimson Centre, Washington, DC.

Special Conference (1994), 'Final Report: Special Conference of the State Parties to the Convention on the Prohibition of the Development, Production and Stockpiling of Bacteriological (Biological) and Toxin Weapons and on Their Destruction (BTWC)', BTWC/SPCONF/1, 19–30 September 1994.

118   *Non-Proliferation Export Controls*

Sweden   (1999),   'Swedish   Review   under   the   Chemical   Weapons
    Convention Paragraph 2(e) of Article XI', C-IV/NAT.1, 16 March 1999,
    <www.opcw.org/html/global/c_series/csp4/civ_nat1.html>.

Toth, T. (1999), 'Time to Wrap Up', *Chemical and Biological Weapons Conventions
    Bulletin*, No.46.

Tucker, J.B. (1998), 'Strengthening the BTWC: Moving Towards a Compliance
    Protocol', *Arms Control Today*, Vol. 28, No. 1.

United Kingdom (1995), 'BTWC Article X: Areas of Biological Activity of Direct
    Relevance to the Convention', BTWC/AD HOC GROUP/WP.7, 28 November
    1995, <www.opbw.org>.

United States of America (1995), 'Discussion of Potential Article X Issues. Working
    Paper Submitted by the United States of America', BTWC/AD HOC GROUP/23,
    13 July 1995, <www.opbw.org>.

—— (1999), 'United States of America Export Controls and the Chemical
    Weapons   Convention',   C-IV/NAT.2,   The   Hague,   29   April   1999,
    <http://www.opcw.org/html/global/c_series/csp4/civ_nat2.html>.

Notes

1.   These were the EC 10 at that time – Belgium, Denmark, France, Germany, Greece,
      Ireland, Italy, Luxembourg, the Netherlands and the United Kingdom – plus Australia,
      Canada, Japan, New Zealand and the US.

2.   This section is based on Kelle (2004).

3.   Quoted in Feakes (2001, 47). Interestingly, while the Australian, Canadian, Swedish
      and US national statements on their review of national regulations to bring them into
      line with Article XI of the CWC are available online on the OPCW webpage, neither
      the draft decision put forward by Iran, Cuba and Pakistan (which is an official OPCW
      document), nor the opening statement of the Director General to the 5th Session of the
      CSP can be accessed online.

4.   This section is based on Kelle (2003).

5.   Parts of this section are based on Kelle (1998).

6.   These Working Papers are Nos 126 (India), 142 (Austria and New Zealand), 147 (Friend
      of the Chair), 148 (Iran), 184 (Austria), 407 (NAM and other states), 424 (UK), 426
      (Iran), 432 (China et al.), 443 (Australia et al.), 444 (UK), 452 (China et al.), and 453
      (China), available at <www.opbw.org>.

Part IV
Missiles

[16]

Emptying the Haunted Air: The Current and Future Missile Control Regime

Scott Jones

Senior Research Associate,
Centre for International Trade and Security,
University of Georgia

Each will have his personal Rocket ... each Rocket will know its intended and hunt him ... through our World, shining and pointed in the sky at his back, his guardian executioner rushing in, *rushing closer.* ...

Thomas Pynchon, *Gravity's Rainbow*

Introduction

On 9 December 2002, a ship operated by a North Korean crew carrying 12 disassembled Scud missiles bound for Yemen was boarded and seized by Spanish and United States military forces in the Arabian Sea (Ricks and Slevin 2002). While the United States had the authority to stop and search the ship, it did not have the authority to seize the vessel, which was later released to the Yemeni government. In response, White House press secretary Ari Fleischer remarked: 'The US inability to prevent the North Korean Scud transfer to Yemen demonstrates a need to improve international regimes against missile proliferation. One thing that this does underscore is the need to take a look [at] – and we will do so with friends and others around the world – whether or not the international regimes that deal with missile proliferation need a second look' (Global Security Newswire 2002). The Yemeni Scuds case represents some of the more salient challenges confronting contemporary missile non-proliferation efforts, undertakings that have traditionally centred upon the Missile Technology Control Regime (MTCR).

Arguably since the inception the International Code of Conduct Against Ballistic Missile Proliferation (ICOC), the MTCR has served as the only international (multilateral) effort to curb missile proliferation.[1] As such, it has been vested with powers and responsibilities beyond its rather modest objectives and institutional design.[2] The establishment of the ICOC – and, in part, the US decision to deploy a National Missile Defence (NMD) system – strongly suggests the inadequacy

Arms Control Law

of the MTCR. Nevertheless, this is not to suggest the 'failure' or, in and of itself, the inadequacy of the MTCR. On the contrary, the MTCR can be duly credited for curtailing several national ballistic programmes and serving, in the absence of a formal prohibitive norm, as the *de facto* standard against missile proliferation.[3] Notwithstanding these more positive attributes, like the other multilateral export control arrangements, the MTCR faces institutional and external challenges to its own long-term viability.

Despite recent alternative missile control efforts, such as the Russian-proposed Global Control System (GCS) and the UN Panel of Experts, and the absence of credible demand-side arms control efforts, the MTCR is still the control standard for missile non-proliferation norms and practices.[4] Unlike these various efforts, the MTCR covers *all* unmanned delivery systems – which include cruise missiles and unmanned aerial vehicles (UAVs) – within a specified performance parameter, the unique challenges these systems pose to the MTCR's effectiveness notwithstanding (Gormley and Speier 2003; see also US GAO 2003). As the international default, the MTCR provides the template for current and future initiatives to stem missile proliferation. To serve in this capacity, however, fundamental adaptations will have to be made to the scope and practices of the MTCR.

This chapter begins by examining the founding and evolution of the MTCR, with particular emphasis on its institutional development and the prominent US engineering and leadership role. Second, we review the internal and external challenges to regime viability in light of the changing nature of the missile proliferation threat. Lastly, we conclude by assessing how effective the MTCR is perceived to be considering the compatibility of members' interests, the degree of export control harmonization and institutional outcomes.

MTCR Origins and Evolution

Initiated by US concerns regarding the proliferation of space launch capabilities and prompted by a series of events in the late 1970s and early 1980s, including South Korea's 1978 ballistic missile test and India's July 1980 SLV-3 tests, the United States and its G7 allies began negotiation on a missile control consortium, negotiations which culminated in the establishment on 16 April 1987 of the Missile Technology Control Regime (MTCR) and the release of its Guidelines.[5] The concept of missile proliferation was first conceived and implemented unilaterally by the United States (see Cooper 2001, 15–20).[6] Until this point, weapons of mass destruction (WMD) and delivery means were issues confined to arms control and disarmament negotiations between the United States and the Soviet Union.[7] The concern that other states – particularly in the developing world – could wed the growing availability of ballistic missile technology with nuclear weapons prompted US-led efforts to coordinate supply-side controls.[8]

The rudiments of the MTCR were enunciated in National Security Decision Directive 70 (NSDD-70) of 30 November 1982.[9] NSDD-70 instructed the relevant

US executive agencies to implement appropriate methods to restrain the spread of nuclear-capable ballistic and cruise missiles. In addition to mandating the immediate implementation of stringent unilateral export controls on missile-related military and dual-use equipment and technology, NSDD-70 also called for simultaneously trying to multilateralize this effort among key western supplier countries, which was successfully accomplished in 1987 (Ozga 1994).

When the first official meeting of the MTCR was convened in 1987, delegates were unanimous in their belief that the principal goal of the organization was best characterized as inhibitory and not as a comprehensive solution to missile proliferation. Other means, such as diplomacy, sanctions, and sundry incentives, were to complement the rather basic, but by no means uncomplicated, instrument of trade controls inherent in the guidelines and control lists.

The Guidelines establish the basis of coordination of export control policies and appropriate procedures in the field of transfers of missile technologies and equipment.[10] The Guidelines emphasize that they are not designed to impede national space programmes for international cooperation in such programmes as long as such programmes could not contribute to delivery systems (other than manned aircraft) for such weapons. The Guidelines, including the Annex, form the basis for controlling transfers to any destination beyond the member-state government's jurisdiction or control of all delivery systems (other than manned aircraft) capable of delivering weapons of mass destruction, and of equipment and technology relevant to missiles whose performance in terms of payload and range exceeds stated parameters.

The Guidelines are implemented in accordance with the national legislation of each member state. The Annex contains 20 item groups divided into two categories. Category I (items 1 and 2) are the items of greatest sensitivity. Category I items include complete systems and major subsystems capable of carrying a payload of 500 kg over a range of at least 300 km, and specifically designed production facilities for such systems.[11] Category II items include other missile defence elements not tightly restricted but requiring case-by-case review including missile-related components such as propellants, avionics equipment and other items used for the production of Category I systems. The regime prohibits the transfer of Category I production facilities; and a 'no undercut' rule prohibits members from exporting anything already denied by another member. Countermeasures to ballistic and cruise missile defence are not covered. Restrictions cover 'transfers to any destination beyond the Government's jurisdiction or control'. If, for example, a system remains under US jurisdiction and control, it is not covered by MTCR.

Category I hardware and technology 'regardless of their purpose' are subject to 'strong presumption to deny' transfers. Category I transfers are 'authorized only on rare occasions and where the government: 1) obtains binding government to government undertakings involving the assurances from the recipient government … and, 2) assumes responsibility for taking all steps necessary to ensure the item is put only to its stated end use'.

Several levels of rules apply to these items:

- *Absolute prohibition (until further notice)* on the transfer of Category I complete production facilities or the technology for such facilities. It obviously does not make sense to have a non-proliferation regime that allows the creation of new suppliers.
- *Strong presumption to deny transfers* of Category I items. This strong presumption of denial also applies to missiles of any range or payload, or any MTCR-controlled item, for which the purpose is deemed to be the delivery of nuclear, biological or chemical payloads. Transfers of Category I items may be made. But they are to be 'rare' and may only be made if there are 1) binding government-to-government assurances with respect to the end-use and end-user and 2) supplier and not just recipient responsibility for the end-use.
- *Case-by-case review* of export applications for all controlled items.
- *No-undercut provision* according to which MTCR partners will respect each others' export denials or consult before undercutting a denial.
- *Information exchanges* to enforce these rules.
- *Catch-all provisions*, observed by most partner governments, under which export reviews will be required for missile-related transfers, whether or not on the MTCR control list, to any destination engaged in Category I programmes.[12]

Recent MTCR Developments

During the August 2002 meeting in Warsaw, parties to the MTCR decided on greater clarity in the definitions of 'range' and 'payload'. Members agreed that the current range of 300 km would be the distance achieved at 'range maximizing' capability. The definition of payload was expanded to include the cover support structures and countermeasures. The new definitions were in response to a controversy over the ambiguity of both range and payload during the late 1990s. At that time, the United Kingdom and France sold *Black Shaheen* cruise missiles, which have a maximum capable range of 500 km, to the United Arab Emirates. Both countries, which are members, argued that the sale was not in violation because the missiles' range was below 300 km when flying at sea level.

Meeting in Buenos Aires in late September 2003, members of the MTCR agreed to add catch-all provisions to the regime's guidelines. Catch-all provisions furnish a legal basis to control items that are not identified in the MTCR annex or national control lists. Such a circumstance would occur if the member state believes that an item is bound for a restricted missile programme, specifically a Category I missile; that is, those exceeding the regime's 300 km and 500 kg range and payload thresholds. Thus, for example, an export licence would be required for *any* trade with an organization involved in producing a Category I missile, such as a Pakistani entity known to be engaged in producing the Ghauri I missile or an Iranian entity supporting the production of the Shahab 3 missile. Before reaching consensus on making catch-all provisions a part of the regime's guidelines, 30 of the 33 member states had already incorporated such measures into their own national control systems. Theoretically, making catch-all regime-wide broadens the effectiveness of this important supply-side control measure.

Also agreed upon in Buenos Aires were restrictions on the transfer of so-called intangible technology, which might include the sending of missile blueprints via email or facsimile. As with catch-all provisions, many of the MTCR member states had already incorporated controls on intangible technology transfers into their own national control regulations. These controls will now become an MTCR-wide requirement. Both the catch-all and intangible technology transfer controls reflect the regime's vigorous attention of late to stanching the flow of equipment and technology integral to either developing a Category I missile or qualitatively improving its performance. Such attention is warranted because missile proliferators have found it difficult to transfer complete missile systems and have turned to transferring dual-use equipment and technology, much of which comprise the critical components of complete missile systems.

In the absence of a missile non-proliferation treaty, the MTCR has been a useful tool in countering the proliferation of missile components, technologies and materials by establishing international norms against missile technology sales. The existence of the MTCR and US sanctions based partly on them has provided a basis for US diplomatic–political efforts to constrain questionable exports from countries such as China and Russia. It has positively impacted export control practices of several European nations and others, likely preventing the 'best teams' from transferring systems and technologies. Although difficult to measure, the growth in the relative sophistication of the missile threat to the United States and its friends and allies from rogue or irresponsible nations has probably been slowed.

As a consequence of the MTCR, proliferators have been forced to indigenize their missile programmes – increasing the difficulties of their programmes and the unreliability of their missiles. Indeed, the greatest source of expanding missile capabilities, especially in relative sophistication and range, has been from countries not party to the MTCR, such as North Korea, which, to date, has been limited to providing systems based on Scud technology (the so-called 'Scud barrier'). Still, the MTCR has not proven to be a panacea. The regime suffers from leakage of technology, inconsistent interpretations of the guidelines, and from the growing problem of secondary and tertiary proliferation. It is important to stress, however, that the MTCR is only one of several 'non-proliferation' tools the United States can use to counter missile export activities.

The current trend is toward a *de facto* multilateral missile non-proliferation standard observed even by some non-members of the MTCR, such as the recent EU-led Hague Code of Conduct on Missile Proliferation and the Russian effort to create a Global Control System (GCS).[13] Some non-member interdictions of transfers violated UN sanctions against Iraq and should have been blocked even in the absence of MTCR. However, the UN missile sanctions against Iraq are based on the technical structure of the MTCR.

Internal and External Challenges

The continuing ability of the MTCR to stem missile proliferation is compromised by a host of internal and external challenges. This section itemizes both the external and internal obstructions. The subsequent section concludes with an examination of options for strengthening the MTCR.

External

The threat of ballistic missile proliferation has been dramatically highlighted over the past few years by a growing number of countries that have tested short-to-intermediate-range ballistic missiles. These include India's Agni-1 and Agni-2; Pakistan's Ghauri-1, Ghauri-2 and Shaheen; North Korea's Taepo Dong-I; China's Dong Feng-31 ICBM; and Iran's Shahab-3.[14] Anxiety over North Korea's much anticipated launch test of the Taepo-Dong-II has caused intense diplomatic and military manoeuvring (Agence France Presse 1999; Struck 1999; Mufson 1999). While the Berlin talks have led to an announced test suspension by Pyongyang, the key elements of North Korean missile programmes, including the DPRK's continued development and sales, remain unaddressed. Missile acquisition and developments efforts are also occurring in other regions of tension and instability, such as the Middle East, the Gulf and South Asia. For example, Iran is developing the Shahab-4, Pakistan is moving ahead with the Shaheen-II, and Syria reportedly is acquiring Chinese M-9 missiles via Pakistan and North Korea (Jones and McDonough 1998; Lackey 1999; Aneja 1999).

Ongoing transfers of missile systems and related technologies to other regions, in particular the highly contentious Gulf region and the Middle East, remain a serious proliferation concern. China and North Korea have over the years been charged with willingly supplying missiles, missile components and relevant technologies to Third World customers. While China has pledged to abide by the MTCR guidelines since 1992 (and indeed Beijing's records in this regard have improved noticeably in recent years), there remain allegations that Chinese missile components and technology continue to be transferred to such countries as Pakistan and Iran. A recently released US intelligence report charges that China may have transferred medium-range missiles to Pakistan (National Intelligence Council 2001; Landay 1999). Beijing has also had to contend with allegations that it has provided assistance to Iran designed to improve the latter's anti-ship missiles, thus violating a Chinese pledge to the United States not to engage in such activities (*The Times of India* 1999b).

North Korea also serves as a source of missile proliferation and is reported to have played a prominent role in Pakistan's missile development (Bermudez 1998, 16–17). Indian authorities have recently intercepted a North Korean ship at *Kandla* port heading for Pakistan, with 177 crates of blueprints, manuals and machine tools for Scud missiles (Reuters 2003). Pyongyang's missile assistance and transfers to Iran are also a matter of concern.

The spread of ballistic missiles around the world was greatly facilitated by the export in the 1970s and 1980s of Scud-B missiles from the former Soviet Union. With an increasing number of countries abiding by the MTCR, the number of potential missile suppliers has declined dramatically. Of the principal missile exporters, only North Korea has not agreed to comply. Moreover, additional countries have learned to copy, modify, extend the range of, and produce their own missiles, and a small number have developed long-range systems, often in conjunction with space-launch programmes and foreign technical assistance. For example, western countries assisted India's space launch vehicle programme in its early stages, and that provided the basis for its missile programme. Indeed, India's missile programme traces its origins to the US-produced Scout Sounding Rocket (Weiss 2001). Western firms, especially in Europe, provided technology for Argentina's Condor II missile programme, which was based on the US Pershing II (Scheffran and Karp 1992, 239–40). Nevertheless, the majority of ballistic missile proliferation involves Scud or Scud-derived materials and technology.[15]

Even so, MTCR constraints have slowed the acquisition by developing countries of technologies associated with more advanced missiles – those having ranges in excess of 1,000 km or guidance errors of less than roughly 0.3 per cent of their range. Given the complex set of technologies and expertise used in advanced aircraft, especially high-performance jet engines, it remains virtually impossible for developing countries to acquire these systems without assistance. However, no internationally binding restrictions limit trade in combat aircraft, and such arms transfers continue to be used as an instrument of foreign policy. Moreover, over capacity in western defence industries, and the economic difficulties facing newly independent Soviet republics and eastern European states, provide great incentive to develop arms export markets.

Secondary Suppliers   In 1987, only six states (the United States, United Kingdom, Russia, China, France and Israel) produced missiles with ranges over 1,000 km. In 2002, eight produced such missiles, the additions being India and Pakistan. Also in 1987, the Treaty on the Elimination of Intermediate-Range and Shorter-Range Missiles (the INF Treaty) required elimination of all Soviet and American longer-range intermediate nuclear force (LRINF) missiles with ranges between 1,000 and 5,500 km, as well as shorter-range intermediate nuclear force (SRINF) missiles with ranges between 500 and 1,000 km.

Traditional export control mechanisms, such as the MTCR, presume a limited number of suppliers, a clear distinction between military and civilian technologies, and a foreign dependence with regard to components, technical know-how and manufacturing technology. However, one of the phenomenal technological developments over the past two decades has been the increasing number of countries that have acquired an indigenous capability to develop missile delivery systems.

Today, a dozen or more non-western countries either already possess short- or medium-range missile systems or have the capability to develop them. Most of them are not MTCR members; some, like North Korea, are active suppliers. Although the most sophisticated ballistic missiles with longer ranges are still difficult to acquire, low-end missiles and the requisite technologies reverse-engineered from the Soviet Scud series are widely available. Denial strategies that rely prominently on export controls will be less effective in stemming the proliferation of missile delivery systems since many of the emerging supplier states do not subscribe to non-proliferation.

Competing Control Initiatives   In contrast to global norms against nuclear, chemical or biological weapons activity, strong norms against missile possession, development and testing do not exist. The international community strongly condemned nuclear tests by China, France, India and Pakistan in the period 1995–8, with some states imposing trade and aid sanctions against them. Yet in 1998 and 1999, missile tests by India, Pakistan and Iran faced far less criticism. Neither the UN General Assembly nor the Security Council passed resolutions condemning these tests. Further, none of these states encountered major aid or trade sanctions (instead incurring only minor US export control sanctions). Eventually, however, three instruments were introduced to address growing concern over missile proliferation: United Nations (UN) initiatives,[16] the Russian-proposed Global Control System (GSK)[17] and the MTCR-initiated Code of Conduct (ICOC), or Hague Code of Conduct.

Of the three, only the International Code of Conduct received a truly international response. Where the MTCR relies on technological criteria to guide policy among a select group of states, the Hague Code of Conduct tries to elevate a single, consistent set of principles to guide all countries in efforts to halt ballistic missile proliferation. The undertaking is all about building moral norms, rules of the road that everyone will accept. Completed in 2002, the Hague Code of Conduct is not a treaty for signature but a text to which states subscribe, pledging cooperation: to prevent and to curb the proliferation of ballistic missile systems capable of delivering weapons of mass destruction; to exercise the 'maximum possible restraint' over their own ballistic missile procurement; not to 'contribute to, support or assist' any ballistic missile programme in countries violating international obligations; and to implement transparency 'to increase confidence and to promote non-proliferation'.[18]

With 119 subscribing states to date, the ICOC is the most important effort to correct the greatest shortcoming of the MTCR: its lack of a unifying normative principle to guide all action against the spread of ballistic missiles (Karp 2005). With its focus on collective ideals, this European initiative represents perhaps the last surviving initiative of universalist arms control and disarmament from the 1990s. Nevertheless, the ICOC's provisions are vague, lack enforcement capabilities, and do not address cruise missiles or UAVs. Furthermore, the competitive nature of parallel groups undermines the *de facto* norm-setting missile proliferation body, the MTCR.

Competing Export Control Objectives   Export control objectives sometimes conflict with other non-proliferation goals. For example, the Bush administration's desire for missile defence cooperation with regional friends and allies continues to be complicated by MTCR restrictions. National Security Presidential Directive 23 (NSPD-23) attempted to de-conflict these two objectives through presidential fiat: 'The goal of the Missile Technology Control Regime (MTCR) is to help reduce the global missile threat by curbing the flow of missiles and related technology to proliferators. The MTCR and missile defences play complementary roles in countering the global missile threat. The United States intends to implement the MTCR in a manner that does not impede missile defense cooperation with friends and allies'. NSPD-23 also ordered the Secretaries of State and Defence to review US commitments under the MTCR in relation to the transfer of missile defence technology, a review which should have been completed by mid-2003.[19] Instead, it appears that internal reviews of the NSPD continue within the departments, and discussions have not yet reached the interagency level. Balancing missile defence cooperation with non-proliferation goals will continue to vex future US administrations.[20]

Internal

Consensus Rules and Growing Membership   The MTCR has expanded nearly five-fold since 1987. Some have argued that membership expansion increases the representational value of the MTCR and nominally broadens the international norm against missile proliferation. Others fear, however, that adding new members with disparate security interests will make it more difficult for the MTCR to reach consensus on addressing emerging challenges, in particular, the need to control new underlying technologies that will enable the growth of missile proliferation in the next two decades.

    MTCR membership criteria, although they have never been officially announced, include like-mindedness and effective export controls (Speier 1997, 6–7). Since 1987, the MTCR has expanded to include 34 countries considered important for controlling missile technology, nearly half of which are not major suppliers of missile systems (see Table 4.1). In addition, a number of other countries (that is, China, Israel and Romania) have made unilateral statements of their intention to adhere to the MTCR Guidelines, with China formally expressing its intent to join the regime in 2004.[21] However, unilateral adoption of export control measures based on MTCR guidelines and lists is not tantamount to actual 'adherent' status, as member states have independent policies for the determination of an official adherence. For example, the United States recognizes adherent states only after a bilateral accord has been reached.

Table 4.1   MTCR Membership

Year	Total members	Members
1987	7	Canada, (West) Germany, France, Italy, Japan, UK, US
1990	13	Spain, Belgium, Luxembourg, Netherlands, Australia, Denmark
1991	18	Norway, New Zealand, Austria, Sweden, Finland
1992	22	Portugal, Switzerland, Ireland, Greece
1993	25	Iceland, Argentina, Hungary
1995	28	Russia, South Africa, Brazil
1997	29	Turkey
1998	32	Czech Republic, Poland, Ukraine
2001	33	South Korea
2004	34	Bulgaria

At its inception, the regime's informal membership criteria emphasized like-mindedness, effective export control laws and enforcement, and a strong non-proliferation track record and counted only exporters as members. As the MTCR has expanded to 34 members, however, its standards have eased, allowing countries to be admitted which are not completely like-minded, do not completely share the same non-proliferation ideals as the original members, and are not even exporters. These have included EU and NATO members such as Norway and Iceland, but also former Soviet republics such as Russia and Ukraine.[22]

Rather than the more standardized criteria of the past, admission of new members to the MTCR today has become a bargaining process involving political and commercial trade-offs and side payments. So, whether or not China, for example, joins the organization is going to depend largely on what demands the current members and Beijing bring to any accession negotiation and the prospects that they can be realized or surrendered (Zaborsky 2004).

Although one of the principal objectives of the regimes is to coordinate or harmonize national policies, it is clear that some countries are not implementing and enforcing export controls in a manner consistent with their non-proliferation objectives. Aside from the United States and some of the larger supplier states, for instance, few countries are actually imposing civil or criminal penalties for export control violations. This suggests that enforcement is lacking. Indeed, various studies of national export control systems continue to show that wide discrepancies among the control systems of regime member countries persist (see, for example, Beck, Cupitt, Gahlaut and Jones 2003).

Inadequate Information Sharing   Information sharing is critical to effective multilateral control efforts. Despite extensive efforts aimed at developing information-sharing networks, MTCR members are not sharing information fully or efficiently. A recent study by the US General Accounting Office (GAO) drew attention in particular to the failure of some states to pool information about denials of export licence applications (US GAO 2002).[23] The GAO found, for example, that 65 per cent of members have never reported export denials (ibid., 12). Many countries provide pre-licence consultations that result in *de facto* denials. These, too, are also almost never reported to other regime members.[24] The failure to share information, or to share it in a timely manner, undercuts the ability of members to assess patterns in technology trading or acquisition and detect activities of proliferation concern. Efforts to strengthen information sharing, including proposals that would have member states report on export approvals, have met with resistance from a few regime members (US GAO 2002,14). The consensus rules cited above have allowed resistance from a determined minority to stall badly needed reforms in this area.

Outmoded Technological Parameters   While the initial focus of the regime was on controlling the proliferation of nuclear-capable systems, its purview was expanded to include missiles for the delivery of chemical or biological weapons (CBW) in 1993. MTCR members have nominally agreed to exercise the most stringent control over what are referred to as Category I systems, or MTCR-class. The technical means – predicated as they are on the physical laws governing ballistic missiles – to determine this category, however, are inadequate for controlling many unmanned systems,[25] such as cruise and loitering missiles and unmanned aerial vehicles (UAVs).[26] Moreover, the underlying technology of cruise missile and UAV systems is nearly identical with that of manned systems and therefore ubiquitous.[27] For example, more than 80 countries today have cruise missiles of some kind. Eighteen of these countries manufacture cruise missiles domestically. The remaining 62 countries import these weapons (International Institute for Strategic Studies, various).

While the MTCR has been relatively effective in limiting the spread and sophistication of ballistic missiles, its ability to control more precisely the proliferation of unmanned systems is insufficient.[28] Although most cruise missile sales to date have been of relatively short-range anti-ship systems, it is clear that ranges are increasing. Moreover, the ease with which anti-ship systems can be converted to the land-attack role suggests that land attack cruise missile (LACM) inventories could readily increase. The land-attack-capable Taiwanese Hsiung Feng II, for example, which has been offered for export, is effectively a reverse-engineered US Harpoon anti-ship cruise missile (ASCM). The relative simplicity of cruise missile technology, and the increasing availability of technologies such as global positioning system (GPS) mean that an increasing number of countries are acquiring the ability to develop land-attack cruise missiles. Category I type controls will be further outstripped by growth in air vehicle types and applications. As a result of the inflexibility of current MTCR controls, proliferators can purposely design systems to circumvent Category I controls, such as the Indo-Russian 'Brahmos' supersonic anti-ship cruise missile (ASCM) (see Eschel 2005).

Abandoned Arms Control Initiative   Originally, the regime required all new members to eliminate any missile or missile development programmes that exceeded the limits of the regime. This restriction, however, did not apply to the originating seven countries. The MTCR was founded in 1987 by the original Group of Seven (G7) partners. Between 1989 and 1993, 16 additional governments were added, all treaty allies of, or linked in security terms to, the original seven. Four additional governments were added in the 1993–5 period – Argentina, Brazil, South Africa and Russia. This was a 'new class' of governments, each having previously engaged in missile activities against which the MTCR had been directed (Mistry 2003a; Speier 2001). Their incorporation helped in some ways, but also presented new problems. They were admitted only after the existing members were satisfied that their objectionable activities – Argentina's *Condor* programme being an example – had been discontinued. But with Brazil's admission in 1995, the MTCR for the first time accepted a new member that was continuing a programme against which the regime had been directed, and even allowed that Brazilian programme to be eligible for assistance. Brazil was developing a space-launch vehicle (called the VLS) capable, in a surface-to-surface mode, of delivering a 500 kg payload to a range of 10,000 km – a true ICBM capability. Within a month of Brazil's admission, South Korea said it would seek membership in order to be able to develop a longer-range missile (Nazarkin 1998).

The regime's terms state that it is not 'designed to impede national space programmes ... as long as such programmes could not contribute to delivery systems for weapons of mass destruction'. MTCR members are expected to take special precautions in such transfers, however, since the technology used in space launch vehicles (SLVs) is virtually identical to that used in ballistic missiles (Zaborsky 2003).

Conclusion

On 14 December 2001, the United States provided formal notification of its withdrawal from the Anti-Ballistic Missile (ABM) Treaty. The US action was designed to remove treaty and other procedural obstacles to implementing a system of national missile defence (NMD). The urgency to pursue such systems was predicated on a ballistic missile threat assessment strongly suggesting the increased likelihood of a strike on the US homeland.[29] In the process of realizing NMD, the Bush administration was careful to articulate its support for the Missile Technology Control Regime (MTCR), arguing that the MTCR was a critical component to the overall non-proliferation regime and served to complement NMD as a countermeasure to actual and future missile proliferation.[30] Both NMD and withdrawal from the ABM Treaty imply the relatively altered nature of the missile proliferation threat, a threat the MTCR was designed to curtail. Furthermore, both issues intimate that supplementary measures to the MTCR are required in order to address more ably the missile proliferation threat.

Much of the current debate over the effectiveness of the MTCR is premised on a *relative* missile proliferation threat perception and, principally, on an unexamined battery of performative expectations. In the case of the former, intelligence estimates themselves have proliferated since the mid-1990s – arguably having been politicized in the process[31] – thereby problematizing any assessment of the state of international missile proliferation. In the case of the latter, *universal* criteria for assessing MTCR effectiveness are absent.[32] On this last point, it is important to note that the relatively modest function of the MTCR has been unofficially empowered beyond its scope and domain, becoming – by default – the primary bulwark against missile proliferation.[33] As noted above, the alternative missile control initiatives are insufficient insofar as they do not address cruise missiles and UAVs. Instead, they should be viewed as part of a larger multilateral dialogue on the proliferation of WMD delivery means.[34]

With respect to the actual missile proliferation threat, the MTCR can be credited with greatly delimiting the spread of ballistic missile systems. Even with an increase in the number of suppliers outside of the regime, the number of ICBM and IRBM producing or holding states has decreased (see Table 4.2), owing in large measure to supplier-side restraint and the prohibitive norm enshrined in 'Category 1' or 'MTCR-class' systems transfers.[35] The results, however, are less sanguine regarding cruise missiles (Gormley 2003).

Table 4.2   Missile/Unmanned Delivery Vehicle Proliferation Trends: 1987 vs 2003[36]

Threat	Status (1987 vs 2005)	Trends
ICBM (>5,500 km)	57% decrease	↓
IRBM (3,000–5500 km)	97% decrease	↓
MRBM (1,000–3,000 km)	3 new national programmes (7 nations total vs 4 then)	↑
SRBM (<1,000 km)	Up, but declining as Scud inventories age	↓
Number of nations with ballistic missile programmes of concern	Fewer, less advanced (11 in mid-1980s, 7 today)	↓
Cruise Missiles (ASCM and LACM)	Inventories of and production capability for both anti-ship and land-attack cruise missiles increase	↑
Unmanned Aerial Vehicles (UAVs)	As with cruise missiles, UAV proliferation and production capabilities increasing	↑

ASCM: Anti-Ship Cruise Missile
ICBM: Intercontinental Ballistic Missile
IRBM: Intermediate-Range Ballistic Missile
LACM: Land-Attack Cruise Missile
MRBM: Medium-Range Ballistic Missile
SRBM: Short-Range Ballistic Missile

The state of missile proliferation today is, by default, commentary on the effectiveness of the MTCR. While some praise the regime's cogency, crediting all manner of agency to the regime, others criticize its exclusivity and failure to address missile proliferation between non-members.[37] In either case, the MTCR is the only enduring international missile non-proliferation standard. As such, it is enlisted to make any number of points about the state of missile proliferation, points which are largely incidental to the basic function of the regime.

Unlike a treaty-based regime, the MTCR is, at its core, simply an association of states seeking to coordinate their export licensing practices relevant to missile technology. In this sense, it acts as a supplier cartel, with all the inherent advantages and problems associated with that type of arrangement. It is this lack of a more formal international legal standing that, to a large extent, drives both praise and criticism of the regime. Its erstwhile legitimacy or image problems, however, are slowly receding.[38] The interest of China, for example, Libya and nine other countries in joining the regime illustrates the global shift in attitudes toward a mechanism previously dismissed as a poorly disguised cartel (Zabrosky 2004, 20–26).

With renewed interest in the MTCR, expressed by the new queue of applicants, a fundamental re-examination of the regime's mandate and scope are necessary. Beyond the institutional and technical issues relevant to the operation of the regime under new constraints, a more basic, substantive question must be addressed: what do we expect the MTCR to do? As noted, the MTCR is nothing more than the sum of national export control systems, coordinated by a mutually agreed upon control list, exporting guidelines and information sharing means. There is little, for example, the regime can do to prohibit North Korean missile sales to Iran. The traditional means of policing such scenarios have resided outside the MTCR.[39]

Because there are extra-MTCR efforts – NMD, GCS, the HCOC and UN Panel of Experts – to stem missile proliferation, the MTCR is not adversely affected or undermined. Although not by design, the emerging international missile non-proliferation architecture evinces a rudimentary division of labour, with the MTCR at its core. Nevertheless, to serve as the international 'linchpin' of international missile non-proliferation, the MTCR will have to modify its structure and rules (Van Diepen 2004). This will involve developing rules and procedures appropriate to an increasingly diverse membership and adapting the guidelines to keep pace with new delivery vehicle technologies, such as UAVs.[40] With respect to procedural modifications, decisions on some issues could be decided by majority or qualified majority vote instead of consensus. Only the most crucial decisions should require a unanimous vote. Only on rare occasions, and only on issues that are non-negotiable, should individual member states be able to bring the work of the MTCR to a standstill.

Perhaps most critically, the essential effectiveness of the MTCR resides in, as noted, the members' respective export control systems. To that extent, regime efficacy is solely dependent upon a relatively uniform approach to implementation amongst the membership. This uniformity may prove elusive with increased membership, especially in the absence a MTCR-level enforcement mechanism. The US interest in missile defence cooperation and the Russian and European interest in exporting sub-Category I cruise missiles are cases in point (see, for example, Graham 2003; Svitak and Ratnam 2003). Widening interpretations of the guidelines amongst an increasingly disparate membership is the central issue to be addressed in reforming the MTCR. A viable reform effort, moreover, will be one based upon cooperation rather than coordination.[41]

To achieve cooperation, among very disparate states with divergent interests, a contract-like agreement may work better than what exists today. Such agreements usually include some type of bargain in which there are direct exchanges between the parties involved. The MTCR began as a mechanism for strong coordination on the export behaviour of the founding supplier states. However, over time, the MTCR has transformed into a cooperation arrangement, where the fundamental security objectives of the regime have broadened in order to accommodate new members. In essence, the regime began admitting non-exporting members and/or members seeking bargains and side-payments. Thus the goals of the regime have changed with changing membership, yet its internal decision rules have lagged behind, giving rise to questions about its current and future effectiveness. This situation should, at least in theory, give rise to new rules or organizing principles.

A completely informal setting is no longer suitable for a regime with mixed membership and static rules. The conditions for membership will need to be precise, coherent, and clearly stated. Binding dozens of diverse members into some informal and generalist arrangement will not make much of a difference in terms of fighting proliferation. The regime of this type will have to be based on a formal agreement, not necessarily as detailed and comprehensive as a treaty, but with clearly determined obligations of the parties. At a minimum, it should clearly define 'violation' to avoid different interpretations of members' behaviour. Ironically, in the current rules structure, meaningful structural reform of the MTCR would require either dissolution of the regime or unanimous consent. In either case, the rules must be changed in order to address the coordination versus cooperation problématique.

References

Agence France Presse (1999), 'S. Korean Defense Minister Seeks Support for Missile Test Halt', *Inside China Today*, 27 August 1999.

Ahlström, C. (2004), 'Arrows for India? Technology Transfers for Missile Defense and the MTCR', *Journal of Conflict & Security Law*, Vol. 9, No. 1 .

Aneja, A. (1999), 'Pakistan Begins Work on Shaheen-II', *The Hindu*, 27 September 1999.

Beck, M., Cupitt, R.T., Gahlaut, S. and Jones, S. (eds) (2003), *To Supply or To Deny: Comparing Non-proliferation Export Controls in Five Key Countries*, Kluwer Law International, New York.

Bermudez, J. (1998), 'A Silent Partner', *Jane's Defence Weekly*, 20 May 1998.

—— (1999), 'A History of Ballistic Missile Development in the DPRK', Occasional Paper No. 2, Centre for Non-Proliferation Studies, Monterrey Institute of International Studies, Monterrey, CA.

Bolkcom, C. and Squassoni, S. (2002), *CRS Report for Congress: Cruise Missile Proliferation*, Congressional Research Service/CRS, Foreign Affairs, Defense, and Trade Division, CRS21252, 3 July 2002, Washington, DC.

Bowen, W.Q. (1996), 'Brazil's Accession to the MTCR', *The Nonproliferation Review*, spring–summer 1996.

—— (1997), 'US Policy on Ballistic Missile Proliferation: The MTCR's First Decade (1987–1997)', *The Nonproliferation Review*, Fall 1997.

—— (2000), *The Politics of Ballistic Missile Nonproliferation*, St Martin's Press, New York.

Centre for Non-Proliferation Studies (2000), 'North Korea: A Second Taepo-dong Test?', Monitoring Proliferation Threat Project, Centre for Non-Proliferation Studies, University of Georgia.

Chellaney, B. (1994), 'An Indian Critique of US Export Controls', *Orbis*, Vol. 25, Summer 1994.

Chengappa, R. (1999), 'Boom for Boom', *India Today*, 26 April 1999.

Cirincione, J. (2000), 'Assessing the Ballistic Missile Threat', Testimony of Joseph Cirincione, Director of the Non-proliferation Programme of the Carnegie Endowment for International Peace, before the Senate Sub-Committee on International Security, Proliferation, and Federal Services, February 2000.

Cooper, D.A. (2001). 'The United States and the Evolution of International Supply-Side Missile Non-Proliferation Controls', in *Missile Proliferation and Defenses: Problems and Prospects*, Occasional Paper No. 7, Centre for Non-Proliferation Studies, May 2001.

Cupitt, R.T. and Khripunov, I. (1997), 'New Strategies for the Nuclear Suppliers Group (NSG)', *Comparative Strategy*, Vol. 16, No. 3, July–September 1997.

Dobbs, M. (2002), 'How Politics Help Define the Threat', *Washington Post*, 14 January 2002.

Eschel, T. (2005), 'Paris Air Show: Israel Extends Missile Offerings within MTCR Limits', *Aerospace Daily and Defense Report*, 14 June 2005.

French Ministry of Defence (2000), 'Maîtrise des Armements, Désarmement, et Non-proliferation: L'Action de la France, Ministère de la Défense', La Documentation Française, Paris.

Gahlaut, S. and Zaborsky, V. (2004), 'Do Export Control Regimes Have Members They Really Need?', *Comparative Strategy*, Vol. 23, No. 1, January/February/March 2004.

Global Security Newswire (2002), 'North Korea: Yemen Expects Fast Return of Scuds Shipment', 12 December 2002.

Gormley, D.M. (1998), 'Hedging Against the Cruise Missile Threat', *Survival*, April 1998.

—— (2003), 'New Developments in Unmanned Air Vehicles and Land-Attack Cruise Missiles', in *SIPRI Yearbook 2003: Armaments, Disarmament and International Security*, Oxford University Press, Oxford.

Gormley, D.M. and Speier, R. (2003), 'Controlling Unmanned Air Vehicles: New Challenges', Paper Commissioned by the Non-Proliferation Education Centre, 19 March 2003, <www.npec-web.org/projects/uavs.pdf>.

Graham, B. (2003), 'US Controls Hamper Foreign Role in Missile Defense', *Washington Post*, 19 October 2003.

Grospeaud, M. (2001), 'Le MTCR Face a La Proliferation des Missiles', Occassional Paper, No. 26, Institut d'Etudes de Sécurité.

Hindustan Times (1999), 'Agni-II Joins Nation's Missile Showcase', 12 April 1999.

International Institute for Strategic Studies (various), *The Military Balance*, Oxford University Press, London.

Isby, D. (1998), 'Barriers to Proliferation and Pathways to Transfer: Building Ballistic Missile Capabilities Under MTCR', in Commission to Assess the Ballistic Missile Threat to the United States, Appendix III, Unclassified Working Papers, July 1998.

Jones, R.W. and McDonough, M.G. (1998), 'Missile Proliferation, 1995–97', with Toby Dalton and Gregory Koblentz, *Tracking Nuclear Proliferation: A Guide in Maps and Charts, 1998*, Carnegie Endowment for International Peace, Washington, DC.

Jones, S. and Zaborsky, V. (eds) (1997), 'Missile Proliferation and MTCR: The Nth Member and Other Challenges', Occasional Paper, Centre for International Trade and Security, June 1997.

Joshi, M. (1998), 'Deadly Option', *India Today*, 4 May 1998.

Karp, A. (1996), *Ballistic Missile Proliferation: The Politics and Technics*, Oxford University Press, Oxford.

—— (2000), 'The Spread of Ballistic Missile Missiles and the Transformation of Global Security', *The Nonproliferation Review*, Spring–Summer 2000.

—— (2005), 'Going Ballistic? Reversing Missile Proliferation', *Arms Control Today*, June 2005.

Kugler, M. (2003), 'International Missile Defense Cooperation and the MTCR', Presentation to the Non-Proliferation Policy Education Centre, 30 June 2003, <www.npec-web.org/projects/kugler.pdf>.

Lackey, S. (1999), 'A Dangerous Race in a Multi-Axial World: The Missile Club in the Middle East', *Al-Wasat*, FBIS translation, 30 August 1999.

Landay, J.S. (1999), 'Missile Issues Put Chill on US–China Thaw', *The Christian Science Monitor*, 17 September 1999.

Mistry, D. (1997). 'Ballistic Missile Proliferation and the MTCR: A Ten-Year Review', *Contemporary Security Policy*, Vol. 18, No. 2.

—— (2003a), *Containing Missile Proliferation: Strategic Technology, Security Regimes, and International Cooperation in Arms Control*, University of Washington Press, Seattle, WA.

—— (2003b), 'Beyond the MTCR: Building a Comprehensive Regime to Contain Ballistic Missile Proliferation', *International Security*, Vol. 27, No. 4.

Mufson, S. (1999), 'Korean Missiles Push US Defense Plans', *Washington Post*, 5 September 1999.

Myers, S.L. (1998). 'Missile Test by North Korea: Dark Omen for Washington', *New York Times*, 1 September 1998.

National Intelligence Council (2001), 'Foreign Missile Developments and the Ballistic Missile Threat to the United States through 2015', National Intelligence Council Report.

Nazarkin, Y. (1998), 'Nonproliferation of Missile Technology', Conference of the PfP Consortium of Defense Academies and Security Studies Institutes, 'Networking the Security Community in the Information Age', October 1998, <www.isn.ethz.ch/3isf/Online_Publications/WS5/WS_5D/Nazarkin2.htm>.

Ozga, D. (1994), 'A Chronology of the Missile Technology Control Regime', *The Nonproliferation Review*, Vol. 1, No. 2.

Reuters (2003), 'North Korea Plans to Sell Missiles to Iran', 6 August 2003.

Ricks, T. and Slevin, P. (2002), 'Spain and U.S. Seize N. Korean Missiles', *Washington Post*, 11 December 2002.

Rodan, S. and O'Sullivan, A. (1998), 'Iran Test-Fires Shahab-3 Missile', *Jerusalem Post*, 24 July 1998.

Sadeh, S. (1999), 'Israel Said To Be Testing Missiles In Lebanon', *Ha'aretz*, June 1999.

Scheffran, J. and Karp, A. (1992), 'National Implementation of the MTCR: The US and German Experiences', in H.G. Brauch, H. van der Graaf, J. Grin and W. Smit (eds), *Controlling the Development and Spread of Military Technology*, VU University Press, Amsterdam.

Smith, M. (2001), 'The MTCR and the Future of Ballistic Missile Non-Proliferation', *Disarmament Diplomacy*, February 2001.

—— (2003), 'Pros and Cons of the MTCR', *Bulletin*, No. 21, International Network of Engineers and Scientists against Proliferation, April 2003, <www.inesap.org/bulletin21/bul21art23.htm>.

Speier, R. (1997), 'Russia, Ukraine, and the Nth Member Problem', in S. Jones and V. Zaborsky (eds), 'Missile Proliferation and MTCR: The Nth Member and Other Challenges', Occasional Paper, Centre for International Trade and Security, June 1997.

—— (2001), 'How Effective Is the Missile Technology Control Regime?', Nonproliferation Brief 4 (7), Carnegie Endowment for International Peace, 12 April 2001.

—— (2004), 'Complementary or Competitive? Missile Controls vs Missile Defense', *Arms Control Today*, June 2004, <www.armscontrol.org/act/2004_06/Speier.asp>.

Struck, D. (1999), 'US, N. Korea to Hold Talks on Missile Test', *Washington Post*, 27 August 1999.

Svitak, A. and Ratnam, G. (2003), 'Missile Defense vs Non-Proliferation: White House Policy Tests International Limits', *Defense News*, 14 July 2003.

Thielman, G. (2003), 'Rumsfeld Reprise? The Missile Report That Foretold the Iraq Intelligence Controversy', *Arms Control Today*, Vol. 33, No. 6.

Times of India (1999a), 'China Tests New Mobile Missile', 1 September 1999.

—— (1999b), 'China Denies Missiles Deal with Iran', 31 August 1999.

United Nations (2002), *The Issue of Missiles in All Its Aspects: Report of the Secretary-General*, A/57/229, 23 July 2002, <http://projects.sipri.se/expcon/UNSG-missile.pdf>.

US General Accounting Office (1996), 'Foreign Missile Threats: Analytical Soundness of Certain National Intelligence Estimates', GAO/NSIAD 96-25, August 1996.

—— (2002), 'Nonproliferation: Strategy Needed to Strengthen Multilateral Export Controls', Report to Congressional Committees, GAO 03-43, October 2002.

—— (2003), 'Nonproliferation: Improvements Needed to Better Control Technology Exports for Cruise Missiles and Unmanned Aerial Vehicles', GAO 04-175, November 2003.

Van Diepen, Vann (2004), 'Controlling the Spread of Ballistic Missiles', Statement by Vann Van Diepen, Director, Office of Chemical, Biological, and Missile Non-Proliferation, US Department of State, Arms Control Association and Embassy of Argentina Press Briefing, 23 November 2004, <www.armscontrol.org/events/20041123_ballistic_missiles_transcript.asp>.

Weiss, K. (2001), 'The Limits of Missile Diplomacy: Missile Proliferation, Diplomacy, and Defense', *World Affairs*, Vol. 163, No. 3.

Yuan, J.-D. (2000), 'The MTCR and Missile Proliferation: Moving Toward the Next Phase', International Security Research and Outreach Programme, International Security Bureau, Department of Foreign Affairs and International Trade, May 2000.

Zaborsky,V. (2003), **'**Missile Proliferation Risks of International Space Cooperation', *World Affairs*, Vol. 165, No. 4.

—— (2004), 'Does China Belong in the Missile Technology Control Regime?', *Arms Control Today*, Vol. 34, No. 8.

Notes

1. The ICOC, or Hague Code of Conduct, Code is a schedule of 'a set of principles, commitments, confidence-building measures and incentives' designed to create a common concept of what is termed 'responsible missile behaviour', to be implemented via a multilateral instrument open to all states. Interestingly, the ICOC is viewed as a completely independent undertaking *vis-à-vis* the MTCR. It is, however, a direct extension of the MTCR, having been discussed, initiated and sponsored by MTCR members. While the ICOC was approved at the 2002 Ottawa Plenary, efforts to construct a demand-side missile non-proliferation vehicle date back to French discussions in 1991. The Office of the President of the French Republic released its 1991 'Plan for Arms Control and Disarmament' in which France recognizes the role of the MTCR in arms control, but points out that the current regime is only a step towards a more general agreement. France calls for a broader agreement with geographic enlargement, increased control, universal applicability to all members, establishment of rules for international cooperation for civilian use of space, and prevention of technology leakage from

civilian to military projects. France proposes the development of confidence-building measures, including the establishment of a 'code of good conduct' and a mechanism for the notification of space launches. See Ozga (1994). See also French Ministry of Defence (2000).

2.   Noted missile proliferation analyst Aaron Karp observes: 'With so much potentially at stake from missile proliferation, it is all the more ironic that its restraint rests on something so modest as the MTCR' (Karp 2000).

3.   With respect to the MTCR's relative success, even a cursory review of the literature covering the MTCR suggests the near-consensus acceptance of the view that in the MTCR's first decade, Argentina, Brazil, Egypt, Iraq, Libya, South Africa, South Korea, Syria and Taiwan were thwarted from advancing their missile ambitions.

4.   On 4 October 2000 Iran introduced a resolution on missiles to the 55th session of the UN First Committee. The resolution emphasizes the 'need for a comprehensive approach towards missiles, in a balanced and non-discriminatory manner, as a contribution to international peace and security'. The resulting UN Panel of Government Experts met to establish such a comprehensive approach. The exercise, however, collapsed with recognition of the impossibility of drafting a consensus report: <www.reachingcriticalwill. org/political/missiles/missilesindex.html>. The Russian- proposed Global Control System (GCS) for the non-proliferation of missiles and missile technology would be, were it realized, a universal transparency regime for launches of ballistic missiles and space delivery vehicles, including, as a component, a multilateral advance notification regime for planned launches of such missiles, as suggested by several states on various occasions: <www.fas.org/nuke/control/mtcr/news/GSC_content.htm>.

5.   American concern intensified primarily because of the progress that several countries were making in developing and producing their own rockets. This centred on the activities of five principal countries, including Israel, Libya, South Korea, Taiwan and India. American concern was exacerbated by each country's simultaneous pursuit of civilian and suspected military nuclear programmes. In short, Washington became anxious about the potential role ballistic missiles might play as delivery vehicles for nuclear weapons in the developing world. The use of ballistic missiles by both sides during the Iran–Iraq War, as well as the use of Scuds in the Afghani and the later Yemeni civil wars, also underscored this proliferation concern. See: Bowen (1997, 22–3).

6.   Cooper notes that the US attempted to instil Coordinating Committee for Multilateral Export Control (COCOM)-like controls in the MTCR's infrastructure, an initiative universally rejected by the member countries.

7.   In the 1950s and 1960s few restrictions were placed on the transfer of nuclear and space technology between states. From the early 1960s onwards the US transferred technical data on sounding rockets and space launch vehicles (the equivalent of short-range and intermediate-range missiles respectively) as well as complete sounding rockets to other NATO members, and to Argentina, Brazil, India, South Korea, Mexico, Pakistan and Taiwan. The former Soviet Union and West European states undertook similar technology transfers. In addition to their space-technology transfers, both superpowers exported short-range ballistic missiles. Washington transferred 120 km range Lance missiles to its North Atlantic Treaty Organization (NATO) allies, and supplied 40 km range Honest John artillery rockets to South Korea and Taiwan, while Moscow supplied Scud missiles to its Warsaw Pact allies and to clients in the Middle East. It should be noted that Washington and Moscow also aided longer-range missile programmes of their close allies. Washington assisted missile projects in Britain and France, and has

actually transferred a strategic missile – the Trident – to the UK. Moscow supplied assistance to Chinese ballistic missile programmes in the 1950s. For more information on early missile transfers, see Scheffran and Karp (1992, 238–40).

8. In the period 1978–81, four events that illustrated the potential of non-industrialized nations to build missiles greatly increased concerns in US policymaking circles about the growing availability of and interest in rocket technology. These events included South Korea's 1978 test of a surface-to-surface missile; Iraq's bid to purchase rocket stages from Italy, discovered in 1979; India's launch of a satellite in 1980; and a German firm's unsuccessful test of a rocket stage in Libya in 1981. See Karp (1996).

9. The Nixon administration's decision to sell production licences of a Delta space launch vehicle to Japan was denounced in Congress as a sacrifice of US technology; the ensuing debate in Congress eventually led to the promulgation of a revised export control policy: National Security Decision Memorandum (NSDM) 187. This Congressional act drastically reduced US cooperation with foreign rocket programmes in order to protect US commercial interests in space launch services and to shield the Space Shuttle project. In the mid-1970s, the US also began limiting missile sales; for example, it denied Israeli requests made after the 1973 Yom Kippur war for the 1,000 km range Pershing I missile, and instead supplied Israel with the 120 km range Lance missile. See Mistry (1997).

10. Specifically, the Guidelines outline the goal of the regime: 'to limit the risks of proliferation of weapons of mass destruction (that is, nuclear, chemical and biological weapons), by controlling transfers that could make a contribution to delivery systems (other than manned aircraft) for such weapons'.

11. The 300 km range limit correlates to the distances, in a majority of strategic theatres of conflict, where nuclear missile use might be considered. This range was also considered to be a convenient, workable and achievable parameter around which international export controls could be established. The 500 kg payload limit recognizes that emerging nuclear states are likely initially to develop relatively crude nuclear weapons. At the 2002 MTCR plenary in Warsaw, the definition of payload was expanded to cover support structures and countermeasures, as well as the warhead itself.

12. Regime members agreed during the 2004 Buenos Aires plenary meeting to make the inclusion of catch-all provisions into national export control regulations a regime-wide requirement.

13. At the October 2000 MTCR Helsinki summit, a draft of a new initiative, Code of Conduct Against Missile Proliferation, was introduced. In July 2000, the European Union (EU), the principal architect of the initiative, adopted a 'Common Position on the Fight Against Ballistic Missile Proliferation' that called for the universal adoption of the new Code of Conduct at a UN Conference in 2002. The 33 nation MTCR, in its plenary session on 24–28 September 2001 in Ottawa, Canada, revisited the idea and augmented the original draft text of the Code of Conduct. Approximately a hundred nations convened in Paris in February and in Madrid in June 2002 to discuss strengths and weaknesses of the Code of Conduct. In their final meeting in The Hague, Netherlands, on 25 November 2002, 92 countries became formal signatories of the International Code of Conduct Against Ballistic Missile Proliferation. The document requires the signatory states to prepare an annual report on their programmes and to signal any upcoming missile tests. However, the Code of Conduct is not legally binding, and it has at least two other serious deficiencies. First, key non-MTCR member states – China, India, Pakistan, Iraq and Iran – have opted to stay outside the framework.

Second, developing a mechanism of space-related incentives to forgo ballistic missile programmes is extremely divisive.

14.   For select coverage, see Joshi (1998); Chengappa (1999); *Hindustan Times* (1999); Myers (1998); *Times of India* (1999a); Centre for Nonproliferation Studies (2000); Rodan and O'Sullivan (1998).

15.   The continued viability of the so-called 'Scud Barrier' is a subject of considerable debate. See Smith (2003), see also Isby (1998).

16.   In accordance with General Assembly Resolution 55/33 of 20 November 2000, the UN Secretary-General was requested to prepare a report on the issue of Missiles in all its aspects. A group of government experts was established to help prepare the report, including representatives from 23 states. The report, which was presented in July 2002, underlined the concern of states about a number of missile-related developments (UN 2002).

17.   In June 1999, Russia proposed a Global Control System (GSK – from Russian *global'naya sistema kontrolya*) at the G8 summit at Cologne, Germany. Later it shaped a more detailed form during two international conferences arranged for governmental representatives by the Russian Ministry of Foreign Affairs, held in Moscow in March 2000 and February 2001. The genealogy of GSK is rooted in 1992, when then Russian President Boris Yeltsin, in his speech given at the UN Security Council on 29 January, proposed a Global System for Protecting the International Community Against Missile Attack. However, by 2001 the idea of the Global Control System had modified into something unique, which would involve the MTCR as well as various existing notification and confidence building measures. Contrary to the 1992 GSK proposal, the GSK does not contain any military enforcement measures. The GSK called for the establishment of an international non-strategic missile defence system, possibly operated by multilateral military contingents. At the same time, initially the GSK proposed only non-military enforcement measures, although its vagueness permitted the inclusion of military options in some other categories. To date, the effort was faltered, becoming a point of departure for missile control discussions rather than an end point. See <www. fas.org/nuke/control/mtcr/news/GSC_content.htm>.

18.   The text is available on the website of the Austrian Ministry of Foreign Affairs at <www.bmaa.gv.at/up-media/114_HCOC.pdf>.

19.   For an unofficial copy of the text of NSPD-23, see <www.fas.org/irp/offdocs/nspd/ nspd-23.htm>. See also Speier (2004).

20.   During the first term, the Bush administration had undertaken extensive legal contortions to justify cooperation on the Israeli Arrow (missile defence) programme. See Kugler (2003).

21.   Author interview with Ambassor Mariusz Handzlik, MTCR Chairman, 2002–2003, April 2004.

22.   At the regime level, there is always the issue of the inevitable trade-off between increased membership and regime efficacy in terms of the agenda, agreement and enforcement issues which would have to be worked out among member states. See, for example, Cupitt and Khripunov (1997, 305–17); Ozga (1994, 68) and Bowen (1996, 86–91). A more recent study is Gahlaut and Zaborsky (2004, 19).

23.   The GAO found that the failure to share information on approvals prevents regime members from determining whether undercutting was taking place (US GAO, 2004).

24.   *De facto* denials refers to the practice in several countries whereby informal consultations between the exporters and the licensing officials help exporters decide whether they

should even bother to apply for a particular export licence. Officials may indicate that a licence for a particular export to an end-user is likely to be denied, discouraging the exporter from even applying. Several regime members have low rates of denial, according to their official statistics, because of such pre-screening. Absent the pre-screening data, fellow members may grant a licence for the same item.

25.   A recent GAO study, for example, highlighted the technical and policy challenge posed by briskly evolving unmanned aerial technologies: 'Distinctions between cruise missiles and UAVs are becoming blurred as the militaries of many nations, in particular the United States, add missiles to traditional reconnaissance UAVs and develop UAVs dedicated to combat missions' (US GAO, 2003). Similarly, a Congressional Research Service (CRS) report notes: 'In contrast to ballistic missile proliferation, cruise missiles present a particular challenge for monitoring and control because they exploit technology that is well understood and well established in the civil aviation industry. Missile airframes, navigation systems, jet engines, satellite maps, and mission planning computers and software all can be purchased on the commercial market. Cruise missile technology "hides in plain sight" – making it difficult to identify a military programme. At the same time, commercial availability generally means relatively low-cost weapons for many nations and, potentially, non-state actors' (Bolkcom and Squassoni 2002, 2; see pp. 3–4 for more information about the MTCR).

26.   The flexibility of cruise missiles to trade off payload and range configurations makes agreement on how to calculate capabilities difficult. Moreover, overlapping military and civilian technology increases pressure to allow technology exports. Ballistic missiles do have a civilian counterpart technology – space launch vehicles – but the technologies are not nearly as ubiquitous as they are for UAV technologies in the aircraft industry. See Gormley and Speier (2003); Gormley (1998); and Bolkcom and Squassoni (2002).

27.   There is no universally accepted definition of cruise missiles, but they can be categorized as unmanned aerial vehicles (UAVs) that are a) continually powered by an air-breathing or rocket engine; b) generally guided for their entire flight; c) weaponized; and d) generally optimized for one-way missions. This contrasts with weaponized UAVs such as the Predator, that can perform multiple missions, but they are treated similarly under the MTCR.

28.   The Wassenaar Arrangement picks up the lower range of the capability spectrum with respect to cruise missile and UAV systems. Wassenaar, which supersedes Cold-War COCOM (Coordinating Committee) export controls, specifically regulates UAVs and UAV technology designed for military purposes. Thus, exports of cruise missiles with ranges shorter than 300 km that can carry warheads weighing less than 500 kg that are not destined for countries with WMD programmes are subject to restrictions under Wassenaar. However, Wassenaar includes exceptions, as does the MTCR, for technologies and components intended for manned aircraft.

29.   The missile threat to the US is based on a series of seemingly contradictory intelligence and task force reports dating back to the early 1990s. The most recent survey, the 1998 'Report of the Commission to Assess the Ballistic Missile Threat to the United States' (or the 'Rumsfeld Report') warns: 'The newer ballistic missile-equipped nations [North Korea, Iran and Iraq] … would be able to inflict major destruction on the US within about five years of a decision to acquire such a capability (10 years in the case of Iraq). During several of those years, the US might not be aware that such a decision had been made'. While National Intelligence Estimate (NIE) on the subject, 'Foreign Missile Developments and the Ballistic Missile Threat to the United States Through 2015', was

released in 1999, it merely confirmed the conclusions of the Rumsfeld Report that the ballistic threat was growing at an alarming rate. An informative survey of the various ballistic missile reports is found in Thielman (2003). See also US GAO (1996).

30.   In National Security Presidential Directive (NSPD) 23, President Bush outlined the rationale behind and nature of NMD cooperation with US allies. In so doing, the administration seeks to preserve, to the extent allowable, the present scope and domain of the MTCR: 'The goal of the Missile Technology Control Regime (MTCR) is to help reduce the global missile threat by curbing the flow of missiles and related technology to proliferators. The MTCR and missile defenses play complementary roles in countering the global missile threat. The United States intends to implement the MTCR in a manner that does not impede missile defense cooperation with friends and allies' (National Security Presidential Directive-23, 16 December 2002). A copy is available on the Federation of American Scientists website: <www.fas.org/irp/offdocs/nspd/nspd-23.htm>.

31.   The US intelligence community had been judged harshly by elements of Congress for the alleged sanguinity of its past assessments of foreign ballistic missile developments. Yet, an attempt to get a more forward-leaning professional assessment on missiles by appointing a commission chaired by former CIA director Robert Gates did not succeed in fundamentally altering previous intelligence judgments that the ballistic missile threat to the United States was not immediate. After passing a new law, which broke with the congressional tradition of naming commission members proportionately between the parties, the Republican majority did succeed in appointing a new commission under Rumsfeld and naming six of its nine members. See Dobbs (2002). Making similar observations, noted missile proliferation analyst, Mark Smith observed: 'Despite the fact that the political impact of ballistic missiles is a considerable distance ahead of technological realities, the strategic implications of proliferation are far-reaching, not least in terms of the impact as a driver of US plans for ballistic missile defense (BMD)'.

32.   A survey of the literature addressing the MTCR reveals the absence of any methodical attempt to assess regime effectiveness. The collective thinking regarding MTCR 'successes' points to curtailment of the Argentine, Brazilian, Egyptian, South African, South Korean and Taiwanese missile programmes. Liabilities include both institutional flaws (for example, decision-making procedures and lack of enforcement mechanisms) and the growth of secondary proliferation (for example, North Korean serial missile proliferation). Representative studies of the MTCR include: Bowen (2000); Mistry (2003a); Weiss (2001); Yuan (2000); Ozga (1994, 66–93).

33.   The MTCR was designed to curb, not end, missile proliferation. Aaron Karp notes: 'With so much potentially at stake from missile proliferation, it is all the more ironic that its restraint rests on something so modest as the MTCR' (Karp 2000, 115).

34.   Aaron Karp notes of the various missile non-proliferation efforts: 'The MTCR, the Hague Code of Conduct, and to a lesser extent the UN Panel of Government Experts dominate multilateral activity (on missile non-proliferation). Although the three are often described as different approaches to a common goal, they actually aim toward distinct objectives. They are based on very different and largely incompatible assumptions. That their divergences have been overlooked is possible only because their progress has been so uneven. None of the three ever claimed to be a comprehensive solution to the global spread of ballistic missiles. Indeed, they are increasingly overburdened by specific missile challenges. Even so, collectively they constitute one of the most

sophisticated international dialogues on arms control and disarmament in the world today' (Karp 2005).

35. 'MTCR-class' has become a term of art regarding missile exports. Israel, for example, has cited MTCR constraints as its reason for not supplying India with the Arrow II theatre missile defence interceptor. See: Ahlström (2004, 103–25).

36. This chart was adapted from Joseph Cirincione's work on assessing the ballistic missile threat. See Cirincione (2000).

37. A representative reading list would include: Bowen (2000); Mistry (2003a); Grospeaud (2001); Jones and Zabrosky (1997); Mistry (2003b); Smith (2001); Speier (2001); Weiss (2001).

38. The various multilateral export control regimes became part and parcel Non-Aligned Movement (NAM) politics in the early 1990s. For example, Brahma Chellaney contends, 'The non-proliferation policies of Western powers are founded on a strategy of preventing Third World development of technologies that might impinge on the Western powers' military and economic interests' (see Chellaney 1994).

39. US MTCR-based missile sanctions, for example, are codified into the Iran Non-Proliferation Act of 2000.

40. Procedural changes may include, for example, a modified voting process. Currently, all decisions within the MTCR are made on a consensus basis. This practice was not so problematic when the members of the regimes were few in number. However, the significant growth in membership in recent years, along with the MTCR decision to co-opt members whose perspectives on security differ from those of the longstanding members, poses a serious functional problem.

41. If the goal is coordination, then the arrangement should be worked out among states with similar political, economic and technological interests. They do not require a treaty, because they can work together quite well in an informal setting. That is, for instance, what we witnessed in the early years of the MTCR. The regime was established by a group of like-minded nations concerned about the spread of missile technologies. Those nations (that is, the G 7) did not require broad bargains to be struck, nor side-payments made, because they had roughly similar interests and objectives. See Jones and Zaborsky (1997).

[17]

THE ABM TREATY: CHANGED CIRCUMSTANCES, EXTRAORDINARY EVENTS, SUPREME INTERESTS AND INTERNATIONAL LAW

REIN MÜLLERSON*

THE Cold War years may have been in a way a good period for international lawyers and other international relations specialists: things were rather predictable and any fundamental change seemed to be out of the question. Today much has changed. What was just recently unforesee-able has become a reality in which unforeseeability is the norm. What about international law in this context?

International law has also changed considerably due to the trans-formed context though legal texts have remained basically the same (for example, the content of one of the central notions of the UN Charter "Threats to International Peace and Security" has undergone radical reinterpretation since the beginning of the 1990s). The professional life of international lawyers has become more difficult, but more interesting at the same time.

Discussions on the ideas underlying the U.S. national missile defence (NMD) and on the Anti-Ballistic Missile (ABM) Treaty[1] highlight several crucial challenges which international law is facing today: stability of law versus fundamental political and military-strategic change; law as an instrument of at least relative predictability versus unforeseen events and developments; essential bilateralism of traditional international law (magnified by the bipolar nature of the international system of the Cold War period) versus both unilateral responses and multilateral (even universal) interests of post-Cold War international society. In such a situation one inevitably starts writing without knowing where one may end or even whether the problem is susceptible to a meaningful legal analysis at all. But is not that exactly what genuine research is all about?

I. "ULTIMATE POWER" AND INTERNATIONAL LAW

United States NMD ideas and proposals and the fate of the ABM Treaty which was signed in 1972 between the U.S. and the Soviet Union (now Russia) have for some time been amongst the most disputed issues of

---

* Professor of International Law, King's College London; *Institut de Droit International*, Member.
1. Source: U.S. Arms Control and Disarmament Agency, *Arms Control and Disarmament Agreements: Texts and Histories of Negotiations*, 1982 ed. (Government Printing Office), pp.139–147.

510   *International and Comparative Law Quarterly*   [Vol. 50

international politics. Politicians, diplomats, specialists in various domains of expertise as well as journalists have commented on practically all aspects of this topic. However, until recently international lawyers have been somewhat peripheral to this discussion.[2] It may be that in this case the moderation shown by lawyers is explained by the consideration well expressed by Dean Acheson after another international controversy involving missiles—the 1962 Cuban crisis: "the power, position and prestige of the United States had been challenged by another State; and law simply does not deal with such questions of ultimate power—power that comes close to sources of sovereignty".[3] However, such self-reserve that lawyers sometimes show *vis-à-vis* politically sensitive issues (and Dean Acheson was not only a prominent diplomat but a lawyer as well) does disservice not only to international law but also to the clarification of political and military-strategic issues which law is supposed to govern.

It has often fallen on international relations specialists to comment on whether concrete NMD aspects violate specific articles or paragraphs of the ABM Treaty and to what extent it is possible to interpret Treaty clauses without stretching them to breaking point.[4] However, these technical (both in legal and physical terms) questions, though necessary for the clarification of concrete details of the ABM Treaty, are of secondary importance today. Moreover, simply juxtaposing various proposed or hypothetical NMD components (for example, boost-phase interception, ground-based or sea-based interceptors, space-based elements, infra-red tracking systems, early warning radars outside the national territory, etc.) with articles of the Treaty and related instruments[5] without corresponding analysis of wider political and military-strategic implications (which themselves are reflected in some important, though rather controversial, legal concepts) does not give answers to fundamental concerns. As in most important international law issues a simple rule-oriented approach[6] reveals its narrow limits.

---

2. The December 2000 issue of the *Journal of Conflict and Security Law* had articles by Ambassador Thomas Graham "Law, Politics and the ABM Treaty" and by Professor Barry Kellman "Missile Defence and the ABM Treaty: Considerations of International Security and Law". John B. Rhinelander's article "The ABM Treaty – Past, Present and Future" (Part I), is forthcoming in the June 2001 issue of the same Journal.

3. *Proceedings of the American Society of International Law*, 1963, p.14.

4. I. H. Daalder, J. M. Goldgeier, J. M. Lindsay, "Deploying NMD: Not Whether, But How", *Survival*, 42, No. 1, Spring 2000; D.A. Wilkening, "Amending the ABM Treaty", *Survival*, 42, No. 1, Spring 2000; R. Garwin, "Cooperative Ballistic Missile Defence", November 1999, http://www.fas.org/rlg; P. Gordon, "Bush, Missile Defence and the Atlantic Alliance", *Survival*, vol. 43, No. 1, Spring 2001.

5. The complex of ABM documents includes besides the 1972 Treaty (with 1974 amendments) seven agreed statements, five common understandings and four unilateral statements. (see J. Rhinelander, p.2).

6. On the nature of international law see R. Higgins, *Problems and Process: International Law and How We Use It*, Clarendon Press, 1994, pp.1–12.

Using a rule-oriented approach, one need not be a Grotius to conclude that most (if not all) proposed or even hypothetical NMD versions come into conflict with at least some concrete provisions of the ABM Treaty, if not with its very object and purpose. At the same time, such a simple analysis also shows quite non-controversially that the U.S. (like Russia) has the right under Article XV of the Treaty to withdraw from it (that is to denounce it in terms provided for in the Treaty).[7]

However, international law is not that simple (or simplistic) and a traffic rules approach is usually quite peripheral in international legal discourse, especially if one reflects or acts upon sensitive issues of international politics. International law attempts, sometimes imperfectly, to take account of and reflect complexities of the real world. That is why the analysis below concentrates on various missile defence ideas and proposals in the light of such legal concepts as the object and purpose of the ABM Treaty; the extent to which events of the last 15 or so years have changed the circumstances in which the ABM Treaty was concluded (i.e. the possible use of the *rebus sic stantibus* clause); how proposed means of creating the NMD system relate to the spirit (the object and purpose) and letter (concrete clauses) of the ABM Treaty; the possibility and conditions of denunciation of the Treaty.[8] Finally, the effect of this important bilateral treaty (or its denunciation) of the bipolar world on third States in

---

7. This issue will be discussed later in detail.

8. There have been some voices in the US claiming that the ABM Treaty has ceased to exist as a legally binding document after one of the Treaty partners – the USSR – disappeared from the political and legal map of the world. So a 1998 letter from the Chairmen of the House International Relations Committee and the Senate Foreign Relations Committee to the President stated: 'If it is unclear as a matter of law whether Russia or any country that emerged from the Soviet Union is today bound by the ABM Treaty, then it should also be unclear whether the United States is so bound' (Quoted by T. Graham, Jr, 'Law, Politics and the ABM Treaty', *Journal of Conflict and Security Law*, 2000, vol. 5, No. 2, p.276). Similar views were expressed by some Senators and legal experts during the hearing on the ABM Treaty in the Senate's Committee on Foreign Relations in May 1999. David B. Rivkin, for example, stated that 'the ABM Treaty no longer binds the United States as a matter of international law and politics' since 'the Soviet Union had disappeared in 1991, rendering performance of the ABM Treaty as originally agreed impossible' (*Committee on Foreign Relations. The Legal Status of the ABM Treaty*, Tuesday, May 25, 1999, http://www.access.gpo.gov/congress/senate). Such views completely misinterpret some elementary points of international law concerning continuity and succession of States especially as applied in cases of fundamental changes which took place in the former USSR, Eastern and Central Europe.

512   *International and Comparative Law Quarterly*   [VOL. 50

a quite different international setting is also studied. It is obvious too that all these issues are intertwined and that none of them is "purely" legal.[9]

Discussions around the possible U.S. withdrawal from the ABM Treaty seem to revolve around two related and sometimes even overlapping political issues and corresponding legal concepts. The first issue—more concrete and imminent—concerns actual or potential ballistic missile threats to the territory of the United States from so-called "rogue" regimes[10] and, as a consequence, the possible denunciation of the ABM Treaty using the withdrawal clause in its Article XV (2) (this may be called the "extraordinary events" and "supreme interests" argument). Secondly, the proliferation of missile technology is not the only, and not even the biggest change,[11] which has happened in the world since the ABM Treaty was negotiated. These changes, which will be analysed further in this article, may point to the possibility of the use of the fundamental change of circumstances argument (*rebus sic stantibus*) for the termination or modification of the ABM Treaty (called in this article the "fundamental change of circumstances" argument).

The United States, if deciding to withdraw from the Treaty or advocating its modification, would hardly resort to the customary law *rebus sic stantibus* argument since the Treaty expressly provides for the possibility of its denunciation. However, it seems that the "fundamental change of circumstances" clause used in combination with the "extraordinary events" and "supreme interests" argument may give Washington a more persuasive and legitimate basis for its initiatives of either agreed modification of the Treaty or of unilateral withdrawal from it.

The point is that though emerging ballistic missile threats from "rogue" regimes referred to by the United States are part of the changed circumstances, the latter notion is obviously much wider. It includes the disappearance of the bipolar world, military-strategic parity between the U.S. and the U.S.S.R. (Russia), struggle between capitalist and commu-

---

9. It is important to note, though only in passing, that 'purity' of intellectual approaches in social sciences, their completeness and non-openendedness seems to be a sign of immaturity. In law a tendency towards 'purely legal' or normative analysis in Kelsen's terms may be explained by the contradiction between the essentially normative character of law and the essentially non-normative nature of any creative process. I believe lawyers (especially academic lawyers) have to constantly balance between being 'too creative' and being too normative. If the first impulse prevails, we become fiction writers (and usually not good at all); if the second tendency gains the upper hand we become technicians (maybe useful but of secondary or even tertiary importance in resolving problems of international relations). See more about this in R. Müllerson, *Ordering Anarchy: International Law in International Society*, Kluwer Law International, 2000, pp.9–86.

10. If one uses the term "rogue" at all in this context, it seems more appropriate to use it in the characterisation of regimes not States, nations or countries.

11. Whenever we speak of changes in geopolitics, ideology or technology it is natural, in the context of this article, that only changes which relate to the circumstances which were essential for the conclusion of the ABM Treaty are taken into account.

nist ideologies and transformation of other political, military-strategic and ideological factors. Changes of such a magnitude may indeed nullify the very *raison d'être* of the ABM Treaty, i.e. its very object and purpose even without new threats from "rogue" regimes.

On the other hand, the emergence of new missile threats to the U.S. (or for some other States for that matter) may not necessarily call for the repudiation of the whole treaty. Its object and purpose may remain, if not in whole then at least partially, valid and it may be possible to face emerging threats in a way which would require modification of only some concrete provisions of the ABM Treaty. Therefore we will analyse, first, circumstances existing at the time of the conclusion of the Treaty which were essential for the consent of the Parties to be bound by the Treaty and whose change may have been so fundamental that it may have radically transformed the scope of obligations still to be performed under the Treaty (Article 62 of the Vienna Convention on the Law of Treaties). Secondly, we will study these extraordinary events related to the subject matter of the ABM Treaty which may have jeopardised the supreme interests of the United States (Article XV of the Treaty) and which may serve as a basis for the denunciation of the Treaty. Finally, the effect of the Treaty (and its denunciation) on third States will be analysed.

II. THE *RAISON D'ÊTRE* OF THE ABM TREATY

The ABM Treaty was part and parcel of the concept and practice of strategic nuclear deterrence, in the form of either mutually assured destruction (MAD) or counterforce (i.e. when strategic forces targeted adversary's offensive weapons) strategy. In more concrete terms the Treaty was one of the core elements of the process of limitation of strategic weapons of the Soviet Union and the United States. The Treaty was signed in Moscow on 26 May 1972 together with the Interim Agreement on Certain Measures with respect to Limitation of Strategic Offensive Arms and they together became known as the SALT I (Strategic Arms Limitation Talks).[12] As John Rhinelander comments, the Treaty "was considered in 1972, and still by many today, the *sine qua non* for limits upon and reduction of U.S. and Soviet strategic offensive weapons whether by formal agreement or otherwise, and a cornerstone of strategic stability".[13]

The ABM Treaty (as amended in 1974) prohibits the Parties from deploying nation-wide ballistic missile defence and limits each Party to one ABM site (100 interceptors). As Article 1 states, "each Party undertakes not to deploy ABM systems for a defence of the territory of its

---

12. For an excellent overview of the content of the Treaty and controversies related to its implementation see J. B. Rhinelander's article in the forthcoming June 2001 issue of the *Journal of Conflict and Security Law*.

13. J. Rhinelander, *op. cit.*, p.2.

514 *International and Comparative Law Quarterly* [VOL. 50

country and not to provide a base for such a defence and not to deploy ABM systems for defence of an individual region except as provided for in Article III of this Treaty". Issues concerning the Treaty compliance, proposed amendments and other concerns related to the implementation of the Treaty are to be discussed in the bilateral Standing Consultative Commission (SCC) set up under the Treaty.[14] The ABM Treaty contains a number of restrictions on the size, type and location of ABM components, including the prohibition on testing and deployment of sea-, air-, or space-based and mobile ABM components. The Parties must not give ABM capabilities to so-called non-ABM facilities like Theatre High Altitude Area Defence (THAAD) or Theatre Missile Defence (TMD) systems.

As President Richard Nixon stated in his communication to the Senate Committee on Foreign Affairs forwarding the ABM Treaty for the ratification, "together the two agreements [the ABM Treaty and the Interim Agreement on Strategic Offensive Arms] provide for a more stable strategic balance in the next several years than would be possible if strategic arms competition continued unchecked. This benefits not only the United States and the Soviet Union, but all the nations of the world".[15] Paul Doty and Antonia Chayes write of the three major premises of the ABM Treaty:

> First, that the only insurance against nuclear war for the foreseeable future remained a stable nuclear deterrent based on invulnerable second-strike forces. Second, that agreed qualitative and quantitative restraints on strategic offensive forces could enhance stability. Third, in the current state of relatively ineffective defences against nuclear weapons, development and testing of air-or space-based antiballistic missile systems would reduce each side's confidence in its retaliatory capability, erode stability, and undermine incentives to limit strategic offensive forces. Since there was little reason to believe that rudimentary ABM technology could provide a cost-effective defence, ABM deployment would stimulate additional offensive deployments and countermeasures, thereby accelerating the arms race.[16]

There were already, during the Cold War, various threats to the ABM Treaty, some of which were discussed in the SCC. Both Parties accused each other of violating Treaty provisions.[17] The Reagan Administration

14. Belarus, Kazakhstan and Ukraine are participating in meetings of the SCC under the Memorandum of Understanding of 1997 signed by the U.S. and Russia. However, this Memorandum has not had the consent of the Senate and therefore is not legally binding. (J. Rhinelander, *op. cit.*, p.14; *The Legal Status of the ABM Treaty, op. cit.*)

15. SALT Agreements. Communication from the President of the United States, Washington, June 13, 1972 (file:///A/SALT Agreements.htm)

16. A. Handler Chayes, P. Doty, *Defending Deterrence: Managing the ABM Treaty Regime into the 21st Century*, Pergamon-Brassey's, 1989, pp.2–3.

17. *Ibid.*, Rhinelander, "The ABM Treaty – Past, Present and Future".

Strategic Defence Initiative (SDI) or the Star Wars project was clearly what the Treaty was meant to prevent from being realised (or even having a basis for the realisation of such a project being created). Had the SDI moved ahead not only the letter but also the very spirit of the Treaty would have been violated. However, unrealistic ambitions of the SDI and the change of the administration in Washington left the idea of the Star Wars in limbo. In the early 1990s, the Bush administration launched another missile defence initiative—Global Protection Against Limited Strikes (GPALS) but the Republicans lost the 1992 elections and the new Democratic administration was initially sceptical about missile defence.

However, at the turn of the Millennium the Clinton administration, being pushed by influential members of Congress, in addition to revelations of the Rumsfeld Report on new missile threats of July 1998[18] and the North Korean test of its Taepo Dong missile in August 1998[19], became quite serious about the idea of a limited national ballistic missile defence. But the realisation of even such a limited or thin ballistic missile defence would have been contrary to, if not always the spirit, then at least the letter of the ABM Treaty.[20] Being regarded as a part (the cornerstone, indeed) of the military-strategic balance between Washington and Moscow, a part and parcel of the concept of Mutually Assured Destruction (MAD) as well as a crucial element of the balance between offensive and defensive weapons, the material violation of the Treaty would have been a fatal blow to all these concepts. The question, however, is how relevant are all these concepts in today's world?

The Bush Administration has so far left little doubt that it will go ahead with NMD. As President Bush stated in his speech on ballistic missile defence on 1 May this year, "we need a new framework that allows us to build defences to counter the different threats of today's world. To do so, we must move beyond the constraints of the 30 year old ABM Treaty".[21]

18. *Executive Summary of the Report of the Commission to Assess the Ballistic Missile Threat to the United States*, 17 July 1998, http://www.fas.org/irp/threat/bm-threat.htm.

19. I. H. Daalder, J. M. Goldgeier, J.M. Lindsay, *op. cit.*, p.9.

20. In the law of treaties instead of the word 'spirit' of the treaty the term 'object and purpose of the treaty' is used. For example, treaties have to be interpreted in the light of their object and purpose, reservations which are contrary to the object and purpose of a treaty are not allowed etc. Article 60 of the Vienna Convention on the Law of Treaties provides that it is only a material breach of a bilateral treaty by one of the parties which entitles the other to invoke the breach as a ground for terminating the treaty or suspending its operation in whole or in part. A 'material breach' is defined as 'a repudiation of the treaty not sanctioned by the Convention, or the violation of a provision essential to the accomplishment of the object or purpose of the treaty' (Article 60(3)). When we speak of the fate of the ABM Treaty in radically changed circumstances, we do not mean so much some specific technical clauses in the Treaty which may be violated in case an NMD programme is developed but the very object and purpose of the Treaty.

21. *Remarks by the President to Students and Faculty at National Defence University*, May 1 2001, http://www.whitehouse.gov/news/releases/2001/05/20010501-10.html.

Sergei Rogov, the Director of the U.S.-Canada Institute of the Russian Academy of Sciences, recognises that "in one form or another, within various timelimits (depending on technical possibilities) Washington may start deploying its anti-missile defence"[22]and Russia need not become hysterical about it "jumping from one extreme to another, announcing of the Russia-U.S. strategic partnership one day, and the next day stating that a new cold war has started".[23]

It seems that Washington's Nato allies which have been hesitant about NMD ideas are, though reluctantly, starting to discuss practicalities of its possible deployment. Russia, the State that in legal terms is somewhere between a successor State to the former U.S.S.R. and its legal continuation, seems to have two basic options: either to continue to object to the deployment of an NMD, regarding it as a clear violation of the ABM Treaty and thereby pushing Washington towards the use of the withdrawal clause, or to start with the United States (and possibly with other interested States as well) the process of renegotiation of the Treaty. The latter option seems to be more in the interest of Russia, if only because it gives Russia some "influence over the character and evolution of U.S. NMD systems".[24]

III. "CHANGED CIRCUMSTANCES", "EXTRAORDINARY EVENTS" AND "SUPREME INTERESTS"

1. Fundamental change of circumstances

(a) The end of the Cold War, bipolar world and U.S.–U.S.S.R. strategic parity

The end of the Cold War, the collapse of one of the superpowers and consequent disappearance of the bipolar world with its military-strategic balance and mutually assured destruction (MAD) as a prevailing doctrine of deterrence, are the most significant changes which have taken place since the 1980s.

The legal and political reflection of the bipolar world was a set of bilateral U.S.-U.S.S.R. treaties and arrangements. The ABM Treaty was a bilateral treaty, which corresponded to that world's essential bipolarity, and it would not be an exaggeration to say that the Treaty reflected the international law of the bipolar international system as a drop of water reflects the whole ocean. The Treaty was considered to be the cornerstone of arms-reduction efforts of the two superpowers whose behaviour and

---

22. S. Rogov, "Words are Strong. What about Deeds?", *Nezavisimoe Voennoe Obozrenie* [The Independent Military Observer], 16 March 2001, p.6.

23. *Ibid.*, p.9.

24. See D. A. Wilkening, "Amending the ABM Treaty", *Survival*, 42, No. 1, Spring 2000, p.38.

relations *inter se* were the axis and determined the main features of Cold War international society.

The Canadian scholar and politician Edward McWhinney, who has written a lot on peaceful co-existence between the East and the West, has well described the character of international law and law-making in the bipolar Cold War world:

> The operational methodology and process of negotiation and international law-making during the Cold War in its post-Stalin, what-might-be-called "mature", period flowed logically and inevitably from its bipolar paradigm or model of world public order: direct, bilateral diplomacy between the two bloc leaders, preferably in summit meetings *a deux*, followed by model treaties reflecting the bloc leaders' bipolar consensus and then presented, after their own bilateral negotiation and drafting, to the lesser, supporting bloc members on either side for signature and ratification, and this normally without the possibility of serious modification or amendment on their part.[25]

Professor McWhinney's observation was meant to apply to international law generally. It was only natural that bilateral U.S.-U.S.S.R. arms-control treaties which, notwithstanding their bilateral character, affected the whole of mankind, were concluded by the superpowers without much, if any (at least in the case of the Soviet Union) consultation even with their respective allies. Not only the process of law making but also the content of law in international society reflected the main characteristics of the bipolar world.[26]

Certainly, the world has ceased to be bipolar with the two superpowers promoting hostile ideologies and vying for world supremacy. This is the most radical change which directly affects the *raison d'être* of the ABM Treaty. Therefore, it is not surprising that today some of such legal instruments are coming under considerable strain. We have seen that international law as a whole is undergoing a period of serious uncertainty (especially in such important areas as sovereignty of States; use of force for humanitarian purposes; sovereign immunities; internal conflicts etc.). International law of peaceful co-existence, as the set of legal principles governing East-West relations was often called,[27] which reflected the

25. E. McWhinney, *The United Nations and a New World Order for a New Millennium: Self-determination, State Succession, and Humanitarian Intervention* by, Kluwer Law International, 2000, p.6.

26. This does not mean that this influence was always direct and visible or that other States (or groups of States) did not exercise any influence. The law of the sea, international environmental law and human rights law may be examples of areas where many States have left their imprint.

27. See, e.g., G.I. Tunkin, *Coexistence and International Law*, RdC, vol. 95 (1958); E. McWhinney, *'Peaceful Coexistence' and Soviet-Western International Law*, Leyden, 1964; E. McWhinney, *The International Law of Détente*, Sijthoff & Noordhoff, 1978; G. Tunkin, *Theory of International Law*, Moscow, 1970, pp.16–56 (in Russian).

essential bipolarity of Cold War international society, is not any more an adequate legal framework for the new world.[28] It is clear that bilateral U.S.-Soviet (Russian) legal relations cannot, by definition, remain the same as they were at the height of the military-strategic competition which was the axis of world politics.

It is not surprising that there are conflicting views as to the polarity of today's international system. Whether the world still has a "unipolar moment",[29] whether it has already passed,[30] or whether we have entered a long, stable and relatively peaceful period of unipolarity[31] may be debatable but one thing seems to be obvious: the world is definitely not bipolar. Notwithstanding the decrease in U.S. military spending in the aftermath of the Cold War, Washington still spends (and can afford to spend) more than the next 10 strongest military powers (China, Japan, Great Britain, France, Germany, Italy, Spain, South Korea, India and Russia) taken together.[32] This factor shows that at least militarily the world is unipolar and will probably stay so at least for a while.

Ambassador Graham is right, in my opinion, in saying that "the U.S. simply does not have competitors in all parameters of power—military, economic, financial, cultural—and there is no one on the horizon. As a result, the ability of the U.S. to form a changing world order is as formidable as never before".[33] It is, probably, impossible to foresee what will be the structure (or polarity) of the international system in, let us say, 30 or 50 years, but for some time, it seems to be safe to predict, it will remain unipolar, at least in its military parameters, not only due to the current huge U.S. superiority but also because most of the militarily advanced States are U.S. allies.

However, the ABM Treaty had also a more concrete purpose: to reduce the risk of the race in strategic offensive arms between the Soviet Union and the United States. As we saw above, the Treaty was concluded as a part of SALT I. Later, other strategic arms limitation treaties (START I, START II) have had the same linkage with the ABM Treaty. It has been noted that:

28. By this I do not mean to say that States should not co-exist or co-operate peacefully. However, the specific Cold War era "struggle and co-operation of states of the two opposing social systems", to use Professor Grigory Tunkin's expression, which expressed the central idea of international law and politics of that period, seems to be over for good.
29. C. Krauthammer, 'The Unipolar Moment', *Foreign Affairs*, Vol. 70, No. 1, 1990/1991.
30. S. Huntington, 'The Lonely Superpower', *Foreign Affairs*, Vol. 78, No. 2, 1999.
31. W. Wohlforth, 'The Stability of a Unipolar World', *International Security*, Vol. 24, No. 1, 1999.
32. Rogov, *op. cit.*, p.3.
33. T. Graham, 'Questions from Washington: Does Russia Have Enough Confidence in Itself to Have a Constructive Dialogue with the US', *Nezavisimaya Gazeta* [The Independent Newspaper], 21 March 2001, pp.1–2.

during the Cold War, a political consensus in missile defence developed around two propositions. First, missile defences that could protect against a large-scale attack would destabilise the strategic balance and raise the risk of war because they undermined each side's confidence in its nuclear deterrent. Second, the deployment of large-scale defences would trigger an offensive arms race as each side sought to prevent the other from making itself invulnerable to attack.[34]

It seems that this purpose too has outlived its usefulness. Washington has no desire to increase its arsenal of strategic offensive weapons while Moscow could hardly afford to do that even if it had such a desire. The United States has decreased its military spending and is planning to reduce unilaterally its strategic ballistic missiles.[35] In his 1 May speech President Bush once again reiterated: "My goal is to move quickly to reduce nuclear forces".[36]

The Soviet-American arms race which was the most significant global factor of world politics for almost half a century has all but disappeared. Russia, though having still almost the same number of strategic weapons as the U.S., does not have the financial and other resources to maintain its strategic forces at the same level.[37]

Anatoli and Alexei Gromyko, for example, write that "by 1999, the United States" defence budget was no more than $270 billion. Russia's defence budget was 60 billion rubles—in purchase equivalence no more than $30 billion. The Pentagon spends about $20 billion annually on its nuclear forces; Russia can barely provide $3 billion".[38] This is an objective reality Russia can do very little about. Efforts to counterbalance the U.S. (or Western) dominance are not only futile, but they would also

34. I. H. Daalder, J.M. Goldgeier, J.M. Lindsay, "Deploying NMD: Not Whether, But How", *Survival*, Vol. 42, No. 1, Spring 2000, p.7.

35. S. Rogov admits that since the mid-1980s the military expenses of the US have decreased by about 40 per cent and that President Bush has plans for unilateral, or in parallel with Russia, limitation of the American strategic nuclear arsenal. Furthermore, George W. Bush has expressed doubts about the 'balance of nuclear terror' (Rogov, *op. cit*, pp.5–6).

36. *Remarks by the President to Students and Faculty at National Defence University, op. cit.*

37. See, e.g., P. Podvig, *Start and the ABM Treaty: Is a Compromise Possible*, Program on New Approaches to Russian Security Policy Memo Series, April 2000, http://www.fas.harvard.edu; C. Wallander, *Russian Policy and Potential for Agreement on Revising the ABM Treaty*, ibid.

38. A. and A. Gromyko, *Russia's Nuclear Imperative*, Global Dialogue, Vol. 1, No. 2, Autumn 1999, p.2.

undermine Russia economically and put it on the wrong side of the road.[39] Taking all this into account one has to agree with John Rhinelander that "the possibility of an action-reaction cycle between the U.S. and Russia involving increased numbers of offensive and defensive strategic weapons does not exist".[40]

Instead of the Cold War balance of terror, other threats, including regional arms races and a threat of proliferation of weapons of mass destruction (WMD) and ballistic missiles, have increased. Therefore, it is possible to conclude that the concept and practice of mutually assured destruction (MAD), of which the ABM Treaty was a part, and which, notwithstanding its immoral nature, served as a deterrence between the two approximately militarily equal superpowers, does not have the same *raison d'être* in today's world. In that respect, at least, the object and purpose of the ABM Treaty has ceased to be relevant in the post-Cold War world.

Keith Payne, asking what factors have led to dramatic changes in prospects for NMD,[41] writes: "first, the ballistic missile threat against which NMD now is expected to play is not remotely comparable to that of the Soviet Union. The Soviet Union mercifully is gone and the probability of a deliberate missile attack from Russia generally is considered to be very low".[42] Secondly, "defending against a small missile threat is well within U.S. technical and budget realities".[43]

This last scientific-technological factor is also rather important in analysing how far the circumstances related to the object and purpose of the ABM Treaty have changed. As we have seen above, one of the rationales of the treaty was that attempts to create an NMD which would be effective against thousands of strategic missiles of the other Cold War adversary would have been technically unfeasible and financially prohibitive. Futile attempts would only have instigated new rounds of the race in offensive weapons. New geopolitical and scientific realities have all but changed that rationale.

---

39. Sergei Karaganov, a prominent Russian political analyst, writes: 'The dilemma is this: If we are to play fourth or even fifth fiddle in the "First World", trying to secure a foothold on its sidelines, then we should move toward greater economic openness, a relatively liberal economy, and democratic society; rapprochement with the EU; integration into the information community; and maintenance of a good relationship with the United States ... This line is feasible but morally difficult. The alternative is to play on the discontent of countries that have fallen by the wayside, trying to knock together a broad, motley coalition which would inevitably be headed by China, Russia coming second, forced to support Beijing in its apparently intensifying rivalry with Washington, including the strategic sphere' (S. Karaganov, *Who Rules the World*, Moscow News, 7 Feb. 2001, p.2).

40. J. Rhinelander, *op. cit.*, p.14.
41. K. B. Payne, "The Case for a National Missile Defence" *Orbis*, Spring 2000.
42. *Ibid.*, p.6.
43. *Ibid.*, p.7.

Moreover, the object and purpose of the ABM Treaty was not to prohibit national missile defence in abstract, for all purposes, against all possible threats. Its purpose was to prohibit such defence against strategic missiles of the other Treaty Party, to secure strategic balance and bilateral nuclear deterrence.

Therefore, the creation of a limited or thin NMD system, though being contrary to several (depending on which version of the NMD the U.S. will choose) concrete clauses of the ABM Treaty, does not necessarily conflict with the object and purpose of the Treaty understood in the proper context. This means that proposed NMD projects may not violate even the outdated object and purpose of the ABM Treaty. As Vladimir Kryazhev, a retired Vice-Admiral of Russia, has recently observed, "the creation of NMD by the Americans has no effect on the ability of Russia to fulfil its purpose of nuclear deterrence even at much lower level (possibly even under 1000 warheads) of nuclear arsenal".[44]

We may conclude that such dramatic changes related to the *raison d'etre* of the ABM Treaty (the disappearance of the bipolar world, military-strategic parity, confrontation of two competing irreconcilable ideologies and the emergence of the technical feasibility of limited national missile defence) have taken place in the world since the Treaty was negotiated that its object and purpose do not any more correspond to the new realities. As Ambassador Graham has put it: "The treaty framework that has governed the American-Russian relations for the last thirty years has become outdated if even only because the strategic stability, due to the proliferation of weapons of mass destruction, is not any more a bilateral issue".[45]

(b) Washington and Moscow today

An arms race, like nuclear deterrence, is not something automatic and inevitable depending merely on some intrinsic nature of weapons. Great Britain and France, for instance, both have nuclear arsenals well below the U.S. level but they are not terribly worried about this strategic imbalance. The nature and intentions of actors matter no less than the nature and number of weapons. If Russia were a mature democracy it would not feel the need for counterbalancing militarily Western democracies through the promotion of the idea of a multipolar international system. Democracies have to join together to meet contemporary challenges such as terrorism, proliferation of weapons of mass destruction and ballistic missiles, drugs and other threats.

44. V. Kryazhev, 'It is possible to break the system of strategic stability', *Nezavissimoe Voennoe Obozrenie,* 2 March 2001.
45. T. Graham, "Questions from Washington", p.4.

Although not allies or friends, the U.S. and Russia do not see each other as enemies either. It is possible to agree with Condoleeza Rice when she referred to the ABM Treaty as a "relic of a profoundly adversarial relationship".[46]

Whether U.S.-Russian relations improve considerably or worsen depends much more on Moscow than on Washington. Washington's foreign policy aims, its alliances and patterns of behaviour, even when administrations in the White House change, are considerably more predictable than those of Russia. The United States has long been a stable, democratic and prosperous society. Its behaviour in international relations has not, of course, always been an example to be blindly followed, and its power may in itself be an irritating factor, especially for those whose relative power has recently drastically decreased. However, the world is lucky that the only remaining superpower is a liberal-democratic State allied with other mature stable democracies. It could have been much worse.

Russia's future, on the contrary, remains a great unknown. Whether Russia chooses a liberal-democratic political regime or slips further into authoritarianism (there are worrying signs in that respect), whether it chooses to ally with democratic States or tries to find its own unique future collaborating closely with "rogue" regimes and attempting to counterbalance "western dominance", are all open questions. If the Russian political and military elites prefer the second option, it would be disastrous for Russia, not at all good for Europe and somewhat irritating for the United States but it would not reverse the international system back to any kind of bipolarity or even multipolarity.

I believe Ambassador Graham has well indicated the main problem of Russia in international affairs, including the current debate on missile defence:

> First, understanding its weakness, Russia hopes to delay the consolidation of a new international system until it will have become more able to participate in the formation of such a system. ... The nuclear parity is the last attribute of Russia's status as a great power. Secondly, the Russian leadership continues to operate within the mental frame of geopolitics of the nineteenth century or that of the Cold War: "either we or they", insisting that Russia is an important geopolitical pole.[47]

There seems sometimes to be a serious misconception in the West about the nature of Russia and where it is going. Indicative in that respect is an article in *The International Herald Tribune* by Ivo Daalder and Fiona Hill from the Brookings Institute who write: "Russians today enjoy the basic

---

46. C. Rice, "Promoting the National Interest", *Foreign Affairs*, Vol. 79, No. 1, Jan/Feb, 2000, p.59.
47. T. Graham, *Questions from Washington*, p.4.

freedoms ... Russia is not the Soviet Union—at home or abroad. It has given up global pretensions. Weapons ... sales to Iran are sources of hard cash, not geostrategic moves to outflank Washington".[48]

This is a one-sided and even naïve view. Of course, Russia is not the Soviet Union but its current political and military leadership (there is a tendency towards militarisation of Russian politics if only because former generals are massively entering politics) have not given up great power ambitions. Equally, the restoration of closer links with the usual suspects—North Korea, Iran and Iraq—is prompted not only by cash considerations. During the March 2001 visit of the President of Iran to Moscow, an influential Russian political analyst commented:

> During the last year President Putin has tried to restore the international subjectivity of Russia, to restore its due place in world society, and to acquire more confidence and freedom of manoeuvre in foreign policy. It is necessary to admit that during the last decade in our relations with America we were in fact not even in the situation of Finland vis-à-vis the U.S.S.R. but rather like that of Poland, Bulgaria or Czechoslovakia whose relations with the Soviet Union were governed by "the Brezhnev doctrine". ... That is why the visit of the Iranian President and an attempt to get free, in Russian-Iranian relations, from U.S. supervision, is a serious test for Russian foreign policy. If we do not have sufficient power and influence Washington will force Russia and other non-western countries not to integrate into but to adapt to the new global order where U.S. dominance is unlimited.[49]

This view is not that of an isolated publicist. It reflects the dominant tendency in the mentality of the current Russian political elite.

Russia is today opposing any possible U.S. withdrawal from or even modification of the ABM Treaty, not because it would affect any concrete Russian strategic interests, but because having lost the empire (i.e. the Soviet Union) and not yet found its role in the world, Russia is constantly trying to box above its weight. As it has been observed, "the Kremlin's expression of fear and dismay concerning the U.S. NMD threat to international 'stability' is mostly rhetoric. ... Russian 'traditionalists', unable to leave the old War behind, continue to call for 'parity' in strategic arms, and demand new offensive capabilities to defeat any U.S. NMD".[50] During the debate between the Minister of Defence Marshal Sergeyev and the Chief of General Staff General Kvashnin on the issue of whether to direct limited financial resources to the maintenance and

48. I. Daalder, F. Hill, "Mr. Bush – the Cold War Has Finished", *The International Herald Tribune*, 24–25 March, 2001, p.10.
49. A. Migranyan, 'Foreign Policy of Russia: the Iranian Test', *Nezavisimaya Gazeta*, 15 March 2001, p.4.
50. K. Payne, Y. Skanikov, A. Shoumikhin, "A 'Grand Compromise' with Russia on National Missile Defence", *Defence News*, May 8, 2000, p.2.

524   *International and Comparative Law Quarterly*   [VOL. 50

development of strategic nuclear forces or to the reform of the Russian ground troops which are in a dismal state, the argument in favour of the strategic forces was usually that without such forces and without upgrading them Russia would completely lose its great power status.[51] As one of the chief negotiators of arms control agreements with the U.S., General Nikolai Chervov, has recently written, "the strategic rocket forces are the main means of defence of the country".[52] Hence, not at all considerations of the practical needs of Russia, including the needs of its military security, but an ambition to be if not one of the two poles then a least one of the few poles in a multipolar world. As the new national security concept of Russia puts it, "Russia opposes all attempts at a creation of the structure of international relations based on the dominance in international relations of developed Western countries led by the United States".[53]

However, there are politicians in Russia who seem to understand that it is not in the national interest of Russia to become involved in military-strategic competition with the U.S. and who understand that Russia may need defence from ballistic missiles no less than the United States. So Grigorii Yavlinsky, the leader of one of the liberal parties in the State Duma (the Lower House of Parliament), writes: "It is necessary to improve the 1972 Treaty. In the near future nuclear technology will be available to many countries, including those which are unpredictable. We have to think today how to guarantee our security in the future. Russia is not less interested in revising the ABM Treaty than the U.S.".[54] Yavlinsky rightly observes that in order to achieve these goals Russia has to co-operate with Europe and Nato and attempts to drive a wedge between the U.S. and Europe is a futile exercise.[55] However, this is exactly what some influential Russian politicians and military leaders are trying to do.

(c) Rebus sic stantibus *in international law*

How can international law respond to seismic geopolitical, military-strategic and ideological changes in the world? How can international law

---

51. See, e.g., *Nezavisimoe Voennoe Obozrenie*, 8 Dec. 2000, p.1. Sergei Karaganov wrote last year that for Russia, because of its current weakness, its nuclear arsenal is the main ground of its political weight and influence. In his opinion, Russia is still listened to in the world 60 per cent because of its nuclear potential, 15 per cent because of its territory and geography, 15 per cent because of its history and 3–4 per cent because of its economy (*Moscow News*, 15 Dec. 2000, http://www.Russian periodicals online).

52. N. Chervov, *Nuclear Vortex: What Was and What will Be*, Moscow, Olma-Press, 2000, pp.171–172 (in Russian).

53. See The Concept of National Security of the Russian Federation, Decree of the President of the Russian Federation, 10 Jan. 2000, No. 24.

54. G. Yavlinsky, 'Umbrella for Europe, Money for Russia, End for Bin Laden', *Argumenty I Facty*, 7 March 2001.

55. *Ibid.*

(and especially its core which in the days of the Cold War governed specific hostile-co-operative superpower relations) adjust to new circumstances?

International society lacks legislative authorities which could react in a timely and authoritative way to radical changes taking place from time to time in what is often, and not without reason, called anarchical society. This means that other, usually less precise and certain, legal mechanisms have to be used to accommodate change. Since customary international law often changes by means of violation of its norms, the Roman law maxim *ex injuria jus non oritur* (a violation of law does not create law) is less absolute in international law than in domestic legal systems. At the same time, another Roman law maxim *ex factis jus oritur* (facts tend to become law) has more relevance in international law than in domestic law. For example, many changes which occurred in the law of the sea (especially the emergence and development of the concept of exclusive economic zones—EEZ – and changes in the legal regime of continental shelves) came about notwithstanding the prior existence of contrary customary and treaty (the 1958 law of the sea conventions) provisions.

Treaties can be renegotiated, cancelled, denounced or they may even fall into desuetude. The principle *pacta sunt servanda* does not and cannot require that treaties remain immutable and in force forever. Moreover, international law contains a concept specifically meant to be a response to changing circumstances—the *rebus sic stantibus* clause. This doctrine is known under different names in many domestic legal systems. Eric Stein and Dominique Carreau wrote of stability and change related to international treaties:

> A basic community policy, reflected in the rule of *pacta sunt servanda* which underlies much of the law of treaties, serves to secure and to protect the shared expectations. The *rebus sic stantibus* doctrine, however, if it is given a broad formulation, unrelated to the expectations of the parties, expresses a different and often competing community policy in favour of peaceful change, that is, in favour of a termination of a treaty obligation that has become unduly burdensome for one of the parties.[56]

Article 62 of the Vienna Convention on the Law of Treaties (1969), which is basically codification of pre-existing customary law,[57] stipulates:

> fundamental change of circumstances which has occurred with regard to those existing at the time of the conclusion of a treaty, and which was not foreseen by the parties, may not be invoked as a ground for terminating or

---

56. E. Stein, D. Carreau, 'Law and Peaceful Change in a Subsystem: "Withdrawal" of France from the North Atlantic Treaty Organisation', *The American Journal of International Law*, 1968, Vol. 62, p.617.

57. See, for example, para. 335 of the *Restatement of the Foreign Relations Law of the United States*, The American Law Institute, 1986, Vol. 1, pp.218–222.

withdrawing from the treaty unless: (a) the existence of those circumstances constituted an essential basis of the consent of the parties to be bound by the treaty; and (b) the effect of the change is radically to transform the extent of obligations still to be performed under the treaty.[58]

As Athanassios Vamvoukos writes, "during the past sixty years or so there have been at least eighty recorded cases where documentary evidence allows for the conclusion either that States ... have invoked the doctrine of *rebus sic stantibus* or have referred to it as a binding rule of international law, or that they have, without mentioning the doctrine by name, advanced the argument of changed circumstances in that sense. In many of these cases, States have formulated a general theory of the doctrine, defining its nature and scope".[59]

In the context of possible termination of the ABM Treaty by the United States, it is interesting to note that Russia—the other Treaty partner—has quite often resorted to references to changed circumstances as a basis for treaty termination or modification. For example, in 1870, Russia used the *rebus sic stantibus* doctrine to terminate the 1856 Treaty of Paris which was concluded at the close of the Crimean War and which, *inter alia*, neutralised the Black Sea. In his famous circular addressed to the Powers party to the Treaty of Paris, Count Alexandre Gorchakov, the Chancellor (Foreign Minister) of the Russian Empire, referred to "the successive alterations which the transactions considered as the foundation of the European Balance of Power have undergone during late years", and which rendered it necessary "to inquire how far their results affect the political position of Russia".[60]

Count Gorchakov had waited for the right moment to start the process of annulment of burdensome clauses of the Treaty of Paris since the time the Treaty was signed in 1856. In his most famous circular note to the Russian embassies and missions abroad he had already alluded to the temporary nature of the clauses on the neutralisation of the Black Sea: "They say, Russia is angry. No, Russia is not angry, it is concentrating".[61] When Prussia had weakened the Austro-Hungarian Empire in the 1866 war, had supported Russia in "putting things in order" in Poland[62] and France was being defeated by Prussia, Gorchakov saw that circumstances which had existed in the aftermath of the Crimean War had changed

---

58. M. Evans (ed.), *International Law Documents* (2nd ed.), Blackstone, 1994, pp.170–171.

59. A. Vamvoukos, *Termination of Treaties in International Law: The Doctrines of Rebus Sic Stantibus and Desuetude*, Clarendon Press, 1985, pp.122–123.

60. Quoted by Vamvoukos, *Ibid.*, p.67.

61. A.V. Ignatieff, I.S. Rybachenok, G.A. Sanin (eds.) *Russian Diplomacy in Portraits* (in Russian), Moscow, International Publishing House, 1992, p.210.

62. R. Albrecht-Carrié, *A Diplomatic History of Europe since the Congress of Vienna*, Methuen & Co., 1958, pp.112–113.

sufficiently to raise the issue of annulment of burdensome clauses of the Treaty of Paris.[63] Therefore Russia, as Count Gorchakov stated, did "not consider itself any more bound by obligations of the Treaty of 18/30 March 1856 to the extent that they limited Russia's sovereignty in the Black Sea".[64]

It is, however, of interest to note that at the same time Gorchakov expressed readiness to negotiate with the Treaty partners in order "either to confirm general clauses, or to renew or substitute them with other equitable arrangements which would be considered appropriate in order to guarantee peace in the East and the European balance of power".[65] It is also important to emphasise that though other powers (especially Great Britain) protested against the unilateral decision of Russia to withdraw from the Treaty of Paris, the London Conference of 1871 nevertheless freed Russia from the Black Sea clauses of the Treaty, affirming at the same time in a special protocol (due to British insistence) that "the Powers recognise that it is an essential principle of the law of nations that none of them can liberate itself from the engagements of a treaty or modify stipulations thereof, unless with consent of the contracting parties by means of amicable understanding".[66]

Athanassios Vamvoukos observes that "this case is of importance because it has become a *locus classicus* on the doctrine of *rebus sic stantibus* and, as such, has frequently been invoked by states and writers alike".[67]

In 1924 the Soviet Government in its note to the British Government stated that it was ready to negotiate on the issue of replacement of old treaties, which had lost their legal force as a result of events taking place during the war and its aftermath: "The question whether previous treaties can be confirmed has to be considered 'from the point of view of the doctrine *rebus sic stantibus* for every state and for every treaty separately'".[68] In 1945 the U.S.S.R. denounced the Soviet-Japanese Treaty of Neutrality. The Soviet declaration emphasised that the Treaty was concluded before the German aggression against the Soviet Union and before the war between Japan, on the one hand, and Great Britain and the U.S., on the other. "Since then, the circumstances have fundamentally changed. Germany attacked the Soviet Union; Japan—an ally of Germany—assists the latter in its war against the U.S.S.R. Moreover,

63. *Russian Diplomacy in Portraits*, pp.218–219.
64. Quoted by W.E. Mosse, *The Rise and Fall of the Crimean System 1855–71. The Story of a Peace Settlement*, Macmillan & Co. Ltd, 1963, p.162.
65. *Correspondence Respecting the Treaty of March 30, 1856,* Parliamentary Papers, C. 245 (1871).
66. Mosse, *op. cit.*, p.191.
67. Vamvoukos, *op. cit.*, p.71.
68. *Documents on Foreign Policy of the USSR*, Vol. V, Moscow, 1961, p.236 (in Russian).

Japan is at war with the U.S. and Britain—both Soviet allies. In such a situation the Treaty of Neutrality has lost its meaning and it has become impossible to keep it in force".[69]

In 1970, commenting on Article 62 of the Vienna Convention on the Law of Treaties, Felix Kovalyov—the then deputy legal adviser to the Foreign Ministry of the U.S.S.R.—wrote: "In the light of facts quoted, it seems impossible to put in doubt the existence of a customary norm in accordance to which a fundamental change of circumstances existing when a treaty was concluded can serve as a basis for its termination".[70]

Of course, Russia is not the only State to have resorted to the *rebus sic stantibus* clause. Withdrawing France from the integrated command of Nato, General de Gaulle declared that "nothing can cause a law that is no longer in accord with custom to remain unamended. Nothing can cause a treaty to remain wholly valid once its purpose has altered. Nothing can cause an alliance to continue as it stands when conditions in which it was created have changed".[71] Stern and Carreau, criticising the procedure (unilateral) followed by France in its reference to the fundamental change of circumstances, comment on the substance of the case: "in the case of the French action, the end of the United States 'impermeability' to nuclear attack and the widely held perception of the change in the nature of the Soviet threat in Europe might arguably be considered as constituting a sufficiently "fundamental" and not 'foreseen' change of circumstances the existence of which was at the basis of the consent".[72]

The International Court of Justice in the *Gabčikovo-Nagymaros Project* case, disagreeing with Hungary that the change of circumstances advanced by the latter was of such a nature as to radically transform the extent of the obligations still to be performed, emphasised that "fundamental change of circumstances must have been unforeseen; the existence of the circumstances at the time of the Treaty's conclusion must have constituted an essential basis of the consent of the parties to be bound by the Treaty. The negative and conditional wording of Article 62 of the Vienna Convention on the Law of Treaties is a clear indication moreover that the stability of the treaty relations requires that the plea of fundamental change of circumstances be applied only in exceptional cases".[73]

Article 62 of the Vienna Convention indeed considers the *rebus sic stantibus* doctrine as an exceptional method of treaty termination.

69. *Foreign Policy of the Soviet Union during the Patriotic War*, Vol. III, Moscow, 1947, p.166 (in Russian).
70. F. Kovalyov, 'Fundamental Change of Circumstances (Doctrine and Practice)', *Soviet State and Law*, 1970, No. 3, p.70.
71. Quoted by Stern and Carreau, *ibid.*, p.577.
72. *Ibid.*, p.639.
73. *Gabčikovo-Nagymaros case*, Judgment, 25 Sept. 1997, para. 104.

Agreeing that this should be really an exceptional method, it seems, however, that the doctrine can be used more flexibly: i.e. not only as a method of terminating treaties but as initiating the process of their renegotiation or modification. The end of the Cold War has already shown the need to renegotiate several important arms-limitation treaties of the bipolar world. For example, the Conventional Forces in Europe (CFE) Treaty of 1990[74] and the Non-Proliferation Treaty (NPT) of 1968[75] both needed to be adjusted to changed political and military-strategic realities.

We can also draw some parallels with State succession which took place after the extraordinary events in the former U.S.S.R., Eastern and Central Europe.[76] Many treaties of predecessor States were succeeded by new States in a modified form (i.e. they were renegotiated between treaty partners) while some were not succeeded at all because of either the impossibility or undesirability of their implementation in new circumstances.[77]

It seems that the fate of the ABM Treaty can be also approached in a more flexible way. An all or nothing approach, i.e. sticking to the Treaty as to a sacred text in which no word can be changed, and equally the complete and unilateral withdrawal from it, are the least preferable ways of responding to changes in the world. The *rebus sic stantibus* doctrine could be used as a legitimate basis for initiating renegotiation or

74. On 19 Nov. 1999, the members of the CFE Treaty signed the Agreement on the Adaptation of the Conventional Forces in Europe (Agreement on Adaptation) in Istanbul. This Agreement removed the outdated bloc-to-bloc structure of the original Treaty. ... Under a special arrangement, Russia can deploy 2,140 armoured combat vehicles in its 'Flank Zones' in North West Russia and the North Caucasus (*The Military Balance 2000–2001*, The International Institute for Strategic Studies, Oxford University Press, 2000, pp.35–36).

75. After the dissolution of the U.S.S.R. on its territory there emerged four (instead of one) independent States which had nuclear weapons on their territory. In accordance with State succession principles, used in the case of dissolution of the USSR, Ukraine, Kazakhstan and Belarus could have become nuclear powers. This, however, would have been contrary to the very object and purpose of the Non-Proliferation Treaty (to limit the number of nuclear States). A Protocol was signed by five States (the US, Russia, Kazakhstan, Ukraine and Belarus) whereby only Russia became a party to the NPT as a nuclear power while Belarus, Kazakhstan and Ukraine joined as non-nuclear States (see Leich Nash, 'Contemporary Practice of the United States Relating to International Law: Arms Control and Disarmament', 86 A.J.I.L. 799–801 (1992).

76. Although State succession and *rebus sic stantibus* are different international law concepts, there is considerable similarity and even overlap between them. Dissolution or unification of States often fundamentally change circumstances under which treaties were concluded by predecessor States. Implementation of treaties of predecessor States may either become impossible or too burdensome. Even Russia which considered itself to be the State-continuation of the former U.S.S.R. (and not simply one of the successor States) chose to renegotiate some treaty obligations (and rights) because circumstances which had existed when treaties had been concluded had fundamentally changed in many respects.

77. R. Müllerson, 'The Continuity and Succession of States', 42 I.C.L.Q. 1993; B. Stern, *La succession d'Etat, RdC,* 1996, tome 261, Martinus Nijhoff Publishers, 2000.

modification of a treaty whose object and purpose (spirit) or important concrete clauses (letter) do not correspond any more to the needs of changed realities. The Russian denunciation of the Treaty of Paris, the French withdrawal from the military structure of Nato, and some other cases show that unilateral initiatives may serve as first steps which lead to negotiated arrangements of relations between the parties.

It may seem that in the presence of an expressly provided possibility of denunciation, references to the *clausula rebus sic stantibus* are superfluous. However, the latter has a different content and context of application. Express provisions providing for the possibility of the denunciation of a treaty do not exclude the use of another concept available for treaty termination—that of changed circumstances (*rebus sic stantibus*).[78]

The U.S. would hardly resort to the *rebus sic stantibus* clause to withdraw from the ABM Treaty. Nor would it be preferable to use Article XV (2) unilaterally for that purpose. Negotiated and agreed upon arrangements are to be preferred to unilateral acts even when law expressly provides for the possibility of the use of the latter. However, Washington could use the *rebus sic stantibus* arguments in combination with references to Article XV (2) in order to convince Russia as its Treaty partner, as well as other interested States, of the legitimacy of its cause.

If we compare political, military-strategic and even ideological changes in the world since the ABM Treaty was concluded with changes referred to by States when resorting to *rebus sic stantibus* arguments, current changes are of such a magnitude and character that if *rebus sic stantibus* can ever be justifiably used this may be one of such cases. Importantly, these changes concern circumstances which were vital for the conclusion of the Treaty and served as a basis for the consent of the Parties to be bound by the Treaty. There is no doubt that today the United States and

---

78. The European Court of Justice in June 1998 considered the *A. Racke GmbH Co.* v. *Hauptzollampt Mianz* case which involved the 1980 Cooperation Agreement between the EEC and the Socialist Federal Republic of Yugoslavia which was concluded for an unlimited period and provided that the Agreement could be denounced only upon six months' notification. However, the EEC Council suspended the trade concessions provided under the Agreement with immediate effect because of *the changed circumstances*. The ECJ, agreeing with the Commission, reasoned that 'the rules of customary international law concerning the termination and the suspension of treaty relations by reason of fundamental change of circumstances are binding upon the Community institutions and form a part of the Community legal order'. And the Court concluded that the Council's assessment that 'the pursuit of hostilities and their consequences on economic and trade relations constitute a radical change' was not manifestly erroneous. (93 A.J.I.L. 206 (1999). It is of interest to note that in this case the EEC Council used the *rebus sic stantibus* clause to suspend a treaty which contained a denunciation clause and the ECJ found that the Council had acted in accordance with customary international law. The ECJ also found that as customary international law does not contain procedural requirements provided for in Article 65 of the Vienna Convention, and since the EEC is not bound by the Convention, the non-observance of these requirements did not prejudice the Community's action.

Russia would not even contemplate the conclusion of such a treaty. In the face of threats coming from the proliferation of weapons of mass destruction and their delivery systems, it is not "manifestly erroneous" (using the words of the ECJ) to conclude that the effect of these changes does radically transform obligations still to be performed under the Treaty. The Treaty, which cannot support the non-existing strategic balance, would, in changed circumstances, obligate the United States (as well as Russia) to give up a realistic opportunity to protect itself and its allies from probable missile blackmail.

Whether the U.S. will or will not start building its national (or global) ballistic missile defence (this will obviously depend on technical, financial and political factors), legal arguments seem to support political and military-strategic initiatives of Washington on the creation of a missile defence system. Such a conclusion gains additional support when we analyse the meaning and implications of the concept of "extraordinary events" and "supreme interests" in Article XV (2) of the ABM Treaty.

2. "Extraordinary events" and "supreme interests"

Article XV(2) of the ABM Treaty, like many other arms-control agreements, explicitly provides that:

> Each Party shall, in exercising its national sovereignty, have the right to withdraw from this Treaty if it decides that *extraordinary events related to the subject matter of this Treaty have jeopardised its supreme interests* (emphasis added). It shall give notice of its decision to the other Party six months prior to withdrawal from the Treaty. Such notice shall include a statement of the extraordinary events the notifying Party regards as having jeopardised its supreme interests.

The reference to a statement of extraordinary events means that, though it is up to the Party which is taking the decision to denounce the Treaty to assess those extraordinary events in the light of its supreme interests, the withdrawing Party has the obligation *vis-à-vis* its Treaty partner to justify in good faith the necessity of withdrawal from the Treaty.

In the case of the use of the concept of *rebus sic stantibus*, considered above, these were fundamental but rather broad circumstances, a change of which may serve as a basis for initiating the process of withdrawal from the Treaty or its modification. The recourse to Article XV (2) of the Treaty, on the contrary, requires the presence of much more concrete threats which put the supreme interests of a Party in jeopardy, though such threats may obviously be part of changed circumstances. As in the case of recourse to the concept of *rebus sic stantibus*, these threats must be of the kind that did not exist when the treaty was concluded and they must have been unforeseen at the time of the conclusion of the treaty.

The United States is referring to missile threats from "rogue" regimes (for the time being, North Korea, Iraq and Iran) in justification of its plans for the creation of national ballistic missile defence which would require withdrawal from the Treaty or its modification. Does this justification sound plausible for a hypothetical impartial third-party body?[79]

It is true that ballistic missiles, potentially with strategic characteristics, have been acquired by quite a few States (for example, India, Pakistan, North Korea, Iran, and Iraq) and the proliferation of missile technology has for years been one of the major security concerns of the world community.[80] There is little doubt that a missile threat to the United States, or to other States for that matter, is not an abstract possibility. Especially deadly is the combination of ballistic missiles and warheads equipped with weapons of mass destruction (WMD) in the hands of unstable authoritarian regimes which are eager to have both.[81]

Keith Payne has put his finger on one of the main reasons why some States crave ballistic missiles and weapons of mass destruction: "One self-expressed reason some regional powers have for seeking long-range missiles and WMD is to deter the United States from intervening against whatever aggressive designs they have in their region. Their logic is simple and possibly accurate: if, by virtue of acquiring long-range missiles and WMD, a regional power can threaten U.S. urban areas, American leaders (who are well-known to be highly sensitive to civilian casualties) are highly unlikely to risk military intervention against that regional power.... The potential for such coercive "asymmetric responses" to U.S. conventional force projection has highlighted the potential value of NMD in the post-Cold War period".[82] Tomorrow, relatively small and weak "rogue" regimes can exercise deterrence against powerful developed states, blackmailing and dictating their conditions to the latter. Such blackmail which may not work against authoritarian regimes can be

79. Existing superpower arms-control agreements do not provide, and in principle could not provide, for any impartial third-party dispute settlement. Therefore, my reference to such a body is just hypothetical. It has been correctly observed that 'international courts and international arbitration have not had, and almost assuredly will not have, any direct role in interpreting arms control obligations of the United States'. (J. B. Rhinelander & S. Wasserman Goodman, "The Legal Environment", in *Defending Deterrence*, p.64). The same can be said of the Soviet Union (Russia).

80. In 1987 the Missile Technology Control Regime (MTCR) was initiated to 'limit the risk of nuclear proliferation by controlling transfers that could make a contribution to nuclear weapons delivery systems other than manned aircraft'. See, e.g., C. Petersen, 'Moscow, Washington and the Missile Technology Control Regime', *Contemporary Security Policy*, vol. 45, 1995; A. Pikayev, L. Spector, E. Kirichenko, R. Gibson, *Russia, the US and the Missile Technology Control Regime, Adelphi Paper 317,* International Institute for Strategic Studies, Oxford University Press, 1998.

81. R. Müllerson, 'Missiles with Non-Conventional Warheads and International Law', *Israel Yearbook on Human Rights,* Vol. 27, 1997, pp.225–250.

82. K. Payne, *op. cit.,* p.14.

effective against liberal-democratic States. As a Russian specialist has put it: "for the United States even one nuclear warhead hitting its territory is unacceptable damage".[83]

One could debate how effective nuclear deterrence was in the form of mutually assured destruction or as a counterforce (i.e. aimed at adversary's strategic offensive forces)[84] in the bipolar world, whether it was morally acceptable or not. However, it seems unreasonable indeed to demand that a State which is able to protect itself (and its allies) against missiles with nuclear warheads (or warheads with other weapons of mass destruction) should not even try to do that. As some experts have emphasised, "the argument that the United States should leave itself defenceless against attacks from Iran or North Korea out of deference to a treaty written in another era simply will not sell".[85] The bipolar world's nuclear deterrence, though morally repugnant and legally dubious (its MAD version, and possibly the counterforce one as well, was based on the acceptance and inevitability of massive violation of basic principles of international humanitarian law in the case of failed deterrence) had at least some practical logic as the best among options which were all bad. Today, instead of the certainty of mutual and general destruction of the bipolar world (certainty as to destruction in the case of failed deterrence and consequently near certainty that both actors would do their utmost to keep deterrence alive) we have the uncertainty of a less suicidal but more volatile world.

Borrowing Anthony Giddens' terminology,[86] we may say that the Cold War nuclear deterrence, of which the ABM Treaty was the cornerstone, was a low-probability high-intensity risk (or threat). The failure of nuclear deterrence between the U.S. and the U.S.S.R. would have had disastrous consequences not only for the Cold War adversaries but for the world as a whole. However, as this risk stemmed from and was a part of the relationship between two rational actors, there was relatively low probability that it would be realised in practice.[87] In a sense, the risk may have been comparable to the possibility of the Earth colliding with a big asteroid. In today's world of proliferation of nuclear weapons, other weapons of mass destruction and missile technology, we face different threats. Their potential consequences for the world, taken individually,

83. V.A. Popov, 'The Range of Parity', *Nezavisimoe Voennoe Obozrenie*, 12 Jan. 2001, p.3.

84. See *Nuclear Deterrence and Moral Restraint* (ed. By H. Shue), Cambridge University Press, 1989.

85. Daalder, Goldgeier, Lindsay, *op. cit.*, p.18.

86. A. Giddens, *Beyond Left and Right: The Future of Radical Politics*, Polity Press, 1996, pp.78–79.

87. However, at least once – during the 1962 Cuban missile crisis – the possible failure of nuclear deterrence was close. See more in A. Fursenko, T. Naftali, *One Hell of a Gamble: Khrushchev, Castro and Kennedy 1958–1964*, W.W. Norton & Co., 1997.

534   *International and Comparative Law Quarterly*   [VOL. 50

may not be so high but at the same time the probability of their realisation in practice is much higher. Hence, we face risks (threats) not of such high consequence as those created by the Cold War nuclear deterrence but of much higher probability.

Deterrence alone, without feasible parallel measures of defence, against multiple threats (especially when the intentions of potential agents of threats are not familiar or are difficult to assess) is a high-probability high-consequence risk that is hardly rational to live with. Keith Payne writes that "the successful exercise of deterrence requires a variety of contextual conditions that generally pertained to U.S.-Soviet relations during much of the Cold War, but are far from ubiquitous. These include well-informed decision-makers, rationality and a degree of mutual familiarity, effective channels of communication, leaders who are sensitive to cost and risk, etc. . . . Defence Department, White House, and Congressional reports acknowledge that the deterrence of regional challengers may not follow Cold War patterns. Given the rogues' relatively unfamiliar goals and values, the success of deterrence will not be predictable in general and may simply fail".[88]

Together with political measures, arms control and disarmament efforts, anti-missile shields may be one of the responses to these new high probability threats. Moreover, as Philip Gordon has shown, deterrence and defence are not mutually exclusive[89] and obviously military deterrence in various forms would remain a factor of world politics.

However, do these new threats justify the use of Article XV (2) of the ABM Treaty? I believe that, taking into account fundamental changes in circumstances which have taken place in the world since 1972 and in view of concrete new threats to the national security of the United States, it is possible to conclude that Washington has a strong case for initiating the process of ABM Treaty revision.

In this process Washington has the duty to negotiate with Russia in good faith the steps it is going to undertake to meet threats from third States' ballistic missiles (of course, only to an extent that these steps contradict some of the provisions of the ABM Treaty). Moscow, in turn,

---

88. K. Payne, *op. cit.*, pp.12–13.
89. P. Gordon, *op. cit.*, pp.32–33. However, I tend to disagree with Philip Gordon that a modified ABM Treaty should ensure 'mutual assured destruction and preventing an armed race'. Preventing an armed race – yes, but it is necessary to avoid slipping back to the situation when the whole world was held hostage to the military balance between the two superpowers, especially since today there are no longer two superpowers. While deterrence has always played a role in international politics, 'mutual assured destruction', as its specific form, had its rationale not simply in the presence of massive nuclear arsenals but also in the competition of two hostile ideologies. It is not only the character and number of weapons that ensure 'mutually assured destruction' but also the hostile relationship between the parties of the equation. Why should the US and Russia remain assured that they can destroy each other and by doing so bring down the whole world?

has the duty to negotiate in good faith with and accommodate Washington's reasonable concerns. If the United States in good faith carries out this obligation and Russia does not fulfil its part of the duty, Washington has the right to unilaterally withdraw from the Treaty. In the absence of a third party dispute-settlement it is especially important that both Parties act in good faith. In this respect, it is encouraging that in its first reaction to President Bush's speech on missile defence the Russian leadership and mass media chose a non-confrontational approach singling out in Bush's speech references to the readiness to consult with friends and allies and the statement that Washington does not consider today's Russia as its enemy. As Foreign Minister Igor Ivanov responded: "Russia is ready for such consultations".[90] *Nezavisimaya Gazeta* even wrote that "readiness to consult shows the strength of the Bush's foreign policy team—the team of well chosen professionals".[91] The Russian Defence Ministry newspaper *Krasnaya Zvezda* (Red Star) emphasises in Bush's speech the idea of further reduction of the U.S. nuclear arsenal and points out that Igor Ivanov had also spoken of the readiness of Russia to cut its strategic nuclear forces down to 1,500 warheads.[92]

However, this is not the end of the story. Though only Russia and the United States are parties to the ABM Treaty, there are other States whose interests may be closely affected by the denunciation of the Treaty.

IV. THE ABM TREATY AND THIRD STATES

Although the 1972 *raison d'être* of the ABM Treaty as an element of strategic balance between Washington and Moscow has ceased to exist, there are other States which have become more Treaty-dependent than the parties to the Treaty. President Nixon himself, let us recall, declared in 1972 that the conclusion of the SALT agreements "benefits not only the United States and the Soviet Union, but all the nations of the world".[93] Getting rid of a bilateral treaty which benefits all the nations of the world should affect, by definition, other nations as well. It is interesting to note that Russia, though a Party to the Treaty, may not have the strongest interest in the existence of the prohibition to build a national missile defence.

If and when the U.S. decides to start the deployment of an NMD system and withdraw from the AMB Treaty (whether unilaterally or having agreed with Russia to modify it) this would raise problems first of all for Washington's allies. Washington will need some components of the

---

90. Nezavisimaya Gazeta, 4 May 2001, p.2.
91. *Ibid.*, p.4.
92. *Krasnaya Zvezda*, 4 May 2001, p.2.
93. SALT Agreements. Communication from the President of the United States, Washington, 13 June, 1972 (file:///A/SALT Agreements.htm)

system located on the territory of other Nato members (Fylingdales in the UK and Thule in Greenland). Moreover, such a decision, if made without consulting U.S. Nato allies, could lead to the "decoupling" of the security interests of Nato Member States. As Philip Gordon writes, "most essential is for all allies—and in particular for the Americans—to realise that it is highly desirable, if not imperative, that Americans and Europeans act in concert"[94] since "deploying without allied agreement could diminish the political legitimacy of the programme, deny the United States valuable resources (in particular forward-based radar sites), make it harder to persuade Russia and China to accept the inevitability of NMD, and perhaps most importantly, leave Europe (with its many U.S. citizens and military bases) vulnerable to missile threat and blackmail".[95]

It is not only political legitimacy that suffers. International law is not only a set of technical rules or "letters" of various unrelated treaties. It is a normative system and as such it can be undermined by acts which for a black-letter lawyer may not violate any specific rules of international law. For example, the "decoupling" of allies' security by creating a missile defence for the American territory only may undermine the very object and purpose of the mutual legal obligations of Nato Member States under the North Atlantic Treaty signed in Washington Treaty in 1949.[96] The unilateral withdrawal of the U.S. from the ABM Treaty without seeking arrangements with Russia may undermine other arms-control agreements etc.

Unilateral acts are prone to affect the legal interests of various States because politically, economically and otherwise, the world is becoming more and more interdependent, and legal principles and norms reflecting, though imperfectly, this interdependence form a relatively coherent normative system. For example, bilateral treaties or multilateral treaties with a limited number of participants governing the regimes of international straits or canals[97] or other waterways have created regimes which cannot be abrogated by States which are party to such treaties.

There are other third States beyond U.S. Nato allies which may be affected by the abrogation of the ABM Treaty. China, whose ballistic missiles are, at least numerically, far inferior to those of Russia, may find that the limited or thin national missile defence that the United States plans to build will bring to naught any deterrence which Chinese strategic missiles may have *vis-à-vis* Washington today. If a thin national missile defence will not serve as an umbrella against 3500 (or even 1500) Russian

94. P. Gordon, *op. cit.*, p.30.
95. *Ibid.*, p.18.
96. 34 UNTS 243.
97. See R. Jennings, A. Watts *Oppenheim's International Law*, Vol. I, parts 2 to 4, pp.591–599, 633–643.

strategic missiles,[98] 20 or so Chinese ICBM[99] could completely lose their ability to threaten U.S. territory. This would mean that the abrogation or even modification of the ABM Treaty, to the extent that it would allow a thin national missile defence of the U.S., would affect China much more than Russia. And this is not the end of the story. If China were to increase its strategic arsenal as a response to a U.S. NMD programme, India might feel threatened; a possible Indian strategic build-up could probably affect Pakistan, and so on.[100]

As a result we may have a curious situation in which some third States may be more interested in the existence of a treaty than treaty-parties. Understanding the wider implications of NMD issues and the ABM Treaty, Washington has started to speak of global or allied missile defence instead of national missile defence.[101] Colin Powell and Condoleeza Rice have emphasised that it is necessary to convince the world that anti-missile defence will support, not undermine, deterrence and that Washington is ready for discussions at all levels with the Russians to find ways of developing new relations.[102] President Bush underlined the same idea in his 1 May speech: "We are not presenting our friends and allies with unilateral decisions already made. We look forward to hearing their views, the views of our friends, and take them into account ... We'll also need to reach out to other interested States, including China and Russia. Russia and the United States should work together to develop a new foundation for world peace and security in the 21st century".[103]

Although treaties are not concluded for the sake of third parties, and they do not give rights to or impose obligations on third States (*pacta tertiis nec nocent nec prosunt*), the denunciation of a treaty which has either benefited third States for years or which has contributed to the creation of a security context on which third States may have started to rely, without genuinely addressing the concerns of those States would be contrary to the spirit of international law.

Sir Robert Jennings and Sir Arthur Watts write of possible obligations which may arise for third States from treaties:

---

98. See, Gromyko & Gromyko, *op. cit.*, p.4.

99. *National Intelligence Council. Foreign Missile Developments and the Ballistic Missile Threat to the United States Through 2015*, September 1999, http://www.cia.gov/cia/publications/nie/nie99msl.html, p.9.

100. Nicholas Barry writes: "China's warnings that it would increase its strategic missile capability would put pressure on India to do the same in order to maintain its minimum deterrence. India realises that to do so would also induce Pakistan to bolster its missile and nuclear programmes in conjunction with Islamabad's traditional military relationship with China" (N. Barry, "U.S. National Missile Defence: Views from Asia", *http:/www. cdi/*, p.6).

101. *http://ww.cdi.org/weekly/2001/issue10.html*.

102. Rogov, *op. cit.*, p.8.

103. *Remarks by the President to Students and Faculty at National Defence University*, *op. cit.*

> The rule that treaties cannot validly impose obligations upon dissenting third states follows clearly from the sovereignty of states and from the resulting fact that there is no international legislative process by which rules of law are imposed upon a dissenting minority of states. However, as international society becomes a more integrated community, a departure from the accepted principle becomes unavoidable, in particular in the sphere of preservation of international peace and security.[104]

As an obvious example, one may refer to Article 2(6) of the UN Charter which provides that the UN "shall ensure that states which are not Members of the United Nations act in accordance with these Principles [principles of the UN Charter] so far as may be necessary for the maintenance of international peace and security". Or let us take some environmental treaties. A single State which is not bound by a specific treaty may, by continuing to pollute contrary to treaty provisions, nullify the efforts of hundreds of treaty parties. For instance, the U.S., with its four per cent of the global population producing nearly a quarter of the world's "greenhouse gas" emissions[105] can bring to naught the efforts of all other States to control global warming.

It seems that in today's world, where the security of one State is increasingly dependent on the security of other States, even bilateral security treaties may create a situation which affects third party security interests to such an extent that the States party to such treaties should neither conclude such treaties nor terminate them without addressing the security concerns of interested third parties. This does not mean that the latter can prevent the States party to a bilateral treaty from terminating it but the treaty parties should address interests which are acquired by third States due to the existence of the treaty.

Such an interpretation of treaty effects on third States would have been out of place in an international society where bilateral legal and political relations prevailed. As Bruno Simma has observed, "traditional international law has been essentially 'bilaterally minded'".[106] However, the more unified the world becomes, the greater the impact of bilateral treaties (especially on issues of peace and security between superpowers) on third States and on international society as a whole. As a consequence, the stronger also become the legitimate interests of other States in the fate of such bilateral treaties. The Parties of the ABM Treaty (and first of

---

104. *Oppenheim's International Law*, ninth ed., Vol. I, parts 2–4, Longman, 1992, p.1262.
105. *The Independent*, 19 March 2001, p.14.
106. B. Simma, *From Bilateralism to Community Interest*, Recuille des Cours de l'Academie de Droit International, 1994, Vol. VI, Martinus Nijhoff Publishers, p.230.

all the U.S.) have at least a political obligation[107] to address the justified concerns of these States. Neither unilateralism, nor even bilateralism, is an acceptable method of decision-making on issues that affect all the nations in the world.

CONCLUSIONS

We may conclude that the circumstances which existed in 1972, when the ABM Treaty was concluded and which served as the *conditio sine qua non* of its conclusion, have changed to such an extent that is possible for the parties to initiate the process of modification or even termination of the Treaty using Article XV (2) of the Treaty, relying, *inter alia*, on the concept of *rebus sic stantibus*. However, in this process it is necessary to take account of legitimate concerns and security interests, not only of the United States and Russia as the Parties to the Treaty, but also of those other States whose security context may have become dependent on the ABM Treaty.

---

107. There are many political (i.e. legally non-binding) obligations in the world which are observed by States not less strictly than legally binding treaties. For example, OSCE obligations and the Nato-Russian Founding Act of 1997 are of such nature (See R. Müllerson, *Nato Enlargement and the Nato-Russian Founding Act: The Interplay of Law and Politics*, I.C.L.Q., 1998, Vol. 47, No. 1). Although such political obligations usually stem from written documents for States which have signed them, there seems to be no reason why political obligations cannot arise from acts of behaviour (like, e.g., customary international law) which other States have started to rely upon.

Part V
The UN Security Council
and Nonproliferation Law

[18]

Developments of the Law of Arms Control as a Result of the Iraq-Kuwait Conflict

Dieter Fleck*

Abstract

Security Council measures against Iraq were hardly indicative of new developments in the law of arms control and disarmament. However, Iraqi threats to use chemical weapons have encouraged consensus among participating states to conclude the 1993 Chemical Weapons Convention and revelations of the advanced nature of Iraq's nuclear programmes might have contributed to the May 1995 decision of states parties to the 1972 Non-Proliferation Treaty to extend the treaty indefinitely. The system of ongoing monitoring and verification introduced under Security Council Resolutions 687 (1991) and 1284 (1999), as well as the practical experience gained through monitoring nuclear, chemical and biological weapons and ballistic missiles have supported efforts to strengthen international verification activities. As a further result of the conflict, increased awareness of the dangers of exporting dual-purpose technologies has led to a review of guidelines and practices for inspections under IAEA safeguards agreements. The problem of enforced verification, however, remains unresolved. This underlines that there is no viable alternative to resolute action by the Security Council. It likewise supports the conclusion that the need for political solutions in post-conflict peace-building, involving and stimulating the participation and cooperation of the state concerned, is even more obvious today than it was a decade ago.

1 Introduction

Arms control initiatives in response to the Iraq-Kuwait conflict were supplementary to a variety of other activities to restore international peace and security, including economic and military sanctions, humanitarian actions and the settlement of claims. These initiatives must all be seen in context with the invasion by Iraq of Kuwait in August 1990, Iraq's declaration of its 'comprehensive, eternal and inseparable

* Director, International Agreements and Policy, Federal Ministry of Defence, Germany; Rapporteur, Committee on Arms Control and Disarmament Law, International Law Association. All opinions expressed in this article are personal.

106   *EJIL* 13 (2002), 105–119

merger' with Kuwait on 7 August 1990,[1] the detention in Iraq and Kuwait of nearly 13,000 third-state nationals (mostly Americans and Europeans, a large number of whom were subsequently placed at strategic sites as 'human shields' against the threat of foreign military attacks),[2] and countless refugees from Iraq and Kuwait (most of them going to or via Jordan).[3]

While arms control decisions normally are a result of negotiations providing for a balance of national interests by the contracting parties, important decisions had to be imposed in the Iraqi case by the Security Council acting under Chapter VII of the Charter. Only a few of these decisions concerned new restrictions for Iraq's armament, while the great majority of them dealt with the implementation and verification of existing obligations under the 1925 Geneva Protocol,[4] the 1972 Biological Weapons Convention[5] and the 1968 Non-Proliferation Treaty (NPT).[6] Indeed, a new quality of verification was established and to a considerable extent also implemented under Chapter VII.

This study will firstly examine the influence played by the Iraq-Kuwait conflict on Iraq's treaty obligations in the field of arms control (Section 1). Section 2 will analyse the problems and opportunities for enforced disarmament as developed during the conflict, and Section 3 will consider certain effects that public awareness of and reactions to the Iraq-Kuwait conflict had on the development of the law of arms control. Finally, the concluding Section 4 will discuss the future success of verification, depending on both the resolved action by the Security Council and the participation and cooperation of Iraq.

2 Iraq's Arms Control Obligations as Derived from Existing Treaties and Measures in Accordance with Chapter VII of the UN Charter

The extent to which international response to the Iraq-Kuwait conflict led to measures supplementing existing treaty obligations can be detected in Security Council Resolution 687 (1991). Section C of this resolution, adopted on 3 April 1991 after a month of negotiations following the successful liberation of Kuwait, summarized Iraq's existing treaty obligations and provided detailed arms control decisions in the field of weapons of mass destruction and certain ballistic missiles.

A Chemical Weapons

Iraq, a party to the 1925 Geneva Protocol, had issued a statement in September 1988 reiterating its attachment and adherence to the provisions of that Protocol. Iraq had

---

[1]   *The United Nations and the Iraq-Kuwait Conflict 1990–1996*, The United Nations Blue Book Series, vol. IX (1996), at 16.

[2]   *Ibid*, at 17.

[3]   *Ibid*, at 19.

[4]   Protocol for the Prohibition of the Use of Asphyxiating, Poisonous or Other Gases, and of Bacteriological Methods of Warfare of 17 June 1925.

[5]   Convention on the Prohibition of the Development, Production and Stockpiling of Bacteriological (Biological) and Toxin Weapons and on Their Destruction of 10 April 1972.

[6]   Treaty on the Non-Proliferation of Nuclear Weapons of 1 July 1968.

also participated in the Conference of States Parties to the 1925 Geneva Protocol and Other Interested States held in Paris on 7–11 January 1989 and had signed the Declaration of the participating states establishing the objective of completely eliminating chemical and biological weapons.[7]

In Resolution 687, the Security Council referred to statements by Iraq threatening to use weapons in violation of its obligations under the Geneva Protocol, and noted its prior use of chemical weapons (preamble, paragraph 8), invited Iraq to reaffirm unconditionally its obligations under the Geneva Protocol (section C7) and decided that Iraq shall accept the destruction, removal or rendering harmless, under international supervision, of all chemical weapons and all stocks of agents and all related subsystems and components and all research, development, support and manufacturing facilities related thereto (section C8a). Chemical weapons had been used previously during the Iran-Iraq war (1980–1988).[8] An investigation team set up in 1984 by the Secretary-General of the United Nations found evidence that these weapons had been produced and used by Iraq.[9]

The decision taken in Resolution 687 went beyond the obligations laid down in the Geneva Protocol in that it confirmed the prohibition of the use of chemical and bacteriological weapons without any qualification and it addressed the problem of existing stockpiles; this latter is not dealt with by the Geneva Protocol.

Several states, including Iraq, had made reservations to the Geneva Protocol, declaring that they shall be bound by its provisions only towards those states which have both signed and ratified it or have acceded thereto. Iraq had expressly stated that it shall not be bound by the Protocol towards any enemy state whose armed forces, or the forces of whose allies, do not respect the provisions of the Protocol.[10] While Resolution 687 might be viewed as an interesting precedent for the Security Council — removing a state's reservations to certain treaty obligations under international humanitarian law and imposing a disarmament obligation in an area where to date only the use of a particular means of warfare has been prohibited — the decision taken under Resolution 687 was less far-reaching than might be assumed. Iraq's reservation to the Geneva Protocol was not even referred to by the Security Council and the use of the word 'unconditionally' in section C7 did not necessarily invalidate it. There was no reason for the Security Council to broach the issue of reciprocity in this context as there was no threat of first use of chemical weapons against Iraq.

As far as the destruction, removal or rendering harmless of chemical weapons is concerned, the Declaration issued at the 1989 Paris conference provided a clear indication, albeit not yet legally binding at the time, of a broad international commitment to the universal elimination of these weapons.

Iraqi threats to use chemical weapons certainly encouraged consensus by

---

[7] Final Declaration of the Paris Conference of States Parties to the 1925 Geneva Protocol and Other Interested States, 11 January 1989 (CD/880, 49; G. Fahl, *International Law of Arms Control*, vol. 1, E/0.4).

[8] Kalshoven, 'Prohibitions or Restrictions on the Use of Methods and Means of Warfare', in I. F. Dekker and H. H. G. Post (eds), *The Gulf War of 1980–1988* (1992) 97, at 112–113.

[9] <http://www.opcw.org/guide.htm>.

[10] <http://www.projects.sipri.se/cbw/docs/cbw-hist-geneva-res.html>.

108   *EJIL* 13 (2002), 105–119

participating states in the then ongoing negotiations which two years later resulted in the Chemical Weapons Convention.[11] The possibility, however, of the Security Council ensuring Iraq's acceptance of this Convention by employing measures under Chapter VII was never pursued. In the Iraqi case, verification under the UNSCOM regime was obviously given exclusive preference to the cooperative and reciprocal system set up under the 1993 Convention. To date Iraq has not signed or acceded to the Convention. Consideration of means to ensure compliance under the Convention[12] are consequently not yet applicable to Iraq.

B *Biological Weapons*

As Iraq had signed, but not yet ratified the 1972 Biological Weapons Convention, the Security Council decision in Resolution 687 (section C7) provided for development in this regard by inviting Iraq to *ratify* the Convention.

This step was taken by Iraq shortly afterwards on 19 June 1991. Too much significance, however, should not be attached to this action on the part of Iraq since it only confirmed the commitment it had already made with its signature to the Convention, no control mechanisms were foreseen under the Biological Weapons Convention, and biological weapons, unlike chemical weapons, did not really present an imminent threat in the region.

C *Nuclear Weapons Programme*

Iraq had been a party to the NPT since 1969, without reservations. At the 1989 Paris Conference, Iraq took a position which was unanimously shared by all Arab countries, namely that all weapons of mass destruction, including nuclear weapons, must be eliminated from the Middle East region.

In Resolution 687, the Security Council, referring to the objective of establishing a nuclear weapons free zone in the region of the Middle East (preamble, paragraph 16), invited Iraq to reaffirm unconditionally its obligations under the NPT (section C11) and decided that Iraq shall unconditionally agree not to acquire or develop nuclear weapons or nuclear-weapon usable material or any subsystems or components or any research, development, support or manufacturing facilities related to the above (section C12). The Security Council thus clarified that Iraq's obligations under the NPT are not limited by any reservations or conditions.

No additional arms control obligation was imposed by the Security Council on Iraq in this field. The Iraq-Kuwait crisis had prompted the Security Council, however, in the preamble of Resolution 687 to recall the objective of the establishment of a nuclear-weapon-free zone in the region of the Middle East. Moreover, and much more importantly, revelations of the advanced nature of Iraq's nuclear programmes may have later contributed to the May 1995 decision on the part of states parties to the NPT to extend the Treaty indefinitely.

---

[11] Convention on the Prohibition of the Development, Production, Stockpiling and Use of Chemical Weapons and on their Destruction of 13 January 1993.

[12] Rosas, 'Reactions to Non-compliance with the Chemical Weapons Convention', in M. Bothe, N. Ronzitti and A. Rosas, *The New Chemical Weapons Convention — Implementation and Prospects* (1998) 415.

D *Ballistic Missiles*

Resolution 687 touched upon new ground in the field of missile restrictions. Iraq had developed extensive missiles and rocket technology, which were used from the beginning of the Iraq-Kuwait crisis to embroil Israel.[13] Several hundred long-range missiles had been used by Iraq earlier during the war with Iran. During the coalition action, which started on 16 January 1991, Iraq launched dozens of surface-to-surface missiles against Saudi Arabia, Israel, and also against Bahrain and Qatar.

In Resolution 687, the Security Council decided that Iraq shall unconditionally accept the destruction, removal, or rendering harmless, under international supervision, of all ballistic missiles with a range greater than 150 km, as well as related major parts and repair and production facilities (section C8b). This decision was indeed a drastic and unprecedented limitation of existing armaments, which was not based on existing treaty law, with the exception of the authority of the Council to take decisions under Article 39 of the UN Charter to maintain or restore international peace and security.

This comparison of the measures taken by the Security Council under Chapter VII with Iraq's existing treaty obligations demonstrates that only very few additional limitations were introduced by the Council in the field of weapons of mass destruction. The limitations on chemical weapons were in line with Iraq's declared commitments made earlier at the 1989 Paris conference, at a time when the 1993 Chemical Weapons Convention was still to be negotiated. No serious attempt was made in later years to invite Iraq to participate in this new convention. As far as the prohibition of biological weapons is concerned, Iraq's signed commitment to the 1972 Convention was strengthened by its subsequent ratification, though this decision provided no imminent threat to Iraq. The prohibition of nuclear weapons for Iraq was underlined, but Iraq was already subject to this same legal situation under the NPT. Only in the case of ballistic missiles were new obligations created by the Security Council, as no treaty obligations previously existed in this field.

Quite differently, however, new obligations were established to ensure notification of existing armaments, to provide for extensive verification activities and to create a strong linkage between arms control and post-conflict peace-building in the region under Security Council Resolutions 687 (1991) and 1284 (1999).

3 Special Decisions and Arrangements and their Implementation

The decisions taken by the Security Council to ensure full implementation of Iraq's obligations in the field of arms control were very far-reaching. They not only defined

[13] Navias, 'The Scud Missile War: A Focus On Iraqi Declaratory Policy', in G. Neuneck and O. Ischebeck (eds), *Missile Proliferation, Missile Defense, and Arms Control, Proceedings of a Symposium Held in Hamburg* (1993) 229.

110   *EJIL* 13 (2002), 105–119

general obligations for Iraq to declare and support the destruction of prohibited weapons, but they also provided organizational mechanisms and working procedures in order to achieve that aim. These decisions need to be assessed before examining the overall results achieved and open issues that are yet to be solved.

A *Declaration and Destruction of Weapons, Demilitarized Zone*

In Resolution 687 (1991), the Security Council decided

> that Iraq shall unconditionally accept the destruction, removal, or rendering harmless, under international supervision, of:
>
> (a) All chemical and biological weapons and all stocks of agents and all related subsystems and components and all research, development, support and manufacturing facilities related thereto;
>
> (b) All ballistic missiles with a range greater than one hundred and fifty kilometres, and related major parts and repair and production facilities (section C8).

Iraq was requested to submit to the Secretary-General, within 15 days, a declaration on the locations, amounts and types of all these items and to agree to urgent, on-site inspection (section C9a). The Security Council also introduced prohibitions against the sale or supply of arms and related matériel to Iraq (section F24) and further asked the Secretary-General to develop a plan for future ongoing monitoring and verification (OMV) of Iraq's compliance with the ban on these weapons and missiles (section C13).

A demilitarized zone (DMZ) was established under section B5 of Resolution 687 (1991), extending 10 km into Iraq and 5 km into Kuwait, to be monitored and controlled by the United Nations Iraq-Kuwait Observation Mission (UNIKOM), in accordance with Resolution 689 (9 April 1991) and the report of the Secretary-General of 5 and 9 April 1991.[14]

Some of the coalition countries created 'no-fly' or 'exclusion' zones in Iraq:[15] the northern zone, covering territory above the 36th parallel, was created in June 1991 to shield the Kurdish population; the southern zone was established in August 1992 and extended the flight ban to territory below the 32nd parallel for the protection of Shiites and to create a buffer zone to ensure the security of Saudi Arabia and Kuwait. The latter was announced by President George Bush and referred to Security Council Resolution 688 (1991) which condemned 'the repression of the Iraqi civilian population in many parts of Iraq, including most recently the Kurdish-populated areas, the consequences of which threaten international peace and security in the region'.[16]

To enforce the no-fly regime, US and UK forces repeatedly attacked various targets in response to Iraqi hostile acts. In none of these cases was there an express and

---

[14] Report of the Secretary-General proposing terms of reference for an observer unit to be known as the United Nations Iraq-Kuwait Observation Mission (UNIKOM), S/22454 (5 April 1991) and addenda S/22454/Add. 1 (5 April 1991), S/22454/Add. 2 (5 April 1991), S/22454/Add. 3 (9 April 1991).

[15] *Supra* note 1, at 41.

[16] US Department of State Dispatch, vol. 3, no. 35, 31 August 1992.

specific authorization by a Security Council decision. In one of these incidents a British government spokesman referred to 'material breaches of Resolution 687', which gave 'other parties to the conflict the right in international law to take necessary and proportionate measures' and to 'action taken to ensure the safety of coalition aircraft patrolling the no-fly-zone in support of UN Security Council Resolution 688'.[17] Evaluation of the legality of the establishment of both of these no-fly zones remains critical.[18] On 14 April 1994 two US F-15 fighters mistakenly shot down two UN helicopters in the northern no-fly-zone.[19] France had terminated its participation in surveillance missions in the northern zone by 1 January 1997,[20] while the US tightened controls there in October 1997.[21]

B *Mechanisms for Implementation*

Unlike the military sanctions as such, which had been carried out by a coalition of the willing in conformity with Resolution 661 (1990), implementation of the arms control decisions under Resolution 687 (1991) was reserved to the Security Council and its subordinate organs.

The Special Commission (UNSCOM) was established by the Security Council under section C9b of Resolution 687 (1991) to carry out immediate on-site inspection of Iraq's biological, chemical and missile capabilities, to take possession for the destruction, removal or rendering harmless of all chemical and biological weapons and related components and all research, development, support and manufacturing facilities, to supervise the destruction by Iraq of all its ballistic missiles with a range greater than 150 km, and to assist and cooperate with the International Atomic Energy Agency (IAEA) in the elimination of Iraq's nuclear-weapon capabilities and in the subsequent monitoring of non-proscribed nuclear activities. The work of UNSCOM was planned and managed from its Headquarters in New York and field offices were established in Bahrain and Baghdad (since 1994, Baghdad Monitoring and Verification Center (BMVC)).[22] Cooperation between UNSCOM and the IAEA, as requested by Resolution 687 (sections C12 and 13), was essential to ensure the assessment of potential dangers related to the export of dual-purpose technologies.

---

[17] Parliamentary Debates (Hansard), Sixth Series, Session 1992–93, 13 January 1993, 21 January 1993, 25 January 1993 (Commons); 26 January 1993 (Lords). Cf. also 'United Kingdom Materials on International Law 1992', 63 *BYbIL* (1992) 824.

[18] Stein, 'No-Fly-Zones', 27 *Israel Yearbook on Human Rights* (1997) 193, at 209–211.

[19] *Archiv der Gegenwart*, 29 May 1994, 3900 4 A.

[20] *Frankfurter Allgemeine Zeitung*, 28 December 1996.

[21] *Financial Times*, 10 October 1997.

[22] R. Butler, *The Greatest Threat: Iraq, Weapons of Mass Destruction, and the Crisis of Global Security* (2000); see the Review Essay by Malone, 'Iraq: No Easy Response to "The Greatest Threat"', 95 *AJIL* (2001) 235; Duelfer, 'Arms Reduction: The Role of International Organizations, The UNSCOM Experience', 5 *Journal of Conflict and Security Law* (2000) 105; 'The Lessons and Legacy of UNSCOM: An Interview with Ambassador Richard Butler', *Arms Control Today*, June 1999, at 3–9.

112   *EJIL* 13 (2002), 105–119

C *Working Procedures*

Under the Guidelines to Facilitate Full International Implementation of section E24, 25 and 27 of Security Council Resolution 687 (1991),[23] research, development, support and manufacturing facilities for nuclear, chemical and biological weapons or weapon-usable material, repair and production facilities for ballistic missiles, related technology and related personnel or materials for training or technical support were also made subject to monitoring. The Security Council Committee, established under Resolution 661 (1990), was requested to report at 90-day intervals on the implementation of the arms and related sanctions against Iraq. States and international organizations were encouraged to cooperate in the implementation of the arms and related sanctions against Iraq. All states were requested to report to the Secretary-General within 45 days on the measures they had instituted to meet the obligations set out in Resolution 687 (para. 24). Detailed work plans were submitted by the Director General of the IAEA[24] and the Secretary-General.[25] They were approved by the Security Council with Resolution 715 (1991) of 11 October 1991, which also authorized UNSCOM, in the exercise of its responsibilities as a subsidiary organ of the Security Council, to continue to take responsibility for designating additional locations for inspections and overflights and to coordinate activities under the work plans in cooperation with the IAEA. A mechanism for export/import monitoring called for in Resolution 715 (para. 7) was proposed by the Chairman of the Committee established under Resolution 661 and approved by the Security Council with Resolution 1051 (1996) of 27 March 1996.

The methods of verification applied by UNSCOM and the IAEA should be seen in context with established principles and rules of verification as developed in various arms control activities. Verification comprises three elements: the establishment of facts, their legal assessment, and the reaction called forth by the determination of any violation.[26] Verification measures include national technical means, national intelligence means, data exchange, notification, on-site inspections, as well as aerial and satellite inspections. As they may vary under different regimes, cooperative, adversarial and coercive methods and techniques may be applied, as exemplified by

---

[23] Annex to the Report of the Secretary-General of 2 June 1991 (S/22660); approved by SC Res. 700 of 17 June 1991.

[24] Revised plan submitted by the Director General of the IAEA for future monitoring and verification of Iraq's compliance with the requirements of Security Council Resolution 687 (1991) for the destruction or removal of specified weapons and with the requirements of Resolution 701 (1991) for full disclosure, access to inspection sites and compliance with international obligations (S/22872/Rev.1, 20 September 1991).

[25] Report of the Secretary-General transmitting the plan, revised pursuant to the adoption of Security Council Resolution 707 (1991), for future monitoring and verification of Iraq's compliance with the destruction or removal of weapons specified in Security Council Resolution 687 (1991), S/22871/Rev. 1, 2 October 1991.

[26] S. Sur, *A Legal Approach to Verification in Disarmament and Arms Limitation* (1988); S. Sur (ed.), *Verification of Current Disarmament and Arms Limitation Agreements: Ways, Means and Practices* (1991); *Verification in All its Aspects, Including the Role of the United Nations in the Field of Verification*. Report of the Secretary-General, UN-Doc A/50377 and Corr. 1.

the CFE Treaty,[27] the Chemical Weapons Convention and the Iraq inspections, respectively.[28] In the Iraqi case, the broad scope of control and its declared aim of ensuring full, final and complete disarmament (FFCD) of all prohibited weapons have led to a new quality of control, which constituted a considerable challenge. Ongoing monitoring and verification (OMV) involves regular inspections of dual-purpose capabilities, maintenance of accurate inventories of all dual-purpose items and close tracking of their real uses.[29] For this purpose, aerial surveillance, remote ground-based sensors, a variety of detection technologies, and export/import controls by other states are all required as necessary components of effective monitoring. To meet this objective, even coercive measures have to rely on a minimum of cooperation with the country involved. It is for this reason that the importance of cooperative verification measures for effective control and confidence-building has been stressed.[30] The Iraqi case has exemplified this need.

D *Open Problems and International Response*

Iraq's refusal, and subsequent acceptance, of its obligations and obstruction of their implementation are documented elsewhere[31] and will be discussed in depth in another context. Iraq clearly voiced its reservations with regard to relevant activities and was reluctant to accept ongoing monitoring and verification measures in accordance with Security Council decisions. Iraq's willingness to support international verification activities has always been connected with the question whether sanctions could be eased or lifted in accordance with section F21 of Resolution 687.

On 5 August 1998 Iraq ended its cooperation, except for monitoring inspections at designated sites. The Security Council condemned this decision by Resolution 1194 of 9 September 1998 and again suspended the sanctions reviews. In late October of the same year, Iraq announced a complete halt of work with UNSCOM and the IAEA. The Council responded by adopting Resolution 1205 on 5 November 1998, condemning Iraq and demanding that it rescind this decision. Military action by the United States was planned, but on 14 November Iraq stated that it would cooperate fully with UNSCOM and the IAEA. The Council indicated that it would conduct a comprehensive review once the Secretary-General confirmed, on the basis of reports from UNSCOM and the IAEA, that Iraq had returned to full cooperation.[32]

Following a report by UNSCOM, which described Iraq's cooperation as inadequate and stated that 'the Commission is not able to conduct the substantive disarmament work mandated to it by the Security Council and, thus, to give the Council the

---

[27] Treaty on Conventional Armed Forces in Europe (CFE) of 19 November 1990, amended on 19 November 1999.

[28] *National and International Verification Measures*, Fifth Report of the ILA Committee on Arms Control and Disarmament Law (Report of the London Conference 2000), at 222–247.

[29] *Supra* note 1, at 79.

[30] 69th ILA Conference, Resolution No. 4/2000, *Arms Control and Disarmament Law*, (Report of the London Conference 2000), at 26.

[31] *Supra* note 1, at 79–94. For developments since 1996, see Butler, Duelfer and Malone, *supra* note 22.

[32] Duelfer, *supra* note 22, at 117.

114 *EJIL* 13 (2002), 105–119

assurance it requires with respect to Iraq's prohibited weapons programmes',[33] the United States and the United Kingdom executed *Operation Desert Fox*, launching military strikes with cruise missile attacks against selected targets in Iraq from 16 to 19 December 1998. American and British planes flew more than 650 strike and strike support sorties. US ships launched more than 325 Tomahawk cruise missiles and Air Force B-52 bombers dropped more than 90 cruise missiles, bombs and missiles. During the four nights of operations 100 Iraqi military targets were struck. These strikes were ordered in response to Iraq's continued failure to comply with Security Council resolutions as well as their interference with UNSCOM inspectors. As Secretary of Defense William S. Cohen stated on 19 December 1998, clear military goals were pursued with this operation: 'We've degraded Saddam Hussein's ability to wage war against his neighbors. Our forces attacked about 100 targets over four nights, following a plan that was developed and had been developed and refined over the past year. We concentrated on military targets and we worked very hard to keep civilian casualties as low as possible. Our goal was to weaken Iraq's military power, not to hurt Iraq's people.'[34]

Secretary of State Madeleine Albright explained the shorter, medium and longer term goals of this campaign: The short-term goals were 'to degrade Saddam Hussein's ability to develop and deploy his weapons of mass destruction, to degrade his command and control of some of his security areas in order to degrade his ability to threaten his neighbors'. A medium-term goal was to have him comply with the Security Council resolutions as a prerequisite for the lifting of sanctions. She then added: 'Longer term, we have come to the determination that the Iraqi people would benefit if they had a government that really represented them. So we know that this is something that cannot be done overnight, and we are working with the various opposition groups on a longer range way of trying to help them help themselves to have a regime that represents them.'[35]

While quite significant results were achieved in respect of the short-term goals,[36] none of the mid- or longer-term aspirations voiced by Secretary Albright have yet been fulfilled. Inspectors from both UNSCOM and the IAEA departed from Iraq on 16 December 1998. As a consequence, Iraq has refused to allow UN inspectors onto its territory as required under Security Council Resolution 687. OMV plans are not operational to date.

In the context of increasing concern regarding the interruption of UN activities in Iraq among Security Council members, a panel under the chairmanship of Ambassador Celso L. N. Amorim of Brazil was constituted, pursuant to a note issued

---

[33] Letter from the Secretary-General transmitting reports of both IAEA and UNSCOM to the Security Council on the Iraqi cooperation from 17 November 1998 to 15 December 1998 (S/1998/1172, 15 December 1998).

[34] DoD News Briefing, 19 December 1998, <http://www.defenselink.mil/news>.

[35] <http://secretary.state.gov/www/statements/1998/981217.html>.

[36] General Anthony C. Zinni, commander of the U.S. Central Command had explained on 8 January 1999 that 'the mission against Iraq's military infrastructure in December was so effective that the time estimate for repair has now been increased from one to two years', <http://www.defenselink.mil/news>.

by the President of the Security Council on 30 January 1999.[37] The panel's task was to assess all existing and relevant information available, including data from ongoing monitoring and verification, relating to the state of disarmament in Iraq. The report produced by this panel[38] developed detailed proposals for further action in relation to remaining questions concerning Iraq's clandestine nuclear weapons programme, Iraq's development and procurement efforts for proscribed missile programmes, discrepancies with remaining stocks of Iraq's chemical weapons, and critical gaps to be filled in in order to obtain a reasonably complete picture of Iraq's biological weapons programme. While accepting that some uncertainty is inevitable in any country-wide verification process, a pragmatic approach was recommended in view of the fact that the extent to which such uncertainty is acceptable is a policy judgement. The report advocated in favour of a reinforced OMV system, stressing the fact, however, that to be effective, any verification system must be deployed on the ground, which could only occur with Iraq's acceptance.

Notwithstanding the severe problems encountered by both UNSCOM and the IAEA in their verification activities, their general achievements should not be diminished. UNSCOM and the IAEA have evaluated extensive information from both international and national sources. The UNSCOM experience has heightened awareness of the dangers of exporting dual-purpose technologies. This has led to a review of existing guidelines and practices for inspections under safeguard agreements with signatories of the NPT.[39] In addition, the Iraq experience has provided useful information regarding ballistic missiles, which could also be used in support of the multilateral Missile Technology Control Regime (MTCR), in which nations possessing certain technologies place various limits on their export.[40]

UNSCOM was officially terminated when the Security Council passed Resolution 1284 (1999), which established, again as a subsidiary body, the United Nations Monitoring, Verification and Inspection Commission (UNMOVIC). This Commission's tasks are to establish and operate a reinforced system of ongoing monitoring and verification to implement the plan approved in Resolution 715 (1991) and to address unresolved disarmament issues. An organizational plan for UNMOVIC was developed[41] and approved by the Security Council.[42]

There is a general understanding that the reinforced OMV envisaged with UNMOVIC must include an integrated system that will also be capable of addressing the outstanding disarmament issues. It cannot be conceived as an enticement for Iraq to invite UNMOVIC into its territory, but rather, if anything, the reinforced OMV must be more intrusive than the one practised to date. Iraq has not yet accepted Resolution

---

[37]　S/1999/100.

[38]　Amorim Report, S/1999/356 of 27 March 1999.

[39]　*Supra* note 1, at 112.

[40]　*Ibid*, at 112.

[41]　S/2000/292 (6 April 2000).

[42]　S/2000/311 (13 April 2000).

116   *EJIL* 13 (2002), 105–119

1284. In spite of ongoing UN efforts[43] to establish a follow-on inspection regime comprising UNMOVIC and the IAEA's Iraq Action Team, no UN inspections have thus far taken place.

4 Assessment of Ongoing Developments

A sound assessment of the ongoing developments in the control of Iraq's armament should of course begin with the question of what is distinctly new in this case and whether comparisons may be drawn with similar challenges the international community has faced in the past.

In the short history of the United Nations no comparable case may be found in which the Security Council acted with similar decisiveness on an issue of international security. Under its predecessor, the League of Nations, only the armed attack against Abyssinia in 1935 had led to the application of sanctions. These remained weak, however, due to their limitation to economic and financial measures short of an oil embargo and short of using military force. The inadequate success of the international community to ensure security for Abyssinia led to the League's decline, followed by its complete inactivity in response to similar armed attacks against China in 1937, against Finland in 1939 and against Poland at the outbreak of World War Two.

As has been suggested elsewhere,[44] and is elaborated by David Bederman in this issue, more relevant parallels might be seen in the measures against Germany instituted at the end of the First World War. But in this case, too, there are strong dissimilarities to the Iraq-Kuwait conflict. The origins of the First World War were much more complex and debatable than those of Iraq's attack against Kuwait, and the outcomes of the two wars also resulted in very different situations. German political leadership underwent a total change after the revolution of 1918 and a democracy was developing under the Weimar Republic; no such change occurred in Iraq after 1991. The limitation of arms and armaments under Part V of the Versailles Treaty of 1919[45] were intended, as declared in its Preamble, as a first step 'in order to render possible the initiation of a general limitation of the armaments of all nations'.[46] No single type of the large quantities of German arms and ammunition, tanks, ships and aircraft rendered under the Versailles Treaty had been prohibited previously under existing law, and it was at least the German understanding that general disarmament

---

[43]   Fifth quarterly report of the Executive Chairman of the United Nations Monitoring, Verification and Inspection Commission under paragraph 12 of Security Council Resolution 1284 (1999), covering the period from 1 March to 31 May 2001 (S/2001/515 of 24 May 2001).

[44]   Duelfer, *supra* note 22, at 109, n.6.

[45]   Treaty between the Principal Allied and Associated Powers of the one part and Germany of the other part, done at Versailles on 28 June 1919, RGBl 1919, 687–1389 [918–961].

[46]   This policy was based on the IVth and XIVth of President Wilson's Fourteen Points: 'IV. Adequate guarantees given and taken that national armaments will be reduced to the lowest point consistent with domestic safety... XIV. A general association of nations must be formed under specific covenants for the purpose of affording mutual guarantees of political independence and territorial integrity to great and small states alike.' It was reflected in Art. 8 of the Covenant of the League of Nations and pursued with little success until its failure at the Conference on Disarmament (1932–1934).

within an appropriate time-frame was an important condition for German disarmament measures.[47] This expectation, however, was not fulfilled. On 16 March 1935, Germany declared Part V as being terminated due to the failed implementation of allied commitments for disarmament, and the last unilateral measures for German disarmament were abolished on 6 March 1936.[48] It is thus only in a very limited sense that similarities may be seen between Germany in 1919 and Iraq in 1991: neither country was occupied and international control in both cases remained limited. International cooperation and support, however, which was severely lacking for the new German government after World War I, was offered to Iraq, albeit in vain, under the Security Council regime.

The Iraq-Kuwait conflict was unique in that no other comparable situation has ever occurred which has met such unanimous, extensive and sustained response from the Security Council. At the same time, this situation has frequently provided a severe challenge for Member States, not only in providing consensus in the Security Council but also in deciding on a national basis on appropriate action in those cases where such consensus could not be established. While some such decisions clearly ensured implementation of Security Council resolutions involving a large group of states acting in solidarity and great coherence, as in the case of *Operation Desert Storm* and Resolution 661 (1990), there remain open questions and even doubts in certain cases where military operations did not enjoy such wide international support.

The continuing situation in the two no-fly zones and the December 1998 *Operation Desert Fox* have already been mentioned above. Similar military operations followed in February 2001, when US and British fighters were screened by Iraqi radars during control flights in the southern zone and, in response, they attacked Iraqi anti-aircraft systems. The Iraqi government, in turn, announced missile attacks against Israel and Saudi Arabia. The results of these operations were assessed by the Pentagon as being mediocre at best, due to the fact that far fewer that half of the targeted radars were damaged.[49] It should also be considered that the success of military operations cannot be judged by military results alone. Political effects, and in particular the consequences for ongoing monitoring and verification in Iraq, remain part of the equation.

Existing verification gaps, which continue to grow under the present situation of Iraq's refusal to permit UN inspections since December 1998, will inevitably lead to further escalation and impose new threats. The automated video monitoring system, installed by the UN at known and suspected facilities for weapons of mass destruction in Iraq, is no longer in operation. Having lost this on-the-ground access, it has become more difficult for the UN or individual Member States to accurately assess the current state of Iraq's weapon programmes. According to the most recent report to Congress of the US Central Intelligence Agency, the risk of diversion of existing equipment for weapons of mass destruction purposes has increased since December 1998, due to

---

[47]   F. Berber, *Lehrbuch des Völkerrechts, III. Band, Streiterledigung, Kriegsverhütung, Integration*, 2. Aufl. 1977, at 128–129.

[48]   *Ibid.*

[49]   *Stars and Stripes*, 23 February 2001, at 7.

118   *EJIL* 13 (2002), 105–119

Iraq's reconstruction efforts on those facilities destroyed by US bombing attacks, including several critical missile production complexes and former dual-use facilities for chemical production. Iraq may still have hidden chemical weapons. The full scope and nature of its biological weapons programme has not been verified. Iraq has continued working on its L-29 unmanned aerial vehicle (UAV) programme, which is believed to have been developed for the delivery of chemical or, more likely, biological warfare agents. Iraq has also probably continued low-level theoretical research and development associated with its nuclear programme, although the still existing lack of a sufficient source of fissile material remains Iraq's most significant obstacle to being able to produce a nuclear weapon.[50]

In comparison with these present and future security risks, some remaining controversial issues from previous military operations may appear less urgent. The latter nevertheless require further careful consideration in view of their potentially long-lasting consequences. The so-called 'Gulf War Syndrome' on soldiers, a previously uncharacterized complex of signs and symptoms which may be related to common wartime experiences rather than to a unique event during the gulf war,[51] has not yet been fully explored. The potential effects of chemical and biological agents, combined with psychological stress situations for soldiers in the field, cannot be neglected as they also influence the legal assessment and bear certain risks of potentially long-term importance. Unsuccessful efforts to provide complete information in these areas could gain political weight and influence public opinion, as is also the case with discussions on the effects of the use of depleted uranium ammunition.

5 Conclusions

The restrictions imposed on Iraq in the field of weapons of mass destruction and ballistic missiles were hardly indicative of new developments in the law of arms control and disarmament. No important obligations have been created by the Security Council that could serve as pace-making examples for the creation of further treaty obligations in this field, although Iraqi threats to use chemical weapons provided support for consensus among participating states in order to conclude the 1993 Chemical Weapons Convention and revelations of the advanced nature of Iraq's nuclear programmes might have contributed to the May 1995 decision by states parties to the NPT to extend the treaty indefinitely.

Nevertheless, the strict determination of the Security Council to introduce a system of ongoing monitoring and verification under Resolutions 687 (1991) and 1284 (1999) and its continuing efforts to make this system fully operational in Iraq might

---

[50]   Unclassified Report to Congress on the Acquisition of Technology Relating to Weapons of Mass Destruction and Advanced Conventional Munitions, 1 January through 30 June 2000, <http://www.cia.gov/cia/publications/bian/bian_fcb_2001.htm>.

[51]   Hyams, Wignall and Roswell, 'War Syndromes and Their Evaluation: From the U.S. Civil War to the Persian Gulf War', *Annals of Internal Medicine*, (1996), 125, at 398–405.

hopefully influence legal responses by the international community to similar situations that may occur in the future. UNSCOM and UNMOVIC, together with the IAEA, have been involved in the most comprehensive international monitoring system ever established in the sphere of arms control. The practical experience gained with regard to nuclear, chemical and biological weapons and ballistic missiles has assisted efforts to strengthen international activities in these areas, most notably with respect to verification. Also as a result of the conflict, awareness of the dangers of exporting dual-purpose technologies has led to a review of guidelines and practices for inspections under IAEA safeguards agreements with signatories of the NPT.

The problem of enforced verification, still unresolved despite the adoption of Resolution 1284 (1999), remains highly critical. This situation keenly underlines the fact that there is no viable alternative to resolute action by the Security Council. It likewise supports the conclusion that the need for political solutions in post-conflict peace-building, involving and stimulating the participation and cooperation of the state concerned, is even more obvious today than it was a decade ago.

[19]

Nuclear non-proliferation and the UN Security Council in a multipolar world

Can international law protect states from the Security Council?

*Daniel H. Joyner**

In this chapter I would like to discuss the United Nations Security Council's efforts to implement, preserve and universalize the obligations of the 1968 Nuclear Non-Proliferation Treaty (NPT). This discussion will lead to questions regarding the Security Council's role and authority in the international legal system, and ultimately to a consideration of how international law can better guarantee that the Council does not exercise an unwarranted degree of legal power at the expense of the member states of the United Nations.

First, however, a word on how this chapter fits in with the title of this volume: *International Law in a Multipolar World*. I take 'multipolarity' as used in this book's title to mean the state of international relations in which there is a distribution of power at the top of the power pyramid, whereby more than two states have relatively equal, or at least not significantly disproportional, amounts of military, cultural, and economic influence. It is likely that this concept of multipolarity has significant explanatory power with reference to the state of international relations today. The United States is the most powerful state in the world by almost any measure. However, it does not enjoy the almost unlimited influence over other states which classic hegemons, or states at the apex of unipolar systems, have historically. A number of other states are either emerging or re-emerging as powers challenging US influence, particularly within their geographical regions. These include China, Russia, India and the European Union.

The first way in which this chapter fits in with the theme of this volume, is that the move from the Cold War system of bipolarity between the US and the USSR, to the modern multipolar reality, was the geopolitical shift which enabled the Security Council to begin the period of relatively effective

* I would like to dedicate this chapter to the memory of Professor Sir Ian Brownlie, who died in a tragic automobile accident in Egypt as this chapter was being written on 3 January 2010. I never had the opportunity to know Sir Ian personally, a fact which I now regret. However, his authoritative presence at the centre of the discipline of international law has been of great value to me, and will endure long after his passing.

44   *International law in a multipolar world*

functioning which it has enjoyed for almost twenty years. Thus, the Security Council can truthfully be said currently to play a meaningful role in international law only because of the multipolarity of the modern state of international relations.

This chapter's focus on the Security Council's efforts in the area of nuclear weapons proliferation is also relevant to the theme of this volume because, quite ironically, the multipolarity of the modern system of international relations – i.e. the dispersal of power among many states and not centralized in one or a few – at the selfsame time makes the Security Council's core mission of maintaining international peace and security, including in the issue area of nuclear weapons proliferation, next to impossible. The arm of the Security Council has been proved over and over again to be of quite limited length, particularly in the face of a recalcitrant target state.

In either blissful or wilful ignorance of these limitations, however, the Security Council continues to see itself at the apex of authority in international security law, and capable of significantly influencing the policies and behaviours of states which its controlling permanent members determine to be a threat to international peace and security. An even more recent phenomenon is the Council's apparent determination that it is empowered not only to act as an executive body, authorizing uses of force to restore international peace and security on an ad hoc basis, but also to act as a legislative body crafting proactive and permanent legal edicts covering important areas of international relations, such as terrorism (Resolution 1373) and weapons of mass destruction (WMD) proliferation (Resolution 1540). Indeed, as we will see in the case studies below on Resolution 1540, Iran and North Korea, the Security Council appears to consider itself to possess ultimate and essentially unlimited legal authority – i.e. to represent something of a legal hegemon – within its broad mandate to maintain and restore international peace and security. Authority, for example, to command a state to re-accede to treaties from which that state has duly withdrawn according to the treaties' terms. Authority to command a state not to take action which is recognized by a broadly subscribed treaty to be that state's 'inalienable right'. Indeed, the Security Council has for the past few years been so bullish in its attitude towards its own authority, and has ostensibly used that authority to trample on so many of the most important underlying principles of the international legal system, that we may need to begin seriously considering how international law can protect states from the authoritarian Security Council which multipolarity has unleashed.

The chapter will proceed with three case studies in the nuclear weapons proliferation issue area in which the Security Council has arguably demonstrated its determination of its own unlimited legal authority by acting in disharmony with fundamental principles of the international legal system. These case studies include the passage of Security Council Resolution 1540 in 2004, and the respective cases of the North Korean and Iranian nuclear programmes. The chapter will then conclude with a consideration of how international law should respond to the Security Council's demonstrated claim to being essentially *legibus solutus* (above the law) in its exercise of its Chapter VII authority to maintain and restore international peace and security.

3.1 Resolution 1540

On 28 April 2004 the Security Council passed Resolution 1540. This resolution was passed, not coincidentally, shortly after the revelation in February 2004 of the existence of a long-standing clandestine nuclear materials-smuggling ring headed by the father of Pakistan's gas centrifuge programme, Dr Abdul Qadeer Khan.[1] In Resolution 1540, the Security Council undertook to address a number of fundamental limitations of the existing WMD non-proliferation treaties and regimes system. In the Security Council meetings leading up to the passage of Resolution 1540, some of which were opened to comment from non-Council members, many states noted the need for such a resolution to close 'gaps' in the coverage of existing non-proliferation treaty instruments. One such gap identified by states during these meetings was the problem of the non-universality of the system, a result of the fact that non-proliferation treaties, as all treaties, have been adopted only voluntarily by states, and that for a variety of reasons many states, including some of significant proliferation concern, have remained outside the non-proliferation system.[2]

A second major challenge to the non-proliferation treaties and regimes system is the fact that all existing restrictions within the regimes upon manufacture, possession and trafficking in weapons-related technologies are addressed to states themselves.[3] Thus at the international level there is no substantive restriction on private parties, including business entities as well as other non-state actors, engaging in any of these activities. The utility of Resolution 1540 in addressing this non-state actor gap in the non-proliferation treaties and regimes system was noted by numerous states, particularly in the context of international efforts to combat terrorism.

The resolution addresses the non-state actor problem described above in operative paragraph 1 in which it provides that 'all States shall refrain from providing any form of support to non-state actors that attempt to develop, acquire, manufacture, possess, transport, transfer or use nuclear, chemical or

---

1 See D. H. Joyner, 'International Legal Responses to WMD Proliferation', in C. W. Hughes and R. Devetak (eds.), *The Globalization of Political Violence: Globalization's Shadow* (London: Routledge, 2007).

2 See S. Gahlaut and V. Zaborsky, 'Do Regimes Have the Members They Need?' (February 2003) Center for International Trade and Security Working Paper (Athens, GA: Center for International Trade and Security, 2003).

3 M. Asada, 'WMD Terrorism and Security Council Resolution 1540: Conditions for Legitimacy in International Legislation', IILJ Working Paper 2007/9 (at: www.iilj.org/publications/2007–9Asada. asp); J. du Preez, 'The 2005 NPT Review Conference: Can It Meet the Nuclear Challenge?' (April 2005) *Arms Control Today* 5.

46   *International law in a multipolar world*

biological weapons and their means of delivery'. Furthermore, operative paragraph 2 provides that:

> all States, in accordance with their national procedures, shall adopt and enforce appropriate effective laws which prohibit any non-State actor to manufacture, acquire, possess, develop, transport, transfer or use nuclear, chemical or biological weapons and their means of delivery, in particular for terrorist purposes, as well as attempts to engage in any of the foregoing activities, participate in them as an accomplice, assist or finance them.

It then addresses in operative paragraph 3 the problem of the non-universality of non-proliferation law by directly imposing an obligation upon states to establish and maintain effective export control laws and regulations at the national level:

> including appropriate laws and regulations to control export, transit, trans-shipment and re-export and controls on providing funds and services related to such export and trans-shipment such as financing...as well as establishing end-user controls; and establishing and enforcing appropriate criminal or civil penalties for violations of such export control laws and regulations.

As in Resolution 1373 on international terrorism, passed in 2001, Resolution 1540 in operative paragraph 4 establishes a Committee of the Security Council to monitor the implementation by states of the obligations imposed by the resolution. Although Resolution 1373 and Resolution 1540 were adopted in very different contexts and are meant to cover quite different, although of course related, areas of law, they share important similarities in structure as well as in legal import. These two resolutions have been claimed by some commentators to have ushered in a new age of Security Council jurisprudence and to have signalled intent by the Council to act as a legislative body, in supplementation of its executive functions.[4]

There had before the passage of Resolution 1373 been other controversial acts of the Security Council which had caused debate on the topic of the proper role and powers of the Council.[5] Notable in this regard were the actions before the International Court of Justice arising out of the explosion of Pan Am flight 103 over Lockerbie, Scotland in 1988. However, although in the *Lockerbie* cases there was an allegation that the Council had overstepped its

---

4 See M. Happold, 'Security Council Resolution 1373 and the Constitution of the United Nations' (2003) 16 LJIL 593; P. Szasz, 'The Security Council Starts Legislating' (2002) 96 AJIL 901–2.

5 See M. Koskenniemi, 'The Police in the Temple: Order, Justice and the UN – A Dialectical View' (1995) 6 EJIL 325; K. Harper, 'Does the United Nations Security Council Have the Competence to Act as a Court and Legislature?' (1994) 27 *NYU J.Int'l Law & Pol.* 103; B. Martenczuk, 'The Security Council, the International Court and Judicial Review: What Lessons from Lockerbie?' (1999) 10 EJIL 517.

prerogatives under the Charter, there was no hint of legislative aspirations in the Council's actions. The resolutions involved were clearly targeted against the acts and omissions of one state, Libya, and they set clear demands which, if met, would bring about the end of the mandate for exercise of Council authority. Thus they were in keeping with the Council's understood role, if perhaps excessively bold in construction.

Because of the predominantly non-legislative characteristics of this and virtually all other Security Council decisions, it can be concluded that at the end of the 1990s, the Security Council had not yet passed a true piece of international legislation.[6] However, in the swelling of outrage and concern following the attacks of 11 September 2001, and, as has been alleged, with little foresight of the legal import of what they were doing, the Council passed Resolution 1373.[7] The Council passed this resolution not only to respond to the 11 September acts of terror themselves, or to mete out any measure of punishment upon its perpetrators, or to target them or those states that aided and abetted them. The attacks served as a backdrop and a catalyst for the establishment of a much broader and temporally indefinite normative regime addressing the issue of international terrorism.

The context of the passing of Resolution 1540 offers even less evidence of a specific situation of threat to international peace and security to which the resolution can be regarded as responding. Again, the revelation of the Khan network provided a circumstantial pretext which seemed to explain the prioritization of the subject of WMD proliferation and its address by the Council in Resolution 1540, but the resolution itself went far beyond simply responding to the existence of this network. It newly imposed a broad set of obligations upon all UN member states which had the purpose of permanently changing the structure and content of national legal systems.

These resolutions, simply put, cannot be described as ad hoc responses to events urgently arising in international politics. They were rather calculated, proactive, forward-looking normative creations. In each case, the Security Council determined that an entire class of actions which had been and which might in the future be committed potentially by any state, constituted a threat to international peace and security. The Council then decided in each case that all UN member states should take extensive measures, broadly prescribed in the resolutions, including changes to their national legal systems, in order to combat these ill-defined present and future threats. The obligations imposed under both Resolutions 1373 and 1540 are not temporally limited, either explicitly or implicitly. Their duration is clearly meant to be indefinite. Moreover, there are no specifically targeted states. The obligations imposed in the resolutions are stated in an abstract manner, so as to make their application universal.

---

6 Szasz (n. 4); Happold (n. 4); M. Koskenniemi, 'International Legislation Today: Limits and Possibilities' (2005) 23 *Wisconsin International Law Journal* 61.

7 Happold (n. 4).

3.2   The UN Charter and WMD non-proliferation law

The United Nations Charter makes no mention of the term 'proliferation' and makes no distinction in the language of its provisions as between conventional and non-conventional (i.e. nuclear, chemical and biological) weapons. The Charter rather uses the terms 'disarmament' and the 'regulation of armaments' in three of its articles: Article 11(1), Article 26 and Article 47. These provisions address the subject of the regulation of military armaments generally through international law, as such technologies existed and were maintained in national arsenals at the time of the drafting of the Charter.[8] The UN Charter system which these provisions comprise was constructed to address issues of international arms control and to facilitate the generation of international law to regulate this issue area.

Article 11(1) is a further specification of the general powers of consideration and recommendation granted to the General Assembly in Article 10.[9] The General Assembly under Article 11(1) is to consider 'general principles of cooperation in the maintenance of international peace and security', a power which should be read to include consideration of abstract, general ideas about how member states should work together, and fundamental principles which should underpin the legal relationships which bind states in this area.[10] This power is apposite to the General Assembly because of its character as the deliberative organ of the United Nations and as the only UN body comprising all members of the organization, thus allowing the broadest possible spectrum of interests and perspectives to have input into the formulation of basic principles governing state cooperation in international arms control efforts.[11]

The role of the Security Council in this system is specified in Article 26, which provides:

> In order to promote the establishment and maintenance of international peace and security with the least diversion for armaments of the world's human and economic resources, the Security Council shall be responsible for formulating, with the assistance of the Military Staff Committee referred to in Article 47, plans to be submitted to the Members of the United Nations for the establishment of a system for the regulation of armaments.

A number of points regarding the Security Council's role under Article 26 bear mention. First is to observe that Article 26, in addition to conferring powers and function upon the Security Council, also establishes responsibilities

---

8 D. Cheever, 'The UN and Disarmament' (1965) 19 *Int'l Org.* 453.

9 B. Simma *et al.* (eds.), *The Charter of the United Nations: A Commentary* (2nd edn, Oxford University Press, 2002), 277–8.

10 *Ibid.* 277–80.

11 L. Sohn, 'Enhancing the Role of the General Assembly of the United Nations in Crystallizing International Law', in J. Makarczyk (ed.), *Theory of International Law at the Threshold of the 21st Century: Essays in Honour of Krzysztof Skubiszewski* (The Hague: Kluwer Law International, 1996), 549–61.

Nuclear non-proliferation and the Security Council 49

for the Council in carrying out its complementary role with the General Assembly in the exercise of its Article 11(1) powers. The Council is given the responsibility, on the basis of the recommendations of 'general principles of cooperation' it receives from the General Assembly, and with the assistance of the Military Staff Committee, to formulate concrete plans in order to implement the general principles recommended by the Assembly. These plans are to compose a coherent 'system' for the regulation of armaments, which would imply that the plans to be authored by the Council using this power are not to be situation specific, as in the case of an ad hoc response to a discrete event in international affairs. Rather, these plans are to form the basis for a universally applicable, enduring system of 'practical and effective' international arms control.[12]

The Security Council under Article 26 only has the power to formulate plans. It must then submit those plans to the member states of the United Nations for their approval and for establishment through multilateral treaty as actual legal principles governing their relationships with each other. The Security Council's plans in and of themselves have no binding force upon members, and are merely hortatory offerings, although endowed with the gravitas of having been generated through the Charter system for creation of arms control law.[13] Members may, however, choose either to accept or reject these plans, in analogous fashion to the ratification of UN-approved treaties by member states. As Hans Kelsen has observed:

> With respect to Article 26 of the Charter . . . the 'plans' formulated by the Security Council 'for the establishment of a system for the regulation of armaments' may provide for reduction of armaments; they must be 'submitted to the members of the United nations'. That means that they are binding upon the members only if accepted by them. The obligation is established by a treaty concluded by the members with the organization. Unlike Article 8, paragraph 4 of the [League of Nations] Covenant, Article 26 does not provide expressly for the 'adoption' of the plan by the members, but if the plan of the Security Council is to be submitted to the members, it can be only for the purpose of being adopted by them.[14]

Thus under the Charter system, member states retain their full sovereignty over decisions to enter into legal relationships in the area of international arms control. This right is not presumptively subsumed under the Council's binding decision-making powers under Article 25, nor under its broad powers

---

12 B. Bechhoefer, *Postwar Negotiations for Arms Control* (Washington, DC: Brookings Institution, 1961); O. Bogdanov, 'Outlawry of War and Disarmament' (1971–2) 133 *Recueil des Cours* 15–42; Simma (n. 9), 466–8.

13 Simma (n. 9), 466–8.

14 H. Kelsen, *Collective Security under International Law* (1957; Union, NJ: Lawbook Exchange, 2001, repr.), 214.

to maintain international peace and security under the articles of Chapter VII.[15]

3.3   The limits of Chapter VII

The UN Charter in Article 24 confers upon the Security Council 'primary responsibility for the maintenance of international peace and security'. In the same paragraph the members of the United Nations 'agree that in carrying out its duties under this responsibility, the Security Council acts on their behalf'. This statement is the closest the Charter comes to attempting to remedy the non-democratic reality, made requisite by geopolitical circumstances in 1945, that the most powerful organ of the United Nations and the only organ capable of issuing decisions binding upon all UN members, is composed of only 15 of those members (who now total 191), five of whom are given permanent status and have an effective veto power over every decision of the Council.

In this language seeming to imply a representative relationship between the Council and the rest of the UN membership, the Charter attempts to legitimize the declaration in Article 25 by the membership, that all UN members 'agree to accept and carry out the decisions of the Security Council in accordance with the present Charter'. Thus, Article 25 establishes the binding character of Security Council decisions upon the entirety of the UN membership.[16]

Although the specific powers granted to the Security Council under the Charter, and particularly in the articles of Chapter VII, are both broadly and vaguely worded, the Charter does however provide limits upon the discretion of the Council in its exercise of these powers. As the Council derives its powers from the Charter's terms, it is by the same process bound by those terms. As the Appeals Chamber of the International Criminal Tribunal for the former Yugoslavia (ICTY) has observed:

> The Security Council is an organ of an international organization, established by a treaty which serves as a constitutional framework for that organization. The Security Council is thus subjected to certain constitutional limitations, however broad its powers under the constitution may be. Those powers cannot, in any case, go beyond the limits of the jurisdiction of the organization at large, not to mention other specific limitations or those which may derive from the internal division of power within the organization. In any case, neither the text

---

15 H. Kelsen, *The Law of the United Nations: A Critical Analysis of Its Fundamental Problems* (London: Stevens, 1951).

16 See the discussion of Article 24 as an independent source of authority for binding decisions of the Security Council in Happold (n. 4), 604–5.

nor the spirit of the Charter conceives of the Security Council as *legibus solutus* (unbound by law).[17]

One such limiting provision upon the Council's power is Article 24(2), which provides that 'In discharging these duties the Security Council shall act in accordance with the purposes and principles of the United Nations'.[18] The purposes and principles of the United Nations are to be found in Articles 1 and 2 of the Charter, and include the right of states to self-determination, respect for human rights, the principle of sovereign equality, an obligation to act in good faith and an obligation not to intervene in matters 'essentially within the domestic jurisdiction' of member states. As the International Court of Justice stated in the *Certain Expenses* advisory opinion in 1962: 'When the organization takes action which warrants the assertion that it was appropriate for the fulfilment of one of the stated purposes of the United Nations, the presumption is that such action is not *ultra vires* the organization'.[19]

Another limiting provision is Article 25. As previously stated, perhaps the greatest import of the text of this article is the establishment of the universally binding character of Security Council decisions.[20] However, the fact that, under this provision, members agree to accept and carry out the decisions of the Security Council 'in accordance with the present charter' suggests that the measure of this obedience should be contingent upon the validity of the Council's decisions and actions as held up to the standard of the provisions of the Charter, and further that it is conceivable that other provisions of the Charter might in some cases take precedence over conflicting Security Council decisions.[21] To paraphrase the article's meaning in this regard, UN members are not obligated to comply with the decisions of the Council one wit further than those decisions themselves comply with the provisions of the Charter.[22]

Although the general purposes and principles of the United Nations are difficult to apply in a meaningful way so as to provide justifiable limitations on the powers of the Security Council under Article 24(2), in the non-proliferation issue area the process for creation of new non-proliferation law contained in Articles 11(1) and 26 described above does provide a clear, authoritative lawmaking procedure which can properly be called the UN Charter system for the creation of non-proliferation law. As this system

17 *Prosecutor* v. *Tadić* (Jurisdiction) ITC-Y94-1-AR72, para. 28 (2 October 1995).

18 See D. Schweigman, *The Authority of the Security Council Under Chapter VII of the UN Charter* (London: Kluwer Law International, 2001), 29–33.

19 *Certain Expenses of the United Nations*, ICJ Reports (1962), 151, 168.

20 See R. Higgins, 'The Advisory Opinion on Namibia: Which UN Resolutions are Binding under Article 25 of the Charter?' (1972) 32 ICLQ 269–86.

21 J. Delbruck, 'Article 25', in B Simma *et al.* (eds.), *The Charter of the United Nations: A Commentary* (Oxford University Press, 1994) 455; E. de Wet, *The Chapter VII Powers of the United Nations Security Council* (Oxford: Hart, 2004), 375–8; P. Rösgen, 'Rechtsetzungakte der Vereinten Nationen und ihrer Sonderorganisationen: Bestandsaufnahme und Volzug in der Bundesrepublik Deutschland' (Ph.D. thesis, University of Bonn, 1985), 157.

22 De Wet (n. 21), 377.

involves a clearly delineated division of roles and authorities between the organs of the UN, it thus comprises a limitation upon the authority of the Security Council deriving from 'the internal division of power within the organization'.[23] This limitation is therefore a part of the substantive law of the Charter in accordance with which, under Article 25, the Security Council is bound to act.[24]

Thus, while the provisions of the Charter in many instances provide limitations upon the powers of the Council which, though valid, are difficult to apply unambiguously, because of the presence of the lawmaking system contained in Articles 11(1) and 26, the non-proliferation law creation issue area does not labour under the same difficulty. I would argue that the Article 25 limitations on the Council's powers can be applied in the non-proliferation law issue area because of the presence of the criteria for legitimate lawmaking by UN bodies contained in Articles 11(1) and 26 of the UN Charter. Accordingly, any act by the Security Council which attempts to create 'a system for the regulation of armaments' outside of the Article 11(1) and Article 26 institutional process is in breach of Article 25, and is thus an act *ultra vires* the Council's authority.[25]

Security Council Resolution 1540 meets this test precisely. The resolution clearly attempts to establish a system for the regulation of WMD, which includes a universalized export control law requirement and a universalized requirement to enact laws on the subject of non-state actors. Therefore, to be valid as a source of binding obligation upon UN member states, I argue that this system of obligations cannot be established through the Council's use of its Chapter VII powers, but must rather be constructed through the procedures provided for in Articles 11(1) and 26.

My essential argument is that in passing what can only be viewed as an ostensible piece of international legislation in Resolution 1540, the Security Council confused the proper scope of its enforcement powers under Chapter VII, with the proper scope of its long unused, limited lawmaking powers under Article 26. Consequently, the Council, by unilateral exercise of its Chapter VII powers, has taken to itself a role which, under the Charter system, it is to share both with the General Assembly in the exercise of its Article 11(1) powers, as well as with the general membership of the United Nations, to whom it is directed under Article 26 to submit proposals for the creation of new international laws in the area of weapons proliferation.

The added political, legal and chronological efficiency of the path chosen by the Security Council is not denied. For the members of the Security Council, the long unused Charter system for the creation of non-proliferation law would certainly have looked less attractive, particularly as the amount of control they would have been able to exercise over the outcome of the approval

---

23   *Prosecutor* v. *Tadić* (n. 17).
24   *Ibid.*
25   Happold (n. 4), 593.

process under the Charter system would have been severely diluted from that they would wield through the Chapter VII process.

However, none of these reasons of expedition and control sufficiently justifies going around the Charter system and assuming a lawmaking authority which was never intended to be exercised by the Council under the Charter. The Charter system in Articles 11(1) and 26 is the authoritative system for the creation of new non-proliferation law for good reasons. The system in Articles 11(1) and 26 divides roles among the political organs of the UN, leaving the final and most important role of actual establishment as law of the principles generated through this institutional process, to the UN member states themselves. This system was created by the Charter framers in maintenance of the classical principles of state sovereignty and sovereign equality in international lawmaking, and was consistent with the positivist tradition that the consent of states to be bound underlies the validity of all of the sources of international law. This system was informed by the understanding that the consent given to Council authority in the first instance by states in Article 25 of the Charter does not equate to direct consent of states at the second instance to every substantive decision of the Council. And while this distinction is less troublesome in the domestic context under most theories of the positivist social compact, it is troubling to states in the international legal system which more jealously guard their sovereign autonomy under the sometimes maligned, but still quite virile Westphalian sovereignty paradigm.

In adopting Resolution 1540, the Security Council, whose role in the Charter system for non-proliferation law creation is really a facilitative and definitional one, effectively bypassed the steps assigned to the General Assembly and to the member states by taking the issue to itself and acting both in the deliberative role assigned to the General Assembly, as well as the law creation role assigned to the members collectively. In doing so, the Council acted in disharmony with the fundamental international legal principle of state sovereignty, and the derivative principle of the consensual foundation of the sources of international law. In short, it acted as a legal hegemon, unbound by the fundamental rules and principles of international law, and the limited nature of its own authority under the Charter.

3.4 Iran

In late 2002, the world learned from Iranian opposition groups in exile that Iran had concealed from the International Atomic Energy Agency (IAEA) the existence of facilities at Natanz and Arak engaged in experiments involving uranium enrichment and plutonium separation for eighteen years. Upon a report by IAEA inspectors detailing their findings of the undeclared activities, the IAEA Board of Governors reached the conclusion in a Resolution passed on 26 November 2003 that, because of this concealment and other reporting omissions, Iran had 'failed in a number of instances...to meet its obligations

54   *International law in a multipolar world*

under its Safeguards Agreement with the agency'.[26] The Board further recognized that Iran had a particular onus of cooperation and transparency in order to 'provide and maintain the assurances required by Member States' and to 'restore confidence'.[27] Iran subsequently agreed upon a temporary suspension of its uranium enrichment activities and in December 2003 signed the IAEA Additional Protocol.

Despite these concessions, Iran has consistently maintained that all of its work with fissile materials and related technologies, including work at these undeclared sites, has been aimed at furthering its capacity to produce civilian nuclear energy. Iran has argued that despite its failure to comply with reporting requirements under its safeguards agreement, it has always been in compliance with its substantive obligations under the NPT. In this argument, Iran has relied specifically upon the 'inalienable right' of all states to engage in peaceful uses of nuclear technologies recognized in Article IV, paragraph 1, of the NPT.[28]

However, suspicions have become widespread, particularly among Western states and Israel, that Iran does indeed have nuclear weapons ambitions, and, in particular, that the uranium enrichment work which Iran has carried out is intended not solely for use in peaceful energy production, but for the creation of nuclear weapons. Notwithstanding these suspicions, IAEA inspectors have to date found no conclusive evidence to support allegations of a clandestine nuclear weapons programme in Iran.[29]

3.5   Resolution 1737

Despite this lack of evidence of a weapons programme, the IAEA Board of Governors took the decision on 4 February 2006 to refer Iran's case to the UN Security Council. This referral, without a supporting report by IAEA inspectors providing evidence that Iran was in breach of its substantive NPT obligations, or that it was in continuing breach of its safeguards agreement, has led some to criticize the Board's decision as premature.[30] Notwithstanding these concerns, on 31 July 2006 the Security Council passed Resolution 1696 in which, acting under Article 40 of Chapter VII of the UN Charter, it demanded that Iran suspend all uranium enrichment-related and reprocessing

---

26 IAEA, 'Implementation of the NPT Standards Agreement in the Islamic Republic of Iran', Doc. GOV/2003/81 (26 November 2003), 2.

27 *Ibid.*

28 For an analysis of the legal arguments surrounding Iran's nuclear programme, see D. H. Joyner, *International Law and the Proliferation of Weapons of Mass Destruction* (Oxford University Press, 2009), 50–5.

29 For a fuller discussion of the question of evidence of an Iranian nuclear weapons programme see D. H. Joyner, 'Why Less is More: Law and Policy Considerations on the Iranian Nuclear Issue', *Harvard Law and Policy Review* (Online) (2010). See also US National Intelligence Estimate, 'Iran: Nuclear Intentions and Capabilities' (November 2007) (at: www.dni.gov/press_releases/20071203_release.pdf).

30 Joyner (n. 29).

activities, and requested a report from the IAEA director-general by 31 August to confirm this suspension. The Council followed up Resolution 1696 on 23 December 2006 with Resolution 1737, in which it acted under Article 41 of the Charter and made binding the demands of Resolution 1696.

Iran's failure to abide by the terms of these resolutions, insisting that its activities are firmly within its rights under NPT Article IV, has led to the adoption of further Security Council resolutions under Chapter VII, including a number of resolutions imposing trade restrictions and other economic sanctions upon Iran and upon specified Iranian individuals and business entities.

3.6 Resolution 1929

Tensions between Iran and Western powers were aggravated by Iran's disclosure in September 2009 that it had for some years been constructing a facility near Qom intended as an additional uranium enrichment facility to supplement its primary enrichment facility at Natanz. Since this disclosure by Iran, one of the points of debate among international observers has been whether in the timing of this disclosure, Iran violated its obligations under its legal agreements with the IAEA.

Iran has argued that its disclosure was perfectly consistent with its legal obligations under its Safeguards Agreement with the IAEA (INFCIRC/214), as implemented through a Subsidiary Arrangements agreement which Iran entered into with the IAEA in 1976.[31] Under the provisions of this Subsidiary Arrangements agreement known as 'Code 3.1', Iran has argued that it is only obligated to disclose the existence of new enrichment facilities 'normally not later than 180 days before the facility is scheduled to receive nuclear material for the first time'.

Some observers, however, argue that Iran did in fact violate its international obligations by not disclosing the existence of the Qom facility earlier.[32] They argue that Iran agreed by exchange of letters with the IAEA in 2003 to a new and revised set of Subsidiary Arrangements, known as 'modified Code 3.1', which provide that preliminary design information on new enrichment facilities is to be provided 'as soon as the decision to construct or to authorize construction has been taken, whichever is earlier'.

The crux of the dispute regarding which of the versions of Code 3.1 is applicable to Iran's actions in and around September 2009 centres on Iran's 29 March 2007 letter to the IAEA in which Iran declared its intention to 'revert' to the original 1976 Code 3.1 formulation. The IAEA Legal Adviser's office issued an opinion in March 2009 in which it rejected Iran's unilateral declaration of reversion, and maintained that the agreed modified Code 3.1

---

31 'IAEA: Iran broke law by not revealing nuclear facility', CNN.com, 30 September 2009.

32 See James Acton, 'Iran Violated International Obligations on Qom Facility' (at: www.carnegieendowment.org/publications/index.cfm?fa=view&id=23884).

56   *International law in a multipolar world*

provisions remained in force between Iran and the IAEA. As the Legal Advisor's office concluded:

> The implementation of the provisions of Subsidiary Arrangements can only be amended or suspended with the agreement of both parties to them. . . The provisions cannot be amended or suspended unilaterally by the state. Thus Iran's failure to provide design information in accordance with the modified Code 3.1 as agreed to by Iran in 2003 is inconsistent with Iran's obligations under the Subsidiary Arrangements to its Safeguards Agreement.

The UN Security Council entered the fray of this essentially legal debate on 9 June 2010 with the passage of Resolution 1929, in which it acted under Article 41 of the Charter and decided that Iran:

> shall without delay comply fully and without qualification with its IAEA Safeguards Agreement, including through the application of modified Code 3.1 of the Subsidiary Arrangement to its Safeguards Agreement . . .

3.7   Legal analysis of Resolution 1737

In consideration of the legal merits of Iran's claim of justification of its activities by reference to Article IV of the NPT, it is important first to note that uranium enrichment, when declared, is not an NPT violation per se. Certainly when uranium is enriched to a U-235 presence of less than 20 per cent, and can thus still be classified as low-enriched uranium (LEU), that enrichment activity is one that falls within the Article IV inalienable right to engage in peaceful uses of nuclear technologies. This understanding was clear at the time of the drafting of the NPT. As the Director of the US Arms Control and Disarmament Agency told the Senate Foreign Relations Committee in 1968:

> It may be useful to point out, for illustrative purposes, several activities which the United States would not consider per se to be violations of the prohibitions in Article II. Neither uranium enrichment nor the stockpiling of fissionable material in connection with a peaceful program would violate Article II so long as these activities were safeguarded under Article III. Also clearly permitted would be the development, under safeguards, of plutonium fuelled power reactors, including research on the properties of metallic plutonium, nor would Article II interfere with the development or use of fast breeder reactors under safeguards.[33]

---

33 W. Foster, 'Extension of Remarks By Mr Foster in Response To Question Regarding Nuclear Explosive Devices' (10 July 1968) US Senate Foreign Relations Committee, Ninetieth Congress, Second Session, Executive H, Treaty on the Non-proliferation of Nuclear Weapons (10, 11, 12, 17 July 1968), 39. Also available from P. K. Kerr, 'Iran's Nuclear Program: Tehran's Compliance with International Obligations' Congressional Research Report for Congress R40094 (31 March 2009), 2.

Japan and a number of other Non-nuclear Weapon State (NNWS) parties to the NPT have carried out enrichment of uranium for the purpose of nuclear power generation for many years without complaint from the IAEA Board of Governors. Japan has in fact separated and stockpiled at least 43.1 tons of plutonium, as well as having a robust and productive gas centrifuge programme for uranium enrichment at its facility in Rokkasho, thus illustrating that even the overproduction and stockpiling of fissile materials is deemed permissible by the IAEA.[34] It is only when this enrichment activity by an NNWS is undeclared to the IAEA that a violation of an IAEA safeguards agreement results. Even this, however, is not a violation of the NPT per se. Only if enrichment proceeds to the production of highly enriched uranium (HEU), at approximately 20 per cent presence of U-235, does it produce weapons-usable material. Undeclared enrichment of weapons-usable HEU would create a prima facie case of breach of Article II of the NPT and such activity would not be justifiable by reference to Article IV.

As a matter of law, therefore, Iran was quite correct in its interpretation that its uranium enrichment activities were covered by Article IV of the NPT at least until 23 December 2006. The basis of its case was not altered by previous IAEA urgings that Iran cease uranium enrichment, as the IAEA's only legal competence is in the administration of safeguards agreements, and the continuation of uranium enrichment in declared sites, under IAEA safeguards, posed no challenge to the provisions of Iran's safeguards agreement. The legal landscape did change, however, on 23 December 2006 with the passage of Security Council Resolution 1737, under which the Council exercised its authority under Chapter VII of the UN Charter to order Iran to cease uranium enrichment

Regardless of the prudence or other merit of this demand by the Council, in passing this resolution the Council likely did change the legal underpinnings of Iran's case for justifying its enrichment activities by reference to NPT Article IV.[35] This issue can be approached legally under a number of different theories. The most often cited theory focuses on the provisions of the UN Charter, which in Article 103 specifies that 'In the event of a conflict between the obligations of the Members of the United Nations under the present Charter and their obligations under any other international agreement, their obligations under the present Charter shall prevail'. By virtue of Article 103, in conjunction with the already-mentioned Article 25, therefore, the obligations of the Charter are declared superior to all other treaty rights and obligations

---

34 See report from Kyodo news agency at: www.redorbit.com/news/science/231519/japans_separated_plutonium_stockpile_increases_to_43_tons/index.html. Uranium enrichment through centrifuge cascade is also carried out, for example, at the Almelo facility in the Netherlands, and at the Gronau facility in Germany.

35 See the discussion of the limits of the Security Council's Chapter VII authority below.

58   *International law in a multipolar world*

Under this analysis, with the passage of Resolution 1737, the Council invoked Iran's obligation as a UN member to abide by the Council's decisions under Article 25, which is an obligation superior to all other treaty obligations pursuant to Article 103, including the rights and duties contained in the NPT. Iran thus became legally obligated to comply with Resolution 1737, as well as with all other resolutions passed by the Security Council under its Chapter VII authority, and unable to rely upon its right to peaceful use of nuclear technologies in NPT Article IV to justify actions in disharmony with such Council decisions.

The problem with this analysis, however, is that it would empower the UN Security Council to trump any of the rights held by states by virtue of their statehood. The implications of this theory are far-reaching and unsettling. Article IV of the NPT, to which 187 states are currently parties, recognizes the residual entitlement of NNWS treaty parties to possess and use nuclear technologies and materials for peaceful purposes, notwithstanding the obligations not to pursue nuclear weapons which they undertook in Article II. This residual entitlement is termed by the treaty to be an 'inalienable right'. This is strong language intended to convey deep legal meaning, analogous to the recognition in Article 51 of the UN Charter of an 'inherent right' of self-defence.[36] The phrasing characterizes the right guaranteed by Article IV not simply as a right created by the NPT, but rather as a pre-existing right independent of the treaty and only recognized by its terms.[37] Like the inherent right to self-defence recognized by the UN Charter, this inalienable right to possess and use nuclear technologies and materials for peaceful purposes would appear to be recognized by the 187 states party to the NPT as comprising one of the bundle of rights inuring to a state by virtue of its statehood, and recognized in both customary and conventional international law.

It can be argued (as I have done elsewhere)[38] that one theory for the superiority of Chapter VII resolutions over the rights of NPT Article IV is to be found in the reasoning that, as noted above, the rights defined in Article IV are not creations alone of the treaty terms of the NPT, but are rather rights recognized by the terms of the treaty yet existing independently within the bundle of rights inherent in the attributes of a state. Under this argument, while the Article IV rights are important features of the sovereign character of all NPT parties, they are nonetheless classifiable along with all other general

---

36 On the recognition of the customary right of self-defence in UN Charter Article 51, see D. Bowett, *Self-Defence in International Law* (Manchester University Press, 1958), 185. ('It is…fallacious to assume that members have only those rights which the Charter accords to them; on the contrary they have those rights which general international law accords to them except in so far as they have surrendered them under the Charter…The view of Committee I at San Francisco was that this prohibition [Article 2(4)] left the right of self-defence unimpaired.')

37 See S. Hall, 'The Persistent Spectre: Natural Law, International Order and the Limits of Legal Positivism' (2001) 12 EJIL 269. On the question of the relationship between this right and Articles I and II of the NPT, see Joyner (n. 28), 45–50.

38 Joyner (n. 28), 54–5.

state rights which are, by a state's consent to the terms of Article 25 of the Charter, made surmountable by and subject to the authority of the Security Council acting under Chapter VII. Thus far this theory may be correct, but it does not fully deal with the central question of the ambit of the Charter's Article 39 grant of authority to the Security Council. Over which of their rights did states contract discretion to the Security Council in exercise of its Article 39 authority, and over which did they not? Space here only permits a superficial answer. However, I will argue that there must be limits to the Council's Article 39 'powers of appreciation' and resulting authoritative discretion, lest the Council become a legal hegemon, unbound by law in the exercise of its Chapter VII powers.[39] The idea of the Security Council, with its unrepresentative make-up and proprietary rights system comprising such a legal hegemon is unlikely to be acceptable to most of the nations of the world.

In summary, then, by trampling upon a right of states recognized in a broadly subscribed treaty to be an 'inalienable right', the Security Council has in its NPT-related dealings with Iran arguably overstepped the bounds of its Chapter VII authority. It has at least, in doing so, pushed the limits of that authority to a point at which serious questions must be asked about what those limits are, and how international law should respond in order to guarantee that there are legal limits placed upon the power of the Security Council, preventing it from becoming a legal hegemon unbound by law.

3.8 Legal analysis of Resolution 1929

Returning to the discussion above in the context of Resolution 1540, of the limits on the Security Council's authority expressed particularly in Article 25 of the Charter, I argue that Resolution 1929 represents yet another occasion on which the Council has acted *ultra vires* its Chapter VII authority. The analysis here is very similar to that conducted above in the case of Resolution 1540. In the case of Resolution 1929, the Security Council considers what is essentially a legal question – i.e. the obligations of Iran under its Safeguards Agreement with the IAEA – and whether those obligations include either the original or the modified Code 3.1 formulation with regard to the disclosure of the existence of new nuclear facilities. The Council makes what can only be

---

39 The term 'powers of appreciation' is taken from Judge Shahabuddeen's searching query in his opinion in the *Lockerbie* case: 'The question now raised…is whether a decision of the Security Council may override the legal rights of states, and, if so, whether there are any limitations on the power of the Council to characterize a situation as one justifying the making of a decision entailing such consequences. Are there any limits to the Council's powers of appreciation? In the equilibrium of forces underpinning the United Nations within the evolving international order, is there a conceivable point beyond which a legal issue may properly arise as to the competence of the Security Council to produce such overriding results? If there are any limits, what are those limits, and what body, if other than the Security Council, is competent to say what those limits are?' *Questions of Interpretation and Application of the 1971 Montreal Convention Arising from the Aerial Incident at Lockerbie (Libyan Arab Jamahiriya v. United Kingdom).* (Request for the Indication of Provisional Measures: Order of 14 April 1992), ICJ Reports [1992], 3, 142.

60   *International law in a multipolar world*

described as a judicial decision, accepting one legal argument or interpretation as more persuasive than another. In unmistakably judicial form, the Council then rules on the legal question by issuing an order that the party in the dock before it must abide by its determination of the law.

Again, under the UN Charter Article 25 analysis adopted above, notwithstanding the Council's broad mandate in Articles 39, 40 and 41, there are limits to the Council's authority to act under Chapter VII. Such limitations can be most clearly determined when the Charter itself provides for an alternative decision-making process or forum. And the Charter is quite clear on the question of which forum, or organ within the institutional structure it creates, is to decide legal disputes, and perform judicial functions.

In Article 92, it provides that the International Court of Justice 'shall be the principal judicial organ of the United Nations'. And even more specifically, in Article 36 it provides this explicit directive and reminder to the Security Council itself:

> In making recommendations under this Article the Security Council should also take into consideration that legal disputes should as a general rule be referred by the parties to the International Court of Justice in accordance with the provisions of the Statute of the Court.

As discussed above the Security Council does have broad authority to act under the Articles of Chapter VII when it determines the existence of a threat to international peace and security. But this authority is not without bounds. The Security Council itself is bound by Article 25 to act in accordance with the Charter. The Council is in this way bound to observe the order and delegations of roles provided for by the instrument from which it draws its own authority. Where, as in Articles 36 and 92, the Charter clearly delegates a role and type of authority to a separate UN organ, the Security Council cannot legally usurp the authority so delegated, and arrogate it to its own use.

I argue that in passing Resolution 1929, the Council did just that. It usurped the role of the International Court of Justice in settling a legal dispute among UN member states, and in exercising an essentially judicial interpretive/ determinative function to do so. This is a role which was never intended by the Charter framers for the Security Council to fulfil. The Council has neither the mandate nor the qualifications to act as an international judicial body. In passing Resolution 1929, therefore, the Council acted in contravention of Article 25 of the Charter. The operative paragraphs in Resolution 1929 which express the determinations of the Council acting in this judicial role, notably paragraph 5 quoted above, are therefore *ultra vires* the Council's authority and, like Resolution 1540, are as a result void *ab initio*.[40]

However, the fact that the Security Council, notwithstanding its lack of authority in the Charter do so, nevertheless is convinced that it can act as an

40 Joyner (n. 28), 195.

international judiciary, in addition to its newly assumed legislative role, gives rise to grave concern that the Council considers itself above the law – a legal hegemon.

3.9   North Korea

United Nations Security Council Resolution 1874 was adopted on 12 June 2009 in response to the nuclear weapon test which had been conducted by the Democratic People's Republic of North Korea (DPRK) on 25 May 2009. This was the second nuclear weapon test conducted by the DPRK, its first having been held on 9 October 2006. The Security Council had responded to the first nuclear test by the adoption of Resolution 1718 on 14 October 2006. Resolution 1874 essentially reiterates the Security Council's previous condemnation of the DPRK's first nuclear test, and further builds upon and supplements the sanctions imposed upon the DPRK in Resolution 1718.

Resolution 1874 represented the latest in a long line of Security Council resolutions focused on the problem of the DPRK's nuclear weapons programme.[41] Long-standing international concern about the DPRK's nuclear weapons programme had been aggravated by three principal events: the first was the DPRK's announcement on 10 January 2003 that it was withdrawing from the NPT, and the second and third were the 2006 and 2009 nuclear weapon tests.

The DPRK's withdrawal from the NPT was significant on a number of levels. It represented the first and only time that a state has withdrawn its membership from the treaty, which is the cornerstone legal instrument in the nuclear non-proliferation normative regime. It also exempted the DPRK from any obligation under either conventional or customary international law prohibiting it from developing or possessing, or even proliferating, nuclear weapons. It is within this context of the DPRK's withdrawal from the NPT, and its evidencing to the world its possession of nuclear weapons, that Resolution 1874 must be understood.

In Resolution 1874, acting under Article 41 of its Chapter VII authority, the Council first condemns 'in the strongest terms' the 25 May 2009 nuclear test. It then demands that the DPRK not conduct any further nuclear weapon tests, or launch of any ballistic missile technology. These injunctions are clearly aimed at reiterating the prohibitions placed upon the DPRK by Resolution 1718, and at addressing the immediate symptoms of the problem of its nuclear weapons programme. The Council then, however, goes on to address the more fundamental legal problem relating to the DPRK's nuclear weapons programme – the current absence of international law prohibiting the DPRK from developing, possessing and proliferating nuclear weapons. In operative paragraphs 5 and 6, the Council demands that North Korea retract

---

41   E.g. UNSC Res. 825 (11 May1993) UN Doc. S/RES/825, UNSC Res. 1695 (4 July 2006) UN Doc. S/RES/1695 and UNSC Res. 1718 (14 October 2006) UN Doc. S/RES/1718.

62   *International law in a multipolar world*

its statement of withdrawal from the NPT, and return 'at an early date' to membership in the NPT and to a safeguards agreement with the IAEA.

Following its demand that the DPRK rejoin the NPT, the Council proceeds in operative paragraph 8 to 'decide' – thus using its most binding and determinative language – that the DPRK shall abandon its nuclear weapons and related development programme, and shall submit itself to the terms of a safeguards agreement administered by the IAEA. The DPRK concluded a safeguards agreement with the IAEA on 30 January 1992 (INFCIRC/403). However, pursuant to the safeguards agreement, its continuance in force was limited to the term of the DPRK's membership in the NPT.[42] Thus, the DPRK's withdrawal from the NPT had as a consequence its simultaneous withdrawal from its safeguards agreement with the IAEA.[43] Operative paragraph 8 of Resolution 1874 thus purports to reverse both the DPRK's withdrawal from the NPT and its withdrawal from its IAEA safeguards agreement, by commanding the state to abide by one of the central obligations of the NPT – i.e. the obligation of non-nuclear weapons States not to develop or possess nuclear weapons – and to abide by the terms of its IAEA safeguards agreement.

This demand and these decisions by the Security Council are singular. First made in Resolution 1718 and then reiterated in Resolution 1874, the Council's demand that the DPRK rejoin the NPT is the only example, to my knowledge, of a Security Council demand that a state re-accede to a treaty from which that state had duly withdrawn according to the treaty's terms. As if that were not enough, the Council in operative paragraph 8 goes one step further, essentially deciding that the DPRK continues to be bound by the central obligation of the NPT and by the terms of its former IAEA safeguards agreement. One might think that there is an element of hypocrisy in a Council decision that a particular state is not allowed, apparently *in perpetuam*, to develop and possess the same weapons technologies which at least eight other states – five of whom have permanent seats on the Council itself – are known to possess.

In its NPT-related decisions concerning North Korea, therefore, the Security Council has determined that it has the authority to contravene a state's decision to withdraw from treaty obligations, according to those treaties' terms. It has further determined that, regardless of the will or contrary actions of the state, it has the authority to impose permanent, substantive obligations on a state with regard to its military capabilities.

These actions of the Security Council would seem to carry serious implications with regard to the consensual nature of all of the sources of international law, which is in turn intimately linked to the sovereign character

---

42 Article 26 of the DPRK's safeguards agreement provides, 'This Agreement shall remain in force as long as the Democratic People's Republic of Korea is party to the Treaty [the NPT]'.

43 See F. Kirgis, 'North Korea's Withdrawal from the Nuclear Nonproliferation Treaty' (January 2003) *ASIL Insight* (at: www.asil.org/insigh96.cfm).

of states in the international legal system. If the Security Council can order a state to enter into, or at least maintain *jus dispositivum* obligations against the will of the state concerned, what indeed can the Security Council not do? From a jurisprudential perspective, by asserting its power over the consent of states to be bound by international law, the Council's actions regarding North Korea represent an even more fundamental 'authority grab' by the Council than do its actions regarding Iran. In its Resolutions 1718 and 1874, the Council appears to consider itself unbound by the fundamental rules and principles of international law and the sovereign character of the member states of the United Nations, and empowered to do anything it deems expedient to bring about international peace and security. In short, it appears to consider itself a legal hegemon.

3.10   How can international law protect states from the Security Council?

The case studies above in the nuclear non-proliferation law issue area, show what I argue to be several examples of the Security Council demonstrating its recent determination that it is essentially unbound by law, whether UN Charter law or otherwise, in its fulfilment of its mandate to maintain and restore international peace and security. I would further argue that it is also clear from the context of these case studies, that in each case it was the permanent five members of the Council, who are also not coincidentally the five Nuclear Weapon State parties to the NPT, who took the initiative in having the relevant Security Council resolutions adopted. This fact has led some in the developing world to charge that the permanent five have hijacked the Security Council in order to use it as an instrument of unbridled legal authority for carrying out their own desires for international lawmaking in this area.[44] As the representative from Indonesia stated at the April 2008 NPT Preparatory Committee meeting:

> [T]he tendency for the Security Council to judge compliance and to act as an enforcer of the NPT needs to be urgently rectified. There is no doubt this inclination has a political motivation, as the Council will not in any way act in a similar manner on non-compliance to Article VI. It has also become a source of concern that the expansion of the Security Council involvement in this field risks to undermine the authority of the IAEA.[45]

---

44 See, e.g., the statements of Egypt, Iran, Mexico, Cuba, India and Namibia in the meetings leading up to the adoption of Resolution 1540 in 2004. In UNSC 4950th Meeting (22 April 2004) UN Doc. S/PV/4950 and UNSC 4950th Meeting (22 April 2004) UN Doc. S/PV/4950 (Resumption 1).

45 IGAW Puja, 'Statement …at the Second Session of the Preparatory Committee for the 2010 Review Conference of the State Parties to the treaty on the Non-proliferation of Nuclear Weapons, Geneva' (29 April 2008) (at: www.un.org/NPT2010/SecondSession/statements.html).

64   *International law in a multipolar world*

Interestingly, the Indonesian Ambassador here argues specifically that the permanent five have used the Security Council to accomplish their own political interests in the name of enforcing NPT law, yet have hypocritically ignored very significant issues of disarmament law under NPT Article VI,[46] because this would not serve their political interests.

This realization of the permanent five's adoption of the Security Council as an instrument for carrying out their own political agendas through international lawmaking in this area, is likely to be quite disconcerting to many smaller, developing countries, who might legitimately worry whether they will be the next target of the Council's attentions. It thus becomes necessary to consider what international law, and the international legal system, can or should do to protect states, particularly smaller and developing states, from the UN Security Council and its demonstrated bullish, near hegemonic attitude towards its own legal authority? I would like to explore one vein of thinking in the remainder of this chapter.[47]

In addition to the hierarchically equal *jus dispositivum* sources of international law (treaties, custom and general principles) it has come to be generally accepted that there are a few 'higher obligations' which are universal and non-derogable for states in the international legal system. These higher-order peremptory rules are termed *jus cogens*. As Ian Brownlie has written:

> In the recent past both doctrine and judicial opinion have supported the view that certain overriding principles of international law exist, forming a body of *jus cogens*...They are rules of customary law which cannot be set aside by treaty or acquiescence but only by the formation of a subsequent customary rule of contrary effect. The least controversial examples of the class are the prohibition of the use of force, the law of genocide, the principle of racial non-discrimination, crimes against humanity, and the rules prohibiting trade in slaves and piracy.[48]

Jus cogens rules are the closest that the current international legal system comes to constitutional or higher-order system rules. As this enumerated list demonstrates, however, the most widely accepted rules of *jus cogens* are prohibitions of certain conduct by states, and in a very few cases by individuals, deemed universally unacceptable by the international community. There have been some indications of principles of law constituting state entitlements, or rights, in customary international law having attained *jus cogens* status, but

---

46 Article VI provides that: 'Each of the Parties to the Treaty undertakes to pursue negotiations in good faith on effective measures relating to cessation of the nuclear arms race at an early date and to nuclear disarmament, and on a Treaty on general and complete disarmament under strict and effective international control.'

47 In a similar vein and from an institutional perspective, I recently argued for a renaissance of attention to the International Court of Justice's role as a judicial check upon the Security Council. To avoid redundancy, I will not pursue that line of thought here. See Joyner (n. 28), ch. 5.

48 I. Brownlie, *Principles of Public International Law* (7th edn, Oxford University Press, 2008), 510–11.

they are considerably more controversial. These include the principle of permanent sovereignty over natural resources, and the principle of self-determination.[49] Indeed, the status and substance of these principles even as rules of customary international law is disputed.[50] Thus, to date, clear *jus cogens* status has been attained almost exclusively by rules of international law which prevent states from using their authority and power to harm individuals.

However, an important new data point was created in this area by the European Court of Justice (ECJ) in its 2008 decision in the *Kadi* case.[51] In this case, the ECJ struck down an EU Council regulation which had frozen the financial assets of Mr Kadi and Mr Al Barakaat. This EU regulation was in direct implementation of UN Security Council resolutions requiring the enforcement by UN member states of financial sanctions against persons designated by the Council's Sanctions Committee as being involved in international terrorism. The ECJ struck down the regulation because it determined that it violated certain fundamental due process rights guaranteed to EU nationals under EU law.

The *Kadi* decision is important because, *inter alia*, it stands for the proposition that the UN Security Council cannot override domestic law when that domestic law contains fundamental legal rights. The case thus establishes an important persuasive precedent of the principle that the power of the Security Council is not, in fact, unlimited.

This landmark case may mark the beginning of attempts by states to create and apply principles of international law which limit the Security Council's Chapter VII authority, and secure to them and their citizens a measure of legal protection from overly aggressive uses of the Council's authority. If so, one avenue to pursue would be the clarification of the basic rights which inure to states by virtue of their sovereignty, and the establishment of these rights as rules of *jus cogens* – supplementing the existing corpus of *jus cogens* rules which, as noted above, currently consist almost exclusively of rules prohibiting state conduct.

This notion of delineating the basic rights which states possess by virtue of their statehood is not new. As Sir Arthur Watts has explained:

---

49 On natural resources, see UNGA Resolutions 3171 (XXVIII) (17 December 1973) and 3281 (XXIX) (12 December 1974). On self-determination, see Judge Ammoun, *Barcelona Traction Case* (Second Phase) (Separate Opinion, 5 February 1970), ICJ Reports 304. The concept of self-determination is not strictly speaking a right of states, but more precisely the right of a people in a particular geographical place to constitute a state. However, it is sufficiently similar to a state entitlement for the analytical purposes herein.

50 On natural resources see, e.g. the Interlocutory Award in the case concerning *SEDCO, Inc.* v. *National Iranian Oil Company and the Islamic Republic of Iran*, Iran–U. Claims Tribunal, 10 Iran–US Cl. Rep. 180 (1986). On self-determination, see, e.g. *Reference re Secession of Quebec* (1998) 2 SCR 217 (Supreme Court of Canada).

51 Joined Cases C-402P and C-415/05P, *Yassin Abdullah Kadi and Al Barakaat International Foundation* v. *Council of the European Union and the Commission of the European Communities* [2008] ECR I-6351.

66   *International law in a multipolar world*

> As international law developed in the second half of the nineteenth
> century and the first half of the twentieth it was thought useful, and
> perhaps even necessary, to consider whether there were some fundamental
> legal principles which were inherent in the relations of States as members
> of the international community. The search for some hierarchical structure
> to the many particular rules of international law seemed to require no less.
> The idea grew that there were certain fundamental rights which were
> essential and self-evident attributes of Statehood, together with certain
> fundamental duties.[52]

In 1949 the newly established International Law Commission (ILC) adopted
a draft Declaration on Rights and Duties of States. This draft Declaration
consisted of 14 draft articles which enunciated, in broad terms, some of the
basic rights and duties of states. The 1949 draft Declaration was never adopted
by the General Assembly, and largely fell by the wayside as geopolitical shifts
over the subsequent decades – notably including the process of decolonization
and the communist–capitalist rivalry between East and West – made
agreement on a statement of states' 'fundamental' rights increasingly difficult.
In 1970, however, a successor statement to the 1949 draft articles was adopted
by the General Assembly, entitled the Declaration on Principles of
International Law concerning Friendly Relations and Cooperation among
States.[53] This 1970 Declaration predominantly discussed states' obligations,
such as the obligation not to use or threaten force against other states, or
otherwise to intervene in the affairs of other states. However, in its discussion
of the principle of the sovereign equality of states, it does delineate some of
the most basic rights of states, including the right of any state 'freely to choose
and develop its political, social, economic and cultural systems'.

Both the 1949 draft Declaration, and the 1970 Declaration can be described
as something of a jumble of proclamations of the rights and duties of states,
with no clear systematic approach to either subject, and certainly no claim to
an exhaustive listing of either rights or duties. The lack of progress since 1970
on a clear and definitive statement of the rights of states inuring to them by
virtue of their statehood is likely explained by a number of factors. The first is
simply the enormity of the task of getting agreement by states as to which
rights are 'fundamental' among the bundle of rights which states inherently
possess. The very notion of fundamental rights of states is likely to be seen
quite differently by developing and developed states, and by states with
different approaches to economics and government.

The second factor is the concern, often present in delineation of entitlements,
that the listing of some rights will appear to prejudice others not listed, and
have a limiting effect upon the subject. This dynamic was analogously present

---

52 A. Watts (ed.), *The International Law Commission: 1949–1998*, vol. 3 (Oxford University Press, 1999),
  1645.
53 UNGA Res. 2625 (XXV) (24 October 1970).

in the deliberations surrounding the drafting of the United States Constitution, and resulted in a compromise approach whereby nine amendments were added to the original document listing the rights of the constituent states of the United States, or in some cases the people of those states, yet a tenth amendment was added to make clear that the enumerated rights were not an exhaustive rendering, and that '[t]he powers not delegated to the United States by the Constitution, nor prohibited by it to the States, are reserved to the States respectively, or to the people'.

However, the Security Council's new interpretation of the extent of its authority, and the arguable use of the Council by the permanent five as an instrument for promoting their own political interests, may make a return to this normative effort advisable. The ILC spent the better part of fifty years developing its Draft Articles on State Responsibility for Internationally Wrongful Acts, which it finally adopted in 2001. The development of a similar set of Draft Articles on the Fundamental Rights of States would seem to be a naturally complementary project for the ILC to now pursue. Such a normative delineation and clarification of the rights of states inherently inuring to them by virtue of their statehood, and recognized in customary international law, would be the first evolutionary step towards those rights eventually achieving *jus cogens* status and thereby constituting a set of needed limitations on the currently seemingly unlimited authority of the United Nations Security Council.

Thus, to return to the case study of Iran, if the inalienable right to peaceful nuclear energy technologies recognized in Article IV of the NPT were to be recognized as among the fundamental rights of states, and thereby achieve the status of a rule of *jus cogens*, this would form an effective legal curtailment of the authority of the Security Council to restrict this fundamental right, and would serve to protect developing countries in their exercise of this right. Other fundamental rights relative to the case studies reviewed herein might include the right not to be bound by international legal obligations to which a state has not expressly or impliedly consented. Such a delineation of the fundamental rights of states and their establishment as rules of *jus cogens* would constitute something of an international 'bill of rights' for states, which could be structured, as the bill of rights in the US Constitution, to expressly provide for the non-exhaustive nature of the delineated rights.

This notion of an international bill of rights for states is of course only one avenue whereby states can begin to draw lines in the sand setting limits upon the authority of the Security Council. Others include the more ad hoc approach adopted by the ECJ in the *Kadi* case, as well as the strengthening of the authority of the International Court of Justice to more effectively act as a co-equal judicial check upon the Council. However it is pursued, it appears that the international legal system must develop effective limits upon the authority of the Security Council, lest the Council become an effective legal hegemon, unbound by law.

Name Index